Street by Street

GW01527047

SHEFFIELD

BARNSLEY, CHESTERFIELD, DONCASTER, ROTHERHAM

Bolsover, Chapeltown, Conisbrough, Dronfield, Maltby, Mexborough, Penistone, Royston, Stocksbridge, Thurnscoe, Wombwell

3rd edition December 2007
© Automobile Association Developments Limited 2007

Original edition printed May 2001

 This product includes map data licensed from Ordnance Survey® with the permission of the Controller of Her Majesty's Stationery Office. © Crown copyright 2007. All rights reserved. Licence number 100021153.

Published by AA Publishing (a trading name of Automobile Association Developments Limited, whose registered office is Fanum House, Basing View, Basingstoke, Hampshire RG21 4EA. Registered number 1878835).

Produced by the Mapping Services Department of The Automobile Association. (A03558)

A CIP Catalogue record for this book is available from the British Library.

Printed by Oriental Press in Dubai

Key to map pages	ii-iii
Key to map symbols	iv-1
Enlarged map pages	2-11
Main map pages	12-197
Index – towns & villages	198
Index – streets	199-235
Index – featured places	236-240
Acknowledgements	241

Scale of enlarged map pages 1:10,000 **6.3 inches to 1 mile**

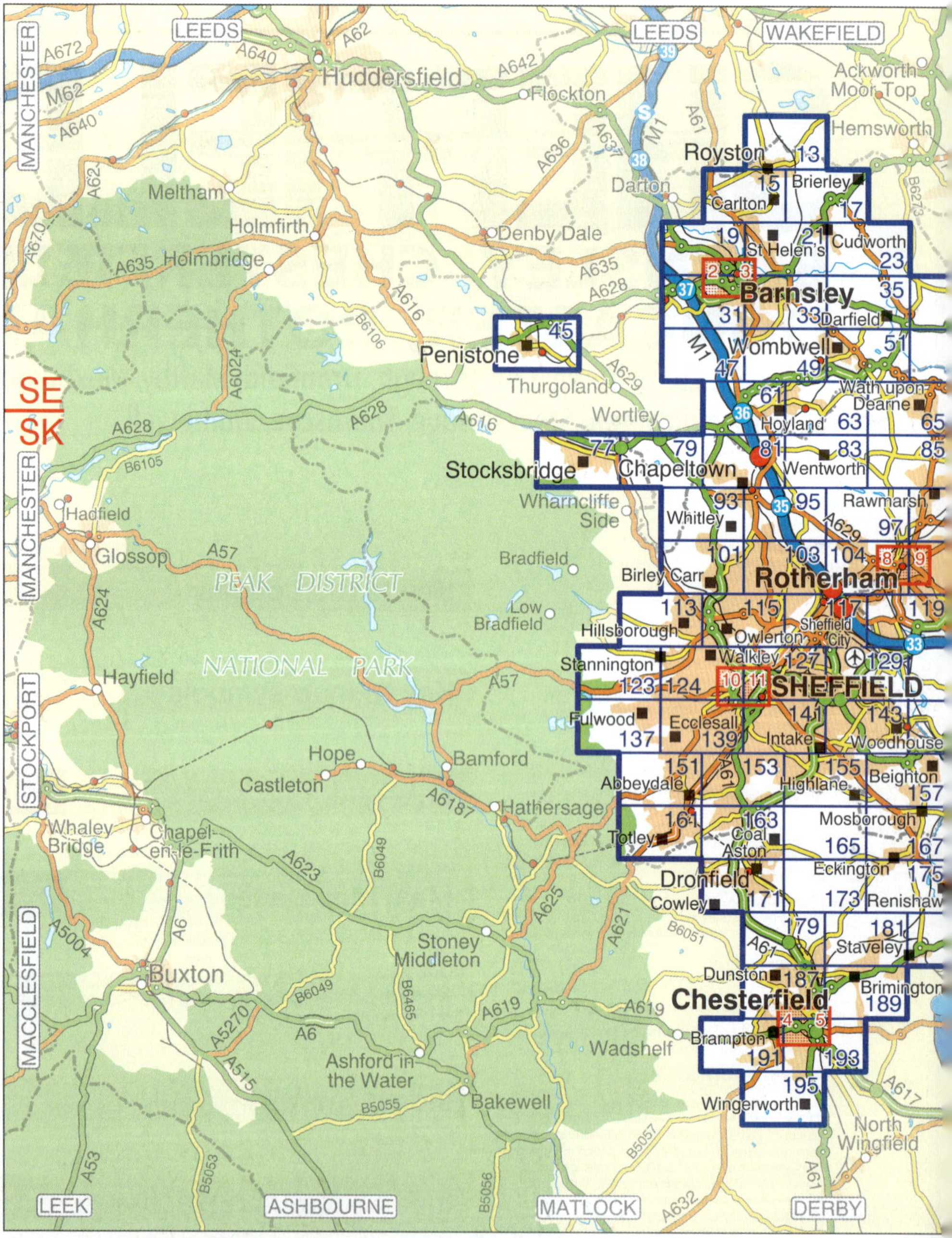

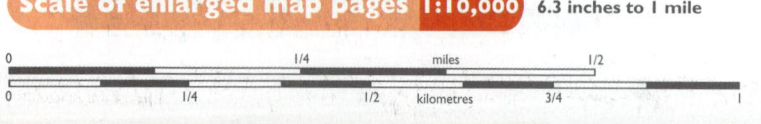

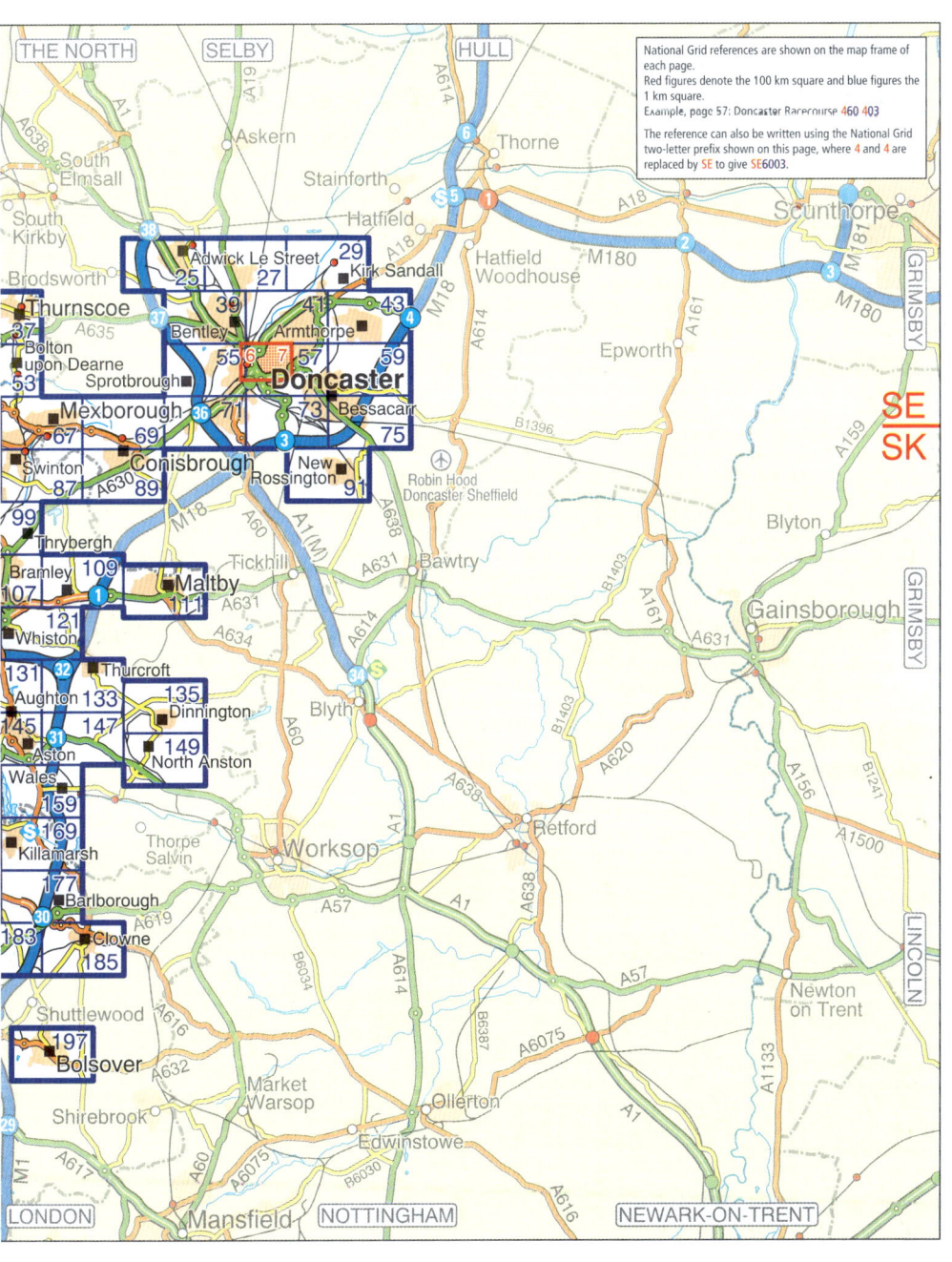

National Grid references are shown on the map frame of each page.
Red figures denote the 100 km square and blue figures the 1 km square.
Example, page 57: Doncaster Racecourse 460 403

The reference can also be written using the National Grid two-letter prefix shown on this page, where 4 and 4 are replaced by SE to give SE6003.

4.2 inches to 1 mile **Scale of main map pages** **1:15,000**

| 0 | | 1/4 | | miles | 1/2 | | 3/4 | | 1 |
| 0 | 1/4 | | 1/2 | kilometres | 3/4 | 1 | | 1 1/4 | 1 1/2 |

iv

Junction 9	Motorway & junction
Services	Motorway service area
	Primary road single/dual carriageway
Services	Primary road service area
	A road single/dual carriageway
	B road single/dual carriageway
	Other road single/dual carriageway
	Minor/private road, access may be restricted
← ←	One-way street
	Pedestrian area
	Track or footpath
	Road under construction
	Road tunnel
P	Parking
P+	Park & Ride
	Bus/coach station
	Railway & main railway station
	Railway & minor railway station
⊖	Underground station
⊖	Light railway & station
+++++++++	Preserved private railway

LC	Level crossing
•—•—•—•	Tramway
– – – – –	Ferry route
....	Airport runway
– · – · – ·	County, administrative boundary
ʸʸʸʸʸʸʸʸʸ	Mounds
17	Page continuation 1:15,000
3	Page continuation to enlarged scale 1:10,000
	River/canal, lake, pier
	Aqueduct, lock, weir
465 ▲ Winter Hill	Peak (with height in metres)
	Beach
	Woodland
	Park
	Cemetery
	Built-up area
	Industrial/business building
	Leisure building
	Retail building
	Other building

City wall		Castle	
A&E	Hospital with 24-hour A&E department		Historic house or building
PO	Post Office	Wakehurst Place (NT)	National Trust property
	Public library	**M**	Museum or art gallery
i	Tourist Information Centre		Roman antiquity
i	Seasonal Tourist Information Centre		Ancient site, battlefield or monument
	Petrol station, 24 hour Major suppliers only		Industrial interest
†	Church/chapel		Garden
	Public toilets		Garden Centre Garden Centre Association Member
	Toilet with disabled facilities		Garden Centre Wyevale Garden Centre
PH	Public house AA recommended		Arboretum
	Restaurant AA inspected		Farm or animal centre
Madeira Hotel	Hotel AA inspected		Zoological or wildlife collection
	Theatre or performing arts centre		Bird collection
	Cinema		Nature reserve
	Golf course		Aquarium
▲	Camping AA inspected	**V**	Visitor or heritage centre
	Caravan site AA inspected		Country park
	Camping & caravan site AA inspected		Cave
	Theme park		Windmill
	Abbey, cathedral or priory		Distillery, brewery or vineyard

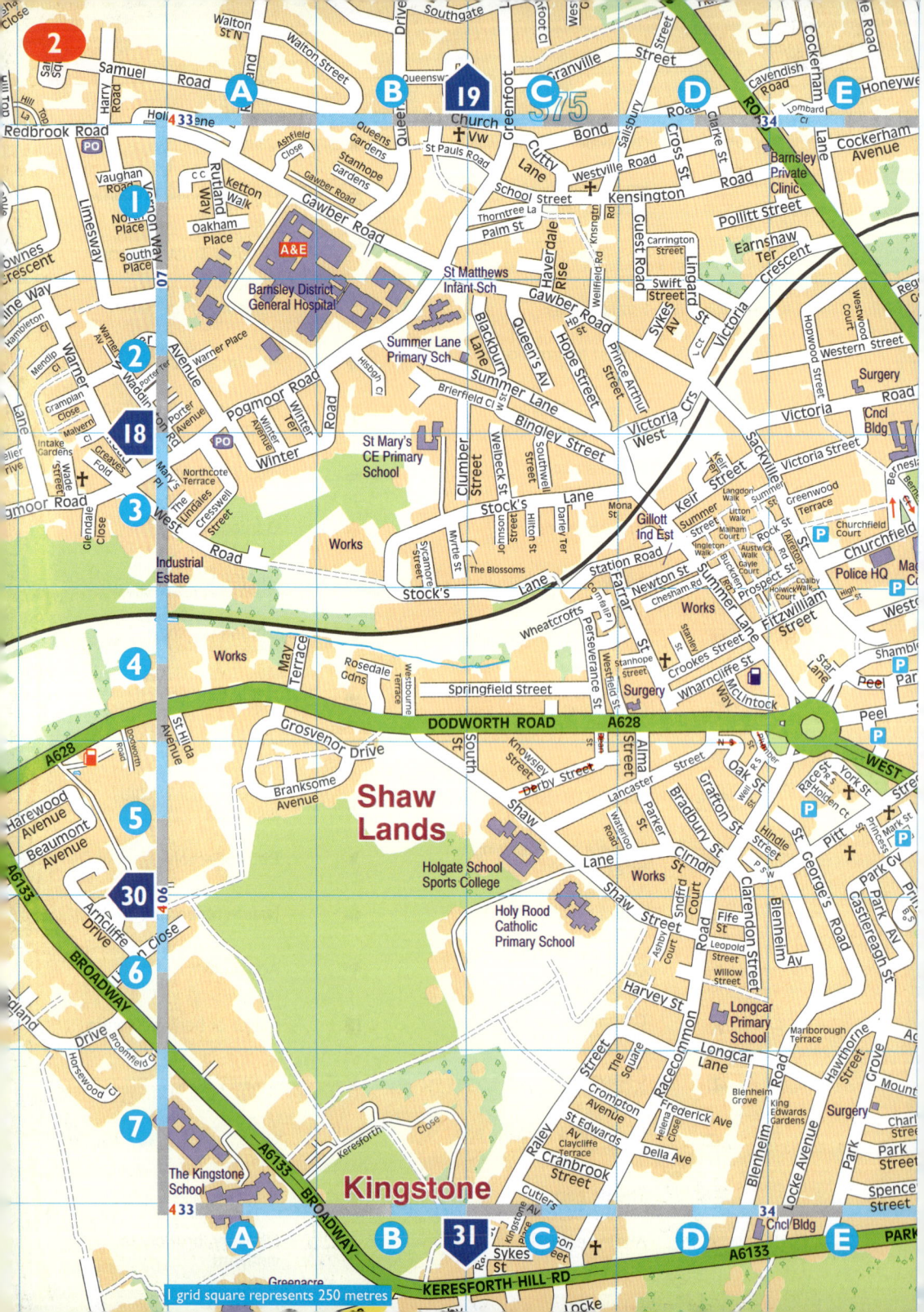

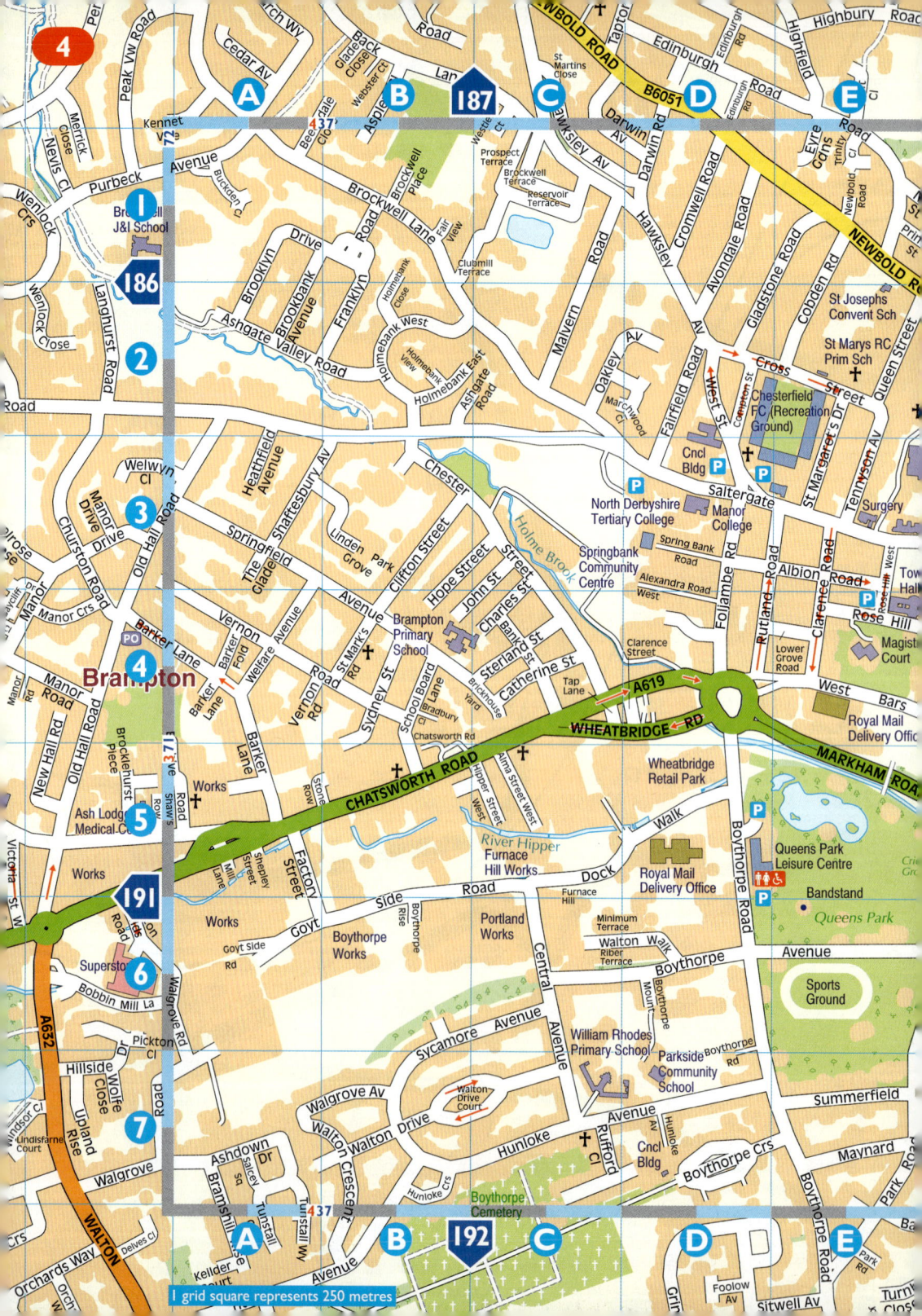

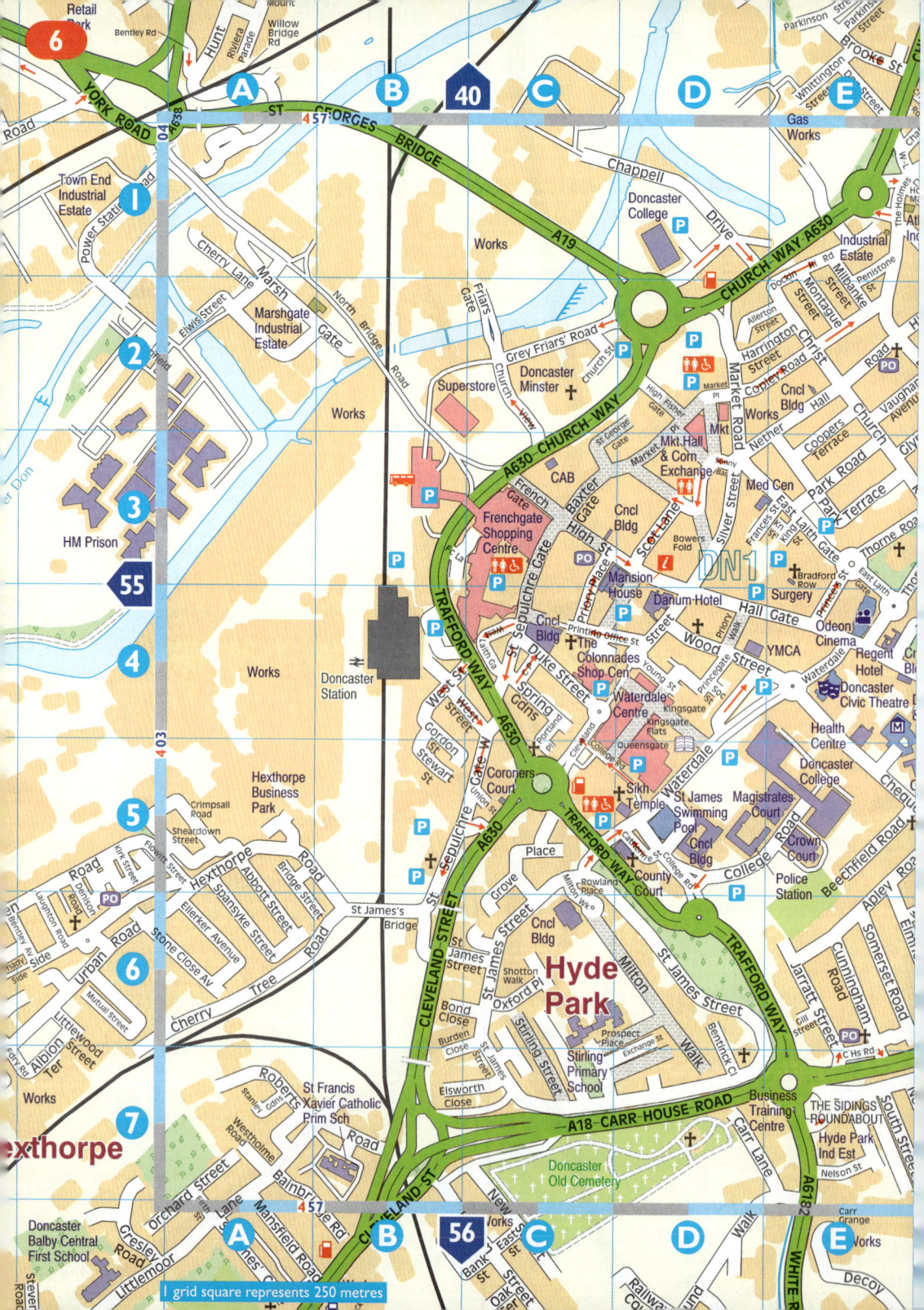

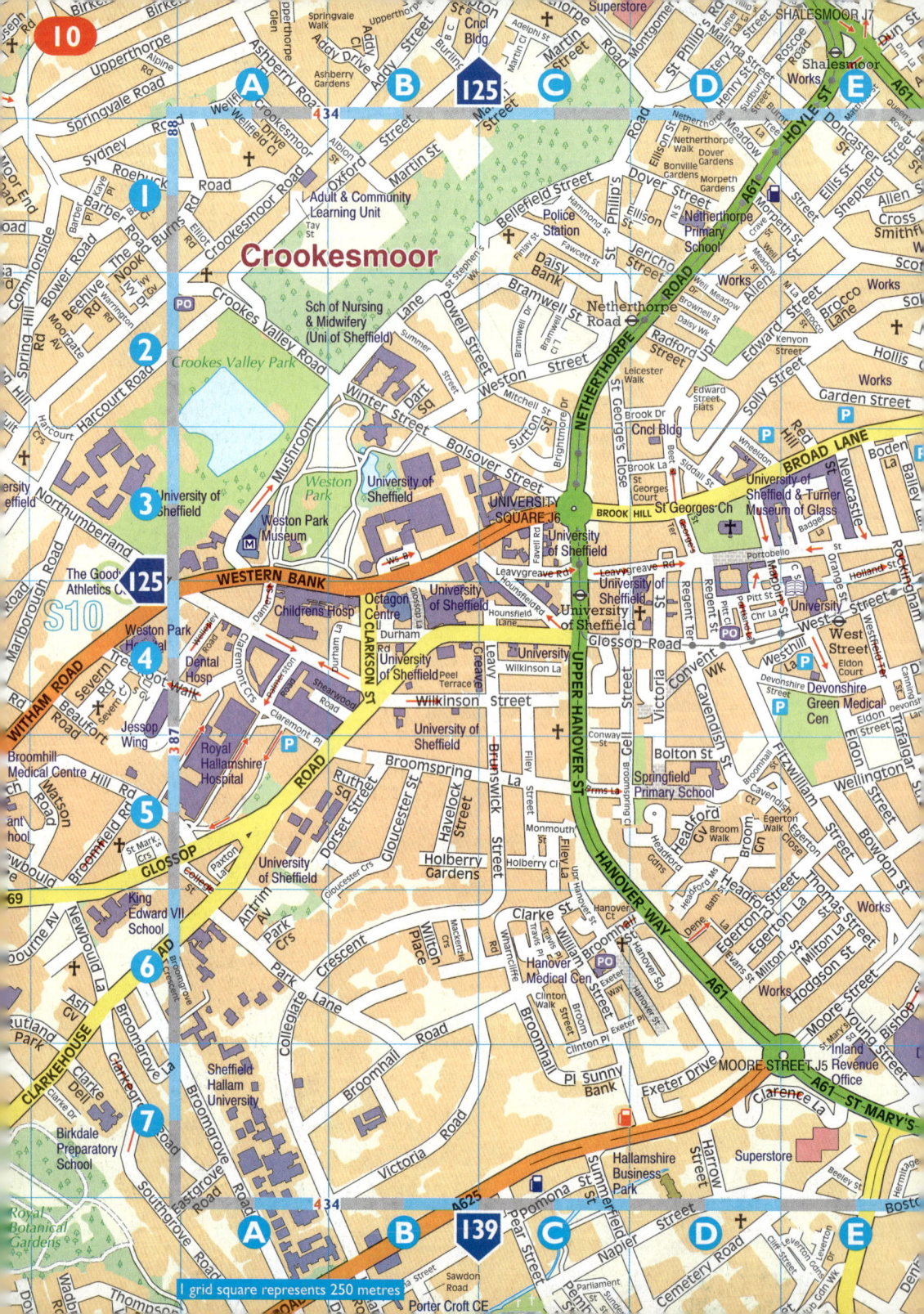

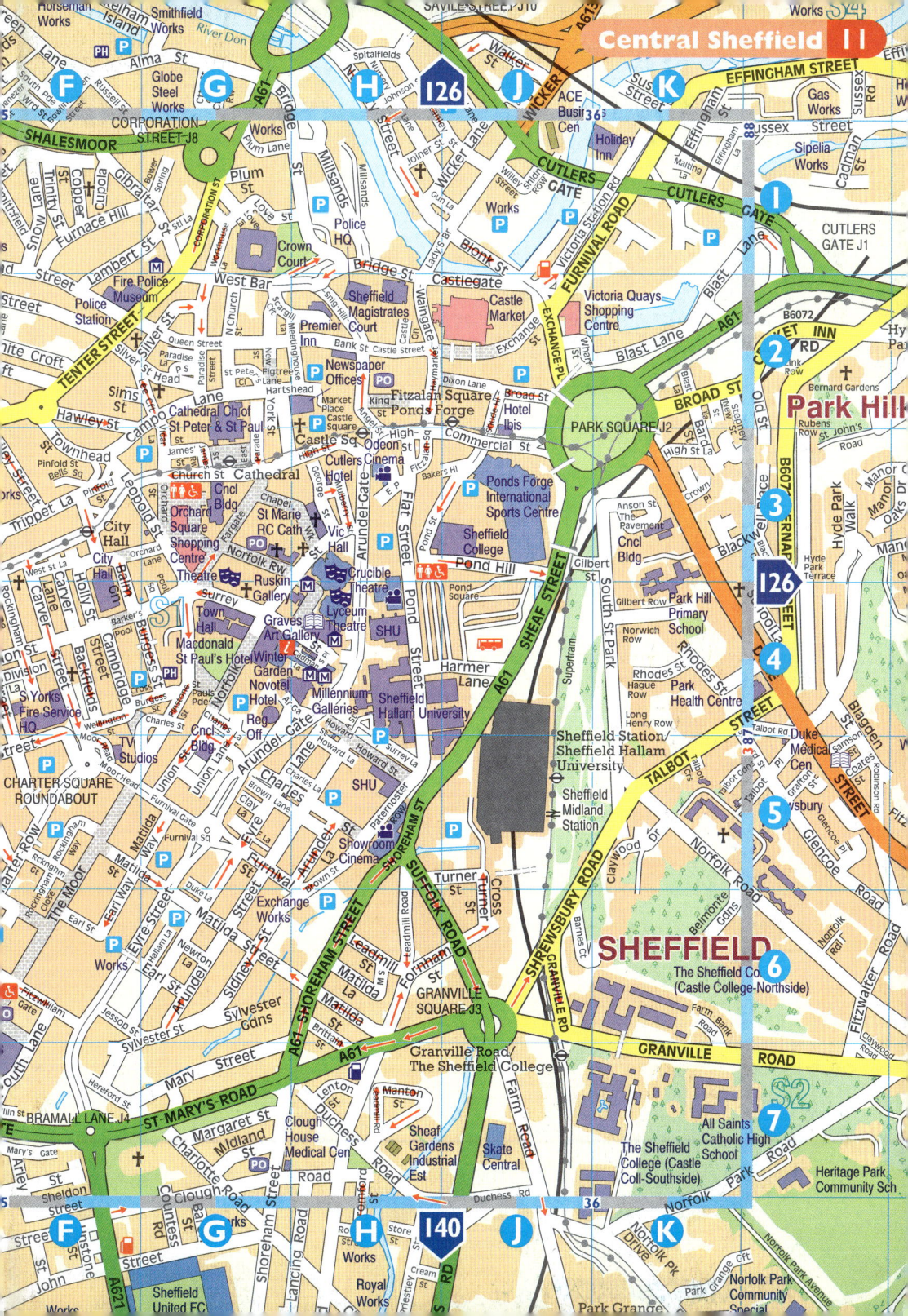

14

A B C D

I

Notton Park

Lee Lane Farm

Golf Course

LEE LANE

Barnsley Wakefield

Warren Lane

BARNS

Spring Lane

4 33

34

Staincross AV

Moorland

LInks VW

Oaklea

Thorne End Rd

Oaklea CI

Orchard CI

New Rd

New Rd

George St

Wellgate

Zion Dr

Crossgate

Wellgate Prim School

New Street AV

TOWNGATE

Mapplewell Health Cen

Bourne Walk

Common

The Balk

Fairway Avenue

Limes Avenue

Close

Fisewil

Surgery

Bourne Ct

SHAW LA

Paddock La

Hornes La

Paddock Road

Barnsley Municipal Golf Club

B6428

GREENSIDE

Hall GV

Greenside AV

Elliston AV

Mapplewell Prim Sch

Green CI

Park CI

Hope St

Park Rd

Cloverlands Drive

Cloudberry Way

Pike Lowe Grove

B6428

SHAW LA

Park La Rd

A61

WAKEFIELD ROAD

Staincross

Works

BLACKER ROAD

salcombe CI

Wentworth Rd

Beaulieu VW

Edward Street

Carron Dr

Spey CI

Carr Green Lane

Spey Road

Hill End

BAR LANE B6131

Eastfield Crs

Eastfield Close

Wentworth Crs

Wentworth Ms

Maple Industrial Estate

WAKEFIELD

Malincroft

Blacker Hill

New Lodge

Kirkstall Road

Beverley Rd

Langsett Rd

Canton

Sherburn Rd

Standhill

New Lodg

Wensley Rd

Newland Crs

Denby Rd

Elland

Mrdc PI

M PI

Stanton

Wollaton CI

Clifton Sheerien CI

Lindhurst Rd

Bramcot

Clifton AV

Clifton Rd

Wakefield Rd

Newstead Rd

Short

Str Rd

Athersley North Primary School

Hill Top AV

Wilford Rd

Greenset View

Warsop Rd

Stoney

Fountain Ct

Raven Royd

N Royds

Royd

Wood Pk VW

Wood

Athersle

Laxton Road

Beeston Sq

Trowell VW

Ollerton

Radclif

Line

Forest Rd

Forest Road

Arnold Avenue

Sutton AV

Upr Bellbank Wy

Sutton AV

Laithes Crs

High Croft Dr

B6132

Richard Newmar Primary School

Regent Park AV

Wakefield Rd

A61

Crescent

Athersley Prim Sch

Maston Crescent

ROAD

PO

4 09

4 33

34

A B **19** C D

River Dear

I grid square represents 500 metres

16

PO

ROAD

A 437 **B** 38 **13** **C** **D**

Railwaymens Sports Club

Shafton

1

Shafton Two Gates

2

Bateman

Weet Shaw Lane

Carlton

3

15

Shaw Lane

Royston Road

Three Nooks

Cudworth Pontefract Road Primary School

4

Cherry Cl

Beech Avenue

Park Av

Oak Tree Av

Rose Tree Av

5

Barnsley Business Innovation Centre

PO

437 **A** 38 **B** **21** **C** BARNSLEY ROAD A628 **D**

Bloemfontein St

Jackson St

West Green

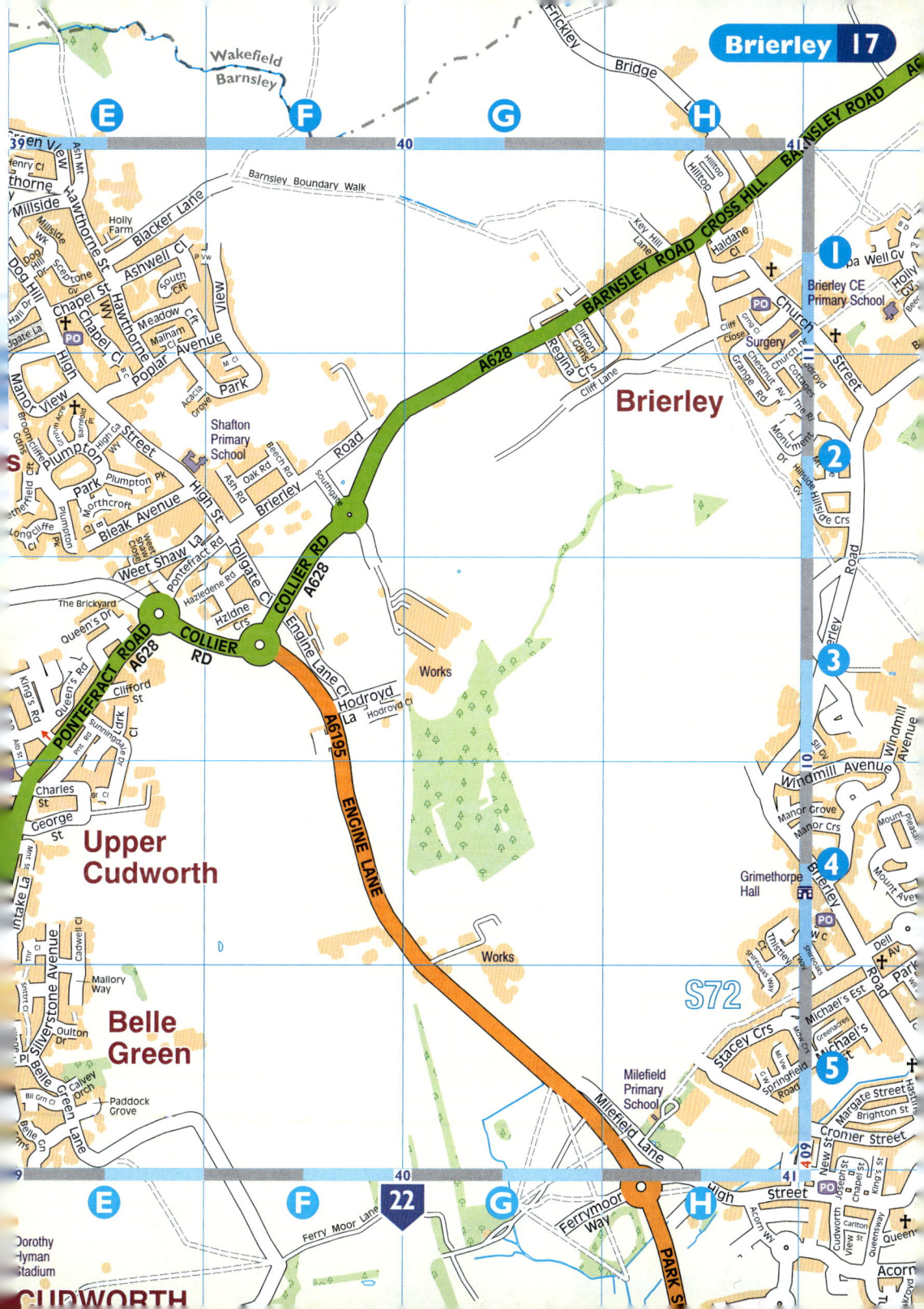

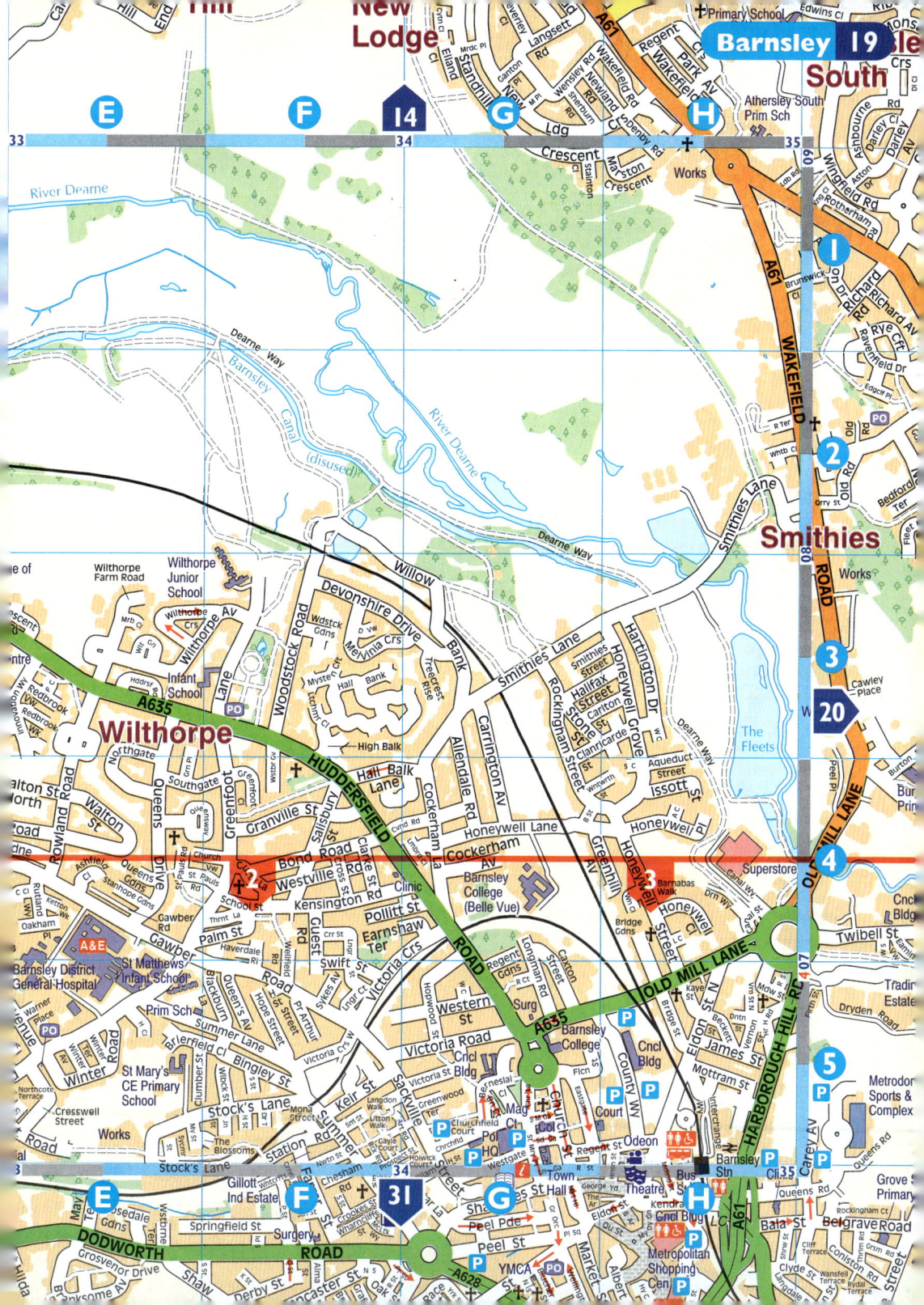

Junction 38

A638

A   B   C   D

451   52

Red House Lane

Ling   Field   Road

A1(M)

Windy
Mount

St Vincent
Lawn Avenue
Great North Rd
Elmwood Avenue
Beaumont Av
Kennington
Av
Harewood
Av
Shaftsbury
Fair Vw Av
The Circuit
Works
Ridge Ba
Balk
Ridge
Marson Avenue
West Avenue
The Cres

Long   Lands   Lane

Doncaster

Road

Ling Field Road

Pickburn

Pickburn   Lane

B6422

1

2

3

4

5

A   B   C   D

451   52

I grid square represents 500 metres

Toll Bar

Rostholme

1 grid square represents 500 metres

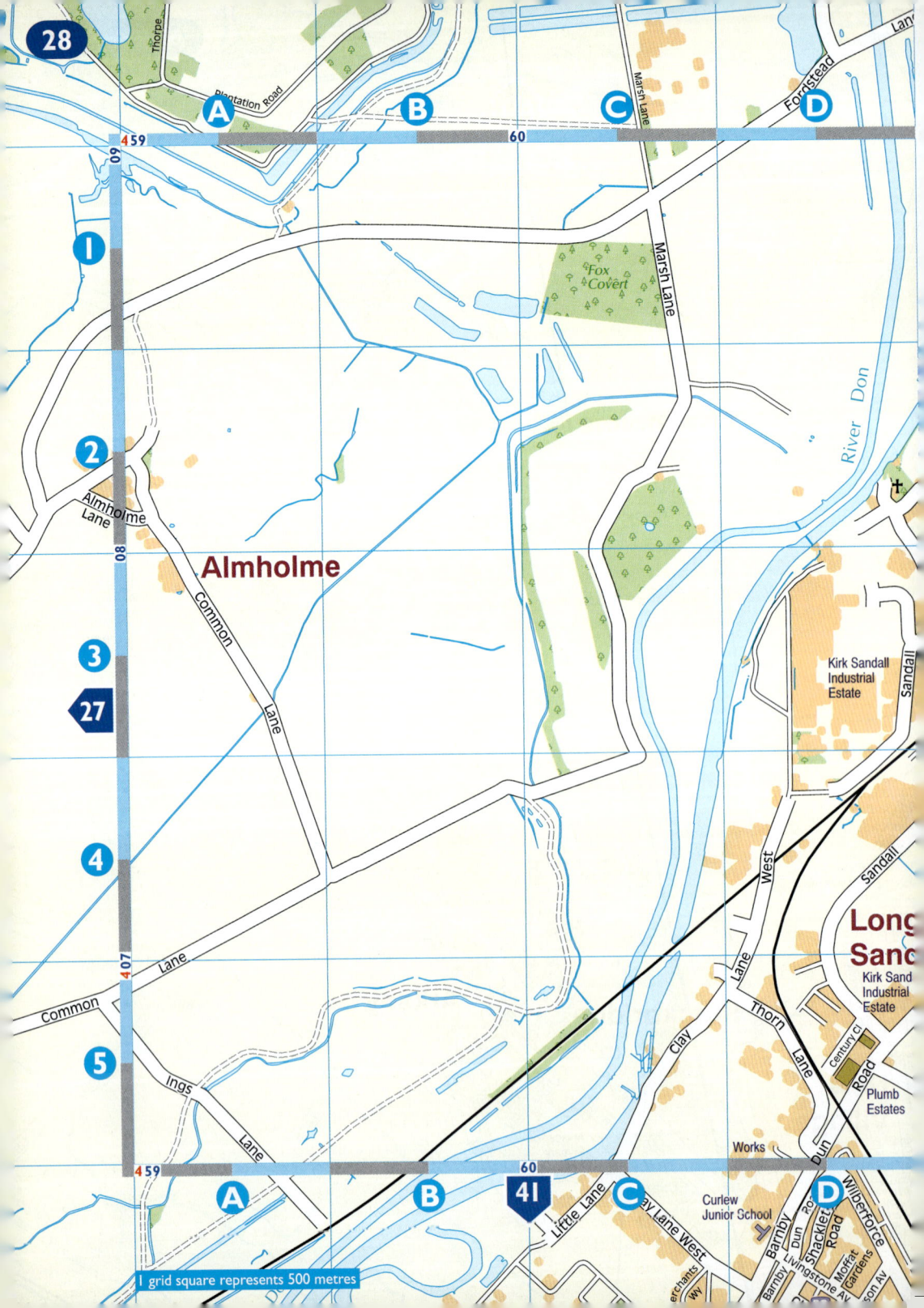

28

459   60

A   Plantation Road   B   C   Marsh Lane   D   Fordstead Lane

1

Fox Covert

River Don

2   Almholme Lane

Almholme

Common Lane

3

27

Kirk Sandall Industrial Estate

Sandall

4

West Lane

Sandall

Common Lane

Long
Sanc

Kirk Sand
Industrial
Estate

Clay Lane

Thorn Lane

Century ci

Road

Plumb
Estates

5   Ings Lane

Dun

Works

459   60

A   B   41   Little Lane   C   Clay Lane West   D   Wilberforce Road

Curlew
Junior School

Barnby   Dun   Road   Livingstone Av   Moffat   Gardens   son Av

Merchants   Wy

Shackle
Gardens

30

A B **18** C D

Higham Common

Pogmoor

Common Rd

Farm House Lane

Pogmoor

St Helier
Walk

St Owns Cl

Glendale Close

Longside Wy

West Moor Crs

Moor Gn Ct

St Martins Cl

I

Golf Course

Higham Lane

M1

Pogmoor Wy

Midhope Wy

Ewden Wy

Crowden Wk

Hunters Rd

Garden

White Hill
Av

Pogmoor Road

Harewood
Avenue

Dodworth Rd

Crown
Hl Rd

A628

Beaumont Av

Arncliffe Dr

A6133 BROADWAY

Horsewood
Close

Horsewood
Close

2

WHINBY ROAD A628

Dodworth
Business
Park

Gt Cliffe
Road

Upr Cliffe Rd

Galpharm Wy

Thornely Av

Barnsley Rd

Hill Pk Grove

Gate Crs

South Road

Wareham Gv

Hollin Cft

PO

Hunter's Avenue

Junction 37

Moorland Av Dr

Woodland
Dr

The Ki
Scho

3

Fall Bank Crescent

Fall Bank
Industrial
Estate

LC

Dodworth
Station

Mitchelson Avenue

Barnsley Road

Brnsl Rd

Clins Cl

Hawthorne
Crescent

Dodworth
Primary
School

South Crs

Birchfield Gv

Queen's
Drive

Bark Mdw

Royd Wd

Low
Pasture
Close

Damsteads

Syke Dr

Farrow
Close

Butterleys

Cinder
Hills Wy

Low

Dark Lane

Cart

4

DODWORTH GREEN ROAD

B6449

Bamford Cl

Haddon Cl

Baslow Crs

Hayfield

Pl Crs

Dodworth
Health
Centre

Pollyfox Wy

Low
Vw

B6099 HIGH STREET

Jermyn Cft

Park Vw

Water Vw

Bowden Gv

Langford Close

Keresforth Rd
Primary
School

Orchard Cft

Woodend Cl

Woodend Cl

KERES

B6099 KERESF

Dodworth

Ratten
Row

Dodworth
CE School

Naylor
Gv

Wentworth
Wy

WP

Strafford Walk

Stainborough
Cl

KERESFORTH ROAD

Locke Road

Green Lane

Low St

**Dodworth
Bottom**

south
St

Stainborough Rd

Silver St

Fairway

The Link

Saville
Road

Ag Cl

Birdwell Rd

Rockingham
Road

Gilroyd Lane

5

Saville Hall

Smithy Wood La

Bradwell Av

Intake
Crs

Calver
Cl

Gilroyd

Trans Pennine Trail

Strafford
Industrial
Park

Rockingham
Road

A B **46** C D

Lowe Lane

Parkdrive

Round
Gree

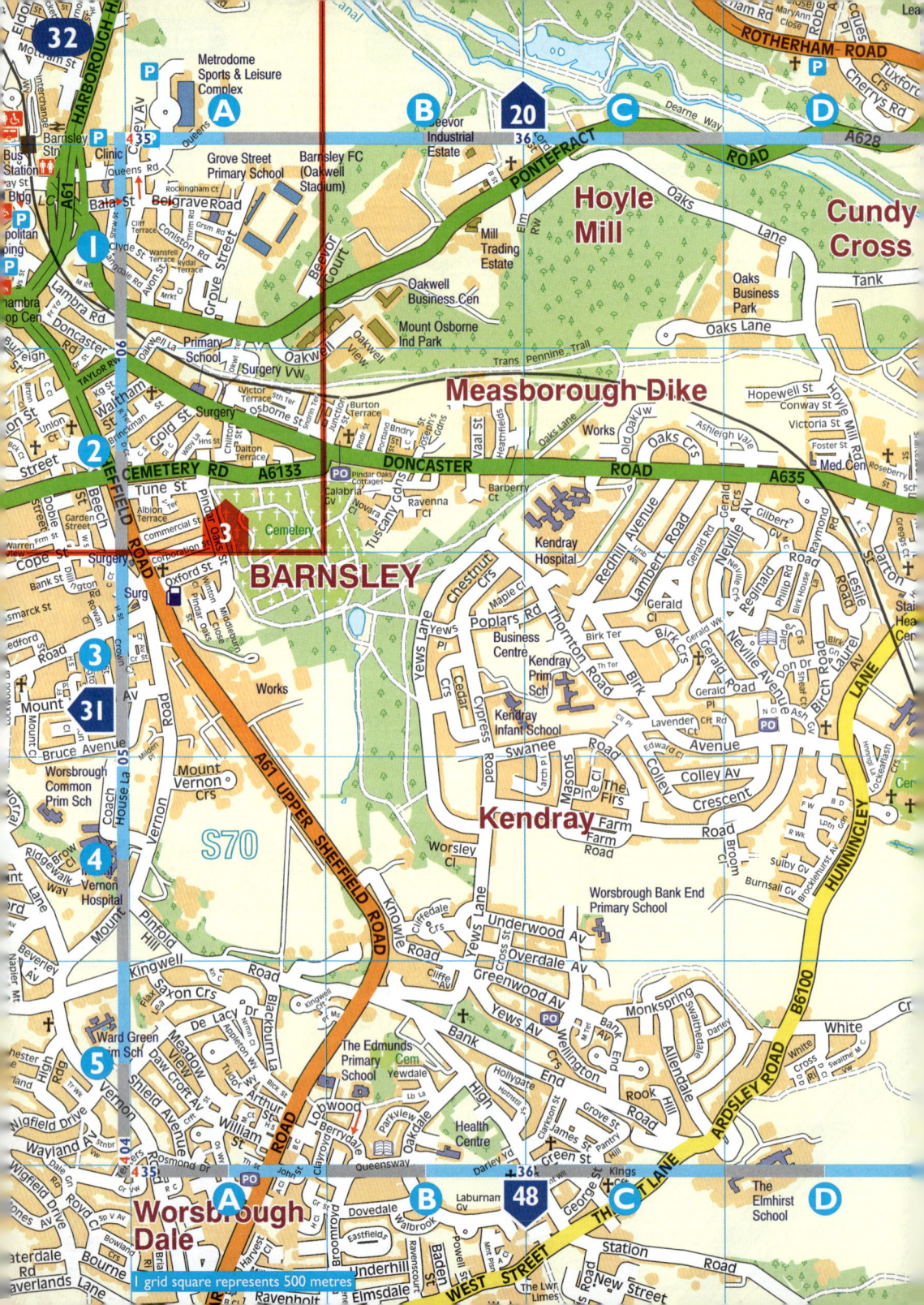

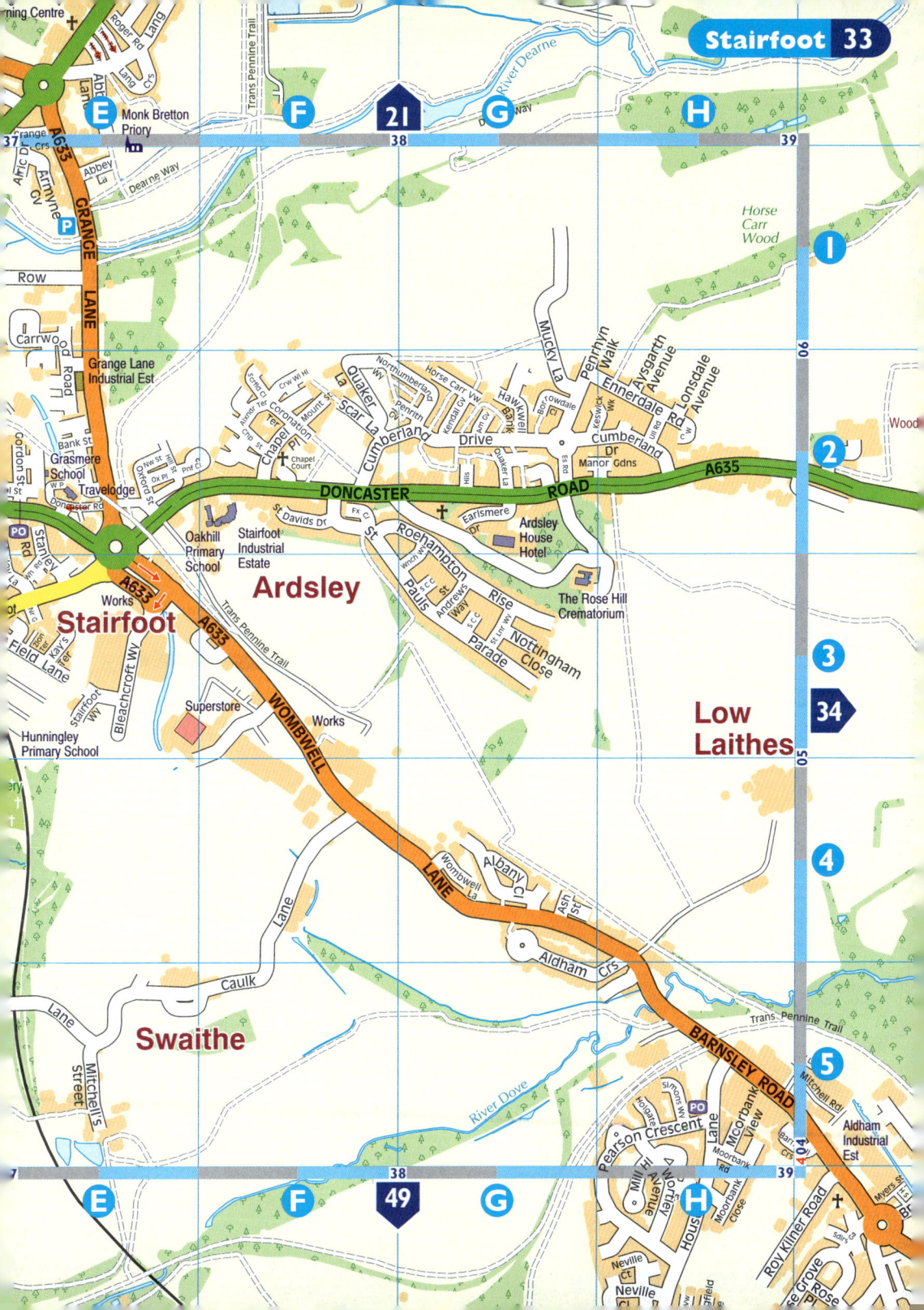

E
Monk Bretton
Priory

F

21

G
River Dearne
Way

H

I

Horse
Carr
Wood

ning Centre

Roger Rd
Lang

Lang Cr
Abb Dr

Row

Trans Pennine Trail

Wood

Carrwood

Carrwood
Road

Grange Lane
Industrial Est

2

A635

Northumberland
Horse Carr Vw
Penrhyn
Walk
Avsgarth
Avenue
Lonsdale
Avenue
Ennerdale Rd

Mucky La

Bank St
Grasmere
School
Travelodge

Quaker
Scar
Cumberland
La
Chapel

Chapel Court
Coronation
Mount St

Penrith
Kendal Gv
Keswick
Cumberland
Drive
Manor Gdns
Dr

A635

DONCASTER ROAD

PO
Rd

Oakhill
Primary
School

Stairfoot
Industrial
Estate

St Davids Dr
Fx Cl
Earismere
Dr

Ardsley
House
Hotel

The Rose Hill
Crematorium

3

34

Stairfoot

A633

Works

Trans Pennine Trail

Ardsley

Roehampton

Pauls
Andrews
Way
St

Nottingham
Close

Rise

Parade

**Low
Laithes**

Field Lane

Hunningley
Primary
School

A633

WOMBWELL

Superstore

Works

4

Lane

Lane

LANE

Wombwell La
Albany
Cl
Ash
St

Aldham Crs

Trans Pennine Trail

Caulk

River Dove

5

BARNSLEY ROAD

Mitchell Rd

Aldham
Industrial
Est

Swaithe

Lane

Mitchell's
Street

Pearson Crescent

PO

Moorbank
View

Moorbank
Rd

Moorbank
Close

Barn Crs

A04

Myers St

E

F

49

G

H

Mill Hill
Avenue

Roy Kilner Road

Neville
Ct

Rose
Grove

37

38

39

06

05

404

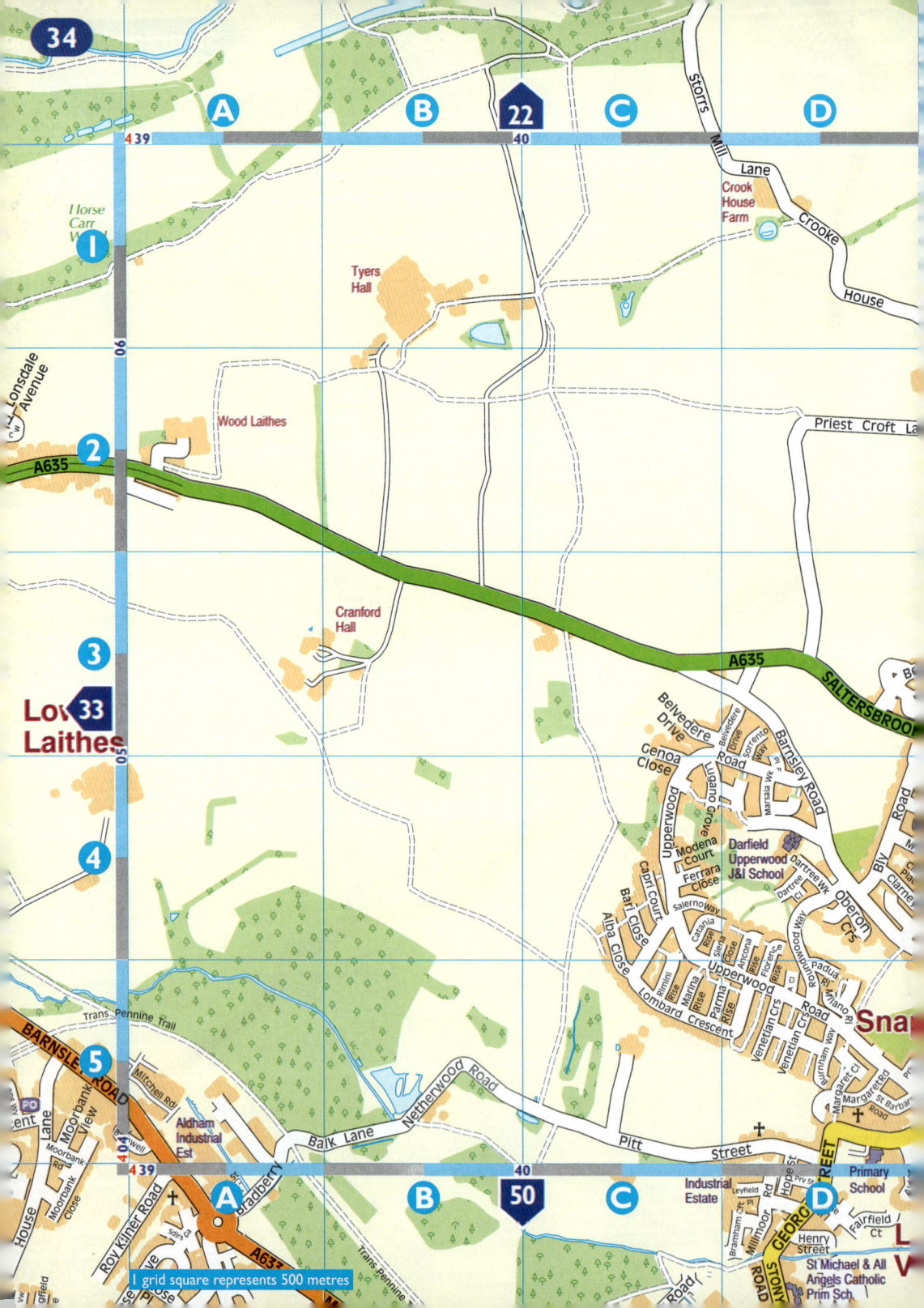

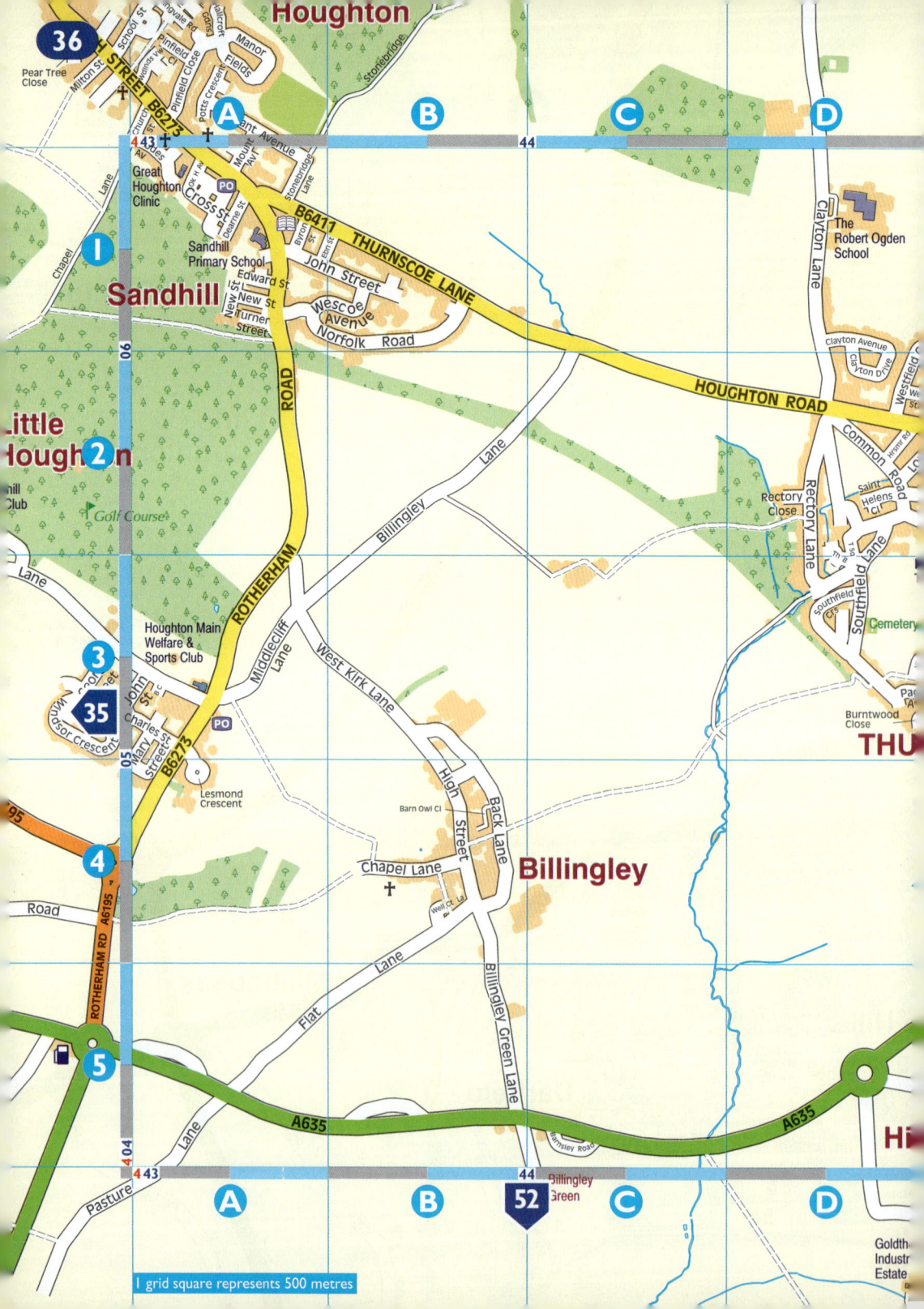

Doncaster
Barnsley

E F G H

45 46 47

Stotfold

Whinside Crs

Gooseacre
Primary
School

Gooseacre
Avenue

Beechlea

Burnside
St. Peter's
Challenger
Crs
Road

Merrill
Road

Pangbourne
Rd
Thornwood

Monsal
street
Richmonde
Road

Lingamore
Leys

Willow
Road

Oak
Road
School
Road

Orchard
Way

Low Grange
Square
A Cl

Garden
Cl
John Street

Holly
Bush
Drive

Whin Gardens

Basildon Road

Deightonby
Street

Briton
Street

Hanover
Street

Lancaster Street

Brunswick
Street

Chapel Lane

Cromwell Street

St. Hildas Cl

York Street

Hanover
Square

Brunswick
Street

Hill
Primary
School

Thurnscoe East

Chapel lane

Roman St

Grange
Crs

Windsor
Square

Windsor
Street

Stuart
Street

Grange
st

Granger
st

Norman
St

Dane
st

Daniel
St

Tudor
Street

Street
North

I

2

Manor
Road

Crescent

Albert
St

Church Street
C B St
Market St

Butcher Street

High
Street

Kingsway
Park Road

Welfare
Road

Pearltree Avenue

HOUGHTON ROAD

STATION ROAD

Shepherd Lane

Farm
Hall
Drive

Br Vw
HI F
Cl

Thurnscoe Station

WC

York
Street

Chapman st

Coronation
st

Saxon Street

Thurnscoe
Business
Centre

Oaklea

George Street

Albion Drive

LIDGET   LANE   B6411

PO

Lansdowne Ct

Hickleton
Court

Walbert Av

Troutbeck
Cl

Springwood GV

Billingley
Hample
Dr

High
Street

Chestnut
street

Hallgate
Grove

Turnescoe
Grove

Lindley
Crescent

Crossdale

King St

Queen St

Princess

Phoenix Lane

Barrowfield   Road

The
Windings

3

RNSCOE

Hillcrest
G Gdns

The
Orch

Derry

Thurnscoe
Bridge Lane

Colliery
Lane

Davey
Rd

A635

Sacred Heart
Catholic Primary
School

Lockwood
Road

St Mary's Rd

Nora Street

Kathleen
Grove

Hamilton Rd

Central St

East St

Doncaster
Surgery

Picknill's
Avenue

4

A635

Gooling Gateway

B6098

Nicholas

Dearne Highgate
Primary School

Goldthorpe
Station

Michaels
Road

Saltersbrook

Cherry
Gv
Rowan
Dr

Holly
Cl

Barnsley
Road

Rosegreave

BARNSLEY ROAD

Dearne
Valley

King Street

M S

Kelly Street

Queen
Street

Elizabeth St

Chri St

Jck St

Main

St

Goldthorpe
Prim Sch

Central
St

Cross St

Co-Operative St

Victoria Rd

Garden street

Beever Street

Dearne

Meltonfield

Parkgate

5

hgate

William Street
Cl

Westmore
Cl

Loscoe
GV

Lawnwood Dr

George Highgate
Court

Probert Avenue

Homecroft Road

Highfield
Avenue

Sankey
Sq

Lnc Gdn

Lesley
Rd

Frederick   Street

Albr Rd

Ppl Av

Wlington St

Flower St

Goldthorpe

404

Barnburgh Lane

E F 53 G H

Commercial Road

Washington Road

GOLDTHORPE

Goldthorpe
Health Centre

Court
Buildings

Dearne
High School

Derwent
Gardens

Lindale
Gardens

Engine Lane

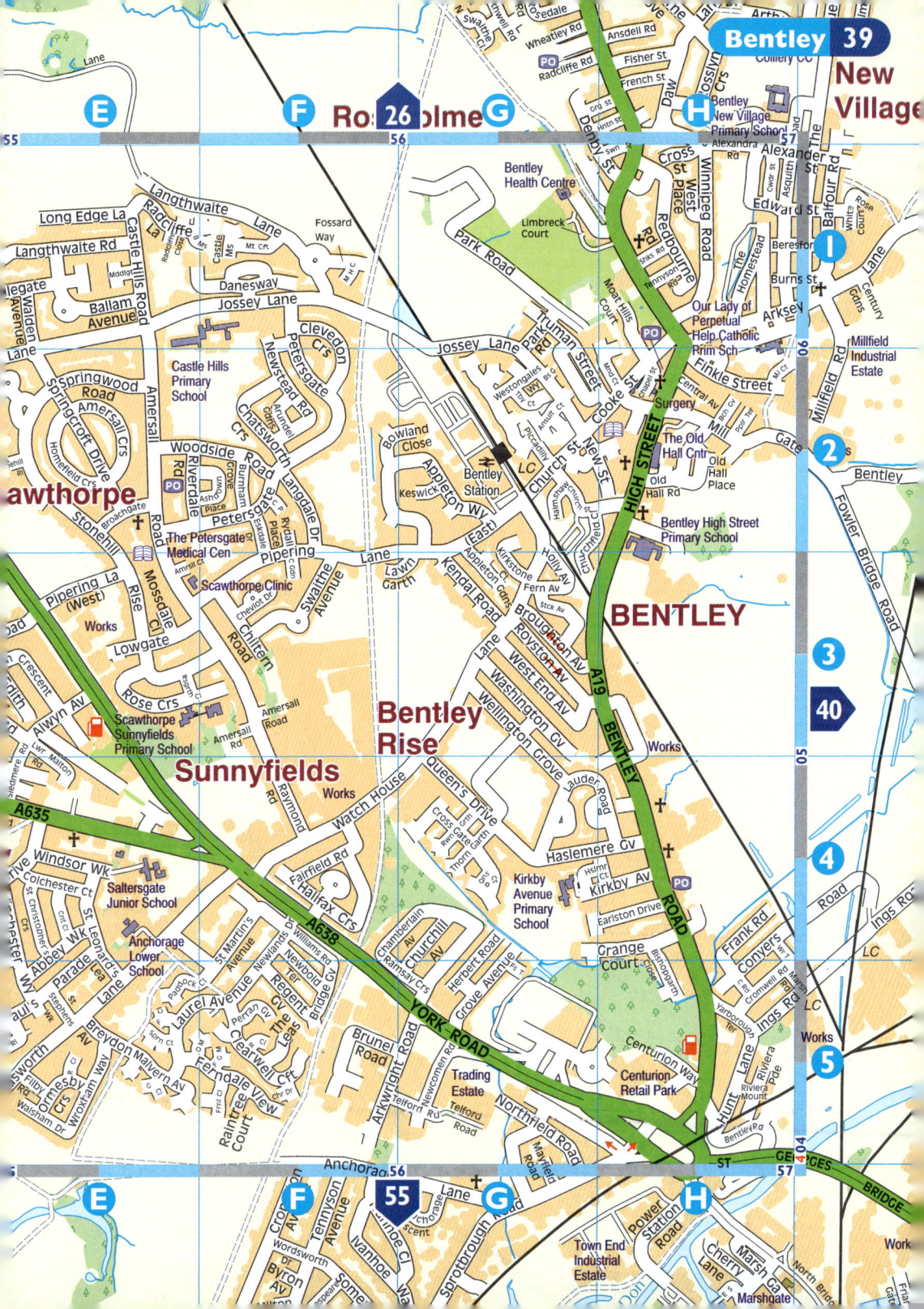

1 grid square represents 500 metres

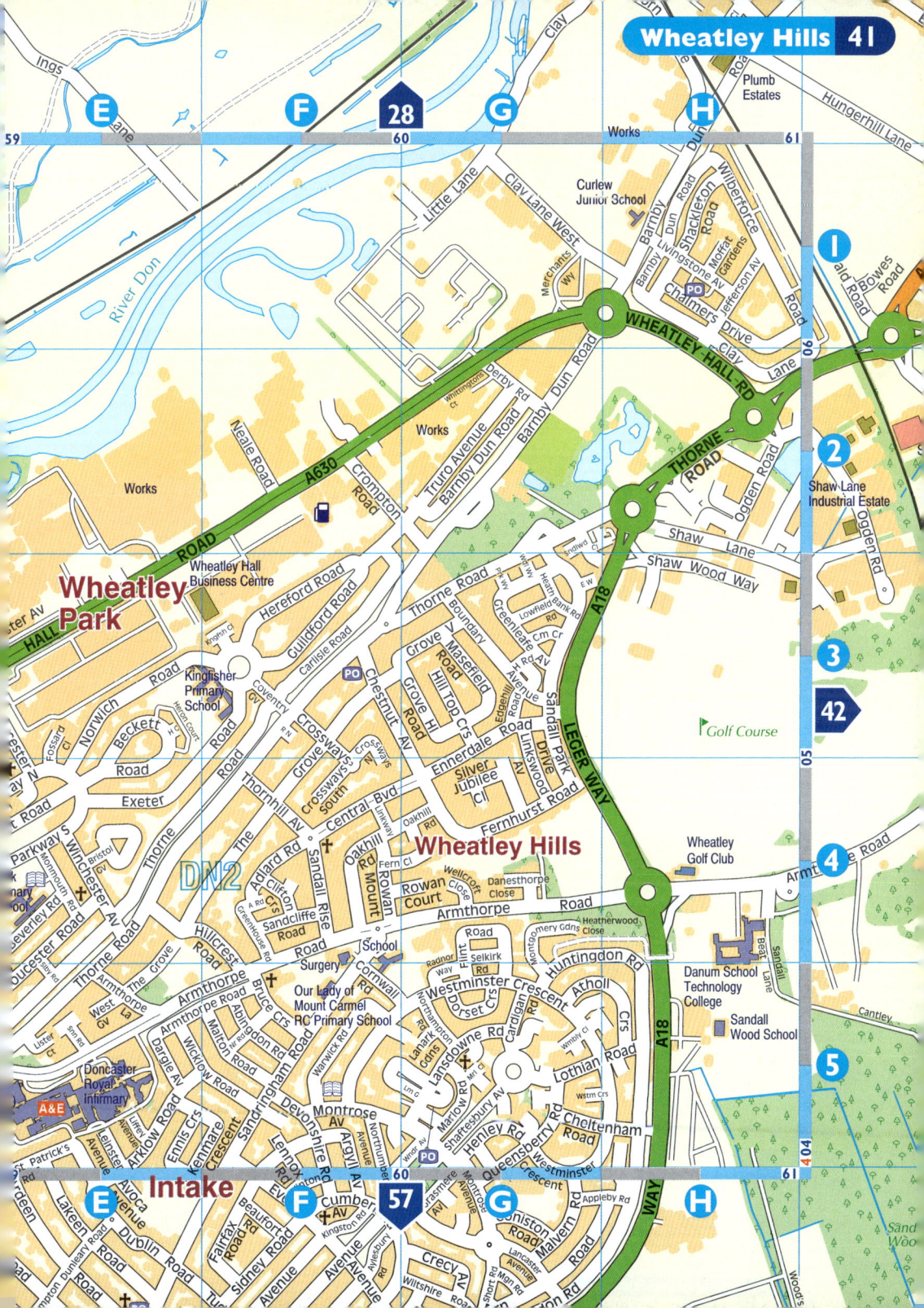

46

4 3 1
04
32

Round Green

Parkdrive

Lowe Lane

I

Lowe Lane

2
03

Wentworth Castle

✝

⚔ ✝

Wentworth Castle College of Education

⚔ Stainborough Castle

Hood Green Road
Castle Drive

Greno View

Hood Green

Road

3

Stainborough

Stainborough Fold

Lane

Broom Royd Wood

4

402

Stainborough

Lane

Manor Farm

5

Gudgeon Hole Lane

4 3 1
32

Dance Lane

A   B   C   D

Cliffe Farm

1 grid square represents 500 metres

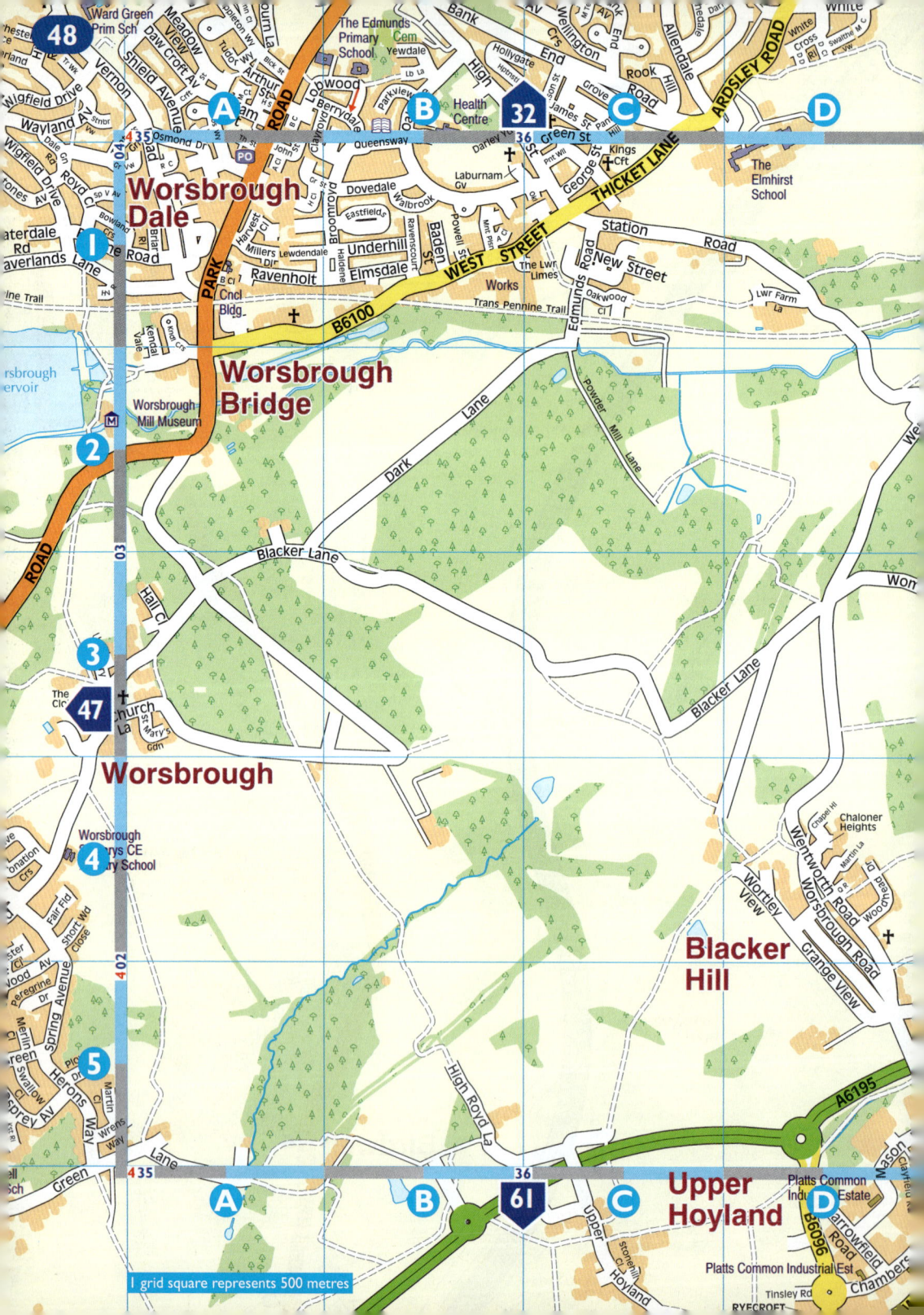

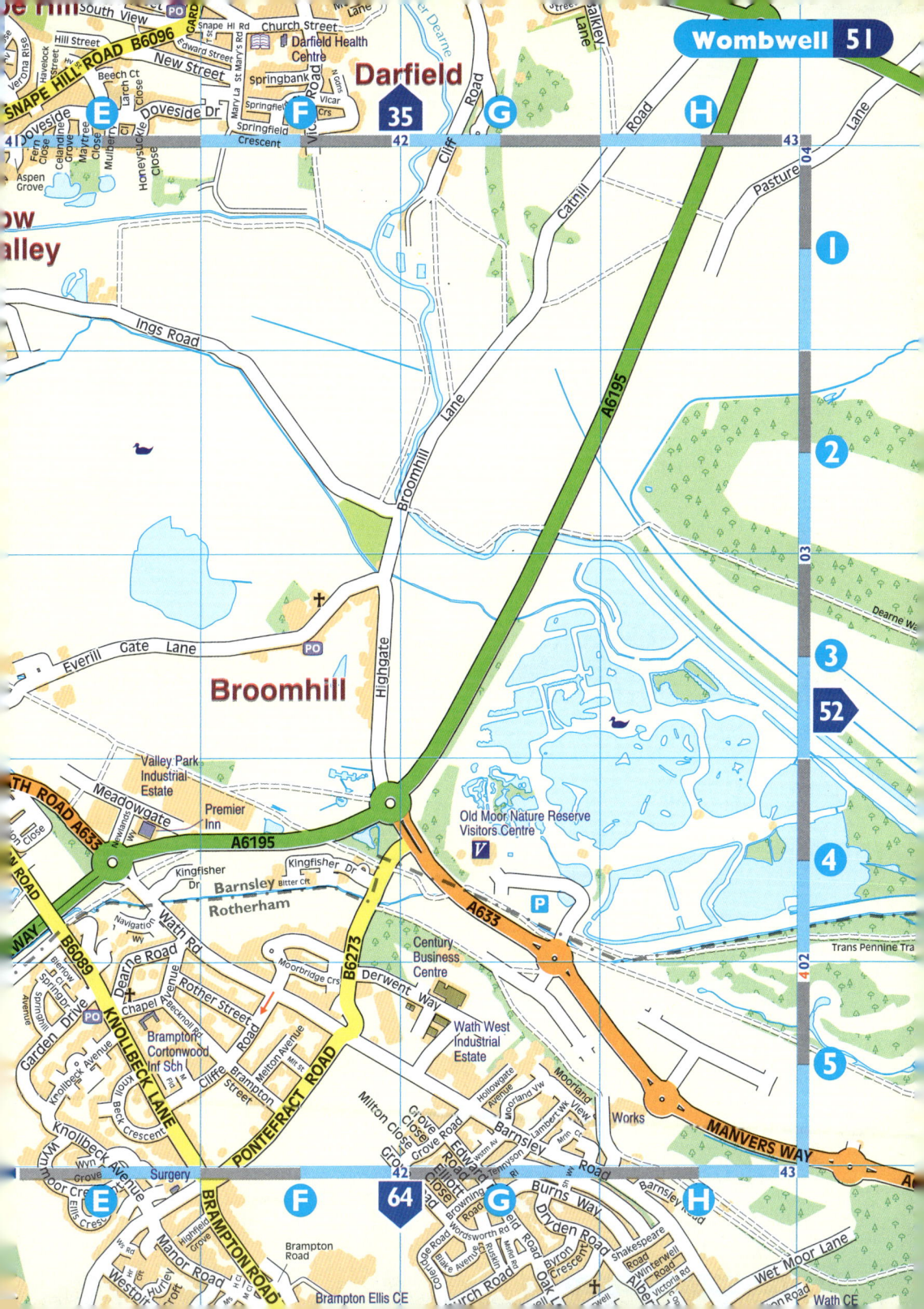

A A635 B 36 C A635 D Hig

Pasture Lane

443
44

Billingley
Green

Goldthorp
Industrial
Estate

I

Heather
Garth Primary
School

Carr

S63

Billingley View

Beckfield

Fairfield

Brow View

Stumpcr
Gdns

2

03

Commonwealth
View

Carr
Head

Ringw

Rise

Ringway

Canberra

Pennyfields

Dearne Way

Ingsfield
Lane

Coronation Dr

Caernarvon Crescent

Prn Cl

Meibourn

Avenue

3

Maori Avenue

Ingsfield

Vancouver Dr

Edinburgh Dr

51

Broadwater

Lane

Dale

GV

Browf

Broomhill

4

River Dearne

Heath
GV

South
Drive

Mill
View

Road

402

Trans Pennine Trail

Dearne

5

Station Rd

MANVERS WAY

443

A633 MANVERS WA
44

A A633 MANVERS WAY B 65 C A6023 D

Wet Moor Lane

Wet Moor
Lane
Works

Road

A633

MANVERS

Hibbard
Works
Green Ings

F PK

Wath CF

Road

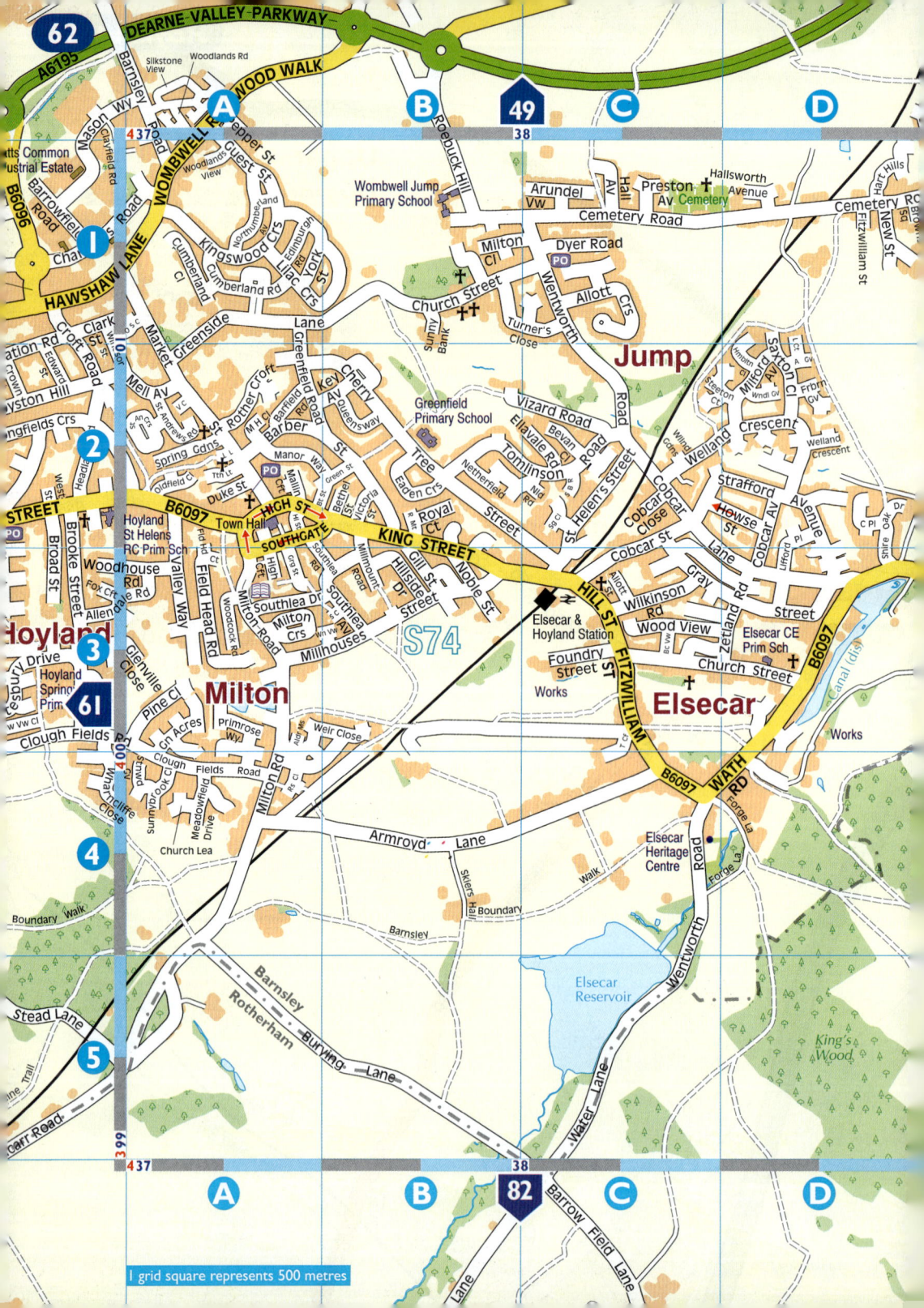

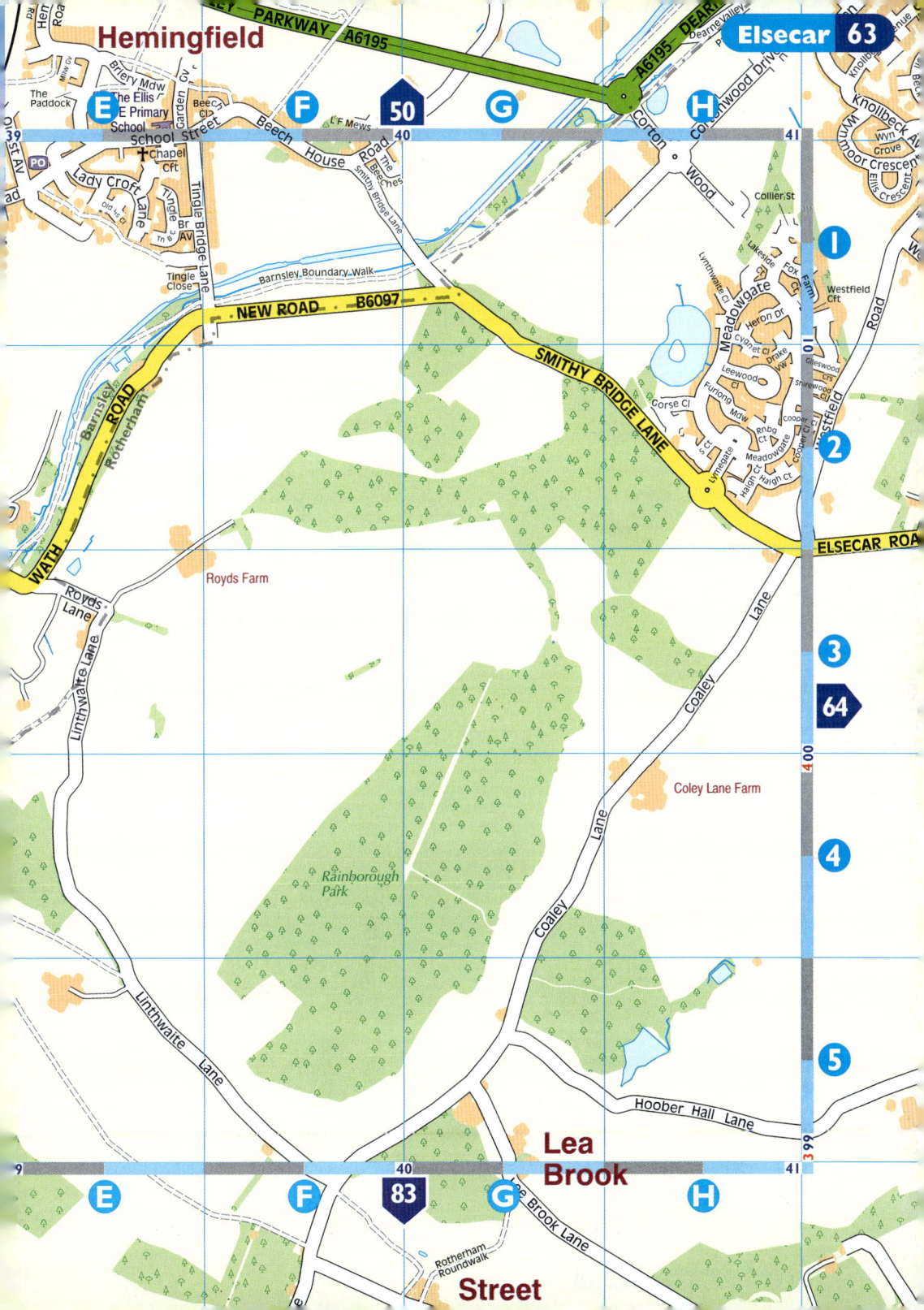

70

A   B   **54**   C   D

4 53   54

I

Laderby Lane   Cadeby Road   Copley Junior School   Nursery Lane   Scott Hi   Boat Lane   Spinney Hi   St Dominic's Close   Side Meadow Croft   A1(M)

Hill Ct   HS Ct   Hill Ct

Mill Lane

10

Kelsol   Ruthven   Guest La   Church   Rd   Grosvenor Crs

River Don   Hyman Close   Oxton Drive   Tenter   Fox Grove   War'en Close   Pamela Drive   Tenter   Beech Grove   Crm Gdn   Cliff Crs   Mill Lane   **2**

Warmsworth   Works   Warmsworth Primary School   **HIGH ROAD A630**   Quaker Lane   Low Rd   Low E   Glebe Street   Jun   Low Road West   Common

69   Mayflower Rd   PO   A630   Wrightson Av   Cecil Avenue   Badsworth Road   Darrington Drive   Low Road West   **3**

SHEFFIELD ROAD   Sheffield Rd   Norbreck Rd   Park Crs   Poplar Grove   Stapleton Road   A630   Lundreck Road   Lord's

4   A630   Oak Dale Road   Asn Dale Road   Hait   Cemetery   Warmsworth Halt Industrial Estate   Lord's

SHEFFIELD   ROAD   Works   Warmsworth   Head Lane   B6376   Lords Cl   Bnd'

69   Sheffield   **5**   Qs Pk   Staveley Street   Wicket Way   Grace Road   Kennington Grove

Edlington Victoria Primary School   Church Road   Victoria Road   **EDLINGTON LANE**   Mullin   Willow Dr   Edgbaston   Wood View   Kennington Grove

Nelson Rd   St   Prince's Crs   King's Crs   Queen's Crescent   The   Shaw Road   Heaton   Arlott Way   Wort View

4 53   Auburn Road   St John's   Main Avenue   **54**   J C   Headingley Dr   Broomhouse Lane Industrial Estate   Broomhouse Lane

A   B   Markham Square   C   D

St Marys Catholic Primary School   Gordon Road   Wellington Road   Hazel Road   Surgery   Bungalow Road   Markham Road   North

I grid square represents 500 metres

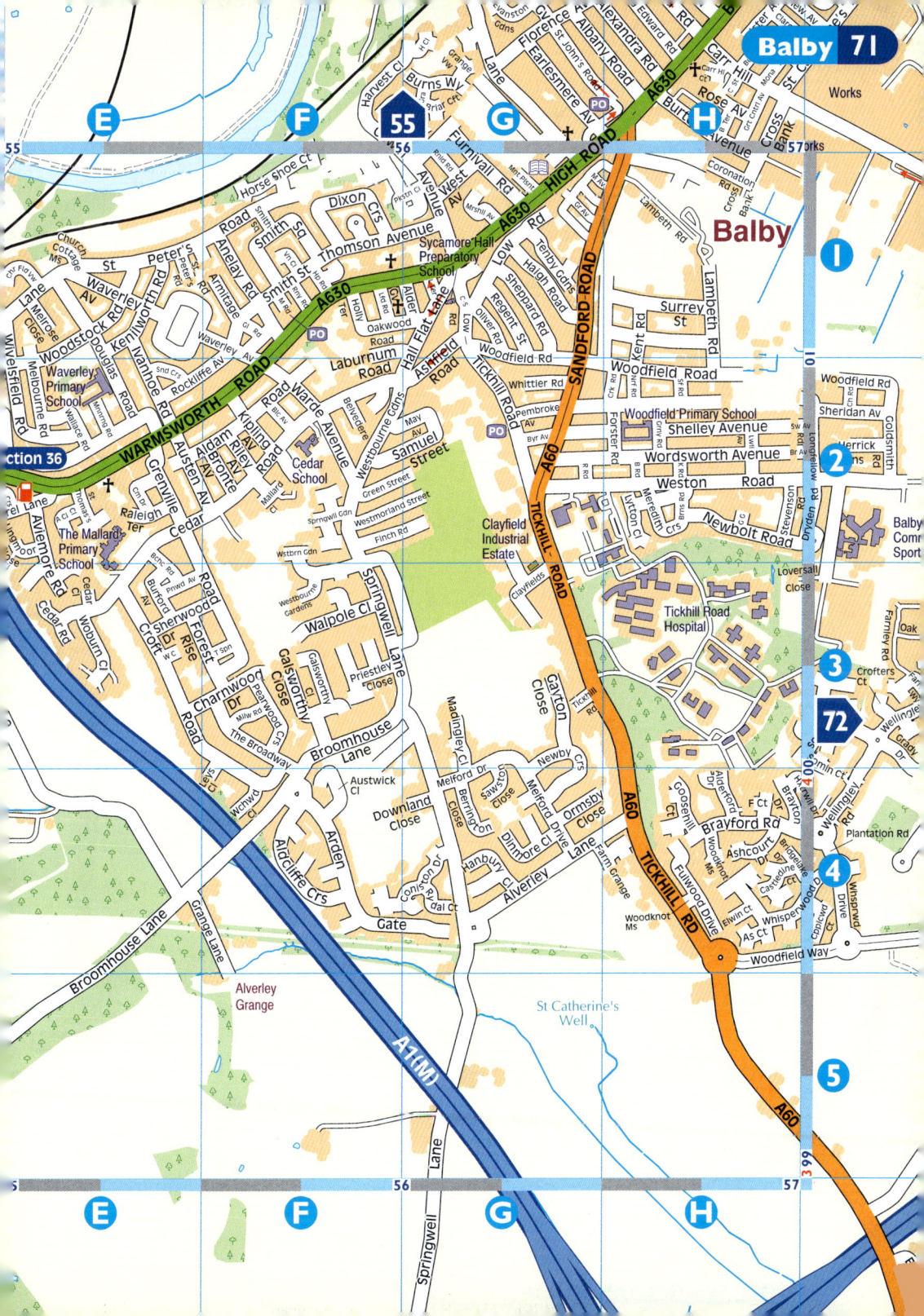

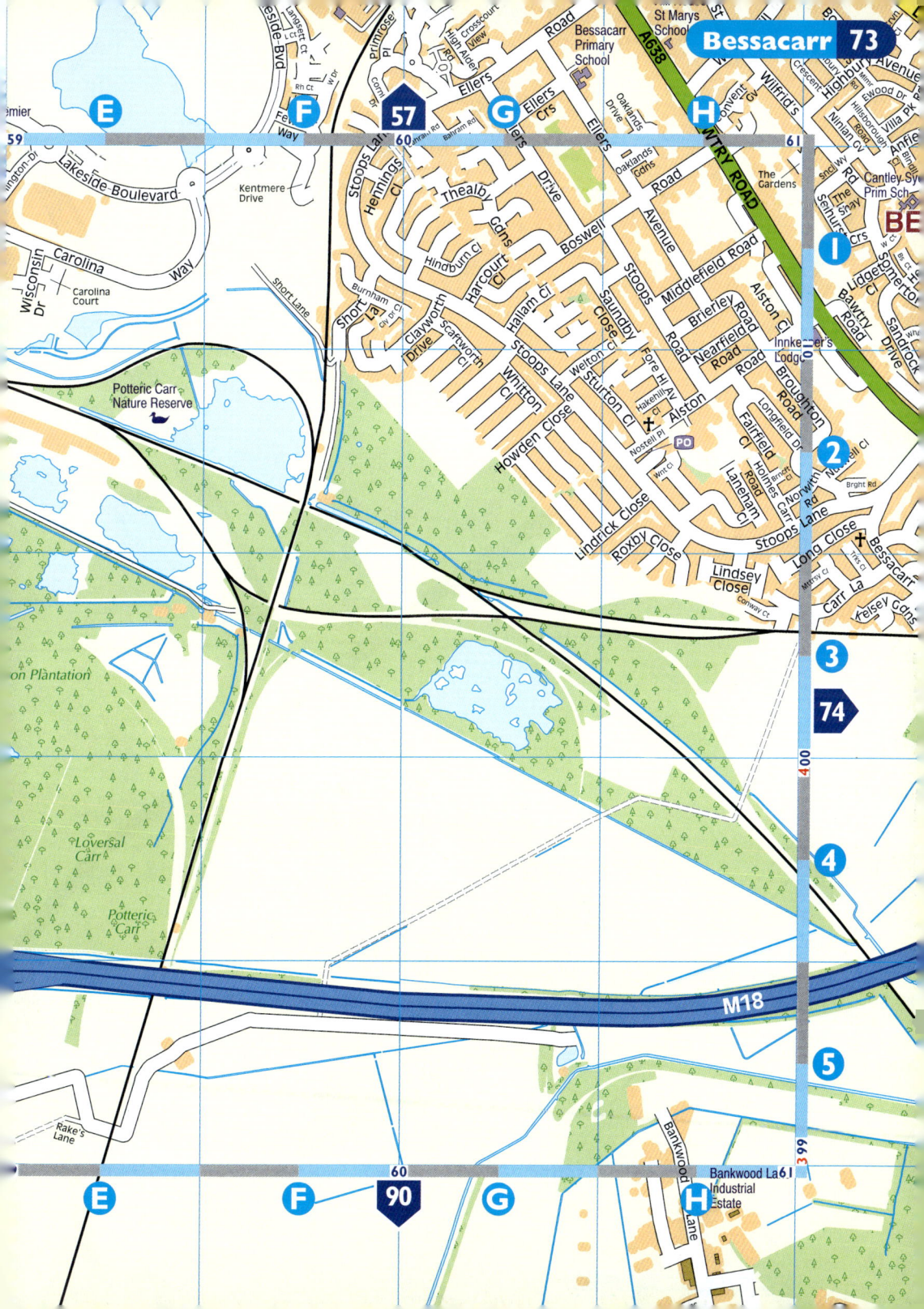

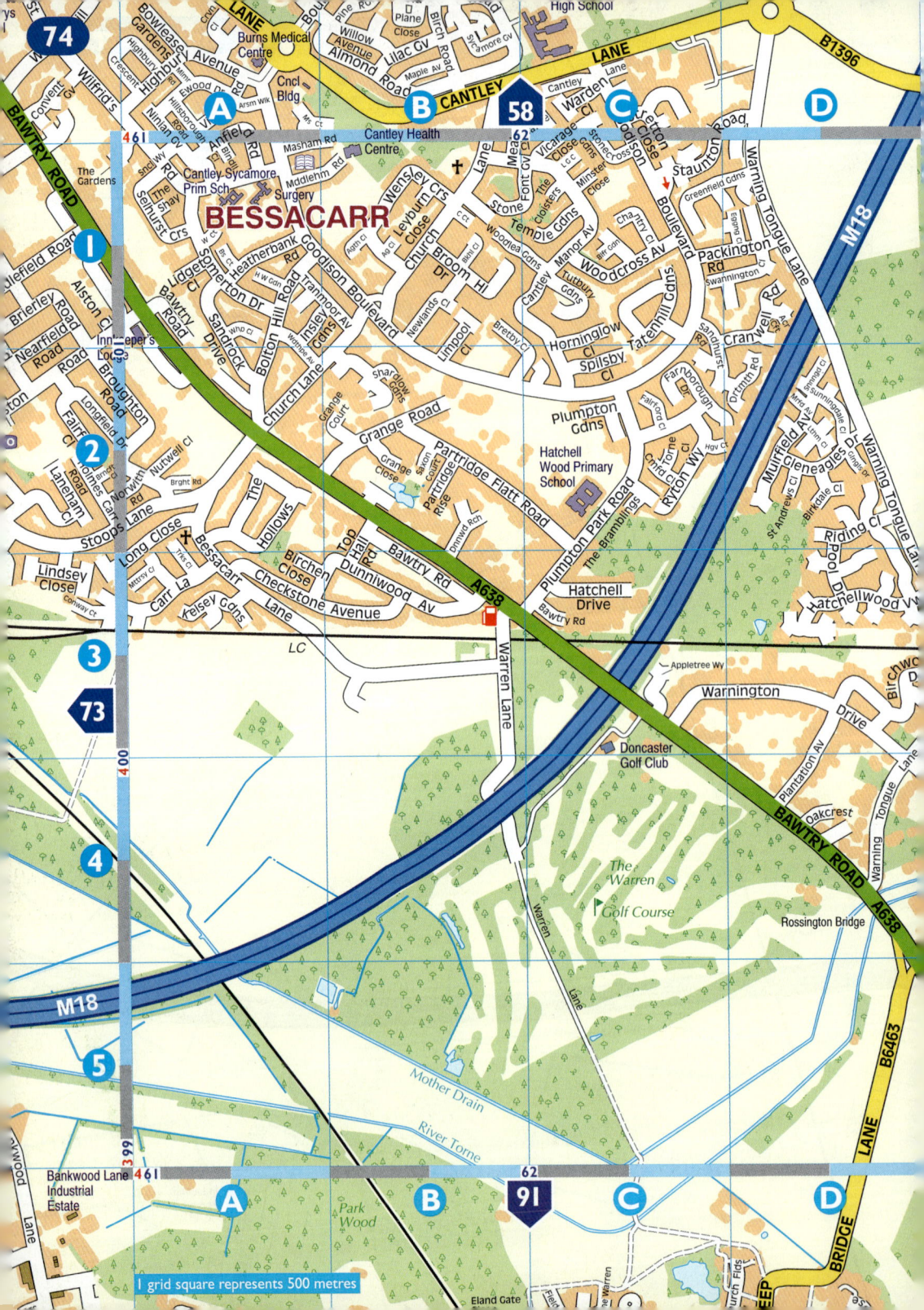

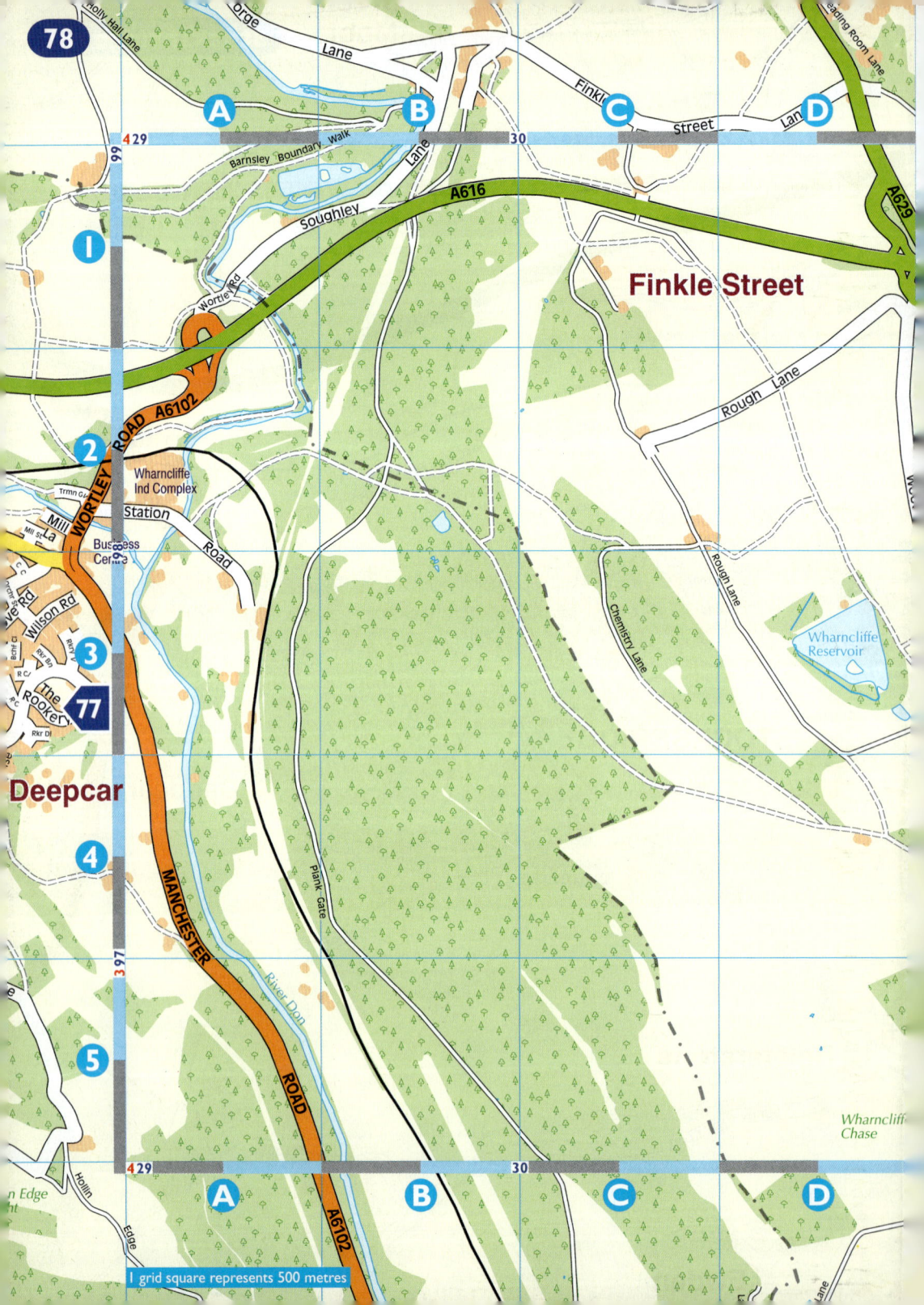

78

Holly Hall Lane
orge Lane
Finkle Street
Leading Room Lane

A **B** **C** **D**

4 29
99

Barnsley Boundary Walk

Soughley Lane

A616

Finkle Street

A629

I

Wortley Rd

ROAD A6102

Rough Lane

2

Wharncliffe
Ind Complex

Station

Trmn Gr

Road

MILL
Mll La

Wilson Rd

Business
Centre

Rough Lane

Chemistry Lane

Wharncliffe
Reservoir

3

R C
The Rookery
Rkr Dl

WORTLEY

77

Deepcar

4

MANCHESTER

Plank Gate

397

ROAD

A6102

River Don

5

Wharncliff
Chase

n Edge
Edge
Hollin

4 29

A **B** **C** **D**

E F G H

Bromley

Trans Pennine Trail

Howbrook Lane

Fields

Pea

Lane

Cross Lane

Storrs Lane

A616

I

Bromley Carr Road

Carr Head Road

Howbrook

2

Hollinberry Lane

Barnsley Boundary Walk

Ashwood Close

3

80

Boswell Close

Renshaw

Ashwood

NEW

WESTW

Furness Road

Tompso

Her

S

Whinmoor

**Cundy
Houses**

A629

Barnsley Boundary Walk

Berry Lane

Bank Lane

Smithy Fold
Lane

Barnsley Boundary Walk

**Potter
Hill**

Tompson H

Boom

Hague La

O

dge Road

Carlthorpe Grove

4

Lodge
Lane

Hazelshaw Farm

A629

A61

5

PENISTONE

HALLW

E F G H

92

84

Hall Lane

A

B

64

C

Golf Cou

D

Watl
Golf

Abdy

1

Hoober
Hall

Hoober Field

America Lane

ROAD

Abdy Road

2

HOOBER   LANE

Hoober

ANGEL LANE

B6089

WENTW

3

83

B6091

CORTWORTH   LANE

STUBBIN   ROAD

Symonds Avenue

Symonds Av

Harding

New Mdw

Ha

4

Rotherham
Roundwalk

Haugh Road

Stubbin Lane

Green Ri

Harding Avenue

**Upper
Haugh**

Raw
Mon
Jun

S62

5

Daniel Lane

Chapel Wy

**Nether
Haugh**

Back Lane

Marriott Place

Hn Rd

A

B

97

C

THE

D

WHIN

1 grid square represents 500 metres

Rake's Lane

459

99

73

60

Bankwood Lane

Bankwood Lane Industrial Estate

Bankwood Crs

Holmes Carr Crs

Holmes Carr

Granby Lane

Henry Lane

King

McConnel

We...

St Catherine's Well Stream

98

Council Building

Council Building

King Georges Cl

Holmes Carr Great Wood

Rutland Lane

Attlee Avenue

George's

Grange Lane Infant School

Grange Lane

Carr Bank

Egg Lane

397

Rossington Grange Farm

Stancil Lane

459

60

Wellingley

1 grid square represents 500 metres

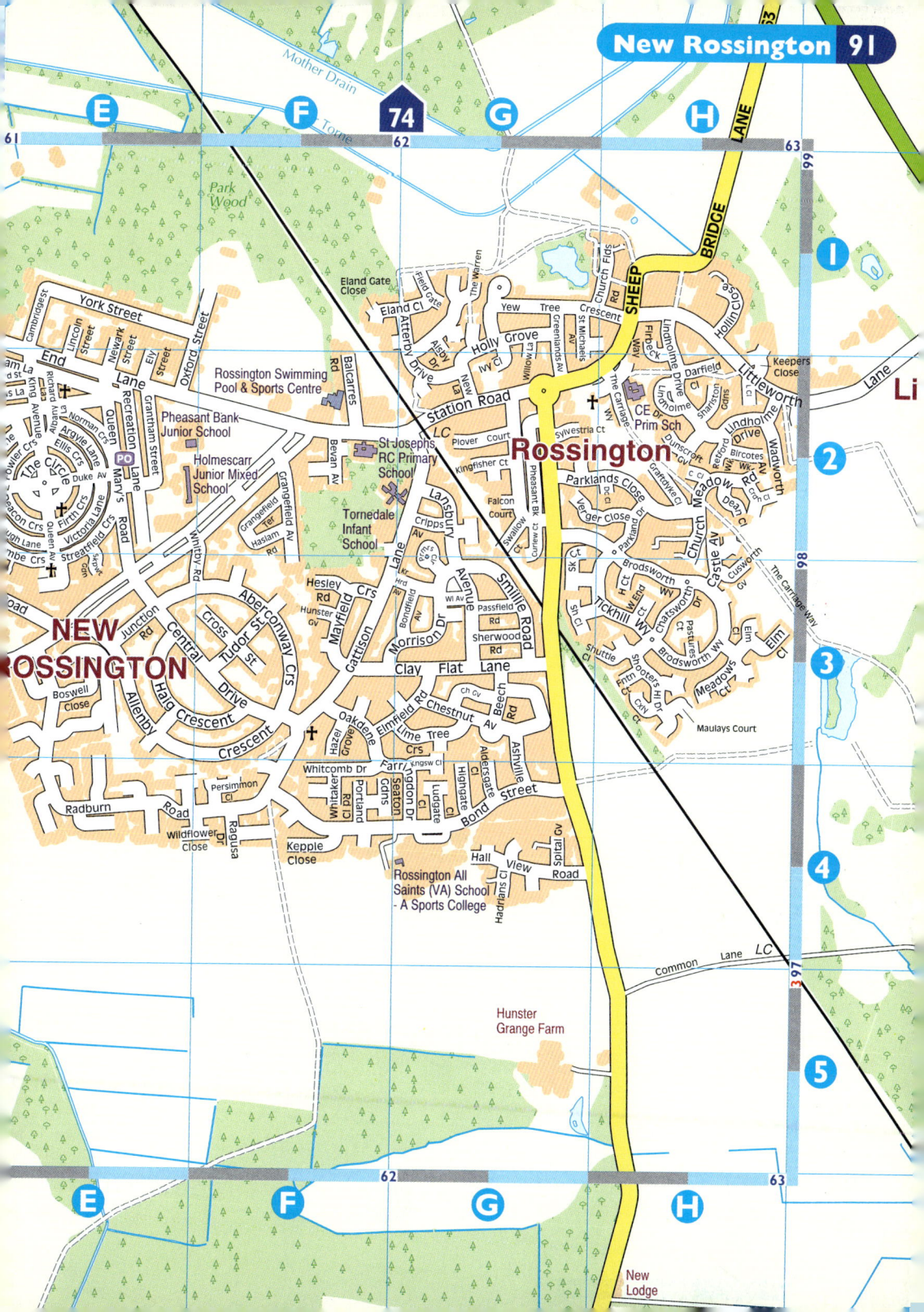

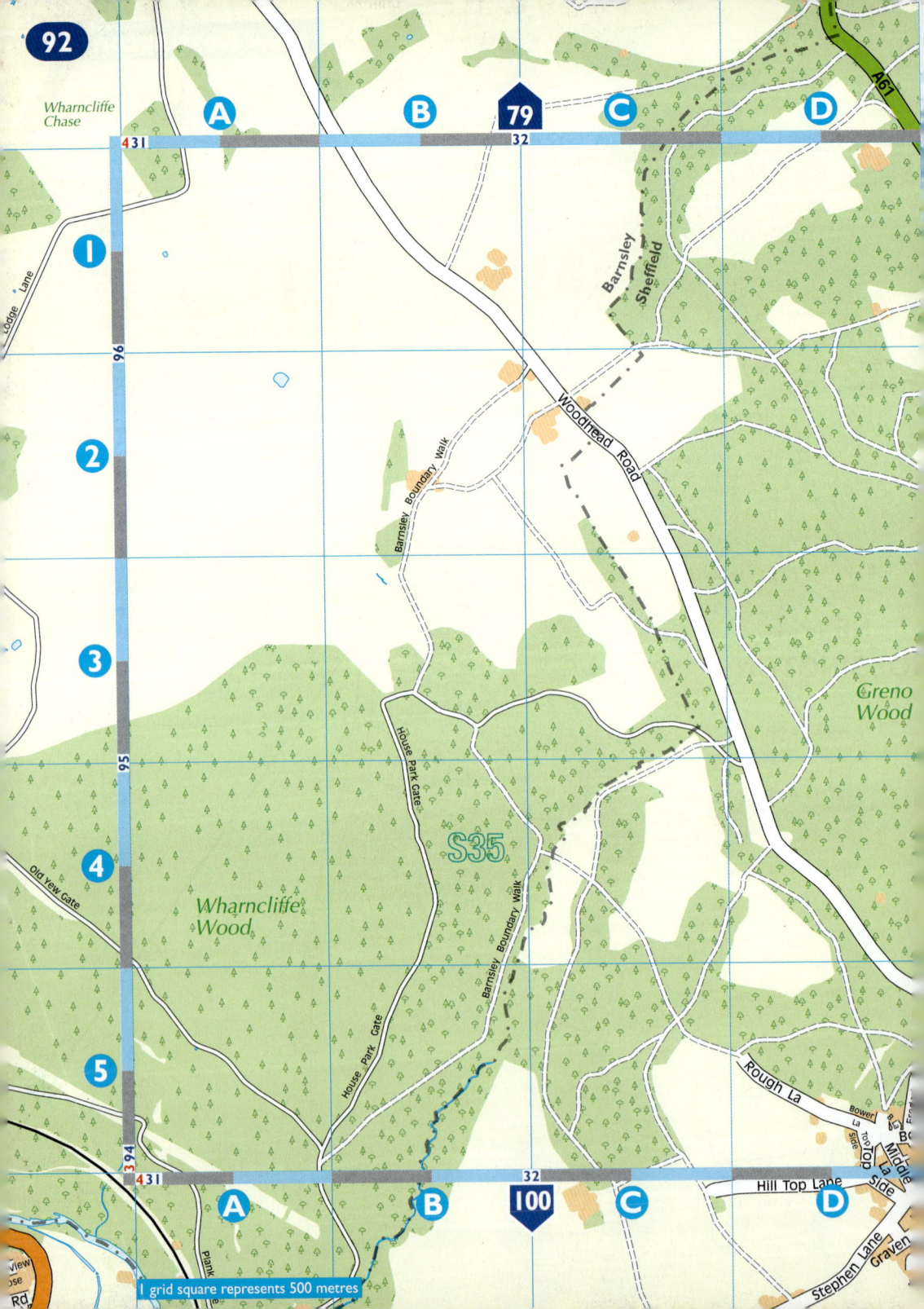

92

Wharncliffe
Chase

A   B   **79**   C   D

4 3 1   32

1

Lodge Lane

96

2

3

95

Barnsley
Sheffield

Woodhead Road

Barnsley Boundary Walk

Greno
Wood

House Park Gate

S35

4

Old Yew Gate

Wharncliffe
Wood

Barnsley Boundary Walk

5

House Park Gate

Rough La

Bower

Top Side

Middle Side

3 9 4

4 3 1   32

A   B   **100**   C   Hill Top Lane   D

Stephen Lane

Craven

view
ose
Rd

Plank

94

Lound Junior School.

Housley Pk **A** Arundel Road **B** CHAPELTOWN **81** **C** **D**

36

Commerce Street

Chapeltown Station

LOUND SIDE

Fairfield

St Giles Sq **1**

Swimming Baths

Smith St

Surgery

Woodburn Drive

Glenwood Crescent

Harvey Rd

Birch Avenue

Chapel Road **2**

Willow Crescent

Park View Road

Hazel Gv

Albany Avenue

Surgery

Hesley Gv

Wood Close

Grove

Cowley Hill A629

Smithy Wood Road

M1

Redwood Glen

Pine Croft

Pinecroft Way

Park Avenue

Coit Primary School

Cowley View Rd

Stuart Road

Broadway Avenue

Westbury Avenue

Cowley La

Wellbourne Close

Cowley Ln

Cowley Dr

3

93

Ecclesfield School

Crakehall Road

Hunshelf Lane

A6135 ECCLESFIELD ROAD

Nether Lane

Whitley Lane **4**

CHAPELTOWN ROAD A6135

Whitley Crt

Shardlows Sports Club

Works

Works

Works

Mellor Lea Farm Garth

Mellor Lea Farm Chase

Whitley View

Mellor Lea Farm Drive

Johnson Lane

Loicher Lane

5

Works

Priory Close

Priory Rd

CHURCH STREET

B6087

Mill Road

THE COMMON A6135

Washington Road

Works

Works

Station Road

Starnhill Close

Atlas Business Park

Cemetery

Surgery

Ecclesfield Health Centre

Linden Road

Ecclesfield

Scholes View

394

Town End Road

STOCKS HILL

Yew La

The Brambles

Scholes Rd

A **B** Minst **102** GREEN LANE **C** Butterthwaite Lane **D**

36

Greaves Road

EPPiC Theatre

High Street

Primrose Drive

Hallam

Hilton

Nurser Dr

Floodgate

Caribbean Sports Club

I grid square represents 500 metres

A
B
83
40
C
D

439

Scholes Lane

Morley Pond

Dog Kennel Pond

I

96

Roundwalk

Rotherham

2

The Paddock

Scholes

Scholes Gn

Town Lane

Cemetery

Lapwater Rd

Rockingham J&I School

Wingfield

Roughwood

Wensleydale Road

Nidderdale

Teesdale

Calder Rd

Eskdale Rd

3

95

Scholes Coppice

S61

Town Lane

Wingfield Rd

4

Keppel Drive

Keppel's Column

Rd

Keppel Ct

Kelvin Ct

Middlewood Dr

Monks Close

Admirals Crest

Hesley Grange

Wrth Pl

Hesley Mews

Cedarwood Ct

The Coppice

Studmoor Road

Pepper Close

Becket Crs

Crumwell Rd

The Willows

Fox Close

Beevers Rd

Maycock Avenue

Town Lane

Oaks La

Remount Rd

Cloverf

Strafford

Ashworth Dr

Asp Cl

Shearman Av

Clover Rd

Roughwood Road

Roughwood Primary School

Jewitt Rd

sd

Crane Road

Lovetot

Hudson Road

Maycock R

Sandbergh Road

Kimberworth Park

Elliott Dr

5

Pennine Trail

Studmoor Rd

Oaks Lane

Abdy Road

Redscope Crs

Rhodes Av

Wellfield Rd

Cinderhill Rd

Kimberworth

Binders Rd

Wheatley Rd

Duke Cs

Sellars Rd

Ox Close

Neville Road

Gloucester Av

Chambers Rd

Habershon Road

Walker Rd

Simmonite Rd

Dropping Well

UPPER WORTLEY ROAD

A629

Hungerhill Road

Grange Rd

Redscope Road

Upper Wortley Road

Drp Fr Cl

Warris Cl

Park Rd

Kimberworth Park Clinic

Birks Rd

PO

Surgery

Leybourne Rd

Byrley Road

Morley Rd

Hutton Road

Bents Rd

Knt Cl

BBC

Barber Balk Road

Wood Rd

Wd Cl

Spr Cft

Ten Acr

3 94

439

A
B
104
40
C
D

Watson Glen

Farm Rd

Webster Rd

Hill Vw Rd

Carr Vw Rd

Keppel Vw Rd

Well Vw Rd

B View Rd

View

H Vw

West View

Great Park

Eilam Road

Kimberworth Park Medical Centre

Warren Hill

Ten Acr

Croft

St.Bedes RC Primary School

PO

Eilam Cl

Manor

WORTLEY

Watson

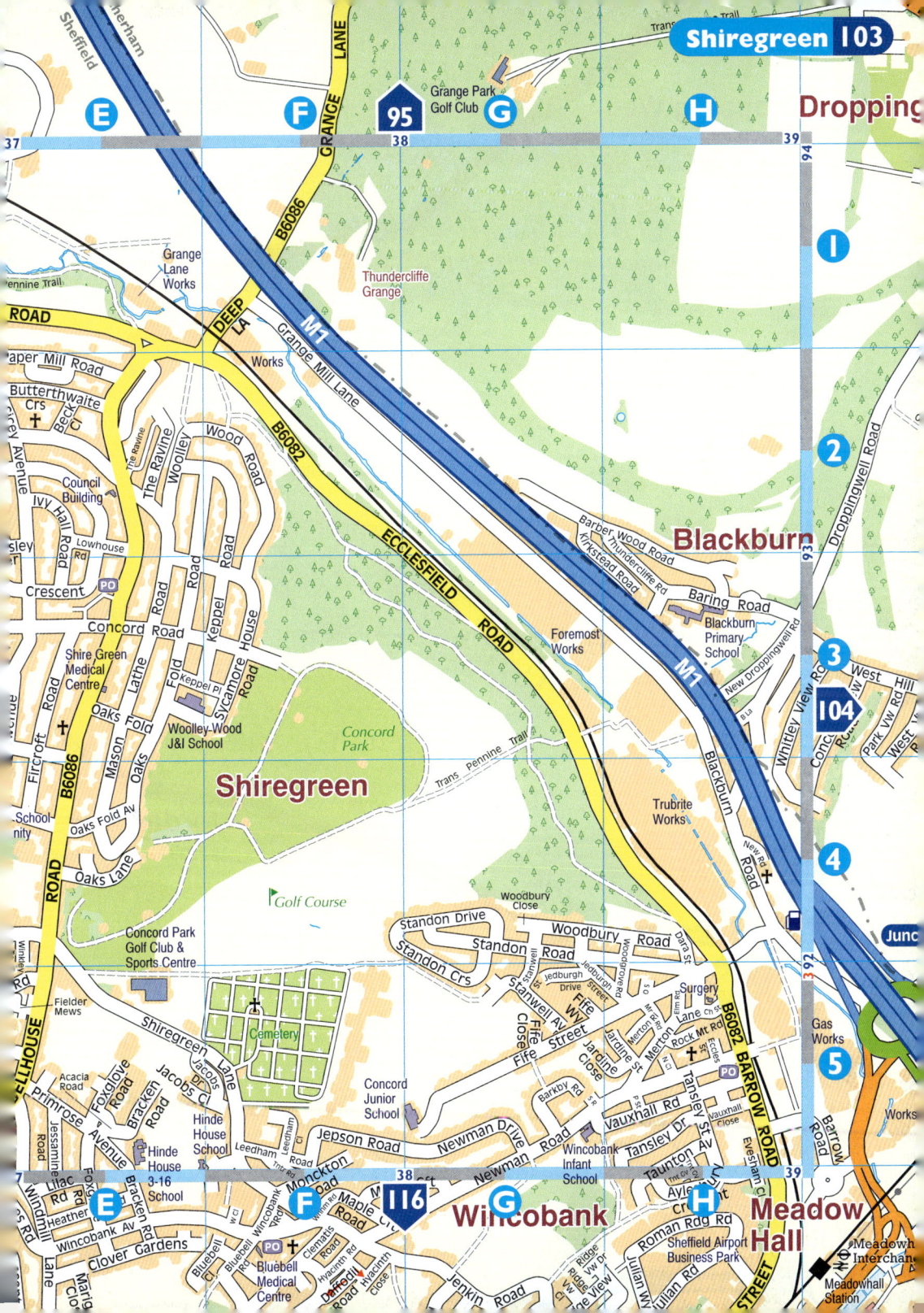

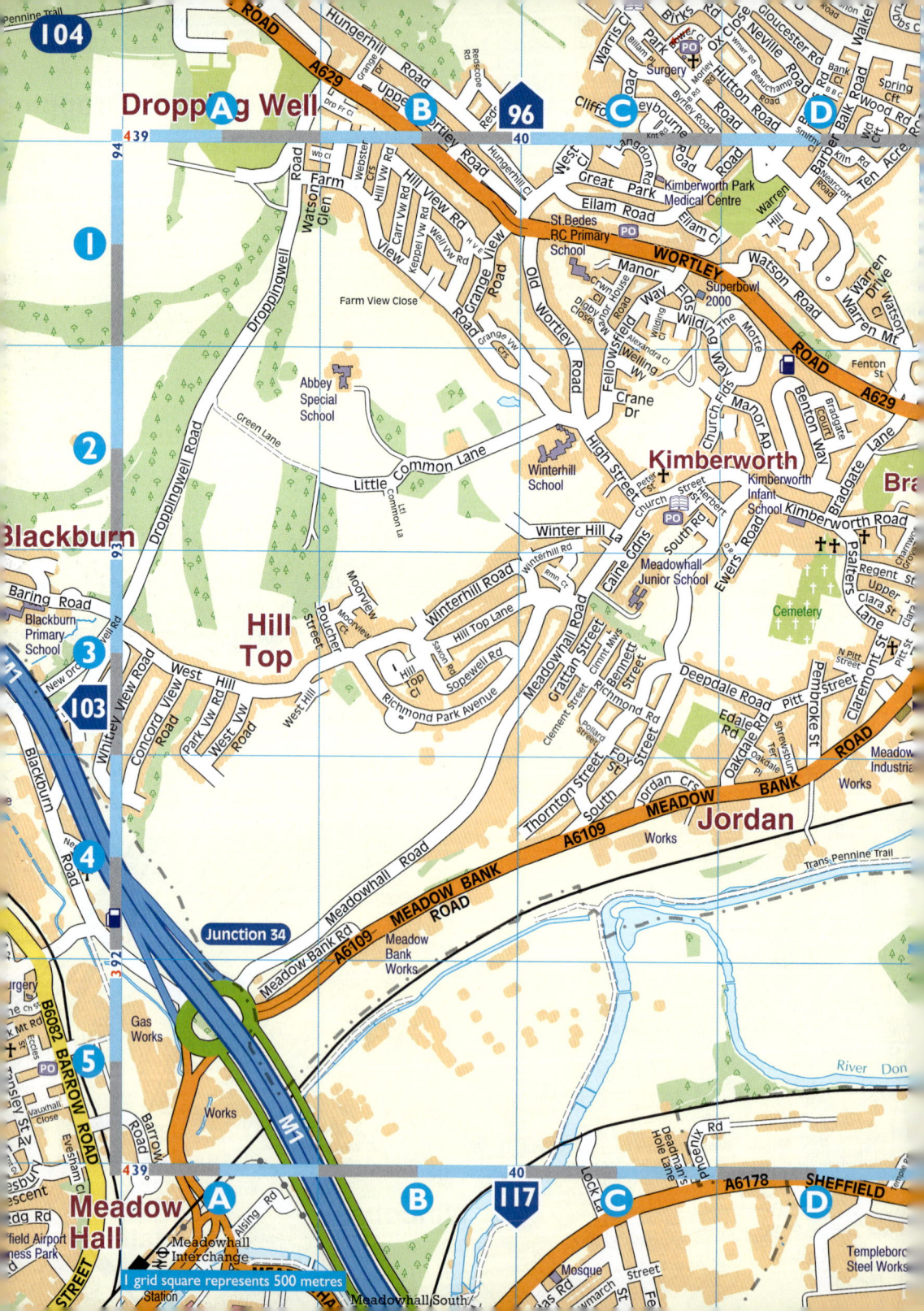

Holdworth

A   B   **Low Ash Farm** C   D

Holdworth Lane

4 29   30

Darwent Lane

Kirk Ed

Yews Day Hospital

Long Lane

Stubbing Lane

Myers Lane

1

Lin House Lane

West Lane

9 91

Loxley Common

2

Stacey Lane

LOXLEY

ROAD

Loxley Chase

Lea Bank Farm

Phillips

Hunters Rd

Gardens

France

Archer Ga

Lee

Stacey Bank

Storrs Bridge Lane

Storrs Bridge

Dunkerley Road

Chase Road

3

9 90

Works

Leaton Cl

Hanson

Loxley Rd

The Cha

Rodney

Loxley

Long Lane

Storrs Green

Carr

Works

Rowell Lane

Wisewood Cemetery

4

Storrs Green

Black

Lane

Greaves Lane

5

Spout La

Storrs

Storrs Lane

Spout Lane

Rowell Lane

Drive

Acorn Cl

Mill Wd Vw

Holme Way

Mdw

Nook Lane

Robin Hood Chase

Greaves Lane

Furness

Acorn Hl

High Matloc

3 89

Lane

Lomas

Nook Lane Junior School

Durmast Grove

Friar Cl

Darley

4 29   30

1 123

Hammoor Road

High Matlock

A   B   Spinney   C   D

Ockside Lane

Spoon Lane

Acornway

Spout Lane

Acorn Dr

Acorn Dr

Hill Cl

Greaves

Friar Cl

Cliff Rd

Falcon Road

Pond Rd

Cliff Road

High Matlock Gdns

St

B6076

1 grid square represents 500 metres

Knowle Close

STANNINGTON

Works

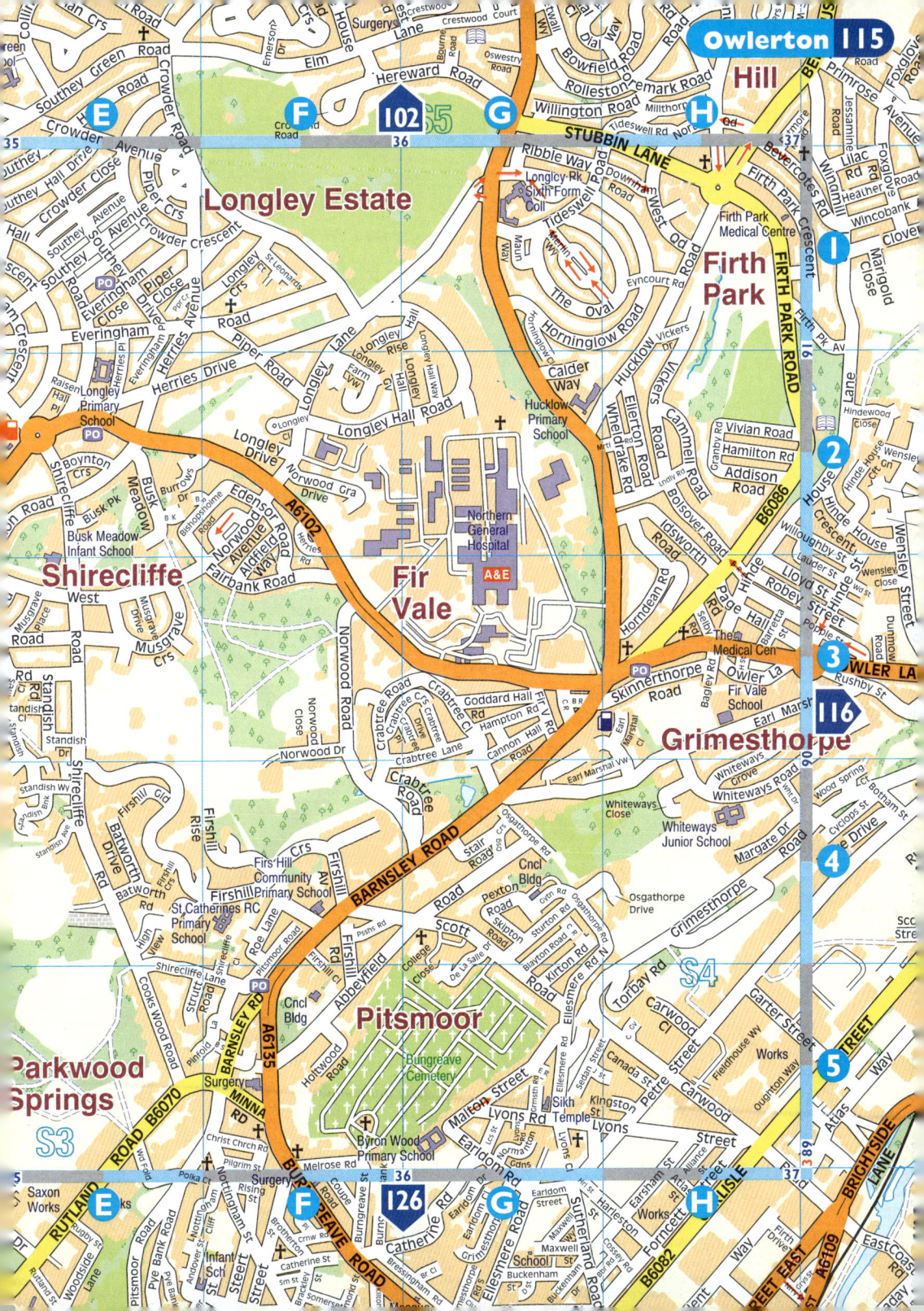

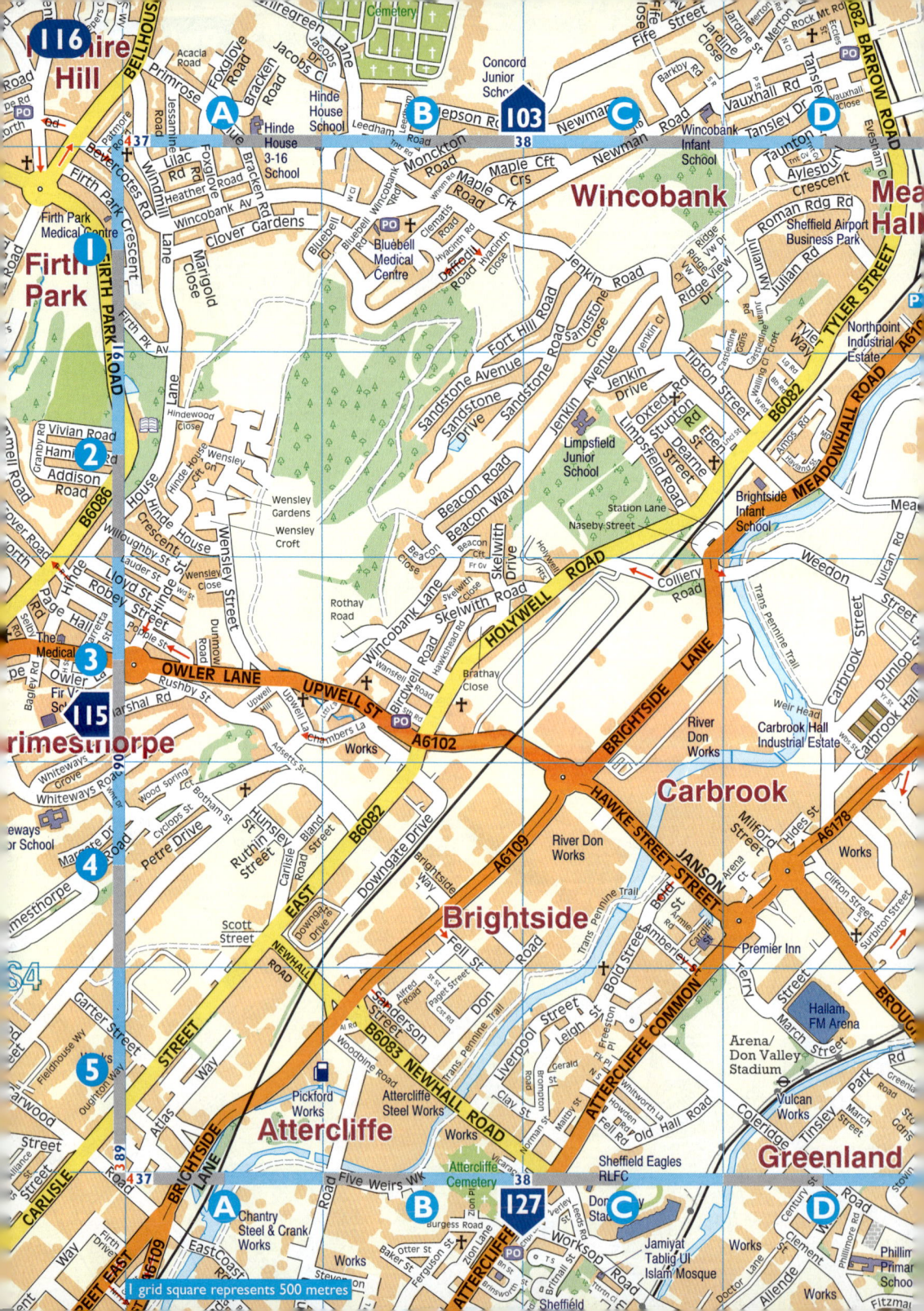

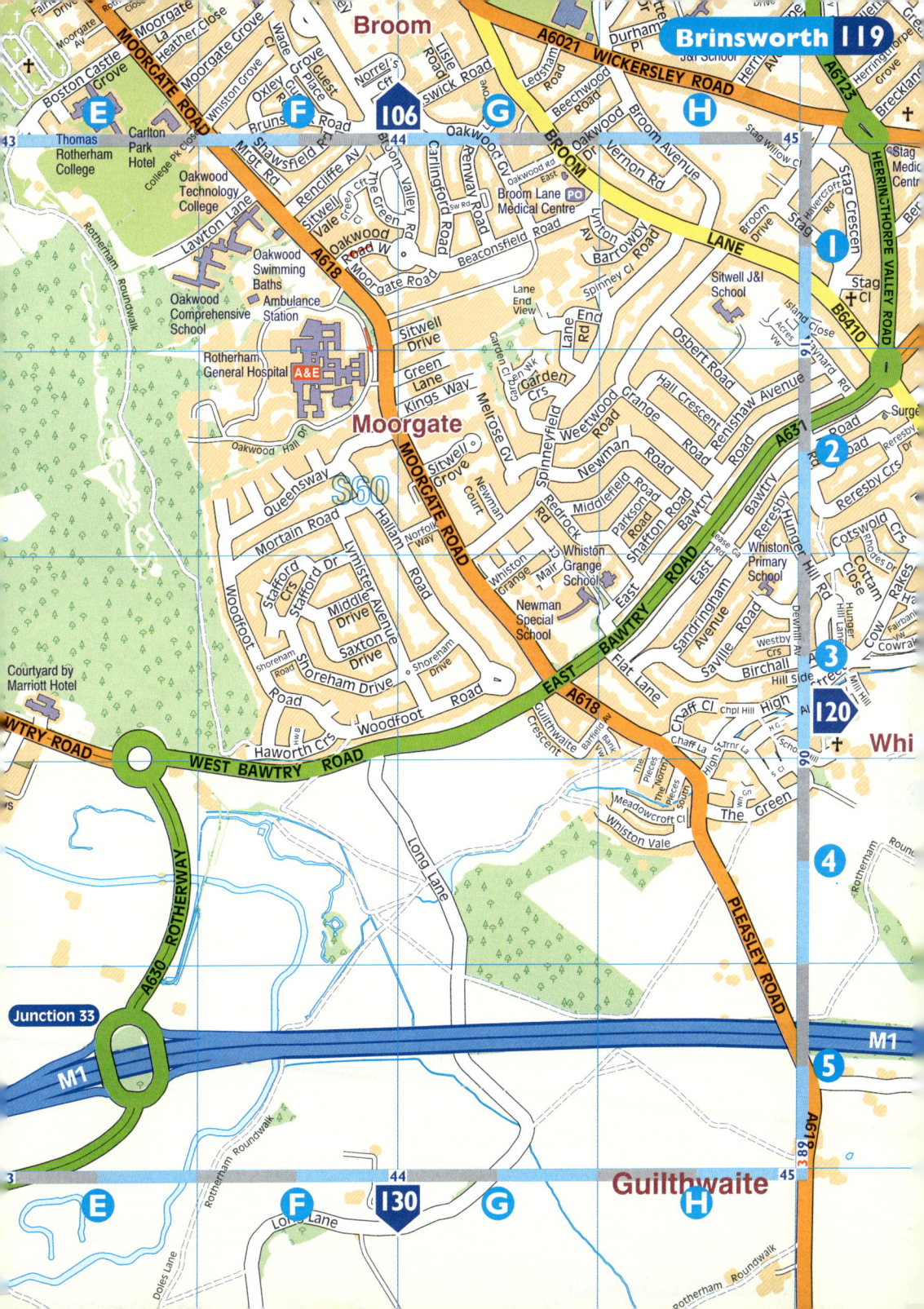

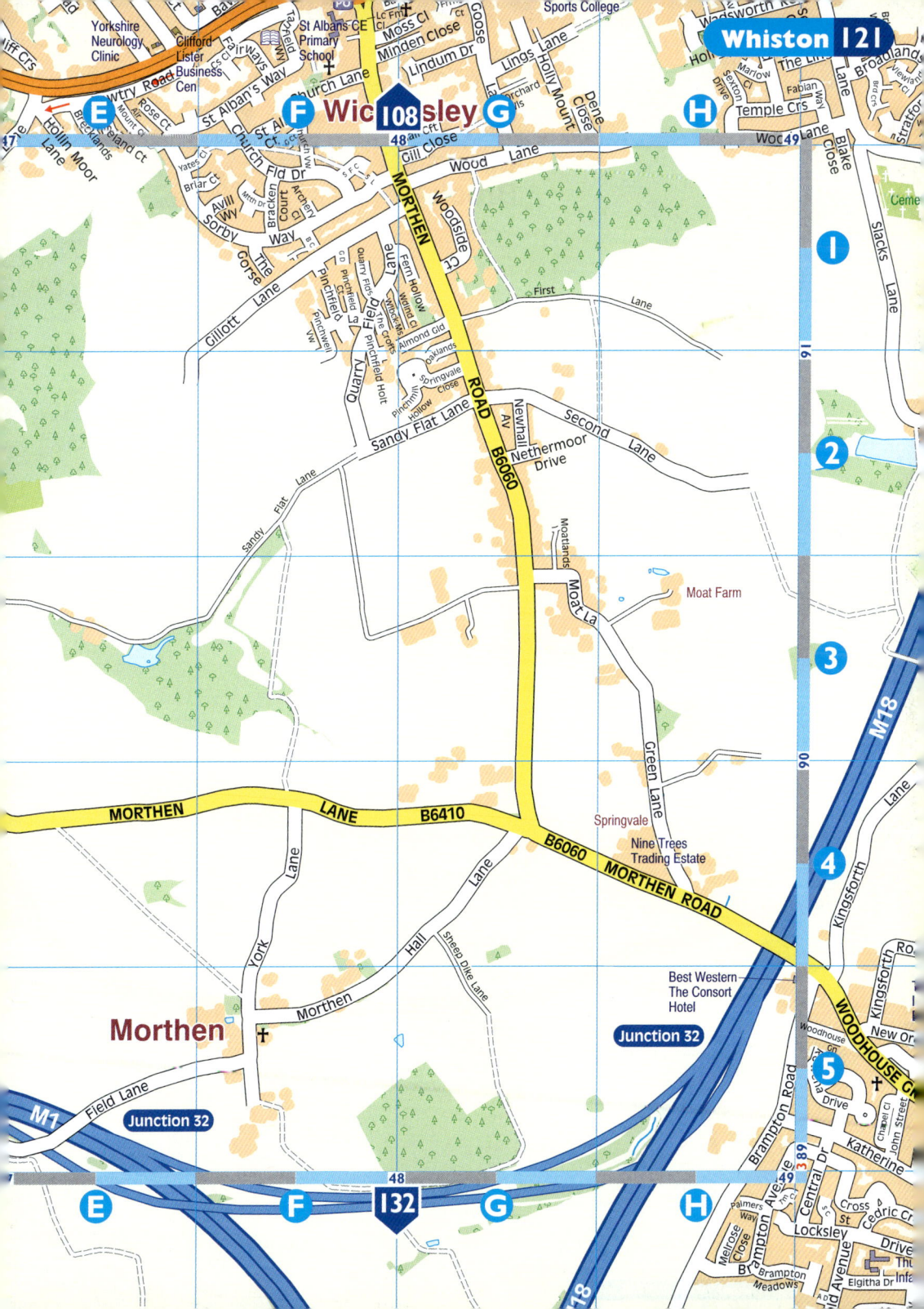

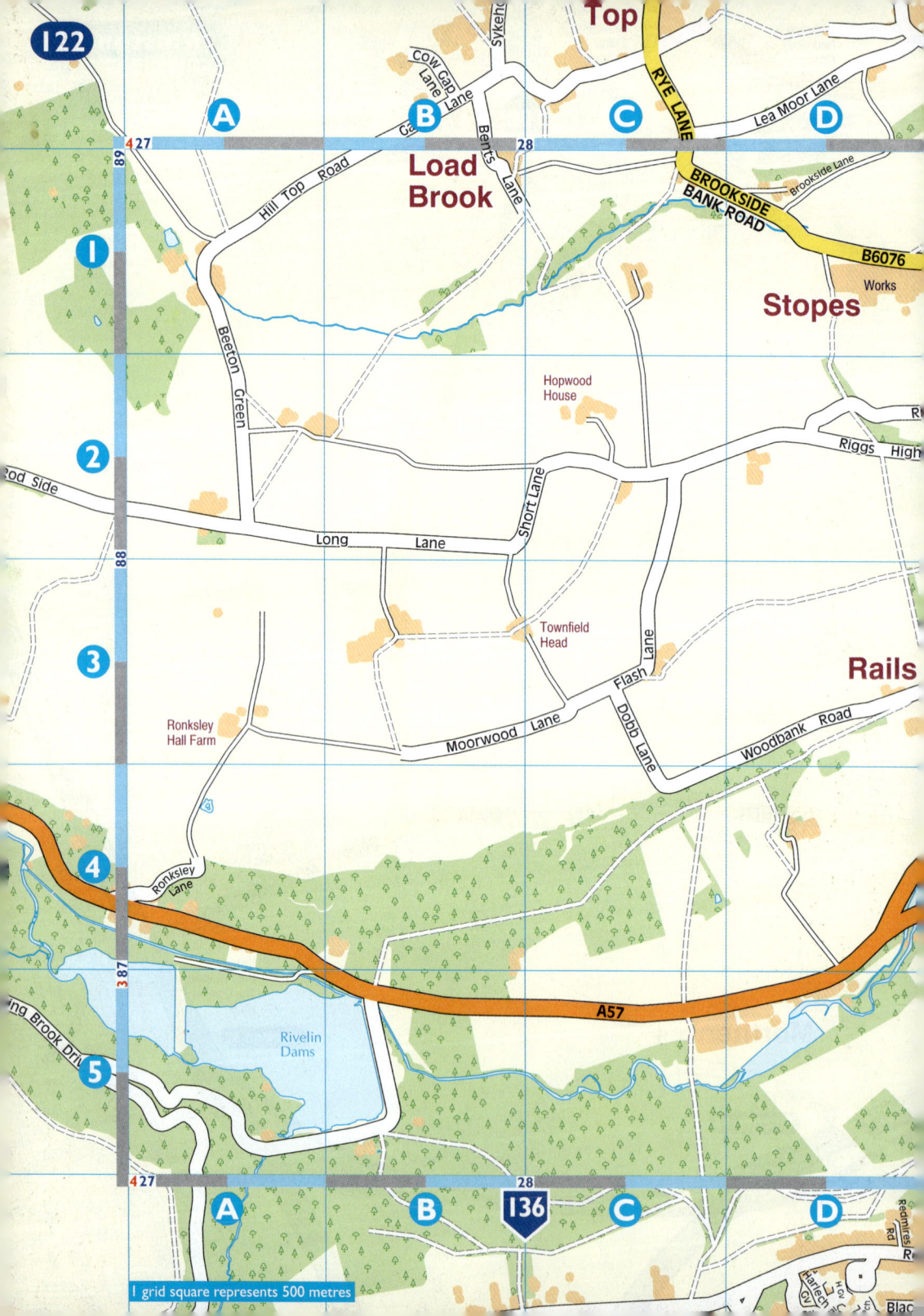

122

A   B   C   D

Top

Cow Gap Lane

Syke...

RYE LANE

Lea Moor Lane

Load Brook

Berts Lane

Hill Top Road

BROOKSIDE BANK ROAD

Brookside Lane

Stopes

Works

B6076

1

Beeton Green

Hopwood House

Riggs High

2

...od Side

Long Lane

Short Lane

3

Townfield Head

Rails

Ronksley Hall Farm

Moorwood Lane

Flash Lane

Dobb Lane

Woodbank Road

4

Ronksley Lane

5

...ing Brook Driv...

Rivelin Dams

A57

Blac...

Redmires R...

Harlech...

A   B   **136**   C   D

1 grid square represents 500 metres

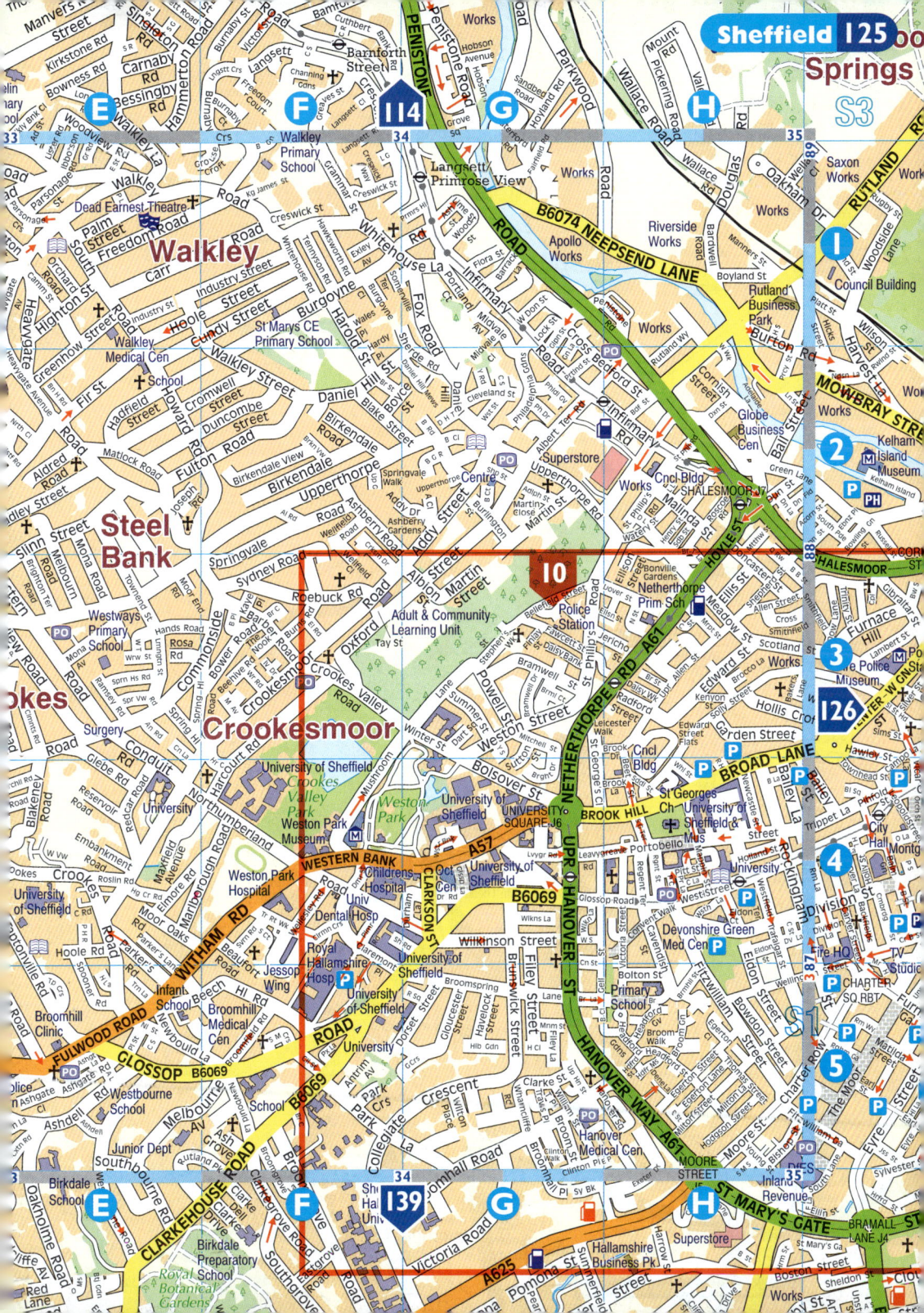

S9

A B 117 C Sheffield Airport Business D

Europa Cl
Europa Cl
Shepcote Way

Europa   Link
Letsby Av
Letsby   Avenue
Sheffield City Airport

Tinsley Pk Rd
Tinsley Pk Close
Huntsmans Gdns
Stevin Street

GREENLAND ROAD
A6371

Phillimore Park Primary School

Fitzmaurice Rd
Jubilee Rd
Chapelwood Rd

Greenland Rd
Greenland Way
Greenland Road
GREENLAND ROAD

Tinsley Industrial Estate

Tinsley Park Cemetery

Works

Tinsley Park

Trans Pennine Trail

I

Stovin Dr
Clipstone Gdns

Pennet

Barleywood Rd

Works

Coleford Road

Works

2

Surgery

Mosque

Darnall Cemetery

Darnall

Catley   Road

Works

Trans Pennine Trail

Balfour Rd
Barnaldiston Road
Main Rd
Fisher Lane
Catley Pl

Darnall Health Centre

Infield   Lane

High Hazels Golf Club

Infield Lane

YORK ROAD A6102

Works

Greenlands J&I School

B6200

Britannia Rd

Senior   Rd

Eslmham   Road

Golf Course

Golf Course

3

Darnall Stn

Cncl Bldg

Poole Road

MAIN   ROAD   B6200

Olivers Dr

Olivers Mount

127

Colister Gdns
Poole Place
James St
Pearce
Halsall Dr

Willow   Drive
Maple   Grove
Hall
Chestnut Avenue
Alder Lane
Larch Hill

Hill Lane

Works

SHEFFIELD PARKWAY A630

4

Hill Primary School

Prince of Wales Road Medical Centre

PRINCE OF WALES RD

Handsworth Avenue
Houstead Road

Handsworth Crescent

Round Road

HANDSWORTH ROAD B6200

Road

Quarry Road
Oakley Rd
Halesworth Road
Hall Road
Finchwell Road
Finchwell Close
Finchwell Rd

387

Mather Road
Mather Av
Goore Av
Goore Rd

A6102

Bowden Wd Rd
Bowden Wd
Bowden Wd Dr

Clifton Crs
Clifton Avenue
Clifton Lane

Trans Pennine Trail

HANDSWORTH ROAD

HANDSWORTH

Handsworth Christian Sch

Enfield Place
St Rd

5

Waltheof School

Bowden Wood Crescent

SHEFFIELD   PARKWAY

Handsworth

Portland Business Park

PO

St Joseph's Rd

Travelodge

439

Pipworth Primary School

A B 142 C Medical Cen D

Castlebeck
Saxonlea Ct
Danewood Gardens
Saxonlea

Richmond Park Rise
Richmond Park Avenue
Richmond Park View
Richmond Park Crescent
Birklands Avenue
Birklands Drive
Athelstan Road
Richmond Park

Ashbourne Road
Parley Hay

Fitzalan Rd
ROAD

BLACK STREET

1 grid square represents 500 metres

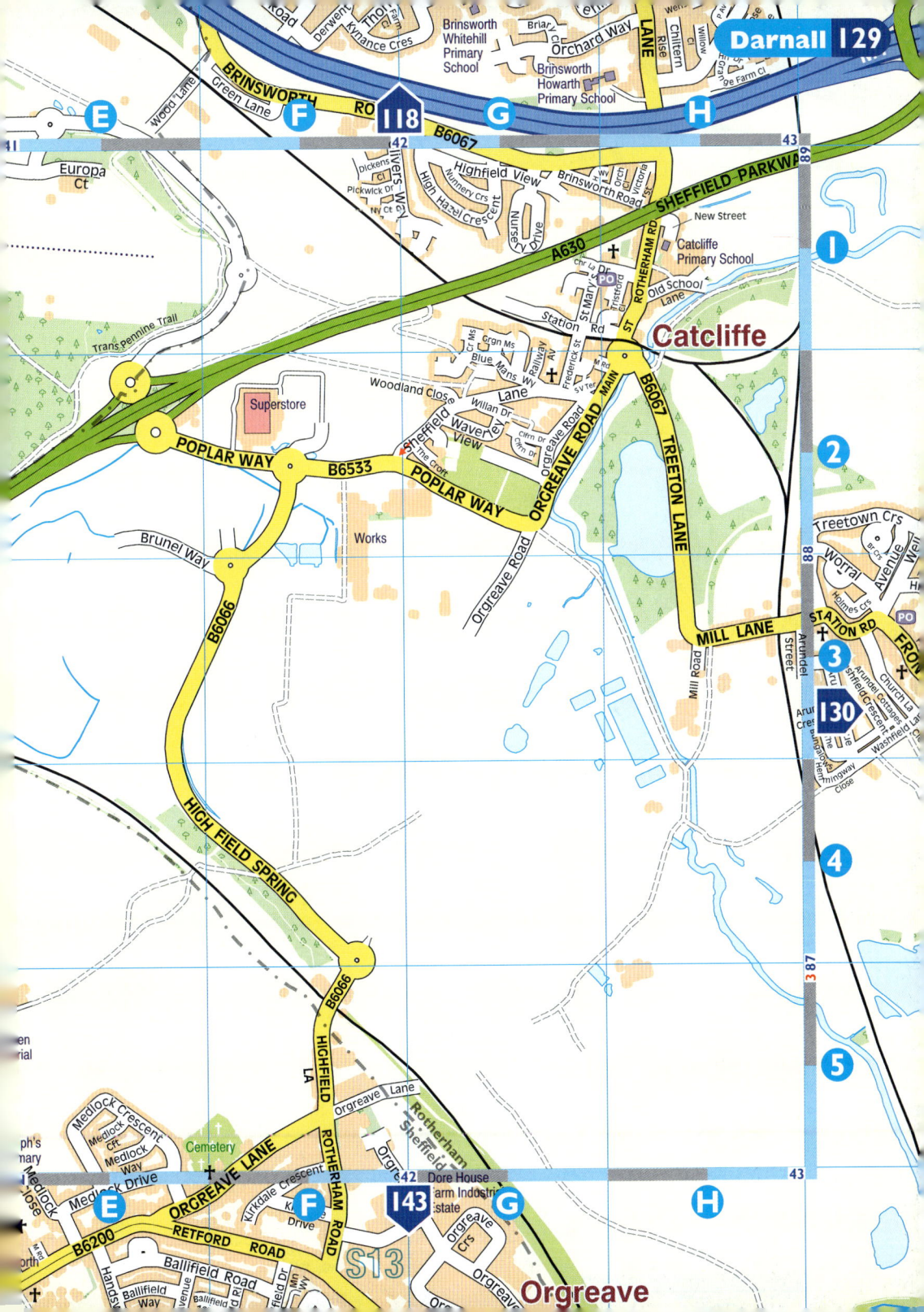

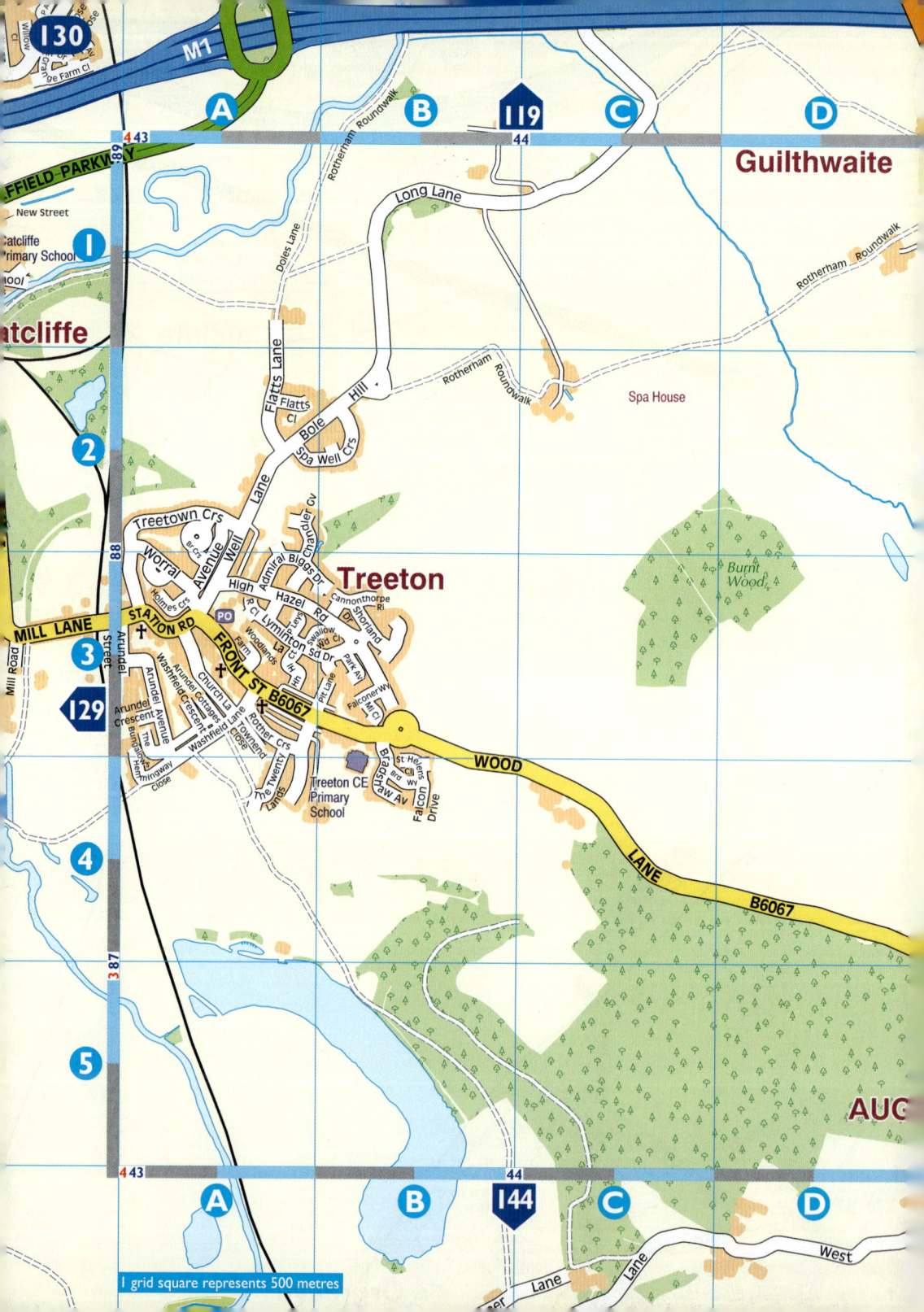

130

M1

New Street

Catcliffe
Primary School

Catcliffe

A

B

119

C

D

Guilthwaite

Long Lane

Doles Lane

Rotherham Roundwalk

Rotherham Roundwalk

Flatts Lane

Flatts Cl

Hill

Bole Lane

Spa Well Crs

Rotherham Roundwalk

Spa House

Burnt Wood

Treetown Crs

Worral

Avenue

Well

High

Admiral Biggs Dr

Chancel Gv

Hazel Rd

Cannonthorpe Ri

Treeton

Holmes Crs

PO

Lymington Dr

Wd Ct

Swallow La Ct

Shortand

Park Av

MILL LANE

STATION RD

Arundel Street

Arundel

Church La

Woodlands

La Ct

In Ct

Pit Lane

WOOD

129

Arundel Crescent

The Bungalows

Minnoway Close

Arundel Cottages

Arundel Avenue

Washfield Crescent

Washfield Lane

Townend Close

Rother Crs

The Twenty Lands

Falconer Wy

Mt Ct

St Helens Brd

St Clms Wy

Badslow Av

Falcon Drive

Treeton CE
Primary School

LANE

B6067

Mill Road

FRONT ST B6067

A

B

144

C

D

AUC

AUG

West

Lane

I grid square represents 500 metres

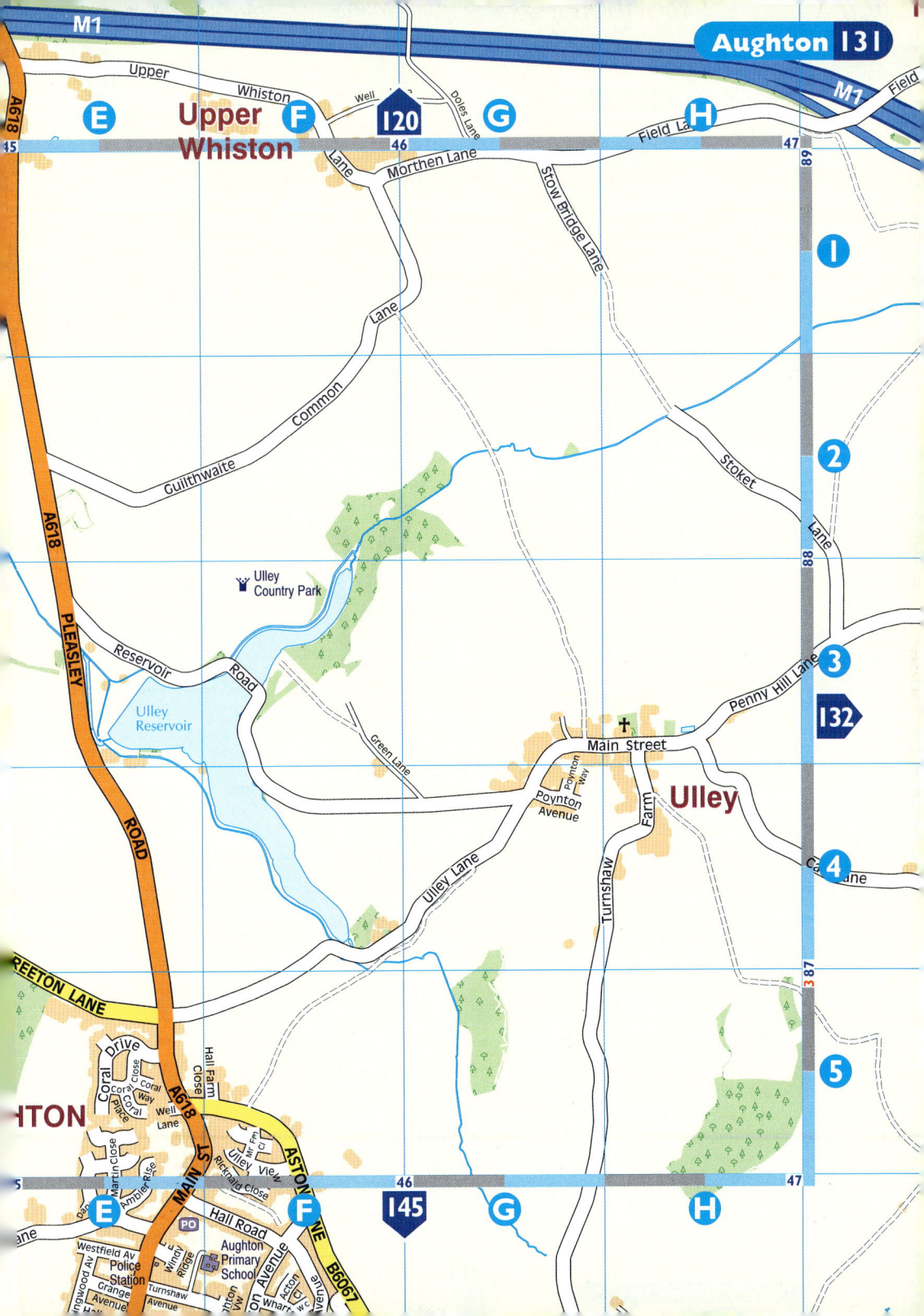

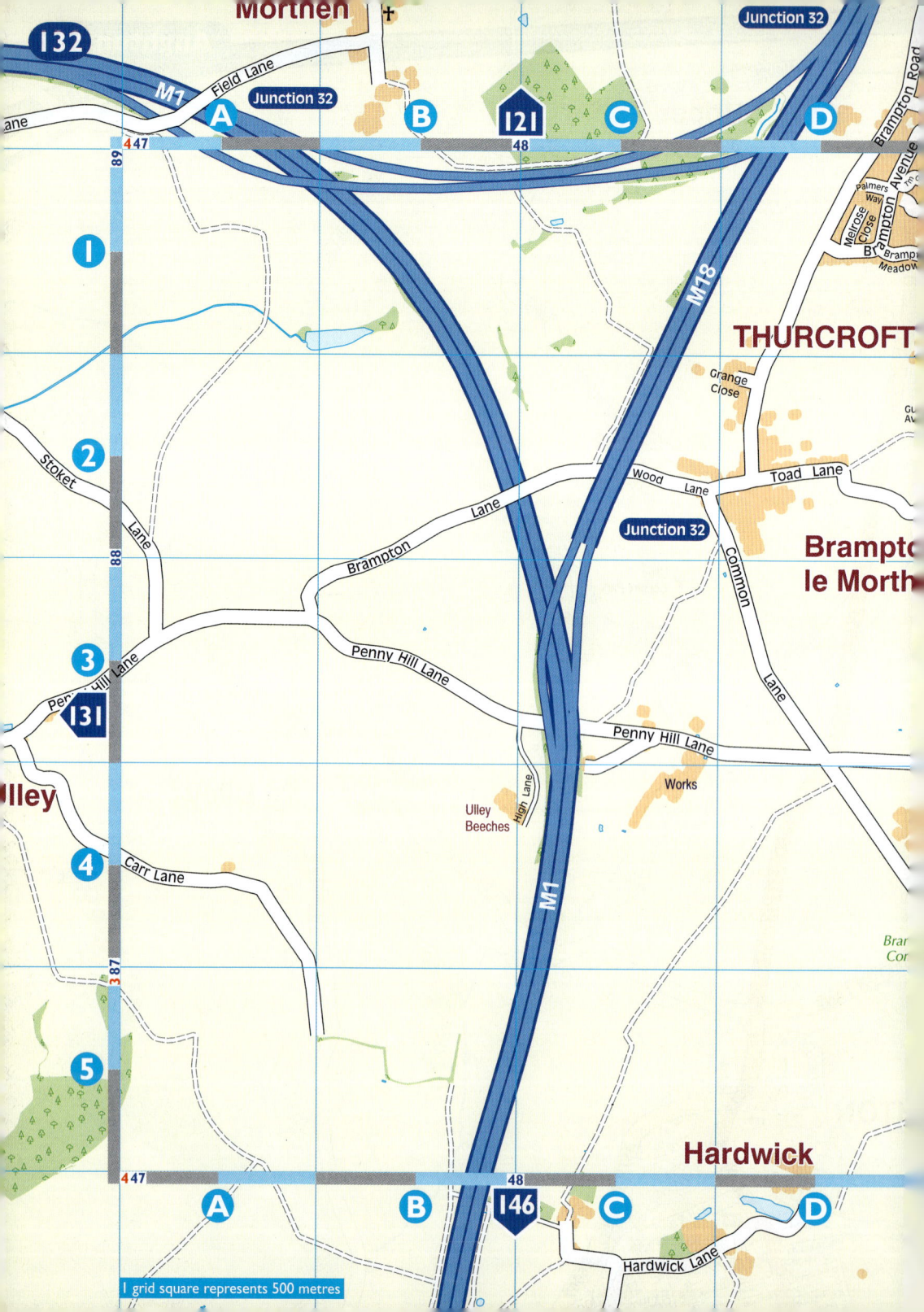

Rivelin
Dams

A   B   122   C   D

4 27   28

I

86

Wyming
Brook Dr

2

Redmires
Lane

Lodge
Moor

Redmires
Rd
Rec

Harlech
GV
H GV
Balmoral

Sandringham Pl
Holyrood Av
Kensington Pk
Kensington
Chatsington Drive

L
Crs
Harlech
Gln
B Ms

Balmoral
Harlech
H VW
Harlow Fold
H Md

Blackb
S
Blac

Lodge
Moor
Road

Knoll
Top Farm

Soughley Lane

Brown Hills Lane

3

Roper Hill

85

Harrison La

Gorse La

4

Fulwood
Head

Harrop
Lane

Foxhall

Douse Croft
Lane

5

Fulwood Lane

Fulwood Head Road

Basset Lane

Andwell
Lane

Greenhouse Lane

Bassett

Brown
Edge
Farm

Porter
Cloug

3 84

4 27   28   Fulwood Lane

A   B   C   D

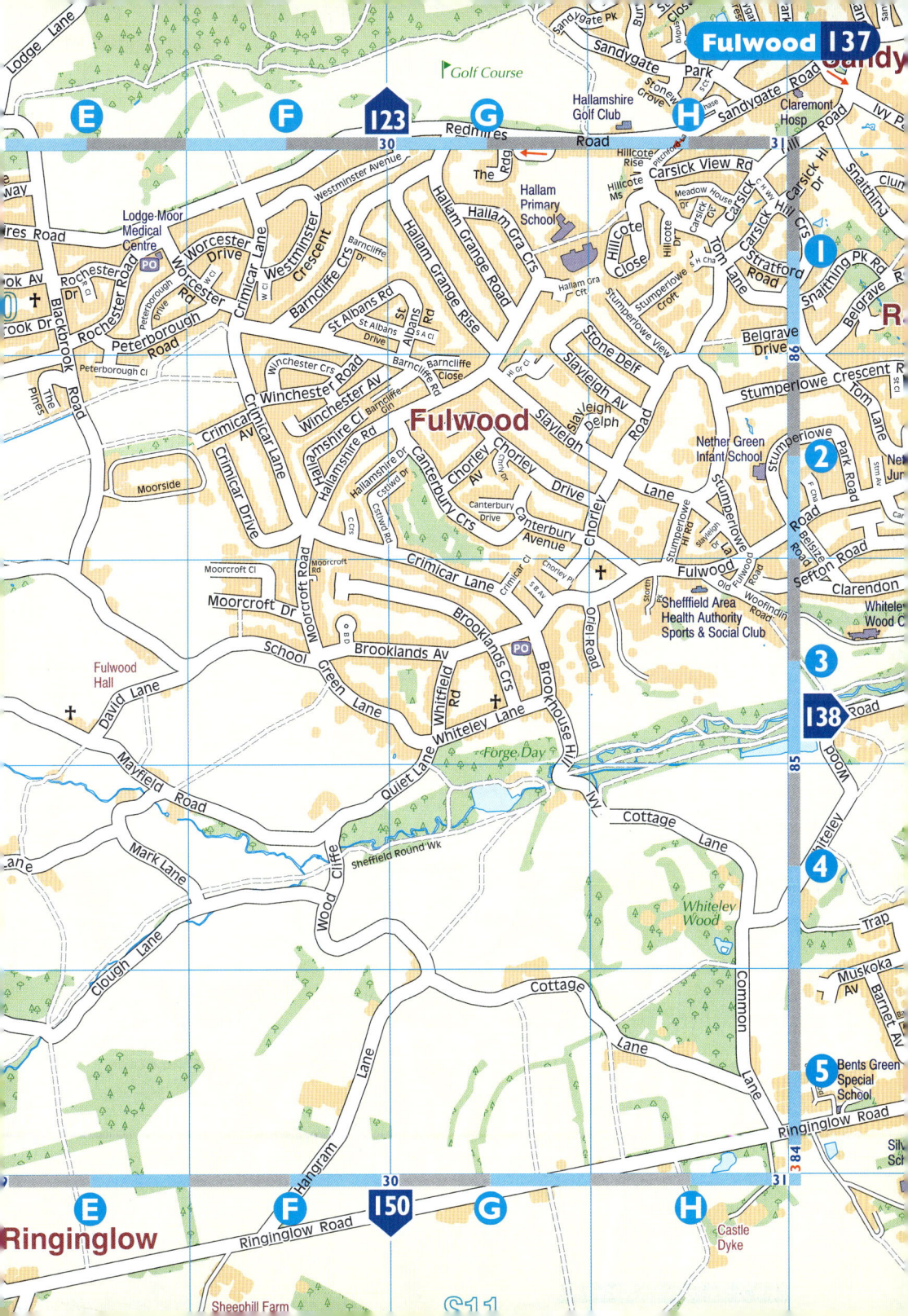

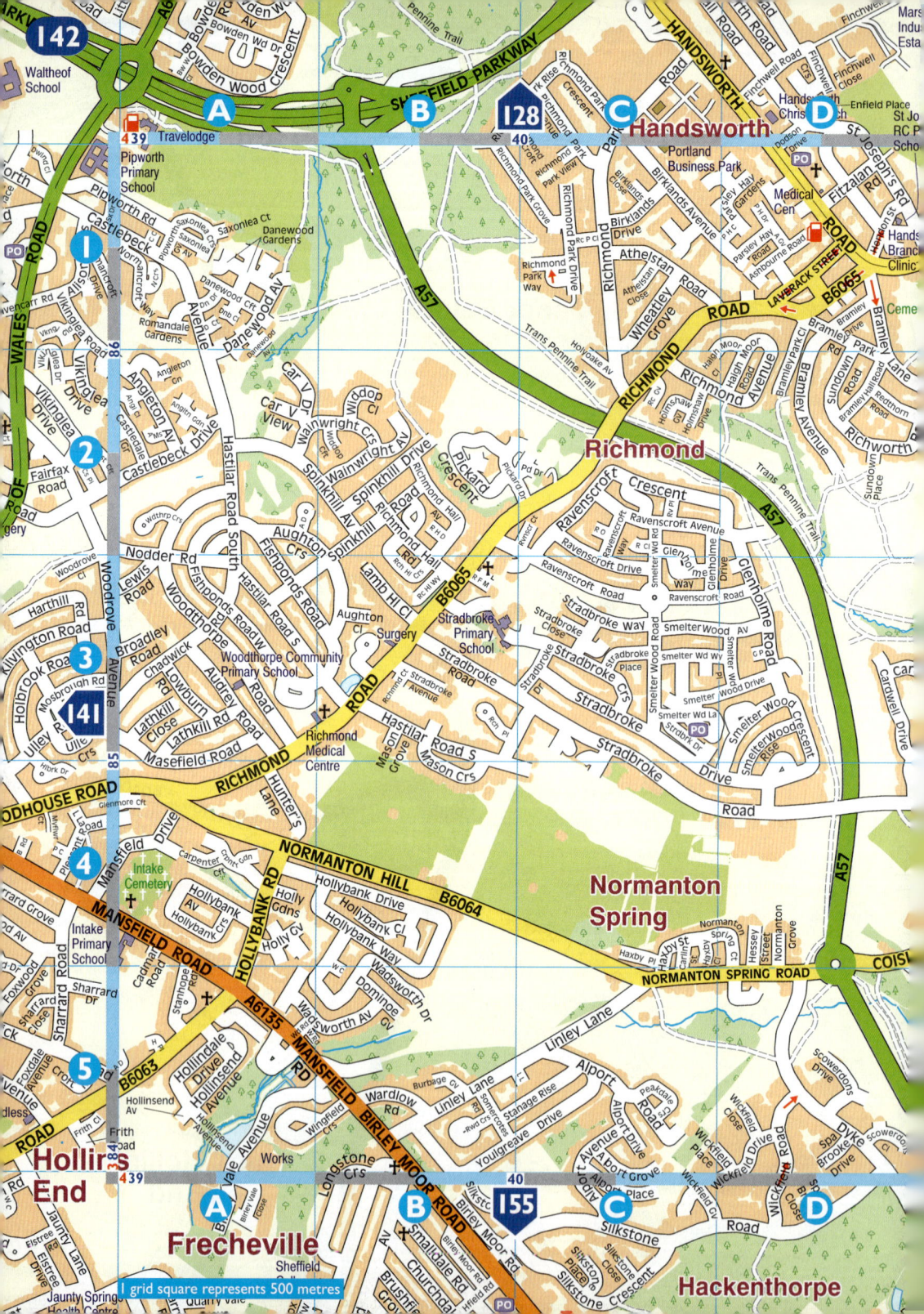

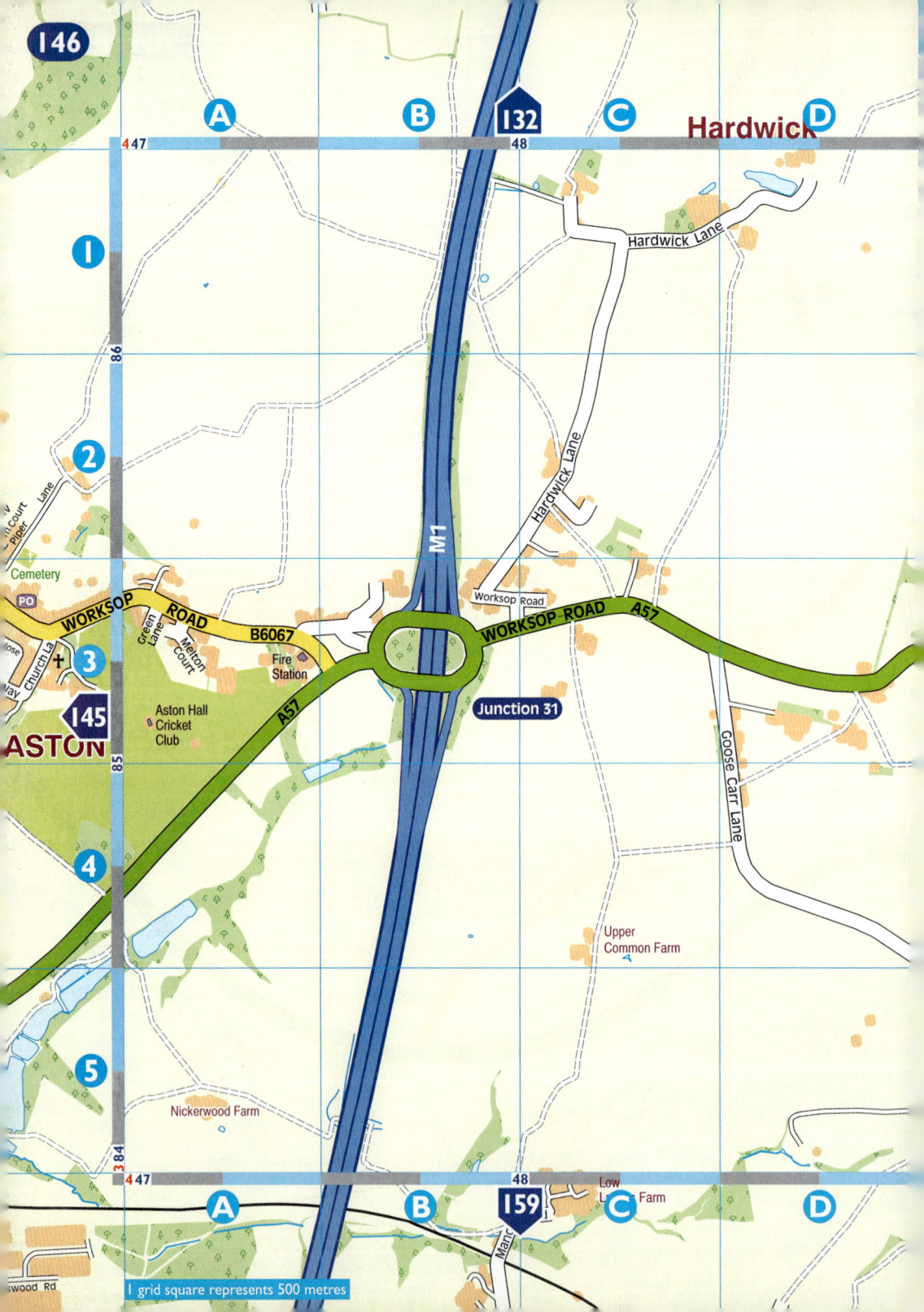

146

A   B   132   C   Hardwick   D

447   48

1

86

2

Piper Lane

Court Lane

Cemetery

PO

WORKSOP   ROAD

Green Lane   B6067

Church La

3

145

ASTON

Aston Hall
Cricket
Club

Melton
Court

85

A57

Fire
Station

M1

Hardwick Lane

Hardwick Lane

Worksop Road

WORKSOP   ROAD   A57

Junction 31

Goose Carr Lane

4

5

Nickerwood Farm

Upper
Common Farm

384

447   48

A   B   159   C   Low   Farm   D

Low

Manc

swood Rd

1 grid square represents 500 metres

133

134

148

Common Farm

Booker's Lane

Works

Bookers Way

Bookers Way

Abbey Way

Common Road

Common Road

Pocket Handkerchief Lane

TODWICK ROAD

B6463

North Anston Trading Estate

Houghton

North Anston Business Centre

Road

Cramf...

Anston Brook

Todwick Grange

Burne Farm

A57

New

Road

Red Lion Hotel

Kiveton Lane

Old Hall

Todwick

Mortains

Todwick JMI School

Osborne Drive

Osborne Road

Ravis Road

Rd

Ravis

Barber Close

The Pastures

PO

Roche End

Paddock View

Manor Way

Church View

Manor Dr

Lindley's Crt

A57

SHEFFIE...

Stortin Lane

Furnival Road

Stanford Cr

St Paul's Close

Th Crescent

The Guildway

Wasteneys Road

Tortmayns

Mill Hills

Sandwith Rd

Rd

Meadows

Rector Gdn

Mill Close

Mill Fields

384

Axle

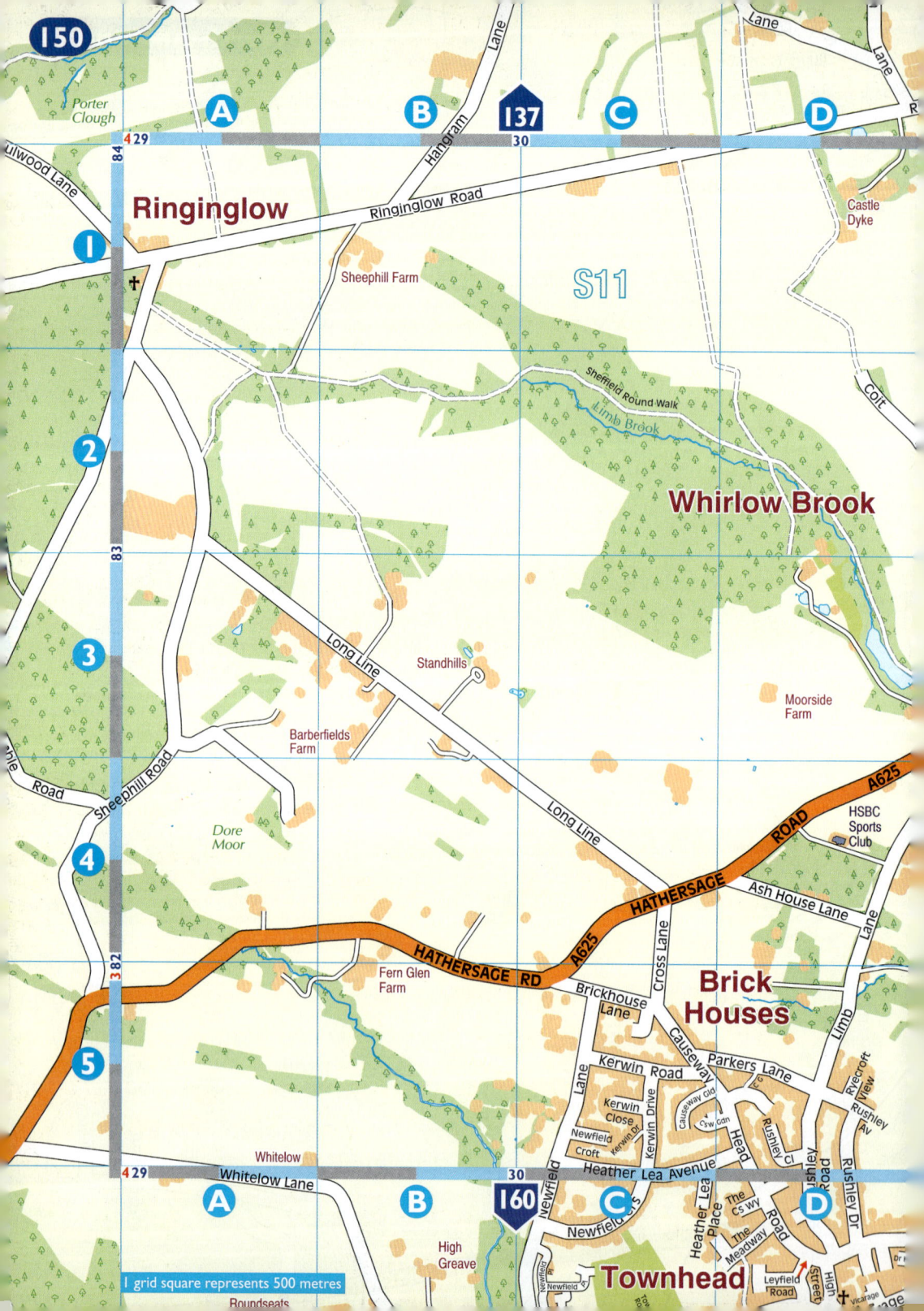

150

Porter
Clough

A   **B**   **137**   **C**   **D**

4 29   30

Ringinglow

Hangram Lane

Ringinglow   Ringinglow Road   Castle
Dyke

ulwood Lane

I   †   Sheephill Farm   **S11**

84

83

2   Sheffield Round Walk   Limb Brook   **Whirlow Brook**

Coit

3   Long Line   Standhills   Moorside
Farm

Barberfields
Farm

Sheephill Road

4   Dore
Moor   Long Line   **A625**   HSBC
Sports
Club

ne
Road   HATHERSAGE   ROAD   Ash House Lane

82

3

5   Fern Glen
Farm   HATHERSAGE RD   A625   **Brick
Houses**

Cross Lane   Brickhouse
Lane   Parkers Lane   Limb

Causeway Head   Rushley Av   Rushley Dr

Kerwin Road   Kerwin Drive   Csw Gdn

Lane   Kerwin
Close   Newfield
Croft

4 29   30

Whitelow   Whitelow Lane   Heather Lea Avenue   Rushley Road   High Street

A   **B**   **160**   **C**   **D**

Newfield   Newfield Cres   Heather Lea Place   The
Meadway   The
Cs Wy   Leyfield
Road   Vicarage

High
Greave   **Townhead**

Roundseats

1 grid square represents 500 metres

158

445 84

A   B   145   C   D

46

A618

Waleswood Rd

MANSFIELD

Wa
Ba

Waleswood Wa

Waleswood Road

Pithouse Lane

Waleswood

Delves Lane

Delves Lane

1

2

83

3

157

Rother Valley Lake

Rother Valley

Rother Valley Country Park

Golf Course

Rother Valley Golf Club

Pithouse Lane

Meadow Gate Lane

Frm Cotn

V Cotts

4

382

Way

Water Sports Centre

ROAD

A618

Works

5

Trans Pennine Trail

cuckoo

Aldred Close

Ellisons Road

Bailey Drive

Way

Bede Ct

Rotherham Ci

Norwood Industrial Estate

Norwoo

445 4

A   B   168   C   D

46

Barber's Lane

Primrose Lane

Primrose Close

Sherwood Road

North Cr's

Rotherwood Rd South

PO

Norwood Crescent

Cross St

Woodside Avenue

Norwood Pl

ROAD

Meadowgate

Parkside Shopping Centre

Nethergreen

Killamarsh County J&I School

B6058

Valley

Pingle

Church

Belvue Drive

Nethergreen Cotn

1 grid square represents 500 metres

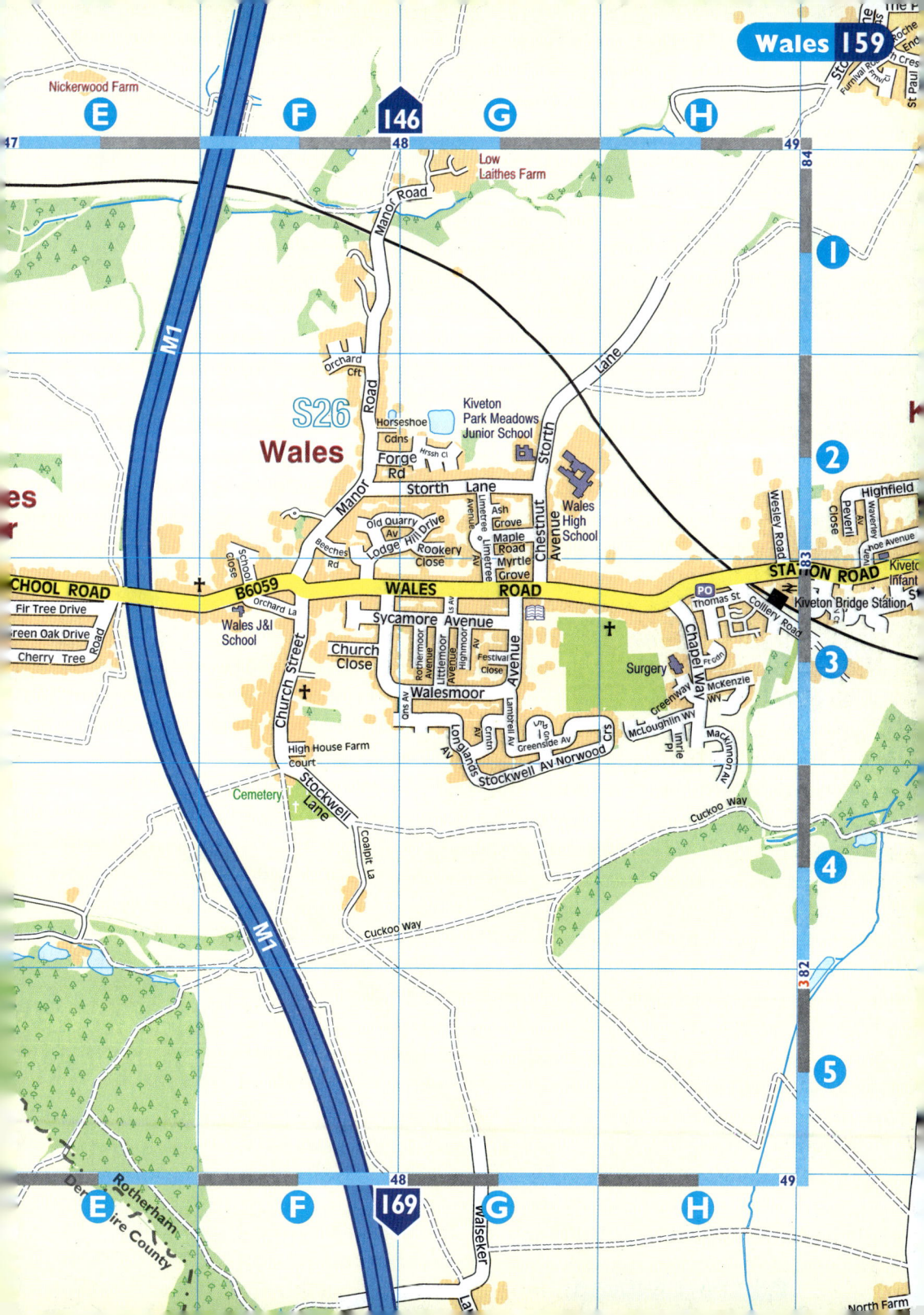

Townhead

Totley

S17

Moor
Edge Farm

I grid square represents 500 metres

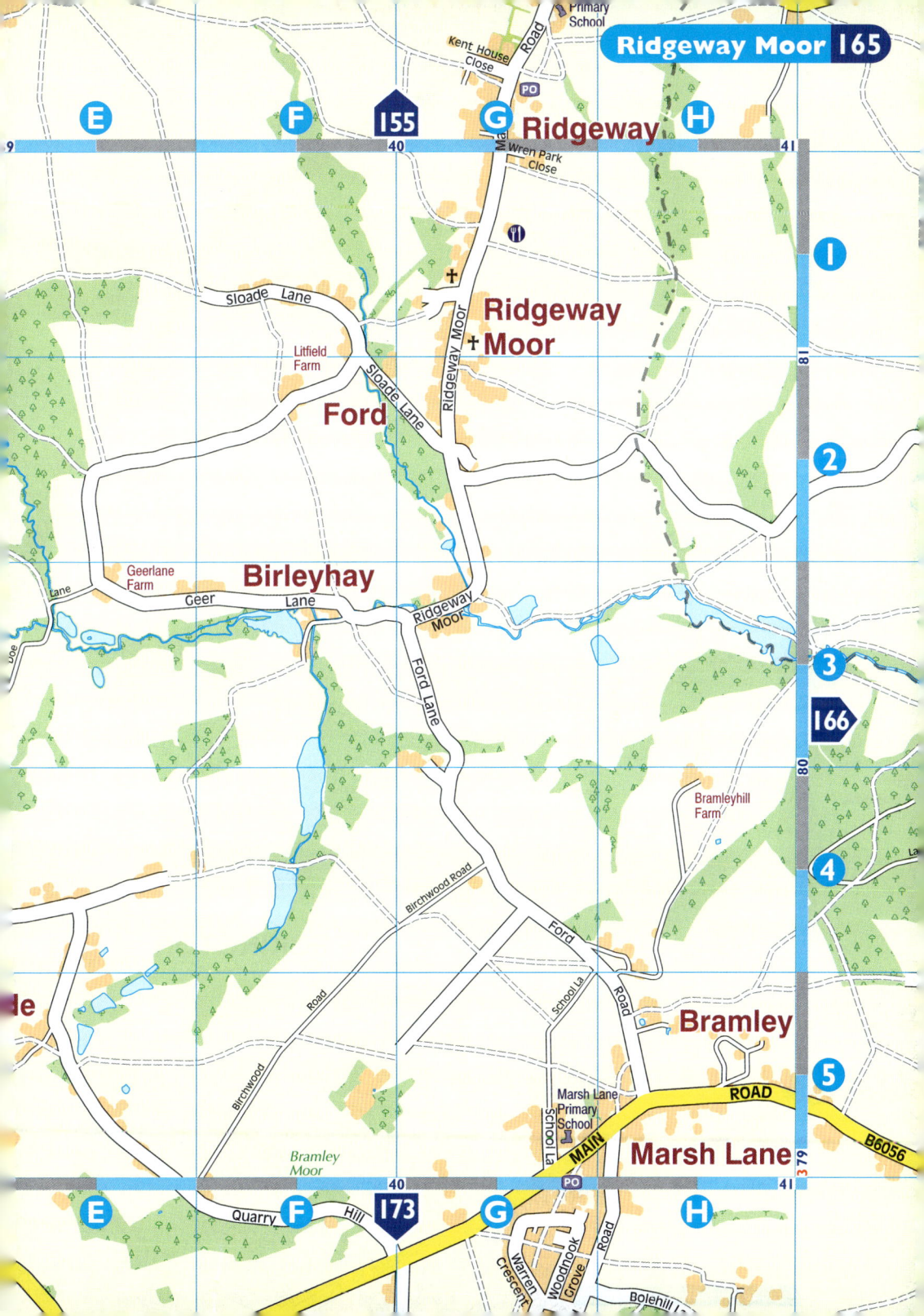

Primary School

Kent House Close

Road

PO

E

F

155

G **Ridgeway**

H

9

40

Wren Park Close

41

I

81

Sloade Lane

Ridgeway Moor

Litfield Farm

Ridgeway Moor

2

Ford

Sloade Lane

Geerlane Farm

Birleyhay

Lane

Geer Lane

Ridgeway Moor

Joe

3

166

Ford Lane

Bramleyhill Farm

80

4

La

Birchwood Road

Birchwood Road

Ford

Bramley

Road

School La

Road

5

ROAD

B6056

Birchwood

Bramley Moor

Marsh Lane Primary School

School La

MAIN

Marsh Lane

3 79

E

F

173

G

H

40

Quarry

Hill

PO

41

Warren Crescent

Wognook Grove

Road

Bolehill La

MOSBOROUGH

MOSBOROUGH MOOR

Owlthorpe Grove

Owlthorpe Rise

Moor Farm Avenue

Moor Farm Rise

Rose Hl Dr
Rose Hill
Rose Hl VC
Rose Hl VW
R Hl Vl AV
R Hl Ms
Rose Hl Av
De Pr Rd

Sycamore Street

Elm Crescent

Westfield Crescent

Oak St
High St Mews
Ash Street

A

B

156

A6135

C

D

Westfield Secondary School

Moor Crescent

HIGH STREET

Ferncroft Avenue

Toll Ho Mead
Toll House Rd

Cragdale Grove
Mossdale
Kl G
Baysdale Croft
Stt Rd

B6058

STATIO

1

Bridle Stile Gdns

New school Rd

Vw Cl
Nw Sl Cl
Nw Sl Rd
Nw Sl Ms

Stone St

PO

Olive Rd

Mosborough Primary School

William Crescent

Oakworth Dr
Oakworth Cl
Oakworth Vw

Plumbley

Bramley Close

Bridle Stile

Queen Street

Cadman St

dman

Duke St

Elmwood Drive

Rai Vw
Rais Cl

Bramley Hall
Carlton Cl
Farm Crs

Plumbley Hall Road

Chapel Street

Westfield Pl

Hollow

2

Plumbley   Lane

Moss View

Plumbley Hall Mews

Marsh Close

South Street

Kelgate

Best Western Mosborough Hall Hotel

A6135

Alu

Hallside Ct

Eckington Hall

Gashouse Lane

3

The Moss

Lady Ida's   drive

165

Eckington Hall

80

Bramleyhill Farm

Lady Ida's Drive

Lady Ida's Drive

Eckington Camms CE Primary School

4

Castle View
Ladybank
Camms Cl

Ida's

Castle

ECKINGTON

Back   Lane

Bramley

Eckington School

Fernbank Drive

Staninforth Avenue

Hayfield Vw
Springfield Close

Martin Rd
Greenhall Road

Green Chase

Castle View
Pinfold St

Stead Street

PINFOLD S

Cosber

5

ROAD

B6056

Fern Way
Fern Cl

Broomhill Close

Road

Ravencar

Aln St
Free Av
S Cl

Hawksway

Kestrel Dr
Curlew Av

Partridge Cary

Highwood Pl
Hunsdon Rd

Berry

Osmund Road

Darcy Road

Wulfric Rd

Sitwell Street

Billam Av

HIGH STREET

Eckington Junior School

John Street

Lansbury Rd

Tertiary College

Mary St
Edward St

Joseph Hardie La

William Lane

Barratt Rd

DRONFIELD ROAD

A

Marsh View

Askmore Avenue

Fenton Street

B

174

C

WEST STREET

Pipeyard Lane

High Street

Lansbury Court

PO

D

Birk Hill Infant School

Hornthorpe Road

Fanshaw Rd
East Vw
Fanshaw Av
Fanshaw Wy
Fns

Pitt St

Setcup

Albert Rd

Chesgate

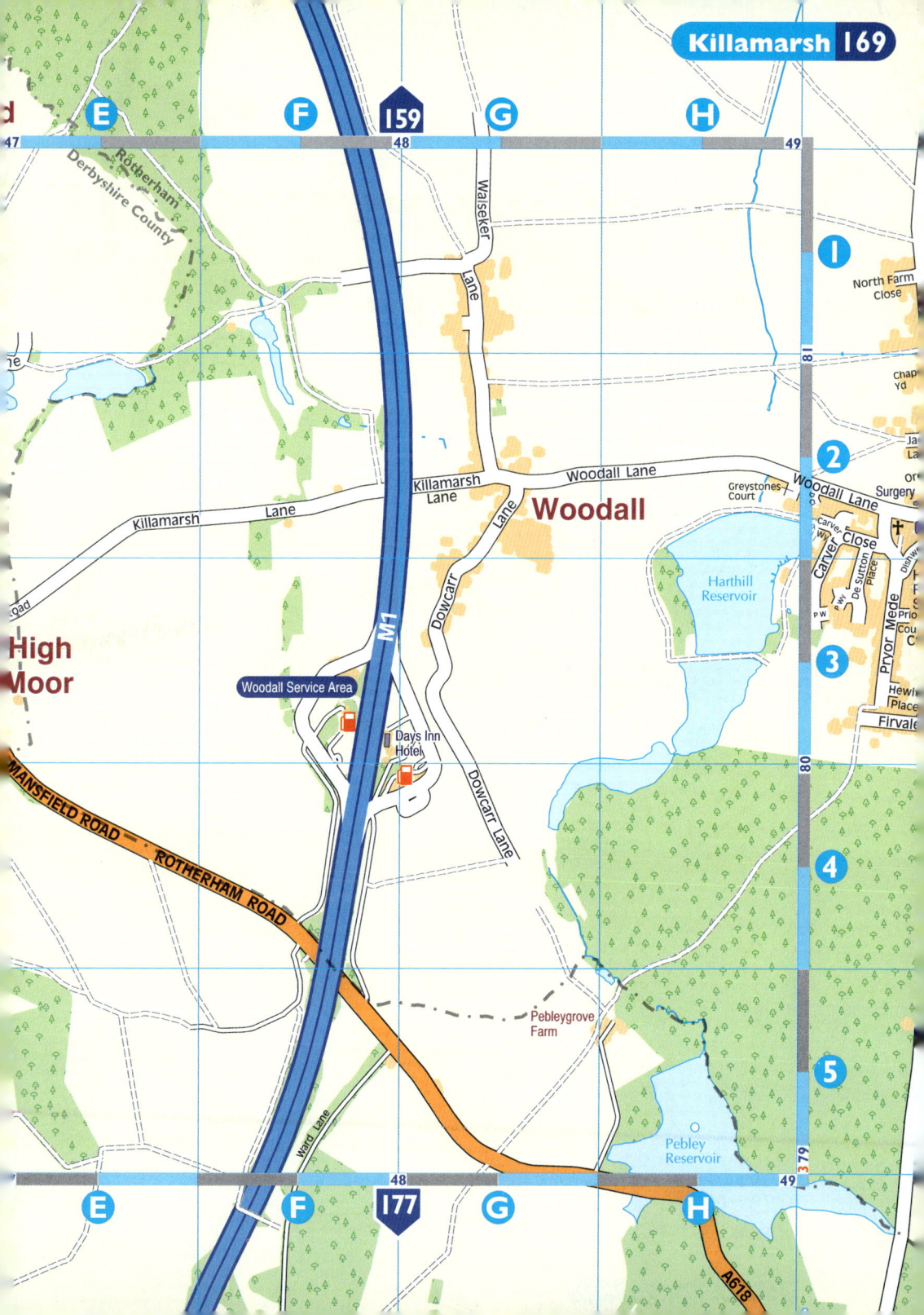

E   F   **159**   G   H

47   48   49

I

North Farm Close

Chap¹ Yd

Walseker Lane

2

Woodall Lane

Greystones Court

Surgery

Woodall Lane

Carver Close

Killamarsh Lane

Killamarsh   Lane

Dowcarr Lane

Woodall

P W   De Sutton Place

Prio   Cou¹

3

Pryor Mede

Hewi¹ Place

Firvale

Harthill Reservoir

High Moor

Road

M1

Woodall Service Area

Days Inn Hotel

4

Dowcarr Lane

MANSFIELD ROAD

ROTHERHAM ROAD

Pebleygrove Farm

5

Pebley Reservoir

Ward Lane

E   F   **177**   G   H

48   49

A618

HOLMLEY

B6158

Lenthall
Infant
School

Warren Rise

Ferndale
Road

Prospect Rd

Falcon
Lane

The Knoll

E Alma Crs · Birchitt View · Cecil · Sycamore Av · Hawthorne Av · Marsh Avenue · Summerfield

F Snape Hill Crs · Linden Av

163

Holmesdale Road

G Northfield Junior School · Oakhill

H Oakdell

Snape Hill

36 Paddock Way

37

Snapehill Crescent · Cecil Road · Thirlmere Dr · Snape Hill · Princess Road · Holburn Av

Hartington Rd · Edgerton Rd · Gn Cross · The Lawn · Hardwick Cl · The Avenue · Hassop Close · Stonelow Crescent

Holmesdale

Gladys Buxton School

Industrial Estate

GREEN

Greendale Shopping Centre

Stonelow Road

Shireoaks Road

Summerley Farm

I

Park Av · Surgery

The Dronfield Henry Fanshawe School

Stonelow Junior School

Fritchwood Dr · Parkgate · Birch House Lane

Civic Cen · Peel Cen & CAB · Shopping Precinct

Wrks · Church St

Dronfield Station

DRONFIELD

Works

House Wy

Works

2

79 78

Dronfield Jun Sch · Gledhill Cl · Fairwinds Cl · Pol Stn · Lea Road · Appletree Drive · Quoit Gn

Works

Callywhite

Industrial Estate

Moonpenny Way · Fletcher Av · Surgery · Cross · Upper School La

Mill Lane

CHESTERFIELD ROAD

Netherdene Rd · Netherdene Road · Hillside · Caldey Road · Pembroke Road · Scarsdale Rd

Fire Stn · Palmer Crescent

B6057

Works

3

Hollins · Spring · Falkand Rise · Geilerd Place · Netherfields Crs · Caernarvon Road · Avenue

Cemetery Road

Westfield Road · Hallowes Rise · Southfield Drive

Works

172 Works

Hill Top

Highfields Road · Hollins · Lundy Road · Shetland Rd

Dale Road · Hazel Court · Hazel Close · Eastfield Rd

Southfield Mount

Hallowes

UNSTONE HILL

Longacre Road · Hilltop Road · Salisbury Avenue · Links Road

Hallowes Drive · Hollies Close · Chestnut Close · Shakespeare Dr · Burns Dr

4 Works PO

Southwood Avenue · Barlow View · Hilltop Way

Hallowes Golf Club

Golf Course

Highgate · Byron Cl · Shelley Dr · Wordsworth Place · Crescent · Chaucer Dr · Kipling Cl

B6057

Un

77

Unstone Green

Highgate Lane

Highfield

5

Brierley Road · Loundes Road

UNSTONE-DRONFIELD-BY-PASS

Bull Close Farm

Birch Holt Grove · Alice Way · Robert Close · Cheeth Avenue

36

178

37

Sylvia Road

A61

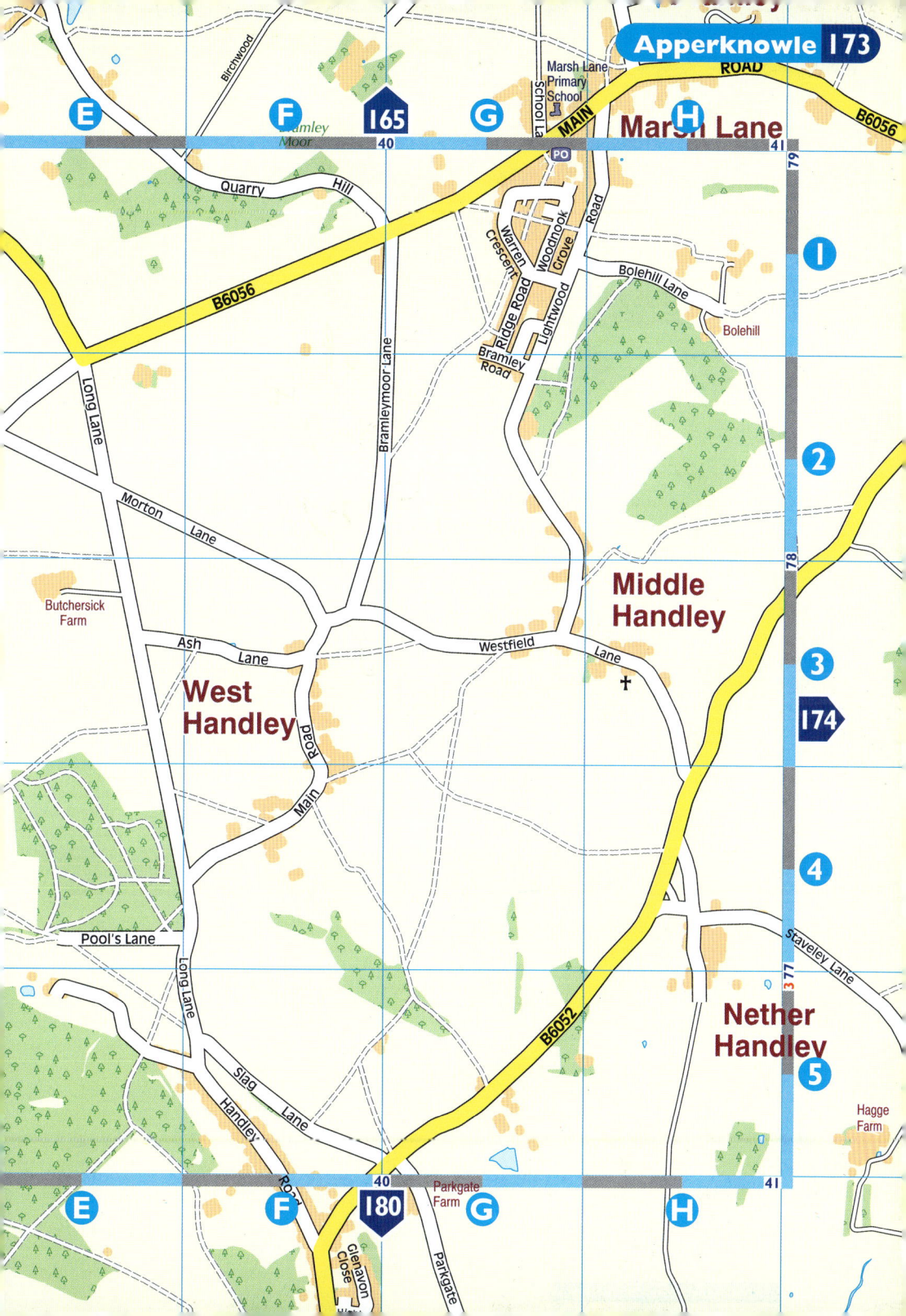

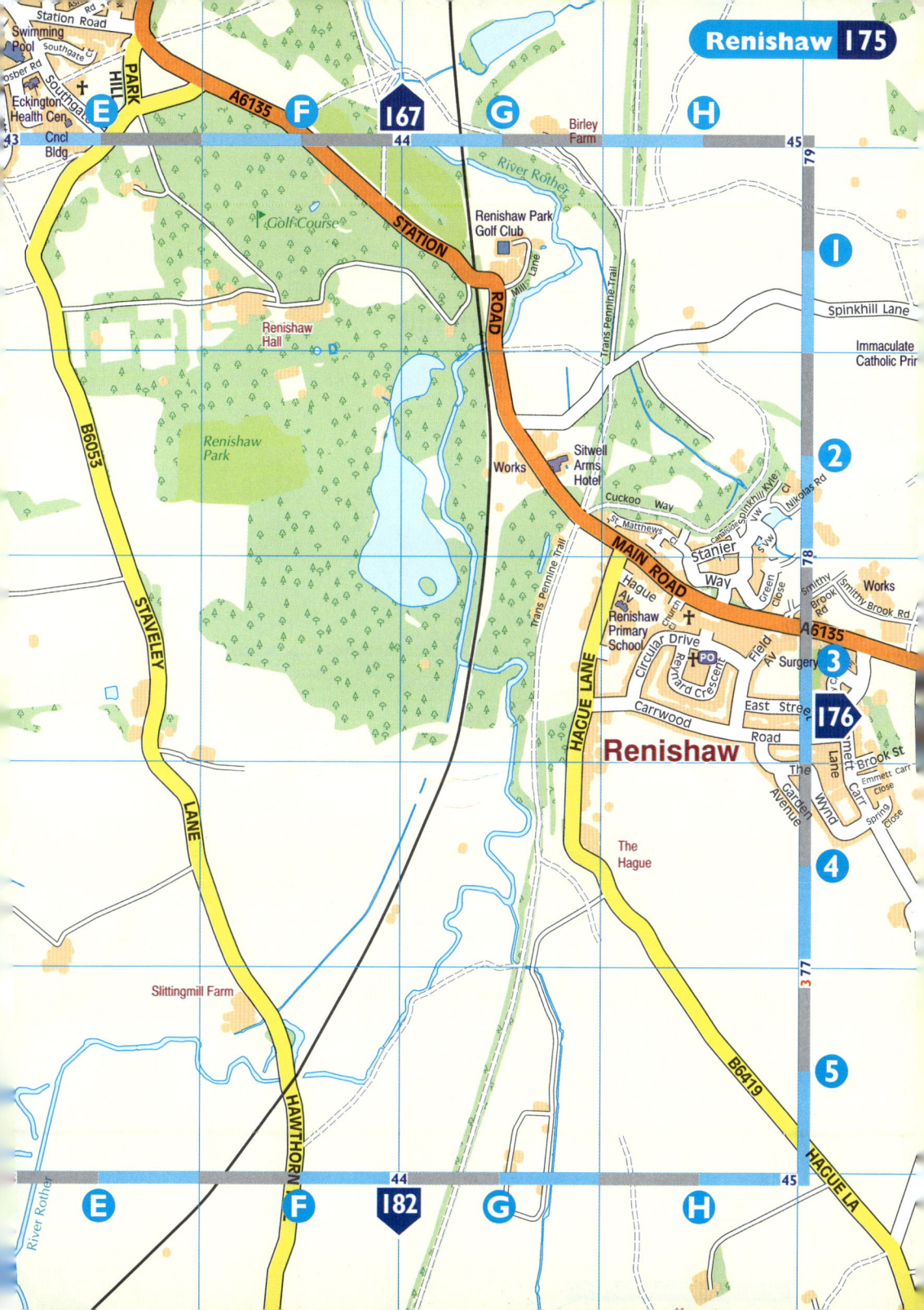

176

A   B   **168**   C   D

4 45
79

Station Rd

46

1

Collage
Road

Mount
St Marys
College

Parkhall Lane

Spinkhill Lane

Spinkhill

Immaculate Conception
Catholic Primary School

College Road

The Lane

The Avenue

The Lane Farm Ms

Park Farm

Syday Lane

High
Wood

2

Cambridge
Spinkhill
Kyle
VW
S VW
Mikolas Rd
Cl VW

Green Close

Stanier
Way

78

Smithy
Brook
Rd

Works

Smithy Brook Rd

Hollinwood
Farm

3

A6135

Surgery

Abbey Crt Rd

Abbey Crt

PO

d Crescent

Street

175

Emmett
Lane

Brook St

Emmett Carr

Emmett Carr
Close

SHEFFIELD

ROAD

Low
Common

Sheffield

Road

**Emmett
Carr**

The
Wynd

Spring Close

Garden
Avenue

4

377

*Barlborough
Low Common*

A6135

Westfield Lane

Junction 30

5

B6419

Beightonfields
Priory

Westfield Farm

HAGUE LA

4 45

A   B   **183**   C   D

46

Woodhouse Lane

Woodhouse
La

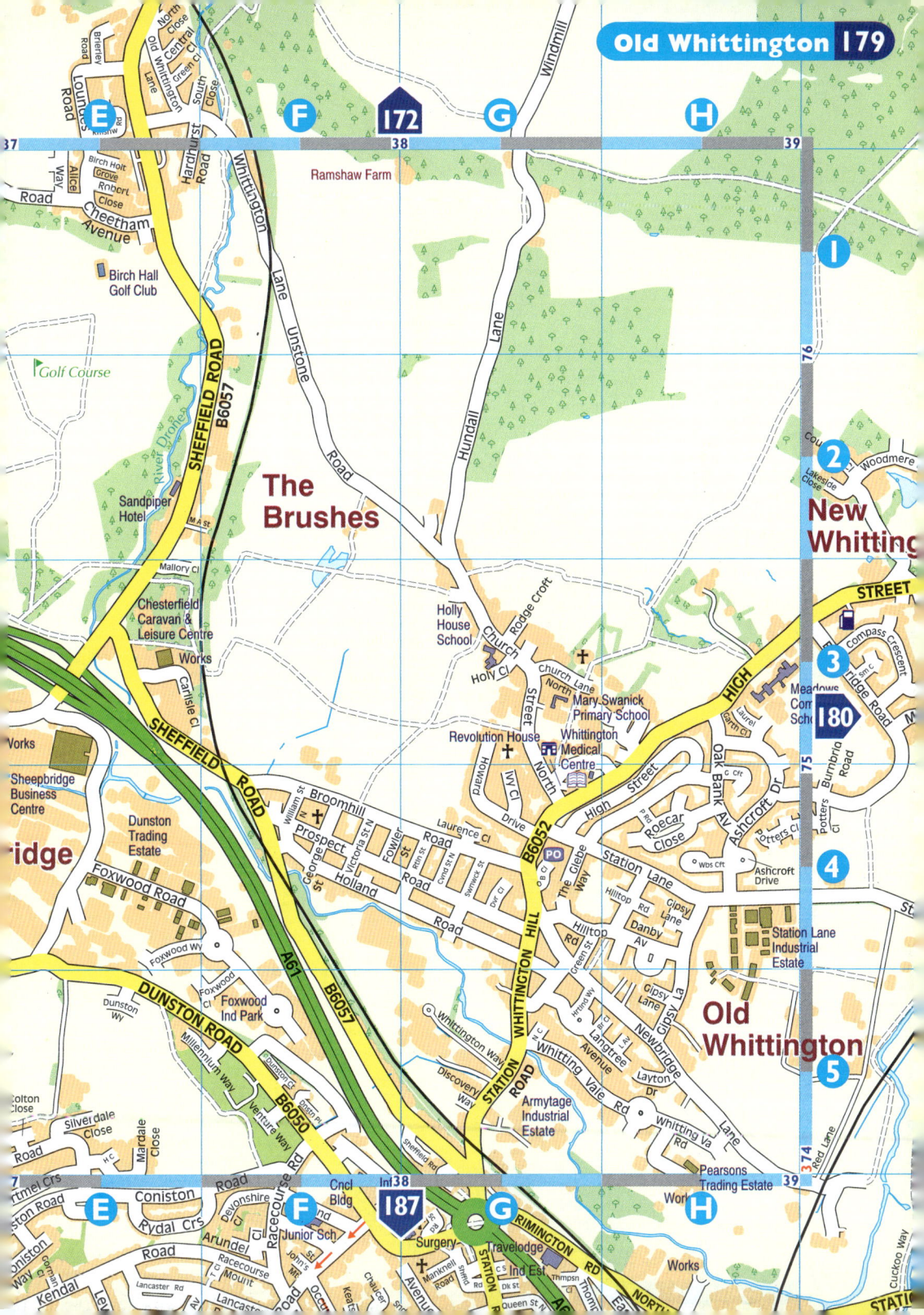

A   B   **173**   C   D

439   40

I

76

2

New Whittington

Slag Lane

Handley Road

Parkgate Farm

Glenavon Close

Highland Road

Dalvey Way

Cairngorm

Cromdale AV

Braemar CI

Cairn Dr

Cairngorm CI

Balmoral Way

Aviemore Close

Whittington Road

Parkgate Lane

Glasshouse Lane

Glasshouse Farm

Infant School

Dixon Cft

Flintson Avenue

Bateman CI

Stone La

HANDLEY ROAD

High Street

South St

Wellington

London St

Back CI

PO

New Whittington Com Prim Sch

Albert Rd

Devonshire AV

Devonshire Rd N

Staveley Road

Handleywood Farm

Coupland CI

Woodmere Dr

Lakeside Close

STREET   **B6052**

Breatley Crescent

Breatley Street

Burnbridge Road

Compass Crescent

May AV

Breatley Road

Durham CI

Fallowfield Rd

Bluebank Avenue

Back St

North

Chesterfield AV

Hardwick AV

3

HIGH

179

Garth CI

Oak Bank AV

Ashcroft Dr

Potters CI

Potters CI

Burnbridge Road

Meadows Community School

Caxton Close

Meadow Close

Station Lane

4

Wbs Cft

Cft

Old Whittington

5

374

Station Lane Industrial Estate

station Lane

Cuckoo Way

Chesterfield Canal (Disused)

Cuckoo Way

Red Lane

Cuckoo Way

Bilby Lane

Cow Lane

Cowpingle Lane

New Brimington

Gregory Lane

Railway Staff Social & Sports Club

Pearsons Trading Estate

439   40

A   B   **188**   C   D

Newbridge Lane

Newbridge Drive

Gregory

Rother AV

Black St

Raveigh AV

View St

Paton Gv

Vale Crescent

Bourne

Peterdale Road

Coronation Road

Summerfield Crescent

Steeping CI

George St

John Street

King Street

Queen Street

Princess Street

Victoria Street

Chapel St

Burnell Street

Devon

Oxford

Henry Bradley Infant School

Hedley Dr

Wilden Av

Wincill

Greave

ROAD

A   B   175   C   D

4 43   44

I

76

2

Works

3

181

75

4

5

3 74

A   B   C   D

4 43   44

River Rother

Huggester Farm

Farndale Road
Hartington Industrial Estate
Deepdale Cl
Hartington View
Hillcrest Grove
Franklyn Drive

ROAD
B6053
HALFORN HILL

Trans Pennine Trail

Cuckoo Way

River Doe Lea

Howells Pl
Wicking Cl
Carpenter Av

Cranleigh Road
Tollbridge Road
Spencer

Hall Lane

ECKINGTON

Hassop Rd
Hayfield Close
Overton Close
Howden Cl
Surgery

Bell House Lane
Wharf La
Pullman Cl

Bent Lane

Victoria Avenue
White Road
Moor View Rd

LOWGATES
PO

Netherthorpe
Netherthorpe School

Church St
Cncl Bldg
High Street Med Cen
Porter St
Rectory
Benfld Cl
Devonshire St
PO
High Street

DUKE STREET

Belmont Dr
Ireland St
Telford Crs
Huntsman Rd
Whitehead St
Bird St
Netherthorpe Rd
Barrow St
Marham Crs

Ralph Road
Milton Pl

Netherthorpe

Marshfield Grove

Bridle Road

MARKET ST

Mill Green

Darley Cl
Barlow Rd
Speedwell Industrial Estate
Brierley Close

Crompton Rd
Brin

Fan Road Industrial Estate
Ireland Close

Road

Fan
Gosborne
Colliery Cl

STAVELEY

Lime Avenue
Staveley Health Clinic
Speedwell Infant School
Cncl Bldg
Staveley Junior School
Cemetery

Inkersall Road
Hayfield Way
Stephenson Road

Cemetery Lane

Ireland Industrial Estate

Frecheville St
Musard Place
St Johns Road
Middlecroft Road
Silver Well Dr
St Josephs RC Primary School
Chatsworth Ct

Griffin Cl
Adelphi Way
Erin Road
Meadows Dr

Poolsbrook Av
Poolsbrook Vw
Erin Road
The Grove
Staveley

1 grid square represents 500 metres

Beightonfields
Priory

Westfield Farm

E   F   **176**   G   H

5   46   47   **I**

HAGUE LA

Woodhouse Lane

Woodhouse
La

A619 WORKSOP ROAD

76

RENISHAW ROAD

M1

2

Hawthorn
Avenue
Willow
Drive   Almond
Crescent   Rose Crs
Miller
AV
Edale   Road
S Pl   PO
Hazel
Drive

✝ **Mastin
Moor**

Royal
Oak Ct

S43

B6419

3

184

WORKSOP ROAD

aveley Norbriggs
ounty Infants School

The
Paddocks

Woodthorpe
Hall Farm

Romeley Hall Farm

Woodthorpe Road

Woodthorpe Road

BOLSOVER

4

75

Bank House

Woodthorpe
✝ CE Primary
School

Seymour Lane

ROAD

M1

5

374

E   F   G   H

46   47

Mill Lane

WOODTHORP

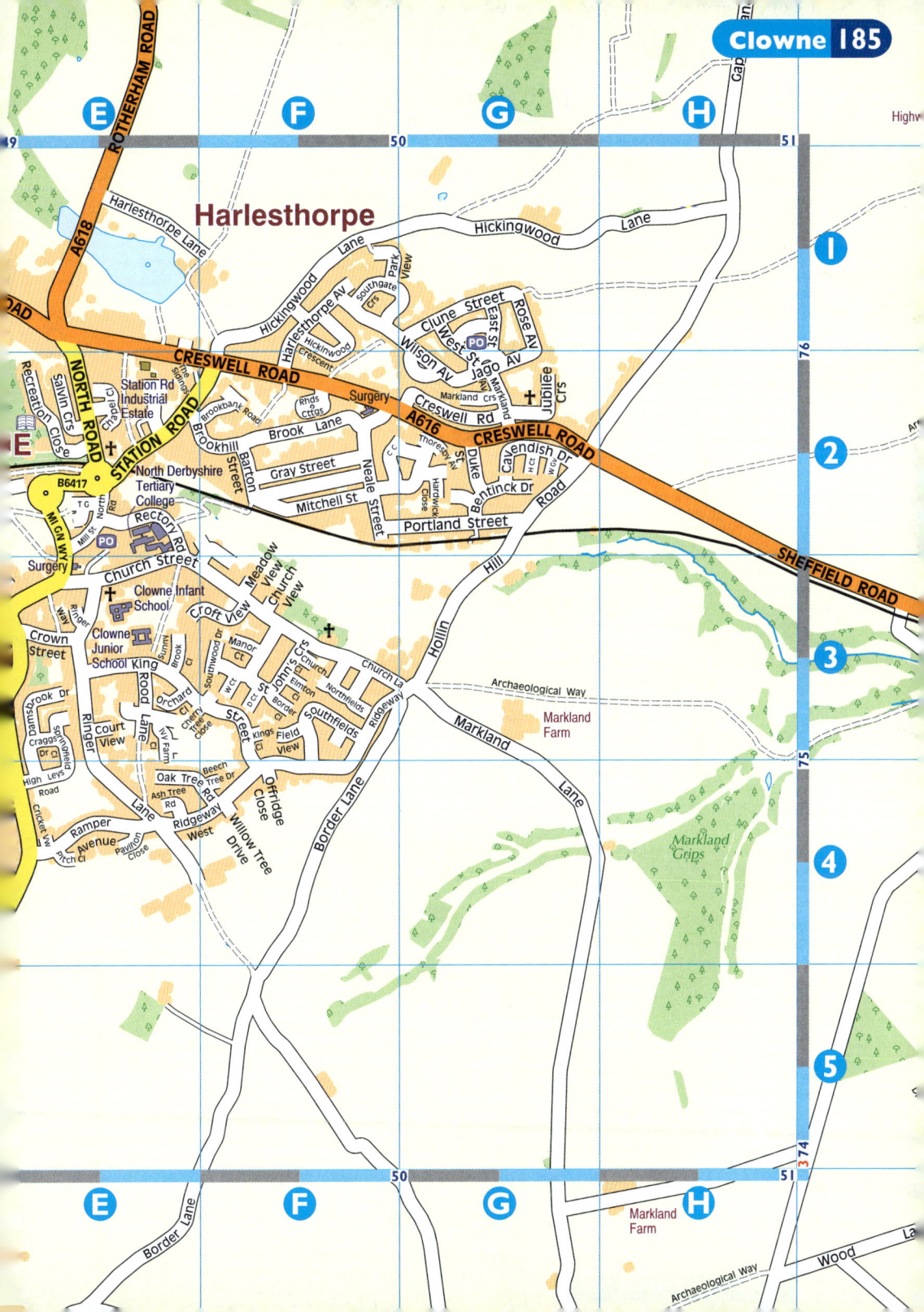

E F G H

Harlesthorpe

ROTHERHAM ROAD

A618

Harlesthorpe Lane

Hickingwood Lane

I

76

Hickingwood Lane

Hickingwood Av

Harlesthorpe Av

Hickinwood Crescent

Park View

Southgate Crs

Clune Street

East St

Rose Av

Wilson Av

West St

Jago Av

PO

Jubilee Crs

CRESWELL ROAD

NORTH ROAD

Recreation Close

Salvin Crs

Chapel Cl

Station Rd Industrial Estate

The Sidings

Brookbank Road

Rnds & Cttgs

Surgery

Creswell Rd

Markland Crs

Markland Cl

Jubilee Crs

Brookhill

Brook Lane

CRESWELL ROAD

A616

Cavendish Dr

2

E

B6417

STATION ROAD

Barton Street

Gray Street

Neale Street

Thoresby Av

St Duke St

Bentinck Dr

Hardwick Close

Hill Road

SHEFFIELD ROAD

North Derbyshire Tertiary College

Mill St North

Rectory Rd

Mitchell St

Portland Street

PO

Surgery

Church Street

Meadow View

Church View

Croft View

Clowne Infant School

Manor Ct

Southwood Dr

St John's Church

St Eimton Border

Church La

Ridgeway

Hollin

Markland Lane

Archaeological Way

Markland Farm

3

75

Crown Street

Clowne Junior School

King

Bunny Brook

Orchard Cl

Cherry Tree Close

Ivy L

Kings Field View

Northfields

Southfields

Ringer Way

Damsbrook Dr

Craggs Dr

Springfield

High Leys Road

Ringer Court View

Oak Tree Rd

Ash Tree Rd

Beech Tree Dr

Offridge Close

Ridgeway West

Border Lane

Markland Grips

4

Cricket Vw

Ramper Avenue

Pitch Cl

Pavilion Close

Willow Tree Drive

5

374

E F G H

Border Lane

Markland Farm

Wood

Archaeological Way

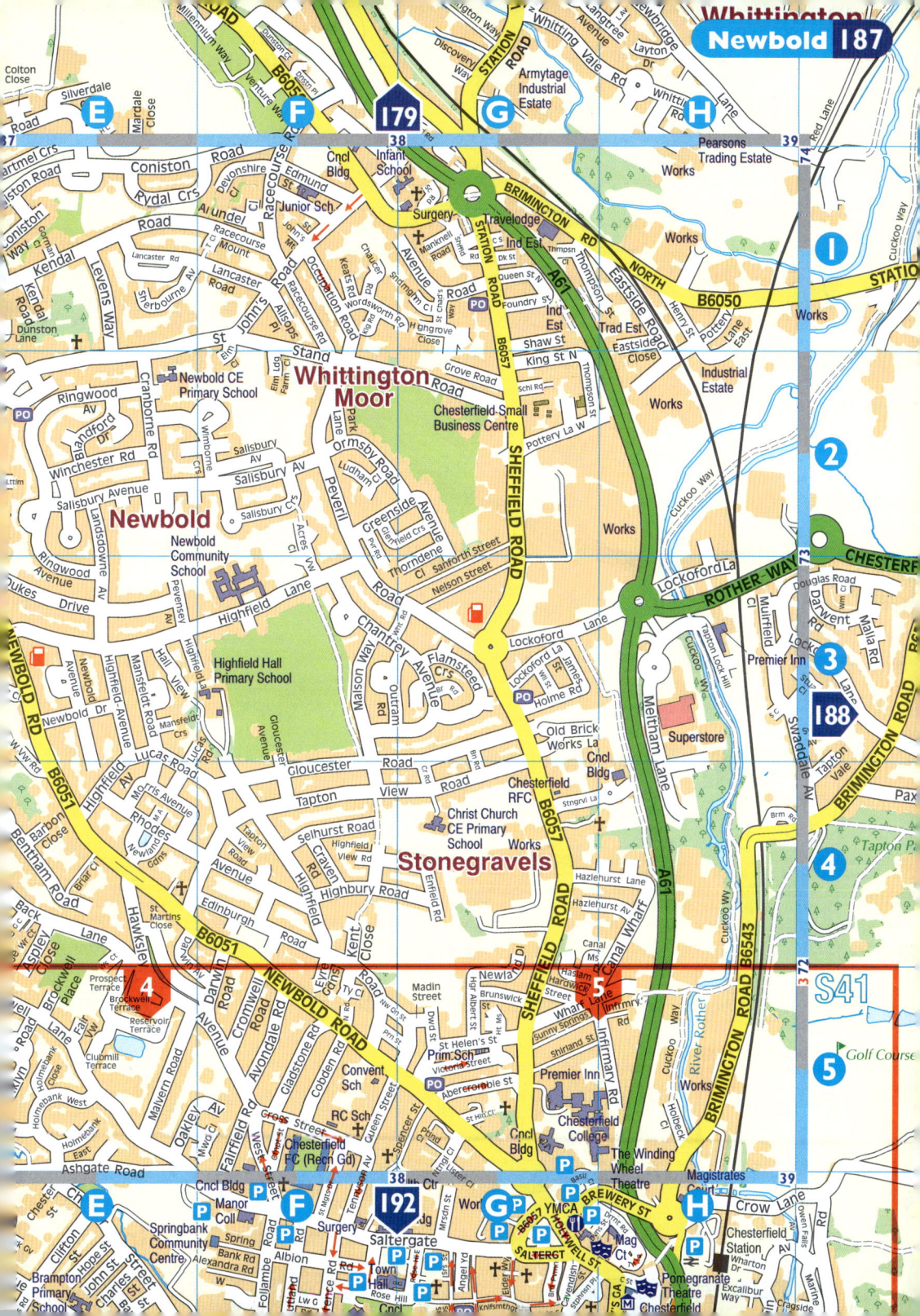

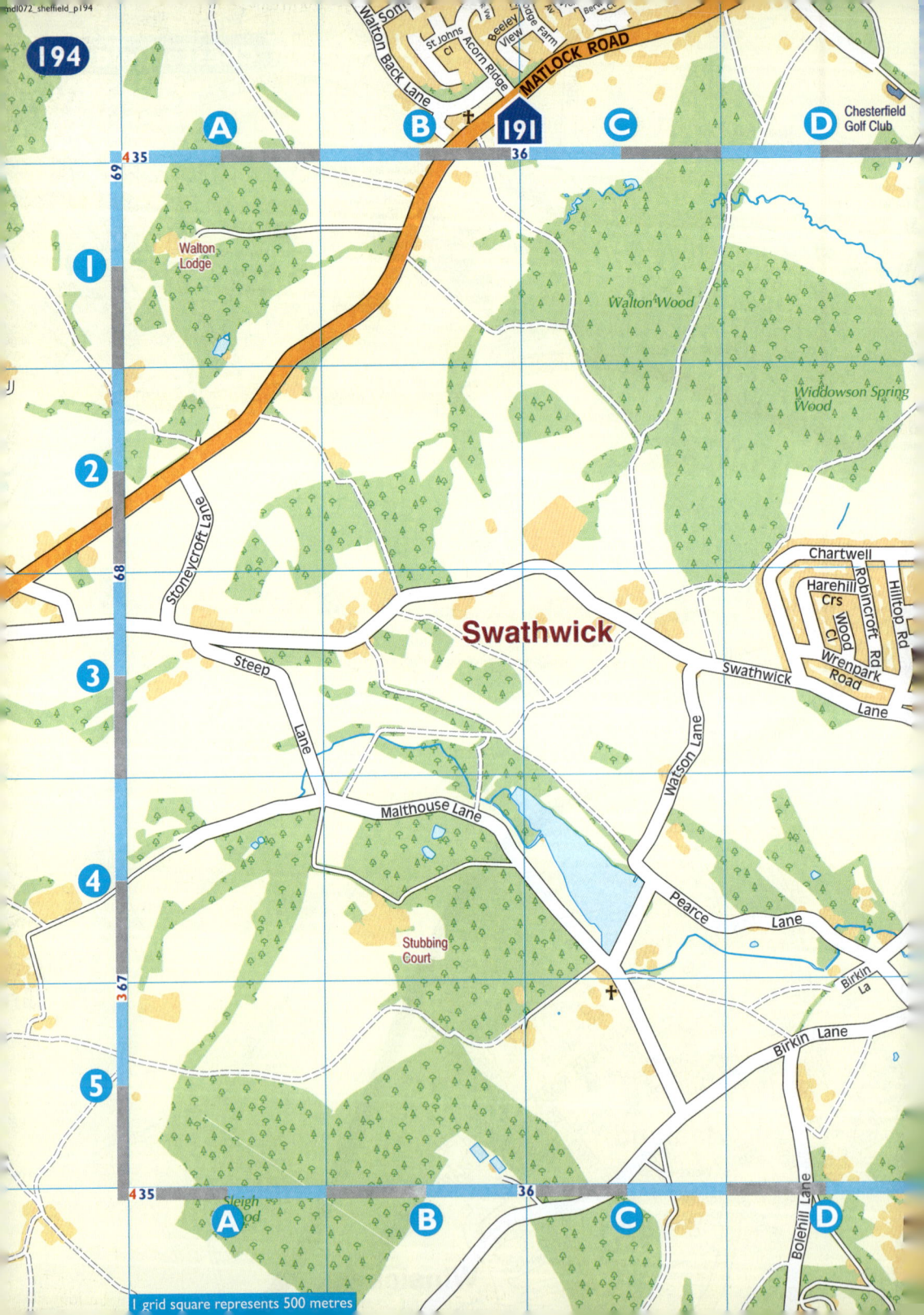

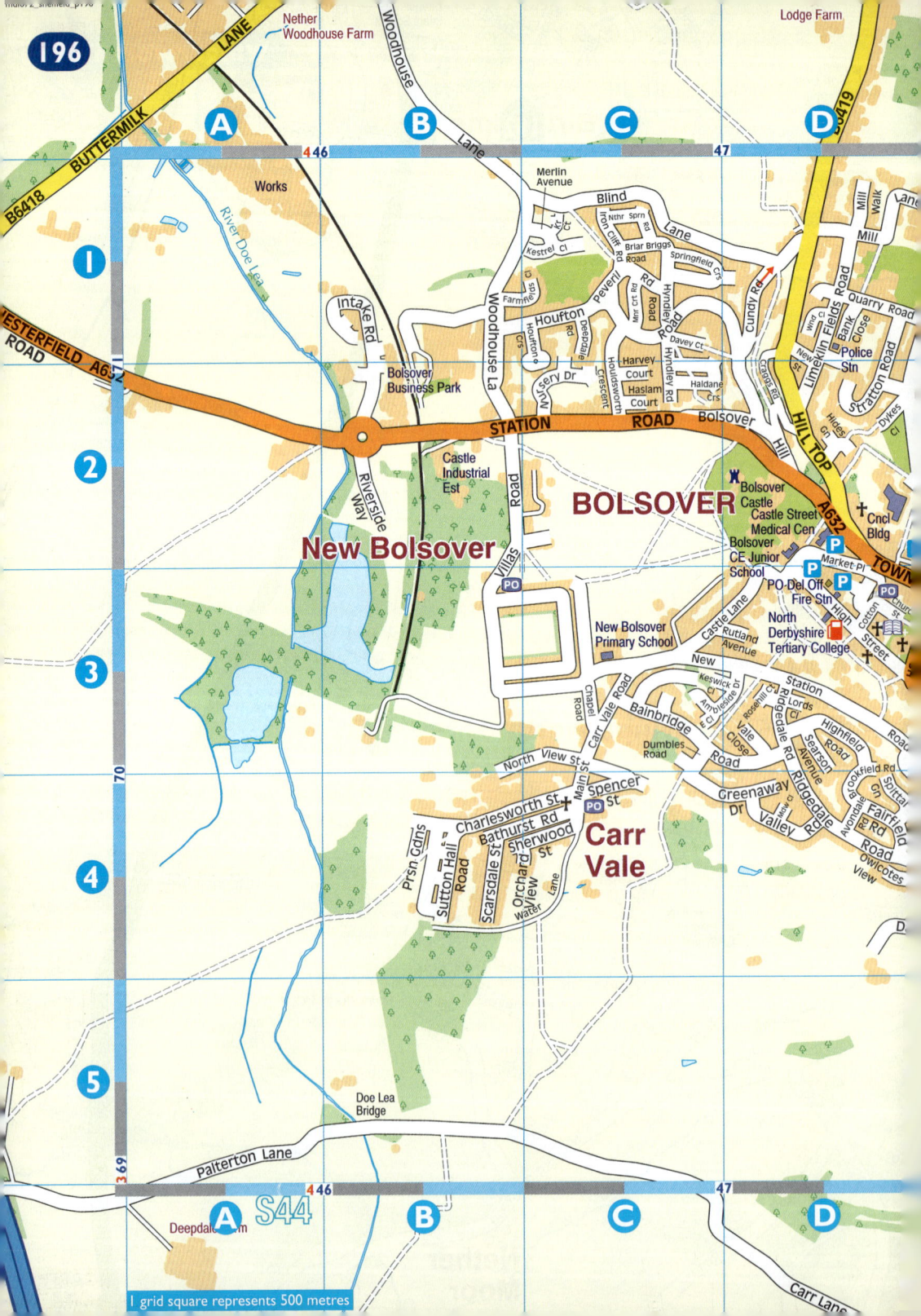

E F G H

48 49

I
71

Limekiln Field

Farnsworth Farm

Bolsover Moor

2

ROTHERHAM ROAD · B6417

Elmton Lane

Welbeck Road

Bolsover Local Hospital

3

70

Cornmill Close

Cedar Park Drive

Beck Close

Meadowlands

Horsehead Lane

Bretton Av

Ridgeway Av

Holbeck Av

SYCM Cl

Horsehead La

Cherry Tree Cl

Rd

Stables Court

Lilac Grove

Elm Close

Steel Lane

Longlands

Welbeck Road

Bolsover Infant School

Bolsover Clinic

The Paddock

Orchard Cl

Sandhills

Laburnum Cl

Langstone Avenue

Moor Lane

Smithson Av

Portland Avenue

Huntington Avenue

Moorfield Av

Moorfield Sq

Moorfield Av

Schoolfield Cl

Portland Crs

Moorfield Avenue

Cavendish Rd

Portland

Tower Crs

Cavendish Road

St. Lawrence Avenue

Cromwell Rd

Eastern Av

Stockley View

Crich View

Lane

Hudson Mt

Victoria St

Cross

Nesbit St

PO

Middle St

Selwyn St

Wells St

Street

A632

LANGWITH ROAD

4

Sutton View

West View

Castle Green

Pleasant Av

Hills Town

Hillstown Business Centre

Mansfield Road

ROTHERHAM ROAD · B6417

5

3 69

Road

48 49

E F G H

Scarcliffe

Langwith

Scarcliffe Primary School

The Elms Farm

Main Street

Abbeydale.....151 H4
Abbeydale Park.....161 E2
Abdy.....84 D1
Adwick Le Street.....25 F2
Aldwarke.....98 C4
Almholme.....28 A3
Apperknowle.....172 C2
Arbourthorne.....140 D2
Ardsley.....33 F3
Arksey.....27 C5
Armthorpe.....42 C4
Ashgate.....191 G1
Aston.....145 H3
Athersley North.....14 D4
Athersley South.....15 E5
Attercliffe.....116 A5
Aughton.....130 C5
Balby.....71 H1
Barlborough.....177 F3
Barnes Hall.....93 F2
Barnsley.....3 J2
Barrow.....82 B2
Barrow Hill.....181 E2
Barugh.....18 A1
Barugh Green.....18 A3
Bassett.....136 B5
Batemoor.....163 E3
Beauchief.....151 H5
Beighton.....157 F1
Belle Green.....17 E5
Belle Vue.....7 J7
Bentley.....39 H3
Bentley Rise.....39 F3
Bessacarr.....74 A1
Billingley.....36 B4
Birdholme.....192 B5
Birdwell.....47 G5
Birley Carr.....100 D4
Birley Edge.....100 D3
Birleyhay.....165 F3
Blackburn.....103 H2
Blacker Hill.....14 A5
Blacker Hill.....48 C4
Bolehill.....153 E3
Bolsover.....196 C2
Bolsterstone.....77 E5
Bolton upon Dearne.....53 F3
Bow Broom.....66 A4
Boythorpe.....192 A3
Bradgate.....104 D2
Bradway.....161 H3
Bramley.....108 C3
Bramley.....165 H5
Brampton.....64 A2
Brampton.....191 H1
Brampton en le Morthen.....132 D2
Branton.....59 F4
Brecks.....107 H5
Brick Houses.....150 C5
Brierley.....17 H2
Brightside.....116 B4
Brimington.....188 D2
Brimington Common.....189 E4
Brincliffe.....139 E4
Brinsworth.....118 B4
Bromley.....79 G1
Brookside.....191 E2
Broom.....106 B5
Broomhill.....51 F3
The Brushes.....179 F2
Burncross.....93 G1
Burngreave.....126 B1
Cadeby.....69 F2
Calow.....193 H1
Canklow.....118 D1
Cantley.....58 D4
Carbrook.....116 C4
Carlton.....15 H3
Carr Vale.....196 C4
Carter Knowle.....139 F5
Castle Green.....45 F4
Catcliffe.....129 H1
Chapeltown.....81 F5
Charltonbrook.....93 E1
Charnock Hall.....154 C3
Chesterfield.....5 F6
Clifton.....9 J5

Clowne.....184 D2
Coal Aston.....163 H4
Coisley Hill.....143 E4
Conanby.....88 B1
Conisbrough.....68 C5
Cortworth.....83 C2
Cowley.....170 B4
Crookes.....124 D3
Crookesmoor.....10 A1
Cudworth.....22 A1
Cudworth Common.....22 B3
Cundy Cross.....32 D1
Cundy Hos.....79 E3
Cusworth.....38 C5
Dalton.....99 F5
Dalton Magna.....107 G2
Dalton Parva.....107 G1
Darfield.....35 F5
Darnall.....128 A2
Dearne.....37 H5
Deepcar.....77 H4
Denaby Main.....68 A4
Dinnington.....134 B4
Dodworth.....30 B3
Dodworth Bottom.....30 A4
Doncaster.....7 G3
Dore.....161 E1
Drakehouse.....156 D2
Dronfield.....171 F2
Dropping Well.....95 H5
Dunston.....186 C1
East Dene.....106 C2
East Herringthorpe.....107 F2
Eastwood.....106 A1
Ecclesall.....138 C5
Ecclesfield.....94 B5
Eckington.....166 C4
Edenthorpe.....42 C1
Elsecar.....62 C3
Emmett Carr.....176 A3
Felkirk.....13 G3
Finkle Street.....78 C1
Firth Park.....115 H1
Fir Vale.....115 F3
Flanderwell.....108 A3
Ford.....165 F2
Frecheville.....155 E1
Fulwood.....137 G2
Garden Village.....76 B2
Gawber.....18 C4
Gilroyd.....30 C5
Gleadless.....154 C1
Gleadless Valley.....154 A2
Goldthorpe.....37 G5
Gosforth Valley.....170 B1
Greasbrough.....97 G2
Greenhill.....162 C1
Greenland.....116 D5
Greenside.....164 D5
The Green.....44 D5
Grenoside.....101 F1
Greystones.....138 A4
Grimesthorpe.....115 H3
Guilthwaite.....130 D1
Hackenthorpe.....155 G1
Hady.....193 F2
Halfway.....167 E1
Hallowes.....171 G3
Handsworth.....128 C5
Hardwick.....132 C5
Harlesthorpe.....185 E1
Harley.....81 H2
Hasland.....193 F5
Hay Field.....75 G4
Heeley.....140 A4
Hellaby.....109 H4
Hemingfield.....50 A5
Hemsworth.....153 H2
Herringthorpe.....107 E4
Hexthorpe.....55 F3
Higham.....18 A4
Higham Common.....18 A5
Highfield.....140 B2
Highfields.....25 G5
Highgate.....36 D5
High Green.....80 B4
Highlane.....155 G5

High Moor.....169 E3
Hillsborough.....113 F2
Hills Town.....197 F4
Hill Top.....104 A3
Hill Top.....88 B4
Hill Top.....171 E4
Hockley.....195 G5
Holbrook.....157 G5
Hollingwood.....181 F5
Hollins End.....141 H5
Holmesdale.....171 G1
Holmley Common.....163 E5
Hoober.....84 A2
Hood Green.....46 A3
Hood Hill.....81 H3
Hooton Levitt.....110 C5
Hooton Roberts.....87 H5
Howbrook.....79 H2
Hoyland.....61 F2
Hoyland Common.....61 F2
Hoyle Mill.....32 C1
Hundall.....172 D4
Hyde Park.....6 C6
Inkersall Green.....189 H3
Intake.....57 E1
Intake.....141 G5
Jordanthorpe.....163 F1
Jordon.....104 C4
Jump.....62 C2
Kendray.....32 B4
Keresforth Hill.....31 E4
Killamarsh.....168 B2
Kilnhurst.....86 B4
Kimberworth.....104 C2
Kimberworth Park.....96 D4
Kingstone.....2 B7
Kirk Sandall.....29 F4
Lane End.....81 E5
Laughton Common.....134 A2
Lea Brook.....54 D5
Lightwood.....154 B5
Limekiln Field.....197 E1
Listerdale.....107 H4
Little Houghton.....35 H2
Load Brook.....122 B1
Lodge Moor.....136 C1
Longley Estate.....115 F1
Long Sandall.....28 D4
Loundsley Green.....186 B3
Low Barugh.....18 B1
Lowedges.....162 D2
Lowfield.....140 A3
Low Laithes.....33 H3
Low Valley.....50 D1
Loxley.....112 C4
Lundwood.....20 D4
Malinbridge.....113 G5
Maltby.....111 E3
Manor Estate.....141 F1
Manor Park.....127 E5
Marsh Lane.....165 H5
Masbrough.....8 A3
Mastin Moor.....183 F2
Meadow Hall.....116 D1
Meadow Head.....152 C4
Measborough Dike.....32 B2
Meersbrook.....140 C5
Mexborough.....67 E1
Mickley.....161 H5
Middlecliffe.....35 G3
Middlecroft.....189 H1
Middle Handley.....173 H5
Middlewood.....100 B5
Millhouses.....151 H2
Millhouses.....35 H5
Milton.....62 A3
Monk Bretton.....20 B3
Moorgate.....119 F2
Moorhole.....156 A4
Morthen.....121 E5
Mortomley.....80 C4
Mosborough.....156 C5
Nether Chanderhill.....190 A3
Nether Edge.....139 G4
Nether Handley.....173 H5
Nether Haugh.....84 B4
Netherthorpe.....182 C4

Newbold.....187 E2
New Bolsover.....196 A2
New Brimington.....180 C5
Newhill.....65 E4
New Lodge.....14 B5
New Rossington.....90 D3
Newton.....55 F2
New Totley.....161 E4
New Village.....27 E5
New Whittington.....180 A2
Normanton Spring.....142 C4
North Anston.....148 A1
Norton.....153 F5
Norton Woodseats.....152 D2
Norwood.....158 D5
Nutwell.....43 F5
Old Denaby.....67 G5
Old Whittington.....179 H5
Orgreave.....143 G1
Oughtibridge.....100 A2
Owlerton.....114 B4
Owlthorpe.....156 B3
Oxclose.....167 G2
Parkgate.....98 B4
Parkhead.....151 F2
Park Hill.....126 D4
Parkwood Springs.....115 E5
Parson Cross.....101 H4
Penistone.....44 B3
Piccadilly.....85 H2
Pickburn.....24 B4
Pilley.....60 A3
Pismire Hill.....102 D5
Pitsmoor.....115 F5
Platts Common.....49 E5
Plumbley.....166 B1
Pogmoor.....18 C5
Potter Hill.....79 H4
Rails.....122 D3
Ranmoor.....138 A1
Rawmarsh.....98 C1
Renishaw.....175 H3
Richmond.....142 C2
Ridgeway.....155 G5
Ridgeway Moor.....165 G1
Ringinglow.....150 A1
Rollestone.....140 C5
Rossington.....91 G2
Rostholme.....26 B5
Rotherham.....8 D6
Royston.....15 H1
Ryecroft.....85 G4
St Helen's.....20 C2
Sandhill.....35 H1
Sandhill.....85 H4
Sandygate.....124 A5
Scawsby.....38 D4
Scawthorpe.....38 D2
Scholes.....96 A2
Shaftholme.....27 E2
Shafton.....16 C1
Shafton Two Gates.....16 C2
Sharrow.....139 F3
Shaw Lands.....2 B5
Sheepbridge.....178 D4
Sheffield.....11 K6
Sheffield Park.....141 E1
Shirecliffe.....115 E3
Shiregreen.....103 F4
Smithies.....19 H2
Smithley.....49 G2
Snape Hill.....34 D5
Snape Hill.....163 E5
Sothall.....157 F4
South Anston.....148 A4
Spital.....193 E3
Spinkhill.....176 B1
Spring Vale.....45 E3
Sprotbrough.....58 A3
Staincross.....14 A3
Stairfoot.....33 E3
Stannington.....123 H1
Staveley.....182 B5
Steel Bank.....125 E2
Stockbridge.....27 E5
Stocksbridge.....77 E3
Stonegravels.....187 F4

Stopes.....122 D1
Storrs.....112 A5
Street.....83 G1
Stubbley.....162 B5
Sunnyfields.....39 E4
Sunnyside.....108 A2
Swaithe.....33 E5
Swallownest.....145 E3
Swathwick.....194 B3
Swinton.....85 H1
Swinton Bridge.....66 C2
Tankersley.....60 C2
Tapton.....188 A3
Tapton Hill.....124 C5
Templeborough.....105 E5
Thorn Hill.....8 D2
Thorpe Hesley.....95 G1
Throapham.....134 D2
Thrybergh.....99 G3
Thurcroft.....132 D1
Thurnscoe.....36 D5
Thurnscoe East.....37 H2
Tinsley.....117 G2
Todwick.....147 F4
Toll Bar.....26 C3
Totley.....160 C4
Totley Brook.....160 D3
Totley Rise.....161 F3
Townhead.....160 C1
Treeton.....130 B3
Troway.....164 C4
Ulley.....131 H4
Under Tofts.....123 G3
Unstone.....172 A4
Unstone Green.....172 A5
Upper Cudworth.....17 E4
Upper Haugh.....84 D4
Upper Hoyland.....61 G1
Upper Newbold.....186 A1
Upper Tankersley.....60 A4
Upperthorpe.....168 A3
Upper Whiston.....120 A5
Wadsley.....113 E2
Wadsley Bridge.....100 D5
Waldershaigh.....76 C5
Wales.....159 F2
Wales Bar.....158 D2
Walkley.....125 E1
Walton.....191 G4
Ward Green.....31 G5
Warmsworth.....70 B3
Warren.....81 F3
Waterthorpe.....156 D3
Wath upon Dearne.....65 G3
Wentworth.....82 D2
Westfield.....167 E1
West Green.....21 F1
West Handley.....173 E3
West Melton.....64 C2
Westthorpe.....168 B4
Wheatley.....40 C5
Wheatley Hills.....41 G4
Wheatley Park.....41 E3
Whinney Hill.....99 F4
Whirlow.....151 F5
Whirlow Brook.....150 C2
Whiston.....120 A3
Whiteley Wood.....138 B3
Whitley.....93 H4
Whittington Moor.....187 F2
Wickersley.....108 B5
Wilthorpe.....19 E3
Wincobank.....116 C1
Windhill.....67 G2
Wingerworth.....195 F3
Wingfield.....96 C3
Wombwell.....50 A4
Woodall.....169 G2
Woodhouse.....143 F3
Woodhouse Mill.....144 A2
Woodlands.....25 F3
Wood Seats.....93 F3
Woodthorpe.....183 E4
Worsbrough.....47 H4
Worsbrough Bridge.....48 A2
Worsbrough Common.....31 H5
Worsbrough Dale.....48 A1

USING THE STREET INDEX

Street names are listed alphabetically. Each street name is followed by its postal town or area locality, the Postcode District, the page number, and the reference to the square in which the name is found.

Standard index entries are shown as follows:

Abbey Brook Cl *SHEFS* S8.....**152** C4

Street names and selected addresses not shown on the map due to scale restrictions are shown in the index with an asterisk:

Adwick Ct *MEX/SWTN* S64 * ...**67** F4

GENERAL ABBREVIATIONS

ACC	ACCESS	CTYD	COURTYARD	HLS	HILLS	MWY	MOTORWAY
ALY	ALLEY	CUTT	CUTTINGS	HO	HOUSE	N	NORTH
AP	APPROACH	CV	COVE	HOL	HOLLOW	NE	NORTH EAST
AR	ARCADE	CYN	CANYON	HOSP	HOSPITAL	NW	NORTH WEST
ASS	ASSOCIATION	DEPT	DEPARTMENT	HRB	HARBOUR	O/P	OVERPASS
AV	AVENUE	DL	DALE	HTH	HEATH	OFF	OFFICE
BCH	BEACH	DM	DAM	HTS	HEIGHTS	ORCH	ORCHARD
BLDS	BUILDINGS	DR	DRIVE	HVN	HAVEN	OV	OVAL
BND	BEND	DRO	DROVE	HWY	HIGHWAY	PAL	PALACE
BNK	BANK	DRY	DRIVEWAY	IMP	IMPERIAL	PAS	PASSAGE
BR	BRIDGE	DWGS	DWELLINGS	IN	INLET	PAV	PAVILION
BRK	BROOK	E	EAST	IND EST	INDUSTRIAL ESTATE	PDE	PARADE
BTM	BOTTOM	EMB	EMBANKMENT	INF	INFIRMARY	PH	PUBLIC HOUSE
BUS	BUSINESS	EMBY	EMBASSY	INFO	INFORMATION	PK	PARK
BVD	BOULEVARD	ESP	ESPLANADE	INT	INTERCHANGE	PKWY	PARKWAY
BY	BYPASS	EST	ESTATE	IS	ISLAND	PL	PLACE
CATH	CATHEDRAL	EX	EXCHANGE	JCT	JUNCTION	PLN	PLAIN
CEM	CEMETERY	EXPY	EXPRESSWAY	JTY	JETTY	PLNS	PLAINS
CEN	CENTRE	EXT	EXTENSION	KG	KING	PLZ	PLAZA
CFT	CROFT	F/O	FLYOVER	KNL	KNOLL	POL	POLICE STATION
CH	CHURCH	FC	FOOTBALL CLUB	L	LAKE	PR	PRINCE
CHA	CHASE	FK	FORK	LA	LANE	PREC	PRECINCT
CHYD	CHURCHYARD	FLD	FIELD	LDG	LODGE	PREP	PREPARATORY
CIR	CIRCLE	FLDS	FIELDS	LGT	LIGHT	PRIM	PRIMARY
CIRC	CIRCUS	FLS	FALLS	LK	LOCK	PROM	PROMENADE
CL	CLOSE	FM	FARM	LKS	LOCKS	PRS	PRINCESS
CLFS	CLIFFS	FT	FORT	LNDG	LANDING	PRT	PORT
CMP	CAMP	FTS	FLATS	LTL	LITTLE	PT	POINT
CNR	CORNER	FWY	FREEWAY	LWR	LOWER	PTH	PATH
CO	COUNTY	FY	FERRY	MAG	MAGISTRATE	PZ	PIAZZA
COLL	COLLEGE	GA	GATE	MAN	MANSIONS	QD	QUADRANT
COM	COMMON	GAL	GALLERY	MD	MEAD	QU	QUEEN
COMM	COMMISSION	GDN	GARDEN	MDW	MEADOWS	QY	QUAY
CON	CONVENT	GDNS	GARDENS	MEM	MEMORIAL	R	RIVER
COT	COTTAGE	GLD	GLADE	MI	MILL	RBT	ROUNDABOUT
COTS	COTTAGES	GLN	GLEN	MKT	MARKET	RD	ROAD
CP	CAPE	GN	GREEN	MKTS	MARKETS	RDG	RIDGE
CPS	COPSE	GND	GROUND	ML	MALL	REP	REPUBLIC
CR	CREEK	GRA	GRANGE	MNR	MANOR	RES	RESERVOIR
CREM	CREMATORIUM	GRG	GARAGE	MS	MEWS	RFC	RUGBY FOOTBALL CLUB
CRS	CRESCENT	GT	GREAT	MSN	MISSION	RI	RISE
CSWY	CAUSEWAY	GTWY	GATEWAY	MT	MOUNT	RP	RAMP
CT	COURT	GV	GROVE	MTN	MOUNTAIN	RW	ROW
CTRL	CENTRAL	HGR	HIGHER	MTS	MOUNTAINS	S	SOUTH
CTS	COURTS	HL	HILL	MUS	MUSEUM	SCH	SCHOOL
						SE	SOUTH EAST
						SER	SERVICE AREA
						SH	SHORE
						SHOP	SHOPPING
						SKWY	SKYWAY
						SMT	SUMMIT
						SOC	SOCIETY
						SP	SPUR
						SPR	SPRING
						SQ	SQUARE
						ST	STREET
						STN	STATION
						STR	STREAM
						STRD	STRAND
						SW	SOUTH WEST
						TDG	TRADING
						TER	TERRACE
						THWY	THROUGHWAY
						TNL	TUNNEL
						TOLL	TOLLWAY
						TPK	TURNPIKE
						TR	TRACK
						TRL	TRAIL
						TWR	TOWER
						U/P	UNDERPASS
						UNI	UNIVERSITY
						UPR	UPPER
						VA	VALE
						VA	VALLEY
						VIAD	VIADUCT
						VIL	VILLA
						VIS	VISTA
						VLG	VILLAGE
						VLS	VILLAS
						VW	VIEW
						W	WEST
						WD	WOOD
						WHF	WHARF
						WK	WALK
						WKS	WALKS
						WLS	WELLS
						WY	WAY
						YD	YARD
						YHA	YOUTH HOSTEL

POSTCODE TOWNS AND AREA ABBREVIATIONS

ABRD	Abbeydale Road	CHSW	Chesterfield south & west	DRON	Dronfield	MEX/SWTN	Mexborough/Swinton
ARMTH	Armthorpe	CLCR	Clay Cross	ECC	Ecclesall	MOS	Mosborough
ATT	Attercliffe	CONI	Conisbrough	ECK/KIL	Eckington/Killamarsh	NROS/TKH	New Rossington/Tickhill
AU/AST/KP	Aughton/Aston/Kiveton Park	CUD/GR	Cudworth/Grimethorpe	EPW	Epworth	OWL	Owlerton
AWLS/ASK	Adwick le Street/Askern	DARN/MH	Darnall/Meadowhall	FUL	Fulwood	RAW	Rawmarsh
BSLY	Barnsley	DEARNE	Wath upon Dearne/Bolton upon Dearne	GLV	Gleadless Valley	RCH	Rural Chesterfield
BSLYN/ROY	Barnsley north/Royston	DIN	Dinnington	HACK/IN	Hackenthorpe/Intake	RHAM	Rotherham
BSVR	Bolsover	DOD/DAR	Dodworth/Darton	HAN/WDH	Handsworth/Woodhouse	RHAM/THRY	Rotherham/Thrybergh
BTLY	Balby	DON	Doncaster Town Centre	HOR/CROF	Horbury/Crofton	SHEF	Sheffield
CHNE	Chesterfield north & east	DONS/BSCR	Doncaster south/Bessacarr	HOY	Hoyland	SHEFN	Sheffield north
CHPT/GREN	Chapeltown/Grenoside			HTFD	Hatfield	SHEFP/MNR	Sheffield Park/Manor
				KIMB	Kimberworth		
				MALT	Maltby		

SHEFS	Sheffield south
ST/HB/BR	Stannington/Hillsborough/Bradfield
STKB/PEN	Stocksbridge/Penistone
STV/CWN	Staveley/Clowne
TOT/DORE	Totley/Dore
WHHL	Wheatley Hills
WKFDW/WTN	Wakefield west/Walton
WMB/DAR	Wombwell/Darfield
WRKN	Worksop north
WRKS	Worksop south

Index - streets — Abb - Alb

A

Abbey Brook Cl SHEFS S8 .....152 C4
Abbey Brook Ct SHEFS S8 ....152 C4
Abbey Brook Dr SHEFS S8 ....152 C4
Abbey Crs ABRD S7 ....151 H4
Abbey Cft ABRD S7 ....151 H4
  CHNE S41 ....186 A2
  ECK/KIL S21 ....176 A3
Abbeydale Pk
  TOT/DORE S17 * 161 G1
Abbeydale Park Crs
  TOT/DORE S17 ....161 F2
Abbeydale Park Ri
  TOT/DORE S17 ....161 E1
Abbeydale Rd ABRD S7 ....152 B2
Abbeydale Rd South
  TOT/DORE S17 ....161 G1
Abbey Farm Vw
  CUD/GR S72 ....21 H2
Abbeyfield Rd ATT S4 ....115 F5
Abbey Gra ABRD S7 ....151 H4
Abbey Gv ABRD S7 ....151 H4
  BSLYN/ROY S71 ....21 E3
Abbey Gv BSLYN/ROY S71.......21 E3
Abbey Lane Dell SHEFS S8 ....151 H4
Abbey Pl ECK/KIL S21 ....176 A3
Abbey Sq BSLYN/ROY S71.......21 E3

Abbey View Rd SHEFS S8 ....153 E2
Abbey Wk BTLY DN5 ....39 E5
Abbey Wy DIN S25 ....147 H1
Abbotsford Dr MALT S66 ....133 E1
Abbots Meadow MOS S20 ......157 G4
Abbots Rd BSLYN/ROY S71 ......21 F4
Abbott St DONS/BSCR DN4 ....6 A5
Abdy Rd KIMB S61 ....96 B4
  RAW S62 ....84 D1
Aberconway Crs
  NROS/TKH DN11 ....91 F3
Abercorn Rd WHHL DN2 ....57 C1
Abercrombie St CHNE S41 ....5 F2
Aberford Gv HOY S74 ....62 D2
Abingdon Gdns KIMB S61 ....97 F3
Abingdon Rd WHHL DN2 ....41 F5
Abney Cl CHSW S40 ....186 C3
  GLV S14 ....140 C4
Abney Dr GLV S14 ....140 C4
Abney Rd GLV S14 ....140 C4
Acacia Av CHPT/GREN S35 ......93 H2
  MALT S66 ....108 C4
  MALT S66 ....110 B3
  STV/CWN S43 ....189 E1
Acacia Ct BTLY DN5 ....26 C5
Acacia Crs ECK/KIL S21 ....167 H3
Acacia Gv CONI DN12 ....88 C3
  CUD/GR S72 ....17 E2
Acacia Rd
  DONS/BSCR DN4 ....58 B5
  SHEFN S5 ....103 E5

Acer Cl DIN S25 ....148 B5
  ECK/KIL S21 ....168 A3
Acer Cft ARMTH DN3 ....42 D5
  DONS/BSCR DN4 ....74 D1
Ackworth Dr
  DARN/MH S9 ....117 H3
Acorn Cft KIMB S61 ....97 F4
Acorn Crs SHEFN S5 ....112 C5
Acorn Dr ST/HB/BR S6 ....112 C5
Acorn HI ST/HB/BR S6 ....112 D5
Acorn Rdg RCH S42 ....191 F5
Acorn St OWL S3 ....125 H2
Acorn Wy CUD/GR S72 ....22 D1
  ST/HB/BR S6 ....123 F1
Acre Cl ARMTH DN3 ....29 F5
  MALT S66 ....110 C1
Acre Ga CHPT/GREN S35 ....80 B5
Acre Rd CUD/GR S72 ....22 A3
Acres Hill La DARN/MH S9 .....127 H4
Acres Hill Rd DARN/MH S9 .....127 H4
Acres Vw RHAM S60 ....119 H1
Acres View Cl CHNE S41 ....187 F2
Acrewood Dr MALT S66 ....108 B2
Acton Cl AU/AST/KP S26 ....145 F1
Adastral Av HACK/IN S12 ....154 C3
Addison Rd MALT S66 ....110 B3
  MEX/SWTN S64 ....55 H2
  SHEFN S5 ....115 H2
Addison Sq DIN S25 ....134 D4
Addy Cl ST/HB/BR S6 ....125 G2
Addy Dr ST/HB/BR S6 ....125 G2
Adelaide La OWL S3 ....125 H2
Adelaide Rd ABRD S7 ....139 F4

Adelaide St MALT S66 ....111 F5
Adelphi St ST/HB/BR S6..........125 G2
Adkins Dr SHEFN S5 ....114 C1
Adkins Rd SHEFN S5 ....114 C1
Adlard Rd WHHL DN2 ....41 F4
Adlington Crs SHEFN S5 ....101 H5
Adlington Rd SHEFN S5 ....101 H5
Admiral Biggs Dr
  RHAM S60 ....130 A3
Admirals Crest KIMB S61 ....95 H4
Adrian Crs SHEFN S5..............102 A5
Adsetts St ATT S4 ....116 A3
Adwick Av BTLY DN5 ....26 B2
Adwick Ct MEX/SWTN S64 * 67 F4
Adwick La AWLS/ASK DN6 ....26 A1
Adwick Pk DEARNE S63 ....66 B3
Adwick Rd MEX/SWTN S64 ....66 D1
Agden Rd ABRD S7 ....139 G2
Agnes Rd BSLY S70 ....2 E6
Agnes Ter BSLY S70 ....3 F1
Ainsdale Av DEARNE S63 ....53 F1
Ainsdale Ct BSLYN/ROY S71.....20 D2
Ainsdale Rd BSLYN/ROY S71 ....12 B4
Ainsley Cl EPW DN9 ....75 H1
Ainsley Rd FUL S10 ....125 E3
Ainsty Rd ABRD S7 ....139 H3
Aintree Av DONS/BSCR DN4 .....57 H3
  ECK/KIL S21 ....166 B5
Aintree Cl BTLY DN5.................38 C5
Aintree Dr MEX/SWTN S64 ....66 C1
Aire Cl CHPT/GREN S35............80 D5
Airedale Rd ST/HB/BR S6 ....113 G2

Aireton Cl MALT S66 ....108 A4
Aireton Rd BSLY S70..................2 E3
Air Mount Cl MALT S66 ....108 A5
Aisby Dr NROS/TKH DN11 ....91 G1
Aisthorpe Rd SHEFS S8 ....152 D2
Aitken Rd MEX/SWTN S64 ....86 B5
Aizlewood Rd ABRD S7 ....139 H4
Albert Bank Cl
  TOT/DORE S17 ....161 F3
Alba Cl WMB/DAR S73 ....34 C4
Albanus Rdg ST/HB/BR S6 .....123 F1
Albany Cl WMB/DAR S73 ....33 G4
Albany La NROS/TKH DN11.......91 E2
Albany Rd ABRD S7 ....139 H3
  DONS/BSCR DN4 ....55 C5
  MEX/SWTN S64 ....86 B2
  STKB/PEN S36 ....76 D2
Albany St RHAM/THRY S65 ....9 H5
Albert Av STV/CWN S43 ....180 C5
Albert Rd DEARNE S63 ....37 C5
  DEARNE S63 ....64 D1
  HACK/IN S12 ....155 C2
  MEX/SWTN S64 ....67 E3
  RAW S62 ....98 B2
  SHEFS S8 ....140 A4
  STV/CWN S43 ....180 B5
Albert St BSLY S70 ....3 C4
  CUD/GR S72 ....17 E3
  DEARNE S63 ....37 E2
  ECK/KIL S21 ....174 D1
  MALT S66 ....111 F4

MEX/SWTN S64 66 B4
RHAM S60 8 C4
Albert Terrace Rd
ST/HB/BR S6 125 G2
Albion Dr DEARNE S63 37 H2
Albion Pl DON DN1 7 F4
Albion Rd BSLYN/ROY S71 15 G4
CHSW S40 4 E3
RHAM S60 9 G5
Albion St ST/HB/BR S6 10 B1
Albion Ter BSLY S70 3 J7
DONS/BSCR DN4 55 H4
Alcester Rd ABRD S7 139 H3
Aldam Cl RHAM/THRY S65 107 F2
TOT/DORE S17 161 E4
Aldam Cft TOT/DORE S17 161 E4
Aldam Rd DONS/BSCR DN4 71 E2
TOT/DORE S17 161 E4
Aldam Wy TOT/DORE S17 161 E4
Aldbury Cl BSLYN/ROY S71 20 B1
Aldcliffe Crs
DONS/BSCR DN4 71 F4
Aldene Av ST/HB/BR S6 113 F3
Aldene Gld ST/HB/BR S6 113 F3
Aldene Rd ST/HB/BR S6 113 F2
Alderford Dr
DONS/BSCR DN4 71 H4
Alder Gv DONS/BSCR DN4 71 F1
WMB/DAR S73 50 D1
Alder Holt Cl ARMTH DN3 43 E5
Alder La DARN/MH S9 128 C4
Alder Ms HOY S74 62 A3
Alderney Rd
SHEFP/MNR S2 140 A3
Aldersgate Cl
NROS/TKH DN11 91 G3
Alderson Av RAW S62 85 F5
Alderson Dr BSLYN/ROY S71 20 A1
WHHL DN2 7 J4
Alderson Pl SHEFP/MNR S2 140 A2
Alderson Rd
SHEFP/MNR S2 139 H2
Alderson Rd North
SHEFP/MNR S2 140 A2
Aldervale Cl MEX/SWTN S64 86 B3
Aldesworth Rd
DONS/BSCR DN4 58 A4
Aldfield Wy SHEFN S5 115 F3
Aldham Cottages
WMB/DAR S73 * 50 A1
Aldham Crs WMB/DAR S73 33 G4
Aldham House La
WMB/DAR S73 49 H1
Aldred Cl ECK/KIL S21 158 C5
MALT S66 108 A4
Aldred Ct RHAM/THRY S65 9 H6
Aldred Rd FUL S10 125 E2
Aldred St RHAM/THRY S65 9 H6
Aldrin Wy MALT S66 110 C2
Aldwarke La
RHAM/THRY S65 98 C4
Aldwarke Rd RAW S62 98 B3
Alexander St BTLY DN5 39 H1
Alexandra Cl KIMB S61 104 C1
Alexandra Gdns ECC S11 139 F4
Alexandra Rd
AU/AST/KP S26 145 E2
AWLS/ASK DN6 25 H1
BTLY DN5 39 H1
DONS/BSCR DN4 55 G5
DRON S18 171 F1
MEX/SWTN S64 67 F3
SHEFP/MNR S2 140 A3
Alexandra Rd East CHNE S41 5 K7
Alexandra Rd West
CHSW S40 4 D3
Alexandra St MALT S66 111 E4
Alexandra Ter
BSLYN/ROY S71 33 F2
Alford Cl CHSW S40 191 G1
DOD/DAR S75 18 D3
Alfred Rd DARN/MH S9 116 B5
Alfred St BSLYN/ROY S71 13 E5
Algar Cl SHEFP/MNR S2 141 E3
Algar Crs SHEFP/MNR S2 141 F3
Algar Dr SHEFP/MNR S2 141 E3
Algar Pl SHEFP/MNR S2 141 E3
Algar Rd SHEFP/MNR S2 141 E3
Alice Rd KIMB S61 8 B3
Alice Wy DRON S18 179 E1
Alison Cl AU/AST/KP S26 145 F3
Alison Crs SHEFP/MNR S2 141 H1
Alison Dr AU/AST/KP S26 145 F3
Allan St RHAM/THRY S65 9 H5
Allatt Cl BSLY S70 3 G7
Alldred Crs MEX/SWTN S64 86 A2
Allenby Cl SHEFS S8 162 C1
Allenby Crs NROS/TKH DN11 91 E3
Allenby Dr SHEFS S8 162 C1
Allendale BSLY S70 32 C5
Allendale Gdns BTLY DN5 55 F2
Allendale Rd BTLY DN5 55 F2
DOD/DAR S75 19 G3
HOY S74 61 H3
RCH S42 195 F4
RHAM/THRY S65 107 E5
Allende Wy DARN/MH S9 127 H1
Allen Gdns CHPT/GREN S35 94 B5
Allen Rd MOS S20 157 F3
Allen St OWL S3 10 F1
Allerton St DON DN1 6 D2
Allestree Dr DRON S18 170 A2
All Hallowes Dr MALT S66 110 C4
Alliance St ATT S4 126 D1
Alliss Rd ARMTH DN3 59 G5
Allott Cl RHAM/THRY S65 108 D1
Allott Crs HOY S74 62 C1
Allott St HOY S74 61 F3
Allpits Rd BSVR S44 193 H1
All Saints Mdw DIN S25 134 A2
All Saints Wy
AU/AST/KP S26 145 G3
All Saints' Sq RHAM S60 9 F4
Allsops Pl CHNE S41 187 F1
Allt St RAW S62 98 B2
Alma Crs DRON S18 163 E5
Alma Rd CHPT/GREN S35 80 B4
RHAM S60 9 F6
Alma Rw RHAM S60 120 A3
Alma St BSLY S70 2 D4
OWL S3 126 A2
WMB/DAR S73 50 B3
Alma St West CHSW S40 4 C5
Almholme La BTLY DN5 27 H2
Almond Av ARMTH DN3 42 D3
CUD/GR S72 16 D5
Almond Cl MALT S66 110 B3
Almond Crs STV/CWN S43 183 E2
Almond Dr ECK/KIL S21 168 A3
Almond Gld MALT S66 121 G1
Almond Pl STV/CWN S43 * 188 C2
Almond Rd
DONS/BSCR DN4 58 B5
Almond Tree Rd
AU/AST/KP S26 158 D3
Alms Hill Crs ECC S11 151 E2
Alms Hill Dr ECC S11 151 F2
Almshill Gld ECC S11 151 F2
Alms Hill Rd ECC S11 151 F2
Alney Pl ST/HB/BR S6 101 F5
Alnwick Dr HACK/IN S12 141 H5
Alnwick Rd HACK/IN S12 141 H5
Alperton Cl BSLYN/ROY S71 21 F2
Alpha Rd RHAM/THRY S65 106 D2
Alpine Cl STKB/PEN S36 76 C2
Alpine Cft STKB/PEN S36 76 C2
Alpine Gv STV/CWN S43 181 E5
Alpine Rd ST/HB/BR S6 125 F2
STKB/PEN S36 76 C2
Alport Av HACK/IN S12 155 G1
Alport Dr HACK/IN S12 142 C5
Alport Gv HACK/IN S12 142 C5
Alport Pl HACK/IN S12 155 G1
Alport Ri DRON S18 170 B1
Alport Rd HACK/IN S12 142 C5
Alric Dr BSLYN/ROY S71 33 E1
RHAM S60 118 B3
Alrich Ms STKB/PEN S36 76 B1
Alsing Rd DARN/MH S9 117 E1
Alston Cl DONS/BSCR DN4 73 H1
Alston Rd DONS/BSCR DN4 73 H2
Alton Cl DRON S18 170 B3
ECC S11 151 G3
RCH S42 191 F4
Alum Chine Cl CHNE S41 193 E4
Alverley La DONS/BSCR DN4 71 G4
Alverley Wy BSLY S70 60 D2
Alwyn Av BTLY DN5 39 E3
Amalfi Cl WMB/DAR S73 34 D5
Ambassador Gdns
ARMTH DN3 43 E5
Amber Crs CHSW S40 191 G3
Amber Cft STV/CWN S43 189 G2
Amberley St DARN/MH S9 116 C4
Ambler Ri AU/AST/KP S26 145 E1
Ambleside Cl CHNE S41 186 C2
MOS S20 167 E2
RHAM S60 * 118 A4
Ambleside Crs BTLY DN5 54 A4
Ambleside Dr BSVR S44 196 C3
Ambleside Gv
BSLYN/ROY S71 33 G2
Ambleside Wk DIN S25 148 C2
Amen Cnr RHAM S60 * 8 E3
America La DEARNE S63 64 C5
Amersall Ct BTLY DN5 39 E3
Amersall Crs BTLY DN5 39 E3
Amersall Rd BTLY DN5 39 E2
Amesbury Cl CHNE S41 * 187 E2
Amory's Holt Cl MALT S66 110 C1
Amory's Holt Dr MALT S66 110 C1
Amory's Holt Rd MALT S66 110 C1
Amory's Holt Wy MALT S66 110 B2
Amos Rd DARN/MH S9 116 D2
Amy Rd BTLY DN5 27 E4
Anchorage Crs BTLY DN5 55 G1
Anchorage La BTLY DN5 55 F1
Ancona Ri WMB/DAR S73 34 D5
Ancote Cl DOD/DAR S75 30 C1
Anderson Cl STV/CWN S43 180 C3
Andover Dr OWL S3 126 A1
Andover St OWL S3 126 A1
Andrew La OWL S3 126 B2
Andrews Pl KIMB S61 105 E1
Andwell La FUL S10 136 C5
Anelay Rd DONS/BSCR DN4 71 F1
Anfield Rd
DONS/BSCR DN4 74 A1
Angel La RAW S62 83 H2
Angel St DEARNE S63 53 F4
SHEF S1 11 H2
Angel Yd CHSW S40 5 F4
Angerford Av SHEFS S8 153 F1
Anglesey Rd DRON S18 171 E3
Angleton Av
SHEFP/MNR S2 142 A2
Angleton Cl
SHEFP/MNR S2 142 A2
Angleton Gdns
SHEFP/MNR S2 142 A2
Angleton Gn
SHEFP/MNR S2 142 A2
Angleton Ms
SHEFP/MNR S2 142 A2
Angram Rd CHPT/GREN S35 80 B3
Annan Cl DOD/DAR S75 18 B2
Annat Pl CHPT/GREN S35 80 A4
Annesley Cl CHNE S41 193 E4
SHEFS S8 162 D1
Annesley Rd SHEFS S8 152 D5
Anne St DIN S25 134 D2
Anns Rd SHEFP/MNR S2 140 A3
Anns Rd North
SHEFP/MNR S2 140 B3
Ann St RAW S62 98 B3
Ansdell Rd BTLY DN5 26 D5
Ansell Rd ECC S11 138 C4
Anson Gv RHAM S60 118 D4
Anson St SHEFP/MNR S2 11 K3
Ansten Crs DONS/BSCR DN4 58 A4
Anston Cl DIN S25 148 B2
Ansult Ct BTLY DN5 39 G2
Antrim Av FUL S10 10 A6
Anvil Cl ST/HB/BR S6 124 A1
Anvil Crs CHPT/GREN S35 102 B1
Apley Rd DON DN1 6 E6
Apollo St RAW S62 85 H4
Apostle Cl DONS/BSCR DN4 71 E2
Appleby Rd WHHL DN2 57 G1
Appleby Wk DIN S25 148 D1
Applegarth Cl HACK/IN S12 141 G4
Applegarth Dr
HACK/IN S12 141 G4
Applehaigh Dr ARMTH DN3 29 E2
Applehaigh Gv
BSLYN/ROY S71 12 A5
Applehaigh La
HOR/CROF WF4 12 A3
Applehaigh Vw
BSLYN/ROY S71 12 A5
Applehurst Bank BSLY S70 * 32 B2
Appleton Gdns BTLY DN5 39 G2
Appleton Wy BSLY S70 32 A5
BTLY DN5 39 G2
Appletree Dr DRON S18 171 E2
Appletree Rd BSVR S44 184 B5
Appletree Wy
DONS/BSCR DN4 74 C3
Apppleton Cl
RHAM/THRY S65 99 F5
April Cl BSLYN/ROY S71 20 C3
April Dr BSLYN/ROY S71 20 D3
Aqueduct St
BSLYN/ROY S71 19 H4
Arbour Crs MALT S66 133 F1
Arbour Dr MALT S66 133 F1
Arbourthorne Rd
SHEFP/MNR S2 141 E4
The Arcade BSLY S70 3 F4
Archaeological Wy
STV/CWN S43 185 G3
Archdale Cl CHSW S40 192 C3
SHEFP/MNR S2 141 H2
Archdale Pl
SHEFP/MNR S2 * 141 G2
Archdale Rd
SHEFP/MNR S2 141 G1
Archer Ga ST/HB/BR S6 112 D3
Archer La ABRD S7 139 F5
Archer Rd ABRD S7 152 B2
SHEFS S8 152 C2
Archery Cl MALT S66 121 F1
Archibald Rd ABRD S7 139 G4
Arcon Pl RAW S62 85 G5
Arcubus Av AU/AST/KP S26 145 F2
Ardeen Rd WHHL DN2 7 K1
Arden Cl CHSW S40 186 C5
Arden Ga DONS/BSCR DN4 71 F4
Ardmore St DARN/MH S9 127 G2
Ardron Wk RAW S62 85 H5
Ardsley Av AU/AST/KP S26 145 G4
Ardsley Cl MOS S20 155 H3
Ardsley Dr MOS S20 155 H3
Ardsley Gv MOS S20 155 H3
Ardsley Rd BSLY S70 32 C5
CHSW S40 191 F1
Arena Ct DARN/MH S9 116 D4
Argyle Cl SHEFS S8 140 B5
Argyle La NROS/TKH DN11 91 E2
Argyle Rd SHEFS S8 140 A5
Argyle St MEX/SWTN S64 67 E3
Argyll Av WHHL DN2 41 F5
Arklow Cl CHNE S41 192 D4
Arklow Rd WHHL DN2 57 E1
Arksey Common La
BTLY DN5 27 G5
Arksey La BTLY DN5 39 H1
Arkwright Rd BTLY DN5 39 F5
Arley St SHEFP/MNR S2 11 F7
Arlington Av
AU/AST/KP S26 145 H2
Arlott Wy CONI DN12 70 C5
Armer St RHAM S60 8 C5
Armitage Rd
DONS/BSCR DN4 71 F1
STKB/PEN S36 77 F3
Armley Rd DARN/MH S9 116 C4
Armroyd La HOY S74 62 B4
Arms Park Dr MOS S20 167 F2
Armstead Rd MOS S20 157 F2
Armstrong Wk MALT S66 110 C2
Armthorpe La ARMTH DN3 29 G2
WHHL DN2 41 E5
Armthorpe Rd ECC S11 138 B2
WHHL DN2 41 E5
Armyne Gv BSLYN/ROY S71 33 E1
Arncliffe Dr BSLY S70 30 D1
CHPT/GREN S35 93 H1
Arnold Av BSLYN/ROY S71 14 D4
HACK/IN S12 154 D4
Arnold Crs MEX/SWTN S64 67 E2
Arnold Rd RHAM/THRY S65 106 D3
Arnold St ST/HB/BR S6 114 A5
Arnside Cl CHNE S41 178 D5
Arnside Rd ABRD S7 139 G5
MALT S66 111 E2
Arran Hl RHAM/THRY S65 99 H3
Arran Rd FUL S10 124 D4
Arras St DARN/MH S9 127 F2
Arthington St SHEFS S8 140 A4
Arthur Av BTLY DN5 26 D5
Arthur Pl BTLY DN5 26 D5
Arthur Rd STKB/PEN S36 76 C2
Arthur St BSLY S70 32 A5
BTLY DN5 26 D4
RAW S62 85 G4
Artisan Vw SHEFS S8 140 A4
Arundel Av RHAM S60 130 A3
RHAM/THRY S65 99 F5
Arundel Cl CHNE S41 187 F1
DRON S18 170 B2
Arundel Cottages
RHAM S60 130 A3
Arundel Crs RHAM S60 129 H3
Arundel Gdns
BSLYN/ROY S71 12 C5
BTLY DN5 39 F2
Arundel Ga SHEF S1 11 G4
Arundel La SHEF S1 11 H5
Arundel Dr BSLYN/ROY S71 21 F2
Arundel Rd CHPT/GREN S35 81 E5
RHAM S60 * 130 A3
RHAM/THRY S65 9 K7
Arundel St RHAM S60 129 H3
SHEF S1 11 G6
Arundel Vw HOY S74 62 C1
Ascension Cl MALT S66 111 E4
Ascot Av DONS/BSCR DN4 57 H4
Ascot Cl MEX/SWTN S64 67 F2
Ascot Dr BTLY DN5 38 D4
DIN S25 134 A3
Ascot St SHEFP/MNR S2 140 A1
Ashberry Cl DEARNE S63 37 F2
Ashberry Gdns
ST/HB/BR S6 125 F2
Ashberry Rd ST/HB/BR S6 125 F2
Ashbourne Cl CHSW S40 186 A4
Ashbourne Gv
HAN/WDH S13 142 D1
Ashbourne Rd
BSLYN/ROY S71 20 A1
HAN/WDH S13 142 D1
Ashburnham Gdns
BTLY DN5 55 E2
Ashburton Cl
AWLS/ASK DN6 25 E1
Ashbury Dr SHEFS S8 153 G3
Ashbury La SHEFS S8 153 G3
Ashby Ct BSLY S70 2 D6
Ash Cl ECK/KIL S21 168 A3
RHAM/THRY S65 107 F5
STV/CWN S43 177 F5
Ash Ct BTLY DN5 54 D4
MALT S66 110 B2
Ashcourt Dr
DONS/BSCR DN4 71 H4
Ash Crs ECK/KIL S21 174 B2
MEX/SWTN S64 66 C2
Ashcroft Dr CHNE S41 179 H4
Ashdale Cl ARMTH DN3 42 B1
Ash Dale Rd
DONS/BSCR DN4 70 B4
Ashdell FUL S10 125 E5
Ashdell La FUL S10 125 E5
Ashdell Rd FUL S10 125 E5
Ashdene Ct MEX/SWTN S64 86 B3
Ashdown Dr CHSW S40 4 A7
Ashdown Gdns MOS S20 157 G2
Ashdown Pl BTLY DN5 39 E2
Asher Rd ABRD S7 139 H2
Ashes La RAW S62 82 B3
Ashfield Cl ARMTH DN3 43 E5
DOD/DAR S75 2 A1
HACK/IN S12 154 B1
Ashfield Ct BSLY S70 * 32 D2
Ashfield Dr HACK/IN S12 154 B1
Ashfield Rd CHNE S41 193 F4
DONS/BSCR DN4 71 G2
STKB/PEN S36 77 F2
Ashfield Wy MALT S66 108 B2
Ashford Ct BSLYN/ROY S71 * 12 B4
Ashford Rd DRON S18 170 B3
ECC S11 * 139 F2
Ashfurlong Cl
TOT/DORE S17 161 F1
Ashfurlong Dr
TOT/DORE S17 161 F1
Ashfurlong Pk
TOT/DORE S17 161 F1
Ashfurlong Rd
TOT/DORE S17 161 E1
Ashgate Av CHSW S40 191 G1
Ashgate Cl FUL S10 125 E5
Ashgate La FUL S10 125 E5
Ashgate Rd CHSW S40 4 B2
FUL S10 125 E5
RCH S42 186 A5
Ashgate Valley Rd
CHSW S40 4 A2
Ash Gv ARMTH DN3 43 E3
AU/AST/KP S26 159 G2
BSLY S70 32 D3
CONI DN12 88 C2
FUL S10 125 F5
MALT S66 108 C4
MALT S66 111 F2
RAW S62 98 C1
STV/CWN S43 182 D2
Ash House La
TOT/DORE S17 150 D4
Ashland Rd ABRD S7 139 G5
ECK/KIL S21 167 E5
Ash La DRON S18 164 B5
ECK/KIL S21 173 E3
STKB/PEN S36 77 G2
Ashleigh Av HACK/IN S12 141 F5
Ashleigh Ct ECK/KIL S21 174 C2
Ashleigh Cft HACK/IN S12 141 F5
Ashleigh Dr HACK/IN S12 141 F5
Ashleigh Gdns KIMB S61 97 F4
Ashleigh Pl HACK/IN S12 141 F5
Ashleigh Rd STV/CWN S43 177 E4
Ashleigh V BSLY S70 32 C2
Ashley Cl ECK/KIL S21 168 B2
Ashley Cft BSLYN/ROY S71 12 B5
Ashley Gv AU/AST/KP S26 145 F3
Ashley La ECK/KIL S21 168 B2
Ashmore Av ECK/KIL S21 174 B1
Ash Mt RAW S62 * 98 B1
RHAM/THRY S65 * 9 G4
Ashopton Rd CHNE S41 186 C3
Ashover Cl BSLY S70 48 A1
Ashover Rd STV/CWN S43 189 G3
Ashpool Cl HAN/WDH S13 143 E4
Ashpool Fold
HAN/WDH S13 143 E4
Ash Rdg MEX/SWTN S64 86 B1
Ash Rd CUD/GR S72 17 F2
DEARNE S63 65 F3
Ash St MOS S20 166 C1
ST/HB/BR S6 125 G1
WMB/DAR S73 33 G4
Ashton Av BTLY DN5 38 D1
Ashton Cl CHSW S40 191 G4
ECK/KIL S21 168 A2
Ashton Dr ARMTH DN3 29 E3
Ash Tree Cl CHSW S40 191 G1
Ash Tree Rd STV/CWN S43 185 E4
Ashurst Cl ST/HB/BR S6 113 E5
Ashurst Dr ST/HB/BR S6 113 E5
Ashurst Pl ST/HB/BR S6 113 E5
Ashurst Rd ST/HB/BR S6 113 E5
Ash V CHSW S40 191 F1
Ash Vw CHPT/GREN S35 93 H2
KIMB S61 97 F3
Ashville NROS/TKH DN11 91 G3
Ashwell Cl CUD/GR S72 17 E1
Ashwell Gv
RHAM/THRY S65 106 C1
Ashwell Rd HAN/WDH S13 143 E4
Ashwood Cl ARMTH DN3 75 E1
BSLY S70 48 B1
CHPT/GREN S35 80 A3
Ashwood Gv CUD/GR S72 23 H4
Ashwood Rd
CHPT/GREN S35 80 A4
RAW S62 98 B2
Ashworth Dr KIMB S61 96 B4
Askam Ct MALT S66 108 D3
Askam Rd MALT S66 108 D3
Askern Rd BTLY DN5 26 C3
Askew Ct STKB/PEN S36 77 E3
Askew Wy CHSW S40 5 G7
Askrigg Cl DONS/BSCR DN4 74 B1
Asline Rd SHEFP/MNR S2 140 A2
Aspen Cl ARMTH DN3 42 B1
ECK/KIL S21 168 A2
Aspen Gv WMB/DAR S73 51 E1
Aspen Rd ECK/KIL S21 174 B2
Aspen Wy MEX/SWTN S64 86 A3
Aspley Cl CHSW S40 4 B1
Asquith Rd BTLY DN5 39 H1
DARN/MH S9 * 103 H5
Astcote Ct ARMTH DN3 29 E3
Aster Cl DIN S25 148 B4
MOS S20 157 F2
Aston Cl DRON S18 163 G5
Aston Dr BSLYN/ROY S71 20 A1
Aston La AU/AST/KP S26 131 F5
Aston St SHEFP/MNR S2 126 D3
Astwell Gdns
CHPT/GREN S35 80 C5
Atebanks Ct
DONS/BSCR DN4 71 H4
Athelstan Cl HAN/WDH S13 142 C1
Athelstane Crs ARMTH DN3 29 F4
Athelstane Dr MALT S66 133 E2
Athelstane Rd CONI DN12 88 D1
Athelstan Rd
HAN/WDH S13 142 C1
Athersley Crs
BSLYN/ROY S71 20 A1
Athersley Gdns MOS S20 156 A3
Athersley Rd
BSLYN/ROY S71 20 A1

Atherton Cl
  SHEFP/MNR S2..............**141** F4
Atherton Rd
  SHEFP/MNR S2..............**141** F4
Athol Cl *RCH* S42..............**191** F4
Atholl Crs *WHHL* DN2..........**41** G5
Athol Rd *SHEFS* S8............**152** C1
Athorpe Gv *DIN* S25..........**134** C4
Athorpe Rd *DIN* S25..........**134** C4
Athron Dr *RHAM/THRY* S65....**107** E5
Athron St *DON* DN1 *..............**6** E1
Atkin Pl *SHEFP/MNR* S2.......**140** A2
Atlantic Dr *SHEFS* S8........**162** C2
Atlantic Rd *SHEFS* S8........**162** C2
Atlantic Wy *SHEFS* S8........**162** C2
Atlas St *ATT* S4..............**126** D1
  RHAM S60..................**118** C3
Atlow Cl *CHSW* S40...........**186** B4
Atterby Dr *NROS/TKH* DN11...**91** G1
Attercliffe Common
  DARN/MH S9................**116** C5
Attercliffe Rd *ATT* S4.......**126** C2
  DARN/MH S9................**127** F1
Attlee Av *NROS/TKH* DN11......**90** D2
Attlee Cl *MALT* S66..........**111** F4
Attlee Crs *WMB/DAR* S73.......**35** G5
Attlee Rd *STV/CWN* S43.......**189** F2
Aubretia Av *RHAM* S60........**118** D5
Auckland Av *ST/HB/BR* S6.....**113** E4
Auckland Dr *MOS* S20.........**166** D2
Auckland Ri *MOS* S20.........**167** E2
Auckland Rd
  MEX/SWTN S64...............**67** F3
  WHHL DN2...................**40** C5
Auckland Wy *MOS* S20........**167** E2
Audrey Rd *HAN/WDH* S13......**142** A3
Aughton Av
  AU/AST/KP S26.............**145** E1
Aughton Cl *HAN/WDH* S13.....**142** B3
Aughton Crs
  HAN/WDH S13..............**142** A3
Aughton Dr *HAN/WDH* S13....**142** A2
Aughton La
  AU/AST/KP S26.............**145** F1
Aughton Rd
  AU/AST/KP S26.............**145** E2
Augustus Rd *RHAM* S60.......**118** C2
Aukley Rd *SHEFS* S8..........**139** H5
Aunby Dr *AU/AST/KP* S26.....**145** F2
Austen Av *DONS/BSCR* DN4....**71** E2
Austen Dr *MALT* S66..........**109** E4
Austin Cl *ST/HB/BR* S6.......**113** E5
Austin Ct *ST/HB/BR* S6.......**113** E5
Austwick Cl
  DONS/BSCR DN4.............**71** E4
Austwick Wk *BSLY* S70..........**2** D3
Autumn Cl *MALT* S66.........**133** G1
Autumn Dr *MALT* S66.........**111** E2
Avenue 1 *CHNE* S41..........**192** D4
Avenue 2 *CHNE* S41..........**192** D4
Avenue 3 *CHNE* S41..........**192** D4
Avenue 4 *CHNE* S41..........**192** D4
Avenue 5 *CHNE* S41..........**192** D4
Avenue 6 *CHNE* S41 *........**192** D4
Avenue 7 *CHNE* S41 *........**192** D4
Avenue 8 *CHNE* S41..........**192** D4
Avenue Rd *ABRD* S7..........**139** H4
  CHNE S41..................**187** G1
  DEARNE S63.................**65** G2
  WHHL DN2...................**30** D1
The Avenue *BSLYN/ROY* S71...**13** E5
  BTLY DN5...................**40** A1
  DARN/MH S9................**128** A3
  DOD/DAR S75................**60** B2
  DONS/BSCR DN4.............**57** G4
  DRON S18..................**171** F1
  ECK/KIL S21...............**176** B1
  MOS S20...................**157** F1
Aviemore Cl *STV/CWN* S43....**180** C2
Aviemore Rd
  DONS/BSCR DN4.............**71** E2
Avill Wy *MALT* S66...........**121** F1
Avisford Dr *SHEFN* S5.......**114** B1
Avisford Rd *SHEFN* S5.......**101** F5
Avoca Av *WHHL* DN2............**57** E1
Avocet Wy *KIMB* S61..........**82** B5
Avon Cl *DOD/DAR* S75.........**18** A4
  DRON S18..................**163** F5
  MALT S66..................**110** D2
  WMB/DAR S73................**50** D4
Avondale Dr
  BSLYN/ROY S71..............**15** G3
Avondale Rd *BSVR* S44.......**196** D4
  CHSW S40....................**4** D2
  KIMB S61..................**105** G2
  ST/HB/BR S6...............**113** H4
  STV/CWN S43...............**189** G2
  WHHL DN2...................**57** E2
Avondale
  BSLYN/ROY S71..............**15** G3
Avon Gv *CHPT/GREN* S35.......**80** C5
Avon Mt *KIMB* S61...........**105** F2
Avonside Cl *STV/CWN* S43....**181** G3
Avon St *BSLYN/ROY* S71........**3** J5
Axholme Ct *WHHL* DN2..........**7** H1
Axholme Rd *WHHL* DN2.........**40** C5
Axle La *DIN* S25.............**148** A4
Aylesbury Crs
  DARN/MH S9................**116** D1
Aylesbury Rd *WHHL* DN2.......**57** F1
Aylesford Cl
  BSLYN/ROY S71..............**19** H4
Aylsham Dr *AU/AST/KP* S26...**145** G3
Aylward Cl *SHEFP/MNR* S2....**141** F3

Aylward Rd
  SHEFP/MNR S2..............**141** F3
Aymer Dr *MALT* S66..........**133** G2
Ayrsome Wk
  DONS/BSCR DN4.............**58** A5
Ayrton Vls *DEARNE* S63 *.....**37** G5
Aysgarth Av *BSLYN/ROY* S71...**33** H2
Aysgarth Ct
  DONS/BSCR DN4.............**74** B1
Aysgarth Ri
  AU/AST/KP S26.............**145** E2
Aysgarth Rd *ST/HB/BR* S6....**101** E5
Ayton Wk *BTLY* DN5...........**26** C4
Azalea Cl *DIN* S25...........**148** B5

B

Babington Cl
  SHEFP/MNR S2..............**141** F3
Babington Ct
  SHEFP/MNR S2..............**141** F3
Babur Rd *ATT* S4..............**28** B1
Backfield Ri *CHPT/GREN* S35..**81** E5
Backfields *SHEF* S1...........**11** F4
Back La *BSLYN/ROY* S71........**20** C2
  BTLY DN5....................**38** C5
  CUD/GR S72..................**36** B4
  DIN S25...................**148** C2
  DRON S18..................**172** B2
  ECK/KIL S21...............**166** C5
  FUL S10...................**124** B3
  RAW S62.....................**84** C5
  RHAM/THRY S65..............**87** H5
  RHAM/THRY S65..............**99** H2
  STKB/PEN S36................**44** C3
  STV/CWN S43...............**185** F2
Back La West
  BSLYN/ROY S71..............**12** A5
Backmoor Crs *SHEFS* S8......**153** G3
Backmoor Rd *SHEFS* S8.......**153** G3
Back Rd *DRON* S18...........**170** D3
Back Rw *NROS/TKH* DN11 *....**91** H2
Back South St
  STV/CWN S43...............**180** B3
Back St *HAN/WDH* S13........**143** G4
Bacon La *DARN/MH* S9........**127** E2
Bacons La *CHSW* S40.........**192** B4
Baden Powell Av
  CHSW S40..................**192** B3
Baden Powell Rd *CHSW* S40....**5** F6
Baden St *BSLY* S70............**48** B1
  RHAM S60....................**8** D2
Badger Cl *HAN/WDH* S13......**143** G3
Badger Dr *HAN/WDH* S13......**143** G3
Badger La *SHEF* S1............**10** E3
Badger Pl *HAN/WDH* S13......**143** G3
Badger Ri *HAN/WDH* S13......**143** G3
Badger Rd *HAN/WDH* S13......**143** G3
Badgers Holt *ARMTH* DN3......**59** F5
Badsley Ct
  RHAM/THRY S65.............**106** C3
Badsley Moor La
  RHAM/THRY S65...............**9** K6
Badsley St *RHAM/THRY* S65.....**9** J5
Badsley St South
  RHAM/THRY S65...............**9** K6
Badworth Cl *MALT* S66.......**109** E4
Badworth Pl *MALT* S66.......**109** E4
Badsworth Rd
  DONS/BSCR DN4.............**70** C3
Badsworth Wy *MALT* S66......**109** E4
Bagley Rd *DIN* S25...........**115** H3
Bagshaw's Rd *HACK/IN* S12...**141** H4
Bagshot St *ECC* S11.........**139** F2
Bahram Rd *DONS/BSCR* DN4....**57** G5
Bailey Dr *ECK/KIL* S21......**158** C3
Bailey La *SHEF* S1............**10** E3
Bailey Ms *BTLY* DN5...........**39** E1
Bailey St *SHEF* S1............**10** E3
Bainbridge Rd *BSVR* S44....**196** C3
  DONS/BSCR DN4...............**6** A7
Baines Wood Cl *CHNE* S41...**186** A7
Bainton Dr *BSLY* S70..........**31** F3
Bakehouse La
  DOD/DAR S75................**18** C4
Baker Dr *ECK/KIL* S21.......**168** A2
Bakers Hl *SHEF* S1...........**11** H5
Bakers La *SHEF* S1...........**10** E2
Baker St *DARN/MH* S9........**127** F1
  DIN S25...................**134** A3
Bakewell Rd
  BSLYN/ROY S71..............**20** A1
  STV/CWN S43...............**189** G4
Bala St *BSLYN/ROY* S71........**3** H4
Balby Carr Bank
  DONS/BSCR DN4.............**73** F1
Balby Rd *DONS/BSCR* DN4.....**55** H5
Balcarres Rd
  NROS/TKH DN11..............**91** F2
Baldwin St *DARN/MH* S9.....**127** E2
Balfour Dr *DARN/MH* S9.....**127** H2
Balfour Rd *BTLY* DN5.........**40** A4
  DARN/MH S9................**127** H2
Balk La *BSLY* S70.............**47** G4
  MALT S66..................**108** D2
Balkley La *WMB/DAR* S73.....**35** G5
The Balk *BTLY* DN5...........**27** C1
  DOD/DAR S75................**14** A2
Ballam Av *BTLY* DN5..........**39** E1

Ballidon Cl *CHSW* S40.......**186** C3
Ballifeld Av *HAN/WDH* S13...**143** H1
Ballifield Cl *HAN/WDH* S13..**143** H1
Ballifield Crs
  HAN/WDH S13..............**143** H1
Ballifield Pl *HAN/WDH* S13..**143** H1
Ballifield Pl *HAN/WDH* S13..**143** H1
Ballifield Ri *HAN/WDH* S13..**143** H1
Ballifield Rd *HAN/WDH* S13..**143** H1
Ballifield Wy
  HAN/WDH S13..............**143** H1
Ball Rd *ST/HB/BR* S6........**113** H5
Ball St *OWL* S3.............**125** H2
Balmain Dr *ST/HB/BR* S6.....**113** H3
Balmain Rd *ST/HB/BR* S6.....**113** H3
Balmer Ri *MALT* S66.........**109** E5
Balm Gn *SHEF* S1.............**11** F3
Balmoak La *CHNE* S41........**188** A4
Balmoral Crs *DRON* S18......**170** B1
  FUL S10...................**136** D1
Balmoral Gln *FUL* S10.......**136** D1
Balmoral Ms *FUL* S10........**136** D1
Balmoral Rd *HAN/WDH* S13...**143** G4
  WHHL DN2....................**7** H1
Balmoral Wy *MALT* S66.......**108** D3
  STV/CWN S43...............**180** C2
Baltic Rd *DARN/MH* S9.......**127** F1
Bamford Av *BSLYN/ROY* S71...**20** A1
Bamford Cl *DOD/DAR* S75......**30** A3
Bamford Rd *STV/CWN* S43.....**189** G4
Bamforth St *ST/HB/BR* S6....**114** B3
Banbury Cl *CONI* DN12........**68** D5
Bank Cl *ABRD* S7............**139** G4
  BSVR S44..................**196** D1
Bank End Av *BSLY* S70........**32** C3
Bank End Cl *DEARNE* S63......**53** E3
Bank End Rd *BSLY* S70........**32** B5
Bankfield La *ST/HB/BR* S6...**123** G1
Bankfield Rd *ST/HB/BR* S6...**113** G5
Bank House Rd
  ST/HB/BR S6...............**125** E2
Bank La *CHPT/GREN* S35.......**79** E4
Bank Rd *CHNE* S41...........**187** G3
  BSLYN/ROY S71..............**33** F3
  CHSW S40....................**4** C4
  CUD/GR S72.................**16** D5
  DIN S25...................**148** B4
  HOY S74.....................**56** A4
  MEX/SWTN S64...............**61** H5
  SHEF S1.....................**11** H2
  STV/CWN S43...............**188** B1
Bank Top Rd
  RHAM/THRY S65.............**107** F5
Bank Vw *RHAM* S60...........**119** H3
Bank Wood Cl *CHNE* S41......**186** B2
Bankwood Cl *GLV* S14........**140** D5
Bankwood Crs
  NROS/TKH DN11..............**90** D1
Bankwood La
  NROS/TKH DN11..............**73** H5
Banner Ct *ECC* S11..........**138** D4
Banner Cross Dr *ECC* S11...**138** D4
Banner Cross Rd *ECC* S11...**138** D4
Bannerdale Cl *ECC* S11......**139** E4
Bannerdale Rd *ECC* S11......**139** E4
Bannerdale Vw *ECC* S11......**139** E4
Bar Av *DOD/DAR* S75..........**14** B4
Barbados Wy *MALT* S66......**109** G4
Bar Balk Cl *KIMB* S61........**96** D5
Barber Balk Cl *KIMB* S61.....**96** C5
Barber Balk Rd *KIMB* S61.....**96** C5
Barber Cl *AU/AST/KP* S26...**147** E5
Barber Crs *FUL* S10.........**125** E3
Barber La *FUL* S10..........**125** E3
Barberry Ct *BSLY* S70........**32** B2
Barberry Wy
  RHAM/THRY S65.............**109** E1
Barbers Av *MEX/SWTN* S64....**66** C3
Barber St *HOY* S74...........**62** A2
Barber's Av *RAW* S62.........**98** B2
Barber's La *ECK/KIL* S21...**158** B5
Barbon Cl *DONS/BSCR* DN4...**187** E4
Barbot Hill Rd *KIMB* S61.....**97** G4
Barcroft *DOD/DAR* S75........**18** C3
Barden Crs *RHAM* S60........**118** C4
Barden Dr *DOD/DAR* S75......**18** C3
Bardolf Rd *DONS/BSCR* DN4...**58** A4
Bardon Rd *ARMTH* DN3.........**59** F5
Bard St *SHEFP/MNR* S2........**11** K2
Bardwell Rd *OWL* S3.........**125** H1
Barfield Rd *HOY* S74.........**62** A2
Barholme Cl *CHNE* S41.......**186** B2
Barholm Rd *FUL* S10.........**124** B5
Baring Rd *KIMB* S61.........**103** G5
Barkby Rd *DARN/MH* S9......**103** G5
Barker Fold *CHSW* S40.........**4** A1
Barker La *CHSW* S40..........**4** A4
Barker St *MEX/SWTN* S64......**66** C3
Barker's Pl *ST/HB/BR* S6....**114** A5
Barker's Pool *SHEF* S1.......**11** F4
Barker's Rd *ABRD* S7........**139** F4

Bark Mdw *DOD/DAR* S75........**30** C3
Barkston Rd
  BSLYN/ROY S71..............**15** G5
Bar La *DOD/DAR* S75..........**14** B4
Barlborough Rd
  STV/CWN S43...............**184** D1
  WMB/DAR S73................**50** C4
Barley Gv *HACK/IN* S12......**154** D2
Barley Cl *BSLY* S70..........**48** A1
Barleycroft La *DIN* S25....**134** D5
Barley La *RCH* S42..........**186** A4
Barley Vw *DEARNE* S63........**37** F3
Barleywood Rd
  DARN/MH S9................**128** A1
Barlow Dr *ST/HB/BR* S6......**124** C1
Barlow Lees La *DRON* S18...**170** D4
Barlow Rd *ST/HB/BR* S6......**113** G5
  STV/CWN S43...............**182** A5
Barmouth Rd *ABRD* S7........**139** G5
Barnabas Wk *BSLYN/ROY* S71...**3** G1
Barnard Av *STV/CWN* S43....**163** H5
Barnardiston Rd
  DARN/MH S9................**127** H2
Barnborough La *DEARNE* S63...**53** C1
Barnby Dun Rd *WHHL* DN2.....**41** G2
Barncliffe Cl *FUL* S10......**137** G2
Barncliffe Crs *FUL* S10.....**137** F1
Barncliffe Dr *FUL* S10......**137** F1
Barncliffe Gln *FUL* S10.....**137** G2
Barncliffe Rd *FUL* S10......**137** G2
Barn Cl *CHNE* S41...........**186** C3
Barnes Av *DRON* S18.........**170** B1
Barnes Ct *SHEFP/MNR* S2......**11** J6
Barnes Hall Rd
  CHPT/GREN S35..............**93** F2
Barnes Gn *DRON* S18.........**161** H4
Barnes Rd *CHNE* S41.........**193** C5
Barnet Av *ECC* S11..........**138** A5
Barnet Rd *ECC* S11..........**138** A5
Barnfield Av *FUL* S10.......**124** A4
  STV/CWN S43...............**182** A4
Barnfield Cl *FUL* S10.......**124** A4
Barnfield Dr *FUL* S10.......**124** A4
Barnham Cl *RCH* S42.........**191** F4
Barn Owl *CUD/GR* S72.........**36** B4
Barnsdale Av *MOS* S20.......**156** A3
Barnside Cl *STKB/PEN* S36...**44** D4
Barnsley Av *CONI* DN12......**88** C1
Barnsley Boundary Wk
  CHPT/GREN S35..............**78** A1
  CUD/GR S72.................**17** F1
  DOD/DAR S75................**60** C5
  DEARNE S63.................**51** G5
  HOR/CROF WF4...............**12** C3
Barnsley Rd *ATT* S4.........**115** F4
  BTLY DN5....................**38** A3
  CUD/GR S72.................**21** G1
  CUD/GR S72.................**36** C5
  DEARNE S63.................**53** E5
  DOD/DAR S75................**30** A3
  HOY S74.....................**48** D5
  KIMB S61....................**82** A4
  OWL S3.....................**115** F5
  SHEFS S8...................**102** C4
  STKB/PEN S36...............**44** D2
  WMB/DAR S73................**33** H5
Barnstone Ct
  DONS/BSCR DN4.............**55** G4
Barnwell Crs *WMB/DAR* S73...**33** H5
Baron St *SHEF* S1...........**140** A1
Barrack La *ST/HB/BR* S6.....**125** C1
Barratt Rd *ECK/KIL* S21....**174** D1
Barrel La *DONS/BSCR* DN4....**70** D2
Barret Rd *DONS/BSCR* DN4....**58** B4
Barretta St *ATT* S4.........**115** H3
Barrie Crs *SHEFN* S5........**114** C1
Barrie Dr *SHEFN* S5.........**114** C1
Barrie Gv *MALT* S66.........**109** H5
Barrie Rd *DONS/BSCR* DN4....**71** H2
Barrie Rd *SHEFN* S5........**114** C1
Barrowby Rd *RAW* S62........**100** D1
Barrow Field La *RAW* S62.....**82** C1
Barrowfield Rd *DEARNE* S63...**37** G5
  HOY S74.....................**61** H1
Barrow Hl *RAW* S62...........**82** B2
Barrow Rd *DARN/MH* S9.......**103** H5
Barrow St *STV/CWN* S43......**182** B4
Barry Rd *STV/CWN* S43.......**188** D5
Bartholomew Cl *MALT* S66...**120** B2
Bartholomew St
  WMB/DAR S73................**50** A2
Bartin Cl *ECC* S11..........**138** C5
Bartle Av *HAN/WDH* S12......**154** D2
Bartle Av *HAN/WDH* S12......**154** B1
Bartle Dr *HACK/IN* S12......**154** B1
Bartlett Cl *ST/HB/BR* S6....**123** C2
Bartlett Rd *SHEFN* S5.......**101** H5
Bartle Wy *HACK/IN* S12......**154** B1
Barton Crs *CHSW* S40........**186** A1
Barton La *ARMTH* DN3.........**42** C4
Barton Pl *CONI* DN12.........**88** C2
Barton St *SHEFS* S8.........**140** A4
Barton St *STV/CWN* S43......**185** F2
Barugh Green Rd
  DOD/DAR S75................**18** A3
Barugh La *DOD/DAR* S75.......**18** A2
Basegreen Av *HACK/IN* S12...**154** D2
Basegreen Cl *HACK/IN* S12...**155** E2
Basegreen Crs
  HACK/IN S12...............**154** D2

Basegreen Dr *HACK/IN* S12...**154** D2
Basegreen Pl *HACK/IN* S12...**154** D2
Basegreen Rd *HACK/IN* S12...**155** E2
Basegreen Wy
  HACK/IN S12...............**155** E2
Basford Cl *DARN/MH* S9.....**127** H2
Basford Dr *DARN/MH* S9.....**128** A2
Basford Ms *DARN/MH* S9.....**128** A2
Basford Pl *DARN/MH* S9.....**127** H2
Basford St *DARN/MH* S9.....**127** H2
Basil Av *ARMTH* DN3..........**42** A3
Basil Cl *CHNE* S41.............**5** C3
Basildon Rd *DEARNE* S63......**37** E1
Baslow Crs *DOD/DAR* S75......**30** A3
Baslow Rd *BSLYN/ROY* S71....**15** F5
  RCH S42...................**190** A3
  TOT/DORE S17..............**160** B5
Bassett La *FUL* S10.........**136** C4
Bassett Pl *SHEFP/MNR* S2...**127** G5
Bassett Rd *SHEFP/MNR* S2...**127** C5
Bassey Rd *ARMTH* DN3.........**59** G5
Bassingthorpe La *KIMB* S61...**97** F4
Bassledene Ct
  SHEFP/MNR S2..............**141** G2
Bassledene Rd
  SHEFP/MNR S2..............**141** G2
Bass Ter *DON* DN1 *...........**7** F3
Bastock Rd *ST/HB/BR* S6.....**114** B3
Bateman Cl *CUD/GR* S72.......**16** C3
  STV/CWN S43...............**180** B2
Bateman La *MALT* S66........**109** G5
Batemoor Cl *SHEFS* S8.......**163** E2
Batemoor Dr *SHEFS* S8.......**163** E2
Batemoor Pl *SHEFS* S8.......**163** E2
Batemoor Rd *SHEFS* S8.......**163** E3
Batesquire *MOS* S20.........**157** F3
Bate Wood Av
  STV/CWN S43...............**189** F4
Bath St *OWL* S3.............**10** D6
Bathurst Rd *BSVR* S44......**196** B4
Battison La *DEARNE* S63......**64** A2
Batt St *ABRD* S7............**140** A2
Batty Av *CUD/GR* S72.........**21** G1
Batworth Dr *SHEFN* S5......**115** E4
Batworth Rd *SHEFN* S5......**115** E4
Baulk Farm Cl *KIMB* S61......**97** F2
Bawtry Ga *DARN/MH* S9.......**117** H3
Bawtry Rd *DARN/MH* S9......**117** H3
  DONS/BSCR DN4.............**57** G3
  MALT S66..................**108** A5
  RHAM S60..................**118** B3
  RHAM/THRY S65.............**107** G5
Baxter Av *WHHL* DN2..........**57** F1
Baxter Cl *DON* DN1 *..........**7** F1
Baxter Dr *ST/HB/BR* S6......**101** E5
Baxter Ga *DON* DN1 *..........**6** C3
Baxter Ms *ST/HB/BR* S6......**101** E5
Baxter Rd *ST/HB/BR* S6......**101** E5
Baycliff Cl *BSLYN/ROY* S71...**15** H5
Baycliff Dr *CHSW* S40.......**191** G4
Bay Ct *ECK/KIL* S21.........**168** A3
Baysdale Cft *MOS* S20.......**166** D1
Bay Tree Av *MALT* S66.......**108** B3
Baytree Gv *EPW* DN9..........**75** H4
Beacon Cl *DARN/MH* S9.......**116** B2
Beacon Cft *ATT* S4..........**116** B2
Beacon Dr *DARN/MH* S9......**116** B2
Beaconsfield Rd
  DONS/BSCR DN4.............**55** G4
  RHAM S60..................**119** G3
Beaconsfield St *BSLY* S70.....**2** E6
  MEX/SWTN S64...............**66** D3
Beacon Vw *HOY* S74...........**56** A4
Beacon Wy *DARN/MH* S9......**116** B2
Beale Wy *RAW* S62............**98** B4
Bear Tree Cl *RAW* S62........**98** B4
Bear Tree Rd *RAW* S62........**98** B3
Bear Tree St *RAW* S62........**98** B3
Beauchamp Rd *KIMB* S61.....**106** D1
Beauchief Abbey La
  SHEFS S8..................**152** A5
Beauchief Cl *STKB/PEN* S36...**77** H3
Beauchief Dr *SHEFS* S8......**162** A1
Beauchief Ri *SHEFS* S8......**152** A4
Beaufort Rd *FUL* S10........**125** F4
  WHHL DN2....................**57** F1
Beaulieu Cl *DOD/DAR* S75.....**14** A4
Beaulieu Vw *DOD/DAR* S75....**14** A4
Beaumont Av
  AWLS/ASK DN6...............**24** D1
  BSLY S70....................**30** D1
  SHEFP/MNR S2..............**127** G5
Beaumont Cl
  SHEFP/MNR S2..............**127** H5
Beaumont Crs
  SHEFP/MNR S2..............**127** G5
Beaumont Dr
  RHAM/THRY S65.............**106** D4
Beaumont Ms
  SHEFP/MNR S2..............**141** H1
Beaumont Rd North
  SHEFP/MNR S2..............**127** G5
Beaumont St *HOY* S74.........**61** G5
Beaumont Wy
  SHEFP/MNR S2..............**127** H5
Beaver Av *HAN/WDH* S13......**143** F2
Beaver Cl *HAN/WDH* S13......**143** F2
Beaver Dr *HAN/WDH* S13......**143** F2
Beaver Hill Rd
  HAN/WDH S13..............**143** F2
Beccles Wy *MALT* S66........**109** G4

Beck Cl *BSVR* S44 ....197 F2
  MEX/SWTN S64 ....86 B2
  SHEFN S8 ....103 E2
Beck Cft *HOY* S74 ....61 C4
Becket Crs *KIMB* S61 ....96 B4
Becket Rd *SHEFS* S8 ....162 C2
Beckett Hospital Ter
  BSLY S70 * 3 H7
Beckett Rd *WHLL* DN2 ....40 C5
Beckett St *BSLYN/ROY* S71 .....3 H2
Beckingham Wy *CHSW* S40 ......5 F5
Becknoll Rd *WMB/DAR* S73.....18 E5
Beck Rd *SHEFN* S5 ....102 D2
Beckton Av *MOS* S20 ....157 E3
Beckton Ct *MOS* S20 ....157 E3
Beckton Gv *MOS* S20 ....157 E3
Beck Vw *HOR/CROF* WF4 ....12 A3
Beckwith Rd *DIN* S25 ....134 A3
  RHAM/THRY S65 ....107 E2
Bedale Ct *RHAM* S60 * 106 B5
Bedale Rd *ABRD* S7 ....139 H4
  BTLY DN5 ....38 D3
Bedford Cl *DIN* S25 ....148 B1
Bedford St *BSLY* S70 ....31 H3
  CUD/GR S72 ....12 E3
  MALT S66 ....111 F4
  ST/HB/BR S6 ....125 H2
Bedford Ter *BSLYN/ROY* S71...20 A2
Bedgebury Cl *MOS* S20 ....157 H4
Bedgrave Cl *ECK/KIL* S21 .....158 D5
Beecham Ct *MEX/SWTN* S64..86 A2
Beech Av *CUD/GR* S72 ....16 D4
  RAW S62 ....98 D1
  RHAM/THRY S65 ....107 C5
Beech Cl *MALT* S66 ....110 B3
  WMB/DAR S73 ....50 A5
Beech Ct *WMB/DAR* S73 ....35 E5
  ECK/KIL S21 ....174 B2
  MEX/SWTN S64 ....66 C3
Beechcroft Rd
  DONS/BSCR DN4 ....71 E2
Beechdale Cl *CHSW* S40 ....4 A1
Beech Dr *ARMTH* DN3 ....59 G4
Beech-en-Hurst
  RHAM S60 * 106 A5
Beeches Bank
  SHEFP/MNR S2 ....140 C2
Beeches Dr *SHEFP/MNR* S2...140 C2
Beeches Gv *MOS* S20 ....157 G2
Beeches Hollow
  SHEFP/MNR S2 ....140 C2
Beeches Rd
  AU/AST/KP S26 ....159 F2
The Beeches *ARMTH* DN3.....29 F3
  AU/AST/KP S26 ....145 F3
  MEX/SWTN S64 ....86 A1
  WMB/DAR S73 ....63 F1
Beechfern Cl
  CHPT/GREN S35 ....80 B3
Beechfield Cl *DEARNE* S63....53 E3
Beechfield Rd *DON* DN1 ....6 E6
Beech Gv *BSLY* S70 ....31 F3
  BTLY DN5 ....39 H2
  CONI DN12 ....88 D2
  DIN S25 ....148 D1
  DONS/BSCR DN4 ....70 C2
  MALT S66 ....108 C4
Beech Hi *CONI* DN12 ....89 E2
Beech Hill Rd *FUL* S10 ....125 E5
Beech House Rd
  WMB/DAR S73 ....50 B5
Beechlea *DEARNE* S63 ....37 E1
Beech Rd *ARMTH* DN3 ....42 D3
  CUD/GR S72 ....17 F2
  DEARNE S63 ....65 C2
  MALT S66 ....110 B3
  NROS/TKH DN11 ....91 C3
Beech St *BSLY* S70 ....3 H7
  STV/CWN S43 ....181 E5
Beech Tree Cl *RHAM/THRY* S65.99 H3
Beech Tree Dr
  STV/CWN S43 ....185 F4
Beech Vls
  RHAM/THRY S65 * 106 C2
Beechville Av
  MEX/SWTN S64 ....86 A2
Beech Wy *AU/AST/KP* S26 ...144 D2
  DRON S18 * 163 E5
Beechwood Cl *ARMTH* DN3...42 C1
  DEARNE S63 ....65 F5
  RAW S62 ....85 H4
Beechwood Ldg
  RHAM/THRY S65 * 9 K3
Beechwood Rd
  CHPT/GREN S35 ....80 C5
  DRON S18 ....170 D2
  RHAM S60 ....105 E5
  ST/HB/BR S6 ....113 H4
  STV/CWN S43 ....76 D3
Beeden Cl *RHAM/THRY* S65...99 H3
Beehive Rd *CHSW* S40 ....4 A5
  FUL S10 ....125 F3
Beeley Cl *STV/CWN* S43 ......189 C3
Beeley St *ECC* S11 ....10 E7
Beeley Vw *RCH* S42 ....191 F5
Beeley Wood La
  CHPT/GREN S35 ....100 C5
Beeley Wood Rd
  ST/HB/BR S6 ....114 A1
Beely Rd *CHPT/GREN* S35 ...100 A3
Beeston Cl *DRON* S18 ....170 A1

Beeston Sq *BSLYN/ROY* S71 ...14 D4
Beeton Gn *ST/HB/BR* S6 ....122 A1
Beeton Rd *SHEFS* S8 ....139 H5
Beet St *OWL* S3 ....10 D3
Beetwell St *CHSW* S40 ....5 G5
Beever La *DOD/DAR* S75 ....18 C4
Beevers Leigh
  RHAM/THRY S65 * 9 H5
Beevers Rd *KIMB* S61 ....96 B4
Beever St *DEARNE* S63 ....37 H5
Beevor Ct *BSLYN/ROY* S71......3 K5
Beevor St *BSLYN/ROY* S71...32 B1
Begonia Cl *DIN* S25 ....148 A4
Beighton Rd *HACK/IN* S12....156 B2
  HAN/WDH S13 ....143 H4
  MEX/SWTN S64 ....64 B4
Beighton Rd East *MOS* S20...156 C2
Belcourt Rd
  RHAM/THRY S65 ....107 F5
Beldon Cl *SHEFP/MNR* S2....140 D3
Beldon Pl *SHEFP/MNR* S2....140 D3
Beldon Rd *SHEFP/MNR* S2...140 D3
Belfit Dr *RCH* S42 ....195 F5
Belford Cl *MALT* S66 ....108 C3
Belford Dr *MALT* S66 ....108 C3
Belfry Gdns
  DONS/BSCR DN4 ....74 C1
Belfry Wy *DIN* S25 ....149 H1
Belgrave Dr *FUL* S10 ....137 H1
Belgrave Pl *AU/AST/KP* S26.145 E3
Belgrave Rd *BSLYN/ROY* S71...3 J4
  FUL S10 ....138 A1
Belgrave Sq
  SHEFP/MNR S2 ....140 A2
Belklane Dr *ECK/KIL* S21 .....168 C1
Bell Bank Vw *BSLY* S70 ....31 H5
Bellbank Wy
  BSLYN/ROY S71 ....14 D4
Bellbrooke Av
  WMB/DAR S73 ....34 D3
Bell Butts La *EPW* DN9 ....75 H2
Bellfield St *OWL* S3 ....10 C1
Belle Green Cl *CUD/GR* S72...17 E5
Belle Green Gdns
  CUD/GR S72 ....17 E5
Belle Green La *CUD/GR* S72...17 E5
Belle Vue Av
  STV/CWN S43 ....188 B1
Belle Vue Cl *STV/CWN* S43 ..188 B1
Belle Vue Rd
  MEX/SWTN S64 ....67 E3
The Bellfields *KIMB* S61 ......95 E1
Bellhagg Rd *ST/HB/BR* S6 ...124 D1
Bell House La
  STV/CWN S43 ....182 B3
Bellhouse Rd *SHEFN* S5 ......103 E5
Bellhouse Vw
  STV/CWN S43 * 182 B3
Bellmer Cl *BSLYN/ROY* S71...20 A2
Bellmer Cft *BSLY* S70 ....60 D2
Bellows Cl *RAW* S62 ....98 B1
Bellows Rd *RAW* S62 ....98 B3
Bellrope Acre *ARMTH* DN3 ...42 D5
Bellscroft Av
  RHAM/THRY S65 ....99 G4
Bells Sq *SHEF* S1 ....11 F3
Bell St *AU/AST/KP* S26 ....145 H3
Bellwood Ct
  RHAM/THRY S65 ....109 E1
Belmont Cl *HOY* S74 ....61 C3
Belmont *CUD/GR* S72 * 22 A3
Belmont Av *BSLYN/ROY* S71...20 B2
  CHPT/GREN S35 ....94 A1
  DONS/BSCR DN4 ....56 A4
Belmont Cl *ARMTH* DN3 ....59 C5
Belmont Crs *CUD/GR* S72 .....36 A3
Belmont Dr *STKB/PEN* S36....77 E2
  STV/CWN S43 ....182 B4
Belmonte Gdns
  SHEFP/MNR S2 ....11 K6
Belmont St *KIMB* S61 ....105 E3
  MEX/SWTN S64 ....66 C3
Belper Rd *ABRD* S7 * 139 H4
Belridge Cl *DOD/DAR* S75 .....18 D3
Belsize Rd *FUL* S10 ....138 A2
Belton Cl *DRON* S18 ....170 A2
Belvedere *DONS/BSCR* DN4...71 F2
Belvedere Av *CHSW* S40 .....191 E4
Belvedere Cl *CHSW* S40 ......191 E4
  CUD/GR S72 ....17 E2
  DIN S25 ....148 D3
Belvedere Dr *WMB/DAR* S73..34 C3
Belvedere Pde *MALT* S66 ....108 C2
Ben Cl *ST/HB/BR* S6 ....124 A3
Beninmoor Wy *CHSW* S40 ...192 A4
Benita Av *MEX/SWTN* S64 ....67 C4
Ben La *ST/HB/BR* S6 ....113 F3
Benmore Dr *MOS* S20 ....157 F4
Bennett Ct *RAW* S62 ....85 H4
Bennetthorpe *WHHL* DN2 ......7 J5
Bennett St *KIMB* S61 ....104 C5
  SHEFP/MNR S2 ....139 H2
Benson Rd *SHEFP/MNR* S2...127 E5
Bentfield Av *RHAM* S60 ....120 A1
Bentham Dr *BSLYN/ROY* S71..14 D3
Bentham Rd *CHSW* S40 ....187 E4
Bentinck Cl *DON* DN1 ....6 D6
Bentinck Dr *STV/CWN* S43...185 C2
Bentinck St *CONI* DN12 ....89 F1
Bent La *STV/CWN* S43 ....182 C3
Bent Lathes Av *RHAM* S60...120 A1
Bentley Av *DONS/BSCR* DN4..55 C3
Bentley Cl *BSLYN/ROY* S71 ...21 E2

Bentley Common La
  BTLY DN5 ....40 A2
Bentley Rd *BTLY* DN5 ....39 H5
  CHPT/GREN S35 ....94 B2
  FUL S10 ....124 C2
  MALT S66 ....109 E5
Bentley St *RHAM* S60 ....118 D1
Benton Ter *MEX/SWTN* S64...86 B2
Benton Wy *KIMB* S61 ....104 D2
Bents Cl *CHPT/GREN* S35 *....94 A1
  ECC S11 ....138 A3
Bents Dr *ECC* S11 ....138 A5
Bents Green Av *ECC* S11 .....138 A4
Bents Green Pl *ECC* S11 ......138 A5
Bents Green Rd *ECC* S11 .....138 A5
Bents La *DRON* S18 ....163 C5
Bents Rd *ECC* S11 ....138 B5
  KIMB S61 ....96 D5
Bent St *SHEFP/MNR* S36 ......44 C2
Bentley La *FUL* S10 ....124 B4
Beresford St *BTLY* DN5 ....39 H1
Berkeley Cft
  BSLYN/ROY S71 * 12 B5
Berkeley Prec *ECC* S11 * 139 F2
Berkley Cl *BSLY* S70 ....31 H5
Bernard St *STV/CWN* S43 ....180 D5
Bernard Gdns
  SHEFP/MNR S2 ....126 C3
Bernard Rd *SHEFP/MNR* S2.126 C3
Bernard St *RAW* S62 ....85 H4
  RHAM S60 ....9 H6
  SHEFP/MNR S2 ....126 C3
Berners Cl *SHEFP/MNR* S2...141 E5
Berners Dr *SHEFP/MNR* S2..141 E4
Berners Pl *SHEFP/MNR* S2...141 E4
Berneslai Cl *BSLY* S70 ....2 C3
Berneslai Ct *BSLY* S70 ....2 A2
Berne Sq *WRKN* S81 ....149 H4
Bernshall Crs *SHEFN* S5 ......102 B2
Berresford Rd *ECC* S11 ....139 F2
Berrington Cl
  DONS/BSCR DN4 ....71 G4
Berry Av *ECK/KIL* S21 ....166 C5
Berry Dr *STV/CWN* S43 ....32 A5
Berry Edge Cl *CONI* DN12 .....89 F2
Berry Holme Cl
  CHPT/GREN S35 * 94 A1
Berry Holme Ct
  CHPT/GREN S35 ....94 A1
Berry Holme Dr
  CHPT/GREN S35 ....94 A1
Berry La *CHPT/GREN* S35 .....79 C3
Berrywell Av *STKB/PEN* S36...45 E4
Bertram Rd
  CHPT/GREN S35 ....100 A3
Berwick Av *RCH* S42 ....191 G5
Berwick Cl *MALT* S66 ....191 G4
Berwick Ct *CHSW* S40 ....191 G5
Berwyn Cl *CHSW* S40 ....186 C4
Bessacarr La
  DONS/BSCR DN4 ....74 A2
Bessemer Pk *RHAM* S60 * ...105 F5
Bessemer Pl *DARN/MH* S9...127 E1
Bessemer Ter *STKB/PEN* S36..76 D1
Bessemer Wy *RHAM* S60 .....105 E4
Bessingby Rd *ST/HB/BR* S6..114 A5
Bethel Rd *RHAM/THRY* S65 *...5 E4
Bethel St *HOY* S74 ....62 B2
Betjeman Gdns *FUL* S10 .....139 E1
Betony Cl *ECK/KIL* S21 ....167 H3
Beulah Rd *ST/HB/BR* S6 ......114 B3
Bevan Av *NROS/TKH* DN11 ...91 F2
Bevan Cl *HOY* S74 ....62 C2
Bevan Dr *STV/CWN* S43 ......189 F2
Bevan Crs *MALT* S66 ....110 D2
Bevan Wy *CHPT/GREN* S35 ...93 H2
Bevercotes Rd *SHEFN* S5 ....115 H1
Beverley Av *BSLY* S70 ....31 H4
Beverley Cl *AU/AST/KP* S26..145 F3
  BSLYN/ROY S71 ....14 C5
Beverley Gdns *BTLY* DN5 .....38 D5
Beverley Rd *WHHL* DN2 ....41 E4
Beverleys Rd *SHEFS* S8 ......153 E1
Beverley St *DARN/MH* S9 ....127 F1
Bevin Pl *RAW* S62 ....85 H5
Bevre Rd *ARMTH* DN3 ....42 D3
Bewicke Av *BTLY* DN5 ....38 D4
Bhatia Cl *MEX/SWTN* S64 .....67 E3
Bickerton Rd *ST/HB/BR* S6...114 A2
Bierlow Cl *WMB/DAR* S73 .....54 E4
Bigby Wy *MALT* S66 ....108 C2
Bignor Pl *ST/HB/BR* S6 ....101 F5
Bignor Rd *ST/HB/BR* S6 ....101 F4
Bilby La *STV/CWN* S43 ....180 C5
Billam Pl *KIMB* S61 ....96 C5
Billam St *ECK/KIL* S21 ....166 B2
Billingley Dr *DEARNE* S63 .....37 E3
Billingley Green La
  CUD/GR S72 ....36 B4
Billingley La *DEARNE* S63 ....36 B2
Bilston St *ST/HB/BR* S6 ....114 B5
Binders Rd *KIMB* S61 ....96 A2
Binfield Rd *SHEFS* S8 ....139 H5
Bingham Park Crs *ECC* S11..138 C2
Bingham Park Rd *ECC* S11..138 C2
Bingham Rd *SHEFS* S8 ....152 D3
Bingley Cl *DOD/DAR* S75 * 2 C2
Bingley La *ST/HB/BR* S6 ......123 F3

Bingley St *DOD/DAR* S75 ....2 C1
Binstead Av *SHEFS* S5 ....101 F5
Binsted Cl *ST/HB/BR* S6 ......114 B1
Binsted Crs *SHEFN* S5 ....114 B1
Binsted Cft *SHEFN* S5 ....114 B1
Binsted Dr *SHEFN* S5 ....114 B1
Binsted Gdns *SHEFN* S5 ......114 B1
Binsted Gld *SHEFN* S5 ....114 B1
Binsted Gv *SHEFN* S5 ....114 B1
Binsted Wy *SHEFN* S5 ....114 B1
Birchall Av *RHAM* S60 ....119 H3
Birch Av *CHPT/GREN* S35 .....93 H2
Birch Cl *BTLY* DN5 ....54 D4
  ECK/KIL S21 ....168 A3
  HOR/CROF WF4 ....13 H1
Birch Crs *MEX/SWTN* S64 .....65 H5
Birchdale Cl *ARMTH* DN3 ......42 B1
Birchen Cl *CHSW* S40 ....186 D4
  DONS/BSCR DN4 ....74 A3
  DRON S18 ....170 B2
Birches Fold *DRON* S18 ....163 C4
Birches La *DRON* S18 ....163 C4
Birch Farm Av *SHEFS* S8 ......92 D3
Birchfield Crs *DOD/DAR* S75..30 B2
Birchfield Wk *DOD/DAR* S75..30 B2
Birch Green Cl *MALT* S66 ....110 B2
Birch Gv *CONI* DN12 ....89 F1
Birch Holt Gv *DRON* S18 ......179 E1
Birch House Wy *DRON* S18...171 G2
Birchitt Cl *TOT/DORE* S17 ....162 A3
Birchitt Pl *TOT/DORE* S17 ...162 A3
Birchitt Rd *TOT/DORE* S17 ..162 A3
Birchitt Vw *DRON* S18 ....163 E5
Birch Kiln Cft
  STV/CWN S43 ....188 D1
Birchlands Dr *ECK/KIL* S21 ..168 B3
Birch Rd *BSLY* S70 ....32 D3
  DARN/MH S9 ....88 B5
  DONS/BSCR DN4 ....74 D3
Birchtree Rd *KIMB* S61 ....95 F5
Birch Tree Rd *STKB/PEN* S36.76 D3
Birchvale Rd *HACK/IN* S12 ...155 F2
Birchwood Av *RAW* S62 ....85 F5
Birchwood Crs *CHSW* S40....192 B5
Birchwood Cft *MOS* S20 ......157 E5
Birchwood Dell
  DONS/BSCR DN4 ....74 D3
Birchwood Dr
  RHAM/THRY S65 ....108 D1
Birchwood Gdns *MOS* S20 ...157 E5
Birchwood Gv *MOS* S20 ....157 E5
Birchwood Ri *MOS* S20 ....157 E5
Birchwood Rd *ECK/KIL* S21..165 F5
Birchwood Vw *MOS* S20 ......157 E5
Birchwood Wy *MOS* S20 ......157 E5
Bircotes Wk
  NROS/TKH DN11 ....91 H2
Bird Av *WMB/DAR* S73 ....50 A3
Birdholme Crs *CHSW* S40 ....192 C4
Bird St *STV/CWN* S43 ....182 B4
Birdwell Rd *ATT* S4 ....116 B3
Birds Royd *SHEFN* S5 ....30 C4
  MEX/SWTN S64 ....86 B3
Birk Av *BSLY* S70 ....32 C3
Birk Crs *BSLY* S70 ....32 C3
Birkdale Av *DIN* S25 ....134 D5
Birkdale Cl *CUD/GR* S72 ....17 E4
  DONS/BSCR DN4 ....74 D2
Birkdale Dr *CHSW* S40 ....191 C4
Birkdale Ri *MEX/SWTN* S64...85 H4
Birkdale Rd *BSLYN/ROY* S71..12 B4
Birkendale Rd
  ST/HB/BR S6 ....125 F2
Birkendale Vw
  ST/HB/BR S6 ....125 F2
Birk Gn *BSLY* S70 ....32 D3
Birkhill Rd *CHNE* S41 ....190 B5
Birkin La *BSLY* S70 ....32 D3
Birkin La *RCH* S42 ....194 D5
Birklands Av
  HAN/WDH S13 ....142 C1
Birklands Cl *HAN/WDH* S13..142 C1
Birklands Dr *HAN/WDH* S13.142 C1
Birks Av *HAN/WDH* S13 ....143 F4
Birks Holt Dr *MALT* S66 ......111 F5
Birks Rd *KIMB* S61 ....96 C5
Birk Ter *BSLY* S70 ....32 C3
Birkwood Av *CUD/GR* S72 .....22 A2
Birley Brook *CHNE* S41 ....186 B2
Birley Cft *CHNE* S41 ....186 B2
Birley La *HACK/IN* S12 ....155 F3
Birley Moor Av
  HACK/IN S12 ....155 G2
Birley Moor Cl *HACK/IN* S12.155 G2
Birley Moor Crs
  HACK/IN S12 ....155 G2
Birley Moor Dr
  HACK/IN S12 ....155 G2
Birley Moor Pl
  HACK/IN S12 ....155 G2
Birley Moor Rd
  HACK/IN S12 ....155 G2
Birley Moor Wy
  HACK/IN S12 ....155 G2
Birley Rise Crs
  ST/HB/BR S6 ....101 E5

Birley Rise Rd
  ST/HB/BR S6 ....101 E5
Birley Spa Cl *HACK/IN* S12..156 B1
Birley Spa Dr *HACK/IN* S12..156 B1
Birley Spa La *HACK/IN* S12..155 H1
Birley Vale Av *HACK/IN* S12.156 B1
Birley Vale Cl *HACK/IN* S12.155 E1
Birstall Cl *CHNE* S41 ....186 C5
Bisby Rd *RAW* S62 ....85 C5
Biscay La *DEARNE* S63 ....65 F2
Biscay Wy *DEARNE* S63 ....65 F2
Bishopdale Ct *MOS* S20 * ...156 A5
Bishopdale Dr *MOS* S20 ......156 A5
Bishopdale Ri *MOS* S20 ....156 A5
Bishop Gdns
  HAN/WDH S13 ....143 E4
Bishopgarth Cl *BTLY* DN5 .....39 H4
Bishop Hl *HAN/WDH* S13.....143 E4
Bishops Ct *SHEFS* S8 ....140 A5
Bishopscourt Rd *SHEFS* S8.140 A5
Bishopsholme Rd
  SHEFN S5 ....115 E2
Bishopstoke Ct
  RHAM/THRY S65 ....106 C2
Bishopston Wk *MALT* S66 ...110 C2
Bishops St *ST/HB/BR* S6 ....10 C6
Bishops Wy *BSLYN/ROY* S71..20 C6
Bisley Cl *BSLYN/ROY* S71 .....13 E5
Bismarck St *BSLY* S70 ....31 H3
Bitter Cft *WMB/DAR* S73 ....51 F4
Bittern Vw *KIMB* S61 ....82 C5
Blacka Moor Crs
  TOT/DORE S17 ....160 C2
Blackamoor Rd *RAW* S62 .....85 F2
Blacka Moor Rd
  TOT/DORE S17 ....160 C2
Blacka Moor Vw
  TOT/DORE S17 ....160 C2
Blackberry Ct
  STV/CWN S43 ....184 D2
Blackbird Av *RHAM* S60 ......118 D4
Blackbrook Av *FUL* S10 ....136 C1
Blackbrook Dr *FUL* S10 ....136 D1
Blackbrook Rd *FUL* S10 ....137 E1
Blackburn Crs
  CHPT/GREN S35 ....80 C5
Blackburn Cft
  CHPT/GREN S35 ....80 D5
Blackburn Dr
  CHPT/GREN S35 ....93 G1
Blackburne St
  ST/HB/BR S6 ....114 B5
Blackburn La *BSLY* S70 ....32 A5
  DOD/DAR S75 ....2 C2
  KIMB S61 ....81 H5
Blackburn Rd *KIMB* S61 ......103 H5
Blackburn St *BSLY* S70 ....32 A5
Black Carr Rd *MALT* S66 .....108 A4
Blackdown Av *CHSW* S40 ....186 B4
  MOS S20 ....156 D3
Blacker La *BSLY* S70 ....38 A3
  CUD/GR S72 ....17 E1
  HOY S74 ....48 C5
Blacker Rd *DOD/DAR* S75 .....14 A4
Blackheath Cl
  BSLYN/ROY S71 ....15 F5
Blackheath Rd
  BSLYN/ROY S71 ....15 F5
Blackheath Wk
  BSLYN/ROY S71 ....15 F5
Black Hill Rd
  RHAM/THRY S65 ....107 F5
Black La *HOY* S74 ....60 D4
  ST/HB/BR S6 ....112 D5
Blackmoor Crs *RHAM* S60 ...118 D2
Blackmore St *ATT* S4 ....126 D2
Blacksmith La
  CHPT/GREN S35 ....101 E1
Blacksmiths Yd *MALT* S66 *.132 D2
Blackstock Cl *GLV* S14 ....153 H3
Blackstock Crs *GLV* S14 ......153 H3
Blackstock Dr *GLV* S14 ....153 H3
Blackstock Rd *GLV* S14 ....153 H3
Blackthorn Av *MALT* S66 ....108 C4
Blackthorn Cl *CHNE* S41 ......195 F3
  STV/CWN S43 ....80 B3
Blackthorn Ri
  RHAM/THRY S65 ....109 E1
Blackwell Cl
  SHEFP/MNR S2 ....11 K3
Blackwell Pl *SHEFP/MNR* S2.11 K3
Blackwood Av
  DONS/BSCR DN4 ....71 F2
Blagden St *SHEFP/MNR* S2..126 C4
Blair Athol Rd *ECC* S11 ....138 D4
Blake Av *DEARNE* S63 ....64 C1
  WHHL DN2 ....40 C4
Blake Cl *MALT* S66 ....109 E5
Blake Grove Rd
  ST/HB/BR S6 ....125 G2
Blakeley Cl *BSLYN/ROY* S71...15 F5
Blakeney Rd *FUL* S10 ....125 E4
Blakeny Ms *DIN* S25 ....134 A3
Blake St *ST/HB/BR* S6 ....125 F2
Blandford Dr *CHNE* S41 ......187 E2
Bland La *ST/HB/BR* S6 ....113 F3
Bland St *ATT* S4 ....116 C3
Blast La *SHEFP/MNR* S2 ....11 K2
Blaxton Cl *MOS* S20 ....156 A3
Blayton Rd *ATT* S4 ....115 C5
Bleachcroft Wy *BSLY* S70 .....33 E3
Bleak Av *CUD/GR* S72 ....17 E2
Bleakley Av *HOR/CROF* WF4..12 B5

Bleakley Cl *CUD/GR S72* 17 E2
Bleakley La *HOR/CROF WF4*..12 B4
Bleakley Ter *HOR/CROF WF4*..12 B1
Bleasdale Gv
  BSLYN/ROY S71 ....20 A3
Blenheim Av *BSLY S70*.........2 E6
Blenheim Cl *DIN S25*.........134 C5
  MALT S66 ....108 C2
Blenheim Crs
  MEX/SWTN S64 ....66 B3
Blenheim Ms *ECC S11*.........138 C5
Blenheim Rd *BSLY S70* 2 D7
  BSLY S70.........31 F3
Blind La *BSVR S44* 196 C1
Bloemfontein St
  CUD/GR S72 ....21 C1
Blonk St *OWL S3* 11 H1
Blossom Crs *HACK/IN S12*..154 D2
The Blossoms *DOD/DAR S75*....2 C3
Blucher St *BSLY S70*.........3 F5
Bluebank Vw
  STV/CWN S43.........180 B3
Bluebell Av *STKB/PEN S36*...44 C3
Bluebell Cl *HOY S74* 61 C4
  SHEFN S5.........
Bluebell Wk *STV/CWN S43* ...177 F5
Bluebell Wood La
  MALT S66 ....108 B2
Blueberry Cl *STV/CWN S43*..189 F4
Blueberry Ct *MALT S66*.........108 B2
Bluebird Hl *AU/AST/KP S26*..145 C4
Blue Boy St *OWL S3* 10 E1
Blue Lodge Cl
  STV/CWN S43.........189 F4
Blue Mans Wy *RHAM S60*...129 G2
Blundell Cl *DONS/BSCR DN4*..74 A1
Blundell Ct *BSLYN/ROY S71*...20 D2
Blunt Av *STV/CWN S43* ...183 E2
Blyde Rd *SHEFN S5*.........115 G3
Bly Rd *WMB/DAR S73*.........34 D4
Blyth Av *RAW S62*.........98 B1
Blyth Cl *STV/CWN S40*.........191 F4
  RHAM S60.........120 B3
Blythe St *WMB/DAR S73*....50 A2
Blyth Rd *MALT S66*.........110 D4
Boardman Av *RAW S62*.........84 C3
Boat La *BTLY DN5*.........54 B5
Bobbin Mill La *CHSW S40*....191 H2
Bochum Pkwy *SHEFS S8*...163 E1
Bocking Cl *SHEFS S8*.........152 B4
Bocking Hl *STKB/PEN S36*....77 F2
Bocking La *SHEFS S8*.........152 B4
Bocking Ri *SHEFS S8*.........152 C5
Boden La *SHEF S1* 10 E5
Boden Pl *DARN/MH S9* 128 A2
Bodmin St *DARN/MH S9* ...127 F1
Bodmin Wy *CHSW S40*.........186 C4
Boggard La *STKB/PEN S36*....44 C4
Boiley La *ECK/KIL S21*.........174 C1
Boland Rd *SHEFS S8*.........162 B3
Bold St *DARN/MH S9*.........116 C4
Bole Cl *WMB/DAR S73* 50 D1
  SHEFS S8.........153 E3
Bole Hill Cl *ST/HB/BR S6* ...124 D1
Bolehill La *ECK/KIL S21*.........173 H1
  FUL S10.........124 C3
Bole Hill Rd *FUL S10*.........124 B3
Bolsover Hl *BSVR S44*.........196 C2
Bolsover Rd *SHEFN S5*.........115 H2
  STV/CWN S43.........183 F4
Bolsover Rd East
  SHEFN S5.........115 H3
Bolsover St *OWL S3*.........10 B3
Bolton Hill Rd
  DONS/BSCR DN4.........74 A2
Bolton Rd *DEARNE S63* 66 B1
Bolton St *CONI DN12*.........88 B1
  OWL S3.........10 D5
Bond Cl *DON DN1*.........6 B6
Bondfield Av
  NROS/TKH DN11.........91 G3
Bondfield Crs
  WMB/DAR S73.........50 A3
Bondfield Rd
  STV/CWN S43.........189 G2
Bond Rd *DOD/DAR S75* 2 C1
Bond St *NROS/TKH DN11*....91 G4
  STV/CWN S43.........189 C1
  WMB/DAR S73.........50 A2
Bonet La *RHAM S60*.........118 A3
Bonington Ri *MALT S66* 110 C2
Bonville Gdns *OWL S3*.........10 D1
Booker Cl *STV/CWN S43*...189 C3
Booker Rd *SHEFS S8*.........152 C5
Bookers Wy *DIN S25*.........147 H1
Booker's La *DIN S25*.........147 H1
Booth Cl *MALT S66*.........133 C1
  MOS S20.........156 D3
Booth Cft *MOS S20*.........156 D3
Booth Pl *RAW S62*.........85 E3
Booth Rd
  CHPT/GREN S35.........80 A4
Booth St *HOY S74*.........
  KIMB S61.........
Border Cl *STV/CWN S43*...185 F3
Border Rd *STV/CWN S43*...185 F4
Borough Rd *ST/HB/BR S6*..114 B4
Borrowdale Av *MOS S20*...167 E2

Borrowdale Cl
  BSLYN/ROY S71 ....33 G2
  MOS S20.........167 E2
Borrowdale Crs *DIN S25*...148 D1
Borrowdale Dr *MOS S20*...167 E1
Borrowdale Rd *MOS S20*...167 E2
Boston Castle Gv
  RHAM S60.........106 A5
Boston St *SHEFP/MNR S2*...139 H1
Bosville Rd *FUL S10*.........138 A4
Bosville St
  RHAM/THRY S65.........107 F1
  STKB/PEN S36.........45 C4
Boswell Cl *BSLYN/ROY S71 **..12 B5
  CHPT/GREN S35.........92 D5
  NROS/TKH DN11.........91 E3
Boswell Rd *DEARNE S63* 65 F4
  DONS/BSCR DN4.........73 C1
Boswell St *RHAM S60*.........9 K7
Bosworth Rd
  AWLS/ASK DN6.........25 E1
Bosworth St *FUL S10*.........124 D3
Botanical Rd *ECC S11*.........139 E1
Botham La *ATT S4*.........116 A4
The Bothy *RAW S62 **.........83 E3
Bottom Rd *RCH S42*.........195 E5
Boughton La *STV/CWN S43*..184 D2
Boulder Bridge La
  BSLYN/ROY S71.........16 B2
The Boulevard *ARMTH DN3* ...29 E5
Boulton Cl *CHSW S40*.........186 A4
Boulton Dr *ARMTH DN3*.........58 D4
Boundary Av *STV/CWN S43*..188 C1
Boundary Cl *CONI DN12*.........70 C5
  STV/CWN S43.........182 C3
Boundary Gn *RAW S62*.........98 B2
Boundary Rd
  SHEFP/MNR S2.........127 E5
Boundary St *BSLY S70*.........32 B2
Boundary Wk *RHAM S60*...118 A4
Bourne Cl *STV/CWN S43*...188 C1
Bourne Ct *DOD/DAR S75*....14 A2
Bourne Mill Cl
  STV/CWN S43.........177 F4
Bourne Rd *BSLY S70*.........47 H1
  SHEFN S5.........102 C5
Bow Bridge Cl *RHAM S60 **..105 C5
Bowbridge Cl *RHAM S60 **..105 C5
Bowden Gv *WMB/DAR S75*....30 B3
Bowden Wood Av
  DARN/MH S9.........128 A3
Bowden Wood Cl
  DARN/MH S9.........128 A3
Bowden Wood Crs
  DARN/MH S9.........128 A3
Bowden Wood Dr
  DARN/MH S9.........128 A3
Bowden Wood Pl
  DARN/MH S9.........128 A3
Bowden Wood Rd
  DARN/MH S9.........128 A3
Bowdon Av *STV/CWN S43*...177 E5
Bowdon St *SHEF S1*.........10 E5
Bowen Dr *RHAM/THRY S65*...99 H4
Bowen Rd *RHAM/THRY S65*...9 K1
Bower Cl *KIMB S61*.........96 C5
Bower La *CHPT/GREN S35*....92 D5
Bower Rd *FUL S10*.........125 F3
  MEX/SWTN S64.........66 B4
Bower Spring *OWL S3*.........11 C1
Bowes Rd *ARMTH DN3*.........42 A1
Bowfell Vw *BSLYN/ROY S71*..20 A3
Bowfield Rd *SHEFN S5*.........102 C5
Bowland Cl *BTLY DN5*.........39 F2
Bowland Crs *BSLY S70*.........47 H1
Bowland Dr *CHPT/GREN S35*..93 C1
  RCH S42.........191 F5
Bowlease Gdns
  DONS/BSCR DN4.........58 A5
Bowling Green St *OWL S3*...11 F1
Bowman Cl *HACK/IN S12*...154 D1
Bowman Dr *HACK/IN S12*...154 D1
  MALT S66.........110 C2
Bowness Cl *CHNE S41*.........186 D2
  DRON S18.........170 C2
Bowness Gv *DEARNE S63*...53 E4
Bowness Rd *CHNE S41*.........186 D2
  ST/HB/BR S6.........114 A5
Bowood Rd *ECC S11*.........139 E4
Bowshaw Av *SHEFS S8*.........163 H4
Bowshaw Cl *SHEFS S8*.........163 H3
Bowshaw Vw *SHEFS S8*.........163 H3
Bow St *CUD/GR S72*.........16 D5
Boyce St *ST/HB/BR S6*.........125 F2
Boyd Rd *DEARNE S63*.........38 A1
Boyland St *OWL S3*.........125 H1
Boynton Crs *SHEFN S5*.........115 C2
Boynton Rd *SHEFN S5*.........114 D3
Boythorpe Av *CHSW S40* 4 D6
Boythorpe Crs *CHSW S40* 4 D7
Boythorpe Mt *CHSW S40* 4 D6
Boythorpe Ri *CHSW S40* 4 C6
Boythorpe Rd *CHSW S40* 4 B6
Brackenberg La *BTLY DN5* ...69 F2
Bracken Cl *ARMTH DN3*.........59 G4
Bracken Ct *MALT S66*.........121 F1
Brackendale Cl
  STV/CWN S43.........188 B2
Brackenfield Gv
  HACK/IN S12.........155 F1
Bracken Hl
  CHPT/GREN S35.........93 F2

Bracken Moor La
  STKB/PEN S36.........77 E3
Bracken Rd *SHEFN S5*.........103 E5
Brackens La *STV/CWN S43*...177 F5
Brackley St *OWL S3*.........126 B1
Bradberry Balk La
  WMB/DAR S73.........50 A1
Bradbourne Cl
  STV/CWN S43.........189 C1
Bradbury Dr *RCH S42*.........194 D3
Bradbury St *SHEFS S8*.........152 D5
  SHEFS S8.........140 A4
Bradbury's Cl *RAW S62*.........98 B3
Bradfield Rd *ST/HB/BR S6*...114 A4
Bradgate Cl *KIMB S61*.........105 E2
Bradgate Ct *KIMB S61*.........104 D2
Bradgate Cft *KIMB S61*.........193 E5
Bradgate La *KIMB S61*.........104 D2
Bradgate Pl *KIMB S61*.........105 E1
Bradgate Rd *KIMB S61*.........105 E1
Bradlea Ri *RAW S62*.........98 B2
Bradley Av *WMB/DAR S73*...50 A2
Bradley St *FUL S10*.........124 D2
Bradley Wy *STV/CWN S43*...188 C2
Bradmarsh Wy *RHAM S60*...105 G5
Bradshaw Av *RHAM S60*....130 B3
Bradshaw Cl *WMB/DAR S75*..18 C1
Bradshaw Rd
  RHAM/THRY S65.........107 E2
Bradshaw Wy *RHAM S60*...130 B4
Bradstone Rd
  RHAM/THRY S65.........107 E2
Bradway Cl *TOT/DORE S17*..161 H3
Bradway Dr *TOT/DORE S17*..161 H3
Bradway Grange Rd
  TOT/DORE S17.........161 H3
Bradway Rd
  TOT/DORE S17.........161 H3
Bradwell Av *DOD/DAR S75*...30 C5
Bradwell Cl *DRON S18*.........170 A2
Bradwell Pl *STV/CWN S43*...189 C2
Bradwell St
  SHEFP/MNR S2.........140 B3
Braeburn Cl *MALT S66*.........110 A1
Braemar Cl *STV/CWN S43*...180 B2
Braemar Rd *WHHL DN2*.........7 K3
Brailsford Av *SHEFN S5*.........102 A1
Brailsford Rd *SHEFN S5*.........102 A1
Braithwell Rd *BTLY DN5*.........26 C5
Braithwell Wy *MALT S66*...109 G3
Bramah St *BSLYN/ROY S71*...15 G3
Bramall St *DARN/MH S9*....140 A2
Bramall La *SHEFP/MNR S2*...140 A2
Bramall Lane Jct
  SHEFP/MNR S2.........11 F7
Bramble Cl *MALT S66*.........121 F1
The Brambles
  CHPT/GREN S35.........102 A1
Bramble Wy *DEARNE S63*...64 B2
Brambling Ct *CHNE S41*....193 E2
The Bramblings
  DONS/BSCR DN4.........74 C3
Bramcote Av
  BSLYN/ROY S71.........14 C4
Brameld Rd *MEX/SWTN S64*..65 H5
  RAW S62.........98 B1
Bramham Cft
  WMB/DAR S73.........50 D1
Bramham Rd
  DARN/MH S9.........127 H2
  DONS/BSCR DN4.........58 B3
Bramley Av *AU/AST/KP S26*..145 C5
Bramley Carr *BSLY S70*.........30 D3
Bramley Cl *MOS S20*.........166 C2
Bramley Dr *HAN/WDH S13*...142 D1
Bramley Grange Crs
  MALT S66.........109 E4
Bramley Grange Dr
  MALT S66.........109 E4
Bramley Grange Ri
  *MALT S66 **.........109 E4
Bramley Grange Vw
  MALT S66.........109 E3
Bramley Grange Wy
  MALT S66.........109 E4
Bramley Hall Rd
  HAN/WDH S13.........142 D2
Bramley La *HAN/WDH S13*..142 D1
  RHAM/THRY S65.........109 G1
Bramley Ms *ECK/KIL S21*....166 D5
Bramleymoor La
  ECK/KIL S21.........173 G2
Bramley Park Cl
  HAN/WDH S13.........142 D2
Bramley Park Rd
  HAN/WDH S13.........142 D1
Bramley Rd *ECK/KIL S21*....173 G2
Bramley Wy *MALT S66*.........109 G3
Bramlyn Cl *STV/CWN S43*...184 D1
Brampton Av *MALT S66*.........132 D1
Brampton Cl *ARMTH DN3*....58 C1
Brampton Ct *MOS S20*.........156 A3
Brampton Crs
  WMB/DAR S73.........50 D4
Brampton La *ARMTH DN3*...42 C5
  AU/AST/KP S26.........132 B3

Brampton Mdw *MALT S66*...132 D1
Brampton Rd *DEARNE S63*...64 B1
  MALT S66.........121 H5
  WMB/DAR S73.........50 D4
Brampton St *WMB/DAR S73*..51 F5
Brampton Vw
  WMB/DAR S73.........50 D4
Bramshill Cl *MOS S20*.........157 C4
Bramshill Dr *MOS S20*.........157 C4
Bramshill Ri *CHSW S40*.........4 A7
Bramwell Dr *OWL S3*.........10 C2
Bramwell Rd *OWL S3*.........10 C2
Bramwell St *ECC S11*.........10 C2
  RHAM/THRY S65.........9 H2
Bramworth Rd
  DONS/BSCR DN4.........55 F4
Brandeth Rd *ST/HB/BR S6*...125 C2
Brandon St *OWL S3*.........115 F5
Brandreth Cl *ST/HB/BR S6*...125 G2
Brand's La *DIN S25*.........149 F1
Branksome Av *BSLY S70*.........2 A5
Bransby St *ST/HB/BR S6*....125 F2
Branstone Rd *BTLY DN5*.........54 B3
Branton Cl *CHSW S40*.........192 B3
Branton Gate Road Or
  Whiphill Top La
  ARMTH DN3.........59 C3
Branton Ter *ARMTH DN3 ** ..59 F5
Brantwood Crs
  DONS/BSCR DN4.........58 B4
Brathay Cl *ATT S4*.........116 B3
Brathay Rd *ATT S4*.........116 B3
Brayford Rd
  DONS/BSCR DN4.........71 H4
Bray St *DARN/MH S9*.........127 H2
Brayton Dr *DONS/BSCR DN4*..71 H4
Brearley Av *STKB/PEN S36*...77 F3
  STV/CWN S43.........180 B3
Brearley St *CHNE S41*.........180 A3
Breckland Cl *CHSW S40*.........191 H4
Brecklands *RHAM S60*.........107 E5
Breck La *DIN S25*.........134 D3
  ECK/KIL S21.........174 C3
Brecks *RHAM/THRY S65*.........107 C4
Brecks La *ARMTH DN3*.........29 C3
  RHAM/THRY S65.........107 H4
Brecon Cl *CHSW S40*.........186 C4
  MOS S20.........157 G3
Brendon Av *STV/CWN S43*...186 C5
Brendon Cl *WMB/DAR S73*....50 D4
Brent Cl *CHSW S40*.........186 D4
Brentwood Cl *HOY S74 **.........61 C4
Brentwood Rd *ECC S11*.........139 F4
Brentwood Vis
  *RHAM/THRY S65 **.........9 H3
Bressingham Cl *ATT S4*.........126 C1
Bressingham Rd *ATT S4*.........126 B1
Bretby Cl *DONS/BSCR DN4*...74 B1
Bretby Rd *CHSW S40*.........186 A3
Brettas Pk *BSLYN/ROY S71*...20 A2
Brett Cl *RAW S62*.........84 C3
Bretton Av *BSVR S44*.........197 F2
Bretton Cl *CHSW S40*.........186 A4
Bretton Gv *HACK/IN S12*....155 F2
Bretton Vw *CUD/GR S72*.........21 C2
Brewery St *CHNE S41*.........5 C3
Breydon Av *BTLY DN5*.........39 E5
Breydon Ct *BTLY DN5 **.........39 F5
Briar Briggs Rd *BSVR S44*...196 C1
Briar Cl *CHSW S40*.........187 E4
Briar Ct *MALT S66*.........121 E1
Briar Cft *DONS/BSCR DN4*....55 C5
Briarfield Av *HACK/IN S12*...154 C3
Briarfield Crs *HACK/IN S12*...154 C3
Briar Gv *STKB/PEN S36*.........44 B4
Briar Ri *BSLY S70*.........31 H1
Briar Rd *ABRD S7*.........139 C4
  ARMTH DN3.........42 C3
Briars Cl *ECK/KIL S21*.........168 B3
Briar Vw *STV/CWN S43*.........188 C2
Briarwood Gdns *MALT S66*..108 B1
Briary Av *CHPT/GREN S35*....80 B4
Briary Ct *MALT S66*.........118 C5
Brick Dr *FUL S10*.........124 C3
Brickhouse La
  TOT/DORE S17.........150 C5
Brickhouse Yd *CHSW S40* 4 A4
Brick St *FUL S10*.........124 D3
The Brickyard *CUD/GR S72*...17 E3
Bricky Cl *STV/CWN S43*.........184 D1
Bridby St *HAN/WDH S13*....143 G4
Bridge Bank Cl *STV/CWN S40*..186 D3
Bridge Gdns *BSLYN/ROY S71*..3 G1
Bridgehouses Jct *OWL S3*...126 B2
Bridge Inn Rd
  CHPT/GREN S35.........81 E5
Bridgelake Dr
  DONS/BSCR DN4.........71 H4
Bridge Rd *DONS/BSCR DN4*...57 C5
Bridge St *ABRD S7 **.........33 E2
  BSLYN/ROY S71.........3 G1
  CHSW S40.........192 C3
  DONS/BSCR DN4.........6 A5
  ECK/KIL S21.........168 B1
  MEX/SWTN S64.........66 C5
  OWL S3.........11 H1
  RHAM S60.........8 E3
  STKB/PEN S36.........44 C2

Bridgewater Wy
  RHAM/THRY S65.........109 E1
Bridle Cl *CHPT/GREN S35*....81 E5
Bridle Crs *CHPT/GREN S35*....81 E5
Bridle Rd *BSVR S44*.........184 B4
  STV/CWN S43.........182 D4
Bridle Stile *MOS S20*.........166 C1
Bridle Stile Cl *MOS S20*.........166 C1
Bridle Stile Gdns *MOS S20*..166 C1
The Bridleway *RAW S62*.........86 A4
Bridport Rd *DARN/MH S9*...127 H2
Brierfield Cl *DOD/DAR S75*....2 B2
Brierfield Rd *HACK/IN S12*...154 C2
Brier La *HOR/CROF WF4*.........13 H1
Brierley Cl *STV/CWN S43*...182 A5
Brierley Rd *CUD/GR S72*.........17 F2
  DONS/BSCR DN4.........73 H1
  DRON S18.........172 A5
Brierly Rd *RHAM/THRY S65*...99 G5
Brier St *ST/HB/BR S6*.........114 A4
Briery Mdw *WMB/DAR S73*...50 A5
Briggs Rd *BSLYN/ROY S71*...15 G3
Bright Meadow *MOS S20*...167 G3
Brightmore Dr *OWL S3*.........10 C3
Brighton Terrace Rd
  FUL S10.........125 E1
Brightside La *DARN/MH S9*..127 E1
Brightside Wy *ATT S4*.........116 B4
Brimington Rd *CHNE S41*.........5 J2
Brimington Rd North
  CHNE S41.........187 C1
Brimmesfield Dr
  SHEFP/MNR S2.........141 E2
Brimmesfield Rd
  SHEFP/MNR S2.........141 E3
Brimmsfield Cl
  SHEFP/MNR S2.........141 F3
Brinckman St *BSLY S70*.........3 H6
Brincliffe Cl *CHSW S40*.........191 F5
Brincliffe Crs *ECC S11*.........139 E3
Brincliffe Edge Cl *ECC S11*..138 D4
Brincliffe Edge Rd *ECC S11*..138 D4
Brincliffe Gdns *ECC S11*.........139 E3
Brincliffe Hl *ECC S11*.........138 D3
Brindley Cl *SHEFS S8*.........153 E1
Brindley Cl *ECK/KIL S21*.........168 A2
Brindley Crs *SHEFS S8*.........153 E1
Brindley Rd *CHNE S41*.........187 C3
Brindley Wy *STV/CWN S43*..182 B4
Brinkburn Cl
  TOT/DORE S17.........161 F2
Brinkburn Dr
  TOT/DORE S17.........161 F2
Brinkburn Vale Rd
  TOT/DORE S17.........161 F2
Brinsford Rd *RHAM S60*.........118 C3
Brinsworth Cra *ARMTH S60*..118 B3
Brinsworth Hall Av
  RHAM.........118 B4
Brinsworth Hall Crs
  RHAM.........118 B4
Brinsworth Hall Dr
  RHAM.........118 B4
Brinsworth Hall Gv
  RHAM.........118 B4
Brinsworth Rd *RHAM S60*...129 G5
Brinsworth St
  DARN/MH S9.........127 F1
  RHAM.........8 D6
Bristol Gv *WHHL DN2*.........4 A1
Bristol Rd *ECC S11*.........139 E1
Britain St *MEX/SWTN S64 **....66 D4
Britannia Cl *BSLY S70*.........3 G6
Britannia Rd *CHSW S40*.........192 D5
  DARN/MH S9.........127 E1
Britland Cl *DOD/DAR S75*....30 C1
Britnall St *DARN/MH S9*.........127 E1
Briton Sq *DEARNE S63*.........37 C1
Briton St *DEARNE S63*.........37 C1
Brittain St *SHEF S1*.........11 H6
Broachgate *BTLY DN5*.........39 E2
Broadcarr Rd *HOY S74*.........81 H1
Broadcroft Cl *MOS S20*.........157 G2
Broad Elms Cl *ECC S11*.........151 F1
Broad Elms La *ECC S11*.........151 E2
Broadfield Cl *SHEFS S8*.........139 H4
Broadfield Rd *SHEFS S8*.........139 H4
Broadfield Wy *ABRD S7*.........139 H4
Broadgate House Cl
  KIMB S61.........104 D3
Broadgorse Cl *CHSW S40*...192 B5
Broadhead Rd
  STKB/PEN S36.........77 F2
Broad Inge Crs
  CHPT/GREN S35.........93 G1
Broadlands *MALT S66*.........109 E5
Broadlands Av *MOS S20*....156 A3
Broadlands Cl *MOS S20*.........156 B3
Broadlands Cl *MALT S66*....109 E5
Broadlands Ri *MOS S20*.........156 B3
Broad La *SHEF S1*.........10 D3
Broad Lane Ct *SHEF S1 **.........10 D3
Bradley Rd
  HAN/WDH S13.........141 H3
Broad Oaks *DARN/MH S9* 5 F2
  DIN S25.........134 C4
Broadoaks Cl *DIN S25*.........134 C5
Broad Pavement *CHSW S40*...5 C4

Broad St *HOY* S74.....................61 H2
  RAW S62.............................98 B3
  SHEF S1.............................11 J2
Broadwater *DEARNE* S63 ......52 C3
Broadway *BSLY* S70...................2 A7
  MEX/SWTN S64................85 H1
  RHAM S60.........................118 B5
  RHAM/THRY S65.............106 D2
Broadway Av
  CHPT/GREN S35...............94 B2
Broadway Cl
  MEX/SWTN S64................85 H1
Broadway East
  RHAM/THRY S65.............106 D2
The Broadway
  DONS/BSCR DN4.............71 F3
Brocco Bank *ECC* S11.............139 E2
Brocco La *SHEF* S11.................10 E2
Brocco St *OWL* S3....................10 E2
Brockfield Cl *BSLY* S70.............32 A5
Brockhole
  DONS/BSCR DN4.............74 B1
Brockholes La *ARMTH* DN3 ....75 F1
Brockhurst Wy
  RHAM/THRY S65................99 H4
Brocklehurst Av *BSLY* S70 ....32 D4
  SHEF S8...........................153 G5
Brocklehurst Piece
  CHSW S40.......................191 H2
Brockwell La *CHSW* S40.............4 C1
  CHSW S40........................186 D4
Brockwell Pl *CHSW* S40..............4 B1
Brockwell Ter *CHSW* S40............4 C1
Brockwood Cl
  HAN/WDH S13 ....143 G3
Brodsworth Wy
  NROS/TKH DN11................91 H3
Bromcliffe Pk
  BSLYN/ROY S71..................21 E2
Bromley Carr Rd
  CHPT/GREN S35................79 H2
Brompton Rd *BTLY* DN5.............54 C4
  DARN/MH S9.....................116 C5
Bromwich Rd *SHEFS* S8..........152 C3
Bronte Av *DONS/BSCR* DN4.....71 E2
Bronte Cl *BSLYN/ROY* S71........20 B4
Bronte Gv *MEX/SWTN* S64.......67 F2
Bronte Pl *RAW* S62....................85 H4
Brookbank Av *CHSW* S40............4 A2
Brookbank Rd
  STV/CWN S43..................185 F2
Brook Cl *AU/AST/KP* S26 ....145 C3
  CHPT/GREN S35................93 E5
  RCH S42...........................190 B5
Brook Crt *DIN* S25..................148 B3
Brookdale Ct
  CHPT/GREN S35................81 E2
Brookdale Rd
  CHPT/GREN S35................81 E2
Brook Dr *OWL* S3......................10 C2
Brooke Dr *DEARNE* S63.............64 D2
  STV/CWN S43..................188 D4
Brooke St *DON* S3.....................40 B5
  HOY S74...........................61 H2
Brook Farm Ms *DEARNE* S63...65 E1
  MEX/SWTN S64................86 B1
Brookfield Cl *ARMTH* DN3 ....42 D5
  RHAM/THRY S65................99 F5
Brookfield Ms *BTLY* DN5...........27 C4
Brookfield Rd *ABRD* S7............139 H3
  BSVR S44.........................196 D4
Brook Gn *HACK/IN* S12............156 B2
Brookhaven Wy *MALT* S66.......109 E5
Brook Hl *KIMB* S61....................95 F1
  OWL S3...........................10 C3
Brookhill *STV/CWN* S43...........185 E2
Brookhouse Cl
  HACK/IN S12.....................156 B2
Brookhouse Dr
  HACK/IN S12.....................156 B2
Brookhouse Hl *FUL* S10..........137 G3
Brookhouse Rd
  AU/AST/KP S26.................145 E4
Brooklands *MALT* S66..............110 A4
Brooklands Av *FUL* S10...........137 F3
Brooklands Crs *FUL* S10..........137 G3
Brooklands Dr *FUL* S10...........137 F3
Brook La *CHPT/GREN* S35.......101 E1
  HACK/IN S12.....................156 B2
  MALT S66.........................108 D3
  OWL S3...........................10 C3
  STV/CWN S43..................185 F2
Brooklyn Dr *CHSW* S40...............4 A1
Brooklyn Rd *SHEFS* S8............140 A4
Brook Ms *DIN* S25...................148 B3
Brook Rd *CHPT/GREN* S35.........89 F1
  CONI DN12.......................89 F1
  RHAM/THRY S65.............106 D1
  SHEFS S8........................139 H5
Brook Rw *STKB/PEN* S36...........77 E3
Brookside *CONI* DN12................89 G2
  MEX/SWTN S64................85 H2
  RHAM/THRY S65.............107 E4
Brookside Bank Rd
  ST/HB/BR S6....................122 C1
Brookside Bar *CHSW* S40.......190 D2
Brookside Cl *HACK/IN* S12 ......156 B2
Brookside Crs *DEARNE* S63......64 B3
Brookside Dr *BSLY* S70.............32 D4
Brookside Gln *CHSW* S40........190 D2

Brookside La *ST/HB/BR* S6.....122 D1
Brooks Rd *STV/CWN* S43........181 F2
Brook St *ECK/KIL* S21..............176 A4
  RHAM S60.........................119 H3
Brookvale *BSLYN/ROY* S71........20 D1
Brook V *CHSW* S40 *.................4 B5
Brookview Ct *DRON* S18..........163 E5
Brook Wy *BTLY* DN5..................40 B1
Brook Yd *CHSW* S40 *................4 D4
Broom Av *RHAM* S60...............106 C5
Broombank Pk *CHNE* S41.........178 D5
Broombank Rd *CHNE* S41.........178 D3
Broom Cha *RHAM* S60.............106 B5
Broomcliffe Gdns
  CUD/GR S72.......................17 E2
Broom Cl *BSLY* S70...................32 D4
  CHNE S41.........................186 D2
  DEARNE S63......................65 G4
  ECC S11...........................139 H1
  MALT S66.........................108 C2
Broom Crs *RHAM* S60..............119 H1
Broomcroft Pk *ECC* S11...........151 F2
Broom Dr *RHAM* S60...............119 H1
Broome Av *MEX/SWTN* S64......66 B5
Broomfield Av *CHNE* S41.........193 F5
Broomfield Cl *BSLY* S70............30 D2
Broomfield Ct
  STKB/PEN S36....................77 F3
Broomfield Gv *RHAM* S60........106 B5
  STKB/PEN S36....................77 E3
Broomfield La
  STKB/PEN S36....................77 F3
Broomfield Rd *FUL* S10...........125 F5
  STKB/PEN S36....................77 F2
Broom Gdns *STV/CWN* S43......188 D2
Broom Gn *OWL* S3.....................10 D5
Broom Gv *DIN* S25...................148 B5
  RHAM S60...........................9 J7
Broomgrove Crs *FUL* S10........125 F5
Broomgrove La *FUL* S10..........125 F5
Broomgrove Rd *FUL* S10..........10 A7
  FUL S10...........................125 F5
Broomhall Pl *FUL* S10...............10 C6
Broomhall Rd *FUL* S10...............10 B7
Broomhall St *OWL* S3................10 C6
Broomhead Rd
  WMB/DAR S73....................50 D4
Broomhill Cl *ECK/KIL* S21........166 B5
Broom Hill Dr
  DONS/BSCR DN4.................74 B1
Broomhill La *WMB/DAR* S73.....51 G2
Broomhill Rd *CHNE* S41..........179 F4
Broomhill Vw *DEARNE* S63.......52 D4
Broomhouse La
  NROS/TKH DN11................71 E5
Broom La *RHAM* S60..................9 K7
Broom Riddings *KIMB* S61........97 F4
Broom Rd *RHAM* S60...................9 K7
Broomroyd *BSLY* S70.................48 B3
Broomspring Cl *OWL* S3............10 C5
Broomspring La *FUL* S10..........10 B5
  OWL S3...........................10 C5
Broom St *FUL* S10.....................10 C6
Broom Ter *RHAM* S60..................9 J7
Broom Valley Rd *RHAM* S60........9 H7
Broomville St
  MEX/SWTN S64................66 C5
Broomwood Cl *MOS* S20.........157 G2
Broomwood Gdns
  MOS S20.........................157 G2
Brotherton St *OWL* S3.............126 B1
Broughton Av *BTLY* DN5...........39 G3
Broughton La
  DARN/MH S9....................116 D5
Broughton Rd
  DONS/BSCR DN4.................73 H2
  ST/HB/BR S6....................114 A3
Brow Cl *BSLY* S70......................31 H4
Brow Crs *MOS* S20...................167 E1
Brow Hill Rd *MALT* S66............110 C2
Brownell St *OWL* S3...................10 D2
Brown Hills La *FUL* S10............136 C2
Browning Av
  DONS/BSCR DN4.................71 H2
Browning Cl *BSLYN/ROY* S71....20 B4
  ST/HB/BR S6....................101 F4
Browning Dr
  RHAM/THRY S65 *.............106 D3
  ST/HB/BR S6....................101 F4
Browning Rd *DEARNE* S63.......64 C1
  MEX/SWTN S64................67 E2
  RHAM/THRY S65.............106 D4
  ST/HB/BR S6....................101 E4
Brown La *DRON* S18................163 G5
  SHEF S1...........................11 G5
Brownroyd Av
  BSLYN/ROY S71..................15 G2
Browns Sq *WMB/DAR* S73........62 D1
Brown St *RHAM* S60...................8 B3
  SHEF S1...........................11 H6
The Brow
  RHAM/THRY S65.............106 D3
Brow Vw *DEARNE* S63...............52 D3
Broxholme La *DON* DN1..............6 E2
Broxholme Rd *SHEFS* S8.........152 D2
Bruce Av *BSLY* S70....................31 H4
Bruce Crs *DEARNE* S63.............65 E4
Bruce Rd *ECC* S11...................139 F2
Bruncroft Cl
  DONS/BSCR DN4.................73 H1
Brunel Cl *BTLY* DN5...................39 F5
Brunel Wy *RHAM* S60..............129 E2

Brunswick Cl
  BSLYN/ROY S71..................19 H1
Brunswick Dr *MALT* S66..........108 B2
Brunswick Rd *OWL* S3.............126 B2
  RHAM S60.........................106 B5
Brunswick St *CHNE* S41.............5 F1
  DEARNE S63......................37 C1
  FUL S10...........................10 C5
  MALT S66.........................111 E4
Brunt Rd *RAW* S62....................85 H5
Brushfield Gv *HACK/IN* S12.....155 F1
Bryn Lea *CHNE* S41.................193 E2
Bryony Cl *ECK/KIL* S21............167 H2
Bubwith Rd *DARN/MH* S9........116 D2
Buchanan Crs *SHEFN* S5........101 G4
Buchanan Dr *SHEFN* S5..........101 G4
Buchanan Rd *SHEFN* S5..........101 H4
Buckden Cl *CHSW* S40................4 A1
Buckden Rd *BSLY* S70................2 D3
Buckenham Cl *CHNE* S41........126 C1
Buckenham St *ATT* S4.............126 C1
Buckingham Cl *DRON* S18.......170 B1
Buckingham Ct
  BSLYN/ROY S71..................12 B5
Buckingham Rd *CONI* DN12......68 D5
  WHHL DN2...........................7 J2
Buckingham Wy
  BSLYN/ROY S71..................12 B5
  MALT S66.........................111 E2
  RHAM S60.........................118 D4
Buckleigh Rd *DEARNE* S63........65 E4
Buckley Ct *BSLY* S70...................3 G6
Buckthorn Cl
  MEX/SWTN S64................86 A3
Buck Wood Vw *GLV* S14..........140 D5
Buck Ct *BSLYN/ROY* S71..........20 C4
Budde Rd *DONS/BSCR* DN4......55 H5
Bullen Rd *ST/HB/BR* S6...........101 E4
Bullfinch Cl *RHAM* S60............118 D4
The Bungalows *CHNE* S41 *........J5
  CHSW S40 *........................4 A4
  ECK/KIL S21 *...................168 A1
  ECK/KIL S21 *...................174 C1
  RAW S62 *.........................85 E4
  RHAM S60.........................130 A3
  STV/CWN S43 *................185 E1
Bunker S Hl *ECK/KIL* S21........168 C2
Bunting Cl *RCH* S42.................191 F3
  SHEFS S8........................153 F4
Bunting Nook *SHEFS* S8..........153 F3
Burbage Cl *DRON* S18.............170 B1
Burbage Gv *HACK/IN* S12.........142 B5
Burbage Rd *STV/CWN* S43......189 G2
Butchill Av *SHEFN* S5..............115 E2
Burcroft Cl *HOY* S74..................62 A5
Burcroft Hl *CONI* DN12..............69 F5
Burden Cl *DON* DN1 *.................4 C4
Burford Av *DONS/BSCR* DN4....71 E3
Burford Crs
  AU/AST/KP S26.................145 C3
Burgen Rd *KIMB* S61.................96 C5
Burgess Cl *CHNE* S41.............193 F5
Burgess Rd *DARN/MH* S9........127 F1
Burgess St *SHEF* S1..................11 F4
Burghley Cl *DIN* S25................148 C4
Burgoyne Cl *ST/HB/BR* S6.......125 F1
Burgoyne Rd *ST/HB/BR* S6......125 F1
Burkinshaw Av *RAW* S62...........85 F3
Burkitt Dr *STV/CWN* S43.........182 D3
Burleigh Cl *BSLY* S70..................3 G5
Burleigh St *BSLY* S70..................3 G6
Burley Cl *CHSW* S40................192 C5
Burlington Av *BSLY* S70..............3 G4
Burlington Ct *ST/HB/BR* S6......125 G2
Burlington Gln
  TOT/DORE S17.................161 E1
Burlington Gv
  TOT/DORE S17.................161 E1
Burlington House
  CHSW S40 *........................5 G4
Burlington Rd
  TOT/DORE S17.................161 E1
Burlington St *CHSW* S40.............5 G4
  ST/HB/BR S6....................125 G1
Burman Rd *WMB/DAR* S73.......62 A2
Burnaby Crs *ST/HB/BR* S6......114 B5
Burnaby Crs *ST/HB/BR* S6......114 B5
Burnaby Grn *ST/HB/BR* S6......125 F1
Burnaby St *DON* DN1 *.............6 B5
  ST/HB/BR S6....................114 B5
Burnaston Cl *DRON* S18..........170 C4
Burnbridge Rd *CHNE* S41........180 A3
Burncross Dr
  CHPT/GREN S35................93 H1
Burncross Gv
  CHPT/GREN S35................93 G1
Burncross Rd
  CHPT/GREN S35................93 G1
Burnell Rd *ST/HB/BR* S6..........114 A4
Burnell St *STV/CWN* S43.........188 D1
Burngreave Bank *ATT* S4.........126 B1
Burngreave Rd *OWL* S3...........115 F5
  OWL S3...........................126 B1
Burn Gv *CHPT/GREN* S35.........94 C2
Burnham Cl
  DONS/BSCR DN4.................73 F1
Burnham Gv *BTLY* DN5.............39 F2
Burnham Wy
  WMB/DAR S73....................34 D5
Burn Pl *BSLYN/ROY* S71...........14 C5
Burnsall Crs *RHAM* S60...........118 C4
Burnsall Gv *BSLY* S70...............32 D4
Burns Cl *CHSW* S40.................192 B5
Cadman St *MOS* S20................166 C2
Cadman La *SHEF* S1..................11 H4
Cadman Rd *HACK/IN* S12........142 A5

Burns Dr *CHPT/GREN* S35 ....93 H1
  DIN S25...........................171 G3
  RHAM/THRY S65.............106 D3
Burnside *DEARNE* S63................37 E1
Burnside Av *SHEFS* S8............140 A5
Burns Rd *DIN* S25...................135 E5
  DONS/BSCR DN4.................71 H2
  FUL S10...........................125 F5
  MALT S66.........................111 E4
  RHAM/THRY S65.............106 C3
Burns St *BTLY* DN5...................39 H1
Burns Wy *DEARNE* S63.............64 C1
Burnt Stones Cl *FUL* S10.........123 H5
Burnt Stones Dr *FUL* S10.........123 H5
Burnt Stones Gv *FUL* S10........123 H5
Burnt Tree La *OWL* S3..............10 B4
Burntwood Cl *DEARNE* S63.......36 D3
Burntwood Crs *RHAM* S60.......130 A2
Burntwood Rd *CUD/GR* S72......23 F1
Burrell St *RHAM* S60...................8 E5
Burrowlee Rd
  BSLYN/ROY S71................114 A3
Burrows Dr *SHEFN* S5.............115 E2
Burrows Gv *WMB/DAR* S73.......49 H3
Burrs Wood Cft *CHNE* S41......186 B2
Bursdon Cl *CHNE* S41.............179 G5
Burton Av *BSLYN/ROY* S71.......20 D3
  DONS/BSCR DN4.................55 H5
Burton Bank Rd
  BSLYN/ROY S71..................20 A4
Burton Rd *BSLYN/ROY* S71.......21 E2
  OWL S3...........................125 H1
Burton St *BSLY* S70...................19 G4
  ST/HB/BR S6......................56 C5
Burton Ter *BSLY* S70..................32 B2
  DONS/BSCR DN4.................55 H5
Burtop Cft *WMB/DAR* S73 *.......63 E1
Burying La *HOY* S74...................62 A5
Bushey Wood Rd
  TOT/DORE S17.................161 E2
Bushfield Rd *DEARNE* S63.......64 D3
Bushy Wood Gv
  TOT/DORE S17.................160 D1
Busk Knoll *SHEFN* S5..............115 E2
Busk Meadow *SHEFN* S5..........115 E2
Busk Pk *SHEFN* S5..................115 E2
Busley Gdns *BTLY* DN5.............39 G2
Butcher St *DEARNE* S63............37 E2
Butchill Av *SHEFN* S5..............115 E2
Bute St *FUL* S10......................124 D4
Butler Wy *ECK/KIL* S21............168 A1
Butterbusk *CONI* DN12..............89 C1
Buttercross Dr *CUD/GR* S72......35 G2
Butterfield Ct
  WMB/DAR S73 *.................51 E5
Butterill Dr *ARMTH* DN3.............43 F5
Butterley Dr *BSLY* S70...............32 D4
Butterleys *DOD/DAR* S75...........30 C3
Buttermere Cl *CHNE* S41.........186 D2
  DEARNE S63......................53 E4
  DIN S25...........................148 C1
Buttermere Dr *DRON* S18.........170 C2
Buttermere Rd *ABRD* S7..........152 C1
Butterthwaite Crs
  SHEFN S5........................103 E2
Butterthwaite La
  CHPT/GREN S35...............102 C1
Butterthwaite Rd
  SHEFN S5........................102 C1
Butterton Cl *DOD/DAR* S75......14 A4
Butterton Dr *CHSW* S40..........186 A4
Butt Hole Rd *CONI* DN12 *........89 C1
Button Hl *ECC* S11..................151 H1
Butts Hl *TOT/DORE* S17...........160 D4
Buxton Rd *BSLYN/ROY* S71.......15 E5
Byland Wy *BSLYN/ROY* S71......20 C5
Byrley Rd *KIMB* S61...................96 C5
Byrne Cl *DOD/DAR* S75.............18 A3
Byron Av *BTLY* DN5....................55 F1
  CHPT/GREN S35................93 H2
  DONS/BSCR DN4.................71 G2
Byron Cl *DRON* S18.................171 G4
Byron Crs *DEARNE* S63............64 C1
Byron Dr *BSLYN/ROY* S71.........20 B3
Byron Rd *ABRD* S7..................139 F4
  CHSW S40.......................186 D3
  DIN S25...........................135 E5
  MALT S66.........................111 E4
  MEX/SWTN S64................67 F3
  MOS S20.........................157 G3
Byron St *CHSW* S40....................5 G7
  CUD/GR S72......................36 A1

C

Cadeby Av *CONI* DN12..............88 C3
Cadeby La *BTLY* DN5................69 F3
Cadeby Rd *BTLY* DN5................54 A5
Caderby La *BTLY* DN5................69 G2
Cadman St *MOS* S20................166 D2
Cadman St *ATT* S4...................126 C3
  DEARNE S63......................52 D3
  MOS S20.........................166 C2
Cadwell Cl *CUD/GR* S72...........18 C1
Caernarvon Cl *CHSW* S40........191 G4
Caernarvon Crs
  DEARNE S63......................52 D3
Caernarvon Rd *DRON* S18.......171 E3
Caine Gdns *KIMB* S61.............104 C3
Cairn Dr *STV/CWN* S43...........180 B2
Cairngorm Cl *STV/CWN* S43...180 B2
Cairns Rd *FUL* S10..................124 B5
  MOS S20.........................157 F1
Caister Av *CHPT/GREN* S35......80 D5
Caistor Av *BSLY* S70..................31 E3
Calabria Gv *BSLY* S70................32 B2
Calcot Park Av
  MEX/SWTN S64................86 B1
Caldbeck Gv
  CHPT/GREN S35................80 B3
Caldbeck Pl *DIN* S25...............148 C1
Calder Av *BSLYN/ROY* S71.......16 A1
Calder Cl *BSLYN/ROY* S71........16 A1
Calder Crs *BSLY* S70.................32 D3
Calder Rd *DEARNE* S63.............53 F4
  KIMB S61.........................96 D4
Calder Ter *CONI* DN12 *.............69 E5
Caldervale *BSLYN/ROY* S71......13 E5
Calder Wy *SHEFN* S5...............115 G2
Caldey Rd *DRON* S18...............171 E3
California Crs *BSLY* S70.............31 G3
California Dr
  CHPT/GREN S35................94 A2
  RHAM S60.........................129 G2
California Gdns *BSLY* S70............3 G7
California La *STV/CWN* S43.......177 E4
California St *BSLY* S70...............31 G3
California Ter *BSLY* S70..............31 G3
Calladine Wy
  MEX/SWTN S64................86 A2
Callis Wy *STKB/PEN* S36..........84 D4
Callow Dr *GLV* S14..................140 C5
Callow Mt *GLV* S14..................140 C5
Callow Rd *GLV* S14..................140 C5
Callywhite La *DRON* S18..........171 G2
Calner Cft *MOS* S20.................157 H3
Calow Brook Dr *CHNE* S41......193 G4
Calow La *CHNE* S41.................193 G4
Calstock Cl *CHSW* S40............186 A5
Calver Cl *DOD/DAR* S75...........30 C5
Calver Crs *STV/CWN* S43........189 H2
Calverley Gdns
  WMB/DAR S73....................50 C3
Calvert Rd *DARN/MH* S9..........128 A1
Calvey Orch *CUD/GR* S72..........17 E5
Camborne Cl *ST/HB/BR* S6......101 C4
Camborne Rd
  ST/HB/BR S6....................101 C4
Camborne Wy
  BSLYN/ROY S71..................20 B4
Cambourne Cl
  AWLS/ASK DN6.....................8 C3
Cambria Dr
  DONS/BSCR DN4.................71 E2
Cambrian Cl *BTLY* DN5.............54 A4
  CHSW S40.......................186 D3
Cambridge Crs
  RHAM/THRY S65.............106 C3
Cambridge Pl
  RHAM/THRY S65.............106 C3
Cambridge Rd *SHEFS* S8........140 B4
  STKB/PEN S36....................77 H3
  STV/CWN S43..................188 D1
Cambridge St
  MEX/SWTN S64................66 D5
  NROS/TKH DN11................91 E1
  RHAM/THRY S65.............107 E4
  SHEF S1...........................11 F4
Cambron Gdns *MALT* S66........108 D4
Camdale Ri *HACK/IN* S12........155 H4
Camdale Vw *HACK/IN* S12.......155 H4
Camden Gv *MALT* S66..............110 D2
Camden Pl *DON* DN1 *...............6 C6
Camellia Cl *CONI* DN12.............89 F2
Camellia Dr *ARMTH* DN3...........29 F4
Camerory Wy
  STV/CWN S43..................180 B1
Camlough Wk *CHNE* S41............5 J5
Cammell Rd *SHEFN* S5...........115 H2
Camms Cl *ECK/KIL* S21...........166 D4
Camm St *FUL* S10....................125 E1
Campbell Cottages
  STV/CWN S43 *................181 E2
Campbell Ct
  STV/CWN S43 *................180 D2
Campbell Dr
  RHAM/THRY S65.............106 D4
  STV/CWN S43..................181 F2
Campbell St *KIMB* S61...............97 G2
Campbell Wy *DIN* S25..............134 B3
Camping La *SHEFS* S8.............152 C3
Campion Cl *DEARNE* S63...........52 D3
Campion Dr *ECK/KIL* S21.........168 A2
  MEX/SWTN S64................86 B2
Campo La *SHEF* S1...................11 F3
Campsall Dr *FUL* S10...............124 C4
Campsall Field Cl
  DEARNE S63......................65 E4
Campsall Field Rd
  DEARNE S63......................65 H5
Canada St *ATT* S4....................115 H5
  BSLY S70.........................31 G3
Canal Br *ECK/KIL* S21..............168 B2

Canal Ms *CHNE* S41..........5 G1
Canalside *ECK/KIL* S21.....175 H2
Canal St *ATT* S4..........126 D3
   BSLYN/ROY S71..........3 H1
Canal Wy *BSLYN/ROY* S71..........3 H1
Canal Whf *CHNE* S41..........5 H1
Canal Wharfe
   MEX/SWTN S64 *..........67 G4
Canary Ct *MALT* S66..........108 B2
Canberra Ri *DEARNE* S63..........52 D3
Candlins Yd
   STV/CWN S43 *..........184 D3
Canklow Hill Rd *RHAM* S60..118 D1
Canklow Rd *RHAM* S60..........8 E6
Canning St *SHEF* S1..........10 E4
Cannock St *ST/HB/BR* S6..114 A4
Cannon Cl *RAW* S62..........85 G5
Cannon Hall Rd *SHEFN* S5..115 G4
Cannonthorpe Ri
   RHAM S60..........130 D3
Cannon Wy *DOD/DAR* S75..145 F2
Canons Wy *BSLYN/ROY* S71..20 C4
Canterbury Av *FUL* S10..........137 G2
Canterbury Cl *BTLY* DN5..........39 E4
   CHSW S40..........192 C4
Canterbury Cr *FUL* S10..........137 G2
Canterbury Dr *FUL* S10..........137 G2
Canterbury Rd *SHEFS* S8..140 B5
   WHHL DN2..........40 D4
Cantilupe Crs
   AU/AST/KP S26..........145 F2
Cantley La *DONS/BSCR* DN4..57 H4
Cantley Manor Av
   DONS/BSCR DN4..........74 C1
Cantley Riding *WHHL* DN2....42 A5
Cantrell Cl *STV/CWN* S43..188 B3
Capel Ri *STV/CWN* S43..........188 B1
Capel St *ST/HB/BR* S6..........114 B5
Caperns Rd *DIN* S25..........148 D3
Capri Ct *WMB/DAR* S73..........34 C4
Caraway Ct *MEX/SWTN* S64..86 B3
Carbis Cl *BSLYN/ROY* S71..........20 B4
Carbrook Hall Rd
   DARN/MH S9..........116 D3
Carbrook St *DARN/MH* S9..116 D3
Cardew Cl *RAW* S62..........98 C1
Cardiff St *DARN/MH* S9..........116 C4
Cardigan Rd *WHHL* DN2........41 G5
Cardinal Cl *NROS/TKH* DN11..91 H2
Cardoness Dr *FUL* S10..........124 A5
Cardoness Rd *FUL* S10..........124 B5
Cardwell Av *HAN/WDH* S13..142 D3
Cardwell Dr *HAN/WDH* S13..142 D3
Carey Av *BSLYN/ROY* S71..........3 J4
Carfield Av *SHEFS* S8..........140 B5
Carfield La *SHEFS* S8..........140 C5
Car Hl *KIMB* S61..........97 G4
Carisbrook Ct *BTLY* DN5..........7 F2
Carisbrooke Rd *WHHL* DN2..7 K3
Carlby Rd *ST/HB/BR* S6..........113 C5
Carley Dr *MOS* S20..........157 F4
Carlingford Rd *RHAM* S60..106 C5
Carlin St *HAN/WDH* S13..........142 C4
Carlisle Cl *CHNE* S41..........179 E3
Carlisle Pl *RHAM/THRY* S65 *..9 F2
   WHHL DN2..........41 F3
Carlisle Rd *ATT* S4..........116 A4
Carlisle St *ATT* S4..........126 D1
   MEX/SWTN S64..........86 B2
   RHAM/THRY S65..........9 G3
Carlisle St East *ATT* S4..126 D1
Carthorpe Gv
   CHPT/GREN S35..........80 A4
Carlton Av *RHAM/THRY* S65..9 J6
Carlton Cl *ARMTH* DN3..........59 G5
   MOS S20..........166 C2
Carlton Rd *BSLYN/ROY* S71..19 G4
   CHSW S40..........195 F1
   DON DN1..........40 C5
   RAW S62..........98 B2
   ST/HB/BR S6..........113 H4
Carlton St *BSLYN/ROY* S71..........19 G4
   CUD/GR S72..........16 D5
   CUD/GR S72..........23 E1
Carlyle Rd *MALT* S66..........111 E3
Carlyle St *MEX/SWTN* S64..67 E3
Carlyon Gdns *CHSW* S40..192 B4
Carnaby Rd *ST/HB/BR* S6..114 A5
Carnarvon St *ST/HB/BR* S6..125 G2
Carnforth Rd
   BSLYN/ROY S71..........20 D2
Carnley St *DEARNE* S63..........64 B2
Carnoustie Av *CHSW* S40..191 G4
Carnoustie Cl
   MEX/SWTN S64..........86 C1
Carolina Ct *DONS/BSCR* DN4..73 E1
Carolina Wy
   DONS/BSCR DN4..........73 E1
Carpenter Av
   STV/CWN S43..........182 D3
Carpenter Cft *HACK/IN* S12..142 A4
Carpenter Gdns
   HACK/IN S12..........142 A4
Carr Bank *NROS/TKH* DN11..90 A4
Carr Bank Cl *ECC* S11..........138 B3
Carr Bank Dr *ECC* S11..........138 A2
Carr Bank La *ECC* S11..........138 A4
Carr Bank Rd *ECC* S11..........118 A4
   STKB/PEN S36..........77 G3
Carrcroft Ct *STKB/PEN* S36..77 H3
Carrfield Dr *SHEFS* S8..........140 B4
Carr Field La *DEARNE* S63..52 D2

Carrfield La
   SHEFP/MNR S2..........140 B4
Carrfield Rd *SHEFS* S8..........140 B4
Carrfield St *SHEFS* S8..........140 B4
Carr Forge Cl *HACK/IN* S12..156 A1
Carr Forge La *HACK/IN* S12..156 A1
Carr Forge Mt *HACK/IN* S12..156 A1
Carr Forge Pl *HACK/IN* S12..156 A1
Carr Forge Rd *HACK/IN* S12..156 A1
Carr Forge Ter
   HACK/IN S12..........156 A1
Carr Forge Vw
   HACK/IN S12..........156 B1
Carr Furlong
   BSLYN/ROY S71..........14 D3
Carr Gra *DONS/BSCR* DN4....56 B4
Carr Gv *DEARNE* S63..........53 E2
Carr Green La
   DOD/DAR S75..........77 G3
Carr Gv *STKB/PEN* S36..........77 G3
Carr Head Rd
   CHPT/GREN S35..........79 H2
Carr Hl *DONS/BSCR* DN4....55 H5
Carr Hill Ct *DONS/BSCR* DN4..55 H5
Carr House Rd *DON* DN1..........6 C7
Carriage Dr
   DONS/BSCR DN4..........56 D5
The Carriage Wy
   NROS/TKH DN11..........91 H3
Carrill Dr *ST/HB/BR* S6..........101 E3
Carrill Rd *ST/HB/BR* S6..........101 E3
Carrington Av
   DOD/DAR S75..........19 G3
Carrington Rd *ECC* S11..........138 D2
Carrington St *DOD/DAR* S75..2 D1
   RHAM/THRY S65 *..........9 J6
Carr La *AU/AST/KP* S26..132 A4
   CHPT/GREN S35..........60 A4
   CONI DN12..........89 C3
   DON DN12..........6 D7
   DONS/BSCR DN4..........74 A3
   DRON S18..........170 A1
   MALT S66..........110 B4
   RHAM/THRY S65..........87 E5
Carr Lane Ms *DRON* S18..170 B1
Carron Dr *DOD/DAR* S75..........14 B4
Carr Rd *DEARNE* S63..........65 G2
   ST/HB/BR S6..........125 E1
   STKB/PEN S36..........77 F4
Carrs La *CUD/GR* S72..........21 H2
Carr St *BSLYN/ROY* S71..........20 D2
Carr Vale Rd *BSVR* S44..........196 C3
Carr View Av
   DONS/BSCR DN4..........55 H5
Carr View Rd *KIMB* S61..........104 B1
Carrville Dr *ST/HB/BR* S6..101 E5
Carrville Rd *ST/HB/BR* S6..101 E5
Carrville Rd West
   ST/HB/BR S6..........101 E5
Carrwell La *ST/HB/BR* S6..114 A1
Carrwood Rd
   BSLYN/ROY S71..........33 E1
   CHNE S41..........178 B3
   ECK/KIL S21..........175 H3
Carsick Gv *FUL* S10..........137 H1
Carsick Hill Crs *FUL* S10..137 H1
Carsick Hill Dr *FUL* S10..........138 A1
Carsick Hill Rd *FUL* S10..........137 H1
Carsick Hill Wy *FUL* S10..........137 H1
Carsick View Rd *FUL* S10..137 H1
Carsington Cl *CHSW* S40..196 B4
Carson Av *DIN* S25..........134 A3
Carson Mt *HACK/IN* S12..154 D2
Carson Rd *HACK/IN* S12..154 D2
Carterhall La *HACK/IN* S12..154 D3
Carterhall Rd *HACK/IN* S12..154 D3
Carter Knowle Av *ECC* S11..138 C5
Carter Knowle Rd *ECC* S11..138 D5
Carter Lodge Av
   HACK/IN S12..........156 A1
Carter Lodge Dr
   HACK/IN S12..........156 B1
Carter Lodge Pl
   HACK/IN S12..........156 B1
Carter Lodge Ri
   HACK/IN S12..........156 B1
Carter Pl *SHEFS* S8..........140 A4
Carter Rd *SHEFS* S8..........140 A4
Cartmel Cl *DRON* S18..........170 C2
   MALT S66..........111 E2
Cartmel Ct *BSLYN/ROY* S71..15 H5
Cartmel Crs *CHNE* S41..........178 D5
Cartmel Crs *SHEFS* S8..........152 C1
Cartmell Hl *SHEFS* S8..........152 C1
Cartmel Wk *DIN* S25..........148 D1
Cart Rd *CHPT/GREN* S35..........60 A2
Car Vale Dr *HAN/WDH* S13..142 A2
Car Vale Vw *HAN/WDH* S13..142 A2
Carver Dr *DIN* S25..........134 C5
Carver La *SHEF* S1..........4 F5
Carver St *SHEF* S1..........4 E4
Carwood Cl *ATT* S4..........115 H5
Carwood Gv *ATT* S4..........115 H5
Carwood Rd *ATT* S4..........115 H5
Cary Gv *SHEFP/MNR* S2..........141 E5
Cary Rd *ECK/KIL* S21..........166 B5
   SHEFP/MNR S2..........141 F2
Castell Crs *DONS/BSCR* DN4..58 A4
Castle Av *CONI* DN12..........89 E1
   NROS/TKH DN11..........91 H3
   RHAM S60..........118 D3

Castlebeck Av
   SHEFP/MNR S2..........141 H1
Castlebeck Cft
   SHEFP/MNR S2..........142 A1
Castlebeck Dr
   SHEFP/MNR S2..........142 A2
Castle Bungalows
   BSVR S44 *..........196 D2
Castle Cl *BSLYN/ROY* S71..........20 B4
   BTLY DN5..........55 E3
   STKB/PEN S36..........45 E4
Castle Crs *CONI* DN12..........69 E5
Castledale Cft
   SHEFP/MNR S2..........141 H2
Castledale Gv
   SHEFP/MNR S2..........141 H2
Castledale Pl
   SHEFP/MNR S2..........141 H2
Castledine Ct
   DONS/BSCR DN4..........71 H4
Castledine Cft
   DARN/MH S9..........116 D2
Castledine Gdns
   DARN/MH S9..........116 C2
Castle Dr *DOD/DAR* S75..........46 A3
Castlegate *OWL* S3..........5 H1
   DIN S25..........134 B1
   S S3..........11 H2
Castle Gv *BTLY* DN5..........54 B4
Castle Grove Ter
   CONI DN12 *..........69 E5
Castle Hl *CONI* DN12..........89 E1
   ECK/KIL S21..........167 H4
Castle Hill Av
   MEX/SWTN S64..........67 G4
Castle Hill Cl *ECK/KIL* S21..166 D4
Castle Hills Rd *BTLY* DN5..........39 E1
Castle La *BSVR* S44..........196 C3
   STKB/PEN S36..........45 E4
Castle Ms *BTLY* DN5..........39 F1
Castlereagh St *BSLY* S70..........2 E5
Castlerigg Wy *DRON* S18 *..170 C2
Castlerow Cl
   TOT/DORE S17..........161 G2
Castlerow Dr
   TOT/DORE S17..........161 H2
Castle Sq *SHEF* S1..........11 H2
Castle St *BSLY* S70..........3 F7
   CONI DN12..........89 E1
   OWL S3..........11 H2
Castle Ter *CONI* DN12..........89 E1
Castleton Gv *STV/CWN* S43..189 F4
Castle Vw *BSLY* S70..........47 C5
   ECK/KIL S21..........166 D5
Castlewood Crs *FUL* S10..137 E2
Castlewood Dr *FUL* S10..........137 F2
Castlewood Rd *FUL* S10..........137 E2
Castor Rd *DARN/MH* S9..........116 B5
Catania Ri *WMB/DAR* S73....34 C4
Catchford Vw *CHNE* S41 *..186 B2
Catcliffe Rd *DARN/MH* S9..128 A3
Catherine Av
   AU/AST/KP S26..........145 E1
Catherine Rd *ATT* S4..........126 D1
Catherine St *CHSW* S40..........4 C4
   DON DN1..........6 C5
   OWL S3..........126 B1
   RHAM/THRY S65..........9 G4
Cathill Rd *WMB/DAR* S73....51 C1
Cat La *GLV* S14..........140 C5
Catley Rd *DARN/MH* S9..........128 A2
Cattal St *DARN/MH* S9..........126 B1
Catterick Cl *CONI* DN12..........88 A1
Cauldon Dr *CHSW* S40..........186 A4
Caulk La *BSLY* S70..........33 F5
Causeway Gdns
   TOT/DORE S17..........150 C5
Causeway Gld
   TOT/DORE S17..........150 C5
Causeway Head Rd
   TOT/DORE S17..........150 C5
The Causeway
   TOT/DORE S17..........160 D1
Cavalier Ct *DONS/BSCR* DN4..72 A3
Cavendish Av *ST/HB/BR* S6..113 C5
   TOT/DORE S17..........161 E1
Cavendish Cl
   RHAM/THRY S65..........107 F5
Cavendish Ct *OWL* S3..........10 D5
Cavendish Dr
   STV/CWN S43..........185 G2
Cavendish Pl *MALT* S66..........111 E2
   STV/CWN S43..........181 F3
Cavendish Ri *DRON* S18..170 D3
Cavendish Rd *BSVR* S44..........197 E4
   BTLY DN5..........26 C3
   DOD/DAR S75..........19 F4
   ECC S11..........138 B1
Cavendish St *CHSW* S40..........10 D4
   OWL S3..........10 D4
   STV/CWN S43..........189 C1
Cavendish St North
   CHNE S41..........179 G4
Cave La *DARN/MH* S9..........127 F2
Cavill Rd *SHEFS* S8..........153 E2
Cawdor Rd *SHEFP/MNR* S2..141 F4
Cawdor St *BTLY* DN5..........39 H1
Cawdron Cl
   RHAM/THRY S65..........99 F5

Cawdron Ri *RHAM* S60..........118 C4
Cawley Pl *BSLYN/ROY* S71....20 A3
Cawston Rd *ATT* S4..........115 C4
Cawthorne Cl *DOD/DAR* S75..36 C4
   RHAM/THRY S65..........107 E2
   SHEFS S8..........152 C2
Cawthorne Rd
   RHAM/THRY S65..........107 E2
Caxton Cl *STV/CWN* S43..180 B4
Caxton La *FUL* S10..........124 C5
Caxton Rd *AWLS/ASK* DN6....25 F2
   FUL S10..........125 E5
Caxton St *BSLY* S70..........3 F2
Caxton Wy *DIN* S25..........134 B4
Caythorpe Cl
   BSLYN/ROY S71..........21 G2
Cayton Cl *BSLYN/ROY* S71....14 C5
Cecil Av *DONS/BSCR* DN4....70 C3
   DRON S18..........171 E1
Cecil Rd *DRON* S18..........163 E5
Cecil Sq *ECC* S11..........139 H1
Cedar Av *CHSW* S40..........186 D4
   MALT S66..........108 C4
   MEX/SWTN S64..........66 D2
Cedar Cl *BSLYN/ROY* S71....12 A5
   DONS/BSCR DN4..........71 E3
   ECK/KIL S21..........168 A3
   ECK/KIL S21..........174 B1
   STKB/PEN S36..........76 D3
Cedar Crs *BSLY* S70..........32 B3
Cedar Dr *MALT* S66..........110 B3
   RHAM/THRY S65..........109 F1
Cedar Gv *CONI* DN12..........88 C3
Cedar Park Dr *BSVR* S44..197 E2
Cedar Rd *ARMTH* DN3..........43 E3
   DONS/BSCR DN4..........71 E2
   STKB/PEN S36..........76 D3
Cedar St *STV/CWN* S43..........181 E5
Cedarwood Ct *KIMB* S61....96 A4
Cedric Av *CONI* DN12..........88 C2
Cedric Crs *MALT* S66..........133 E1
   ARMTH DN3..........29 F5
Celandine Ct
   TOT/DORE S17..........161 G2
Celandine Gdns
   TOT/DORE S17..........161 G3
Celandine Gv *WMB/DAR* S73..51 E1
Celandine Ri *MEX/SWTN* S64..86 B3
Cemetery Av *ECC* S11..........139 F1
Cemetery La *STV/CWN* S43..182 A5
Cemetery Rd
   AWLS/ASK DN6..........25 E3
   BSLY S70..........3 K5
   CHNE S41..........5 K5
   CUD/GR S72..........23 F1
   DEARNE S63..........56 B5
   DRON S18..........171 F3
   ECC S11..........139 G2
   HOY S74..........62 C1
   MEX/SWTN S64..........67 E3
Cemetery Ter
   STV/CWN S43..........188 C2
Centenary Wy *RHAM* S60........8 D6
Central Av *AWLS/ASK* DN6....25 E3
   BTLY DN5..........39 H2
   CHSW S40..........5 C4
   DIN S25..........134 D5
   MALT S66..........108 B2
   MEX/SWTN S64..........85 H1
   RHAM/THRY S65..........106 D2
Central Bvd *WHHL* DN2..........2 A4
Central Dr *BTLY* DN5..........55 C1
   CONI DN12..........70 C5
Central Dr *BSLYN/ROY* S71....15 C1
   BSVR S44..........193 H1
   CHNE S41..........193 E5
   MALT S66..........133 E1
   NROS/TKH DN11..........91 E5
   RAW S62..........84 C3
   RCH S42..........195 H4
Central Ms *DIN* S25..........135 E5
Central Pde
   RHAM/THRY S65 *..........106 D3
Central Pavement *CHSW* S40..5 C4
Central St *CHNE* S41..........193 E3
   DEARNE S63..........37 G4
   HOY S74..........63 F3
Central Wk *STV/CWN* S43..188 B3
Centurion St *RHAM* S60..105 E4
Centurion Wy *BTLY* DN5..........39 H5
Century Cl *ARMTH* DN3..........28 D5
Century Ct *CONI* DN12..........70 C5
Century Gdns *BTLY* DN5..........40 A1
Century St *DARN/MH* S9..........127 E4
Century Wy *RHAM* S60..........118 A4
Chadbourne Cl *ARMTH* DN3..42 C5
Chaddesden Cl *DRON* S18..170 A2
Chadwick Dr *MALT* S66..........110 D2
Chadwick Rd
   AWLS/ASK DN6..........25 E3
   BTLY DN5..........39 H5
   HAN/WDH S13..........142 A3
Chaff Cl *RHAM* S60..........119 H3
Chaffinch Av *RHAM* S60..........118 D4
Chaff La *RHAM* S60..........119 H3
Chalbury Cl *DOD/DAR* S75..18 D3
Challands Cl *CHNE* S41..........193 E4
Challands Wy *CHNE* S41..193 E4
Challenger Crs *DEARNE* S63..37 E2

Challenger Dr *BTLY* DN5..........55 E2
Challiner Ms *RHAM* S60..129 C2
Challoner Gn *MOS* S20..........157 E5
Challoner Wy *MOS* S20..........157 E5
Chalmers Dr *WHHL* DN2..........41 H1
Chaloner Hts *HOY* S74..........63 F4
Chamberlain Av *BTLY* DN5....39 F4
Chamberlain Ct
   CHPT/GREN S35..........80 D5
Chambers Av *CONI* DN12..88 C1
Chambers Dr
   CHPT/GREN S35..........81 E4
Chambers Gv
   CHPT/GREN S35..........81 E4
Chambers La *ATT* S4..........116 A3
Chambers Rd *HOY* S74..........61 H1
   KIMB S61..........96 D5
Chambers Valley Rd
   CHPT/GREN S35..........81 E4
Chambers Vw
   CHPT/GREN S35..........81 E4
Champion Cl *SHEFN* S5..102 D3
Champion Rd *SHEFN* S5..102 C3
Chancel Wy *BSLYN/ROY* S71..20 C4
Chancery Pl *DON* DN1..........6 C4
Chancet Wood Cl *SHEFS* S8..152 D5
Chancet Wood Dr
   SHEFS S8..........152 D5
Chancet Wood Ri *SHEFS* S8..152 D5
Chander Hill La *RCH* S42..190 A4
Chandler Gv *RHAM* S60..130 A3
Chandos Crs *ECK/KIL* S21..168 A5
Chandos St *FUL* S10..........125 E5
Chaneyfield Wy *CHNE* S41..186 D2
Channing Gdns
   ST/HB/BR S6..........114 B5
Channing St *ST/HB/BR* S6..114 B5
Chantrey Av *CHNE* S41..........187 F3
Chantrey Rd *SHEFS* S8..........152 D2
Chantry Cl *DONS/BSCR* DN4..74 C1
Chantry Gv *BSLYN/ROY* S71..15 C1
Chapel Av *BSLYN/ROY* S71....50 C1
   WMB/DAR S73..........51 E5
Chapel Cl *BSLY* S70 *..........60 C1
   CHPT/GREN S35..........93 C1
   CUD/GR S72..........17 E1
   FUL S10..........138 D1
   STV/CWN S43..........185 E2
Chapel Ct *BSLY* S70 *..........60 C1
   BSLYN/ROY S71..........33 F2
Chapel Cft *WMB/DAR* S73....63 E1
Chapelfield Crs *KIMB* S61..95 F1
Chapelfield La *KIMB* S61..95 F1
Chapel Field La
   STKB/PEN S36..........44 C4
Chapelfield Mt *KIMB* S61..95 F1
Chapelfield Pl *KIMB* S61..95 F1
Chapelfield Rd *KIMB* S61..82 A5
Chapel Field Wk
   STKB/PEN S36..........44 C4
Chapelfield Wy *KIMB* S61..95 F1
Chapel Hl *HOY* S74..........48 D4
   MEX/SWTN S64..........66 C1
   RHAM S60..........119 H3
Chapel La *ARMTH* DN3..........59 C5
   BSLYN/ROY S71..........15 G4
   CONI DN12..........89 E2
   CUD/GR S72..........35 G2
   DARN/MH S9..........127 G1
   DEARNE S63..........37 G1
   DRON S18..........172 C2
   RAW S62..........8 E6
   STKB/PEN S36..........44 C4
   TOT/DORE S17..........160 C4
Chapel La East *CHNE* S41..193 F5
Chapel La West *CHNE* S41..191 G2
Chapel Pl *BSLYN/ROY* S71....33 F2
Chapel Ri *DIN* S25..........148 B3
Chapel Rd *BSVR* S44..........196 C3
   CHPT/GREN S35..........93 C2
   DOD/DAR S75..........60 A2
   BSLYN/ROY S71..........33 F2
   BTLY DN5..........39 H2
   CHNE S41..........187 C1
   CUD/GR S72..........17 E1
   DARN/MH S9..........127 G1
   DEARNE S63..........37 G1
   HAN/WDH S13..........143 F4
   KIMB S61..........97 F2
   MEX/SWTN S64..........66 C3
   MOS S20..........157 G5
   RAW S62..........98 B1
   STV/CWN S43..........188 D1
Chapel Ter *FUL* S10..........138 B1
Chapeltown Rd
   CHPT/GREN S35..........94 B4
Chapel Wk *RAW* S62..........84 D4
   RHAM S60..........8 C4
   RHAM S60 *..........129 G2
   S S3..........11 G5
Chapel Wy *AU/AST/KP* S26..159 H3
   RAW S62..........84 D4
Chapelwood Rd
   DARN/MH S9..........127 H1
Chapel Yd *DRON* S18..........171 H3
Chapman St *DARN/MH* S9..103 H5
   DEARNE S63..........37 F3
Chappell Dr *DON* DN1..........6 C1
Chapter Wy *BSLYN/ROY* S71..20 C4
Charity St *BSLYN/ROY* S71..21 F1
Charles Ashmore Rd
   SHEFS S8..........152 D5

Charles Crs *ARMTH* DN3..........42 B3
Charles La *SHEF* S1..............11 G4
Charles Rd *DEARNE* S63..........65 F3
Charles St *BSLY* S70...............2 E7
  BSLY S70 *................48 A1
  CHSW S40.....................4 C4
  CUD/GR S72..................17 E4
  CUD/GR S72..................35 H3
  DEARNE S63..................37 F5
  DIN S25.....................134 D3
  DON DN1.......................6 E1
  MEX/SWTN S64..............133 E1
  MEX/SWTN S64...............86 B1
  RAW S62......................85 H4
  SHEF S1......................11 G4
Charlesworth St *BSVR* S44.....196 B4
Charlotte La *SHEF* S1...........10 D4
Charlotte Rd *SHEF* S1...........11 G7
  SHEFP/MNR S2...............140 B1
Charlton Brook Crs
  CHPT/GREN S35...............80 C5
Charlton Clough
  CHPT/GREN S35...............93 F1
Charlton Dr *CHPT/GREN* S35...80 D3
Charlton Hill Ri
  CHPT/GREN S35...............93 F1
Charnell Av *MALT* S66..........111 E3
Charnley Av *ECC* S11...........139 E5
Charnley Cl *ECC* S11...........138 D4
Charnley Dr *ECC* S11...........139 E5
Charnley Ri *ECC* S11...........139 E5
Charnock Av *HACK/IN* S12.....154 D3
Charnock Crs *HACK/IN* S12....154 C3
Charnock Dale Rd
  HACK/IN S12................154 C3
Charnock Dr *BTLY* DN5.........39 F5
  HACK/IN S12................154 C2
Charnock Gv *HACK/IN* S12....154 D3
Charnock Hall Rd
  HACK/IN S12................154 C3
Charnock View Rd
  HACK/IN S12................154 C3
Charnock Wood Rd
  HACK/IN S12................154 D3
Charnwood Ct *MOS* S20.........157 G3
Charnwood Dr
  DONS/BSCR DN4...............71 E3
Charnwood Gv *KIMB* S61.......104 D3
Charnwood St
  MEX/SWTN S64...............66 B5
Charter Dr *BTLY* DN5............38 C2
Charter Rw *SHEF* S1............11 F6
Charter Square Rbt *SHEF* S1..11 F5
Chartwell Av *RCH* S42.........194 D2
Chasecliff Cl *CHSW* S40........186 D4
Chase Rd *ST/HB/BR* S6.........112 D4
The Chase *AU/AST/KP* S26.....145 G4
  ST/HB/BR S6................112 D4
Chatfield Rd *SHEFS* S8.........152 C3
Chatham St *OWL* S3............126 A2
  RHAM/THRY S65...............9 G4
Chatsworth Av *CHSW* S40.....191 F2
  MEX/SWTN S64...............67 H3
Chatsworth Cl
  AU/AST/KP S26..............145 H3
  BSVR S44...................197 F2
Chatsworth Ct
  STV/CWN S43................189 H1
Chatsworth Crs *BTLY* DN5......39 F2
Chatsworth Dr
  NROS/TKH DN11...............91 H3
Chatsworth Park Av
  HACK/IN S12................141 G5
Chatsworth Park Dr
  HACK/IN S12................141 G5
Chatsworth Park Gv
  HACK/IN S12................141 G5
Chatsworth Park Ri
  HACK/IN S12................141 G5
Chatsworth Pl *DRON* S18.......170 B1
Chatsworth Ri
  DOD/DAR S75 *...............30 B4
  RHAM S60...................118 D4
Chatsworth Rd
  BSLYN/ROY S71..............20 A1
  CHSW S40......................4 B4
  CHSW S40...................191 E2
  TOT/DORE S17...............161 E2
Chatterton Dr
  RHAM/THRY S65.............105 D5
Chaucer Cl *SHEFN* S5..........101 F3
Chaucer Dr *DRON* S18..........171 G4
Chaucer Rd *CHNE* S41..........187 F1
  MEX/SWTN S64...............67 H3
  RHAM/THRY S65.............106 D5
  SHEFN S5...................101 F3
Cheadle St *ST/HB/BR* S6.......114 A4
Cheapside *BSLY* S70...............3 G4
Checkstone Av
  DONS/BSCR DN4..............74 A3
Cheedale Av *CHSW* S40.........186 D4
Cheedale Cl *CHSW* S40.........186 D5
Cheetham Av *DRON* S18........179 E1
Cheetham Dr *MALT* S66........111 E4
Chelmsford Av
  AU/AST/KP S26..............145 G2
Chelmsford Dr *WHLL* DN2......40 D4
Chelsea Ct *ECC* S11............139 E3
Chelsea Ri *ECC* S11............139 E3
Chelsea Rd *ECC* S11...........139 E4
Cheltenham Ri *BTLY* DN5.......38 D5
Cheltenham Rd *WHLL* DN2......41 G5
Chemist La *RHAM* S60 *..........8 D3

Chemistry La
  CHPT/GREN S35...............78 C3
Chepstow Cl *CHSW* S40.........192 B4
Chepstow Dr
  MEX/SWTN S64...............67 F2
Chepstow Gdns *BTLY* DN5......38 D5
Chequer Av
  DONS/BSCR DN4................7 F6
Chequer Rd *DON* DN1.............6 E5
Cheriton Av
  AWLS/ASK DN6................25 E1
Cherry Bank Rd *SHEFS* S8....153 E2
Cherry Brook
  RHAM/THRY S65.............106 D1
Cherry Cl *BSLYN/ROY* S71.....12 A5
  CUD/GR S72..................16 D4
Cherry Garth *BTLY* DN5.........26 D4
Cherry Gv *CONI* DN12............88 B3
  DEARNE S63..................37 E5
  NROS/TKH DN11..............91 C3
Cherry La *BTLY* DN5..............6 C3
Cherrys Rd *BSLYN/ROY* S71....20 D5
Cherry St *SHEFP/MNR* S2......140 A1
Cherry St South
  SHEFP/MNR S2..............140 A2
  DOD/DAR S75 *...............14 A3
Cherry Tree Cl *BSVR* S44.....197 F3
  ECC S11....................139 F3
  RHAM S60...................118 D4
  STV/CWN S43................185 C3
Cherry Tree Crs *MALT* S66....105 C4
Cherry Tree Dell *ECC* S11.....139 F3
Cherry Tree Dr *ECC* S11.......139 F3
  ECK/KIL S21................168 A3
Cherry Tree Gv
  STV/CWN S43................183 E3
Cherry Tree Pl *DEARNE* S63....65 F3
Cherry Tree Rd *ARMTH* DN3....42 D4
  AU/AST/KP S26..............159 E3
  DONS/BSCR DN4................6 A6
  ECC S11....................139 F3
  MALT S66...................110 B4
Cherry Tree St *HOY* S74.........62 B2
Cherry Wk *CHPT/GREN* S35.....94 A2
Chertsey Cl *CHSW* S40.........192 B4
Cherwell Cl *STV/CWN* S43.....180 C5
Chesham Rd *BSLY* S70............2 D4
Chessel Cl *SHEFS* S8..........153 E1
Chester Ct *ECK/KIL* S21.......174 B1
Chesterfield Av
  STV/CWN S43................180 C3
Chesterfield Rd
  AU/AST/KP S26..............144 D5
  CHNE S41...................188 A3
  DRON S18...................171 F2
  ECK/KIL S21................174 A2
  SHEFS S8...................152 D1
  SHEFS S8...................189 E1
Chesterfield Rd South
  SHEFS S8...................163 E2
Chesterhill Av
  RHAM/THRY S65...............99 G5
Chester St *WHHL* DN2...........40 D3
  CHSW S40.....................4 B3
Chesterton Cl
  STV/CWN S43................188 D5
Chesterton Rd
  DONS/BSCR DN4..............72 A2
  RHAM/THRY S65.............106 C1
Chesterton Wy
  DONS/BSCR DN4..............98 D5
Chesterwood Dr *FUL* S10 *....124 D5
Chestnut Av *ARMTH* DN3.......42 D4
  AU/AST/KP S26..............159 G3
  CUD/GR S72..................17 H1
  DARN/MH S9................128 C4
  DEARNE S63..................65 F4
  ECK/KIL S21................167 H3
  ECK/KIL S21................174 B1
  MOS S20....................144 B5
  NROS/TKH DN11..............91 G3
  RHAM/THRY S65.............106 D2
  STKB/PEN S36................76 D5
  WHHL DN2....................41 F3
Chestnut Ct *BSLY* S70...........31 H5
  BTLY DN5 *...................26 C5
  RHAM/THRY S65...............99 H3
Chestnut Crs *BSLY* S70...........32 B3
Chestnut Dr
  CHPT/GREN S35...............93 G2
  STV/CWN S43................184 D2
Chestnut Gv *BTLY* DN5..........54 B5
  CONI DN12...................88 C2
  DEARNE S63..................37 F3
  DIN S25....................134 D3
  MALT S66...................110 B2
Chestnut Rd
  AU/AST/KP S26..............144 D2
Chestnut St *CUD/GR* S72........16 D4
Chevet La *HOR/CROF* WF4......12 F1
Chevet Ri *BSLYN/ROY* S71......12 A5
Chevet Vw *BSLYN/ROY* S71......12 A5
Cheviot Dr *BTLY* DN5............39 F3
Chevril Ct *MALT* S66...........108 A5
Chichester Rd *FUL* S10.........124 D3
Chigwell Wy *STV/CWN* S43....181 F3
Chilcombe Pl *BSLY* S70..........60 D2
Childers St *DONS/BSCR* DN4.....7 F7
Chiltern Cl *CHSW* S40..........186 C5
Chiltern Crs *BTLY* DN5..........54 A1

Chiltern Ri *RHAM* S60..........118 D5
Chiltern Rd *BSLYN/ROY* S71.....39 F3
  ST/HB/BR S6................113 H4
Chilton St *BSLY* S70............184 B5
Chilwell Cl *BSLYN/ROY* S71.....14 D3
Chilwell Ms *BSLYN/ROY* S71...14 D3
Chinley St *DARN/MH* S9........127 G2
Chippingham Pl
  DARN/MH S9................127 F1
Chippingham St
  DARN/MH S9................127 G1
Chippinghouse Rd
  SHEFS S8...................139 H3
Chippingham St
  DARN/MH S9................127 F1
Chiverton Cl *DRON* S18........171 E1
Chorley Av *FUL* S10............137 G2
Chorley Dr *FUL* S10............137 G2
Chorley Pl *FUL* S10............137 G3
Chorley Ri *FUL* S10............137 H2
Christchurch Av
  AU/AST/KP S26..............145 G2
Christchurch Rd
  DEARNE S63..................64 C1
Christ Church Rd *DON* DN1......6 C2
  OWL S3.....................115 F5
Christchurch Ter *DON* DN1 *....7 C5
Church Av *RAW* S62..............98 A2
Church Balk *ARMTH* DN3........29 F4
Church Balk Gdns
  ARMTH DN3....................29 F4
Church Cl *AU/AST/KP* S26.....159 F3
  ECK/KIL S21................175 H3
  MALT S66...................110 D4
  MEX/SWTN S64...............66 A5
  RCH S42....................195 G3
  STV/CWN S43................185 F3
  STV/CWN S43................189 G2
Church Cottage Ms
  DONS/BSCR DN4..............71 E1
Church Ct *DIN* S25.............148 C4
  DONS/BSCR DN4..............74 B1
Church Cft *ARMTH* DN3..........29 E4
  RAW S62.....................98 A2
Churchdale Ms
  HACK/IN S12................155 F1
Churchdale Rd
  HACK/IN S12................155 F1
Church Dr *CUD/GR* S72..........17 H2
  RAW S62.....................82 C2
Churchfield Av *CUD/GR* S72....21 H1
Churchfield Cl *BTLY* DN5........39 G3
Church Field Dr *MALT* S66....108 D5
Churchfield Gdns
  BSLYN/ROY S71..............15 H3
Church Field La *RAW* S62.......82 B3
Church Flds *KIMB* S61..........104 C2
Churchfields Cl *BSLY* S70........3 F3
Church Fields Rd
  NROS/TKH DN11..............91 H1
Church Field Vw
  DONS/BSCR DN4..............71 E1
Church Fold *ST/HB/BR* S6.....113 C4
Church Glebe *ST/HB/BR* S6....113 C1
Church Gn *DEARNE* S63..........65 E2
Church Gv *BSLYN/ROY* S71.....20 C3
Church La *BSLYN/ROY* S71......15 F1
Church Houses
  STV/CWN S43................181 E5
Churchill Av *BTLY* DN5..........39 G5
Churchill Rd *DON* DN1...........40 C4
  FUL S10....................124 D4
  STKB/PEN S36................76 B1
Churchill Wy
  CHPT/GREN S35...............80 D3
Church La *AU/AST/KP* S26.....145 H3
  AWLS/ASK DN6................25 C1
  BSLY S70.....................3 F3
  BSLY S70....................47 H3
  CHSW S40...................193 H1
  CHSW S40.....................5 D4
  CUD/GR S72..................13 G5
  DIN S25....................134 B4
  DOD/DAR S75.................60 C5
  DONS/BSCR DN4..............70 D2
  DONS/BSCR DN4..............74 A2
  ECK/KIL S21................168 C2
  HACK/IN S12................156 C2
  HAN/WDH S13...............143 F4
  HOR/CROF WF4...............13 E2
  MALT S66...................108 B5
  MALT S66...................110 D4
  MOS S20....................157 G2
  MOS S20....................166 D1
  MOS S20....................129 G1
  STV/CWN S43................185 F3
  TOT/DORE S17..............160 D2
Church Lane Ms *MALT* S66....108 B5
Church La North *CHNE* S41....179 G3
Church Lea *HOY* S74.............62 A4
Church Meadow Rd
  NROS/TKH DN11..............91 H3
Church Mdw *BSVR* S44.........193 H1
Church Ms *DEARNE* S63..........53 E4
  ECK/KIL S21................168 C1
  MEX/SWTN S64...............67 H4
  MOS S20....................166 D1

Church Rein Cl
  DONS/BSCR DN4..............70 C2
Church Rd *ARMTH* DN3..........29 F3
  BSVR S44...................184 B5
  CONI DN12...................68 C4
  CONI DN12...................70 B5
Church Side *BSVR* S44.........193 H1
Church St *ARMTH* DN3..........42 C4
  AU/AST/KP S26..............159 F3
  BSLY S70.....................3 F3
  BSLYN/ROY S71..............15 G1
  BSVR S44...................193 H1
  BSVR S44...................184 B5
  BTLY DN5....................39 G2
  CHPT/GREN S35...............94 A5
  CONI DN12...................89 E1
  CUD/GR S72..................37 E2
  DEARNE S63..................37 E2
  DOD/DAR S75.................18 C4
  DON DN1......................6 C2
  DRON S18...................171 G2
  ECK/KIL S21................167 E4
  HOY S74.....................62 B1
  KIMB S61...................104 C2
  MALT S66...................133 F1
  MEX/SWTN S64...............66 A5
  RAW S62.....................98 A2
  RHAM S60.....................9 F4
  SHEF S1.....................11 G3
  ST/HB/BR S6................125 G2
  STKB/PEN S36................44 A5
  STV/CWN S43................177 F4
  STV/CWN S43................182 A4
  STV/CWN S43................185 E3
  WMB/DAR S73................50 B3
Church St North *CHNE* S41....179 G3
Church St South *CHSW* S40....192 C5
Church St West *CHSW* S40....191 G2
Church Vw *AU/AST/KP* S26.....145 H3
  ECK/KIL S21................147 F5
  CUD/GR S72..................21 H2
  CHSW S40..................191 G2
  DOD/DAR S75.................19 E4
  DON DN1......................6 C2
  ECK/KIL S21................168 C1
  HAN/WDH S13...............143 H4
  HOY S74.....................61 F3
  MALT S66...................110 D4
  RHAM/THRY S65...............99 H3
  ST/HB/BR S6................113 G1
  STV/CWN S43................177 E4
  STV/CWN S43................185 E3
  WMB/DAR S73................35 G5
Church View Crs
  STKB/PEN S36................44 D3
Church View Rd
  STKB/PEN S36................44 D3
Church Wk *CONI* DN12...........68 C4
Church Wy *CHSW* S40............5 G4
  DON DN1......................6 C3
  DON DN1......................6 C3
Churcroft *DOD/DAR* S75........18 C3
Churston Rd *CHSW* S40.........191 E1
Cinder Bridge Rd *KIMB* S61....97 G2
Cinder Hill La
  CHPT/GREN S35..............101 F1
Cinderhilla La *SHEFS* S8.......153 G5
Cinderhill Rd *KIMB* S61.........96 D5
Cinder Hills Wy
  DOD/DAR S75.................30 C3
Cinder La *ECK/KIL* S21........168 C4
Circle Cl *SHEFP/MNR* S2......141 H2
The Circle *NROS/TKH* DN11....91 E2
  SHEFP/MNR S2..............141 H2
The Circuit *AWLS/ASK* DN6.....24 D1
City Rd *SHEFP/MNR* S2........141 E1
Clanricarde St
  BSLYN/ROY S71..............19 G4
Clara Pl *KIMB* S61.............104 D3
Clarehurst Rd
  WMB/DAR S73................35 E4
Clarel Cl *STKB/PEN* S36........44 C4
Clarell Gdns
  DONS/BSCR DN4..............58 A4
Clarel St *STKB/PEN* S36........44 C4
Claremont Crs *FUL* S10.........10 A4
Claremont Pl *FUL* S10..........10 A4
Claremont St *KIMB* S61........104 D3
Clarence Av
  DONS/BSCR DN4..............55 H5
Clarence La *ECC* S11..........10 D7
Clarence Pl *MALT* S66.........111 G4
Clarence Rd *BSLYN/ROY* S71...20 B3
  CHSW S40.....................4 D4
  ST/HB/BR S6................113 H4
Clarence Sq *DIN* S25..........135 E4
Clarence St *CHSW* S40...........4 D4
  DEARNE S63..................64 C1
  DIN S25....................135 E4
Clarendon Rd *FUL* S10.........138 A3
  RHAM/THRY S65...............9 J2
  STV/CWN S43................189 G2
Clarendon St *BSLY* S70...........2 D5
Clark Av *DONS/BSCR* DN4.......7 G6
Clarke Av *DIN* S25............134 A2
  MALT S66...................133 G1

Clarke Ct *DIN* S25.............134 D3
Clarke Dell *FUL* S10...........139 F1
Clarke Dr *FUL* S10.............139 F1
Clarkegrove Rd *FUL* S10.......125 F5
Clarkehouse Rd *FUL* S10......139 F1
Clarkes Cft *WMB/DAR* S73......50 B2
Clarke Sq *ECC* S11.............139 H2
Clarke St *DOD/DAR* S75........19 F4
  FUL S10.....................10 C6
Clark Gv *ST/HB/BR* S6.........123 G1
Clarks Ct *AWLS/ASK* DN6......25 F1
Clarkson St *BSLY* S70...........32 C5
  FUL S10.....................10 B4
Clark St *HOY* S74...............61 H1
Clarney Av *WMB/DAR* S73......34 D4
Clarney Pl *WMB/DAR* S73......34 D4
Claycliffe Av *DOD/DAR* S75....18 B3
Claycliffe Rd *DOD/DAR* S75....18 B2
Claycliffe Ter *BSLY* S70..........2 C7
Clayfield La *MEX/SWTN* S64...67 G3
Clayfield La *MEX/SWTN* S64...82 D2
Clayfield Rd *HOY* S74...........48 D5
  MEX/SWTN S64...............67 G3
Clayfields *DONS/BSCR* DN4.....71 G3
Clayfield Vw
  MEX/SWTN S64...............67 H3
Clay Flat La
  NROS/TKH DN11..............91 F3
Clay La *SHEF* S1...............11 C5
  WHHL DN2....................41 H2
Clay La West *WHHL* DN2.......28 C5
Clay Pit La *RAW* S62............98 C1
Clay Pits La *STKB/PEN* S36....76 A1
Clay Pit Wy *STV/CWN* S43.....177 G5
Clayroyd *BSLY* S70..............48 A1
Clay St *DARN/MH* S9...........116 B5
Clayton Av *DEARNE* S63........36 D1
Clayton Crs *MOS* S20..........157 E3
Clayton Dr *DEARNE* S63........36 D2
Clayton Hollow *MOS* S20.......157 E3
Clayton La *DEARNE* S63........36 D1
Clayton St *CHNE* S41............5 J6
Clay Wheels La
  ST/HB/BR S6................100 D5
Claywood Dr
  SHEFP/MNR S2...............11 K5
Claywood Rd
  SHEFP/MNR S2..............126 C3
Clayworth Dr
  DONS/BSCR DN4..............73 F1
Clearwell Cft *BTLY* DN5.........39 F5
Cleeve Hill Gdns *MOS* S20....156 D3
Clematis Rd *SHEFN* S5.........116 B1
Clement Ms *KIMB* S61.........104 C3
Clementson Rd *FUL* S10.......125 E3
Clement St *DARN/MH* S9......127 H1
  KIMB S61...................104 C3
Clevedon Crs *BTLY* DN5.........39 F1
Clevedon Wy
  BSLYN/ROY S71..............12 B2
Cleveland Rd *ARMTH* DN3......43 E4
Cleveland St *DON* DN1..........6 B5
  ST/HB/BR S6................125 G2
Cleveland Wy *CHSW* S40......186 B5
Cliff Cl *CUD/GR* S72.............17 H1
Cliff Crs *DONS/BSCR* DN4.......70 C2
Cliff Dr *WMB/DAR* S73..........35 G5
Cliffe Av *BSLY* S70..............32 B5
Cliffe Bank *MEX/SWTN* S64....66 B5
Cliffe Cl *BSLYN/ROY* S71........20 C4
Cliffe Crs *DOD/DAR* S75.........30 A3
Cliffedale Crs *BSLY* S70.........32 B4
Cliffe Farm Dr *ECC* S11........138 C3
Cliffefield Rd
  MEX/SWTN S64...............86 B1
  SHEFS S8...................139 H5
Cliffe House Rd *SHEFN* S5....102 C4
Cliffe La *BSLYN/ROY* S71.......20 C5
Cliffe Rd *ST/HB/BR* S6.........124 C2
  WMB/DAR S73................51 F5
Cliff Hl *MALT* S66.............110 B3
  STV/CWN S43................184 C3
Cliff Hills Cl *MALT* S66........110 C3
Cliff La *CUD/GR* S72............17 G2
Clifford Cl *CHSW* S40..........191 F2
Clifford Rd *ECC* S11...........139 E3
  KIMB S61....................96 C5
  MALT S66...................109 G5
Clifford St *CUD/GR* S72.........17 E3
Clifford Wk *CONI* DN12.........68 A5
Cliff Rd *ST/HB/BR* S6.........123 H1
  WMB/DAR S73................51 G1
Cliff St *ECC* S11..............139 H1
  MEX/SWTN S64...............67 G4
Cliff Ter *BSLYN/ROY* S71.........3 J4
Cliff Vw *CONI* DN12.............68 A5
Clifton Av *BSLYN/ROY* S71......14 C4
  DARN/MH S9................128 C4
  RHAM/THRY S65.............106 C3
  STV/CWN S43................177 E4
Clifton Bank *RHAM* S60...........9 G5
Clifton Crs *RHAM/THRY* S65.....9 J5
Clifton Crs North
  RHAM/THRY S65...............9 J5
Clifton Crs South
  RHAM/THRY S65...............9 J5
Clifton Dr *BTLY* DN5.............39 E1
Clifton Gdns *CUD/GR* S72.......17 G1
Clifton Gv
  RHAM/THRY S65...............9 K4
Clifton Hl *CONI* DN12...........89 F2

Clifton La DARN/MH S9.......128 C5
  RHAM/THRY S65.......9 H5
Clifton Mt RHAM/MH S9.......9 H5
Clifton Rd MALT S66.......110 C2
  DONS/BSCR DN4.......5 J7
Clifton St BSLY S70.......3 J7
  CHSW S40.......4 B4
  DARN/MH S9.......116 D4
Clifton Ter RHAM S60.......9 H5
Clinton Pl FUL S10.......10 C7
Clinton Wk FUL S10.......10 C6
Clipstone Av
  BSLYN/ROY S71.......14 D4
Clipstone Gdns
  DARN/MH S9.......128 A1
Clipstone Rd DARN/MH S9.......128 A1
The Cloisters BSLY S70.......47 H5
  DONS/BSCR DN4.......74 C1
Cloisters Wy
  BSLYN/ROY S71.......20 D5
Cloonmore Cft SHEFS S8.......153 E4
Cloonmore Dr SHEFS S8.......153 C4
The Close ARMTH DN3.......59 F5
  BSLYN/ROY S71.......15 C3
  BSLYN/ROY S71.......21 E4
  DIN S25.......134 D5
Cloudberry Wy
  DOD/DAR S75.......14 B4
Clough Bank KIMB S61.......8 A2
  SHEFP/MNR S2.......140 B2
Clough Flds FUL S10.......124 B3
Clough Fields Rd HOY S74.......61 G3
Clough Gn KIMB S61.......8 A2
Clough Gv CHPT/GREN S35.......100 A2
Clough Head STKB/PEN S36...44 D5
Clough La FUL S10.......137 E4
Clough Rd HOY S74.......61 H3
  KIMB S61.......8 B2
  SHEF S1.......140 A1
Clough St KIMB S61.......8 B5
The Clough CHNE S41.......193 C3
Clovelly Rd ARMTH DN3.......29 F5
Clover Gdns SHEFN S5.......116 A1
Clover Gn KIMB S61.......96 B4
Cloverlands Dr
  DOD/DAR S75.......14 A4
Clowne Rd DONS/BSCR S44.....184 A5
  STV/CWN S43.......177 G5
Club Garden Rd ECC S11.......139 F2
Club Garden Wk ECC S11.......139 F1
Club Mill Rd ST/HB/BR S6.....114 C4
Clubmill Ter CHSW S40.......4 B3
Club St BSLYN/ROY S71.......20 C3
  ECC S11.......139 H2
  HOY S74.......61 H3
Clumber Cl STV/CWN S43.....185 F2
Clumber Pl STV/CWN S43.....189 C3
Clumber Ri AU/AST/KP S26...145 H3
Clumber Rd DONS/BSCR DN4....7 J7
  FUL S10.......138 A1
Clumber St DOD/DAR S75.......2 B3
Clune St STV/CWN S43.......177 H5
Clun Rd ATT S4.......126 C1
Clun St ATT S4.......126 C1
Clyde Rd SHEFS S8.......139 H4
Clyde St BSLYN/ROY S71.......3 H5
Coach House Dr BTLY DN5.......38 D5
Coach House La BSLY S70.......31 H4
The Coach Houses
  FUL S10 *.......125 F3
Coach Rd KIMB S61.......97 F2
  RAW S62.......81 H3
Coalbrook Av
  HAN/WDH S13.......143 H2
Coalbrook Gv
  HAN/WDH S13.......143 H2
Coalbrook Rd
  HAN/WDH S13.......143 H2
Coalby Wk BSLY S70.......2 E3
Coaley La RAW S62.......96 D5
Coalpit La AU/AST/KP S26...159 G4
Coal Pit La CUD/GR S72.......22 A2
  STKB/PEN S36.......76 D4
Coalpit Rd CONI DN12 *.......84 B5
Coates St SHEFP/MNR S2 *...126 C5
Cobb Ct MEX/SWTN S64.......86 B2
Cobb Dr MEX/SWTN S64.......86 A2
Cobcar Av HOY S74.......62 D3
Cobcar Cl HOY S74.......62 C2
Cobcar La HOY S74.......62 C2
Cobcar St HOY S74.......62 C2
Cobden Av MEX/SWTN S64...67 F3
Cobden Pl FUL S10.......125 E3
Cobden Rd CHSW S40.......4 E2
Cobden View Rd FUL S10.....124 D3
Cobnar Av SHEFS S8.......153 E3
Cobnar Dr CHNE S41.......186 D1
  SHEFS S8.......153 E3
Cobnar Gdns SHEFS S8.......152 D3
Cobnar Rd SHEFS S8.......152 D3
Cobnar Wood Cl CHNE S41...178 B3
Cockayne Pl SHEFS S8.......152 D1
Cockerham Av
  DOD/DAR S75.......2 E1
Cockshot La STKB/PEN S36....77 E4
Cockshutt Av SHEFS S8.......152 B5
Cockshutt Dr SHEFS S8.......152 B5
Cockshutt Rd SHEFS S8.......152 B5
Coggin Mill Wy RHAM S60...105 E4
Coisley Hill HAN/WDH S13...142 D5
Coisley Rd HAN/WDH S13...143 E4
Coit La ECC S11.......150 D2

Coke Hl RHAM S60.......9 F6
Coke La RHAM S60.......9 F6
Colbeck Cl ARMTH DN3.......42 C4
Coley Pl ST/HB/BR S6.......124 B2
Colchester Cl BTLY DN5.......39 F4
Colchester Rd FUL S10.......124 D3
Coldstream Av
  DONS/BSCR DN4.......70 D2
Coldwell La FUL S10.......124 A4
Coleford Rd DARN/MH S9...128 B2
Coleman St RAW S62.......98 B3
Coleridge Av
  BSLYN/ROY S71.......20 B3
Coleridge Rd DARN/MH S9...116 D5
  DEARNE S63.......64 C1
  MALT S66.......111 E4
  RHAM/THRY S65.......9 J2
Colister Dr DARN/MH S9.....127 H3
Colister Gdns
  DARN/MH S9.......127 H4
Collage Rd ECK/KIL S21.....176 B1
College Av STV/CWN S43.....181 H5
College Cl ATT S4.......115 G5
College Ct MEX/SWTN S64...67 F3
College La RHAM/THRY S65.....9 F4
College Park Cl RHAM S60...119 E1
College Rd DON DN1.......6 C5
  ECK/KIL S21.......176 A4
  MEX/SWTN S64.......67 F3
  RHAM S60.......9 F5
College Road Rbt RHAM S60....8 C3
College St FUL S10.......125 F5
  RHAM/THRY S65.......9 F4
College Wk RHAM S60 *.......9 F3
Collegiate Crs FUL S10.......10 A7
Colley Av BSLY S70.......32 C3
  SHEFN S5.......102 A3
Colley Cl SHEFN S5.......102 A3
Colley Crs SHEFN S5.......102 A3
Colley Dr SHEFN S5.......102 B3
Colley Pl BSLY S70.......32 C3
Colley Rd SHEFN S5.......102 A3
Collier Gv CUD/GR S72.......17 E5
Colliers Cl HAN/WDH S13...143 F4
Collier St WMB/DAR S73.......63 H1
Colliers Trek STV/CWN S43...184 C1
Colliery Cl DIN S25.......134 C3
  STV/CWN S43.......182 B5
Colliery La DEARNE S63.......37 F4
Colliery Rd ATT S4.......115 F2
  AU/AST/KP S26.......159 H3
Colliery Yd DOD/DAR S75.......60 B4
Collin Av SHEFS S8.......113 C3
Collindridge Rd
  WMB/DAR S73.......50 B3
Collingbourne Av MOS S20..157 G4
Collingbourne Dr
  MOS S20 *.......157 G4
Collingham Rd
  AU/AST/KP S26.......145 E4
Collins Cl DOD/DAR S75.......30 A3
Collinson Rd SHEFN S5.......102 A5
Collishaw Cl CHNE S41.......193 H4
Colonel Ward Dr
  MEX/SWTN S64.......66 C5
The Colonnades DON DN1 *....6 C4
Colster Cl DOD/DAR S75.......18 C5
Coltfield BSLY S70.......47 H4
Coltishall Av MALT S66.......109 E3
Colton Cl CHNE S41.......179 E5
Coltsworth La
  STV/CWN S43.......177 H3
Columbia St BSLY S70.......31 H3
Columbus Wy MALT S66.....110 B2
Colver Rd SHEFP/MNR S2...140 A2
Colvin Cl BTLY DN5.......40 C1
Colwall St DARN/MH S9.....127 F1
Commerce St
  CHPT/GREN S35.......94 A1
Commercial Rd
  DEARNE S63.......52 D2
Commercial St BSLY S70.......3 F7
  SHEF S1.......11 J5
Common Farm Cl
  RHAM/THRY S65.......108 D1
Common La BSLYN/ROY S71...15 H5
  BTLY DN5.......28 A5
  CONI DN12.......89 F4
  DEARNE S63.......65 H2
  DONS/BSCR DN4.......70 D3
  ECC S11.......137 H5
  MALT S66.......132 D2
  NROS/TKH DN11.......91 H5
  STKB/PEN S36.......77 G4
Common Rd
  AU/AST/KP S26.......147 G1
  CONI DN12.......89 F4
  DEARNE S63.......36 D2
  DIN S25.......135 E5
Commonside FUL S10.......125 E3
The Common
  CHPT/GREN S35.......94 B4
Commonwealth Vw
  DEARNE S63.......51 E5
Companions Cl MALT S66...108 B5
Compass Crs CHNE S41.......180 A3
Compton St CHSW S40.......4 D2
Conalan Av TOT/DORE S17...161 H3
Conan Rd CONI DN12.......88 D1
Concorde Ms DON DN1 *.......6 E2
Concord Rd SHEFN S5.......103 E3

Concord View Rd
  KIMB S61.......104 A4
Conduit La FUL S10.......125 E3
Conduit Rd BSVR S44.......196 D4
  FUL S10.......125 E3
Coney St FUL S10.......26 C3
Congress St SHEF S1.......10 E3
Coningsburgh Rd
  ARMTH DN3.......29 F5
Coningsby Rd SHEFN S5.....115 G3
  STKB/PEN S36.......115 G4
Coniston Cl DIN S25.......148 D2
Coniston Dr DEARNE S63.......53 E4
  DONS/BSCR DN4.......71 G4
Coniston Pl BTLY DN5.......39 F2
Coniston Rd ARMTH DN3.......25 J4
  BSLYN/ROY S71.......186 D1
  CHNE S41.......186 D1
  DRON S18.......170 C2
  MEX/SWTN S64.......67 G2
  SHEFS S8.......139 G5
  WHHL DN2.......57 G1
Coniston Ter SHEFS S8.......139 G5
Coniston Wy CHNE S41.......187 E1
Connaught Dr MALT S66.......110 C2
Connelly Ct CHSW S40 *.......4 C3
Conrad Dr MALT S66.......110 C2
Constable Cl DRON S18.......170 C3
  GLV S14.......153 H3
Constable Dr GLV S14.......153 H3
Constable La DIN S25.......134 C4
Constable Pl DEARNE S63.......65 E2
  GLV S14.......154 A3
Constable Rd GLV S14.......153 H3
Constable Wy GLV S14.......153 H4
  RHAM/THRY S65.......99 E5
Convent Gv
  DONS/BSCR DN4.......57 H5
Convent Pl OWL S3 *.......10 D4
Convent Wk OWL S3.......10 D4
Conway Ct DONS/BSCR DN4..73 H5
Conway Crs
  RHAM/THRY S65.......107 E1
Conway Dr ARMTH DN3.......39 F5
Conway Pl WMB/DAR S73.......50 D4
Conway St BSLY S70.......3 G5
  OWL S3.......10 C5
Conway Ter MEX/SWTN S64...67 F2
Conyers Dr AU/AST/KP S26...145 F2
Conyers Rd BTLY DN5.......39 H5
Cook Av MALT S66.......110 C2
Cooke St BTLY DN5.......39 G2
Cookson Cl SHEFN S5.......101 F5
Cookson Rd SHEFN S5.......114 B1
Cookson St
  DONS/BSCR DN4.......55 H5
Cooks Rd MOS S20.......157 G3
Cooks Wood Rd OWL S3.......9 K1
Coombe Pl FUL S10.......124 D4
Coombe Rd FUL S10.......124 D4
Co-operative St
  CUD/GR S72.......21 G1
  DEARNE S63.......37 G5
  DEARNE S63.......64 D1
Cooper St DONS/BSCR DN4...63 H2
Coopers Ter DON DN1.......6 F7
Cooper St DONS/BSCR DN4...7 F7
Copeland Rd WMB/DAR S73..50 A2
Cope St BSLY S70.......31 H3
Copley Av CONI DN12.......88 C1
Copley Crs BTLY DN5.......58 C4
Copley Gdns BTLY DN5.......58 C4
Copley Pl KIMB S61.......105 E2
Copley Rd DON DN1.......6 E1
Copper Beech Cl MOS S20...157 C2
Copper Beech Crs
  MALT S66.......110 C5
Copper Cl BSLY S70.......3 H6
Copper St OWL S3.......11 F1
Coppice Av DOD/DAR S75...14 B4
Coppice Cl STKB/PEN S36.......76 B1
Coppice Gdns RAW S62.......81 F2
  ST/HB/BR S6.......107 H2
Coppice Ri AWLS/ASK DN6...25 F5
Coppice Rd CHPT/GREN S35...81 F5
  AWLS/ASK DN6.......25 F5
The Coppice KIMB S61.......96 A4
Coppice Vw STV/CWN S43.....185 E4
Coppicewood Ct
  DONS/BSCR DN4.......72 A4
Coppins Cl MALT S66.......108 D3
Coppin Sq SHEFN S5.......101 F4
The Copse MALT S66.......108 D5
Coquet Av MALT S66.......108 D5
Coral Cl RAW S62.......81 H2
Coral Dr AU/AST/KP S26...131 E5
Coral Pl AU/AST/KP S26...131 E5
Coral Wy AU/AST/KP S26...131 E5
Corby St ATT S4.......126 D1
Cordwell Av CHNE S41.......186 C1
Cordwell Cl STV/CWN S43...180 C5
Corker Bottoms La
  SHEFP/MNR S2.......127 F4
Corker Rd HACK/IN S12.......141 G4
Cornfail Pl BSLY S70.......3 G5
Cornfield Cl RCH S42.......196 B4
Cornflower Dr
  DONS/BSCR DN4.......57 F5
Corn Hl CONI DN12.......89 F2
Cornish St OWL S3.......125 H2

Cornish Wy RAW S62.......98 A4
Cornmill Cl BSVR S44.......197 F2
Cornwall Av STV/CWN S43...188 D3
Cornwall Cl BSLYN/ROY S71...20 B3
  STV/CWN S43.......188 D1
  STV/CWN S43.......188 D1
Cornwall Rd WHHL DN2.......41 F5
Cornwell Ct RAW S62.......84 C4
Coronation Av
  AU/AST/KP S26.......159 G3
  CUD/GR S72.......16 D1
  CUD/GR S72.......23 E1
  DIN S25.......134 D3
Coronation Dr KIMB S61.......8 A5
Coronation Crs BSLY S70.......47 H4
Coronation Dr BSLYN/ROY S71..47 H4
  DEARNE S63.......52 D3
Coronation Gdns
  DONS/BSCR DN4.......70 C2
Coronation Rd DEARNE S63...65 G2
  DONS/BSCR DN4.......71 H1
  HOY S74.......61 H2
  MEX/SWTN S64.......66 C5
  RAW S62.......86 A5
  STKB/PEN S36.......76 D2
  STV/CWN S43.......188 C1
Coronation St
  BSLYN/ROY S71.......20 C3
  DONS/BSCR DN4.......37 G3
  WMB/DAR S73.......35 F4
Coronation Ter
  BSLYN/ROY S71.......33 F2
  CONI DN12 *.......89 E1
Corporation St BSLY S70.......32 A3
  CHNE S41.......5 H3
  OWL S3.......11 G1
  RHAM S60.......8 E4
Corporation St Jct OWL S3...11 G1
Cortina Ri WMB/DAR S73 *...34 C4
Corton Wd WMB/DAR S73.......50 D5
Cortonwood Dr
  WMB/DAR S73.......63 H1
Cortworth La RAW S62.......83 F2
Cortworth Pl HOY S74.......62 C2
Cortworth Rd ECC S11.......151 G1
Corwen Pl HAN/WDH S13...143 E4
Cosgrove Ct ARMTH DN3.......29 C5
Cossey Rd ATT S4.......126 C1
Coterel Crs DONS/BSCR DN4..58 A4
Cotleigh Av HACK/IN S12...156 A4
Cotleigh Cl HACK/IN S12...156 A4
Cotleigh Crs HACK/IN S12...156 A4
Cotleigh Dr HACK/IN S12...156 A4
Cotleigh Gdns HACK/IN S12..156 A4
Cotleigh Pl HACK/IN S12...156 A4
Cotleigh Rd HACK/IN S12...156 A4
Cotleigh Wy HACK/IN S12...156 A4
Cotswold Av
  CHPT/GREN S35.......93 G1
Cotswold Cl DOD/DAR S75...18 D5
Cotswold Crs RHAM S60.......120 A2
Cotswold Dr
  AU/AST/KP S26.......145 G3
  BTLY DN5.......54 A4
Cotswold Gdns BTLY DN5.......39 F3
Cotswold Rd ST/HB/BR S6...113 E4
Cottage La ECC S11.......137 C5
Cottam Cl RHAM S60.......120 A3
Cottam Dr STV/CWN S43.....177 F5
Cottenham Rd
  RHAM/THRY S65.......9 J2
Cotterdale Gdns
  STV/CWN S43.......50 D2
Cotterhill La STV/CWN S43..188 C2
Cottesmore Cl
  DOD/DAR S75.......2 A1
Cottingham St
  DARN/MH S9.......127 F3
Cotton Mill Hl RCH S42.......190 D5
Cotton St BSVR S44.......196 D5
  OWL S3.......126 A2
Coultas Av STKB/PEN S36...77 F3
Countess Rd SHEF S1.......11 G7
County Wy SHEFS S8.......3 G2
Coupe Rd OWL S3.......126 B1
Coupland Cl CHNE S41.......180 A2
Coupland Rd
  RHAM/THRY S65.......107 E1
Court Cl BTLY DN5.......38 D4
Court Pl STV/CWN S43.......189 C1
Court Vw STV/CWN S43.......185 E3
The Courtyard CONI DN12...67 C5
Coventry Gv WHHL DN2.......41 F5
Coventry Rd
  DARN/MH S9.......128 A2
Cover Cl RAW S62.......81 H2
Coverdale Rd ABRD S7.......139 C5
Cover Dr WMB/DAR S73.......35 F4
Coverleigh Rd DEARNE S63...65 F4
Cow House La ARMTH DN3...43 E4
Cow La ECC S11.......151 G2
  STV/CWN S43.......180 C5
Cowley Bottom DRON S18...170 B4
Cowley Cl CHNE S41.......5 H5
Cowley Dr CHPT/GREN S35...94 A2
Cowley Gdns MOS S20.......157 E5
Cowley Hl CHPT/GREN S35...94 A2
Cowley La CHPT/GREN S35...94 B1
  DRON S18.......170 B4
Cowley Pl ARMTH DN3.......29 F3

Cowley View Cl
  CHPT/GREN S35.......94 A3
Cowley View Rd
  CHPT/GREN S35.......94 B3
Cowlishaw Rd ECC S11.......139 E2
Cowood St
  MEX/SWTN S64 *.......66 D3
Cowper Av ST/HB/BR S6.......101 F3
Cowper Crs ST/HB/BR S6...101 F3
Cowper Dr
  RHAM/THRY S65.......106 D5
  ST/HB/BR S6.......101 F3
Cowper Rd MEX/SWTN S64...67 G3
Cowpingle La
  STV/CWN S43.......180 C5
Cowrakes Cl RHAM S60.......120 A3
Cow Rakes La RHAM S60.......120 A3
Coxley Ct NROS/TKH DN11...91 H3
Cox Pl ST/HB/BR S6.......113 F4
Cox Rd ST/HB/BR S6.......113 F4
Crabtree Cl SHEFN S5.......115 G3
Crabtree Crs SHEFN S5.......115 F3
Crabtree Dr CUD/GR S72.......23 H4
  SHEFN S5.......115 G3
Crabtree La SHEFN S5.......115 F3
Crabtree Pl SHEFN S5.......115 F3
Crabtree Rd SHEFN S5.......115 F3
Cradley Dr AU/AST/KP S26...145 G3
Cradock Ms
  SHEFP/MNR S2.......141 E3
Cradock Rd
  SHEFP/MNR S2.......141 E3
Cragdale Gv MOS S20.......166 D1
Craggon Dr STV/CWN S43...180 B2
Craggs Dr STV/CWN S43.....185 E3
Craggs Rd BSVR S44.......196 D1
Craglands Gv CHSW S40.....186 A5
Cragside Cl CHNE S41.......5 J4
Crags Rd CONI DN12.......68 C3
Craigholme Crs WHHL DN2...41 F3
Craithie Rd WHHL DN2.......7 J1
Crakehall Rd
  CHPT/GREN S35.......94 A3
Cramfit Cl DIN S25.......148 B2
Cramfit Crs DIN S25.......134 B5
Cramfit Rd DIN S25.......148 A1
Cramlands DOD/DAR S75.......30 C3
Cranborne Rd CHNE S41.....187 E2
Cranbrook St ATT S4.......40 C5
Cranbrook St BSLY S70.......2 C7
Crane Dr KIMB S61.......104 C2
Crane Rd KIMB S61.......96 C4
Crane Well La DEARNE S63...53 C3
Cranfield Cl ARMTH DN3.......42 D5
Cranford Ct MOS S20.......156 A3
Cranford Dr MOS S20.......156 A2
Cranford Gdns
  BSLYN/ROY S71.......12 B5
Cranleigh Gdns
  AWLS/ASK DN6.......25 E2
Cranleigh Rd
  STV/CWN S43.......182 D4
Cranston Cl BSLYN/ROY S71...20 D3
Cranwell Ct DEARNE S63.......53 E1
Cranwell Rd
  DONS/BSCR DN4.......74 D2
Cranworth Cl
  RHAM/THRY S65.......9 K2
  RHAM/THRY S65.......106 C2
Cranworth Pl OWL S3.......126 B1
Cranworth Rd OWL S3.......126 B1
Craven Cl BSLYN/ROY S71...12 B5
  DARN/MH S9 *.......128 A2
  DONS/BSCR DN4.......58 A5
Craven Rd CHNE S41.......187 E3
Craven St OWL S3.......10 D1
  RAW S62.......98 B3
Craven Wood Cl
  DOD/DAR S75.......18 C4
Crawford Rd SHEFS S8.......152 B1
Crawshaw Av SHEFS S8.......152 B5
Crawshaw Gv SHEFS S8.......152 B5
Crawshaw Rd
  DONS/BSCR DN4.......55 G3
Cream St DARN/MH S2 *...140 B1
Crecy Av WHHL DN2.......57 G1
Creighton Av RAW S62.......98 D1
The Crescent East
  MALT S66.......108 C2
The Crescent East MALT S66..133 F1
Crescent Rd ABRD S7.......139 C3
  RCH S42.......190 D5
The Crescent ARMTH DN3...29 F5
  AWLS/ASK DN6.......70 B5
  CONI DN12.......70 B5
  CONI DN12 *.......16 D5
  CUD/GR S72 *.......16 D5
  DEARNE S63.......53 E2
  DIN S25.......135 E4
  MALT S66.......133 C1
  MEX/SWTN S64.......85 H1
  RCH S42.......190 B5
The Crescent West
  MALT S66.......108 B2
Cresswell Rd DARN/MH S9...128 A3
  MEX/SWTN S64.......66 B4

Cresswell St DOD/DAR S75....2 A3
MEX/SWTN S64......66 D4
Crest Rd SHEFN S5......102 B5
Crestwood Cl SHEFS S5....102 C5
Crestwood Gdns SHEFN S5..102 C5
Creswell Rd STV/CWN S43...185 E2
Creswick Av SHEFN S5......101 H2
Creswick Cl RCH S42......191 F1
RHAM/THRY S65......107 F1
Creswick Greave
CHPT/GREN S35......101 G2
Creswick Greave Cl
SHEFN S5......101 H1
Creswick La
CHPT/GREN S35......101 G1
Creswick Rd
RHAM/THRY S65......107 F1
Creswick St ST/HB/BR S6...125 F1
Creswick Wy STV/CWN S43..125 F1
Crich Av BSLYN/ROY S71...15 E5
Crich Cl STV/CWN S43......189 G2
Crich Vw BSVR S44......197 G3
Cricket Inn Crs
SHEFP/MNR S2......127 E3
Cricket Inn Rd
DARN/MH S9......127 E3
SHEFP/MNR S2......127 E3
Cricket Vw STV/CWN S43...185 E4
Cricket View Rd RAW S62...81 H2
Crimicar Av FUL S10......137 F2
Crimicar Cl FUL S10......137 F2
Crimicar Dr FUL S10......137 F2
Crimicar La FUL S10......137 F1
Crimpsall Rd
DONS/BSCR DN4......6 A5
Cripps Av NROS/TKH DN11..91 G2
Cripps Cl MALT S66......111 F4
Crispin Cl HACK/IN S12....154 C1
Crispin Gdns HACK/IN S12.154 C1
Crispin Rd HACK/IN S12...154 C1
Crochley Cl
DONS/BSCR DN4......58 B4
Croft Av BSLYN/ROY S71...15 F1
Croft Cl ECC S11 *......151 F2
WMB/DAR S73......50 D4
Croft Ct ARMTH DN3......29 F4
Crofters Cl ECK/KIL S21...168 D1
Crofters Ct DONS/BSCR DN4..72 A3
Croft La ECC S11......151 F2
Croft Lea DRON S18......170 A1
Crofton Av ST/HB/BR S6...113 H2
Crofton Cl DRON S18......170 D2
Crofton Dr DEARNE S63....53 E2
Crofton Ri CHPT/GREN S35..80 B5
DRON S18......170 D2
Croft Rd BSLY S70......32 C3
DONS/BSCR DN4......71 E5
HACK/IN S12......141 H5
HOY S74......61 H1
RHAM S60......118 B3
Crofts Dr RHAM/THRY S65..99 C4
The Crofts MALT S66......121 F1
RHAM......9 F5
Croft St BSLY S70......32 A5
KIMB S61......97 F3
The Croft BTLY DN5......27 F5
CONI DN12......89 E2
DOD/DAR S75......18 A2
HOY S74......62 C2
MEX/SWTN S64......85 H1
RAW S62......81 H2
Croft Vw STV/CWN S43....185 E3
STV/CWN S43......189 G4
Cromarty Ri DRON S18....170 B1
Cromdale Av STV/CWN S43..180 B2
Cromer Cl RAW S62 *......85 F5
Cromer Rd WHHL DN2......57 G1
Cromford Dr
BSLYN/ROY S71......20 B1
Cromford Cl
DONS/BSCR DN4......74 C2
Cromford Dr STV/CWN S43..189 F1
Cromford St
SHEFP/MNR S2......140 B1
Crompton Av BSLY S70....2 C7
BTLY DN5......55 F1
Crompton Rd
STV/CWN S43......182 B4
WHHL DN2......41 F2
Cromwell Dr BTLY DN5....55 E3
Cromwell Mt STV/CWN S43..31 G4
Cromwell Rd BSVR S44....197 E4
BTLY DN5......39 H5
CHSW S40......4 D1
MEX/SWTN S64......66 B3
Cromwell St DEARNE S63...37 G1
ST/HB/BR S6......125 E2
Cromwell Vls
MEX/SWTN S64 *......67 E4
Crookhill La BSLYN/ROY S71..15 H3
Crooked La
RHAM/THRY S65......87 H3
Crooke House La
BSLYN/ROY S71......34 D1
Crookes FUL S10......124 D3
Crookes La BSLYN/ROY S71..15 G3
Crookes Rd
DONS/BSCR DN4......71 H2
FUL S10......125 E4

Crookes St BSLY S70......2 D4
Crookes Valley Rd FUL S10..10 A2
Crookhill Rd CONI DN12...89 F1
Cropston Cl CHNE S41....193 E5
Cropton Rd BSLYN/ROY S71..15 F1
Crosby Av MALT S66......109 E4
Crosby Ct BSLYN/ROY S71..20 D2
Crosby Rd SHEFS S8......152 C3
Crosby St CUD/GR S72....16 D4
Cross Allen Rd MOS S20...157 F1
Cross Bank DONS/BSCR DN4..55 H5
Cross Bedford St
ST/HB/BR S6......125 G1
Cross Burgess St SHEF S1..11 F4
Cross Butcher St
DEARNE S63......37 E2
Cross Chantrey Rd
SHEFS S8......153 E2
Crosscourt Vw
DONS/BSCR DN4......57 G5
Cross Dr HAN/WDH S13 *..143 F4
Crossfield Dr DEARNE S63..65 E3
Cross Ga BTLY DN5......39 G4
Crossgate DEARNE S63....37 F3
Cross Ga MEX/SWTN S64...67 G4
Cross Hi CHPT/GREN S35...102 C2
CUD/GR S72......17 H1
Cross Hill Cl
CHPT/GREN S35......102 C2
Cross House Cl
CHPT/GREN S35......100 D1
Cross House Rd
CHPT/GREN S35......101 E1
Cross Keys La HOY S74....61 G2
Crossland Dr HACK/IN S12.154 C2
Crossland Pl HACK/IN S12.154 C2
Crossland St MEX/SWTN S64..86 B1
Cross La BSLYN/ROY S71...16 A1
CHPT/GREN S35......79 H1
DRON S18......171 E2
FUL S10......124 D4
STKB/PEN S36......44 A4
STKB/PEN S36......76 A1
TOT/DORE S17......150 C5
Crossley Cl MALT S66.....110 C2
Cross London St
STV/CWN S43......180 B3
Cross Myrtle Rd
SHEFP/MNR S2......140 B3
Cross Park Rd SHEFS S8...140 A5
Cross Riding WHHL DN2...58 A1
Cross Smithfield OWL S3...10 E1
Cross South St KIMB S61...97 E3
Cross St BSLY S70......32 B5
BSLYN/ROY S71......20 C3
BSVR S44......197 E4
BTLY DN5......39 H1
CHSW S40......4 D2
CUD/GR S72......36 A1
DEARNE S63......37 E3
DEARNE S63......65 E2
DOD/DAR S75......19 F4
DONS/BSCR DN4......71 C1
ECK/KIL S21......168 D1
HAN/WDH S13......143 F4
HOY S74......61 F3
KIMB S61 *......97 G3
MALT S66......108 D4
MALT S66......111 E5
NROS/TKH DN11......91 F3
RAW S62......98 B3
RHAM/THRY S65......99 G4
STV/CWN S43......188 C1
Cross Turner St
SHEFP/MNR S2......11 J5
Crossway MEX/SWTN S64...85 H1
Crossways DEARNE S63....52 D2
WHHL DN2......41 F3
Crossways North
WHHL DN2......41 F3
Crossways South
WHHL DN2......41 F4
The Crossways
SHEFP/MNR S2......141 G1
Cross Wellington St
STV/CWN S43 *......180 B3
Crowden Wk DOD/DAR S75..30 C1
Crowder Av SHEFN S5.....102 A5
Crowder Cl SHEFN S5.....115 E1
Crowder Crs SHEFN S5....115 E1
Crowder Rd SHEFN S5....102 A5
Crowgate DIN S25......148 A5
Crowland Rd SHEFN S5....102 B5
Crow La CHNE S41......5 J3
DRON S18......172 A4
Crowley Dr DEARNE S63...65 E4
Crown Av BSLY S70......32 A3
CUD/GR S72......22 A3
Crown Cl BSLY S70......31 H5
KIMB S61......104 C1
STV/CWN S43......189 G1
Crown Hill Rd BSLY S70...50 D5
Cronhill Rd RHAM S60....118 A3
Crown Pl SHEFP/MNR S2...11 K3
Crown Rd CHNE S41......187 G4
Crown St BSLY S70......32 A3
HOY S74......61 G2
MEX/SWTN S64......66 B5
Crown Well Hl
BSLYN/ROY S71......33 F2
Crowther Pl ABRD S7....139 H4

Crow Tree La
MEX/SWTN S64......66 D1
Croydon St ECC S11......139 H2
Cruck Cl DRON S18......170 C1
Cruise Rd ECC S11......138 B2
Crummock Rd ABRD S7 *..139 G5
Crummock Wy
BSLYN/ROY S71......33 H2
Crumpsall Dr SHEFN S5...114 D3
Crumpsall Rd SHEFN S5...114 D3
Crumwell Rd KIMB S61....96 B4
Crusader Dr BTLY DN5....55 E2
Cubley Rise Rd
STKB/PEN S36......44 C5
Cuckoo Wy AU/AST/KP S26..159 F4
CHNE S41......175 H1
ECK/KIL S21......175 H2
STV/CWN S43......180 B4
STV/CWN S43......182 B3
STV/CWN S43......188 A1
Cudworth Vw CUD/GR S72..23 E1
Cullabine Rd
SHEFP/MNR S2......141 G3
Cumberland Av WHHL DN2..57 F1
Cumberland Cl BSLY S70...31 H5
HOY S74......62 A1
Cumberland Crs
CHPT/GREN S35......94 B2
Cumberland Dr
BSLYN/ROY S71......33 F2
Cumberland Rd HOY S74...62 A1
Cumberland Wy
DEARNE S63......53 E4
Cundy Rd BSVR S44......196 D1
Cundy St ST/HB/BR S6....125 E2
Cunliffe St DRON S18....163 G4
Cunningham Rd DON DN1...6 E6
Cupola OWL S3......11 F5
Cupola La CHPT/GREN S35..93 E5
Cupola Yd RHAM S60....117 H3
Curbar Curve STV/CWN S43..189 F3
Curlew Av ECK/KIL S21...166 B5
Curlew Cl NROS/TKH DN11..91 G2
Curlew Rdg
SHEFP/MNR S2......126 D5
Curlew Ri KIMB S61......82 C5
Curzen Crs ARMTH DN3....29 G3
Curzon Av DRON S18.....170 D3
Curzon Cl ECK/KIL S21...168 B2
Cusworth Gv
NROS/TKH DN11......91 H3
Cusworth La BTLY DN5....39 E5
Cuthbert Bank Rd
ST/HB/BR S6......114 B5
Cuthbert Rd ST/HB/BR S6..114 B5
Cutler Cl ECK/KIL S21...167 H1
Cutlers Av BSLY S70......2 C7
Cutlers Ga ATT S4......11 L1
OWL S3......11 L1
Cutlers Gate Jct ATT S4...126 C3
Cuttholme Rd CHSW S40..186 B5
Cuttholme Wy CHSW S40..186 C5
Cutthorpe Gra CHNE S41..186 A2
Cutts Av DEARNE S63....64 D3
Cutts Field Vw
BSLYN/ROY S71 *......12 B4
Cutts Ter SHEFS S8......139 H3
Cutty La DOD/DAR S75....2 C1
Cyclops St ATT S4......116 A4
Cygnet Cl DEARNE S63....63 H1
Cypress Av EPW DN9.....75 H4
SHEFS S8......153 C4
Cypress Cl ECK/KIL S21...168 A3
Cypress Ga CHPT/GREN S35..93 E2
Cypress Gv CONI DN12....88 B3
Cypress Rd BSLY S70......32 B3
Cyprus Rd SHEFS S8......140 A5

D

Dade Av STV/CWN S43....189 F3
Daffodil Rd SHEFN S5....116 B3
Dagnam Cl SHEFP/MNR S2.141 F4
Dagnam Crs
SHEFP/MNR S2......141 F3
Dagnam Dr SHEFP/MNR S2.141 F3
Dagnam Pl SHEFP/MNR S2.141 F4
Dagnam Rd
SHEFP/MNR S2......141 F3
Daisy Bank OWL S3......10 C1
Daisy Wk MOS S20......157 E2
OWL S3......10 D2
Dalby Cft STKB/PEN S36...45 E3
Dalby Gdns MOS S20.....157 G4
Dalby Gv MOS S20......157 G3
Dale Av RHAM/THRY S65..107 E4
Dale Bank Crs
STV/CWN S43......180 B3
Dale Cl BSLYN/ROY S71...15 E5
Dale Ct RAW S62......98 B1
Dale Green Rd BSLY S70...15 H1
Dale Gv DEARNE S63.....52 D4
Dale Hill Cl MALT S66....110 D2
Dale Hill Rd MALT S66....110 C1
Dale Rd CONI DN12......89 E1
DRON S18......171 F3
ECK/KIL S21......168 C2
MALT S66......108 A5
RAW S62......85 F5
RHAM/THRY S65......107 E4

Dale Rd RAW S62......85 F5
Dalestorth Av BSLY S70...3 K7
Daleswood Av BSLY S70...2 A7
Daleswood Dr BSLY S70...32 D5
The Dale SHEFS S8......152 D2
Daleview Av SHEFS S8....152 B3
Dalewood Av SHEFS S8...151 H4
Dalewood Cl CHNE S41...193 G3
Dalewood Dr SHEFS S8...152 A4
Dalewood Rd SHEFS S8...152 A4
Dalmore Rd ABRD S7....139 E5
Dalton Ct SHEFS S8......139 H3
Dalton La RHAM/THRY S65.107 F1
Dalton Ter BSLY S70......3 K7
Dalvey Wy STV/CWN S43..180 B2
Damer St FUL S10......10 A4
Damon Dr STV/CWN S43...188 D1
Damsbrook Dr
STV/CWN S43......185 E3
Damson Cft STV/CWN S43..181 E5
Damsteads DOD/DAR S75...30 C3
Danby Av CHNE S41......179 H4
Danebrook Cl
SHEFP/MNR S2......142 A1
Danebrook Ct
SHEFP/MNR S2......142 A1
Danebrook Dr
SHEFP/MNR S2......142 A1
Danesthorpe Cl WHHL DN2..41 G4
Dane St DEARNE S63.....37 G2
Dane St North DEARNE S63.37 G2
Dane St South DEARNE S63.37 G2
Danesway BTLY DN5......39 F1
Danethorpe Wy CONI DN12..88 C3
Danewood Av
SHEFP/MNR S2......142 A2
Danewood Cft
SHEFP/MNR S2......142 A1
Danewood Gdns
SHEFP/MNR S2......142 A1
Daniel Hill ST/HB/BR S6...125 G2
Daniel Hill Ct
ST/HB/BR S6 *......125 F2
Daniel Hill Ms ST/HB/BR S6.125 F2
Daniel Hill St ST/HB/BR S6.125 F2
Daniel Hill Ter
ST/HB/BR S6......125 G2
Daniel La RAW S62......84 B5
Daniels Dr AU/AST/KP S26.145 E1
Dannemora Dr
DARN/MH S9......117 E5
Danum Dr RHAM/THRY S65..9 K3
Danum Rd DONS/BSCR DN4..7 H6
Dara St DARN/MH S9.....103 H4
Darcy Cl AU/AST/KP S26..145 F1
Darcy Rd ECK/KIL S21....166 C5
Daresbury Dr
SHEFP/MNR S2......140 D4
Daresbury Pl
SHEFP/MNR S2......140 D4
Daresbury Rd
SHEFP/MNR S2......140 D4
Daresbury Vw
SHEFP/MNR S2......140 D4
Darfield Av MOS S20.....155 H3
NROS/TKH DN11......91 H2
Darfield Cl CUD/GR S72...22 A2
Dargle Av WHHL DN2.....57 E1
Dark La BSLY S70......30 D3
BSLY S70......48 B2
BSVR S44......195 H2
STV/CWN S43......188 C5
Darley BSLY S70......32 C5
Darley Av BSLY S70.....31 G4
BSLYN/ROY S71......20 A1
Darley Cl BSLYN/ROY S71..20 A1
STV/CWN S43......182 A4
Darley Gv ST/HB/BR S6...112 D5
Darley Ter DOD/DAR S75...2 E3
Darley Yd BSLY S70......48 B1
Darnall Dr DARN/MH S9...127 H2
Darnall Rd DARN/MH S9...127 H2
Darnley Dr SHEFP/MNR S2.141 G2
Darrington Dr
DONS/BSCR DN4......70 D3
Darrington Pl
BSLYN/ROY S71......21 E4
Dartmouth Rd
DONS/BSCR DN4......74 D2
Darton St BSLY S70......32 D2
Dartree Cl WMB/DAR S73..34 D4
Dartree Wk WMB/DAR S73..34 D4
Dart Sq OWL S3......10 D2
Darwall Cl CHPT/GREN S35..82 A5
Darwent Rd CHNE S41....188 A3
Darwin Av CHNE S41.....187 E4
Darwin Cl FUL S10......124 B5
Darwin La FUL S10......137 E3
Darwin Rd CHSW S40.....4 D1
ST/HB/BR S6......124 B5
Darwood La BSVR S44....196 D4
Darwynn Av
MEX/SWTN S64......65 G5
Davey Ct BSVR S44......196 C1
Davey Rd DEARNE S63....37 F4
Davian Wy CHSW S40....192 A4
David Cl HAN/WDH S13...143 H1
David La FUL S10......137 E3
Davids Dr RCH S42......106 C2
Davies Dr MEX/SWTN S64..86 B2
Davis St RHAM/THRY S65.106 C2
Davy Dr MALT S66......108 A2
MALT S66......110 D2

Davy Rd CONI DN12......68 A5
Dawber La ECK/KIL S21...168 D1
Daw Croft Av BSLY S70...32 A5
Dawlands Cl
SHEFP/MNR S2......127 H5
Dawlands Dr
SHEFP/MNR S2......141 H1
Daw La BTLY DN5......26 D5
Dawson Av RAW S62.....84 C3
Dawson Cft RHAM S61 *...97 F2
Dawson La DEARNE S63...65 E4
Daw Wd BTLY DN5......26 D4
Dayhouse Ct DOD/DAR S75..18 D3
Dayhouse Wy DOD/DAR S75.18 D3
Daylands Av CONI DN12...88 C2
Day St BSLY S70......3 F7
Deacon Cl NROS/TKH DN11..91 H2
Deacon Crs MALT S66....111 E4
NROS/TKH DN11......91 E2
Deacons Wy
BSLYN/ROY S71......20 C4
Deadman's Hole La
DARN/MH S9......104 C5
Deakins Wk FUL S10.....138 D1
Dean Cl BTLY DN5......54 D3
NROS/TKH DN11......91 H2
Deane Field Vw MOS S20..156 D5
Deanhead Dr MOS S20....155 H3
Deanhead Dr MOS S20....155 H3
Dean Rd RHAM/THRY S65.107 G3
Deansfield Cl ARMTH DN3..42 D5
Dean St BSLY S70......2 C4
Deans Wy BSLYN/ROY S71.20 C3
Dearden Ct
CHPT/GREN S35......102 B3
Dearne Bc BTLY DN5.....68 B1
Dearne Cl WMB/DAR S73..50 D4
Dearne Hall Fold
DOD/DAR S75......18 B1
Dearne Hall Rd
DOD/DAR S75......18 B1
DEARNE S63......53 D5
WMB/DAR S73......51 E5
Dearne St CONI DN12....69 F5
CUD/GR S72......36 A1
DARN/MH S9......116 C2
Dearne Valley Pkwy
HOY S74......61 E2
WMB/DAR S73......50 A5
Dearne Vw DEARNE S63...37 F5
Dearneway DEARNE S63...36 C4
Dearne Wy BSLYN/ROY S71..19 F1
BTLY DN5......68 A1
CUD/GR S72......22 B4
WMB/DAR S73......52 A3
Dearnley Vw DOD/DAR S75.19 F1
Deben Cl STV/CWN S43...191 G4
Decoy Bank North
DONS/BSCR DN4......56 B4
Decoy Bank South
DONS/BSCR DN4......56 C5
Deepcar La CUD/GR S72...22 A3
Deepdale Cl STV/CWN S43.182 A3
Deepdale Cft DOD/DAR S75.18 B2
Deepdale Rd BSVR S44....196 C1
KIMB S61......104 C3
Deep La SHEFN S5......103 F1
Deepwell Av MOS S20....167 F2
Deepwell Bank MOS S20..167 F2
Deepwell Ct MOS S20....167 F2
Deepwell Vw MOS S20....167 F2
Deerlands Av SHEFN S5...101 F3
Deerlands Cl SHEFN S5...101 G3
Deerlands Mt SHEFN S5...101 G3
Deerlands Rd CHSW S40..101 G3
RCH S42......195 F4
Deer Park Cl ST/HB/BR S6.124 B1
Deerpark Crs RCH S42....195 F4
Deer Park Pl ST/HB/BR S6.124 B1
Deer Park Rd ST/HB/BR S6.124 B1
Deer Park Vw
ST/HB/BR S6......124 B1
Deer Park Wy
ST/HB/BR S6......124 B1
De Houton Cl
AU/AST/KP S26 *......147 E5
Deightonby St DEARNE S63.37 G2
De Lacy Dr BSLY S70.....32 A5
Delamere Cl MOS S20....157 G3
De La Salle Dr ATT S4....115 G5
Delf Cottages BSLY S70 *..31 F5
Delf St SHEFP/MNR S2....140 B3
Della Av BSLY S70......32 C5
Dell Crs DONS/BSCR DN4..55 F4
The Dell CHSW S40......191 H1
MALT S66......108 C1
Delmar Wy MALT S66....108 A3
Delph Bank CHSW S40...192 A4
Delph House Rd FUL S10..124 B4
Delta Pl RHAM/THRY S65..106 D2
Delta Wy MALT S66......111 F2
Delves Av HACK/IN S12...156 C2
Delves Cl CHSW S40......191 H5
HACK/IN S12......156 C2
Delves Dr HACK/IN S12...156 C2
Delves La AU/AST/KP S26.158 B2
Delves Pl HACK/IN S12....156 C2
Delves Rd ECK/KIL S21...168 A2
HACK/IN S12......156 C2
Delves Ter HACK/IN S12...156 C2
Denaby Av CONI DN12....88 C1
Denaby La CONI DN12....87 F2
Den Bank Av FUL S10....124 A4

Den Bank Cl FUL S10 ....124 B4
Den Bank Crs FUL S10 ....124 A4
Den Bank Dr FUL S10 ....124 A4
Denby Rd BSLYN/ROY S71 ...14 D5
  STV/CWN S43 ....189 G3
Denby St BTLY DN5 ....26 C5
Denby Rd CHSW DN5 ....139 H1
Denby Wy MALT S66 ....109 G3
Dene Cl MALT S66 ....108 C5
Dene Crs RHAM/THRY S65 ...106 D1
Denehall Rd ARMTH DN3 ....29 G4
Dene La OWL S5 ....10 D6
Dene Rd RHAM/THRY S65 ....106 D1
Denham Rd ECC S11 ....139 C1
Denholme Cl OWL S5 ....126 B2
Denison Cl BSLY S70 ....3 H7
Denison Rd
  SHEFP/MNR S2 ....140 B4
Denman La DEARNE S63 ....64 D2
Denman St RHAM/THRY S65 ....9 H1
Denmark Rd
  SHEFP/MNR S2 ....140 B4
Dent La HACK/IN S12 ....155 H3
Denton Rd SHEFS S8 * 152 D2
Dentons Green La
  ARMTH DN3 ....29 F3
Denton St BSLYN/ROY S71 ....3 H2
Derby Rd SHEFP/MNR S2 ....140 C4
Derby Rd CHSW S40 ....195 C1
  WHHL DN2 ....40 A1
Derbyshire Ct ARMTH DN3 ....43 F3
Derbyshire La SHEFS S8 ....153 E2
Derby St BSLY S70 ....2 C5
  SHEFP/MNR S2 ....140 B4
Derby Ter SHEFP/MNR S2 ...140 C4
Derriman Av ECC S11 ....151 H1
Derriman Cl ECC S11 ....151 H1
Derriman Dr ECC S11 ....151 H1
Derriman Gln ECC S11 ....151 H1
Derriman Gv ECC S11 ....151 H1
Derry Gv DEARNE S63 ....37 G3
Derwent Cl BSLYN/ROY S71 ...15 F5
  DIN S25 ....148 D1
  DRON S18 ....163 F5
Derwent Crs
  BSLYN/ROY S71 ....15 F5
  CHNE S41 ....186 D2
  RHAM S60 ....118 B5
Derwent Dr ARMTH DN3 ....29 F4
  CHPT/GREN S35 ....93 G1
  MEX/SWTN S64 ....67 G2
  RAW S62 ....98 B2
Derwent Pl BTLY DN5 * 54 B4
  WMB/DAR S73 ....50 D4
Derwent Rd BSLYN/ROY S71 ..15 F5
  DRON S18 ....163 F5
  KIMB S61 ....97 E3
  MEX/SWTN S64 ....67 G2
Derwent St SHEFP/MNR S2 ..126 C3
Derwent Ter
  MEX/SWTN S64 ....67 E2
Derwent Vw
  STV/CWN S43 ....183 G3
Derwent Wy WMB/DAR S73 ...51 F5
Deveron Rd MOS S20 ....167 F1
Devizes Cl CHSW S40 ....192 B1
Devon Dr STV/CWN S43 .....188 D1
Devon Park Vw
  STV/CWN S43 ....188 D1
Devonshire Av East
  CHNE S41 ....193 E4
Devonshire Av North
  STV/CWN S43 ....180 B3
Devonshire Cl CHNE S41 ....187 F1
  DRON S18 ....170 D3
  STV/CWN S43 ....182 A4
  TOT/DORE S17 ....161 F2
Devonshire Ct
  STV/CWN S43 ....188 B2
Devonshire Dr DIN S25 .....134 C5
  DOD/DAR S75 ....19 F3
  TOT/DORE S17 ....161 E1
Devonshire Gln
  TOT/DORE S17 ....161 F2
Devonshire Gv
  TOT/DORE S17 * 161 E2
Devonshire La SHEF S1 ....10 E4
Devonshire Rd MALT S66 ....111 E2
  TOT/DORE S17 ....161 E1
  WHHL DN2 ....41 F5
Devonshire Rd East
  CHNE S41 ....193 E4
Devonshire Rd North
  STV/CWN S43 ....180 B3
Devonshire St KIMB S61 ....8 A4
  OWL S3 ....10 D4
  STV/CWN S43 ....182 A4
  STV/CWN S45 ....188 C1
Devonshire Vis CHNE S41 * ..187 F1
Dewar Dr ABRD S7 ....152 A1
Dewhill Av RHAM S60 ....119 H3
Dial Cl CHSW S40 ....102 C5
Dial House Rd
  ST/HB/BR S6 ....113 G4
Dial Wy SHEFS S8 ....102 C5
Diamond St WMB/DAR S73 ....50 B2
Dickan Gdns ARMTH DN3 ......43 F5
Dickens Cl RHAM S60 ....129 F1
Dickenson Ct
  CHPT/GREN S35 ....93 H1
Dickenson Rd CHNE S41 ....5 J7
Dickens Rd RAW S62 ....85 H4

Dickinson Pl BSLY S70 ....31 H3
Dickinson Rd BSLY S70 ......31 H3
  SHEFN S5 ....102 D2
Didcot La CHSW S40 ....192 B4
Dike Hl RAW S62 ....82 A1
Dikelands Mt
  CHPT/GREN S35 ....80 B5
Dillington Rd BSLY S70 ......31 H3
Dillington Sq BSLY S70 ......31 H3
Dillington Ter BSLY S70 * 31 H3
Dingle La CHNE S41 ....103 C3
Dinmore Cl
  DONS/BSCR DN4 ....71 G4
Dinnington Rd SHEFS S8 ....152 C1
  WRKN S81 ....149 H4
Dirleton Dr
  DONS/BSCR DN4 ....70 D2
Discovery Wy CHNE S41 ....179 G5
  MALT S66 ....110 B3
Disraeli Gv MALT S66 ......110 C2
Ditchingham St ATT S4 .....126 C1
Division La SHEF S1 ....11 F4
Division St SHEF S1 ....10 E4
  STV/CWN S45 ....189 G1
Dixon Crs DONS/BSCR DN4 ...71 F1
Dixon Cft STV/CWN S43 ....180 B2
Dixon La SHEF S1 ....11 J2
Dixon Rd ST/HB/BR S6 ......113 H3
Dixon St RHAM/THRY S65 .....9 G3
  ST/HB/BR S6 ....125 H2
Dixon's Rd CHNE S41 ....5 H4
Dobbin Hl ECC S11 ....138 C4
Dobbin La DRON S18 ....170 A5
Dobb La ST/HB/BR S6 ....122 C3
Dobcroft Av ABRD S7 ....151 H5
Dobcroft Cl ECC S11 ....151 G1
Dobcroft Rd ECC S11 ....151 G1
Dobie St BSLY S70 ....3 H7
Dobson Hl STV/CWN S43 ....189 H5
Dobsyke Cl BSLY S70 ....32 D5
Dockin Hill Rd DON DN1 ......4 C5
Dock Wk CHSW S40 ....4 C5
Doctor La DARN/MH S9 .....127 C1
Dodds Cl RHAM S60 ....105 C5
Dodd St ST/HB/BR S6 ....114 A5
Dodson Dr HAN/WDH S13 ...142 D1
Dodsworth St
  MEX/SWTN S64 ....66 D4
Dodworth Rd BSLY S70 ....2 B4
Doe La BSLY S70 ....47 G2
  ECK/KIL S21 ....164 D4
  HACK/IN S12 ....165 E3
Doe Lea Br BSVR S44 ....196 B5
Doe Quarry La DIN S25 .....134 D3
Doe Quarry Pl DIN S25 .....135 E4
Doe Royd Crs SHEFN S5 ....101 F4
Doe Royd Dr SHEFN S5 .....101 G4
Doe Royd La SHEFN S5 .....101 F5
Dog Hl CUD/GR S72 ....16 D1
Dog Hill Dr CUD/GR S72 .....17 E1
Dolcliffe Rd MEX/SWTN S64 ..67 E4
Doles Av BSLYN/ROY S71 .....15 F1
Doles Crs BSLYN/ROY S71 ....15 F1
Doles La BSLYN/ROY S71 .....15 F1
  RHAM S60 ....120 C5
Doleswood Dr DIN S25 .....134 C1
Domine La RHAM S60 ....130 A1
Dominoe Gv HACK/IN S12 ...142 B5
Don Av ST/HB/BR S6 ....113 C1
Doncaster Ga
  RHAM/THRY S65 ....9 F4
Doncaster La
  AWLS/ASK DN6 ....25 G4
Doncaster Pl
  RHAM/THRY S65 ....106 C2
Doncaster Rd ARMTH DN3 ....42 A4
  BSLY S70 ....3 H5
  BSLYN/ROY S71 ....33 F2
  BTLY DN5 ....24 B3
  BTLY DN5 ....26 B1
  CONI DN12 ....68 B4
  CONI DN12 ....89 E1
  DEARNE S63 ....37 H4
  DEARNE S63 ....65 G2
  MEX/SWTN S64 ....67 F4
  RHAM/THRY S65 ....106 C5
  WMB/DAR S73 ....35 F4
Doncaster St OWL S3 ....125 H2
Don Dr BSLY S70 ....32 D3
Donetsk Wy HACK/IN S12 ...156 B3
  MOS S20 ....156 A2
Donnington Rd
  MEX/SWTN S64 ....67 H2
  SHEFP/MNR S2 ....140 D1
Donovan Cl SHEFN S5 ......114 C1
Donovan Rd SHEFN S5 ......114 C1
Don Pottery Yd
  MEX/SWTN S64 ....66 D5
Don Rd DARN/MH S9 ....116 B5
Donstone Vw DIN S25 ......134 D5
Don St CONI DN12 ....69 F5
  DON DN1 ....40 B5
  RHAM S60 ....8 E6
  STKB/PEN S36 ....45 F4
Dorchester Pl BSLY S70 .....31 H5
Dore Cl TOT/DORE S17 .....161 G1
Dore Hall Cft
  TOT/DORE S17 ....160 D1
Dore Rd TOT/DORE S17 .....151 E5
Dorking St ATT S4 ....126 C2
Dorothy Rd ST/HB/BR S6 ...113 H3
Dorothy V CHSW S40 ....186 C5

Dorset Av STV/CWN S43 ....188 D1
Dorset Crs WHHL DN2 ....41 G5
Dorset Dr STV/CWN S43 ....188 D1
Dorset St FUL S10 ....10 A5
Douglas Rd CHNE S41 ......187 H3
  DONS/BSCR DN4 ....71 E1
  OWL S3 ....125 H1
Douglas St RHAM S60 ....9 F5
Douse Croft La FUL S10 ....136 D2
Dovebush Wy DOD/DAR S75 ..18 A2
Dovecliffe Rd BSLY S70 .....49 E2
  WMB/DAR S73 ....49 G4
Dove Cl DEARNE S63 ....53 F4
  WMB/DAR S73 ....50 D4
Dovecote Ms
  BSLYN/ROY S71 ....20 C3
Dovecott Lea MOS S20 .....157 H2
Dovedale Rd SHEFS S8 ......48 D1
Dovedale Av STV/CWN S43 ..189 F4
Dovedale Rd ABRD S7 ......139 F5
  RHAM/THRY S65 ....107 E5
Dove La AU/AST/KP S26 ....145 G5
Dovercourt Rd KIMB S61 ....105 E2
  SHEFP/MNR S2 ....141 E1
Dover Gdns OWL S3 ....10 C1
Doveridge Cl OWL S3 ......179 C4
Dove Rd WMB/DAR S73 ....50 D4
Dover Rd ECC S11 ....139 E1
Dover St OWL S3 ....10 C1
Doveside Dr WMB/DAR S73 ...35 E5
Dowcar La AU/AST/KP S26 ..169 G3
Dowdeswell St CHNE S41 ......5 F1
Dowland Av
  CHPT/GREN S35 ....80 B3
Dowgate Dr ATT S4 ....116 A4
Downham Rd SHEFN S5 .....115 H1
Downing La OWL S3 ....125 H2
Downing Rd SHEFS S8 ......152 C5
Downing Sq STKB/PEN S36 ...44 D4
Downland Cl
  DONS/BSCR DN4 ....71 F4
Downlands STV/CWN S43 ...188 B2
Down's Rw RHAM S60 ....9 F5
Drake Cl CHPT/GREN S35 ....93 C1
Drake Head La CONI DN12 ...89 C1
Drake House La MOS S20 ...157 F2
Drake House La West
  MOS S20 ....157 E2
Drake House Wy MOS S20 ..156 D2
Drake Rd WHHL DN2 ....40 C4
Drake Ter STV/CWN S43 * ..188 A1
Drake Vw DEARNE S63 ....53 F4
Dransfield Av STKB/PEN S36 ..44 D4
Dransfield Cl FUL S10 .....124 B5
Dransfield Rd FUL S10 .....124 A5
Draycott Pl DRON S18 .....170 B3
Drill Hall Sq CHSW S40 * 4 D6
Driver St HAN/WDH S13 ....143 H3
The Drive ARMTH DN5 ....29 G5
Dronfield Rd ECK/KIL S21 ..174 A1
Droppingwell Farm Cl
  KIMB S61 ....96 B5
Droppingwell Rd KIMB S61 ..104 A2
Drover Cl CHPT/GREN S35 ...80 C1
Droves Dale Rd DEARNE S63 ..37 F5
Drummer Av BTLY DN5 ....38 C3
Drummond Crs SHEFN S5 ...102 B4
Drummond St RHAM S60 ......9 F1
Drury Farm Ct
  DOD/DAR S75 ....30 C1
Drury La DRON S18 ....163 G5
  TOT/DORE S17 ....160 D1
Dryden Av CHSW S40 ......192 B4
  SHEFN S5 ....101 G5
Dryden Dr SHEFN S5 ......101 G5
Dryden Rd BSLYN/ROY S71 ...3 J1
  DEARNE S63 ....64 C1
  MEX/SWTN S64 ....72 A2
  RHAM/THRY S65 ....106 D5
  SHEFN S5 ....101 G5
Dryden Wy SHEFN S5 ......101 G5
Dublin Rd WHHL DN2 ....57 E1
Duchess Rd SHEFP/MNR S2 ..11 H7
Duckham Dr
  AU/AST/KP S26 ....145 G4
Ducksett La ECK/KIL S21 ...166 D5
Dudley Rd ST/HB/BR S6 ....113 H2
  WHHL DN2 ....40 C5
Dudley St RAW S62 * 98 B3
Duftons Cl CONI DN12 ....69 F5
Dugdale Dr SHEFN S5 .....101 H1
Dugdale Rd SHEFN S5 .....101 H2
Duke Av MALT S66 ....111 E4
Duke Crs BSLY S70 ....3 G6
  KIMB S61 ....96 C5
Duke La SHEF S1 ....11 G5
Duke of Norfolk La
  MALT S66 ....107 G5
Dukeries Ct STV/CWN S43 ..185 F5
Dukeries Dr DIN S25 ....148 C1
Dukes Dr CHNE S41 ....187 E3
Dukes Pl RHAM/THRY S65 ..106 D5
Duke St BSLY S70 ....3 G7
  CHNE S41 ....187 G1

  CUD/GR S72 ....23 E1
  DIN S25 ....134 D3
  DON DN1 ....6 C4
  HOY S74 ....62 A2
  MEX/SWTN S64 ....66 B4
  MOS S20 ....166 D2
  SHEFP/MNR S2 ....126 C4
  STV/CWN S43 ....182 A4
  STV/CWN S43 ....185 G2
Duke's Crs CONI DN12 ....70 B5
Dumbles Rd BSVR S44 ......196 C5
Dumbleton Br ECK/KIL S21 ..168 C3
Dumble Wood Gra
  CHNE S41 ....186 C2
Duncan Rd FUL S10 ....124 D3
Duncan St RHAM S60 ....118 C3
Duncombe St ST/HB/BR S6 ..125 F2
Dundas Rd DARN/MH S9 ....117 C1
  WHHL DN2 ....40 C5
Dunedin Cl MOS S20 ....167 E2
Dunedin Gv MOS S20 ....167 E2
Dunella Dr ST/HB/BR S6 ....113 H3
Dunella Pl ST/HB/BR S6 ....113 G3
Dunella Rd ST/HB/BR S6 ....113 G3
Dun Flds OWL S3 ....125 H2
Dunford Cl DEARNE S63 .....55 G3
Dunkeld Rd ECC S11 ....138 D5
Dunkerley Rd ST/HB/BR S6 ..112 D3
Dun La OWL S3 ....125 H2
Dunleary Rd BSLYN/ROY S71 ..20 A2
Dunlin Cl KIMB S61 ....82 B5
Dunlop St DARN/MH S9 ....116 B3
Dunmere Cl BSLYN/ROY S71 ..20 A2
Dunmow Rd ATT S4 ....116 A3
Dunninc Rd SHEFN S5 .....102 D2
Dunninc Ter SHEFN S5 .....102 D2
Dunniwood Av
  DONS/BSCR DN4 ....74 B3
Dunniwood Reach
  DONS/BSCR DN4 ....74 B3
Dunns Dl MALT S66 ....111 F3
Dunscroft Gv
  NROS/TKH DN11 ....91 H2
Dunstan Rd MALT S66 ......110 C4
Dunston Ct CHNE S41 ......179 F5
Dunston La CHNE S41 ......178 D5
Dunston Pl CHNE S41 ......179 F5
Dunston Rd CHNE S41 ......178 D5
Dunston Wy CHNE S41 .....179 G5
Dun St MEX/SWTN S64 ......86 C1
  OWL S3 ....125 H1
Durham Cl STV/CWN S43 ...180 B3
Durham La ARMTH DN3 ......43 F3
  FUL S10 ....10 B4
Durham Pl
  RHAM/THRY S65 ....106 D5
Durham Rd FUL S10 ....10 B4
  WHHL DN2 ....40 C3
Durham St MALT S66 ....110 C4
Durley Chine Dr CHNE S41 ..193 E4
Durlstone Cl HACK/IN S12 ..141 G5
Durlstone Crs HACK/IN S12 ..141 F5
Durlstone Dr HACK/IN S12 ..141 F5
Durlstone Gv HACK/IN S12 ..141 F5
Durmast Gv HACK/IN S12 ..141 G5
Durnan Gv RAW S62 ....84 C3
Durnford Rd WHHL DN2 ......40 C5
Durrant Rd CHNE S41 ....5 G3
Dursley Ct CHNE S41 * 193 E4
Durvale Ct TOT/DORE S17 ..161 E2
Dutton Rd ST/HB/BR S6 ....114 B3
Dyche Cl SHEFS S8 ....163 F2
Dyche Dr SHEFS S8 ....163 F2
Dyche La DRON S18 ....163 E5
  SHEFS S8 ....163 E5
Dyche Pl SHEFS S8 ....163 F2
Dyche Rd SHEFS S8 ....163 F2
Dycott Rd KIMB S61 ....104 D2
Dyer Rd HOY S74 ....62 C1
Dykes Hall Gdns
  ST/HB/BR S6 ....113 H4
Dykes Hall Pl ST/HB/BR S6 ..113 H3
Dykes Hall Rd
  ST/HB/BR S6 ....113 G3
Dykes La ST/HB/BR S6 .....113 G4
  ECK/KIL S21 ....175 H5
  STV/CWN S43 ....185 G1
  WMB/DAR S73 ....35 E4
Dyke Vale Av HACK/IN S12 ..156 A1
Dyke Vale Cl HACK/IN S12 ..156 A1
Dyke Vale Pl HACK/IN S12 ..156 A1
Dyke Vale Rd HACK/IN S12 ..142 D5
Dyke Vale Wy HACK/IN S12 ..155 H1
Dykewood Dr
  ST/HB/BR S6 ....113 H1
Dyson Pl ECC S11 ....139 F2
Dyson St BSLY S70 ....31 F3

E

Eaden Crs HOY S74 ....62 B2
Eagleton Br
  CHPT/GREN S35 ....80 C3
Eagleton Ri CHPT/GREN S35 ..80 C3
Eagle Vw AU/AST/KP S26 ..145 G4
Eaming Vw BSLYN/ROY S71 ...3 K1
Earl Av MALT S66 ....111 E4
  NROS/TKH DN11 ....90 D2
Earldom Cl ATT S4 ....126 C1
Earldom Dr ATT S4 ....126 C1
Earldom Rd ATT S4 ....126 C1
Earldom St ATT S4 ....115 G5
Earlesmere Av
  DONS/BSCR DN4 ....55 C5
Earl Marshal Cl ATT S4 ....115 H3
Earl Marshal Dr ATT S4 * ..115 H4
Earl Marshal Rd ATT S4 ...115 H3
Earl Marshal Vw ATT S4 ...115 G4
Earlsmere Dr
  BSLYN/ROY S71 ....33 G2
Earlston Dr BTLY DN5 ....39 H4
Earl St SHEF S1 ....11 F6
Earl Wy SHEF S1 ....11 F6
earsham st ATT S4 ....126 C1
East Av BSVR S44 ....184 B5
  MEX/SWTN S64 ....85 H1
  RAW S62 ....85 F5
  WMB/DAR S73 ....49 H2
East Bank Pl
  SHEFP/MNR S2 ....140 D4
East Bank Rd
  SHEFP/MNR S2 ....140 D4
East Bank Wy
  SHEFP/MNR S2 ....140 D4
East Bawtry Rd RHAM S60 ..119 G5
East Cl STKB/PEN S36 ....45 G5
East Coast Rd
  DARN/MH S9 ....127 C1
East Crs RHAM/THRY S65 ..106 D2
  STKB/PEN S36 ....76 C2
East Cft DEARNE S63 ....53 E3
Eastcroft Cl MOS S20 .....157 F5
Eastcroft Dr MOS S20 .....167 E1
Eastcroft Gln MOS S20 ....157 F5
Eastcroft Gv MOS S20 .....167 E1
Eastcroft Vw MOS S20 ....157 F5
Eastcroft Wy MOS S20 ....157 F5
East End Crs
  BSLYN/ROY S71 ....16 A1
Eastern Av BSVR S44 ......197 E4
  DIN S25 ....135 E4
Eastern Cl DIN S25 ....135 E4
Eastern Crs SHEFP/MNR S2 ..140 D3
Eastern Dr SHEFP/MNR S2 ..140 D3
Eastern Wk
  SHEFP/MNR S2 ....140 D3
Eastfield Av HACK/IN S12 ..155 G2
Eastfield Cl DOD/DAR S75 ...14 B4
Eastfield Crs DOD/DAR S75 ..14 B4
Eastfield Pl RAW S62 ....86 A4
Eastfield Rd ARMTH DN3 ....42 D5
  DRON S18 ....125 E2
  FUL S10 ....125 E2
Eastfields BSLY S70 ....48 B1
Eastgate BSLY S70 ....3 F5
  ST/HB/BR S6 ....113 C1
East Glade Av HACK/IN S12 ..155 G2
East Glade Cr HACK/IN S12 ..155 G2
East Glade Crs
  HACK/IN S12 ....155 G1
East Glade Dell
  HACK/IN S12 ....155 G1
East Glade Pl HACK/IN S12 ..155 G2
East Glade Rd HACK/IN S12 ..155 G2
East Glade Sq
  HACK/IN S12 * 155 G2
East Glade Wy
  HACK/IN S12 ....155 G1
Eastgrove Rd FUL S10 .....139 F1
East Laith Ga DON DN1 ......6 E3
East Ms MI MOS S20 * 157 E5
Eastmoor Gv
  BSLYN/ROY S71 ....15 E5
Eastmoor Rd STV/CWN S43 ..188 D3
East Pde SHEF S1 ....11 H4
East Pinfold BSLYN/ROY S71 ..15 G1
East Rd RHAM/THRY S65 ...106 D2
  SHEFP/MNR S2 ....140 B3
  STKB/PEN S36 ....45 G5
Eastside Cl CHNE S41 .....187 H1
East Side CHNE S41 ....187 H1
East St DEARNE S63 ....37 H4
  DIN S25 ....134 D4
  DON DN1 ....56 A4
  ECK/KIL S21 ....175 H5
  STV/CWN S43 ....185 G1
  WMB/DAR S73 ....35 E4
East Vale Dr
  RHAM/THRY S65 ....99 H4
East Vw CUD/GR S72 ....16 D5
  MALT S66 ....109 H4
East View Av ECK/KIL S21 ..174 C1
East View Ter ST/HB/BR S6 ..114 A4
Eastwell Gv WMB/DAR S73 ...50 D4
Eastwood Av DIN S25 ......148 C3
Eastwood Cl CHNE S41 ....193 E4
Eastwood La
  RHAM/THRY S65 ....9 G4
Eastwood Mt
  RHAM/THRY S65 ....106 C3
Eastwood Rd ECC S11 .....139 F2
Eastwood V
  RHAM/THRY S65 ....106 C3
Eastwood Park Dr
  CHNE S41 ....193 E4
Eastwood Vw
  RHAM/THRY S65 ....106 D1
Eaton Pl SHEFP/MNR S2 ...126 D3
Ebenezer Pl OWL S3 ....126 A2
Ebenezer St CUD/GR S72 ....36 A1
  OWL S3 ....126 A2
Eben St DARN/MH S9 ......116 C2

Ecclesall Rd ECC S11.............138 D4
Ecclesall Rd South ECC S11..151 E3
Ecclesfield Rd
CHPT/GREN S35 ....94 B2
SHEFN S5.........................102 D1
Eccles St RHAM S60.............103 H5
Eccleston Rd ARMTH DN3......29 G2
Eckington Rd DRON S18......163 H5
MOS S20.............................157 F5
STV/CWN S43...................182 B4
Eckington Wy MOS S20.......156 D1
Ecton Ar ARMTH DN3............29 E2
Edale Ri DOD/DAR S75..........30 A3
Edale Rd ECC S11................138 C4
KIMB S61...........................104 C3
STV/CWN S43...................183 E3
Edderthorpe La
WMB/DAR S73...................35 E2
Eddyfield Rd STKB/PEN S36...45 G4
Eden Cl DOD/DAR S75............18 A2
MALT S66...........................109 H4
Edencroft Dr ARMTH DN3.......29 E4
Eden Dr ST/HB/BR S6...........113 E4
Edenfield Cl BSLYN/ROY S71...20 D1
Eden Field Rd ARMTH DN3....29 G4
Eden Gdl AU/AST/KP S26.....145 F3
Eden Gv AU/AST/KP S26......145 F3
DONS/BSCR DN4................55 G3
Eden Grove Rd ARMTH DN3...29 G5
Edenhall Rd
SHEFP/MNR S2.................141 F3
Edensor Rd SHEFN S5..........115 H2
Eden St RCH S42.................195 E4
Eden Ter WHHL DN2...............67 E2
Edenthorpe Dell MOS S20...156 C3
Edenthorpe Gv MOS S20......156 C3
Edgar La ATT S4...................115 G5
Edgbaston Wy CONI DN12 ...70 C5
Edgcliffe Rd ECC S11...........139 F4
Edgecliffe Pl
BSLYN/ROY S71................20 A2
Edge Cl ST/HB/BR S6.........101 E3
Edgedale Rd ABRD S7..........139 F5
Edge Gn ARMTH DN3.............29 F3
Edgehill Rd ECC S11...........139 E4
WHHL DN2.........................41 G3
Edgelands Ri CUD/GR S72....21 H2
Edge La ST/HB/BR S6.........100 D3
Edgemount Rd ABRD S7......139 G5
Edge Well Cl ST/HB/BR S6...101 E3
Edge Well Crs ST/HB/BR S6..101 E3
Edge Well Dr ST/HB/BR S6...101 E4
Edge Well Pl ST/HB/BR S6...101 E3
Edge Well Ri ST/HB/BR S6...101 E3
Edinburgh Av DEARNE S63....52 D3
Edinburgh Cl
RHAM/THRY S65..................9 K5
Edinburgh Dr DIN S25.........148 C1
Edinburgh Rd CHNE S41......187 F4
HOY S74..............................62 A1
RCH S42.............................195 E3
Edith Ter BTLY DN5...............38 D3
Edlington La CONI DN12........70 C5
Edmonton Cl
DOD/DAR S75 * 18 D5
Edmund Av RHAM S60.........118 D5
Edmund Cl TOT/DORE S17...162 B2
Edmund Dr TOT/DORE S17...162 A2
Edmund Rd
SHEFP/MNR S2.................140 B2
Edmund St CHNE S41..........187 F1
Edna St DEARNE S63.............53 E3
Edward Cl BSLY S70...............32 C3
Edward Rd AWLS/ASK DN6...25 H1
DEARNE S63.......................51 G5
DEARNE S63........................53 E1
Edward St ARMTH DN3...........42 B3
BTLY DN5............................39 H1
CUD/GR S72.......................36 A1
DEARNE S63 * 37 E2
DIN S25.............................134 D4
DOD/DAR S75....................18 A4
ECK/KIL S21.......................166 D5
HOY S74..............................61 H2
MEX/SWTN S64....................64 B4
NROS/TKH DN11..................90 D2
SHEF S1..............................10 D2
STKB/PEN S36.....................77 E2
STV/CWN S43....................189 G1
WMB/DAR S73.....................50 C2
Edward Street Flats
OWL S3...............................10 D2
Edwin Av CHSW S40...........191 H4
Edwin Rd AWLS/ASK DN6.....25 E3
SHEFP/MNR S2.................140 C4
Edwins Cl BSLYN/ROY S71 ...14 D5
Effingham La ATT S4.............11 K1
Effingham Rd ATT S4..........126 C2
Effingham Sq RHAM S60 ....9 F3
Effingham St ATT S4...............11 K1
RHAM/THRY S65...................9 F3
Egerton Cl OWL S3................10 E5
Egerton La OWL S3................10 D6
Egerton Rd AU/AST/KP S26..145 F3
DRON S18.........................171 F1
Egerton St OWL S3................10 D6
Egerton Wk OWL S3...............10 D5
Eggington Cl
DONS/BSCR DN4................74 D1
Egmanton Rd
BSLYN/ROY S71................14 D3

Egremont Ri MALT S66.........110 B1
Eilam Cl KIMB S61...............104 C1
Eilam Rd KIMB S61..............104 C1
Ekin St RHAM S60................117 H1
Eland Cl NROS/TKH DN11.....91 F1
Eland Gate Cl
NROS/TKH DN11................91 F1
Eland Rd CONI DN12.............67 H5
Elcroft Gdns MOS S20........157 F2
Elder Av DIN S25.................148 D3
Elder Cl ECK/KIL S21...........168 A3
Elder Dr MALT S66..............166 B3
Elder Gv CONI DN12.............88 C2
Eldertree Rd KIMB S61..........95 F3
Elder Wy CHSW S40...............5 G3
Eldon Ar BSLY S70...................3 G4
Eldon Ct SHEF S1..................10 D4
Eldon Rd RHAM/THRY S65..106 B1
Eldon St BSLY S70...................3 G4
SHEF S1..............................10 E4
Eldon St North BSLY S70........3 G3
Eleanor Ct ARMTH DN3..........42 A1
Eleanor St DARN/MH S9......127 H1
Elgar Dr MALT S66..............111 G4
Elgin Cl CHSW S40.............191 G5
Elgin St FUL S10.................124 B2
Egitha Dr MALT S66.............133 E1
Eliot Cl STV/CWN S43........188 D4
Elizabeth Av ARMTH DN3......29 G3
Elizabeth Rd
AU/AST/KP S26.................145 F3
Elizabeth St CUD/GR S72......23 E1
DEARNE S63........................37 G5
Elizabeth Wy RHAM S60..........8 C4
Elkstone Rd CHSW S40........186 A4
Elland Cl BSLYN/ROY S71.....14 C5
Ella Rd ATT S4....................115 G5
Ellavale Rd HOY S74..............62 B2
Ellenboro Rd ST/HB/BR S6..113 H4
Elm Tree Cl RHAM S60.........118 B3
Ellerker Av DONS/BSCR DN4...6 A6
Ellers Av DONS/BSCR DN4....57 G5
Ellers Crs DONS/BSCR DN4...57 G5
Ellers Dr DONS/BSCR DN4....57 G5
Ellershaw La CONI DN12........88 C2
Ellershaw Rd CONI DN12.......88 D2
Ellers Rd DONS/BSCR DN4....57 G5
Ellerton Gdns
DONS/BSCR DN4................58 A4
Ellerton Rd SHEFN S5.........115 H2
Ellesmere Rd ATT S4..........126 C1
Ellesmere Rd North
ATT S4..............................115 G5
Ellesmere Ter
RHAM/THRY S65...................9 K5
Ellington Ct BSLY S70............31 F3
Ellin St SHEFP/MNR S2.........11 F7
Elliot Rd ST/HB/BR S6...........10 A1
Elliott Av WMB/DAR S73........50 B4
Elliott Cl DEARNE S63..............6 A2
Elliott Ct RHAM/THRY S65.......9 G3
Elliott Dr KIMB S61................96 D4
Elliott La CHPT/GREN S35.....93 G3
Elliottville St ST/HB/BR S6...125 E1
Ellis Av DEARNE S63..............64 D4
Ellis Crs NROS/TKH DN11......91 E2
WMB/DAR S73.....................64 A1
Ellisons Rd ECK/KIL S21......158 C5
Ellison St OWL S3.................10 C1
Ellis St OWL S3.....................10 E1
RHAM S60.........................118 C3
Elliston Av DOD/DAR S75......14 A3
Ellorslie Dr STKB/PEN S36....77 F2
Ellwood BSLYN/ROY S71........21 E3
Elmbridge Cl
BSLYN/ROY S71................16 A1
Elm Cl BSVR S44.................197 F3
CHNE S41..........................187 F2
ECK/KIL S21.......................168 A3
NROS/TKH DN11................91 H3
MOS S20...........................156 C5
Elmdale La MEX/SWTN S64...86 B3
Elmdale Dr ARMTH DN3.........42 B1
Elm Dr ECK/KIL S21.............168 A3
Elmfield Av SHEFS S8..........102 B5
Elmfield Rd DON DN1..............6 E6
NROS/TKH DN11................91 F3
Elm Green La CONI DN12......89 E1
Elm Gv KIMB S61...................97 F3
Elmham Rd DARN/MH S9.....128 B3
DONS/BSCR DN4................58 A4
Elmhirst Dr
RHAM/THRY S65..............107 G5
Elm La SHEFS S5.................102 B5
Elm Lodge Farm Cl
CHNE S41..........................187 F2
Elmore Rd FUL S10.............125 E4
Elm Pl ARMTH DN3...............42 C3
BSLYN/ROY S71..................20 D2
CHSW S40 * 4 B5
RAW S62..............................98 C1
Elm Ri CHPT/GREN S35.........93 H2
Elm Rd ARMTH DN3...............42 C3
ECK/KIL S21.......................174 C1
EPW DN9..............................75 H5
MEX/SWTN S64....................66 D2
MOS S20...........................157 G1
Elm Rw BSLYN/ROY S71........32 C1
Elmsdale BSLY S70................48 B1

Elm St HOY S74.....................61 F3
STV/CWN S43....................181 E5
Elmton Cl STV/CWN S43......185 F3
Elmton La BSVR S44............197 E2
Elm Tree Cl DIN S25............148 D3
Elm Tree Crs DRON S18......163 E5
Elm Tree Dr RCH S42...........195 F5
Elm Tree Rd KIMB S61...........95 F3
MALT S66...........................110 B3
Elmview Rd DARN/MH S9....103 H5
Elmville Av MEX/SWTN S64...86 A2
Elm Wy DEARNE S63.............53 E3
Elmwood Av AWLS/ASK DN6..24 D1
Elmwood Crs ARMTH DN3......42 C4
Elmwood Dr MOS S20..........166 D2
Elsecar Rd RAW S62..............64 A3
Elsham Cl MALT S66............108 D2
Elstead Cl DOD/DAR S75.......18 A2
Elstree Dr HACK/IN S12.......154 D1
Elstree Rd HACK/IN S12......154 D1
Elsworth Cl DON DN1..............6 B7
Elton La MALT S66...............108 B2
Elton St CHSW S40..................5 F6
Elton Vw STV/CWN S43.......189 H1
Elwin Ct DONS/BSCR DN4.....71 H4
Elwis St BTLY DN5...................6 A2
Elwood Rd TOT/DORE S17...162 A2
Ely Rd WHHL DN2.................40 D3
Ely St NROS/TKH DN11.........91 E2
Embankment Rd FUL S10....125 E4
Emerson Cl SHEFN S5.........102 B4
Emerson Crs SHEFN S5.......102 B5
Emerson Dr SHEFN S5.........102 B5
Emily Cl BSLYN/ROY S71......20 D5
Emley Dr BTLY DN5................38 C3
Emmet Carr Cl CHSW S40......5 F6
Emmet Carr Dr
ECK/KIL S21 * 176 A3
Emmet Carr La
ECK/KIL S21.....................176 A3
Empire Dr MALT S66............110 B1
Empire Rd ABRD S7.............139 H3
Emsley Av CUD/GR S72..........22 A3
Endcliffe Av FUL S10............138 D1
Endcliffe Crs FUL S10..........124 D5
Endcliffe Edge FUL S10.......138 D1
Endcliffe Glen Rd ECC S11..139 E1
Endcliffe Grove Av
FUL S10.............................138 C1
Endcliffe Hall Av FUL S10....138 C1
Endcliffe Rise Rd ECC S11...139 E1
Endcliffe Terrace Rd
FUL S10.............................139 E1
Endcliffe Vale Av ECC S11...139 E2
Endcliffe Vale Rd FUL S10...138 D1
Endcliffe Wy WHHL DN2.......41 G3
Endfield Rd SHEFN S5.........101 H2
Endowood Rd ABRD S7.......151 H3
Enfield Pl HAN/WDH S13.....128 D5
Enfield Rd CHNE S41...........187 G4
Engine La CUD/GR S72..........17 F4
Engine Lane Cl CUD/GR S72..17 F3
Ennerdale Av MOS S20........167 E2
Ennerdale Cl DIN S25..........148 C1
DRON S18..........................170 C2
MEX/SWTN S64...................67 G2
Ennerdale Crs CHNE S41....186 C2
Ennerdale Dr MOS S20........167 E2
Ennerdale Rd
BSLYN/ROY S71..................33 H2
WHHL DN2...........................41 G4
Ennis Crs WHHL DN2............41 E5
Entwhistle Rd
CHPT/GREN S35..................80 C4
Epping Gdns MOS S20.........157 G3
Epping Gv MOS S20.............157 G3
Epsom Cl MEX/SWTN S64.....67 F2
Epsom Rd DONS/BSCR DN4..57 H5
Epworth Ct BTLY DN5.............39 F2
Erringrton Av
SHEFP/MNR S2.................141 E3
Erringrton Cl
SHEFP/MNR S2.................141 E4
Erringrton Crs
SHEFP/MNR S2.................141 E4
Erringrton Rd CHSW S40.....191 H4
DONS/BSCR DN4................74 C2
Erringrton Wy
SHEFP/MNR S2.................141 E3
Erskine Crs SHEFP/MNR S2.140 C3
Erskine Rd RHAM/THRY S65...9 G1
SHEFP/MNR S2.................140 C3
Erskine Vw SHEFP/MNR S2.140 C4
Eshton Wk BSLY S70 * 2 D4
Eskdale Cl BSVR S44...........196 C3
DRON S18..........................170 C2
ST/HB/BR S6.....................114 H4
Eskdale Dr BTLY DN5.............39 F2
Eskdale Rd BSLYN/ROY S71..33 C2
KIMB S61.............................96 D3
ST/HB/BR S6.....................114 A2
Eslaforde Dr
RHAM/THRY S65 * 106 C1
Esperanto Pl SHEF S1...........11 H3
Essendine Crs SHEFS S8.....153 F2
Essex Av WHHL DN2.............57 F2
Essex Rd BSLY S70 * 31 H5
SHEFP/MNR S2.................140 D1
Essoldo Chambers
RHAM S60 * 9 F4

Estate Rd RAW S62................85 E4
Estone Dr AU/AST/KP S26...145 F2
Ettrick Cl CHSW S40...........186 C4
Etwall Cl CHSW S40............186 A3
Etwall Wy SHEFN S5...........102 C5
Europa Cl DARN/MH S9......117 F5
Europa Dr DARN/MH S9......129 C1
Europa Dr DARN/MH S9......117 F5
Europa Link STV/CWN S43..128 C1
Euston Wy DIN S25.............134 A3
Evans St OWL S3...................10 D6
Evanston Gdns
DONS/BSCR DN4................55 G5
Eveline St CUD/GR S72.........21 H1
Evelyn Av WHHL DN2............57 F1
Evelyn Rd FUL S10.............124 C4
Evelyn St RAW S62................85 H5
Evelyn Ter BSLY S70................3 K6
Everard Av TOT/DORE S17...161 G2
Everard Dr TOT/DORE S17...161 G3
Everard Gld TOT/DORE S17.161 G3
Everett Cl STV/CWN S43.....188 C2
Everill Cl WMB/DAR S73........50 D4
Everill Gate La
WMB/DAR S73.....................50 D3
Everingham Cl SHEFN S5....115 E1
Everingham Crs SHEFN S5..114 D1
Everingham Pl SHEFN S5....115 E2
Everingham Rd
DONS/BSCR DN4................58 A4
SHEFN S5..........................115 E1
Everson Cl MALT S66...........110 C1
Everton Rd ECC S11............139 E2
Evesham Av DARN/MH S9...103 H5
Ewden Rd WMB/DAR S73......50 D4
Ewden Wy DOD/DAR S75......30 C1
Ewers Rd KIMB S61.............104 D3
Ewood Dr DONS/BSCR DN4..58 A5
Excalibur Wy CHNE S41..........5 J4
Exchange Pl SHEFP/MNR S2.11 J2
Exchange St DON DN1............6 D7
SHEFP/MNR S2.....................11 J2
Exeter Dr OWL S3..................10 D7
Exeter Pl FUL S10.................10 C6
Exeter Rd WHHL DN2.............41 E4
Exeter Wy OWL S3.................10 C6
Exley Av ST/HB/BR S6.........125 F1
Eyam Cl DOD/DAR S75...........30 A3
Eyam Rd FUL S10................124 D4
Eyecourt Rd SHEFN S5........115 H1
Eyre La SHEF S1...................11 G5
Eyre St SHEF S1.....................11 G5
Eyre St East CHNE S41........193 E5

F

Fabian Wy MALT S66...........108 D5
Factory La DON DN1................6 B3
Factory St CHSW S40...............4 A5
Fairbank Rd SHEFN S5.........115 F3
Fairbank Vw RHAM S60........120 A3
Fairbarn Cl ST/HB/BR S6....124 C4
Fairbarn Dr ST/HB/BR S6....124 C4
Fairbarn Pl ST/HB/BR S6....124 C4
Fairbarn Rd ST/HB/BR S6...124 C4
Fairbarn Wy ST/HB/BR S6...124 C4
Fairburn Croft Crs
STV/CWN S43....................185 F3
Fairburn Gdns RHAM S60....118 D4
Fairburn Gv HOY S74..............62 D2
Fairfax Dr SHEFP/MNR S2...141 F2
Fairfax Rd SHEFP/MNR S2...141 F2
WHHL DN2...........................57 F1
Fair Fld BSLY S70..................32 D5
Fairfield Cl DONS/BSCR DN4..73 H2
DEARNE S63........................52 D2
Fairfield Cl ARMTH DN3.........42 D5
MALT S66...........................108 C2
STV/CWN S43....................188 B1
Fairfield Ct ARMTH DN3.........42 D5
WMB/DAR S73.....................50 D1
Fairfield Rd BSVR S44..........196 D4
CHNE S41............................39 F4
CHSW S40............................4 D5
OWL S3..............................125 G1
Fairford Cl CHSW S40.........192 B5
DONS/BSCR DN4................74 C2
Fairholme Hts
CHPT/GREN S35..................80 C4
Fair Holme Vw ARMTH DN3...43 F5
Fairleigh SHEFP/MNR S2.....141 G2
Fairleigh Dr RHAM S60........106 A5
Fairmount Gdns
HACK/IN S12.....................156 A2
Fairthorn Rd SHEFN S5.......102 D5
Fair Vw CHSW S40...............192 B5
Fair View Av AWLS/ASK DN6..24 D2
Fairview Cl HOY S74...............61 G3
Fairview Ct ARMTH DN3.........29 F1
Fair View Dr
AU/AST/KP S26.................145 F3
Fairview Rd DRON S18.........163 E5
Fairview Ter ARMTH DN3.......29 F1
Fairway DOD/DAR S75...........30 C4
Fairway Av DOD/DAR S75......14 A2
Fairways MALT S66..............108 B5
The Fairway FUL S10...........137 G1
Fairwinds Cl DRON S18........171 E2
Faith St BSLYN/ROY S71.......11 F1
Falcon Cl AWLS/ASK DN6.....25 F1

Falcon Ct NROS/TKH DN11....91 G2
Falcon Dr BSLY S70...............47 H5
RHAM S60.........................130 B4
Falconer La HAN/WDH S13..144 B1
Falconer Wy RHAM S60.......130 B3
Falcon Ri DRON S18............163 H5
Falcon St BSLY S70..................3 F3
Falcon Wy DIN S25.............148 C1
Falding St CHPT/GREN S35...94 B1
RHAM S60..............................8 C4
Falkland Ri DRON S18.........171 E3
Falkland Rd ECC S11...........138 C4
Fallon Rd ST/HB/BR S6.......123 H1
Fallowfield Rd
STV/CWN S43....................180 B3
Falmouth Cl
BSLYN/ROY S71..................20 B5
Falmouth Rd ABRD S7.........139 C5
Falstaff Crs SHEFN S5.........101 H5
Falstaff Rd SHEFN S5..........101 H5
Fane Crs AU/AST/KP S26.....145 F2
Fanny Av ECK/KIL S21.........168 C3
Fan Rd STV/CWN S43..........182 B5
Fanshaw Av ECK/KIL S21....174 C1
Fanshaw Bank DRON S18....171 E2
Fanshaw Dr ECK/KIL S21....174 C1
Fanshaw Rd DRON S18.......171 E2
ECK/KIL S21.......................174 C1
Fanshaw Wy ECK/KIL S21...174 C1
Faraday Rd DARN/MH S9....127 E1
Faranden Rd DARN/MH S9...127 G2
Farcliff BTLY DN5...................54 B4
Far Crs RHAM/THRY S65.....106 D2
Far Cft DEARNE S63...............53 E3
Farcroft Gv ATT S4..............115 H5
Far Dalton La
RHAM/THRY S65..............107 G1
Fardell Gdns MALT S66.......108 D5
Far Field Cl ARMTH DN3.......29 G4
Far Field La BSLYN/ROY S71..16 A5
Far Field Pk DEARNE S63......65 H1
Far Field Rd ARMTH DN3......29 G4
RHAM/THRY S65..............107 E5
Fargate SHEF S1....................11 G3
Far Golden Smithies
MEX/SWTN S64...................66 A3
Farish Pl SHEFP/MNR S2 *..140 B2
Far La RHAM/THRY S65.......106 D2
ST/HB/BR S6.....................113 H3
Far Lawns BSLYN/ROY S71...15 H3
Farlawns Ct
DONS/BSCR DN4................71 H4
Farlow Cft CHPT/GREN S35...80 A3
Farm Bank Rd
SHEFP/MNR S2...................11 K6
Farm Cl ARMTH DN3..............42 C1
BSLYN/ROY S71..................20 C3
CHSW S40.........................195 F1
DRON S18..........................163 H4
HACK/IN S12.....................154 C3
RHAM S60.........................118 B3
Farm Crs AWLS/ASK DN6.....25 G1
Farm Crs MOS S20..............166 C2
Farmfields Cl BSVR S44......196 B1
Farm Fields Cl MOS S20.....156 D4
Farmhill Cl BTLY DN5.............39 E5
Farm House La
DOD/DAR S75.....................18 C5
Farmoor Gdns MOS S20.....157 H4
Farm Rd BSLY S70.................32 C4
SHEFP/MNR S2...................11 K6
Farmstead Cl GLV S14.........140 D5
Farm View Cl HACK/IN S12..156 B2
KIMB S61...........................104 B1
Farm View Dr HACK/IN S12.156 B2
Farm View Gdns
HACK/IN S12.....................156 B2
Farm View Rd KIMB S61......104 B1
Farm Wy WMB/DAR S73........35 E4
Farnaby Gdns
CHPT/GREN S35..................80 B3
Farnaby Rd CHPT/GREN S35..80 B3
Farnborough Dr
DONS/BSCR DN4................74 C2
Farndale Rd BTLY DN5..........38 D3
ST/HB/BR S6.....................114 A2
STV/CWN S43....................182 A2
Farnham Av DIN S25...........134 A3
Farnley Av ST/HB/BR S6......101 F5
Farnley Rd
DONS/BSCR DN4................72 A3
Farnon Cl CHSW S40...........192 D3
Farnsworth Rd
RHAM/THRY S65..............107 E2
Farnsworth St CHNE S41....195 E4
Far Pl RHAM/THRY S65.......106 D2
Farquhar Rd MALT S66........111 F3
Farrar Rd ABRD S7..............139 H5
Farrar St BSLY S70..................2 C3
Farrier Ga CHPT/GREN S35...80 C5
Farriers Wy
DONS/BSCR DN4................72 A3
Farrington Dr
NROS/TKH DN11................91 F4
Farrington Cl MALT S66......108 C5
Farrow Cl DOD/DAR S75.......30 C3
Farthing Gale Ms BTLY DN5..39 F5
Farr Townend
DOD/DAR S75 * 30 B3
Far View Rd SHEFN S5.........102 B5
Farwater Cl DRON S18 * 171 G3

Farwater La DRON S18 ....170 D2
Fathers Gdns
  AU/AST/KP S26 ....159 H5
Favell Rd OWL S3 ....10 C3
  RHAM/THRY S65 ......107 F2
Fawcett St OWL S3 ....10 C1
Fawn Cl RCH S42 ....195 F4
Fearheough St
  DARN/MH S9 ....127 F2
Fearn House Crs HOY S74 .....61 G3
Fearnley Rd HOY S74 ....61 H3
Fearnville Gv
  BSLYN/ROY S71 ....15 C1
Feeman Gdns
  CHPT/GREN S35 ....80 B5
Felkirk Vw CUD/GR S72 ....16 D1
Fellbrigg Rd
  SHEFP/MNR S2 ....140 D3
Fellowsfield Wy KIMB S61 ...104 C2
Fell Rd DARN/MH S9 ....116 C5
Fell St DARN/MH S9 ....116 B4
Fenland Wy CHSW S40 ....192 A4
Fenney La ECC S11 ....151 E3
Fenn Rd DOD/DAR S73 ....60 D3
Fensome Wy WMB/DAR S73 ...34 D4
Fenton Cl ARMTH DN3 ....42 D5
Fenton Cft OWL S3 ....105 E1
Fenton Flds KIMB S61 ....105 E1
Fenton Rd KIMB S61 ....105 E1
Fenton St BSLY S70 * 2 E4
  ECK/KIL S21 ....174 B1
  KIMB S61 ....104 D2
Fentonville St ECC S11 .....139 G2
Fenton Wy KIMB S61 ....105 E1
Feoffees Rd
  CHPT/GREN S35 * 102 B1
Ferguson St DARN/MH S9 .....127 F1
Ferham Cl KIMB S61 ....105 E3
Ferham Park Av KIMB S61 ....105 E3
Ferham Rd KIMB S61 ....105 E3
Fern Av BTLY DN5 ....39 G3
  MOS S20 ....157 F1
  STV/CWN S43 ....99 G5
Fern Bank AWLS/ASK DN6 ......25 F1
  KIMB S61 ....104 C2
Fernbank Cl BSLY S70 * 31 G3
Fernbank Dr ARMTH DN3 ....42 D2
  ECK/KIL S21 ....166 B5
Fern Cl ECK/KIL S21 ....166 B5
  WHHL DN2 ....41 F4
  WMB/DAR S73 ....51 E1
Ferncroft Av MOS S20 ....166 C1
Ferndale Cl DRON S18 ....163 H5
Ferndale Dr MALT S66 ....108 C3
Ferndale Ri DRON S18 ....163 H5
Ferndale Rd CONI DN12 ......88 D1
  DRON S18 ....163 H5
Ferndale Vw BTLY DN5 ....39 G3
Fernhall Cl ARMTH DN3 ......29 G4
Fernhall Cft WMB/DAR S73 ...50 C2
Fern Hollow MALT S66 ....121 G1
Fernhurst Rd WHHL DN2 ......41 G4
Fernlea Cl BTLY DN5 ....39 G3
Fernlea Gv CHPT/GREN S35 ...102 A1
Fernlea Rd DEARNE S63 ......52 D4
Fernleigh Dr RHAM S60 ......118 B2
Fern Rd ST/HB/BR S6 ....124 D1
Fernvale Wk
  MEX/SWTN S64 ....86 B3
Fern Wy ECK/KIL S21 ....166 B5
Ferrand St BSLY S70 ....20 D2
Ferrars Cl WMB/DAR S73 .....34 C4
Ferrars Ct DARN/MH S9 ......117 H2
Ferrars Dr DARN/MH S9 ......117 H3
Ferrars Rd DARN/MH S9 ......117 G1
Ferrars Wy DARN/MH S9 ......117 H3
Ferrers Rd WHHL DN2 ....40 D5
Ferriby Rd ST/HB/BR S6 .....113 H2
Ferry Boat La CONI DN12 ....67 G5
Ferry La CONI DN12 ....69 E5
Ferry Moor La CUD/GR S72 ...22 D1
Ferrymoor Wy CUD/GR S72 ....22 C1
Ferry Ter CONI DN12 * 69 E5
Ferry Vls CONI DN12 * 69 E5
Festival Cl AU/AST/KP S26 ..159 E3
Festival Rd DEARNE S63 .....65 F3
Fewton Wy
  DONS/BSCR DN4 ....57 F5
Fiddlers Dr ARMTH DN3 ......59 E1
Field Av ECK/KIL S21 ....175 H3
Field Cl DRON S18 ....170 A1
  WMB/DAR S73 ....35 E4
Field Dr CUD/GR S72 ....21 H2
Fielder Ms SHEFN S5 ....103 E5
Fielders Wy CONI DN12 ......70 C5
Field Ga NROS/TKH DN11 .....91 G1
Field Head Cl HOY S74 ......62 A2
Field Head Rd HOY S74 ......62 A3
Fieldhead Rd SHEFS S8 * 140 A3
Fieldhead Wy CHNE S41 ......186 C3
Field House Rd BTLY DN5 ....54 B5
Fieldhouse Wy ATT S4 ....115 H5
Fielding Dr MALT S66 ....108 D5
Fielding Gv RAW S62 ....85 F4
Fielding Rd ST/HB/BR S6 ....114 A2
Field La BSLY S70 ....33 E3
  ECK/KIL S21 ....167 H3
  MALT S66 ....121 G5
Fieldside ARMTH DN3 ....42 B5
  STV/CWN S43 ....185 F3
Field Vw RHAM S60 ....118 C3
Fieldview Pl CHNE S41 ......186 C3

Field Wy RHAM S60 ....8 E1
Fife Cl DARN/MH S9 ....103 G5
Fife St BSLY S70 ....2 D6
  DARN/MH S9 ....103 G5
Fife Wy DARN/MH S9 ....103 G5
Fifth Av AWLS/ASK DN6 ......25 F4
Figtree La SHEF S1 ....11 G2
Filby Rd BTLY DN5 ....39 E5
Filey Av BSLYN/ROY S71 .....12 D5
Filey La OWL S3 ....10 C5
Filey St FUL S10 ....10 C1
Finch Cl RHAM/THRY S65 .....99 H4
Finch Gdns MALT S66 ....109 E5
Finch Ri AU/AST/KP S26 ....145 G4
Finch Rd DONS/BSCR DN4 ....71 F2
Finchwell Cl HAN/WDH S13 ..128 D5
Finchwell Crs
  HAN/WDH S13 ....128 D5
Finchwell Rd
  HAN/WDH S13 ....128 D5
Findon Crs ST/HB/BR S6 ....113 G4
Findon Pl ST/HB/BR S6 .....113 G4
Findon Rd ST/HB/BR S6 .....113 G4
Findon St ST/HB/BR S6 .....113 H4
Finkle St BTLY DN5 ....39 H2
Finlay Rd RHAM/THRY S65 ...106 C1
Finlay St OWL S3 ....10 C1
Finsbury Cl DIN S25 ....134 A2
Firbeck Av DIN S25 ....134 C1
Firbeck Rd
  DONS/BSCR DN4 ....7 H6
  SHEFS S8 ....152 C2
Firbeck Wy
  NROS/TKH DN11 ....91 H1
Fir Cl DEARNE S63 ....65 F3
Fircroft Av SHEFN S5 ......102 D4
Fircroft Rd SHEFN S5 ......103 E4
Firethorn Ri
  RHAM/THRY S65 ....109 F1
Firham Cl BSLYN/ROY S71 ...12 A5
Fir Pl ECK/KIL S21 ....168 A3
Fir Rd ECK/KIL S21 ....174 B1
Firsby La CONI DN12 ....88 A4
Firshill Av ATT S4 ....115 F4
Firshill Cl ATT S4 ....115 F4
Firshill Crs ATT S4 ....115 F4
Firshill Gld SHEFN S5 .....115 F4
Firshill Ri ATT S4 ....115 F4
Firshill Rd ATT S4 ....115 F4
First Av AWLS/ASK DN6 .....25 G3
  RHAM/THRY S65 ....106 C1
The Firs BSLY S70 ....32 C4
  BSLYN/ROY S71 ....12 A5
First La DIN S25 ....148 C5
  MALT S66 ....121 G1
Fir St ST/HB/BR S6 ....125 E2
  STV/CWN S43 ....181 F5
Firth Av CUD/GR S72 ....21 G2
Firth Ct STV/CWN S43 * 180 B2
Firth Crs MALT S66 ....111 E4
  NROS/TKH DN11 ....91 E2
Firth Dr ATT S4 ....126 D1
Firth Park Av SHEFN S5 ....115 H1
Firth Park Crs SHEFN S5 ...115 H1
Firth Park Rd SHEFN S5 ....115 H1
Firth Rd DEARNE S63 ....64 B2
Firth St BSLYN/ROY S71 .....3 F2
  DONS/BSCR DN4 ....6 A7
  KIMB S61 ....97 G3
Firthwood Av DRON S18 .....163 H5
Firthwood Cl DRON S18 .....163 H5
Firthwood Rd DRON S18 .....163 H5
Fir Tree Dr AU/AST/KP S26 ..159 E3
Firtree Ri CHPT/GREN S35 ...94 A2
Fir Vale Pl SHEF S8 * 115 G3
Firvale Rd RCH S42 ....191 F4
Fir Vale Rd SHEFN S5 ......115 G3
Fish Dam La BSLYN/ROY S71 ..20 D2
Fisher Cl CHSW S40 ....192 B5
  RHAM S60 ....8 C4
Fisher La DARN/MH S9 ......103 G5
Fisher Rd MALT S66 ....111 F3
Fisher St BTLY DN5 ....26 D5
Fisher Ter BTLY DN5 ....39 G5
Fishponds Cl RCH S42 ......195 F5
Fishponds Rd
  HAN/WDH S13 ....142 A2
Fishponds Rd West
  HAN/WDH S13 ....142 A3
Fitzalan Rd HAN/WDH S13 ...142 D1
Fitzalan Sq SHEF S1 ....11 H3
Fitzgerald Rd FUL S10 .....124 D3
Fitzhubert Rd
  SHEFP/MNR S2 ....141 G2
Fitzmaurice Rd
  DARN/MH S9 ....127 H1
Fitzroy Rd SHEFP/MNR S2 ...140 B4
Fitzwalter Rd
  SHEFP/MNR S2 ....126 D5
Fitzwilliam Av CONI DN12 ...88 D1
Fitzwilliam Ga SHEF S1 .....11 F6
Fitzwilliam Rd
  RHAM/THRY S65 ....9 H2
  WMB/DAR S73 ....35 G4
Fitzwilliam Sq KIMB S61 ....97 F2
Fitzwilliam St BSLY S70 ....2 D4
  DEARNE S63 ....65 E3
  HOY S74 ....61 F3
  MEX/SWTN S64 ....86 A1
  OWL S3 ....10 D5
  RAW S62 ....98 A3
  WMB/DAR S73 ....62 D1

Five Oaks BTLY DN5 ....27 G4
Five Trees Cl
  TOT/DORE S17 ....161 C2
Five Trees Dr
  TOT/DORE S17 ....161 C2
Five Weirs Wk
  DARN/MH S9 ....127 F1
Flamsteed Crs CHNE S41 ....187 C3
Flanders Cl KIMB S61 ....95 F1
Flanderwell Av MALT S66 ...108 C4
Flanderwell Ct MALT S66 ...108 C3
Flanderwell Gdns
  MALT S66 ....108 C3
Flanderwell La MALT S66 ...108 A3
Flash La MALT S66 ....109 E5
  ST/HB/BR S6 ....122 C3
Flask Vw ST/HB/BR S6 ......112 C5
Flat La CUD/GR S72 ....36 A5
  RHAM S60 ....119 H3
Flat St SHEF S1 ....11 H3
Flatts Cl RHAM S60 ....130 A2
Flatts La DEARNE S63 ....64 D2
  RHAM S60 ....130 A2
Flaxby Rd DARN/MH S9 ......127 H2
Flax Lea BSLY S70 ....32 A5
Fleet Cl DEARNE S63 ....64 A1
Fleet Hill Crs
  BSLYN/ROY S71 ....20 C2
Fleetwood Av
  BSLYN/ROY S71 ....20 C2
Fleming Gdns MALT S66 .....108 B3
Fleming Pl BSLY S70 * 3 F6
Fleming Sq DEARNE S63 .....65 E2
Fleming Wy MALT S66 ....108 A4
Fletcher Av DRON S18 ......171 E2
Fleury Cl GLV S14 ....154 A1
Fleury Pl GLV S14 ....154 A1
Fleury Ri GLV S14 ....154 A1
Fleury Rd GLV S14 ....154 A1
Flint Rd WHHL DN2 ....41 G5
Flintson Av STV/CWN S43 ...180 B2
Flintway DEARNE S63 ....65 F5
Flockton Av HAN/WDH S13 ..143 F2
Flockton Crs
  HAN/WDH S13 ....143 F2
Flockton Dr HAN/WDH S13 ..143 F2
Flockton Rd HAN/WDH S13 ..143 G2
Flodden St ST/HB/BR S6 ....124 D1
Floodgate Dr
  CHPT/GREN S35 ....102 B1
Flora St ST/HB/BR S6 ......125 C1
Florence Av
  AU/AST/KP S26 ....145 F3
  DONS/BSCR DN4 ....55 G5
Florence Cl CHNE S41 ......195 H1
Florence Ri WMB/DAR S73 ...34 D5
Florence Rd RCH S42 ......195 G3
  SHEFS S8 ....152 C3
Flower St DEARNE S63 ......37 H5
Flowitt St DONS/BSCR DN4 ..55 H3
  MEX/SWTN S64 ....86 A2
Folderings La STKB/PEN S36 ..77 E5
Folder La BTLY DN5 ....54 A4
Folds Crs SHEFS S8 ....152 A4
Folds Dr SHEFS S8 ....152 A4
Folds La SHEFS S8 ....152 A4
The Fold RHAM/THRY S65 ...107 F1
Foley St WMB/DAR S73 ......50 A3
Foljambe Av CHSW S40 .....191 H4
Foljambe Crs
  NROS/TKH DN11 ....90 D2
Foljambe Dr
  RHAM/THRY S65 ....99 G5
Foljambe Rd CHSW S40 .....106 D1
  RHAM/THRY S65 ....106 D1
  STV/CWN S43 ....188 C1
Foljambe St RAW S62 ....98 B2
Folkwood Gv ECC S11 ......138 A5
Follett Rd SHEFN S5 ....102 A5
Fontwell Dr MEX/SWTN S64 ..67 F2
Foolow Av CHSW S40 ....192 B3
Forbes Rd ST/HB/BR S6 .....126 D2
Foley St HACK/IN S12 ......165 C3
  STKB/PEN S36 ....77 E1
Ford Rd ECC S11 ....138 D4
  ECK/KIL S21 ....165 G5
Fore Hill Av
  DONS/BSCR DN4 ....73 H2
Foremark Rd SHEFN S5 .....102 D5
Forest Ct STV/CWN S43 ....177 F5
Forest Edge ECC S11 ....151 F4
Forest Gra DONS/BSCR DN4 ..71 E3
Forest Ri DONS/BSCR DN4 ...71 E3
Forest Rd BSLYN/ROY S71 ...14 D4
Forge Dr CHSW S40 ....5 G7
Forge La ECK/KIL S21 ......167 H1
  HOY S74 ....62 C4
  RHAM S60 ....8 E4
  SHEFP/MNR S2 ....11 F7
Forge Rd AU/AST/KP S26 ...159 F2
Formby Ct BSLYN/ROY S71 ...20 D1
Forncett St ATT S4 ....126 D1
Fornham St SHEF S1 ....11 H6
Forres Av FUL S10 ....124 C5
Forres Rd FUL S10 ....124 C5
Forrester Cl MALT S66 .....108 B3
Forrester's La DRON S18 ...163 H4
Forster Rd DONS/BSCR DN4 ..71 H2
Forth Av DRON S18 ....170 A1
Fort Hill Rd DARN/MH S9 ...116 B2
Fortway Rd RHAM S60 ......118 C2

Fossard Cl WHHL DN2 ....41 E4
Fossard Wy BTLY DN5 ....39 F1
Fossdale Rd ABRD S7 ......139 F5
Foster Rd MALT S66 ....108 B4
Foster St BSLY S70 ....32 D2
Foster Wy CHPT/GREN S35 ...80 B5
Foster's Cl MEX/SWTN S64 ..66 A5
Foston Dr CHSW S40 ....186 B4
Fothergill Dr ARMTH DN3 ...29 G4
Foulstone Rw
  WMB/DAR S73 ....50 C3
Foundry Ga WMB/DAR S73 ...49 H4
Foundry St BSLY S70 ....3 F6
  CHNE S41 ....187 C1
  HOY S74 ....62 C3
  RAW S62 ....98 B3
Fountain Ct BSLYN/ROY S71 ..14 C3
  NROS/TKH DN11 ....91 H3
Fountain Prec SHEF S1 * 11 F3
Fountains Cl ARMTH DN3 ....29 E3
Fountains Wy
  BSLYN/ROY S71 ....20 D2
Four Lands Cl DOD/DAR S75 ..18 A2
Fourth Av AWLS/ASK DN6 ....25 F4
Four Wells Dr HACK/IN S12 ..156 A4
Fowler Bridge Rd BTLY DN5 ..40 A2
Fowler Crs NROS/TKH DN11 ..91 E2
Fowler St CHNE S41 ....179 F4
Foxbrook Cl CHSW S40 .....191 F4
Foxbrook Dr CHSW S40 .....191 F4
Fox Cl KIMB S61 ....96 B4
Foxcote Wy RCH S42 ....191 F4
Fox Ct MEX/SWTN S64 ....86 B2
Fox Covert Cl DEARNE S63 * ..53 E1
Fox Cft HOY S74 ....61 H3
Foxcroft Cha ECK/KIL S21 ..168 A2
Foxcroft Cl ECK/KIL S21 ...168 A2
Foxcroft Gv ECK/KIL S21 ...168 A2
Foxcroft Mdw MALT S66 ....111 E4
Foxdale Av HACK/IN S12 ....141 H5
Fox Farm Ct DEARNE S63 ...63 H1
Foxfields STKB/PEN S36 ....45 G5
Foxfield Wk BSLY S70 ......32 D4
Fox Glen Rd STKB/PEN S36 ...77 F3
Foxglove Rd SHEFN S5 .....103 E5
Fox Gv DONS/BSCR DN4 .....70 C2
Foxhall La FUL S10 ....136 D4
Fox Hill Av ST/HB/BR S6 ...101 E4
Fox Hill Cl ST/HB/BR S6 ...101 E4
Fox Hill Crs ST/HB/BR S6 ..101 E4
Fox Hill Dr ST/HB/BR S6 ...101 E4
Fox Hill Pl ST/HB/BR S6 ...101 E4
Fox Hill Rd ST/HB/BR S6 ...101 E3
Fox Hill Wy ST/HB/BR S6 ...101 E3
Fox La AU/AST/KP S26 .....147 G3
Fox La HACK/IN S12 ....155 G2
Fox Lane Ct HACK/IN S12 ...155 G1
Fox Lane Vw HACK/IN S12 ...155 G1
Fox Rd ST/HB/BR S6 ....125 C1
Foxroyd Cl BSLYN/ROY S71 ..33 F2
Foxton Ct STV/CWN S43 ....189 H1
Fox St KIMB S61 ....104 C3
  OWL S3 ....126 B1
Foxwood Av HACK/IN S12 ...141 H4
Foxwood Dr HACK/IN S12 ...141 H5
Foxwood Gr HACK/IN S12 ...141 H5
Foxwood Rd CHNE S41 ......179 E4
  HACK/IN S12 ....141 H4
Foxwood Wy CHNE S41 ......179 E4
Foyers Wy CHNE S41 ....5 J4
Framlingham Pl
  SHEFP/MNR S2 ....140 D3
France Rd ST/HB/BR S6 ....112 D3
Frances Dr RCH S42 ....195 E3
Frances St DON DN1 ....6 D5
  9 H6
France St RAW S62 ....98 B3
Francis Crs North
  RHAM S60 ....120 B1
Francis Crs South
  RHAM S60 ....120 B1
Francis Dr RHAM S60 ....120 B1
Francis Gv CHPT/GREN S35 ...80 B3
Francus Royd
  BSLYN/ROY S71 ....15 G3
Franklin Crs WHHL DN2 .....7 J4
Franklyn Dr STV/CWN S43 ...182 B3
Franklyn Rd CHSW S40 .....4 B2
Frank Pl DARN/MH S9 ......116 C5
Fraser Cl SHEFS S8 ....152 C2
Fraser Crs SHEFS S8 ......152 C2
Fraser Dr SHEFS S8 ....152 D2
Fraser Rd RHAM S60 ....9 J7
  SHEFS S8 ....152 C2
Frecheville St
  STV/CWN S43 ....181 H5
Frederick Dr
  CHPT/GREN S35 ....92 D5
Frederick St DARN/MH S9 ...127 H3
  DEARNE S63 ....37 G5
  DEARNE S63 ....64 D1
  MEX/SWTN S64 ....66 C3
  RHAM S60 ....8 B5
  RHAM S60 ....129 G2
  WMB/DAR S73 ....50 A2
Frederic Pl BSLY S70 ......31 H3
Fred Mulley Rd ATT S4 .....126 D2

Freebirch Vw CHNE S41 ....186 B2
Freedom Ct ST/HB/BR S6 ...114 B5
Freedom Rd ST/HB/BR S6 ...125 E1
Freeman Rd MALT S66 ......108 B4
Freemans Yd BSLY S70 ....3 H7
Freeman St BSLY S70 ....3 H5
Freesia Cl DIN S25 ....148 A4
Freeston Pl DARN/MH S9 ...116 C5
French Ga DON DN1 ....6 C3
French St BTLY DN5 ....26 D6
Frenson Cl ST/HB/BR S6 * ..141 G2
Fretson Gn
  SHEFP/MNR S2 ....141 G2
Fretson Rd SHEFP/MNR S2 ..141 G2
Fretson Road S
  SHEFP/MNR S2 ....141 G3
Fretwell Cl MALT S66 ......109 E4
Fretwell Rd MALT S66 ......109 H4
  RHAM/THRY S65 ....107 E1
Friar Cl ST/HB/BR S6 ......123 H1
Friars Ga DON DN1 ....6 C1
Friars Rd BSLYN/ROY S71 ...21 E4
Frickley Rd ECC S11 ....138 B2
Frinton Cl CHSW S40 ......192 B5
Frithbeck Cl ARMTH DN3 ....42 D4
Frith Cl HACK/IN S12 ......141 H5
Frithhall La RCH S42 ......190 A2
Frith Rd HACK/IN S12 ......141 H5
Frithwood Dr DRON S18 ....171 C1
Frobisher Gv MALT S66 ....110 C2
Froggatt Cl STV/CWN S43 ...5 K1
Froggatt La SHEF S1 ....11 F6
Frogmore Cl MALT S66 .....108 D3
Front Rw NROS/TKH DN11 * ..91 H2
Front St RHAM S60 ....130 A3
Frostings Cl CHPT/GREN S35 ..93 E5
The Frostings
  CHPT/GREN S35 ....93 E5
Fulford Cl CHSW S40 ......191 G4
  DARN/MH S9 ....128 A2
Fulford Pl DARN/MH S9 ....128 A2
Fuller Dr CHNE S41 * 188 A3
Fullerton Av CONI DN12 ....88 B1
Fullerton Crs
  RHAM/THRY S65 ....99 G4
Fullerton Dr RHAM S60 ....118 B4
Fullerton Rd RHAM S60 ....118 C1
Fulmar Wy KIMB S61 ....82 C5
Fulmer Cl BSLYN/ROY S71 ...20 B1
Fulmere Crs SHEFN S5 .....101 G3
Fulmere Rd SHEFN S5 ......101 G3
Fulney Rd ECC S11 ....138 B2
Fulton Rd ST/HB/BR S6 ....125 E2
Fulwood Cha FUL S10 ......138 C4
Fulwood Dr
  DONS/BSCR DN4 ....71 H4
Fulwood Head Rd FUL S10 ..136 C4
Fulwood La FUL S10 ....136 B4
Fulwood Rd FUL S10 ....137 H3
Furlong Ct DEARNE S63 .....53 F2
Furlong Mdw DEARNE S63 ...63 H2
Furlong Rd DEARNE S63 .....53 F2
Furnace Hl CHSW S40 ....4 C5
  OWL S3 ....11 F1
Furnace La HAN/WDH S13 ...145 H3
  STV/CWN S43 ....188 D3
Furness Dene
  BSLYN/ROY S71 ....20 D2
Furness Rd CHPT/GREN S35 ..80 A4
Furniss Av TOT/DORE S17 ..160 D2
Furniss Ms TOT/DORE S17 ..161 E2
Furnival Cl AU/AST/KP S26 .147 E5
Furnival Ga SHEF S1 ....11 G5
Furnival Rd
  DONS/BSCR DN4 ....55 G5
  SHEFP/MNR S2 ....11 J2
Furnival Sq SHEF S1 ....11 G6
Furnival St SHEF S1 ....11 G6
Furnival Wy RHAM S60 .....120 B3
Future Wk CHSW S40 * 4 E4
Fylde Cl BSLYN/ROY S71 ....20 D1

G

Gainsborough Cl MALT S66 ..108 B4
Gainsborough Rd
  DRON S18 ....170 C3
  ECC S11 ....139 F3
Gainsborough Wy
  BSLYN/ROY S71 ....20 B3
Gainsford Rd DARN/MH S9 ..128 A3
Gaitskell Cl DEARNE S63 ...53 F2
Gala Crs MALT S66 ....110 B2
Gallery La RCH S42 ....190 A5
Galley Dr MOS S20 ....156 D4
Gallow Tree Rd
  RHAM/THRY S65 ....107 F5
Galpharm Wy
  DOD/DAR S75 ....30 A2
Galsworthy Av SHEFN S5 ...114 D1
Galsworthy Cl
  DONS/BSCR DN4 ....71 F3
Galsworthy Rd SHEFN S5 ...114 D1
Galway Cl BSLYN/ROY S71 ...12 C5
  RAW S62 ....85 G5
Gamston Rd SHEFS S8 ......139 H5
Gander La STV/CWN S43 ....184 B1

Gannow Cl ECK/KIL S21....168 D1
Ganton Pl BSLYN/ROY S71....14 C5
Ganton Rd ST/HB/BR S6....113 H2
Garbroads Crs
  RHAM/THRY S65....99 G4
Garbutt St DEARNE S63....53 F4
Garden Av ECK/KIL S21....175 H4
Garden Cl RHAM S60....119 G1
  STV/CWN S43....180 B3
Garden Ct BSLY S70....30 D1
Garden Crs RHAM S60....119 G2
Garden Dr WMB/DAR S73....51 E5
Gardeners Cl BSVR S44....196 D2
Garden Gv WMB/DAR S73....50 A5
Garden House Cl
  BSLYN/ROY S71....20 C2
Gardenia Rd ARMTH DN3....29 E4
Garden La BTLY DN5....69 F1
  RHAM S60....162 B1
Gardens La CONI DN12....88 D1
The Gardens
  DONS/BSCR DN4....73 H1
Garden St BSLY S70....3 H7
  DEARNE S63....37 F2
  DEARNE S63....64 D1
  KIMB S61....8 A3
  MEX/SWTN S64....66 D3
  SHEF S1....10 E2
  WMB/DAR S73....35 E5
Garden Wk RHAM S60....119 G2
Gardom Cl DRON S18....170 D2
Garfield Mt
  RHAM/THRY S65....9 H6
Garland Cl STV/CWN S43....167 E1
Garland Ct MOS S20....167 E1
Garland Dr ST/HB/BR S6....112 D3
Garland Mt MOS S20....167 E1
Garland Wk MOS S20....167 E1
Garry Rd ST/HB/BR S6....124 B1
Garter St ATT S4....115 H5
Garth Cl DARN/MH S9....127 G2
Garth Wy DRON S18....170 D2
Gartrice Gdns MOS S20....167 G3
Gartrice Gv MOS S20....167 G3
Gashouse La MOS S20....166 D3
Gate Crs DOD/DAR S75....30 D2
Gatefield Cl CHNE S41....186 C2
Gatefield Rd ABRD S7....139 G4
Gateway Cl RAW S62....98 A4
Gateway Ct RAW S62....98 A4
The Gateway RAW S62....98 A4
Gate Wood La ARMTH DN3....59 H3
Gattison La
  NROS/TKH DN11....91 F3
Gatty Rd SHEFN S5....102 D2
Gaunt Cl ECK/KIL S21....168 A2
  GLV S14....153 H1
  MALT S66....108 D3
Gaunt Dr GLV S14....153 H1
  MALT S66....108 D3
Gaunt Pl GLV S14....153 H1
Gaunt Rd GLV S14....153 H1
  MALT S66....108 D3
Gawber Rd DOD/DAR S75....2 A1
Gawtress Rw DEARNE S63....65 G2
Gayle Ct BSLY S70....4 A4
Gayton Cl DONS/BSCR DN4....71 G3
Gayton Rd ATT S4....115 G4
Geer La HACK/IN S12....165 E3
Gelderd Pl DRON S18....171 E3
Gell St OWL S3....8 B5
Genn La BSLY S70....31 F4
Genoa Cl WMB/DAR S73....34 C3
Genoa St MEX/SWTN S64....67 F3
The Gentre MALT S66....108 D4
George Pl RAW S62....98 B1
George Sq BSLY S70 *....3 F5
George St ARMTH DN3....42 B3
  BSLY S70....3 G5
  BSLY S70....48 A1
  CHNE S41....26 C5
  CHNE S41....179 F4
  CUD/GR S72....17 E4
  CUD/GR S72....35 H5
  DEARNE S63....37 E5
  HOY S74....62 A3
  RHAM S60....8 E3
  SHEF S1....11 H3
  STV/CWN S43....188 C1
  WMB/DAR S73....50 B3
George Yd BSLY S70....3 F4
Georgian Ms RHAM S60....129 G3
Gerald Cl BSLY S70....32 C3
Gerald Crs BSLY S70....32 D2
Gerald Pl BSLY S70....32 C3
Gerald Rd BSLY S70....32 C3
Gerald St DARN/MH S9....116 C5
Gerald Wk BSLY S70....32 C3
Gerard Cl CHSW S40....191 G3
  SHEF S8....140 B4
Gerard Rd RHAM S60....9 G7
Gerard St SHEFS S8....140 B4
Gervase Av SHEFS S8....162 C2
Gervase Dr SHEFS S8....162 C2
Gervase Pl SHEFS S8....162 C2
Gervase Rd SHEFS S8....162 C2
Gibbing Greaves Rd
  RHAM/THRY S65....107 G5
Gibbons Dr GLV S14....154 A3
Gibbons Wy GLV S14....154 A3
Gibraltar St OWL S3....11 F1
Gibson La STKB/PEN S36....77 E1
Gifford Dr DONS/BSCR DN4....70 D2

Gifford Rd SHEFS S8 *....140 A3
Gilbert Av CHSW S40....191 H4
Gilbert Gv BSLY S70....32 D2
Gilberthorpe Dr
  RHAM/THRY S65....106 C3
Gilberthorpe Rd
  DONS/BSCR DN4....71 F1
Gilberthorpe St
  RHAM/THRY S65....9 K5
Gilbert Rw SHEFP/MNR S2....11 K4
Gilbert St SHEF S1....11 J3
Gildhurst Ct BSLY S70....60 D2
Giles Av DEARNE S63....64 A2
Gileswood Crs DEARNE S63....64 A2
Gill Cl MALT S66....121 G1
Gill Cft ST/HB/BR S6....123 G1
Gilleyfield Av
  TOT/DORE S17....161 E1
Gill Mdw ST/HB/BR S6....123 G1
Gillot Dell MALT S66....121 F1
Gillott La MALT S66....121 F1
Gillott Rd ST/HB/BR S6....101 E5
Gill St DON DN1....6 E6
  HOY S74....62 A3
Gilpin La ST/HB/BR S6....125 G2
Gilpin St ST/HB/BR S6....125 G2
Gilroyd La DOD/DAR S75....30 D5
Ginhouse La MALT S66....105 G1
Gipsy Green La DEARNE S63....65 H4
Gipsy La CHNE S41....179 H4
  DRON S18....172 C2
Gisborne Rd ECC S11....151 E1
Gisbourne Cl STV/CWN S43....182 B5
Glade Cl CHSW S40....187 E4
Glade Cft HACK/IN S12....141 G5
Glade Lea HACK/IN S12....141 G5
The Glade CHSW S40....4 A3
Glade Vw ARMTH DN3....29 F5
Gladstone Ms FUL S10....138 A1
Gladstone Rd CHSW S40....4 D2
  DONS/BSCR DN4....71 G4
  FUL S10....138 A1
  MALT S66....110 C2
Gladwin Gdns CHSW S40....191 H4
Gladys St RHAM/THRY S65....106 C3
Glaisdale Cl DIN S25....134 A2
Glamis Rd WHHL DN2....57 E2
Glasshouse La
  STV/CWN S43....180 B1
Glasshouse Rd
  MEX/SWTN S64....86 C4
Glasshouse St RHAM S60....8 D3
Glastonbury Ga BTLY DN5....38 D5
Gleadless Av HACK/IN S12....154 B1
Gleadless Bank
  HACK/IN S12....154 B1
Gleadless Common
  HACK/IN S12....141 F5
Gleadless Ct
  SHEFP/MNR S2....140 B4
Gleadless Dr HACK/IN S12....154 B1
Gleadless Mt HACK/IN S12....154 C2
Gleadless Ri HACK/IN S12....141 F5
Gleadless Rd GLV S14....141 E5
  HACK/IN S12....154 C2
  SHEFP/MNR S2....140 B4
Gleadless Vw HACK/IN S12....141 F5
Glebe Cl MEX/SWTN S64....86 A2
Glebe Ct CHNE S41....179 G4
Glebe Crs RHAM/THRY S65....99 G5
Glebe Farm Cl ARMTH DN3....42 C4
Glebeland Cl RAW S62....85 E3
Glebelands Rd
  STKB/PEN S36....77 E3
Glebe Rd FUL S10....125 E3
  MEX/SWTN S64....86 A2
Glebe St DONS/BSCR DN4....70 D2
Glebe Vw STV/CWN S43....177 F5
The Glebe Wy CHNE S41....179 G4
Gledhill Av STKB/PEN S36....44 C5
Gledhill Cl STV/CWN S43....171 E2
Glenalmond Rd ECC S11....138 D3
Glenavon Cl STV/CWN S43....180 B1
Glencoe Dr SHEFP/MNR S2....126 C5
Glencoe Pl
  SHEFP/MNR S2....126 C5
Glencoe Rd SHEFP/MNR S2....126 C5
Glencoe Wy CHSW S40....186 B5
Glendale Cl DOD/DAR S75....30 D1
Glendale Rd BTLY DN5....54 B4
Gleneagles Cl CHSW S40....191 G4
Gleneagles Dr
  DONS/BSCR DN4....74 D2
Gleneagles Ri
  MEX/SWTN S64....86 B1
Gleneagles Rd DIN S25....134 D5
Glen Field Av
  DONS/BSCR DN4....55 G4
Glenfield Crs CHNE S41....187 F2
Glenholme Dr
  HAN/WDH S13....142 C3
Glenholme Pl
  HAN/WDH S13....142 C3
Glenholme Rd
  HAN/WDH S13....142 C3
Glenholme Wy
  HAN/WDH S13....142 C2
Glenmoor Av BSLY S70....30 D2
Glenmore Cl STV/CWN S43....189 E4
Glenmore Cft HACK/IN S12....141 H4
Glenmore Ri
  WMB/DAR S73....50 C4
Glenorchy Rd ABRD S7....139 F5

Glen Rd ABRD S7....139 G4
  ARMTH DN3....59 C5
The Glen FUL S10....138 D1
Glenthorne Cl CHSW S40....191 G2
Glentilt Rd ABRD S7....139 F5
Glen V DRON S18....170 B2
Glen View Rd SHEFS S8....152 C5
Glenville Cl HOY S74....61 H3
Glenwood Ct ST/HB/BR S6....113 F1
Glenwood Crs
  CHPT/GREN S35....94 B1
Glenwood Dr ST/HB/BR S6....113 F1
Gliwice Wy DONS/BSCR DN4....57 H4
Glossop La FUL S10....10 B4
Glossop Rd FUL S10....10 C4
Glossop's Cft CHNE S41....179 H4
Glumangate CHSW S40....5 F3
Glyn Av DON DN1....6 E3
Goathland Dr
  HAN/WDH S13....143 G3
Goathland Pl
  HAN/WDH S13....143 H3
Goathland Rd
  HAN/WDH S13....143 H3
Goddard Av STKB/PEN S36....76 B1
Goddard Hall Rd SHEFN S5....115 G3
Godley St BSLYN/ROY S71....12 D5
Godric Dr RHAM S60....118 B3
Godric Gn RHAM S60....118 B3
Godric Rd SHEFN S5....102 C2
Godstone Rd RHAM S60....9 G6
Goldcrest Wk KIMB S61....95 C1
Gold Cft BSLY S70....3 J7
Golden Smithies La
  MEX/SWTN S64....65 H5
Goldsborough Rd WHHL DN2....7 K3
Goldsmith Dr
  RHAM/THRY S65....106 C3
Goldsmith Rd
  DONS/BSCR DN4....72 A2
  RHAM/THRY S65....106 D3
Gold St BSLY S70....3 J6
Goldthorpe Rd DEARNE S63....53 F1
Gomersal La DRON S18....171 G2
Gomersall Av CONI DN12....88 B1
Gooder Av BSLYN/ROY S71....15 G1
Goodison Bvd
  DONS/BSCR DN4....74 A1
Goodison Crs ST/HB/BR S6....124 B1
Goodison Ri ST/HB/BR S6....124 B1
Goodwin Av RAW S62....85 F5
Goodwin Crs
  MEX/SWTN S64....66 B4
Goodwin Rd KIMB S61....97 E2
  SHEFS S8....140 A4
Goodwood Gdns
  DONS/BSCR DN4....57 H3
Goodyear Crs
  WMB/DAR S73....50 B3
Goore Av DARN/MH S9....127 E5
Goore Dr DARN/MH S9....127 H4
Goore Rd DARN/MH S9....127 H5
Gooseacre Av DEARNE S63....37 E1
Goosebutt St RAW S62....98 B2
Goose Carr La
  AU/AST/KP S26....146 D3
Goosecroft Av
  RHAM/THRY S65....99 G4
Goosehill Ct
  DONS/BSCR DN4....71 H4
Goose La MALT S66....108 C5
Gordon Av SHEFS S8....153 E3
Gordon Rd ECC S11....139 F2
Gordon St BSLY S70....33 E2
  DON DN1....6 B4
Gordon Ter
  RHAM/THRY S65 *....9 K5
Gorehill Cl DEARNE S63....65 G2
Gorman Cl CHNE S41....187 E1
Gorse Cl DEARNE S63....63 H2
Gorse St RHAM/THRY S65....109 F1
Gorse Dr ECK/KIL S21....168 B3
Gorseland Ct MALT S66....108 A5
Gorse La FUL S10....136 D3
The Gorse MALT S66....121 F1
Gorse Rd RHAM/THRY S65....107 E4
Gorse Valley Rd CHNE S41....193 C5
Gorse Valley Wy CHNE S41....193 C5
Gorsey Brigg DRON S18....170 B2
Gosber Rd ECK/KIL S21....166 C5
Gosber St ECK/KIL S21....166 C5
Gosforth Cl DRON S18....170 D2
Gosforth Crs DRON S18 *....170 D2
Gosforth Dr DRON S18....170 B3
Gosforth Gn DRON S18....170 D2
Gosforth La DRON S18....170 D2
Gosling Gate Rd
  DEARNE S63....37 G5
Gotham Rd RHAM S60....118 C3
Gough Cl RHAM/THRY S65....107 E5
Goulding St MEX/SWTN S64....66 D4
Gowdall Gn BTLY DN5....26 C4
Gower Crs CHSW S40....186 C4
Gower St ATT S4....126 C1
  WMB/DAR S73....50 C3

Goyt Side Rd CHSW S40....4 A6
Goyt Ter CHSW S40 *....4 A6
Grace Rd CONI DN12....70 C5
Grace St BSLYN/ROY S71....21 F5
Grady Dr DONS/BSCR DN4....72 A3
Graftdyke Cl
  NROS/TKH DN11....91 H2
Grafton St BSLY S70....2 D5
  SHEFP/MNR S2....126 C5
Grafton Wy
  RHAM/THRY S65....9 G2
Graham Av RHAM S60....118 D5
Graham Rd ARMTH DN3....29 F4
  FUL S10....138 A2
Graham's Orch BSLY S70....3 F4
Grammar St ST/HB/BR S6....125 F1
Grampian Cl BTLY DN5....39 G5
  DOD/DAR S75....18 D5
Grampian Crs CHSW S40....186 B5
Granary Ct RCH S42....186 A1
Granary Ct DIN S25....148 B2
Granby Ct ARMTH DN3....43 E5
Granby Crs WHHL DN2....7 J5
Granby La NROS/TKH DN11....90 D2
Granby Rd SHEFN S5....115 H2
Grange Av AU/AST/KP S26....145 E1
  DONS/BSCR DN4....71 G1
  DRON S18....170 C2
Grange Cliffe Cl ECC S11....151 H1
Grange Cl CUD/GR S72....17 H1
  DONS/BSCR DN4....74 B1
  MALT S66....132 C2
Grange Ct BTLY DN5....39 G4
  DONS/BSCR DN4....74 B1
  MALT S66....108 B5
Grange Crs BSLYN/ROY S71....21 E5
  DEARNE S63....37 G2
  ECC S11....139 G2
Grange Crescent Rd
  ECC S11....139 G2
Grange Dr KIMB S61....96 B5
  MALT S66....109 H5
Grange Farm
  DONS/BSCR DN4....71 G4
Grange Farm Cl RHAM S60....118 D5
Grange Farm Dr
  AU/AST/KP S26....145 G4
Grange Mill La
  DARN/MH S9....103 F1
Grangemill Pl
  STV/CWN S43....189 G1
Grange Pk ARMTH DN3....29 G2
Grange Park Av
  STV/CWN S43....188 D5
Grange Rd AWLS/ASK DN6....25 G4
  BSLYN/ROY S71....15 E1
  BTLY DN5....26 C3
  CUD/GR S72....17 H2
  DEARNE S63....64 D3
  DONS/BSCR DN4....74 B2
  ECC S11....139 G2
  MEX/SWTN S64....85 H1
  MOS S20....157 G2
  RAW S62....85 G4
  RHAM S60....118 D5
Grange St DEARNE S63....37 G2
The Grange KIMB S61....96 B4
Grange Vw DEARNE S63 *....37 E2
  DONS/BSCR DN4....55 G5
  HOY S74....48 B3
Grange View Crs KIMB S61....104 B1
Grange View Rd KIMB S61....104 B1
Grangewood Rd CHSW S40....192 B5
  DIN S25....134 C2
Granham Acre CUD/GR S72....17 E2
Grantham St
  NROS/TKH DN11....91 E2
Grantley Cl WMB/DAR S73....50 D5
Granville Cl CHNE S41....193 F4
Granville Rd
  SHEFP/MNR S2....11 J6
  SHEFP/MNR S2....140 D1
Granville Sq Jct
  SHEFP/MNR S2....11 J6
Granville St DOD/DAR S75....19 F4
Granville Ter
  RHAM/THRY S65....9 K5
Grasby Cl MALT S66....108 B2
Grasmere Av WHHL DN2....57 G1
Grasmere Cl CHNE S41....193 E4
  DIN S25....148 C2
  STKB/PEN S36....44 D2
Grasmere Rd ABRD S7....139 G5
  BSLYN/ROY S71....3 J4
  CONI DN12....88 D1
  DRON S18....170 C2
Grassdale Vw HACK/IN S12....155 H2
Grassington Cl
  HACK/IN S12....156 B2
Grassington Dr
  HACK/IN S12....156 A2
Grassington Wy
  CHPT/GREN S35....80 D5

Grassmoor La HACK/IN S12....141 F4
Grassthorpe
  HACK/IN S12....154 C1
Grattan St KIMB S61....154 B4
Graven Cl CHPT/GREN S35....100 D1
Gray Av AU/AST/KP S26....145 G4
Gray Gdns
  DONS/BSCR DN4....71 H2
Grays Ct CONI DN12....68 C4
Gray La
  RHAM/THRY S65....108 D1
  STKB/PEN S36....77 E3
Grayson Cl
  RHAM/THRY S65....108 D1
Gray St HOY S74....62 C3
  MOS S20....166 C1
  OWL S3....126 B1
  STV/CWN S43....185 F2
Gray's Rd BSLYN/ROY S71....15 G3
Greasbro Rd DARN/MH S9....117 F2
Greasbrough La RAW S62....97 H1
Greasbrough Rd KIMB S61....97 H5
  RAW S62....98 A3
  RHAM S60....8 E1
Greasbrough St RHAM S60....8 D2
Great Bank Rd
  RHAM/THRY S65....107 E5
Great Broading
  DOD/DAR S75....18 D2
Great Central Av
  DONS/BSCR DN4....55 H5
Great Cliffe Rd
  DOD/DAR S75....30 A2
Great Common Cl
  STV/CWN S43....177 F4
Great Cft DRON S18....170 D1
Great Eastern Wy RAW S62....98 B4
Great North Rd
  AWLS/ASK DN6....24 D1
Great Park Rd KIMB S61....104 C1
Greaves Cl ST/HB/BR S6....123 G1
Greaves Fold DOD/DAR S75....18 D5
Greaves La CHPT/GREN S35....80 B1
  ST/HB/BR S6....123 G1
Greaves Rd KIMB S61....105 E2
  SHEFN S5....102 A1
Greaves St ST/HB/BR S6....123 G1
Greave Wy STV/CWN S43....188 A1
Green Acres HOY S74....62 A3
  RAW S62....98 C1
  STKB/PEN S36....45 E3
Greenacres Cl DRON S18....171 G4
Green Arbour Rd MALT S66....133 E1
Greenaway Dr BSVR S44....196 C4
Greenbank BSLYN/ROY S71....14 D5
Greenbank Dr CHSW S40....186 C5
Green Bank Dr MALT S66....108 C2
Greenbank Wk CUD/GR S72....17 G1
Green Boulevard
  DONS/BSCR DN4....58 A5
Green Brook Pl
  STKB/PEN S36....44 D4
Green Cha ECK/KIL S21....166 C5
Green Cl DRON S18....172 A5
  ECK/KIL S21....175 H3
  STV/CWN S43....189 G3
Green Ct MALT S66....108 C2
Green Croft Cl RHAM S60....119 F1
Green Cross DRON S18....171 F1
Grendale Av RCH S42....190 C4
Green Farm Cl CHSW S40....186 C5
Green Farm Hamlet
  STKB/PEN S36....76 A2
Greenfield RAW S62....98 B1
Greenfield Cl ARMTH DN3....29 C1
  ARMTH DN3....43 E5
  RHAM/THRY S65....107 F1
  SHEFS S8....162 D1
Greenfield Ct MALT S66....108 B3
  MEX/SWTN S64....53 H5
Greenfield Dr SHEFS S8....162 D1
Greenfield Gdns
  DONS/BSCR DN4....74 C1
  MALT S66....108 B3
Greenfields ECK/KIL S21....166 C5
Green Finch Cl RHAM S60....118 D4
Greenfoot Cl DOD/DAR S75....19 F4
Greenfoot La DOD/DAR S75....19 F4
Greengate Cl CHSW S40....191 G2
Green Gate Cl DEARNE S63....53 F2
Greengate La
  CHPT/GREN S35....80 B5
  HAN/WDH S13....143 G4
Greengate Rd
  HAN/WDH S13....143 H4
Green Gln CHSW S40....191 G2
Greenhall Rd ECK/KIL S21....166 C5
Greenhead Gdns
  CHPT/GREN S35....94 A1
Greenhead La
  CHPT/GREN S35....81 E5
Greenhill Av BSLYN/ROY S71....19 G4
  MALT S66....109 H5
  SHEFS S8....152 C5
Greenhill Main Rd
  SHEFS S8....162 C1
Greenhill Pkwy SHEFS S8....162 B2
Greenhill Rd SHEFS S8....152 C5

Greenhouse La FUL S10 ....136 D5
Greenhouse Rd WHHL DN2 ....41 F4
Greenhow St ST/HB/BR S6 ..125 E2
Green Ings La DEARNE S63 ....65 G1
Greenland Av MALT S66 ....111 E1
Greenland Av South
  MALT S66 ....111 E2
Greenland Cl DARN/MH S9 ..128 A2
  DIN S25 ....148 B2
Greenland Dr DARN/MH S9 ..128 A1
Greenland Rd
  DARN/MH S9 ....116 D5
Greenlands Av
  NROS/TKH DN11 ....91 G1
Greenland Vw BSLY S70 ....47 H1
  DARN/MH S9 ....128 A2
Greenland Wy
  DARN/MH S9 ....128 A1
  MALT S66 ....111 E2
Green La ARMTH DN3 ....58 D4
  AU/AST/KP S26 ....131 F3
  AWLS/ASK DN6 ....25 E3
  BSLY S70 ....31 E5
  BTLY DN5 ....38 B1
  CHNE S41 ....188 D5
  CHPT/GREN S35 ....102 C1
  DOD/DAR S75 ....30 C4
  DRON S18 ....171 F1
  ECK/KIL S21 ....168 A4
  HOR/CROF WF4 ....12 A3
  HOY S74 ....61 E4
  KIMB S61 ....104 A2
  MALT S66 ....121 H3
  RAW S62 ....64 D5
  RAW S62 ....98 B1
  RHAM S60 ....118 B5
  ST/HB/BR S6 ....125 H2
  STKB/PEN S36 ....76 A1
Green Lea DRON S18 ....170 A1
Greenleafe Av WHHL DN2 ....41 F3
Green Oak Av
  TOT/DORE S17 ....161 E4
Green Oak Crs
  TOT/DORE S17 ....161 E4
Green Oak Dr
  AU/AST/KP S26 ....159 E3
  TOT/DORE S17 ....161 E4
Green Oak Gv
  TOT/DORE S17 ....161 E4
Green Oak Rd
  TOT/DORE S17 ....161 E4
Greenock St ST/HB/BR S6 ..113 H4
Green Pastures
  TOT/DORE S17 ....161 E1
Green Rd BSLY S62 ....84 D4
Green Rd STKB/PEN S36 ....44 D4
Greenset Vw
  BSLYN/ROY S71 ....14 C3
Greenside CUD/GR S72 ....13 H5
  DOD/DAR S75 ....14 A3
  HOR/CROF WF4 ....13 H1
  KIMB S61 ....97 F3
Greenside Av
  AU/AST/KP S26 ....159 G3
  CHNE S41 ....187 F2
  DOD/DAR S75 ....14 A3
Greenside Cl STV/CWN S43 ..184 C2
Greenside La HOY S74 ....62 A2
Greenside Ms HACK/IN S12 ..156 A4
Green Spring Av BSLY S70 ....47 H5
Greens Rd RHAM/THRY S65 ..106 D3
Green St BSLY S70 ....48 C1
  CHNE S41 ....179 C5
  DONS/BSCR DN4 ....71 F2
  HOY S74 ....62 B2
  KIMB S61 ....97 F2
  STKB/PEN S36 ....77 F2
The Green CHNE S41 ....193 F5
  CONI DN12 ....67 G5
  DEARNE S63 ....53 E2
  DIN S25 ....148 B2
  MALT S66 ....108 C2
  MEX/SWTN S64 ....85 H1
  RHAM S60 ....119 F1
  STKB/PEN S36 ....44 A2
  STV/CWN S43 ....185 E2
  TOT/DORE S17 ....160 D4
The Green Vw CUD/GR S72 ..13 H5
Greenway AU/AST/KP S26 ..159 H3
Greenways CHSW S40 ....191 C4
The Greenway SHEFS S8 ....152 D5
Greenwood Av BSLY S70 ....32 B5
  DARN/MH S9 ....127 G4
  DONS/BSCR DN4 ....55 F5
Greenwood Cl
  DARN/MH S9 ....127 H4
Greenwood Crs
  DARN/MH S9 ....127 G4
  MALT S66 ....108 C4
Greenwood Dr
  DARN/MH S9 ....127 H4
Greenwood La
  HAN/WDH S13 ....143 H3
Greenwood Ter BSLY S70 ....2 E3
Greenwood Wy
  DARN/MH S9 ....127 G4
Greeton Dr
  CHPT/GREN S35 ....100 A3

Gregg House Crs
  SHEFN S5 ....102 D4
Gregg House Rd SHEFN S5 ..102 D3
Greggs Ct BSLY S70 ....32 D2
Gregory Cl STV/CWN S43 ..188 B1
Gregory La STV/CWN S43 ..180 B5
Gregory Rd SHEFS S8 ....140 A4
Grendon Vls
  RHAM/THRY S65 * 106 C2
Grenfell Av STV/CWN S64 ..187 F3
Grenfolds Rd
  CHPT/GREN S35 ....101 F1
Grenobank Rd
  CHPT/GREN S35 ....101 F1
Greno Crs CHPT/GREN S35 ..101 F1
Greno Ga CHPT/GREN S35 ..93 E5
Grenomoor Cl
  CHPT/GREN S35 ....101 E2
Greno Rd MEX/SWTN S64 ....86 B2
Grenoside Mt
  CHPT/GREN S35 ....101 F2
Greno Vw DOD/DAR S75 ....46 A3
  HOY S74 ....61 G3
Greno View Rd
  CHPT/GREN S35 ....80 B4
Greno Wood Ct
  CHPT/GREN S35 ....93 E5
Grenville Rd
  DONS/BSCR DN4 ....71 E2
Gresham Av RHAM S60 ....118 C3
Gresham Rd ST/HB/BR S6 ..125 E2
Gresley Rd DONS/BSCR DN4 ..55 H4
  SHEFS S8 ....162 B3
Grey Friars' Rd DON DN1 ....6 C2
Greystock St ATT S4 ....126 C1
Greystones Av BSLY S70 ....47 H1
  ECC S11 ....138 C3
Greystones Cl ECC S11 ....138 C3
Greystones Ct
  AU/AST/KP S26 ....169 H2
Greystones Crs ECC S11 ....138 C3
Greystones Dr ECC S11 ....138 C3
Greystones Grange
  ECC S11 ....138 C3
Greystones Grange Rd
  ECC S11 ....138 C3
Greystones Hall Rd
  ECC S11 ....138 C3
Greystones Ri ECC S11 ....138 C3
Greystones Rd ECC S11 ....138 C3
  RHAM S60 ....120 B3
Grice Cl DONS/BSCR DN4 ..58 B5
Griffin Rd MEX/SWTN S64 ....65 H5
Griffiths Cl RAW S62 ....98 B2
Griffiths Rd CHPT/GREN S35 ..80 C5
Grimesthorpe Rd ATT S4 ....126 C1
Grimesthorpe Rd South
  ATT S4 ....126 C1
Grimpit Hl HOR/CROF WF4 * ..12 A3
Grimsell Cl ST/HB/BR S6 ..101 F2
Grimsell Crs ST/HB/BR S6 ..101 F2
Grimsell Dr ST/HB/BR S6 ..101 F2
Grindlow Av CHSW S40 ....140 B3
Grindlow Cl GLV S14 ....140 C4
Grindon Cl CHSW S40 ....186 C4
Grizedale Av MOS S20 ....157 C3
Grizedale Cl MOS S20 ....157 C3
Grosvenor Crs BTLY DN5 ....27 F5
  DONS/BSCR DN4 ....70 D2
Grosvenor Dr BSLY S70 ....2 A4
Grosvenor Rd
  AWLS/ASK DN6 ....25 F2
  RHAM/THRY S65 ....9 H1
Grosvenor Sq
  SHEFP/MNR S2 ....139 H2
Grosvenor Ter
  DONS/BSCR DN4 ....70 D2
Grouse Cft ST/HB/BR S6 ..125 E4
Grove Av BTLY DN5 ....39 G5
  ST/HB/BR S6 ....113 G2
Grove Bank RHAM S60 * 106 A5
Grove Cl DEARNE S63 ....51 G5
  STKB/PEN S36 ....44 D5
Grove Cottages
  CHSW S40 * 191 H2
Grove Farm Cl
  STV/CWN S43 ....188 C2
Grove Gdns DEARNE S63 ....37 E3
  STV/CWN S43 ....188 D5
Grove Hill Rd WHHL DN2 ....41 G3
Grove House Ct
  TOT/DORE S17 * 161 E3
Grove Pl DON DN1 ....6 C5
Grove Rd ABRD S7 ....152 A2
  CHNE S41 ....187 G2
  DEARNE S63 ....51 F5
  RHAM S60 ....9 F6
  STKB/PEN S36 ....77 H3
  STV/CWN S43 ....188 B3
  TOT/DORE S17 ....161 E3
Grove Sq ST/HB/BR S6 ....114 C5
Grove St BSLY S70 ....32 C5
  BSLYN/ROY S71 ....3 H3
  CHNE S41 ....193 E4
The Grove CUD/GR S72 ....16 D5
  MALT S66 ....108 B4
  RAW S62 ....98 C1
  RHAM/THRY S65 ....106 D2
  ST/HB/BR S6 ....113 G4
  TOT/DORE S17 ....160 D3
  WHHL DN2 ....41 E5

Grove V WHHL DN2 ....41 G3
Grove Wy STV/CWN S43 ....188 D4
Guernsey Rd
  SHEFP/MNR S2 ....140 A3
Guest La DONS/BSCR DN4 ....70 D1
Guest Pl RHAM S60 ....106 B5
Guest Rd DOD/DAR S75 ....2 D1
  ECC S11 ....139 E2
  RHAM S60 ....106 B5
Guest St HOY S74 ....62 A1
Guilbert Av MALT S66 ....132 D2
Guildford Av CHSW S40 ....191 H4
  SHEFP/MNR S2 ....140 D2
Guildford Ri
  SHEFP/MNR S2 ....140 D2
Guildford Rd
  BSLYN/ROY S71 ....12 B4
  WHHL DN2 ....41 F3
Guildford Wy RHAM/THRY S65 ..106 D3
Guildway AU/AST/KP S26 ....147 E5
Guilford Wy
  SHEFP/MNR S2 ....141 E3
Guilthwaite Common La
  AU/AST/KP S26 ....131 E2
Guilthwaite Crs RHAM S60 ..119 G3
Gullane Dr DONS/BSCR DN4 ..70 D2
Gunhills La ARMTH DN3 ....43 E3
Gun La OWL S3 ....111 H1
Gurney Rd RHAM S60 ....71 H2
Gurth Av ARMTH DN3 ....29 G4
Gurth Dr MALT S66 ....133 E2
Gwendoline Ms
  DEARNE S63 ....65 F3
Gypsy La WMB/DAR S73 ....50 C4

H

Habershon Dr
  CHPT/GREN S35 * 80 D5
Habershon Rd KIMB S61 ....96 D5
Hackings Av STKB/PEN S36 ..44 C5
Hackness La RHAM S60 ....118 B5
Hackthorn Rd SHEFS S8 ....152 D2
Haddon Pl STV/CWN S43 ..191 C2
  DOD/DAR S75 ....30 A3
  DRON S18 ....171 F1
Haddon Ri MEX/SWTN S64 ....67 H2
Haddon Rd BSLYN/ROY S71 ..20 B3
Haddon St OWL S3 ....125 H1
Haddon Wy
  AU/AST/KP S26 ....145 H3
Haden St ST/HB/BR S6 ....114 A4
Hadfield St ST/HB/BR S6 ..125 E2
  STV/CWN S43 ....50 C4
Hadleigh Cl RAW S62 ....98 B2
Hadrian Rd RHAM S60 ....118 C2
Hadrians Cl
  NROS/TKH DN11 ....91 G4
Hady Crs CHNE S41 ....193 E1
Hady Hl CHNE S41 ....5 K5
Hady La CHNE S41 ....193 F2
Haggard Rd ST/HB/BR S6 ..114 B4
Hagg Hl ST/HB/BR S6 ....96 D4
  ST/HB/BR S6 ....124 B2
Hagg La FUL S10 ....123 H4
Hague Av ECK/KIL S21 ....175 H3
  RAW S62 ....85 E3
Hague La ARMTH DN3 ....80 A4
  ECK/KIL S21 ....175 G3
  KIMB S61 ....80 A4
  STV/CWN S43 ....176 A5
Hague Rw SHEFP/MNR S2 ....11 K4
Haids Cl MALT S66 ....110 D1
Haids Rd MALT S66 ....110 D1
Haig Crs NROS/TKH DN11 ....91 E3
Haigh Ct DEARNE S63 ....63 H2
Haigh Cft BSLYN/ROY S71 ....12 B5
Haigh Moor Cl
  HAN/WDH S13 ....142 C2
Haigh Moor Dr DIN S25 ....134 A4
Haigh Moor Rd
  HAN/WDH S13 ....142 D2
Haigh Moor Wy
  AU/AST/KP S26 ....144 C3
  BSLYN/ROY S71 ....12 B5
Haigh Rd DONS/BSCR DN4 ..71 G1
Hail Mary Dr
  HAN/WDH S13 ....143 H2
Hakehill Cl DONS/BSCR DN4 ..73 H2
Halcyon Cl HACK/IN S12 ....155 H2
Haldane Cl CUD/GR S72 ....17 H1
Haldane Dr
  RHAM/THRY S65 ....106 C1
Haldane Rd
  HAN/WDH S13 ....128 A4
Hale St SHEFS S8 ....139 H4
Halesworth Cl STV/CWN S40 ..191 F4
Halesworth Rd
  HAN/WDH S13 ....128 C5
Half Acre La DRON S18 ....171 H3
Half Cft STV/CWN S43 ....188 D2
Halfway Dr MOS S20 ....167 E1
Halfway Gdns MOS S20 ....167 E1
Halifax Av CONI DN12 ....88 C1
Halifax Crs BTLY DN5 ....39 F4
Halifax Rd ST/HB/BR S6 ....101 H4
Halifax St BSLYN/ROY S71 ....19 G3
Hallam Cha FUL S10 ....123 H5

Hallam Cl AU/AST/KP S26 ....145 E1
  DONS/BSCR DN4 ....73 G1
Hallam Ct DEARNE S63 * 52 D4
Hallamgate Rd FUL S10 ....124 D5
Hallam Grange Cl FUL S10 ..137 G2
Hallam Grange Crs FUL S10 ..137 G1
Hallam Grange Cft FUL S10 ..137 G1
Hallam Grange Ri FUL S10 ..137 G1
Hallam Grange Rd FUL S10 ..137 G1
Hallam La SHEF S1 ....11 G6
Hallam Pl RAW S62 ....98 C1
Hallam Rd RHAM S60 ....119 F2
Hallamshire Cl FUL S10 ....137 F2
Hallamshire Dr FUL S10 ....137 F2
Hallamshire Rd FUL S10 ....137 F2
Hallam Wy CHPT/GREN S35 ..102 B1
Hall Av HOY S74 ....62 C1
  MEX/SWTN S64 ....67 F3
Hall Balk La DOD/DAR S75 ..19 F4
  NROS/TKH DN11 ....72 A5
Hall Bank DOD/DAR S75 ....19 F5
Hall Broome Gdns
  DEARNE S63 ....53 E2
Hallcar St ATT S4 ....126 C2
Hall Cl BSLY S70 ....48 A3
  DEARNE S63 ....64 B1
  DIN S25 ....148 B2
  RHAM S60 ....170 A1
Hall Close Av RHAM S60 ....120 A3
Hall Crs RHAM S60 ....119 H2
Hall Cft MALT S66 ....108 C5
Hallcroft Dr ARMTH DN3 ....59 E1
Hallcroft Ri BSLYN/ROY S71 ..15 F1
Hall Cross Av WMB/DAR S73 ..50 D4
Hall Dr DEARNE S63 ....64 D3
Haller Cl ARMTH DN3 ....42 B4
Hall Farm Cl
  AU/AST/KP S26 ....131 E5
  CHNE S41 ....193 F5
Hall Farm Dr DEARNE S63 ....37 E3
Hall Farm Ri DEARNE S63 ....37 E3
Hallfield Cl RCH S42 ....195 D5
Hall Field La HOR/CROF WF4 ..13 C2
Hall Flat La DONS/BSCR DN4 ..71 G2
Hallgate DEARNE S63 ....37 E3
Hall Ga DON DN1 ....6 D4
  MEX/SWTN S64 ....67 G3
  STKB/PEN S36 ....44 D3
Hallgate Rd FUL S10 ....124 C5
Hall Gv DOD/DAR S75 ....14 A3
  RHAM S60 ....9 G7
Halliwell Cl SHEFN S5 ....114 B1
Halliwell Crs SHEFN S5 ....114 C1
Hall La STV/CWN S43 ....181 G2
Hall Meadow Cft MOS S20 ..167 F3
Hall Meadow Gv MOS S20 * ..167 F3
Hallowes Ct DRON S18 ....171 F3
Hallowes Dr DRON S18 ....171 F3
Hallowes La DRON S18 ....171 F3
Hallowmoor Rd
  ST/HB/BR S6 ....113 G4
Hall Park Head
  CHNE S41 ....123 H2
Hall Park Hl ST/HB/BR S6 ..124 A2
Hall Park Mt ST/HB/BR S6 * ..124 A2
Hall Pl BSLYN/ROY S71 ....20 C3
Hall Rd AU/AST/KP S26 ....145 F1
  HAN/WDH S13 ....128 C5
  RHAM S60 ....9 F7
  WMB/DAR S73 ....50 C3
Halls Ct SHEFS S8 ....152 D2
Hallside Ct ARMTH DN3 ....58 D4
  MOS S20 ....166 D2
Halls Rw CHSW S40 * 4 A5
Hall St BSLY S70 ....53 C1
  HOY S74 ....62 A2
  RHAM S60 ....8 D4
  WMB/DAR S73 ....50 C3
Hallsworth Av
  DARN/MH S9 ....128 C1
Hall Vw CHNE S41 ....187 E3
Hall View Rd
  NROS/TKH DN11 ....91 G4
Hallwood Rd
  CHPT/GREN S35 ....93 F1
Halsall Rd
  CHPT/GREN S35 ....93 E1
Hallyburton Cl
  SHEFP/MNR S2 ....140 C4
Hallyburton Dr
  SHEFP/MNR S2 ....140 C4
Hallyburton Rd
  SHEFP/MNR S2 ....140 C4
Halmshaw BTLY DN5

Hamilton Ms
  DONS/BSCR DN4 ....7 J6
Hamilton Park Rd BTLY DN5 ..38 D4
Hamilton Rd DEARNE S63 ....37 H4
  DONS/BSCR DN4 ....7 H7
  MALT S66 ....111 F4
  SHEFN S5 ....115 H2
Hammerton Rd
  ST/HB/BR S6 ....114 A5
Hammerton St
  WMB/DAR S73 ....50 A1
Hammond St OWL S3 ....10 C1
Hampden Rd
  MEX/SWTN S64 ....67 E4
Hamper La STKB/PEN S36 ....45 F1
Hampole Dr DEARNE S63 ....37 E3
Hampson Gdns ARMTH DN3 ..29 G4
Hampton Rd SHEFN S5 ....115 G3
  WHHL DN2 ....7 J3
Hampton St CHNE S41 ....193 F5
Hanbury Cl BSLYN/ROY S71 ..20 D3
  CHSW S40 ....186 A4
  DONS/BSCR DN4 ....71 G4
  DRON S18 ....170 D2
Handby St CHNE S41 ....126 C2
Handley Cl STV/CWN S43 ..180 B2
Handley Rd STV/CWN S43 ..180 B2
Handley St ATT S4 ....126 B2
Handley St RHAM S60 ....125 E3
Handsworth Av
  DARN/MH S9 ....128 A4
Handsworth Crs
  DARN/MH S9 ....128 B4
Handsworth Gdns
  ARMTH DN3 ....43 E4
Handsworth Grange Cl
  HAN/WDH S13 ....143 E2
Handsworth Grange Crs
  HAN/WDH S13 ....143 E1
Handsworth Grange Rd
  HAN/WDH S13 ....143 E1
Handsworth Rd
  DARN/MH S9 ....138 B4
Hanging Water Rd FUL S10 ..138 B3
Hangingwater Rd ECC S11 ..138 B3
Hangram La ECC S11 ....150 B1
Hangsman La DIN S25 ....134 A2
Hangthwaite La
  AWLS/ASK DN6 ....25 H4
Hanley Cl HACK/IN S12 ....156 B2
Hanmoor Rd ST/HB/BR S6 ..123 G1
Hannah Rd HAN/WDH S13 ..143 H3
Hannas Royd DOD/DAR S75 ..30 C3
Hanover Ct OWL S3 ....10 C6
Hanover Sq DEARNE S63 ....37 G2
  OWL S3 ....10 D6
Hanover St DEARNE S63 ....37 G2
  OWL S3 ....10 C6
Hanover Wy OWL S3 ....10 C5
Hanslope Vw ARMTH DN3 ....29 E2
Hanson Rd ST/HB/BR S6 ....112 D4
Hanson St BSLY S70 ....3 G4
Hanwell Cl CHPT/GREN S35 ..102 B1
Harbord Rd SHEFS S8 ....152 C3
Harborough Av
  SHEFP/MNR S2 ....141 G1
Harborough Cl
  SHEFP/MNR S2 ....127 G2
Harborough Dr
  SHEFP/MNR S2 ....127 G5
Harborough Hill Rd
  BSLYN/ROY S71 ....3 H4
Harborough Ri
  SHEFP/MNR S2 ....127 G5
Harborough Rd
  SHEFP/MNR S2 ....127 G5
Harborough Wy
  SHEFP/MNR S2 ....141 G1
Harbury St SHEF 189 H1
  DONS/BSCR DN4 ....73 G1
Harcourt Crs FUL S10 ....125 F4
Harcourt Ri
  CHPT/GREN S35 ....94 B2
Harcourt Rd FUL S10 ....125 F4
Harcourt Ter
  RHAM/THRY S65 ....9 K5
Hardcastle Dr
  HAN/WDH S13 ....143 E4
Hardcastle Gdns
  HAN/WDH S13 ....143 E3
Hardcastle Rd
  HAN/WDH S13 ....143 E4
Harden Cl DOD/DAR S75 ....18 C5
  STKB/PEN S36 ....44 D4
Hardhurst Rd DRON S18 ....179 F1
Hardie Cl MALT S66 ....111 F4
Hardie Pl RAW S62 ....85 F5
  STV/CWN S43 ....189 H1
Hardie St ECK/KIL S21 ....174 D1
Harding Av RAW S62 ....84 D3
Harding Cl RAW S62 ....84 D3
Harding St DARN/MH S9 ....127 H1
Hardwick Av STV/CWN S43 ..180 B3
Hardwick Cl
  AU/AST/KP S26 * 145 H3
  BSLY S70 ....48 A1
  DRON S18 ....171 F1
  HOR/CROF WF4 ....13 G1
  STV/CWN S43 ....185 G2
Hardwick Crs
  BSLYN/ROY S71 ....15 E5
  ECC S11 ....139 E3

Hardwicke Rd
  RHAM/THRY S65 ....9 H1
Hardwick Gv *DOD/DAR* S75....30 B4
Hardwick La
  AU/AST/KP S26 ....146 C2
Hardwick St *CHNE* S41 ....5 C1
  RHAM/THRY S65 ....107 F1
Hardwicks Yd *CHSW* S40 *........4 B5
Hardy Pl *ST/HB/BR* S6...........125 F2
Hardy Rd *WHHL* DN2 ....40 C4
Hardy St *RHAM* S60 ....8 C2
Harefield Rd *ECC* S11 ....139 F1
Harehill Crs *RCH* S42 ....194 D3
Harehill Rd *CHSW* S40...........192 B5
Harehills Rd *RHAM* S60 ....9 H6
Harewood Av *ARMTH* DN3 .....29 F3
  AWLS/ASK DN6 ....24 D2
  BSLY S70.............................30 D1
Harewood Ct
  NROS/TKH DN11 ....91 H3
Harewood Gv *MALT* S66........108 D3
Harewood Rd *WHHL* DN2 ....7 K3
Harewood Wy *ECC* S11 ....151 G3
Hargrave Pl
  RHAM/THRY S65 ....99 H4
Harland Rd *ECC* S11 ....139 G1
Harlech Cl *CHPT/GREN* S35....80 D5
Harlech Fold *FUL* S10 ....136 D1
Harlech Gn *FUL* S10 ....136 D1
Harlech Gv *FUL* S10...............136 D1
Harlech Md *FUL* S10 ....136 D1
Harlesthorpe Av
  STV/CWN S43.....................185 F2
Harlesthorpe La
  STV/CWN S43.....................185 E1
Harleston St *ATT* S4..............126 C1
Harley Rd *ECC* S11 ....138 B5
  RAW S62.............................81 H2
Harlington Ct *CONI* DN12......68 C4
Harlington Rd
  MEX/SWTN S64 ....53 H5
Harmer La *SHEF* S1 ....11 H4
Harmony Wy *RHAM* S60 ....129 G1
Harney Cl *DARN/MH* S9 ....128 A2
Harold Av *AWLS/ASK* DN6 .....25 G2
  BSLYN/ROY S71 ....19 F5
Harold Cft *KIMB* S61..............97 G2
Harold St *ST/HB/BR* S6.........125 F1
Harperhill Cl *CHSW* S40........192 B5
Harriet Cl *BSLY* S70 *.............32 A3
Harrington Ct
  BSLYN/ROY S71 ....21 E5
Harrington Rd
  SHEFP/MNR S2 ....140 A2
Harrington St *DON* DN1 ....6 D2
Harrison La *FUL* S10 ....136 D3
Harrison Rd *ST/HB/BR* S6.....113 H5
Harrison St *KIMB* S61 ....105 E4
Harris Rd *ARMTH* DN3 ....42 B4
  ST/HB/BR S6....................113 H2
Harrogate Rd *CONI* DN12......68 A5
Harrogate Rd
  AU/AST/KP S26 ....145 E4
Harrop Dr *MEX/SWTN* S64.....86 A2
Harrop La *FUL* S10 ....136 D4
Harrowden Rd
  DARN/MH S9 ....117 G2
  WHHL DN2 ....40 D4
Harrow Rd *ARMTH* DN3 ....43 E3
Harrow St *ECC* S11 ....10 C7
Harry Firth Cl *DARN/MH* S9..127 G2
Harry Rd *DOD/DAR* S75..........14 B5
Hartcliff Av *STKB/PEN* S36 ....44 C3
Hartfield Cl *CHNE* S41...........192 D5
Hartford Cl *SHEFS* S8.............84 D3
Hartford Rd *SHEFS* S8 ....153 E2
Hart Hl *RAW* S62 ....84 D3
Harthill Rd *CONI* DN12...........88 C2
  HAN/WDH S13 ....141 H3
Hart Hills *WMB/DAR* S73........62 D1
Hartington Av *ABRD* S7.........152 A2
Hartington Cl *KIMB* S61 ....105 E3
Hartington Ct
  STV/CWN S43.....................185 G2
Hartington Dr
  BSLYN/ROY S71 ....19 H3
Hartington Rd *ABRD* S7........152 A2
  DRON S18........................171 F1
  KIMB S61 ....105 E3
Hartington Vw
  STV/CWN S43.....................182 B3
Hartland Av *MOS* S20 ....157 G3
Hartland Ct *MOS* S20 *..........157 G3
Hartland Crs *ARMTH* DN3 .....29 F5
Hartland Dr *MOS* S20 ....157 G3
Hartland Wy *CHNE* S41........179 G5
Hartley Brook Av
  SHEFN S5.........................102 C3
Hartley Brook Rd
  SHEFN S5.........................102 C3
Hartley Cl *MEX/SWTN* S64.....86 B2
Hartley La *KIMB* S61 ....8 C2
Hartley St *MEX/SWTN* S64 .....66 D4
  SHEFP/MNR S2 ....140 A3
Hartopp Av
  SHEFP/MNR S2 ....140 C4
Hartopp Cl *SHEFP/MNR* S2 ...140 C4
Hartopp Dr
  SHEFP/MNR S2 ....140 C4
Hartopp Rd
  SHEFP/MNR S2 ....140 C4
Hartshead *SHEF* S1 ....11 G2

Hartshead Sq *SHEF* S1 *.........11 H2
Hartside Cl *CHSW* S40...........186 D3
Harvest Cl *ARMTH* DN3 ....29 G4
  BSLY S70.............................48 A1
  DONS/BSCR DN4 ....55 F5
  MALT S66 ....110 A4
Harvest La *OWL* S3................126 A1
Harvest Rd *MALT* S66 ....108 B4
Harvest Wy *RCH* S42 ....186 A4
Harvey Clough Ms
  SHEFS S8 ....153 E2
Harvey Clough Rd
  SHEFS S8 ....153 E2
Harvey Ct *BSVR* S44 ....196 C2
Harvey Rd *CHNE* S41............193 G2
  CHPT/GREN S35 ....94 A1
Harvey St *BSLY* S70 *.............7 D6
  STKB/PEN S36 ....77 F2
Harwell Rd *SHEFS* S8............139 H3
Harwich Rd
  SHEFP/MNR S2 ....141 E1
Harwood Cl
  SHEFP/MNR S2 ....139 H2
Harwood Dr *MOS* S20 ....156 D4
Harwood Gdns *MOS* S20......157 E4
Harwood St
  SHEFP/MNR S2 ....140 A2
Harwood Ter
  BSLYN/ROY S71 ....21 E5
Haslam Ct *BSVR* S44 ....196 C2
  CHNE S41 ....5 C1
Haslam Crs *SHEFS* S8 ....162 B2
Haslam Pl *MALT* S66.............111 F2
Haslam Rd *NROS/TKH* DN11...91 F2
Hasland Rd *CHNE* S41...........193 E3
  CHNE S41 ....193 E4
  CHSW S40 ....5 H7
Haslehurst Rd
  SHEFP/MNR S2 ....127 E5
Haslemere Ct *BTLY* DN5.........39 G4
Haslemere Gv *BTLY* DN5........39 G4
Hassop Cl *CHSW* S40............186 C3
  DRON S18........................171 G1
Hassop Rd *STV/CWN* S43.....182 B4
Hastilar Cl *SHEFP/MNR* S2 ...141 H2
Hastilar Rd *SHEFP/MNR* S2 ..141 G2
Hastilar Rd South
  HAN/WDH S13 ....142 A3
Hastings Cl *CHNE* S41...........186 D3
Hastings Mt *ABRD* S7...........152 A1
Hastings Rd *ABRD* S7 ....152 A1
Hatchell Dr *DONS/BSCR* DN4..74 C3
Hatchellwood Vw
  DONS/BSCR DN4 ....74 D3
Hatfield Cl *BSLYN/ROY* S71 ...14 C5
Hatfield Crs *DIN* S25.............134 A3
Hatfield Gdns
  BSLYN/ROY S71 ....12 B5
Hatfield House Ct
  SHEFN S5 * 102 D4
Hatfield House Cft
  SHEFN S5..........................102 D4
Hatfield House La
  SHEFN S5..........................102 D4
Hatfield La *ARMTH* DN3 ....29 H5
Hatherley Rd *DARN/MH* S9...117 F1
  MEX/SWTN S64 ....66 B3
  RHAM/THRY S65 ....9 H1
Hathern Cl *STV/CWN* S43.....188 D5
Hathersage Rd
  TOT/DORE S17..................150 B4
Hatton Cl *DRON* S18.............170 B3
Hatton Dr *CHSW* S40............186 B4
Hatton Rd *ST/HB/BR* S6........114 A5
Haugh Gn *RAW* S62 ....84 C3
Haugh La *ECC* S11 ....138 B5
Haugh Rd *RAW* S62 ....84 C3
Haughton Rd *SHEFS* S8........152 D3
Havelock St *BSLY* S70 * 2 D6
  FUL S10 ....10 B5
  WMB/DAR S73 ....35 E5
Havercroft Rd *RHAM* S60.....120 A1
Havercroft Ter *ECK/KIL* S21..167 H1
Haverdale Ri *DOD/DAR* S75....2 C2
Haverhill Gv *WMB/DAR* S73....50 C2
Havercroft La *BSLY* S70..........47 F1
Haverlands Rdg *BSLY* S70.......47 H1
Hawes Cl *MEX/SWTN* S64......67 G2
Hawfield Cl
  DONS/BSCR DN4 ....55 G4
Hawke Cl *RAW* S62 ....84 B3
Hawke Rd *WHHL* DN2 ....40 D5
Hawke St *DARN/MH* S9.........116 C2
Hawk Hill La *MALT* S66..........133 E4
Hawkins Av *CHPT/GREN* S35..93 G1
Hawkshead Av *DRON* S18.....170 B2
Hawkshead Crs *DIN* S25.......148 D2
Hawkshead Rd *ATT* S4..........116 B3
Hawksley Av *CHSW* S40...........4 F1
  ST/HB/BR S6....................114 A4
Hawksley Cl *ARMTH* DN3 ......42 D3
Hawksley Ct *ARMTH* DN3 ......42 D5
Hawksley Ms *ST/HB/BR* S6...114 A4
Hawksley Rd *ST/HB/BR* S6....114 A4
Hawksway *ECK/KIL* S21.........166 B5
Hawksworth Cl
  RHAM/THRY S65 ....107 H3
Hawksworth Rd
  RHAM/THRY S65 ....107 H2
  ST/HB/BR S6....................125 F1
Hawkwell Bank
  BSLYN/ROY S71 ....33 G2

Hawley St *DRON* S18.............172 C2
  RAW S62.............................98 B1
  SHEF S1 ....11 F2
Haworth Bank *RHAM* S60.....119 F3
Haworth Cl *BSLYN/ROY* S71 ...20 B4
Haworth Crs *RHAM* S60........119 F3
Hawshaw La *HOY* S74 ....61 G2
Hawthorn Av *ARMTH* DN3......42 D2
  MALT S66 ....110 B3
  MOS S20 ....156 D4
  STV/CWN S43...................185 E2
Hawthorn Cl *STV/CWN* S43...184 D2
  DRON S18........................163 E5
  RAW S62.............................98 C1
  STKB/PEN S36 ....76 B1
Hawthorne Cha
  MEX/SWTN S64 ....66 A5
Hawthorne Cl *ECK/KIL* S21...168 B3
  STV/CWN S43...................177 E5
Hawthorne Crs
  DOD/DAR S75....................30 A2
  MEX/SWTN S64 ....66 A5
Hawthorne Cft
  DEARNE S63 ....37 E5
Hawthorne Dr *DEARNE* S63...53 F3
Hawthorne Gv *BTLY* DN5........26 D5
Hawthorne Pl
  AU/AST/KP S26 ....145 G3
Hawthorne Rd *DEARNE* S63...65 G3
The Hawthornes *MOS* S20....157 F1
Hawthorne St *BSLY* S70...........2 F7
  CHSW S40 ....192 C3
  CUD/GR S72 ....17 E1
  ST/HB/BR S6....................124 D1
Hawthorne Wy *CUD/GR* S72...17 F1
Hawthorn Gv *CONI* DN12.......88 C3
Hawthorn Hl *STV/CWN* S43...175 F5
Hawthorn Rd
  CHPT/GREN S35 ....95 E4
  ECK/KIL S21.....................174 B1
  STKB/PEN S36 ....76 B1
Haxby Cl *HAN/WDH* S13.......142 C4
Haxby Pl *HAN/WDH* S13.......142 C4
Haxby St *HAN/WDH* S13.......142 C5
Haybrook Ct
  TOT/DORE S17..................161 E3
Haydn Rd *MALT* S66.............111 F4
Haydock Cl *MEX/SWTN* S64...67 F2
Haydon Gv *MALT* S66...........108 B3
Hayes Ct *MOS* S20 ....167 E2
Hayes Cft *BSLY* S70 ....3 C5
Hayes Dr *MOS* S20 ....166 D1
Hayfield Cl *DOD/DAR* S75 ......30 A3
  DRON S18........................170 B2
  RCH S42...........................195 F4
  STV/CWN S43...................188 D5
Hayfield Crs *HACK/IN* S12 ....155 F2
Hayfield Dr *HACK/IN* S12......155 F2
Hayfield La *EPW* DN9 ....118 B1
Hayfield Pl *HACK/IN* S12.......155 F2
Hayfield Vw *ECK/KIL* S21......155 F2
Hayford Wy *STV/CWN* S43....182 A5
Hay Green La *BSLY* S70 ....60 D1
Hayhurst Crs *MALT* S66........111 E4
Hayland St *DARN/MH* S9......116 D2
Haylock Cl *DOD/DAR* S75 ......18 A4
Haymarket *SHEF* S1 ....11 H2
Haythorne Wy *MEX/SWTN* S64..86
Haywood Av
  STKB/PEN S36 ....77 F2
Haywood Cl
  RHAM/THRY S65 ....107 E2
Haywood La *STKB/PEN* S36 ...77 F2
Hazel Av *ECK/KIL* S21...........168 A3
Hazelbadge Crs
  HACK/IN S12 ....155 G2
Hazel Cl *DRON* S18...............171 G3
Hazel Ct *DRON* S18...............171 F3
  RHAM/THRY S65 ....109 E1
Hazel Dr *CHSW* S40...............191 H4
  RCH S42...........................195 H4
Hazel Gv *ARMTH* DN3 ....43 E5
  CHPT/GREN S35 ....94 A2
  CONI DN12 ....88 D2
  MALT S66 ....108 C4
  NROS/TKH DN11 ....91 H3
  STV/CWN S43...................183 E2
Hazel Rd *ECK/KIL* S21...........174 C1
  MALT S66 ....110 B3
Hazelshaw *DOD/DAR* S75 ......30 C4
Hazelwood *BSLYN/ROY* S71...20 A2
Hazelwood Cl *DRON* S18.......170 A2
Hazelwood Dr
  MEX/SWTN S64 ....86 B3
Hazelbarrow Cl *SHEFS* S8.....163 F1
Hazelbarrow Ct *SHEFS* S8.....163 F1
Hazelbarrow Crs *SHEFS* S8....163 F1
Hazelbarrow Dr *SHEFS* S8.....163 G1
Hazelbarrow Gv *SHEFS* S8.....163 G1
Hazelbarrow Rd *SHEFS* S8.....163 G1
Hazledene Cl *CUD/GR* S72.....17 F5
Hazledene Rd *CHNE* S41.......187 G4
Hazlehurst Cl
  RHAM/THRY S65 ....99 F5
Hazlehurst La *CHNE* S41........187 G4
  SHEFS S8 ....162 A5
Hazlewood Dr
  STV/CWN S43...................177 F5
Headford Gdns *OWL* S3 ....10 D5
Headford Gv *OWL* S3.............10 D5

Headford Ms *OWL* S3 ....10 D6
Headford St *OWL* S3...............10 D5
Headingley Cl *ARMTH* DN3....29 F2
Headingley Wy *CONI* DN12....70 C5
Headland Cl *STV/CWN* S43...188 C2
Headland Dr *FUL* S10............124 C4
Headland Rd *FUL* S10...........124 C4
Headlands Rd *HOY* S74..........61 H2
Heads La *STKB/PEN* S36........76 C5
Heath Av *ECK/KIL* S21...........168 B3
Heath Bank Rd *WHHL* DN2....41 G3
Heathcote Dr *CHNE* S41........193 G4
Heathcote St *ATT* S4.............115 H3
Heath Ct *DONS/BSCR* DN4....70 D1
Heatherbank Rd
  DONS/BSCR DN4 ....74 A1
Heather Cl *RHAM* S60...........106 A5
Heather Ct *WHHL* DN2 *.........41 G3
Heatherdale Rd *MALT* S66....111 F3
Heather Gdns *CHNE* S41 *.....193 G5
Heather Knowle
  DOD/DAR S75....................30 C3
Heather Lea Av
  TOT/DORE S17..................160 C1
Heather Lea Pl
  TOT/DORE S17..................160 C1
Heather Rd *SHEFN* S5...........116 A1
Heather Vale *CHNE* S41........193 G5
Heather Vale Rd *CHNE* S41...193 G5
Heather Wy *RCH* S42............190 B5
Heatherwood Cl *WHHL* DN2...41 G4
Heathfield Cl *ARMTH* DN3 .....29 G1
  DRON S18........................170 D2
  RCH S42...........................195 F4
Heathfield Rd *HACK/IN* S12..155 F1
Heathfields *BSLY* S70..............32 B2
Heath Gv *DEARNE* S63............52 D4
Heath Rd *ST/HB/BR* S6.........101 F5
  STKB/PEN S36 ....77 F3
Heaton Cl *DRON* S18.............170 B2
Heatons Bank *RAW* S62..........85 G5
Heaton St *CHSW* S40............191 G2
Heavens Wk
  DONS/BSCR DN4 ....56 B4
Heavygate Av *FUL* S10..........125 E1
Heavygate Rd *FUL* S10..........125 E1
Hedgehill Rd *STKB/PEN* S36...44 B3
Hedge Hill Rd
  STKB/PEN S36 ....44 A3
Hedley Dr *STV/CWN* S43......188 B1
Heeley Bank Rd
  SHEFP/MNR S2 ....140 B3
Heeley Gn *SHEFP/MNR* S2 ...140 B4
Heelis St *BSLY* S70 ....3 G6
Heighton Vw
  AU/AST/KP S26 ....145 F1
Helena Cl *BSLY* S70 ....2 B2
Helena St *MEX/SWTN* S64......67 E3
Helensburgh Cl
  DONS/BSCR DN4 ....2 B2
Hellaby Hall Rd *MALT* S66....109 H5
Hellaby La *MALT* S66............109 H4
Hellaby Vw *MALT* S66...........108 D2
Helliwell La *STKB/PEN* S36.....77 G4
Helmsley Av *MOS* S20...........166 D1
Helmsley Cl
  AU/AST/KP S26 ....145 E4
  CHNE S41 ....186 C2
Helmton Dr *SHEFS* S8 ....153 E2
Helmton Rd *SHEFS* S8 ....153 D3
Helston Cl *CHNE* S41............192 D4
Helston Crs *BSLYN/ROY* S71...20 B4
Helston Ri *ABRD* S7..............152 A1
Hemingfield Rd
  WMB/DAR S73 ....49 H4
Hemmingway Cl
  RHAM S60........................130 A4
Hemper Gv *SHEFS* S8............162 B1
Hemper La *SHEFS* S8.............162 B2
Hemp Pits Rd *BTLY* DN5.........40 B1
Hemsworth Rd *SHEFS* S8 .....153 F3
Henderson Gln
  BSLYN/ROY S71 ....15 E1
Hendon St *HAN/WDH* S13....142 D1
Hengist Rd *BTLY* DN5.............55 E3
Henley Av *SHEFS* S8 ....153 F5
Henley Grove Rd *KIMB* S61.....8 A2
Henley Ri *KIMB* S61..............105 E1
  KIMB S61 ....105 E1
Henley Rd *WHHL* DN2...........41 G5
Henley Wy *KIMB* S61............105 E2
Hennings Cl
  DONS/BSCR DN4 ....73 F1
Henry Cl *CUD/GR* S72............16 D1
Henry Ct *RAW* S62 ....98 B3
Henry La *NROS/TKH* DN11.....90 D2
Henry Pl *MEX/SWTN* S64.......67 G4
Henry Rd *DEARNE* S63............65 F2
Henry St *BSLY* S70 ....32 A5
  CHNE S41 ....187 H1
  CHPT/GREN S35 ....88 A3
  ECK/KIL S21.....................166 D5
  OWL S3 ....125 H2
  RHAM/THRY S65 ....9 F5
  SHEFN S5...........................50 D1
Henshall St *BSLY* S70 ....3 J7
Heppenstall La
  DARN/MH S9 ....127 F1
Heptinstall St *BSLY* S70..........32 B5
Hepworth Dr
  AU/AST/KP S26 ....145 F3

Hepworth Rd
  DONS/BSCR DN4 ....71 F1
Herald Rd *WHHL* DN2 ....42 A1
Herbert Rd *ABRD* S7.............139 G4
  BTLY DN5...........................39 G5
Herbert St *KIMB* S61............104 C2
  MEX/SWTN S64 ....67 F3
Herdings Ct *SHEFS* S12........154 C2
Herdings La *HACK/IN* S12.....154 C2
Herdings Vw *HACK/IN* S12....154 C2
Hereford Dr *STV/CWN* S43...188 D1
Hereford Rd *WHHL* DN2........41 F3
Hereford St *SHEF* S1..............11 F7
Hereward Ct *CONI* DN12........89 G1
Hereward Rd *SHEFN* S5.........102 B5
Hereward's Rd *SHEFS* S8......153 H4
Heritage Dr *STV/CWN* S43....184 D1
Hermitage St
  SHEFP/MNR S2 ....60 A2
Hermit Hl *DOD/DAR* S75........60 A2
Hermit La *DOD/DAR* S75........18 B5
Heron Ct *CONI* DN12.............89 G1
  WHHL DN2 ....41 E3
Heron Dr *DEARNE* S63............63 H1
Heron Hl *AU/AST/KP* S26.....145 G4
Heron Mt *SHEFP/MNR* S2....127 E5
Herons Wy *BSLY* S70 ....47 H5
  DONS/BSCR DN4 ....72 B1
Herrick Gdns
  DONS/BSCR DN4 ....72 A2
Herries Av *SHEFN* S5............115 E2
Herries Dr *SHEFN* S5 ....115 E2
Herries Pl *SHEFN* S5 ....115 E2
Herries Rd *ST/HB/BR* S6.......114 A2
Herringthorpe Av
  RHAM S60........................106 D5
Herringthorpe Cl
  RHAM/THRY S65 ....107 E5
Herringthorpe Gv
  RHAM/THRY S65 ....107 E5
Herringthorpe La
  RHAM/THRY S65 ....107 E4
Herringthorpe Valley Rd
  RHAM S60........................120 A1
  RHAM/THRY S65 ....107 E4
Herriot Dr *CHSW* S40............192 D3
Herschell Rd *ABRD* S7..........139 H3
Hesketh Dr *ARMTH* DN3........29 C3
Hesley Bar *KIMB* S61..............94 D2
Hesley Ct *MEX/SWTN* S64......86 A2
Hesley Gra *KIMB* S61..............95 H4
Hesley Gv *CHPT/GREN* S35 ....94 C2
Hesley La *KIMB* S61 ....95 H4
Hesley Ms *KIMB* S61...............96 A4
Hesley Rd *NROS/TKH* DN11 ...91 F2
  SHEFN S5.........................102 D2
Hesley Ter *SHEFN* S5............102 D3
Heslow Gv *KIMB* S61...............95 E1
Hessey St *HAN/WDH* S13.....142 D4
Hessle Rd *ST/HB/BR* S6........113 H2
Hewers Holt *STV/CWN* S43...177 F5
Hewitt St *MEX/SWTN* S64......67 G3
Hexthorpe Rd
  DONS/BSCR DN4 ....6 A5
Heyhouse Dr
  CHPT/GREN S35 ....81 E4
Heyhouse Wy
  CHPT/GREN S35 ....80 D4
Heysham Gn
  BSLYN/ROY S71 ....20 D2
Heywood St *STV/CWN* S43...188 C1
Heywood Vw
  STV/CWN S43...................177 G5
Hibberd Pl *ST/HB/BR* S6.......113 G4
Hibberd Rd *ST/HB/BR* S6.....113 G4
Hibbert Ter *BSLY* S70 * 31 H3
Hickingwood La
  STV/CWN S43...................185 F1
Hickinwood Crs
  STV/CWN S43...................185 F1
Hickleton Ct *DEARNE* S63......53 F1
Hickleton St *CONI* DN12........68 B5
Hickmott Rd *ECC* S11 *.........139 F2
Hickson Dr *BSLYN/ROY* S71...21 E3
Hicks St *OWL* S3...................126 A1
Hides St *DARN/MH* S9..........116 D4
High Alder Rd
  DONS/BSCR DN4 ....57 G5
Higham Common Rd
  DOD/DAR S75....................18 A5
Higham La *DOD/DAR* S75.......30 A1
High Ash Dr *DIN* S25.............148 B5
High Balk *DOD/DAR* S75........19 F3
High Bank
  RHAM/THRY S65 *..............99 G4
Highbury Av
  DONS/BSCR DN4 ....58 A5
Highbury Crs
  DONS/BSCR DN4 ....58 A5
Highbury Rd *CHNE* S41........187 F4
Highcliffe Ct
  MEX/SWTN S64 ....66 C5
Highcliffe Dr *ECC* S11 ....138 B3
  MEX/SWTN S64 ....66 C5
Highcliffe Pl *ECC* S11 ....138 B4
Highcliffe Rd *ECC* S11 ....138 B3
High Cft *HOY* S74 ....62 A3
High Croft Dr
  BSLYN/ROY S71 ....14 D5
Higher Albert St *CHNE* S41......5 F1
Highfield Av *BSLY* S70 ....31 H4
  BSLYN/ROY S71 ....20 A1

CHNE S41 ....187 E3
DEARNE S63 ....37 F5
Highfield Cottages
 MEX/SWTN S64 * 66 D4
Highfield Ct *WMB/DAR S73*....50 A2
Highfield Gv *DEARNE S63*....64 A1
Highfield La *CHNE S41*.........187 E3
 HAN/WDH S13 ....129 F5
Highfield Pk *MALT S66*........111 F4
Highfield Pl
 SHEFP/MNR S2..........140 A2
Highfield Range
 WMB/DAR S73..........35 E3
Highfield Ri *ST/HB/BR S6*....123 F2
Highfield Rd *BSVR S44*........196 D3
 CHNE S41.........187 F4
 CONI DN12..........89 F2
 DON DN1..........6 E2
 KIMB S61..........97 G4
 MEX/SWTN S64 ....65 H5
 WMB/DAR S73 ....35 E4
Highfields Crs *DRON S18*....171 E3
High Field Spring
 HAN/WDH S13 ....129 E4
Highfields Rd *DRON S18*....171 E5
Highfield Ter *CHNE S41* * 187 F4
Highfield Vw *RHAM S60*......129 G1
Highfield View Rd
 CHNE S41.........187 F4
Highfield Vls
 CHNE S41.........99 G3
High Fisher Ga *DON DN1*....6 D2
Highgate *DARN/MH S9*......117 C2
 WMB/DAR S73..........51 F3
Highgate Cl
 NROS/TKH DN11..........91 C4
Highgate Ct *DEARNE S63*....37 E5
Highgate Dr *DRON S18*....171 C4
Highgate La *DEARNE S63*....53 E1
 DRON S18..........171 C4
High Gate Wy *CUD/GR S72*....17 E2
Highgreave *SHEFN S5*........102 C3
High Greave Av *SHEFN S5*....102 B2
High Greave Ct *SHEFN S5*....102 C2
High Greave Pl
 RHAM S60..........107 E2
High Greave Rd
 RHAM/THRY S65 ....107 E2
Highgrove Cl *CHNE S41*......187 G1
Highgrove Ct
 DONS/BSCR DN4..........74 C2
High Hazel Cl *RHAM S60*....130 A3
High Hazel Crs *RHAM S60*....129 C1
High Hazel Rd *RHAM S60*....130 A3
High Hazels Cl
 DARN/MH S9 * 128 B3
High Hazels Md
 WMB/DAR S73..........128 B3
High Hazels Rd
 STV/CWN S43..........184 A1
High House Farm Ct
 AU/AST/KP S26..........159 F3
High House Ter
 ST/HB/BR S6..........123 H1
Highland Rd *STV/CWN S43*....180 B1
High La *HACK/IN S12*........155 C4
 MALT S66..........132 C4
High Lee La *STKB/PEN S36*....45 F1
High Leys Rd *STV/CWN S43*..185 E4
Highlow Cl *CHSW S40*........4 B4
Highlow Vw *RHAM S60*......118 C3
High Matlock Av
 ST/HB/BR S6..........123 H1
High Matlock Rd
 ST/HB/BR S6..........112 D5
Highmill Av *MEX/SWTN S64*....65 G5
Highmoor Av
 AU/AST/KP S26..........159 G5
Highnam Crescent Rd
 FUL S10..........125 E4
High Nook Rd *DIN S25*........135 C5
High Pavement Rw
 SHEFP/MNR S2..........126 C3
High Rdg *BSLY S70*..........31 H5
Highridge Cl *CONI DN12*......89 F2
High Rd *DONS/BSCR DN4*....70 C2
High Royd Av *CUD/GR S72*....21 H1
High Royd La *HOY S74*........48 D5
 STKB/PEN S36..........45 G1
Highroyds *BSLY S70*..........31 H5
Highstone Av *BSLY S70*......31 G3
Highstone Crs *BSLY S70*......31 G3
Highstone La *BSLY S70*......31 H4
Highstone Rd *BSLY S70*......31 G3
Highstone V *BSLY S70*........31 G3
High Storrs Cl *ECC S11*......138 B4
High Storrs Crs *ECC S11*......138 C3
High Storrs Dr *ECC S11*......138 B4
High Storrs Ri *ECC S11*......138 C3
High Storrs Rd *ECC S11*......138 B4
High St *AU/AST/KP S26*......145 G2
 BSLY S70..........2 E4
 BSLY/ROY S71..........15 F1
 BSLYN/ROY S71..........20 D2
 BSVR S44..........196 D3
 BTLY DN5..........39 H2
 CHNE S41..........179 G4
 CHPT/GREN S35..........102 B1
 CHSW S40..........5 F4
 CONI DN12..........89 E1
 CUD/GR S72..........17 E2
 DEARNE S63..........65 F2

DIN S25 ....148 B4
DOD/DAR S75 ....30 B3
DON DN1..........6 C3
DRON S18..........170 D1
DRON S18..........172 C2
ECK/KIL S21..........166 C5
HOY S74..........62 A2
KIMB S61..........104 C2
MALT S66..........111 E3
MEX/SWTN S64 ....67 E4
MOS S20..........166 C1
RAW S62..........98 B2
RHAM S60..........9 F4
RHAM S60..........119 H5
SHEF S1..........11 H5
STKB/PEN S36..........46 D4
STV/CWN S43..........177 E4
STV/CWN S43..........180 B3
STV/CWN S43..........182 A4
STV/CWN S43..........184 D3
STV/CWN S43..........188 D1
TOT/DORE S17..........160 D1
WMB/DAR S73..........35 E3
High Street La
 SHEFP/MNR S2..........11 K3
High Street Ms *MOS S20*....166 C1
Highthorn Rd
 MEX/SWTN S64 ....86 B2
Highthorn Vls
 MEX/SWTN S64 ....86 C2
Highton St *ST/HB/BR S6*....125 E1
High Trees *RHAM S60* * 119 H1
 TOT/DORE S17..........160 D1
High Vw *BSLYN/ROY S71*....15 F1
 SHEFN S5..........115 E4
High View Cl *CHNE S41*......193 F2
 WMB/DAR S73..........35 F3
Highwood Pl *ECK/KIL S21*....166 C5
Highwoods Crs
 MEX/SWTN S64 ....66 C3
Highwoods Rd
 MEX/SWTN S64 ....66 C3
High Wood Wy
 STV/CWN S43..........184 C1
High Wray Cl *ECC S11*........151 H1
Hilary Wy *AU/AST/KP S26*....145 F3
Hild Av *CUD/GR S72*..........22 B3
Hillberry Ri *CHSW S40*......195 F1
Hill Cl *RHAM/THRY S65*....107 F5
 ST/HB/BR S6..........123 C1
Hillcote Cl *FUL S10*..........137 H1
Hillcote Dr *FUL S10*..........137 H1
Hillcote Ms *FUL S10*..........137 H1
Hillcote Ri *FUL S10*..........137 H1
Hillcrest *DEARNE S63*........37 E3
Hill Crest *HOY S74*..........61 C3
 RHAM/THRY S65 * 99 G4
Hillcrest Dr *DIN S25*........148 B4
Hillcrest Gv *STV/CWN S43*....182 B3
Hillcrest Ri *STKB/PEN S36*....77 H3
Hill Crest Rd
 CHPT/GREN S35..........93 H1
 RHAM/THRY S65..........106 D2
Hillcrest Rd *CHNE S41*......193 F5
 STKB/PEN S36..........77 H3
 WHHL DN2..........41 E4
Hillcrest Wy *MALT S66*......108 B1
Hill End Rd *DOD/DAR S75*....14 A5
Hill Farm Cl *DEARNE S63*....36 D3
Hillfoot Ct *TOT/DORE S17*....160 D4
Hillfoot Rd *TOT/DORE S17*....160 C3
Hill Fold *STV/CWN S43*......181 F2
Hillhouses La *ECC S11*......195 E4
Hillman Dr *STV/CWN S43*....189 C3
Hill Park Gv *DOD/DAR S75*....30 B2
Hillsborough Barracks
 ST/HB/BR S6 * 114 B5
Hillsborough Pl
 ST/HB/BR S6..........114 A4
Hillsborough Rd
 DONS/BSCR DN4..........58 A5
 ST/HB/BR S6..........114 A4
Hills Cl *DIN DN5*..........55 E3
 MEX/SWTN S64 ....66 D3
Hillside *BSLYN/ROY S71*......33 G2
 DIN S25..........148 B2
 MOS S20..........166 C1
Hill Side *RHAM S60*..........119 H3
Hillside Av *DRON S18*......171 E3
 SHEFN S5..........102 B3
Hillside Ct *BTLY DN5*........54 B5
 KIMB S61..........97 H5
Hillside Dr *CHSW S40*........191 H5
 HOY S74..........62 C3
 STV/CWN S43..........183 G3
Hillside Gv *CUD/GR S72*....17 F4
Hillside Rd *WHHL DN2*........41 C3
Hill St *BSLYN/ROY S71*........33 G2
 HOY S74..........62 C3
 SHEFP/MNR S2..........139 H1
 WMB/DAR S73..........35 E5
Hill Top *RHAM S60*..........196 D2
Hilltop *CUD/GR S72*..........17 H1
Hill Top Av *BSLYN/ROY S71*....14 C3
Hill Top Cl *HOR/CROF WF4*....12 B3
 KIMB S61..........104 B3
Hilltop Cl *MALT S66*..........110 B2
Hill Top Cm *BSLY S70*......118 A3
Hill Top Crs *MOS S20*......156 D4
 WHHL DN2..........41 G3
Hilltop Gdns *CONI DN12*......88 B1
Hilltop Gn *SHEFN S5*........114 D1

Hill Top La *CHPT/GREN S35*..100 D1
 DOD/DAR S75 ....18 D4
 KIMB S61..........104 B3
 RHAM/THRY S65..........107 H2
Hill Top Rd *CHPT/GREN S35*..101 F2
Hill Top Rd *CHPT/GREN S35*..101 F1
 CONI DN12..........88 B2
 ST/HB/BR S6..........122 A1
 BSLY S70..........47 H5
Hilltop Rd *CHNE S41*......179 C4
 DRON S18..........171 E3
 RCH S42..........194 D5
Hilltop Wy *DRON S18*......171 E4
Hill Turrets Cl *ECC S11*....151 F1
Hill Vw East *KIMB S61*......104 B1
Hill View Rd *KIMB S61*......104 B1
 STV/CWN S43..........188 C1
Hilton Dr *CHPT/GREN S35*..102 B1
Hilton St *DOD/DAR S75*......2 C3
Hindburn Cl
 DONS/BSCR DN4..........73 C1
Hinde House Crs *ATT S4*....116 A2
Hinde House Cft *ATT S4*....116 A2
Hinde House La *ATT S4*....115 H3
Hinde St *ATT S4*..........116 A3
Hindewood Cl *ATT S4*......116 A2
Hindle St *BSLY S70*..........2 D5
Hind Rd *RHAM S60*..........120 A2
Hipley Cl *CHSW S40*........186 B4
Hipper St *CHSW S40*..........5 G5
Hipper St South *CHSW S40*....5 G5
Hipper St West *CHSW S40*....4 C5
Hirst Common La
 SHEFN S5..........100 C3
Hirst Dr *RHAM/THRY S65*....107 F2
Hirst Ga *MEX/SWTN S64*....67 C3
Hobart St *ECC S11*..........139 H2
Hobson Pl *ST/HB/BR S6*....114 C5
Hobson Pl *ST/HB/BR S6*....114 C5
Hockley La *RAW S62*........195 C5
Hodder Ct *CHPT/GREN S35*..80 D5
Hodgkinson Av
 STKB/PEN S36..........44 D3
Hodgson St *OWL S3*..........10 E6
Hodroyd Cl *CUD/GR S72*....17 F3
Hodroyd Cottages
 CUD/GR S72..........17 H2
Hodroyd La *CUD/GR S72*....17 F3
Hogarth Ri *DRON S18*......170 D2
Holbeach Dr *CHSW S40*....192 A4
Holbeck Rd *BSVR S44*......197 F2
Holbeck Cl *CHNE S41*........5 H2
Holbein Cl *DRON S18*......170 D3
Holberry Cl *FUL S10*..........10 C5
Holberry Gdns *FUL S10*......10 B5
Holbourne Gv
 CHPT/GREN S35..........80 B2
Holbrook Av *MOS S20*......157 F5
Holbrook Cl *CHSW S40*....191 G4
 MOS S20..........157 F5
Holbrook Dr
 HAN/WDH S13..........141 H4
Holbrook Gn *MOS S20*......157 F5
Holbrook Pl *STV/CWN S43*..189 C2
Holbrook Ri *MOS S20*......157 F4
Holbrook Rd
 HAN/WDH S13..........141 H3
Holburn Av *DRON S18*......171 H4
Holden Ct *BSLY S70*..........2 E5
Holderness Dr
 AU/AST/KP S26..........145 F2
Holdings Rd
 SHEFP/MNR S2..........140 D1
Hole House La
 STKB/PEN S36..........76 D2
Holgate *WMB/DAR S73*......33 H5
Holgate Crs *SHEFN S5*......101 H3
Holgate Dr *SHEFN S5*......102 A3
Holgate Mt *BSLY S70*........31 H4
Holgate Rd *SHEFN S5*......102 A3
Holiwell Cl *MALT S66*......111 F2
Holkham Ri *ECC S11*........151 H3
Holland Cl *DEARNE S63*......85 F4
Holland Pl
 SHEFP/MNR S2 * 140 A2
Holland Rd *CHNE S41*......179 F4
 CHPT/GREN S35..........80 B4
 SHEFP/MNR S2..........140 A2
Holland St *SHEF S1*..........10 E5
Hollies Cl *DRON S18*......171 G3
Hollinberry La
 CHPT/GREN S35..........79 H2
Hollin Busk La
 STKB/PEN S36..........77 E4
Hollin Busk Rd
 STKB/PEN S36..........77 E5
Hollin Cl *CHNE S41*..........186 C1
 NROS/TKH DN11..........91 H1
Hollin Cft *DOD/DAR S75*......30 C2
Hollin Cft *STKB/PEN S36* * 77 C2
Holling Hill La *MALT S66*....107 H5
Hollingswood Wy
 MALT S66..........108 C2
Hollingwood Crs
 STV/CWN S43..........181 E5
Holling's La *RHAM S60*......108 C1
 RHAM/THRY S65..........99 H4
Hollin Hill Rd *STV/CWN S43*..185 C3
Hollin Moor La *MALT S66*....108 A5
Hollins Cl *ST/HB/BR S6*....124 B2

Hollins Dr *ST/HB/BR S6*....124 B2
Hollinsend Av *HACK/IN S12*..142 A5
Hollinsend Pl *HACK/IN S12*..142 A5
Hollinsend Rd *HACK/IN S12*..154 C2
Hollins La *CHNE S41*........124 C1
Hollins Spring Av *DRON S18*..171 E3
Hollins Spring Rd
 DRON S18..........171 E3
The Hollins *DOD/DAR S75*....30 C4
Hollins Wood Gv
 CUD/GR S72..........22 A3
Holly Av *BTLY DN5*..........39 C3
Hollybank *CHSW S40*........4 C2
Hollybank Crs *HACK/IN S12*..142 A4
Hollybank Dr *HACK/IN S12*..142 A4
Hollybank Rd *HACK/IN S12*..142 A5
Hollybank Wy *HACK/IN S12*..142 A4
Holly Bush Dr *BSVR S44*....37 F2
Hollybush St *RAW S62*......98 B3
Holly Cl *CHPT/GREN S35*....93 H2
 ECK/KIL S21..........167 H3
Holly Crs *MALT S66*........108 C3
Holly Dene *ARMTH DN3*....42 C2
Holly Dr *BTLY DN5*..........26 D5
Holly Farm *CUD/GR S72*....17 E1
Holly Gdns *HACK/IN S12*....142 A4
Hollygate *BSLY S70*..........32 B5
Holly Gv *DEARNE S63*........37 E5
 DEARNE S63..........65 F4
 NROS/TKH DN11..........91 C2
Holly La *SHEF S1* * 1 F3
Holly Mt *MALT S66*..........108 C5
Holly St *DON DN1*..........56 A4
 SHEF S1..........11 F3
Holly Ter *AU/AST/KP S26*....144 D2
Holme Cl *CHPT/GREN S35*..101 F2
 ST/HB/BR S6..........113 H5
Holme Oak Wy
 ST/HB/BR S6..........113 H5
Holme Park Av *CHNE S41*....186 C5
Holme Rd *CHNE S41*......187 C3
Holmes Carr Crs
 NROS/TKH DN11..........90 D2
Holmes Carr Rd
 DONS/BSCR DN4..........73 H2
 NROS/TKH DN11..........90 D1
Holmes Ct *KIMB S61*........8 A5
Holmes La *RHAM S60*......130 A3
Holmesdale Cl *DRON S18*..163 G5
Holmesdale Rd *DRON S18*..163 F5
Holmesfield *KIMB S61* * 104 C2
 KIMB S61..........8 A5
Holmes Market *DON DN1*....6 E1
Holmes Rd *MALT S66*......108 C5
The Holmes *DON DN1*......6 E1
Holme Wood Cl
 ARMTH DN3 * 29 G4
Holme Wood Gdns
 DONS/BSCR DN4..........74 A1
Holme Wood La
 ARMTH DN3..........43 F4
Holm Flatt St *RAW S62*....98 A3
Holmhirst Cl *SHEFS S8*....152 C3
Holmhirst Dr *SHEFS S8*....152 C2
Holmhirst Rd *SHEFS S8*....152 C2
Holmhirst Wy *SHEFS S8*....152 C3
Holmley Bank *DRON S18*..163 E5
Holmley La *DRON S18*......163 E5
Holmoak Cl *MEX/SWTN S64*..86 B2
Holmshaw Cl *ARMTH DN3*....29 G4
Holmshaw Dr
 HAN/WDH S13..........142 C2
Holmshaw Gv
 HAN/WDH S13..........142 C2
Holt House Gv *ABRD S7*....152 B1
Holtwood Rd *ATT S4*......115 F3
Holwick Ct *BSLY S70*......32 E4
Holy Cl *CHNE S41*..........179 G3
Holymoor Rd *RCH S42*......190 B5
Holyoake Av
 HAN/WDH S13..........142 C1

Holyrood Av *FUL S10*........136 D1
Holyrood Ri *MALT S66*......108 D3
Holyrood Rd *WHHL DN2*....7 K3
Holyrood Vw *FUL S10*......136 D1
Holywell Hts *ATT S4*......116 C2
Holywell La *CONI DN12*......89 E2
Holywell Pl
 RHAM/THRY S65 * 9 G3
Holywell Rd *ATT S4*........116 B3
 MEX/SWTN S64 ....86 B2
Holywell St *CHNE S41*......5 G3
Hnmecroft Rd *BSVR S44*....37 F5
Homefield Crs *BTLY DN5*....39 E2
Homeport Ms *CHNE S41*....5 G1
Homestead Cl *SHEFS S5*....102 D4
Homestead Dr *RAW S62*....85 F4
 RHAM S60..........118 B3
Homestead Rd *SHEFN S5*....102 C5
The Homestead *BTLY DN5*....39 H1
Honeysuckle Cl
 DONS/BSCR DN4..........57 G5
 WMB/DAR S73..........51 E1
Honeysuckle Rd
 SHEFS S5 * 116 B1
Honeywell Cl
 BSLYN/ROY S71..........3 G1
Honeywell Gv
 BSLYN/ROY S71..........19 H3
Honeywell La *DOD/DAR S75*..19 G4
Honeywell Pl
 BSLYN/ROY S71..........19 H4
Honeywell St
 BSLYN/ROY S71..........19 H4
Honister Cl *DEARNE S63*......64 A1
Hoober Av *ECC S11*........138 C5
Hoober Ct *RAW S62*........84 B3
Hoober Fld *DEARNE S63*....84 B1
Hoober Hall La *RAW S62*....83 H5
Hoober La *RAW S62*........84 A2
Hoober Rd *ECC S11*........138 C5
Hoober St *DEARNE S63*......64 B2
Hoober Vw *RAW S62*........84 D3
 WMB/DAR S73..........50 D4
Hood Green Rd
 DOD/DAR S75..........46 A3
Hoodhill Rd *RAW S62*......81 H2
Hoole La *FUL S10*..........125 E5
Hoole St *CHNE S41*........193 F4
 ST/HB/BR S6..........125 E1
Hooton La *MALT S66*......86 D4
Hooton Rd *MEX/SWTN S64*....86 D4
Hope Av *DEARNE S63*........53 F1
Hopedale Rd *HACK/IN S12*..155 F1
Hopefield Av *HACK/IN S12*..155 F1
Hope Rd *CHPT/GREN S35*..100 A3
Hope St *BSLYN/ROY S71*......21 F1
 CHSW S40..........4 B4
 DOD/DAR S75..........2 C2
 DOD/DAR S75..........14 A4
 MEX/SWTN S64..........67 E4
 RHAM S60..........8 D2
 STKB/PEN S36..........77 E2
 WMB/DAR S73..........50 C3
Hope Street Extension
 RHAM S60..........8 D2
Hopewell St *BSLY S70*........32 D2
Hopwood La *ST/HB/BR S6*....123 E3
Hopwood St *BSLY S70*........2 E2
Horace St *RHAM S60*........9 H6
Horbiry End
 AU/AST/KP S26..........147 E5
Horbury La *CHPT/GREN S35*..93 G2
Horbury Rd *CUD/GR S72*....16 D4
Hornbeam Cl
 CHPT/GREN S35..........93 H2
 STV/CWN S43..........181 E4
Hornbeam Rd *MALT S66*....108 B5
Hornby St *BSLY S70*..........31 H3
Horndean Rd *SHEFN S5*......115 H3
Horner Cl *STKB/PEN S36*....76 D2
Horner Rd *ABRD S7*..........139 H3
Hornes La *DOD/DAR S75*....14 A3
Horninglow Cl
 DONS/BSCR DN4..........74 C2
 SHEFN S5..........115 G1
Horninglow Rd *SHEFN S5*..115 G1
Hornsby Rd *ARMTH DN3*....43 E5
Hornscroft Rd *BSVR S44*....196 D3
Hornthorpe Rd
 ECK/KIL S21..........174 B1
Hornthwaite Hill Rd
 STKB/PEN S36..........44 A3
Horse Car Vw
 BSLYN/ROY S71..........33 G2
Horse Chestnut Cl *CHSW S40*....5 F7
Horsefair Cl *MEX/SWTN S64*....66 C1
Horsehead La *BSVR S44*....197 F2
Horsehills La *ARMTH DN3*....42 C5
Horsemoor Rd *DEARNE S63*..36 D2
Horseshoe Cl
 AU/AST/KP S26..........159 C2
Horse Shoe Ct
 DONS/BSCR DN4..........71 F1
Horseshoe Gdns
 AU/AST/KP S26..........159 F2
Horsewood Cl *BSLY S70*....30 D2
Horsewood Rd
 HAN/WDH S13..........143 H2
 RCH S42..........191 F4
Horsley Cl *CHSW S40*......186 A4
Horton Cl *MOS S20*..........167 E1
Horton Dr *MOS S20*..........167 E1

Horton Vw ARMTH DN3.........29 E2
Houfton Crs BSVR S44.........196 C1
Houfton Rd BSVR S44.........196 C1
Hough Cl CHSW S40.........5 C7
Hough La WMB/DAR S73.........49 H4
Houghton Rd DEARNE S63.........36 C2
  DIN S25.........147 H2
Houldsworth Crs BSVR S44.........196 C1
Houldsworth Dr CHNE S41.........193 C2
Hound Hill La BSLY S70.........31 F5
  DEARNE S63.........66 B1
Hounsfield Crs
  RHAM/THRY S65.........107 F2
Hounsfield La FUL S10.........10 C4
Hounsfield Rd OWL S3.........10 C5
  RHAM/THRY S65.........107 F2
House Park Ga
  CHPT/GREN S35.........92 B5
Housley La CHPT/GREN S35.........30 C1
Housley Pk CHPT/GREN S35.........81 E5
Houstead Rd DARN/MH S9.........128 B4
Howard Dr CHNE S41.........179 C3
Howard La SHEF S1.........11 H5
Howard Rd MALT S66.........108 D4
  MALT S66.........111 F3
  ST/HB/BR S6.........125 E2
Howards Cl MALT S66.........133 C1
Howard St BSLY S70.........31 H3
  DIN S25.........135 E4
  RHAM/THRY S65.........9 F3
  SHEF S1.........11 H4
  WMB/DAR S73.........35 C5
Howarth Dr RHAM S60.........118 D5
Howarth Rd RHAM S60.........118 C5
Howse St HOY S74.........62 C2
Howson Cl
  RHAM/THRY S65.........109 E1
Howson Rd STKB/PEN S36.........77 F2
Hoylake Av CHSW S40.........191 G5
Hoylake Dr MEX/SWTN S64.........86 B2
Hoyland Av HOY S74.........61 F3
  OWL S3.........114 C5
Hoyland St MALT S66.........111 F3
  WMB/DAR S73.........50 B3
Hoyle Mill Rd BSLY S70.........32 D2
Hoyle St OWL S3.........118 C5
Hucklow Av CHSW S40.........192 B3
  STV/CWN S43.........189 C2
Hucklow Rd SHEFN S5.........115 H2
Hucknall Av CHSW S40.........186 C5
Huddersfield Rd
  DOD S75.........19 E3
  STKB/PEN S36.........44 C2
Hudson Av HOR/CROF WF4.........12 B3
Hudson Hvn
  WMB/DAR S73 *.........49 H1
Hudson Mt BSVR S44.........197 E4
Hudson Rd HAN/WDH S13.........144 A2
  KIMB S61.........96 C4
Humberside Wy
  BSLYN/ROY S71.........20 D1
Humphrey Rd SHEFS S8.........152 C5
Humphries Av RAW S62.........84 D4
Hundall La CHNE S41.........179 C2
  DRON S18.........172 B4
Hungerhill Cl KIMB S61.........104 B1
Hungerhill La ARMTH DN3.........29 E5
Hunger Hill La DEARNE S63.........120 A3
Hungerhill Rd KIMB S61.........96 B5
Hunger Hill Rd RHAM S60.........119 H2
Hunloke Av CHSW S40.........4 C7
  CHSW S40.........191 H3
Hunloke Crs CHSW S40.........4 B7
Hunloke Vw RCH S42.........195 H3
Hunningley Cl BSLY S70.........32 D3
Hunningley La BSLY S70.........32 D5
Hunsdon Rd ECK/KIL S21.........166 C5
Hunshelf La
  CHPT/GREN S35.........94 B4
Hunshelf Pk STKB/PEN S36.........77 F1
Hunshelf Rd
  CHPT/GREN S35.........93 H1
  STKB/PEN S36.........76 D1
Hunsley St ATT S4.........116 A4
Hunster Gv
  NROS/TKH DN11.........91 F3
Hunstone Av SHEFS S8.........163 E1
Hunt Cl BSLYN/ROY S71 *.........20 C3
Hunter Hill Rd ECC S11.........139 E5
Hunter House Rd ECC S11.........138 D3
Hunter Rd ST/HB/BR S6.........113 H4
Hunters Cha DIN S25.........134 D3
Hunters Cl DIN S25.........134 D2
Hunters Cottages
  DOD S75 *.........30 C1
Hunters Ct DIN S25.........134 D2
Hunters Dr DIN S25.........134 D2
Hunters Gdns DIN S25.........134 D2
  ST/HB/BR S6.........112 D3
Hunters Gn DIN S25.........134 D2

Hunters Pk DIN S25.........134 D2
Hunters Ri DOD/DAR S75.........30 C1
Hunters Wy DIN S25.........134 D2
Hunter's Av BSLY S70.........30 C2
Hunter's La
  HAN/WDH S13.........142 A4
Huntingdon Av BSVR S44.........197 E3
Huntingdon Crs ECC S11.........139 G2
Huntingdon Rd WHHL DN2.........57 G1
Huntington St BTLY DN5.........26 D5
Huntington Wy MALT S66.........110 C1
Huntingtower Rd ECC S11.........138 D3
Hunt La BTLY DN5.........39 H5
Huntley Cl STV/CWN S43.........189 F1
Huntley Gv ECC S11.........138 D4
Huntley Rd ECC S11.........138 C4
Huntsman Rd
  DARN/MH S9.........128 B3
  STV/CWN S43.........182 A4
Huntsmans Gdns
  DARN/MH S9.........117 E5
Hunt St HOY S74.........61 F3
Hurl Dr HACK/IN S12.........141 F5
Hurley Cft DEARNE S63.........64 A1
Hurlfield Av HACK/IN S12.........141 F4
Hurlfield Ct HACK/IN S12.........141 F4
Hurlfield Dr HACK/IN S12.........141 F4
  MALT S66.........108 D2
Hurlfield Rd HACK/IN S12.........141 F5
Hurlingham Cl ECC S11.........152 A1
Hurlstone Cl ARMTH DN3.........29 G4
Hursley Cl MOS S20.........157 G4
Hursley Dr MOS S20.........157 G4
Hurst Gn CHPT/GREN S35.........80 B4
Hurst La EPW DN9.........75 H5
Hutchings Crs
  STV/CWN S43.........184 D1
Hutchinson La ABRD S7.........152 B2
Hutchinson Rd ABRD S7.........152 B2
  RAW S62.........85 G5
Hutcliffe Dr SHEFS S8.........152 B3
Hutcliffe Wood Rd
  SHEFS S8.........152 B3
Hutcliffe Wood Vw
  SHEFS S8.........152 B4
Hut La ECK/KIL S21.........168 C4
Hutton Rd KIMB S61.........96 C5
Huxterwell Dr
  DONS/BSCR DN4.........71 H4
Hyacinth Cl SHEFN S5.........116 B1
Hyacinth Rd SHEFN S5.........116 B1
Hyde Park Ter
  SHEFP/MNR S2.........126 C4
Hyde Park Wk
  SHEFP/MNR S2.........126 C4
Hyland Crs DONS/BSCR DN4.........70 D2
Hyman Cl DONS/BSCR DN4.........70 D1
Hyndley Rd BSVR S44.........196 C1

I

Ians Wy CHSW S40.........186 C5
Ibbotson Rd ST/HB/BR S6.........125 E1
Ickles Wy RHAM S60.........105 F5
Icknield Wy RHAM S60.........118 C4
Ida Gv MALT S66.........110 B2
Ida's Rd ECK/KIL S21.........166 D4
Idsworth Rd SHEFN S5.........115 H2
Ilam Cl STV/CWN S43.........189 C3
Ilkley Crs AU/AST/KP S26.........145 E4
Ilkley Rd SHEFN S5.........115 H2
Ilsley Cl SHEFN S5.........115 H2
Ilsley Rd WMB/DAR S73.........35 E4
Imperial Buildings
  RHAM S60 *.........9 F4
Imperial Crs WHHL DN2.........7 J2
Imrie Pl AU/AST/KP S26.........159 H3
Indstry Rd BSLYN/ROY S71.........15 G5
Industry Rd
  BSLYN/ROY S71.........15 G5
  DARN/MH S9.........128 A2
Industry St ST/HB/BR S6.........125 E1
Infield La DARN/MH S9.........128 A3
Infirmary Rd CHNE S41.........5 H1
  RAW S62.........98 C3
  ST/HB/BR S6.........125 G1
Ingbirchworth Rd
  STKB/PEN S36.........44 A2
Ingelow Av SHEFN S5.........102 B4
Ingfield Av DARN/MH S9.........117 G2
Ingleborough Cft
  CHPT/GREN S35.........80 D5
Ingleborough Dr BTLY DN5.........55 E3
Ingleby Cl DRON S18.........170 A2
Ingle Gv BTLY DN5.........55 E3
Ingleton Rd CHNE S41.........192 D5
Ingleton Wk BSLY S70.........2 D3
Inglewood Av MOS S20.........157 G4
Inglewood Crs MOS S20 *.........157 G4
Inglewood Dell MOS S20.........157 G4
Ingram Ct
  SHEFP/MNR S2.........126 D5
Ingram Rd
  SHEFP/MNR S2.........126 D5
Ingsfield La DEARNE S63.........52 C3
Ingshead Av RAW S62.........98 C3
Ings La BTLY DN5.........27 G5
  BTLY DN5.........35 F3
  CUD/GR S72.........35 F3
Ings Rd BTLY DN5.........39 H5
  BTLY DN5.........69 F2
  WMB/DAR S73.........51 E1

Ings Wy BTLY DN5.........27 F5
Inkerman Cottages
  CHSW S40 *.........191 C1
Inkerman Rd
  WMB/DAR S73.........35 E5
Inkersall Dr MOS S20.........157 E5
Inkersall Green Rd
  STV/CWN S43.........189 F1
Inkersall Rd STV/CWN S43.........182 A5
Innovation Wy
  DOD S75.........19 E3
Insley Gdns
  DONS/BSCR DN4.........74 A1
Intake Crs DOD/DAR S75.........30 B4
Intake Gdns DOD/DAR S75.........18 D5
Intake La CUD/GR S72.........17 E4
  DOD/DAR S75.........30 B4
Intake Rd BSVR S44.........196 B1
Interchange Wy
  BSLYN/ROY S71.........3 H3
Ireland St STV/CWN S43.........182 B5
Ireland St STV/CWN S43.........182 B4
Iron Cliff Rd BSVR S44.........196 C1
Irongate CHSW S40.........5 C4
Ironside Cl GLV S14.........153 H3
Ironside Pl GLV S14.........154 A2
Ironside Rd GLV S14.........153 H3
Ironstone Crs
  CHPT/GREN S35.........80 D4
Ironstone Dr
  CHPT/GREN S35.........80 D4
Irving St DARN/MH S9.........128 A3
Irwell Gdns
  DONS/BSCR DN4.........57 H3
Island Cl RHAM S60.........119 H1
Islay St FUL S10.........124 D4
Issott St BSLYN/ROY S71.........19 H4
Ivan Brook Cl DRON S18 *.........170 A2
Ivanhoe Cl BTLY DN5.........55 F1
Ivanhoe Ms
  AU/AST/KP S26.........145 E2
Ivanhoe Rd ARMTH DN3.........42 B1
  CONI DN12.........88 D1
  DONS/BSCR DN4.........71 G1
  MALT S66.........133 E1
  ST/HB/BR S6.........124 C1
Iveagh St BTLY DN5.........55 F1
Ivor Gv DONS/BSCR DN4.........55 C5
Ivy Cl CHNE S41.........179 C4
  NROS/TKH DN11.........91 G2
Ivy Cottage La FUL S10.........137 G4
Ivy Ct CUD/GR S72.........21 H1
  SHEFS S8.........153 C3
Ivy Dr FUL S10.........125 F3
Ivy Farm Cft
  RHAM/THRY S65.........99 F5
  STV/CWN S43.........185 E3
Ivy Gv FUL S10 *.........125 F3
Ivy Hall Rd SHEFN S5.........103 E2
Ivy House Ct EPW DN9.........75 H1
Ivy La MOS S20.........157 G1
Ivy Park Rd FUL S10.........124 A5
Ivy Side Cl ECK/KIL S21.........168 B2
Ivyside Gdns ECK/KIL S21.........168 B2
Ivy Spring Cl RCH S42.........195 H3
Ivy Ter BSLY S70.........3 K6

J

Jack Close Orch
  BSLYN/ROY S71.........12 C5
Jackson Crs RAW S62.........84 D4
Jackson St CUD/GR S72.........21 C1
  DEARNE S63.........37 G5
Jacksons Yd BSLY S70 *.........2 E7
Jacobs Cl SHEFN S5.........103 E5
Jacobs Dr SHEFN S5.........103 E5
Jacques Pl BSLYN/ROY S71.........20 D5
Jago Av STV/CWN S43.........185 G2
Jamaica St ATT S4.........115 C5
James Andrew Cl
  SHEFS S8.........162 D1
James Andrew Crs
  SHEFS S8.........162 C1
James Andrew Cft
  SHEFS S8.........162 D1
James St BSLY S70.........32 C5
  BSLYN/ROY S71.........3 H2
  CHNE S41.........187 G3
  DARN/MH S9.........128 A4
  MEX/SWTN S64.........67 F2
  RHAM S60.........8 B4
James Walton Dr MOS S20.........167 F1
James Walton Pl MOS S20.........167 F1
James Walton Vw
  MOS S20.........167 F1
Janson St DARN/MH S9.........116 C4
Jardine Cl DARN/MH S9.........103 H5
Jardine St DARN/MH S9.........103 H5
Jarratt St DON DN1.........6 E6
Jarrow Rd ECC S11.........139 F2
Jasmine Av MOS S20.........157 F2
Jasmine Cl CONI DN12.........89 F2
Jaunty Av HACK/IN S12.........154 D2
Jaunty Cl HACK/IN S12.........154 D2
Jaunty Crs HACK/IN S12.........154 D2
Jaunty Dr HACK/IN S12.........154 D2
Jaunty La HACK/IN S12.........154 D1
Jaunty Mt HACK/IN S12.........155 E2

Jaunty Pl HACK/IN S12.........154 D2
Jaunty Rd HACK/IN S12.........155 E2
Jaunty Vw HACK/IN S12.........155 E2
Jaunty Wy HACK/IN S12.........154 D1
Jay La AU/AST/KP S26.........145 G4
Jebb Gdns CHSW S40.........191 G2
Jedburgh Dr DARN/MH S9.........103 G5
Jedburgh St DARN/MH S9.........103 G5
Jeffcock Rd
  CHPT/GREN S35.........80 C4
  DARN/MH S9.........128 A3
Jefferson Av WHHL DN2.........41 H1
Jeffery Crs STKB/PEN S36.........77 F3
Jeffery St
  SHEFP/MNR S2 *.........140 B4
Jenkin Av DARN/MH S9.........116 C2
Jenkin Cl DARN/MH S9.........116 C1
Jenkin Dr DARN/MH S9.........116 C2
Jenkin Rd DARN/MH S9.........116 C1
Jenkinson Gv ARMTH DN3.........42 B4
Jenkin Wood Cl MALT S66.........108 C2
Jennings Cl
  RHAM/THRY S65.........9 H1
Jepson Rd CHNE S41.........193 E5
  SHEFN S5.........103 F5
Jericho St OWL S3.........10 C1
Jermyn Av HACK/IN S12.........155 G1
Jermyn Cl HACK/IN S12.........155 H2
Jermyn Cft DOD/DAR S75.........30 B3
Jermyn Crs HACK/IN S12.........155 H2
Jermyn Dr HACK/IN S12.........155 H2
Jermyn Wy HACK/IN S12.........155 G2
Jersey Rd SHEFP/MNR S2.........140 A3
Jervis Pl STV/CWN S43.........189 F3
Jesmond Av
  BSLYN/ROY S71.........15 F1
Jesop Ct DIN S25.........135 F1
Jessamine Rd SHEFN S5.........103 E5
Jessell St DARN/MH S9.........127 F2
Jessop St SHEF S1.........11 F6
Jewitt Rd HAN/WDH S13.........144 C4
Joan La MALT S66.........110 C4
Joan Royd La
  STKB/PEN S36.........44 B5
Jockell Dr RAW S62.........98 B1
Jockey Rd STKB/PEN S36.........45 H4
John Calvert Rd
  HAN/WDH S13.........143 H4
John Hibbard Av
  HAN/WDH S13.........144 A3
John Hibbard Cl
  HAN/WDH S13.........144 A3
John Hibbard Crs
  HAN/WDH S13.........144 A3
John Hibbard Ri
  HAN/WDH S13.........144 A3
Johnson Cl CONI DN12.........70 C5
  RHAM/THRY S65.........9 H3
Johnson La CHPT/GREN S35.........94 B5
Johnson St DOD/DAR S75.........2 C3
  OWL S3.........126 B2
  STKB/PEN S36.........76 D2
Johnstone Cl CHSW S40.........192 B3
John St AWLS/ASK DN6.........25 C1
  BSLY S70.........3 G5
  BSLY S70.........48 A1
  CHSW S40.........4 B4
  CUD/GR S72.........35 H3
  ECK/KIL S21.........166 D5
  MEX/SWTN S64.........67 G2
  RHAM S60.........8 G5
  SHEFP/MNR S2.........140 A1
  STV/CWN S43.........184 D3
  STV/CWN S43.........188 C1
  WMB/DAR S73.........50 A2
John Ward St
  HAN/WDH S13.........143 H3
John West St STKB/PEN S36.........76 D3
Joiner St OWL S3.........11 H1
Jones Av WMB/DAR S73.........49 H2
Jordan Crs KIMB S61.........104 C4
Jordanthorpe Gn SHEFS S8.........163 G2
Jordanthorpe Pkwy
  SHEFS S8.........163 G3
Jordanthorpe Vw
  SHEFS S8.........163 G1
Joseph Fletcher Dr
  RCH S42.........195 F5
Josephine Rd KIMB S61.........105 E3
Joseph Rd FUL S10.........125 E2
Joseph St BSLY S70.........3 G6
  CUD/GR S72.........23 E1
  ECK/KIL S21.........166 D5
  RHAM S60.........8 C2
Joshua Rd ABRD S7.........139 G3
Josselin Ct CHPT/GREN S35.........93 H1
Jossey La BTLY DN5.........38 D2
Jowitt Cl MALT S66.........111 F5
Jowitt Rd ECC S11.........138 D4
Jubb Cl RHAM/THRY S65.........107 F5
Jubilee Cottages
  RHAM S60 *.........118 B3
Jubilee Crs ECK/KIL S21.........168 C1
  STV/CWN S43.........185 G2
Jubilee Gdns
  BSLYN/ROY S71.........12 D5
Jubilee Rd DARN/MH S9.........127 H1
  DON DN1.........40 C5
Jubilee St RHAM S60.........105 H5
Judith Rd AU/AST/KP S26.........145 F4
Judy Rw BSLYN/ROY S71.........20 C3
Julian Rd DARN/MH S9.........116 D1

Julian Wy DARN/MH S9.........116 D1
Jumble La KIMB S61.........95 E4
Junction Cl WMB/DAR S73.........50 D4
Junction Rd ECC S11.........139 E2
  HAN/WDH S13.........143 H3
  NROS/TKH DN11.........91 E3
Junction St BSLY S70.........32 B2
  WMB/DAR S73.........50 B2
June Rd HAN/WDH S13.........143 H4
Juniper Cl STV/CWN S43.........181 E4
Juniper Ri ECK/KIL S21.........168 A3

K

Kariba Cl CHNE S41.........5 J4
Kashmir Gdns
  DARN/MH S9.........127 H2
Katherine St MALT S66.........133 E1
Kathleen Gv DEARNE S63.........37 H4
Kay Crs RAW S62.........84 C3
Kaye Pl FUL S10.........125 F3
Kaye St BSLYN/ROY S71.........3 G2
Kay St HOY S74.........61 F3
Kay's Ter BSLY S70.........33 E3
Kea Park Cl MALT S66.........109 G4
Kearsley Rd CONI DN12.........88 D3
Kearsley Rd
  SHEFP/MNR S2.........140 A2
Keats Dr DIN S25.........135 F5
Keats Gv STKB/PEN S36.........44 D2
Keats Rd CHNE S41.........187 F1
  DONS/BSCR DN4.........71 H2
  ST/HB/BR S6.........101 F3
Keble Martin Wy
  DEARNE S63.........64 D2
Keble Sq DEARNE S63.........64 C2
Kedleston Cl CHNE S41.........186 C2
Keepers Cl NROS/TKH DN11.........91 H2
  SHEFN S5.........102 D5
Keetons Hl SHEFP/MNR S2.........139 H2
  ECC S11.........139 H2
Keilder Ct CHSW S40.........191 H5
Keir Pl RAW S62.........85 H5
Keir St BSLY S70.........2 D3
Keir Ter BSLY S70.........2 D3
Kelburn Av CHSW S40.........191 G3
Kelby Cft DOD/DAR S75.........18 B2
Kelgate MOS S20.........166 D2
Kelham Bank DON DN1.........56 A4
Kelham Island OWL S3.........126 A2
Kelham St DON DN1.........5 E3
Kelly St DEARNE S63.........37 G5
Kelsey Gdns
  DONS/BSCR DN4.........74 A3
Kelsey Ter BSLY S70.........31 H3
Kelso Dr DONS/BSCR DN4.........70 D1
Kelvin Cl KIMB S61.........96 A4
Kelvin Gv WMB/DAR S73.........50 C3
Kendal Av DIN S25.........134 C3
Kendal Cl BTLY DN5 *.........54 A4
Kendal Crs BSLY S70.........48 A1
  CONI DN12.........89 F1
Kendal Dr DEARNE S63.........53 E4
  DRON S18.........170 C2
Kendal Green Rd BSLY S70.........47 G1
Kendal Gv BSLYN/ROY S71.........33 G2
Kendal Rd BTLY DN5.........39 G3
  CHNE S41.........187 E1
  ST/HB/BR S6.........113 H4
Kendal V BSLY S70.........48 A1
Kendray St BSLY S70.........3 G4
Kenilworth Cl ECC S11.........139 E5
Kenilworth Rd
  DONS/BSCR DN4.........71 E1
Kenmare Crs WHHL DN2.........57 E1
Kennedy Dr DEARNE S63.........53 F2
Kennedy Rd SHEFS S8.........152 C3
Kenneth St
  RHAM/THRY S65.........9 G2
Kennet V STV/CWN S40.........186 D5
Kenning Hall Cl
  SHEFP/MNR S2.........140 D3
Kenninghall Dr
  SHEFP/MNR S2.........140 D3
Kenninghall Mt
  SHEFP/MNR S2.........140 D3
Kenninghall Rd
  SHEFP/MNR S2.........140 D3
Kennington Av
  AWLS/ASK DN6.........24 D2
Kennington Gv CONI DN12.........70 C5
Kenrock Cl BTLY DN5.........40 C1
Kensington Av
  STKB/PEN S36.........44 A2
Kensington Cha FUL S10.........136 A3
Kensington Gdns DIN S25.........134 A3
Kensington Gv FUL S10.........136 A3
Kensington Dr FUL S10.........136 D1
Kensington Pk FUL S10.........136 C2

Kensington Rd
 DOD/DAR DN75 ....2 D1
Kent Av RAW S62 ....85 E4
Kent Cl BSLYN/ROY S71 .....12 C5
 CHNE S41 ....187 F4
Kent House Cl
 HACK/IN S12 ....155 G5
Kentmere Cl DRON DN18...170 C2
Kentmere Dr
 DONS/BSCR DN4 ....73 F1
Kentmere Wy
 STV/CWN S43 ....189 C1
Kent Rd DONS/BSCR DN4 ...71 H2
 KIMB S61 ....96 C5
 SHEFS S8 ....140 B4
Kent St CHNE S41 ....193 E4
Kenwell Dr TOT/DORE S17..161 H3
Kenwood Av ABRD S7 ....139 C3
Kenwood Bank ECC S11 .....139 F2
Kenwood Cl BSLY S70 ....32 D2
 ABRD S7 ....139 C3
Kenwood Ri MALT S66 ....108 C3
Kenwood Rd ABRD S7 ....139 F3
Kenworthy Rd BSLY S70 ....31 G3
 STKB/PEN S36 ....76 D3
Kenyon Av CHNE S41 ....193 C5
Kenyon St SHEF S1 ....10 C1
Keppel Dr KIMB S61 ....95 H4
Keppel Pl SHEFN S5 ....95 H4
 SHEFN S5 ....103 F5
Keppel View Rd KIMB S61..104 B1
Kepple Cl NROS/TKH DN11..91 F4
Keresforth Cl BSLY S70 ....2 B7
Keresforth Hall Rd
 BSLY S70 ....31 F3
Keresforth Hill Rd BSLY S70..30 D3
Keresforth Rd
 DOD/DAR DN75 ....30 B4
Kerwin Cl TOT/DORE S17...150 C5
Kerwin Dr TOT/DORE S17...150 C5
Kerwin Rd TOT/DORE S17...150 C5
Kestrel Av KIMB S61 ....95 C1
Kestrel Cl BSVR S44 ....196 C1
 ECK/KIL S21 ....167 H1
Kestrel Dr AWLS/ASK DN6...25 F1
 ECK/KIL S21 ....166 B5
Kestrel Gn SHEFP/MNR S2...127 E5
Kestrel Ri AU/AST/KP S26..144 C3
 BSLY S70 ....47 H5
Keswick BTLY DN5 ....39 C2
Keswick Cl BSVR S44 ....196 C3
 ST/HB/BR S6 ....113 E4
Keswick Crs RHAM S60 ....118 B5
Keswick Dr CHNE S41 ....186 C2
Keswick Pl DRON DN18 ....170 B2
Keswick Wk
 BSLYN/ROY S71 ....33 H2
Keswick Wy DIN S25 ....148 D2
Kettlebridge Rd
 DARN/MH S9 ....127 C4
Ketton Av SHEFS S8 ....153 E2
Ketton Wk DOD/DAR DN75 ....2 A1
Kevin Gv MALT S66 ....109 H4
Kew Ct MEX/SWTN S64 ....86 A2
Kew Crs HACK/IN S12 ....154 B3
Key Av HOY S74 ....62 A2
Key Hill La CUD/GR S72 ....17 H1
Keyworth Pl
 HAN/WDH S13 ....143 E4
Keyworth Rd ST/HB/BR S6...114 A3
Khartoum Rd ECC S11 ....139 F2
Kibworth Cl CHNE S41 ....193 E5
Kidsley Cl CHSW S40 ....186 A4
Kier Hardie Av
 NROS/TKH DN11 ....91 G3
Kilburn Rd DRON DN18 ....170 A2
Kildale Gdns MOS S20 ....166 D1
Kildonan Gv HACK/IN S12...155 G2
Kilham La ARMTH DN3 ....59 H4
Killamarsh La ECK/KIL S21..169 E2
Kilner Wy ST/HB/BR S6 .....114 D1
 RHAM/THRY S65 ....87 E5
Kiln Rd KIMB S61 ....104 D1
Kilton Hl OWL S3 ....126 B1
Kilton Pl OWL S3 ....126 B1
Kilvington Av
 HAN/WDH S13 * 141 H3
Kilvington Crs
 HAN/WDH S13 ....141 H3
Kilvington Rd
 HAN/WDH S13 ....141 H3
Kimberley St DARN/MH S9..127 F1
Kimberworth Park Rd
 KIMB S61 ....96 C5
Kimberworth Rd KIMB S61..104 D3
Kinder Cl MALT S66 ....102 B4
Kinder Rd STV/CWN S43...189 F3
King Av MALT S66 ....111 H4
 NROS/TKH DN11 ....91 E2
King Edgert Rd
 TOT/DORE S17 ....161 E2
King Edward Rd
 DONS/BSCR DN4 ....55 H5
King Edwards
 Gdns BSLY S70 ....2 E7
King Edward St
 BSLYN/ROY S71 ....20 D1
Kingfield Rd ECC S11 ....139 D1
Kingfisher Cl WHHL DN2 .....41 F3

Kingfisher Ct BSVR S44......196 C1
 NROS/TKH DN11 ....91 G2
Kingfisher Dr WMB/DAR S73..51 E4
Kingfisher Gv
 AU/AST/KP S26 ....144 C3
Kingfisher Ri KIMB S61......82 C5
Kingfisher Rd
 AWLS/ASK DN6 ....25 F1
King Georges Cl
 NROS/TKH DN11 ....90 D3
King George Sq ARMTH DN3..29 F3
King George Ter BSLY S70 *..32 B2
King George's
 NROS/TKH DN11 ....90 D2
King James St
 ST/HB/BR S6 ....125 F1
Kings Ar DON DN1 * 6 C4
Kings Cl STV/CWN S43 .....185 F3
Kings Coppice
 TOT/DORE S17 ....160 D2
Kings Cft BSLY S70 ....48 C1
Kingscroft Cl
 TOT/DORE S17 ....151 E5
Kingsgate DON DN1 ....6 D4
Kingsgate Flats DON DN1......6 D4
Kingsley Av BTLY DN5 ....55 F1
 CHSW S40 ....188 A3
Kingsley Cl BSLYN/ROY S71..20 A1
Kingsley Crs ARMTH DN3......42 D4
Kingsley Dr
 RHAM/THRY S65 ....109 F1
Kingsley Park Av ABRD S7...151 H1
Kingsley Park Gv ABRD S7 *.151 H1
Kingsley Rd AWLS/ASK DN6..25 E2
Kingsmead Dr ARMTH DN3....59 F5
Kingsmede Av CHSW S40...191 H3
Kings Ms ECK/KIL S21 ....167 E5
Kings Rd WMB/DAR S73 ....51 E5
Kingstone Pl BSLY S70 ....31 F3
Kingston Rd WHHL DN2 ....57 F1
Kingston St ATT S4 ....115 C5
King St AU/AST/KP S26 .....145 C2
 BSLY S70 ....3 H6
 CHPT/GREN S35 ....81 E5
 DEARNE S63 ....37 G5
 DON DN1 ....6 E3
 HOY S74 ....62 B2
 MEX/SWTN S64 ....66 B5
 SHEF S1 ....11 H2
 STV/CWN S43 ....180 D5
 STV/CWN S43 ....185 E3
King St North CHNE S41 .....187 G2
King St South CHSW S40 ....192 C5
Kingsway DEARNE S63 ....37 E2
Kings Wy RHAM S60 ....119 G2
Kingsway Cl NROS/TKH DN11..91 G3
Kingsway Gv DEARNE S63......37 E2
Kingswood Av CHNE S41 .....186 D1
 MOS S20 ....156 A3
Kingswood Cl CHNE S41......186 D1
 MOS S20 ....155 H5
Kingswood Crs HOY S74 ....62 A1
Kingswood Cft MOS S20 .....156 A3
Kingswood Gv MOS S20 .....156 A3
Kingwell Crs BSLY S70 ....31 H4
Kingwell Cft BSLY S70 ....32 A5
Kingwell Rd BSLY S70 ....32 A5
King's Crs CONI DN12 ....70 B5
King's Rd CUD/GR S72 ....17 E3
 DON DN1 ....7 F2
 MEX/SWTN S64 ....67 F3
King's St CUD/GR S72 ....23 E1
Kinharvie Rd SHEFN S5 .....114 D1
Kinnaird Av SHEFN S5 ....102 C4
Kinnaird Pl SHEFN S5 ....102 C4
Kinnaird Rd SHEFN S5 ....102 C4
Kinsey Rd CHPT/GREN S35...80 A4
Kipling Av DONS/BSCR DN4..71 F2
Kipling Cl DRON DN18 ....171 G4
Kipling Rd CHNE S41 ....187 F1
Kirby Cl CHNE S41 ....193 E5
Kirby La CHPT/GREN S35 .....81 H4
Kirby Rw KIMB S61 * 95 E1
Kirby St MEX/SWTN S64 ....66 C5
Kirk Balk HOY S74 ....62 A1
Kirkby Av BSLYN/ROY S71 .....15 E4
 BTLY DN5 ....39 G3
 HACK/IN S12 ....154 C1
Kirkby Dr HACK/IN S12 .....154 C1
Kirkby Rd HACK/IN S12 .....154 C1
Kirkby Vw HACK/IN S12 .....154 C2
Kirkcroft Av ECK/KIL S21...168 B1
 KIMB S61 ....95 C1
Kirkcroft Cl KIMB S61 ....95 G1
Kirkcroft Dr ECK/KIL S21...168 B2
Kirkcroft La ECK/KIL S21...168 B2
Kirk Cross Crs
 BSLYN/ROY S71 ....15 G2
Kirkdale Cl CHSW S40 ....192 D4
Kirkdale Crs HAN/WDH S13..143 F1
Kirkdale Dr HAN/WDH S13...143 F1
Kirkfield Wy BSLYN/ROY S71..15 G2
Kirkham Cl ARMTH DN3 ....43 E5
Kirkham Ct BSLYN/ROY S71..15 G1
Kirkland Gdns
 BSLYN/ROY S71 ....20 A2
Kirklands Dr RAW S62 ....85 E5
Kirkstall Cl BTLY DN5 ....38 D5
 DIN S25 ....148 B5
 RHAM S60 ....118 A3

Kirkstall Rd BSLYN/ROY S71..14 C5
 ECC S11 ....139 E2
Kirkstead Abbey Ms
 KIMB S61 ....95 G4
Kirkstead Gdns
 HAN/WDH S13 ....144 A3
Kirkstead Rd KIMB S61 .....103 G2
Kirkstone Cl BTLY DN5 ....39 G2
Kirkstone Rd CHNE S41 .....186 C1
 ST/HB/BR S6 ....114 A5
Kirk St ATT S4 ....126 C1
 DONS/BSCR DN4 ....55 H3
Kirk Wy BSLYN/ROY S71 .....20 D4
Kirkwood Cl STKB/PEN S36...45 F4
Kirton Rd ATT S4 ....115 C5
Kitchen Wood La
 DRON S18 ....170 A3
Kitchin Rd WMB/DAR S73 .....49 H2
Kitson Dr BSLYN/ROY S71 .....20 D4
Riverton La AU/AST/KP S26..147 F4
Knab Cl ABRD S7 ....139 E5
Knab Cft ABRD S7 ....139 E5
Knab Ri ABRD S7 ....139 E5
Knab Rd ABRD S7 ....139 E5
Knapton Av RAW S62 ....85 E5
Knaresboro Rd ABRD S7 .....152 A2
Knaresborough Cl
 AU/AST/KP S26 ....145 E3
Knaresborough Rd
 CONI DN12 ....88 B2
Knaves Mire Av DIN S25....134 A3
Knavesmire Gdns
 DONS/BSCR DN4 ....57 H3
Knifesmithgate CHSW S40.....5 F4
Knighton Cl CHNE S41 ....192 D5
Knollbeck Av WMB/DAR S73..51 E3
Knoll Beck Cl DEARNE S63...53 E1
Knoll Beck Crs
 WMB/DAR S73 ....51 E5
Knollbeck La WMB/DAR S73..51 E5
Knoll Cl STKB/PEN S36 ....77 E2
Knoll Cottages
 DOD/DAR DN75 * 60 C3
Knoll Drift DOD/DAR DN75 *..60 B3
The Knoll CHSW S40 ....190 D1
 DRON S18 ....163 H5
Knowle Cl ST/HB/BR S6 .....123 C1
Knowle Cft ST/HB/BR S6 .....123 C1
Knowle Gn TOT/DORE S17...160 C4
Knowle La ECC S11 ....138 B5
 SHEFN S5 ....102 B3
Knowles Av STKB/PEN S36......77 F4
Knowles St STKB/PEN S36 .....45 F4
Knowle Top MOS S20 ....167 E1
Knowsley St BSLY S70 ....2 C5
Knutton Crs SHEFN S5 ....101 G3
Knutton Ri SHEFN S5 ....101 G3
Knutton Rd SHEFN S5 ....101 G3
Kyle Cl ECK/KIL S21 ....175 H1
Kyle Crs SHEFN S5 ....101 C5
Kynance Crs RHAM S60 .....118 B5

L

Laburnam Gv BSLY S70 ....48 B1
Laburnam Av MALT S66 .....108 B3
Laburnam Cl BSVR S44 ....197 E3
 CHPT/GREN S35 ....94 A2
 DIN S25 ....148 B2
Laburnam Dr ARMTH DN3 .....43 E3
Laburnam Gv CONI DN12 .....88 C2
 ECK/KIL S21 ....168 A3
 STKB/PEN S36 ....76 D3
Laburnam Pde MALT S66 ...110 B3
Laburnam Pl BTLY DN5 ....26 C5
Laburnam Rd
 DONS/BSCR DN4 ....71 F2
 MALT S66 ....110 B3
 MEX/SWTN S64 ....86 B3
Laburnam St STV/CWN S43...181 E5
Laceby Cl MALT S66 ....108 D2
Laceby Ct BSLY S70 ....31 E3
Ladies Spring Gv
 TOT/DORE S17 * 161 C1
Ladock Cl BSLYN/ROY S71 .....20 B4
Lady Bank Dr
 DONS/BSCR DN4 ....56 C4
Ladybank Rd MOS S20 ....166 D2
Ladybank Vw ECK/KIL S21...166 D4
Ladybower La
 STV/CWN S43 ....189 H1
Ladycroft DEARNE S63 ....53 E3
Lady Cft DEARNE S63 ....65 E2
Lady Croft La
 WMB/DAR S73 ....63 E1
Ladycroft Rd ARMTH DN3 .....58 D1
Lady Ida's Dr ECK/KIL S21...166 A4
Ladymead BSLYN/ROY S71 .....20 B3
Lady Oak Rd
 RHAM/THRY S65 ....107 E1
Ladyroyd Cft CUD/GR S72 .....21 H1
Ladysmith Av ABRD S7 ....139 F5
Ladywood Dr CHNE S41 ....186 C2
Ladywood Rd CHNE S41 ....23 F1
Lady's Br OWL S3 ....11 H1
Laird Av ST/HB/BR S6 ....113 C4
Laird Dr ST/HB/BR S6 ....113 C4
Laird Rd ST/HB/BR S6 ....113 C4
Lairds Wy STKB/PEN S36 .....45 E3

Laithe Cft DOD/DAR DN75 .....30 B3
Laithes Cl BSLYN/ROY S71 .....15 F5
Laithes Crs BSLYN/ROY S71..14 D5
Laithes La BSLYN/ROY S71 .....14 D5
Lakeen Rd WHHL DN2 ....7 H1
Lakeland Cl CUD/GR S72 ....21 H2
Lakeland Dr DIN S25 ....148 C2
Lake Lands RCH S42 ....195 F5
Lakeside RCH S42 ....195 F5
Lakeside Bvd
 DONS/BSCR DN4 ....73 E1
Lakeside Cl CHNE S41 ....180 A2
Lakeside Ct DEARNE S63 ....63 H1
Lake View Av CHSW S40 .....191 G3
Lambcote Wy MALT S66 .....111 F2
Lambcroft Vw
 HAN/WDH S13 ....143 G4
Lamb Dr SHEFN S5 ....114 B1
Lambcroft BSLYN/ROY S71 .....15 G3
Lambert Fold DOD/DAR DN75..30 C3
Lambert Rd BSLY S70 ....32 C3
Lamberts La
 RHAM/THRY S65 ....99 G3
Lambert St OWL S3 ....11 F2
Lambert Wk BSLY S70 ....32 C2
 DEARNE S63 ....51 G5
Lambeth Rd
 DONS/BSCR DN4 ....71 H1
Lamb Hill Cl HAN/WDH S13..142 B3
Lamb La BSLYN/ROY S71 .....20 C2
Lambra Rd BSLY S70 ....35 C1
Lambreli Av
 AU/AST/KP S26 ....159 G3
Lambrell Gn
 AU/AST/KP S26 ....159 G3
Lamb Rd SHEFN S5 ....114 B1
Lanark Dr MEX/SWTN S64......67 C1
Lanark Gdns WHHL DN2 ....41 G5
Lancar Ct BSLYN/ROY S71 .....20 A3
Lancaster Av ARMTH DN3 .....29 F3
 WHHL DN2 ....57 G1
Lancaster Ga BSLY S70 ....3 F4
Lancaster St CHNE S41 .....187 E1
 STKB/PEN S36 ....76 D2
Lancaster St BSLY S70 ....2 C5
 DEARNE S63 ....51 C5
 OWL S3 ....125 H2
Lancelot Cl CHSW S40 ....191 H4
Lancing Rd SHEFP/MNR S2..140 A2
Landsdowne Av CHNE S41 ...187 E2
Landseer Cl DRON S18 ....170 C3
 GLV S14 ....153 H3
Landseer Ct MALT S66 ....108 B3
Landseer Dr GLV S14 ....153 H3
Landseer Pl GLV S14 ....154 A3
Lane End CHPT/GREN S35 .....80 D4
Lane End Rd RHAM S60 ....119 C1
Lane End Vw RHAM S60 ....119 C1
Laneham Cl
 DONS/BSCR DN4 ....73 H2
Lane Head Cl RAW S62 * 85 G5
Lane Head Rd
 TOT/DORE S17 ....160 C4
Laneside Cl DONS/BSCR DN4..55 C4
The Lanes RHAM/THRY S65..106 D2
The Lane ECK/KIL S21 ....176 B2
Lang Av BSLYN/ROY S71 .....21 E5
Lang Crs BSLYN/ROY S71 .....21 E5
Langdale Dr BTLY DN5 ....39 F2
 DRON S18 ....163 G5
Langdale Rd ABRD S7 ....139 C5
 BSLYN/ROY S71 ....3 H5
 DOD/DAR DN75 ....18 A2
Langdale Sq STV/CWN S43..188 B1
Langdale Wk BSLY S70 ....2 D3
Langdon Rd KIMB S61 ....104 C1
Langdon St ECC S11 ....139 H2
Langer Field Av CHSW S40..192 C5
Langer La RCH S42 ....195 E3
Langford Cl DOD/DAR DN75..30 C3
Langford Cft CHSW S40 ....5 C7
Langhurst Rd CHNE S41 .....186 D5
Langley Cl CHSW S40 ....186 A4
 RHAM/THRY S65 ....107 F2
Langsett Av ST/HB/BR S6...113 G2
Langsett Cl ST/HB/BR S6 ...114 B5
Langsett Ct
 DONS/BSCR DN4 ....57 F5
Langsett Crs ST/HB/BR S6...114 B5
Langsett Gv ST/HB/BR S6 ...125 E5
Langsett Ri ST/HB/BR S6 ...125 F1
Langsett Rd
 BSLYN/ROY S71 ....3 H5
 ST/HB/BR S6 ....114 B5
Langsett Rd South
 CHPT/GREN S35 ....100 A3
Langstone Av MALT S66 .....197 F3
Langthwaite La BTLY DN5 .....25 H5
Langthwaite Rd BTLY DN5 .....25 H5
Langton Gdns ARMTH DN3 .....59 C5
Langtree Av CHNE S41 ....179 C5
Lansbury Rd BSVR S44 ....196 C5
Lansbury Av
 CHPT/GREN S35 ....93 H1
 MALT S66 ....111 F5
 NROS/TKH DN11 ....91 G2
 STV/CWN S43 ....182 D2
Lansbury Ct ECK/KIL S21...166 D5

Lansbury Pl RAW S62 ....86 A5
Lansbury Rd ECK/KIL S21...166 D5
Lansdowne Cl DEARNE S63 .....37 E3
Lansdowne Crs
 MEX/SWTN S64 ....86 B1
Lansdowne Rd
 STV/CWN S43 ....188 B2
 WHHL DN2 ....41 G5
Lanyon Wy BSLYN/ROY S71...20 B4
Lapwater Rd KIMB S61 ....96 B5
Lapwing V KIMB S61 ....82 C5
Larch Av ECK/KIL S21 ....168 A3
 EPW DN9 ....75 H5
 MALT S66 ....108 C4
Larch Cl WMB/DAR S73 ....35 E5
Larch Dr ARMTH DN3 ....42 D4
The Larches
 MEX/SWTN S64 ....86 A1
Larchfield Pl
 BSLYN/ROY S71 ....20 D2
Larchfield Rd
 DONS/BSCR DN4 ....71 F1
Larch Gv AU/AST/KP S26....145 H1
 CHPT/GREN S35 ....94 A2
 CONI DN12 ....88 B2
Larch Hl DARN/MH S9 ....128 C4
Larch Ms RHAM/THRY S65...106 D1
Larch Pl BSLY S70 ....32 C4
Larch Rd ECK/KIL S21 ....174 B1
 MALT S66 ....110 B2
Larch Wy CHSW S40 ....186 D4
Larkhill Cl RAW S62 ....98 C3
Larkspur Cl ARMTH DN3 ....42 B1
 MEX/SWTN S64 ....86 A3
Lark St ST/HB/BR S6 ....128 C1
Larwood Gv CONI DN12 ....70 C5
Latchmoor Ct DOD/DAR DN75..19 F5
Latham Sq ARMTH DN3 ....29 F2
 ECC S11 ....138 A3
Lathe Rd RHAM S60 ....120 A2
Lathkill Av STV/CWN S43...189 C1
Lathkill Cl HAN/WDH S13...142 A3
Lathkill Rd HAN/WDH S13...142 A3
Latin Gdns BTLY DN5 ....38 C3
Lauder Rd BTLY DN5 ....39 C4
Lauder St ATT S4 ....115 H3
Laudsdale Cl
 RHAM/THRY S65 ....107 F2
Laudsdale Rd
 RHAM/THRY S65 ....107 E1
Laughton Common Rd
 MALT S66 ....133 G3
Laughton Mdw DIN S25 ....134 G3
Laughton Rd DARN/MH S9...116 D2
 DIN S25 ....134 D5
 DONS/BSCR DN4 ....55 H3
 MALT S66 ....133 F3
Launce Rd SHEFN S5 ....101 H3
Laurel Av BSLY S70 ....32 C3
 BTLY DN5 ....39 F5
 MALT S66 ....108 C4
Laurel Cl DIN S25 ....148 B5
 ECK/KIL S21 ....167 G5
Laurel Crs STV/CWN S43 ...181 E5
Laurel Dr ECK/KIL S21 ....168 A4
Laurel Garth Cl CHNE S41 ...179 H3
Laurel Rd ARMTH DN3 ....42 D3
Laurel Ter DONS/BSCR DN4 ...71 G1
Laurence Cl CHNE S41 ....179 G4
Lavender Cl CONI DN12 ....89 F2
Lavender Dr BSLY S70 ....32 C3
Laverack St HAN/WDH S13..142 D1
Laverdene Av
 TOT/DORE S17 ....161 E4
Laverdene Cl
 TOT/DORE S17 ....161 E4
Laverdene Dr
 TOT/DORE S17 ....161 E4
Laverdene Rd
 TOT/DORE S17 ....161 E4
Laverdene Wy
 TOT/DORE S17 ....161 E4
Laverock Wy SHEFN S5 ....102 D4
Lavinia Rd CHPT/GREN S35..101 F2
Lawn Av AWLS/ASK DN6 ....24 D1
 DON DN1 ....7 F3
Lawn Garth BTLY DN5 ....39 F3
Lawn Rd DON DN1 ....7 F3
The Lawns ECC S11 ....138 D4
The Lawn DRON S18 ....171 H1
Lawnwood Dr DEARNE S63 .....37 E5
Lawrence Cl DOD/DAR DN75..38 A4
 MALT S66 ....108 B4
Lawrence Dr
 MEX/SWTN S64 ....86 A1
Lawson Rd FUL S10 ....124 D5
Lawton La RHAM S60 ....119 E1
Laxey Rd ST/HB/BR S6 ....124 A2
Laxfield Cl CHSW S40 ....191 G4
Laxton Cl MALT S66 ....110 B2
Laxton Rd BSLYN/ROY S71 .....14 C5
Laycock Av AU/AST/KP S26..145 C3
Layden Dr BTLY DN5 ....38 C2
Layton Dr CHNE S41 ....179 H5
Leabrook Rd DRON S18 ....170 A2
Leach La MEX/SWTN S64 .....67 F2
Leadbeater Dr
 HACK/IN S12 ....141 G5
Leadbeater Rd
 HACK/IN S12 ....141 F5
Leader Rd ST/HB/BR S6 .....113 H3
Leadhill Rd CHSW S40 ....186 A5
Leadley St DEARNE S63 ....37 G5

Leadmill Rd SHEFP/MNR S2 ...11 H6
Leadmill St SHEF S1 ...11 H6
Leaf Cl MALT S66 ...111 F2
Leaholme BSVR S44 * ...196 A2
Leake Rd ST/HB/BR S6 ...114 A2
Leamington Gdns
　WHHL DN2 ...41 G5
Leamington St FUL S10 ...125 E3
Leander Ct STV/CWN S43 *...182 B4
Lea Rd BSLYN/ROY S71 ...15 F5
　DRON S18 ...171 E2
Lease Gate Rd RHAM S60 ...119 H2
The Leas BTLY DN5 ...39 F5
The Lea MEX/SWTN S64 ...85 H2
　MOS S20 ...156 D3
Leaton Cl ST/HB/BR S6 ...112 D3
Leavy Greave FUL S10 ...10 C4
Leavygreave Rd OWL S3 ...10 C3
Leawood Pl ST/HB/BR S6 ...123 H1
Ledbury Gdns BTLY DN5 ...10 D5
Ledbury Rd BSLYN/ROY S71...19 H1
Ledsham Ct HOY S74 ...62 D1
Ledsham Rd RHAM S60 ...106 C5
Ledstone Ct SHEFS S8 ...152 C1
Lee Av STKB/PEN S36 ...77 F2
Leebrook Av MOS S20 ...156 B4
Leebrook Ct MOS S20 ...156 B4
Leebrook Dr MOS S20 ...156 B4
Lee Brook La RAW S62 ...83 G1
　SHEF S1 ...11 F2
Leedham Cl SHEFN S5 ...103 F5
Leedham Rd
　RHAM/THRY S65 ...107 E5
　SHEFN S5 ...103 F5
Leeds Av DIN S25 ...148 C1
Leeds Rd DARN/MH S9 ...127 G1
Lee House La STKB/PEN S36...76 D3
Lee La BSLYN/ROY S71 ...14 C2
Lee Rd CHNE S41 ...193 G2
　ST/HB/BR S6 ...112 D3
Lees Av STKB/PEN S36 ...44 D3
Lees Hall Av SHEFS S8 ...153 E1
Lees Hall Pl SHEFS S8 ...140 B5
Lees Hall Rd SHEFS S8 ...140 B5
Lees House Ct SHEFS S8 *...153 E1
Leeswood Cl CHNE S41 ...186 D1
Leeswood Ct SHEFS S8 ...63 H2
Leger Ct WHHL DN2 *...7 G5
Leger Wy WHHL DN2 ...57 E2
Legion Dr AU/AST/KP S26 ...145 G3
Leicester Av WHHL DN2 ...57 E2
Leicester Rd DIN S25 ...135 E4
Leicester Wk OWL S3 ...10 C2
Leigh St DARN/MH S9 ...115 H3
Leighton Cl BSLYN/ROY S71 ...3 G1
Leighton Dr GLV S14 ...154 B2
Leighton Pl GLV S14 ...154 B2
Leighton Rd GLV S14 ...154 B2
Leighton Vw GLV S14 ...141 G5
Leinster Av WHHL DN2 ...41 E5
Lemont Rd TOT/DORE S17 ...161 E4
Lennox Rd ST/HB/BR S6 ...113 H5
　WHHL DN2 ...41 E5
Lenton St SHEFP/MNR S2 ...11 H7
Leonard Cl SHEFP/MNR S2 ...141 G3
Leopold Av DIN S25 ...134 D5
Leopold St BSLY S70 ...2 D6
　DIN S25 ...134 D4
　SHEF S1 ...11 F3
Leppings La ST/HB/BR S6 ...114 A2
Lepton Gdns BSLY S70 ...32 D4
Lescar La ECC S11 ...139 E2
Lesley Rd DEARNE S63 ...37 G5
Leslie Av CONI DN12 ...88 C1
　MALT S66 ...110 B4
Leslie Rd BSLY S70 ...32 D3
　ST/HB/BR S6 ...113 G3
Lesmond Crs CUD/GR S72 ...36 A4
Lestermoor Av
　AU/AST/KP S26 ...159 G3
Letard Dr RHAM S60 ...118 C3
Letsby Av DARN/MH S9 ...128 C1
Levens Wy CHNE S41 ...187 E1
Leverick Dr RHAM S60 ...86 A4
Leverton Dr ECC S11 ...139 H1
Leverton Gdns ECC S11 * ...139 H1
Leverton Wy
　RHAM/THRY S65 ...99 G5
Leveson St ATT S4 ...126 D2
Levet Rd DONS/BSCR DN4 ...58 B4
Lewdendale BSLY S70 ...48 A1
Lewden Garth BSLY S70 *...48 A1
Lewes Rd CONI DN12 ...88 D2
Lewis Rd BSLYN/ROY S71 ...21 G3
　HAN/WDH S13 ...141 F2
Lewyns Dr DONS/BSCR DN4...58 B4
Leybourne Rd KIMB S61 ...96 C5
Leyburn Cl CHSW S40 ...186 A4
　DONS/BSCR DN4 ...74 B1
Leyburn Dr AU/AST/KP S26 .145 E2
Leyburn Gv ABRD S7 ...139 H4
Ley End BSLY S70 ...47 H1
Leyfield Ct ARMTH DN3 ...43 F4
Leyfield Rd TOT/DORE S17 ...160 D1
The Leylands DOD/DAR S75...18 C3
Leys Cl DONS/BSCR DN4 ...71 F4
Leys La DIN S25 ...135 F4
Liberty Cl ST/HB/BR S6 ...124 A3
Liberty Dr ST/HB/BR S6 ...124 A2

Liberty Hl ST/HB/BR S6 ...124 A2
Liberty Pl ST/HB/BR S6 ...124 A2
Liberty Rd ST/HB/BR S6 ...124 A2
Library Cl KIMB S61 ...97 E3
Lichen Cl ARMTH DN3 ...42 B1
Lichfield Rd CHSW S40 ...191 G4
　WHHL DN2 ...40 D4
Lichfield Wy RHAM S60 ...118 D3
Lichford Rd
　SHEFP/MNR S2 ...140 C4
Lidgate La CUD/GR S72 ...16 D1
Lidget Cl AU/AST/KP S26 ...144 D4
　DONS/BSCR DN4 ...74 A1
Lidget La DEARNE S63 ...37 H3
　DOD/DAR S75 ...60 B3
　RHAM/THRY S65 ...109 E3
Lidget Gra HOY S74 ...81 G1
Lidgett La DIN S25 ...134 D5
Lidgett Wy BSLYN/ROY S71 ...12 C5
Listers La DIN S25 ...148 C4
Liffey Av RHAM S60 ...41 E5
Lifford Pl HOY S74 ...62 D3
Lifford Rd WHHL DN2 ...40 D5
Lifford St DARN/MH S9 ...117 C1
Lightwood Rd ECK/KIL S21...173 G1
Lilac Av STKB/PEN S36 ...76 D3
Lilac Cl DIN S25 ...148 B4
Lilac Crs HOY S74 ...62 A1
Lilac Farm Cl MALT S66 ...108 B5
Lilac Gv BSVR S44 ...197 F3
　CONI DN12 ...88 C2
　DONS/BSCR DN4 ...58 B5
　MALT S66 ...110 B3
Lilac Rd ARMTH DN3 ...43 E3
　MOS S20 ...157 F2
　SHEFN S5 ...116 A1
Lilac St STV/CWN S43 ...181 G5
Lilian St RHAM S60 ...9 H6
Lilian St South RHAM S60 ...9 H6
Lilford Rd ARMTH DN3 ...59 G5
Lilly Hall Cl MALT S66 ...110 B2
Lilly Hall Rd MALT S66 ...110 C3
Lillymede Cl CHSW S40 ...195 F1
Limb La TOT/DORE S17 ...150 D5
Limbreck Ct BTLY DN5 ...39 F3
Limbrick Ct ST/HB/BR S6 ...113 H5
Limbrick Rd ST/HB/BR S6 ...114 A5
Lime Av STV/CWN S43 ...182 A5
Lime Ct BTLY DN5 ...54 D4
Limecroft Vw MEX/SWTN S64...195 G4
Limedale Vw ARMTH DN3 ...43 H3
Limegrove RHAM S60 ...107 E3
Lime Gv BSLYN/ROY S71 ...15 G3
　CHPT/GREN S35 ...94 A2
　MALT S66 ...111 F3
　MEX/SWTN S64 ...86 B2
　STKB/PEN S36 ...76 C3
Limekiln Fields Rd
　BSVR S44 ...196 D2
Limekilns DIN S25 ...148 B2
Limekiln Wy STV/CWN S43 ...177 F5
Limelands Rd DIN S25 ...134 C5
Lime Rd ECK/KIL S21 ...174 B2
Limes Av DOD/DAR S75 ...14 A2
　DOD/DAR S75 ...18 D4
Limes Cl DOD/DAR S75 ...14 A2
Limestone Cottage La
　ST/HB/BR S6 ...100 D5
Lime St MOS S20 ...157 F1
　ST/HB/BR S6 ...125 G1
Limesway DOD/DAR S75 ...18 D4
　MALT S66 ...110 D3
Lime Tree Av ECK/KIL S21 ...168 A3
　ARMTH DN3 ...42 D3
Limetree Av
　AU/AST/KP S26 ...159 G2
Lime Tree Av
　DONS/BSCR DN4 ...7 G6
Limetree Av MALT S66 ...133 F1
Limetree Cl STV/CWN S43 ...188 D4
Lime Tree Ct
　DONS/BSCR DN4 ...7 H7
Lime Tree Crs
　NROS/TKH DN11 ...91 G3
　RAW S62 ...85 H5
Limpool Cl DONS/BSCR DN4...74 B2
Limpsfield Rd
　DARN/MH S9 ...114 B3
Linacre Rd CHSW S40 ...186 B3
Linaker Rd ST/HB/BR S6 ...124 D2
Linburn Cl BSLYN/ROY S71 ...12 A5
Linburn Rd SHEFS S8 ...152 D5
Linby Rd BSLYN/ROY S71 ...14 D4
Lincoln Gdns DEARNE S63 ...37 F5
Lincoln Rd WHHL DN2 ...40 D4
Lincolnshire Wy
　ARMTH DN3 ...43 F4
Lincoln St CHSW S40 ...192 C4
　KIMB S61 ...116 D2
　MALT S66 ...111 E4
　NROS/TKH DN11 ...91 E2
　RHAM S60 ...8 E1
Lincroft Dr RAW S62 ...98 B3
Lindale Ct DIN S25 ...134 D5
Lindale Gdns DEARNE S63 ...53 H1
Lindale Rd CHNE S41 ...186 D2
The Lindales DOD/DAR S75 ...2 A3
Linden Av CHSW S40 ...191 F3
　DRON S18 ...168 C2
　MALT S66 ...108 C4
　SHEFS S8 ...152 C4

Linden Ct CHPT/GREN S35...94 B5
Linden Crs STKB/PEN S36 ...76 D2
Linden Gv DIN S25 ...110 B3
Linden Park Gv CHSW S40...4 B3
Linden Rd CHPT/GREN S35 ...94 B5
　DEARNE S63 ...64 B2
Linden Wk BTLY DN5 ...26 C3
Lindholme Dr
　NROS/TKH DN11 ...91 H1
Lindholme Gdns MOS S20 ...156 C3
Lindhurst Rd
　BSLYN/ROY S71 ...14 C4
Lindisfarne Ct CHSW S40 ...191 G3
Lindisfarne Rd DRON S18 ...171 F3
Lindley Crs DEARNE S63 ...37 F3
Lindley Rd SHEFN S5 ...115 H2
Lindley St RHAM/THRY S65 ...9 G2
Lindley's Cft
　AU/AST/KP S26 ...147 F5
Lindrick Av MEX/SWTN S64...86 C1
Lindrick Cl CUD/GR S72 ...17 E3
　DONS/BSCR DN4 ...73 G3
Lindrick Dr ARMTH DN3 ...42 D5
Lindrick Gdns CHSW S40 ...191 G4
Lindrick Wy STV/CWN S43 ...184 B1
Lindsay Av SHEFN S5 ...102 B4
Lindsay Cl SHEFN S5 ...102 B4
Lindsay Crs SHEFN S5 ...102 B4
Lindsay Dr SHEFN S5 ...102 B4
Lindsay Pl AU/AST/KP S26 ...145 F5
Lindsay Rd SHEFN S5 ...102 B4
Lindsey Cl DONS/BSCR DN4...73 H3
Lindum Dr MALT S66 ...108 C5
Lindum Ter
　RHAM/THRY S65 * ...9 H4
Lingamore Leys
　DEARNE S63 ...37 F1
Lingard Ct DOD/DAR S75 ...2 D2
Lingard St DOD/DAR S75 ...2 D1
Lingfield Cl MALT S66 ...109 E5
Lingfield Dr BTLY DN5 ...38 D5
Ling Field Rd BTLY DN5 ...24 A2
Lingfoot Av SHEFS S8 ...163 F2
Lingfoot Cl SHEFS S8 ...163 F2
Lingfoot Crs SHEFS S8 ...163 F2
Lingfoot Dr SHEFS S8 ...163 F2
Lingfoot Pl SHEFS S8 ...163 F2
Lingmoor Cl
　DONS/BSCR DN4 ...71 E2
Lingodell Cl DIN S25 ...134 C1
Ling Rd CHSW S40 ...191 H4
Lings La MALT S66 ...108 C5
The Lings ARMTH DN3 ...43 F5
　MALT S66 ...108 D5
Lingthwaite DOD/DAR S75...30 C3
Link Rw SHEFP/MNR S2 ...126 C3
Links Rd DRON S18 ...171 F3
Linkswood Av WHHL DN2 ...41 G3
Linkswood Rd
　RHAM/THRY S65 ...99 F3
The Link DOD/DAR S75 ...30 C4
Linkway DARN/MH S9 ...127 G1
Linley Cl RAW S62 ...98 B3
Linley La HACK/IN S12 ...142 B5
Linnet Mt KIMB S61 ...95 F1
Linscott Cl CHNE S41 ...186 D2
Linscott Rd SHEFS S8 ...152 C3
Linthwaite La RAW S62 ...63 E5
Linton Cl BSLY S70 ...30 D2
Linton Rd CHSW S40 ...191 C4
Lipp Av ECK/KIL S21 ...166 C5
Liskeard Pl AWLS/ASK DN6...25 E2
Lisle Rd RHAM S60 ...106 C5
Lismore Rd SHEFS S8 ...140 B5
Lister Av DONS/BSCR DN4 ...55 H5
　HACK/IN S12 ...154 D1
　RAW S62 ...85 E4
Lister Cl CHNE S41 ...95 F3
　HACK/IN S12 ...154 D2
Lister Ct WHHL DN2 ...41 E5
Lister Crs HACK/IN S12 ...154 D2
Lister Dr HACK/IN S12 ...154 D2
Lister La OWL S3 ...125 H2
Lister Rd HACK/IN S12 ...154 D2
Lister St RHAM/THRY S65 ...9 K5
Lister Wy HACK/IN S12 ...154 D1
Little Brind Rd CHNE S41 ...181 F5
Little Common La ECC S11...151 F2
　KIMB S61 ...104 B2
　RHAM S60 ...106 C5
Little Cft DARN/MH S9 *...127 H5
Littlefield La WMB/DAR S73...50 B2
Littlefield Rd DIN S25 ...134 C4
Little Haynooking La
　MALT S66 ...110 D3
Littlehey Cl MALT S66 ...108 C5
Little La ATT S4 ...116 B3
　BTLY DN5 ...54 A1
　HACK/IN S12 ...141 H4
　KIMB S61 ...82 A5
　WHHL DN2 ...41 G1
Little Leeds HOY S74 ...62 A2
Little London Pl SHEFS S8 ...139 H4
Little London Rd SHEFS S8...139 G5
Little Matlock Gdns
　ST/HB/BR S6 ...123 H1
Little Matlock Wy
　ST/HB/BR S6 ...123 H1
Littlemoor CHNE S41 ...186 D2
　ECK/KIL S21 ...167 E5
Littlemoor Av
　AU/AST/KP S26 ...159 G3
Littlemoor Crs CHNE S41 ...186 D2

Littlemoor La
　DONS/BSCR DN4 ...55 H4
Littlemoor St
　DONS/BSCR DN4 ...55 H3
Little New Cl DOD/DAR S75...18 D4
Little Norton Av SHEFS S8...163 E1
Little Norton Dr SHEFS S8 ...153 E5
Little Norton La SHEFS S8 ...153 E5
Little Norton Wy SHEFS S8...163 E1
Little Westfields
　BSLYN/ROY S71 ...12 A5
Little Wood Dr
　HACK/IN S12 ...154 B2
Little Wood Rd
　HACK/IN S12 ...154 C2
Littlewood St
　DONS/BSCR DN4 ...55 H3
Littlewood Wy MALT S66 ...111 F2
Littleworth Cl
　NROS/TKH DN11 ...91 H2
Littleworth La
　BSLYN/ROY S71 ...20 A4
　NROS/TKH DN11 ...91 H2
Litton Cl STV/CWN S43 ...189 G1
Litton Wk BSLY S70 ...2 D3
Liverpool Av DARN/MH S9 ...40 D4
Liverpool St DARN/MH S9 ...116 B5
Livesey St DARN/MH S9 ...116 B4
Livingstone Av WHHL DN2...41 H1
Livingstone Crs
　BSLYN/ROY S71 ...20 B2
Livingstone Rd
　DARN/MH S9 ...127 E1
　RAW S62 ...98 B3
Livingstone Ter BSLY S70 *...3 F6
Livingston Rd
　CHPT/GREN S35 ...80 C5
Lloyd St ATT S4 ...115 H3
Loakfield Dr SHEFN S5 ...101 H2
Lobelia Cl DIN S25 ...148 B3
Lobelia Crs ARMTH DN3 ...29 F4
Lobwood BSLY S70 ...32 A5
Lobwood La BSLY S70 ...32 B5
Lockeaflash Crs BSLY S70...32 D4
Locke Av BSLY S70 ...31 G3
Locke Rd DOD/DAR S75 ...30 C4
Lockesley Av CONI DN12 ...88 C1
Locke St BSLY S70 ...31 F3
Lock House Rd
　DARN/MH S9 ...117 E3
Locking Dr ARMTH DN3 ...43 E5
Lock La DARN/MH S9 ...117 G1
Lockoford La CHNE S41 ...187 G3
Locksley Av ARMTH DN3 ...29 F5
Locksley Dr MALT S66 ...132 D1
Lock St ST/HB/BR S6 ...125 G1
Lockton Cl CHPT/GREN S35...80 A3
Lockwood Av DIN S25 ...148 B5
Lockwood Cl
　RHAM/THRY S65 ...107 E2
Lockwood La BSLY S70 ...31 H3
Lockwood Rd DEARNE S63 ...37 G4
　DON DN1 ...40 C5
　RHAM/THRY S65 ...107 E2
Lodge Cl STV/CWN S43 ...189 E5
Lodge Dr RAW S62 ...81 H2
Lodge Farm Cl DIN S25 ...148 B2
　RCH S42 ...195 G3
Lodge Hill Dr
　AU/AST/KP S26 ...159 F3
Lodge La AU/AST/KP S26 ...145 F4
　CHPT/GREN S35 ...79 E5
　DIN S25 ...135 F4
　FUL S10 ...137 E2
　SHEFS S8 ...95 F3
Lodge Moor Rd FUL S10 ...136 C2
Lodge Pl STV/CWN S43 ...189 G3
Lodge Wy RHAM S60 ...118 C3
Loganberry Ct MALT S66 ...108 B2
Logan Rd DARN/MH S9 ...128 B3
Loicher La CHPT/GREN S35...94 D5
Lomas Cl ST/HB/BR S6 ...112 C5
Lombard Cl DOD/DAR S75...14 A4
Lombard Crs WMB/DAR S73...34 C5
London Cft BSLYN/ROY S71...20 B3
London Rd SHEFP/MNR S2 ...139 H1
London Rd South
　SHEFS S8 ...140 A3
London St STV/CWN S43 ...180 B3
London Wy KIMB S61 ...95 E2
Long Acre BSLYN/ROY S71 ...15 F3
Longacre Cl MOS S20 ...157 G4
Long Acre Vw MOS S20 ...157 G5
Longacre Wy MOS S20 ...157 G5
Longcar La BSLY S70 ...2 B7
Long Cswy BSLYN/ROY S71...20 C4
Longcliffe Cl CUD/GR S72 ...17 E2
Longcliff Wk CHSW S40 ...186 C5
Longcroft Crs DRON S18 ...170 A1
Longcroft Rd DRON S18 ...170 A1
Longedge Gv RCH S42 ...195 H4
Longedge La RCH S42 ...195 G5
Longedge Ri RCH S42 ...195 G3
Longfellow Dr
　RHAM/THRY S65 ...106 D4
Longfellow Rd
　DONS/BSCR DN4 ...72 A2
Longfield Cl WMB/DAR S73...49 H1

Long Field Dr ARMTH DN3 ...29 G5
Longfield Dr
　DONS/BSCR DN4 ...73 H2
　RHAM/THRY S65 ...108 D1
Longfield Gra CHNE S41 ...186 C5
Long Field Rd ARMTH DN3 ...29 G4
Longfield Rd FUL S10 ...124 D2
Longfields Crs HOY S74 ...61 H2
Longfields Rd
　BSLYN/ROY S71 ...15 F4
Longford Cl
　TOT/DORE S17 * ...161 G3
Longford Crs
　TOT/DORE S17 ...161 G3
Longford Dr
　TOT/DORE S17 ...161 F4
Longford Rd
　TOT/DORE S17 ...161 F4
Longford Spinney
　TOT/DORE S17 ...161 F4
Long Henry Rw
　SHEFP/MNR S2 ...11 K4
Longlands BSVR S44 ...197 E2
Longlands Dr
　AU/AST/KP S26 ...159 G3
Long Lands La BTLY DN5 ...24 B3
Long La BTLY DN5 ...54 B1
　ECK/KIL S21 ...168 C2
　ECK/KIL S21 ...173 E2
　FUL S10 ...124 B3
　RHAM S60 ...130 B1
　ST/HB/BR S6 ...122 D2
　ST/HB/BR S6 ...123 H2
　STKB/PEN S36 ...45 F5
　STV/CWN S43 ...173 G4
Longley Av West SHEFN S5...114 D2
Longley Cl DOD/DAR S75 ...18 A3
　SHEFN S5 ...115 F2
Longley Crs SHEFN S5 ...115 F1
Longley Dr SHEFN S5 ...115 F2
Longley Farm Vw
　SHEFN S5 ...115 F2
Longley Hall Gv SHEFN S5...115 F2
Longley Hall Ri SHEFN S5 ...115 F2
Longley Hall Rd SHEFN S5 ...115 F1
Longley Hall Wy SHEFN S5...115 G1
Longley Ings STKB/PEN S36...45 G4
Longley La SHEFN S5 ...115 F2
Longley Spring HOY S74 ...61 G1
Longley St DOD/DAR S75 ...18 A3
Long Line ECC S11 ...150 B3
Longman Rd BSLY S70 ...3 F1
Longridge Rd
　BSLYN/ROY S71 ...20 D1
Long Rd MALT S66 ...108 D5
Longshaw Cl STV/CWN S43...189 H2
Longside Wy DOD/DAR S75...18 C5
Longstone Crs
　HACK/IN S12 ...155 F1
Longthwaite Cl DIN S25 ...134 C1
Longton Rd ARMTH DN3 ...29 G2
Longwood Cl MALT S66 ...108 B1
Lonsdale Av MALT S66 *...33 H2
　WHHL DN2 ...57 F2
Lonsdale Cl DIN S25 ...148 C2
Lonsdale Rd ST/HB/BR S6 ...114 A5
Loosemore Dr
　HACK/IN S12 ...141 F5
Lopham Cl OWL S3 ...126 B3
Lopham St OWL S3 ...126 B3
Lordens Hl DIN S25 ...135 E4
Lord Roberts Rd CHSW S40...192 C3
Lords Cl BSVR S44 ...196 D3
　CONI DN12 ...70 C4
Lordsmill St CHNE S41 ...5 H6
Lorna Rd MEX/SWTN S64 ...67 E3
Lorne Cl DRON S18 ...170 B1
Lorne Rd DEARNE S63 ...36 D2
Loscoe Gv DEARNE S63 ...37 F2
Lothian Rd WHHL DN2 ...41 G5
Louden Cl KIMB S61 ...95 H4
Louden Rd KIMB S61 ...95 H4
Lounde Cl BTLY DN5 ...54 C4
Loundes Rd DRON S18 ...172 A3
Loundes Wood Av
　CHNE S41 ...186 C1
Lound Rd DARN/MH S9 ...128 B4
Lound Side CHPT/GREN S35...94 B1
Loundsley Green Rd
　CHSW S40 ...186 B5
Louth Rd ECC S11 ...138 D3
Love La OWL S3 ...11 G1
Lovell St ATT S4 ...126 D2
Loversall Cl
　DONS/BSCR DN4 ...71 H3
Love St OWL S3 ...11 G2
Lovetot Av AU/AST/KP S26...145 F2
Lovetot Rd DARN/MH S9 ...127 E2
　KIMB S61 ...96 C4
Lowburn Rd HAN/WDH S13...142 A3
Low Common Rd DIN S25 ...134 B4
Low Cft BSLYN/ROY S71 ...15 H1
Lowcroft Rd DOD/DAR S75 ...50 D2
Low Cudworth CUD/GR S72...21 H2
Lowedges Cl SHEFS S8 ...162 C2
Lowedges Crs SHEFS S8 ...162 C2
Lowedges Dr SHEFS S8 ...162 D2
Lowedges Pl SHEFS S8 *...163 E2

Lowedges Rd *SHEFS* S8 ......162 B3
Lowe La *DOD/DAR* S75......46 B2
Lowell Av *DONS/BSCR* DN4 ....71 H2
Lower Castlereagh St
BSLY S70.....................................3 F5
Lower Dolcliffe Rd
MEX/SWTN S64 ....66 D3
Lower Farm La *BSLY* S70 ....48 D1
Lower Grove Rd *CHSW* S40 .....4 E4
The Lower Limes *BSLY* S70 ....48 D1
Lower Malton Rd *BTLY* DN5....39 E3
Lower Mill Cl *DEARNE* S63 ......53 E1
Lower Thomas St *BSLY* S70......3 F6
Lower Unwin St
STKB/PEN S36 ....44 D4
Lower York St
WMB/DAR S73 * 50 B2
KIMB S61 ....97 G3
Lowfield Av *HACK/IN* S12.....155 G4
Lowfield Cl *ARMTH* DN3.........29 C1
Lowfield Farm
DEARNE S63 * 53 G1
Lowfield Gv *DEARNE* S63 ......53 G1
Lowfield Mdw *DEARNE* S63 ....53 F4
Lowfield Rd *DEARNE* S63........53 F5
WHHL DN2 ....41 G3
Lowfields *STV/CWN* S43 ......182 C4
Lowgate *BTLY* DN5 ....39 E3
Lowgates *STV/CWN* S43 ....182 B4
Low Golden Smithies
MEX/SWTN S64 ....66 A4
Low Grange Rd *DEARNE* S63..37 G2
Low Grange Sq *DEARNE* S63 ..37 G2
Lowhouse Rd *SHEFN* S5.......103 E2
Low Laithes Vw
WMB/DAR S73 ....50 A5
Lowlands Cl *BSLYN/ROY* S71 ..20 D2
BTLY DN5...................................26 D4
Low La *KIMB* S61 ....105 E1
Low Matlock La
ST/HB/BR S6.........................113 E5
Low Pasture Cl
DOD/DAR S75 ....30 C3
Low Riddings *MALT* S66.......108 C5
Low Rd *BSVR* S44 ....184 B4
CONI DN12 ....89 E1
DONS/BSCR DN4 ....71 C1
RHAM S60...............................124 C1
Low Rd East
DONS/BSCR DN4 ....70 C2
Low Rd West
DONS/BSCR DN4 ....70 C3
Lowry Dr *DRON* S18..............170 D2
Low St *DOD/DAR* S75...............80 A2
Lowther Rd *DON* DN1 ....40 C5
ST/HB/BR S6.........................114 B3
Lowton Wy *MALT* S66...........109 G4
Low Vw *DOD/DAR* S75 ....30 A3
Low Wood Cl
MEX/SWTN S64 * 86 A2
Loxley Av *WMB/DAR* S73 ....50 A3
Loxley Cl *CHSW* S40 ....191 H4
Loxley New Rd
ST/HB/BR S6.........................113 H5
Loxley Pk *ST/HB/BR* S6........113 G5
Loxley Rd *BSLYN/ROY* S71 ....21 F4
ST/HB/BR S6.........................112 A2
Loxley View Rd *FUL* S10 .....124 D2
Loy Cl *KIMB* S61.......................97 E3
Lucas Cl *ATT* S4.....................187 E4
Lucas St *ATT* S4.....................115 G3
Ludgate Cl *CHNE* S41 ....187 F2
Lugano Cv *WMB/DAR* S73 .....34 C4
Luke La *ST/HB/BR* S6............113 F5
Lulworth Cl *BSLY* S70...............32 B2
Lumley Crs *MALT* S66...........111 G3
Lumley St *ATT* S4 ....126 D3
Lump La *CHPT/GREN* S35.......93 E5
Lumsdale Rd *STV/CWN* S43..189 G1
Lundy Rd *DRON* S18 ....171 E3
Lunn Rd *CUD/GR* S72..............21 H1
Lupton Crs *SHEFS* S8............162 D2
Lupton Dr *SHEFS* S8 ....162 D2
Lupton Rd *SHEFS* S8.............162 D2
Luterell Dr *AU/AST/KP* S26 ..145 F2
Lutterworth Dr
AWLS/ASK DN6 ....25 E1
Lych Gate Cl
DONS/BSCR DN4 ....74 C1
Lydden Cl *STV/CWN* S43 ......188 C1
Lydford Av *CHNE* S41 ....179 H5
Lydgate Ct *FUL* S10 ....124 C4
Lydgate Hall Crs *FUL* S10 ....124 C4
Lydgate La *FUL* S10...............124 C4

Lymegate *DEARNE* S63 ....63 H2
Lyme St *RHAM* S60....................8 C5
Lyminster Rd *ST/HB/BR* S6...101 E4
Lyminton La *RHAM* S60...........130 A3
Lymister Av *RHAM* S60..........119 F2
Lyncroft *RHAM* S60 * 118 D4
Lyndale Av *ARMTH* DN3..........42 A1
Lynden Av *AWLS/ASK* DN6 .....25 E2
Lyndhurst Bank
STKB/PEN S36 ....44 D4
Lyndhurst Cl *ECC* S11............139 E4
Lyndhurst Crs *ARMTH* DN3....29 E4
Lyndhurst Rd *ECC* S11...........139 E4
Lynham Av *BSLY* S70................50 D2
Lynmouth Rd *ABRD* S7...........139 G5
Lynn Pl *DARN/MH* S9 ....116 D4
Lynthwaite Cl
WMB/DAR S73........................63 H1
Lynton Av *RHAM* S60.............119 G1
Lynton Dr *ARMTH* DN3............29 E5
Lynton Rd *ECC* S11................139 F2
Lynwood Cl *DRON* S18...........170 B2
Lynwood Dr *BSLYN/ROY* S71 ..15 G4
MEX/SWTN S64 ....66 D3
Lyons Cl *ATT* S4.....................115 G5
Lyons Rd *ATT* S4....................115 G5
Lyons St *ATT* S4 ....115 G4
Lytham Av *BSLYN/ROY* S71 ....20 D2
Lytham Cl *DONS/BSCR* DN4....74 D2
Lyttleton Crs *STKB/PEN* S36....44 C5
Lytton Av *SHEFN* S5...............101 G5
Lytton Cl *DONS/BSCR* DN4 .....71 H2
Lytton Crs *SHEFN* S5..............101 G4
Lytton Dr *SHEFN* S5................101 G4
Lytton Rd *SHEFN* S5...............101 G4

M

Mabel St *RHAM* S60 ....9 J6
Macaulay Crs *ARMTH* DN3.......43 H4
Machin Dr *RAW* S62 ....84 C3
Machins Ct *DRON* S18............171 E1
Mackenzie Crs
CHPT/GREN S35 ....93 F2
FUL S10 ....10 B6
Mackenzie St *ECC* S11...........139 G2
Mackinnon Av
AU/AST/KP S26.....................159 H3
Macmanus Av *RAW* S62..........85 F3
Macnaghten Rd
DOD/DAR S75 ....60 D3
Macro Rd *WMB/DAR* S73 ......50 C4
Madehurst Gdns
SHEF/MNR S2........................140 B3
Madehurst Ri
SHEF/MNR S2........................140 B3
Madehurst Rd
SHEF/MNR S2........................140 B3
Madehurst Vw
SHEF/MNR S2........................140 B3
Madin Dr *STV/CWN* S43 ....189 F3
Madingley Cl
DONS/BSCR DN4 ....71 G3
Madin St *CHNE* S41....................5 F1
Mafeking Pl
CHPT/GREN S35 ....81 E5
Magellan Rd *MALT* S66..........110 C2
Magna Cl *MALT* S66 ....108 A3
Magna Crs *MALT* S66 ....108 A3
Magna La *RHAM/THRY* S65....99 F5
Magnolia Cl *ARMTH* DN3 ....29 F4
CUD/GR S72..............................17 F2
DIN S25 ....148 B5
Magpie Gv *SHEF/MNR* S2 .....127 E5
Mahon Av *RAW* S62..................85 F5
Maidstone Rd
ST/HB/BR S6.........................101 F5
Maidwell Wy *ARMTH* DN3......29 E3
Main Av *CONI* DN12..................70 B5
TOT/DORE S17 ....161 E4
Main La *DARN/MH* S9 ....128 A2
DRON S18 ....172 A4
ECK/KIL S21 ....173 F4
ECK/KIL S21 ....175 H2
HACK/IN S12 ....165 G1
Main St *ARMTH* DN3 ....58 D4
AU/AST/KP S26 ....145 E3
BSVR S44 ....196 C4
BTLY DN5................................54 B5
CHPT/GREN S35 ....101 E1
DEARNE S63 ....37 G5
DIN S25 ....148 B3
EPW DN9 ....75 H1
HACK/IN S12 ....156 B1
KIMB S61 ....97 G3
MALT S66 ....108 D4
MEX/SWTN S64 ....66 D4
RAW S62 ....82 C2
RAW S62 ....85 G5
RHAM S60 ....129 H2
RHAM S60 ....50 A2
Mair Ct *RHAM* S60 ....119 G3
Makin St *MEX/SWTN* S64 ....67 E3
Malcolm St *BSLY* S70 ....32 D2
Malham Ct *CHSW* S40............186 D4
CUD/GR S72..............................17 E1
Malham Ct *BSLY* S70 ....2 B3

Malham Gdns *MOS* S20.........166 D1
Malham Gv *MOS* S20 ....167 E1
Malham Pl *CHPT/GREN* S35 ...80 D5
Malham Tarn Ct
DONS/BSCR DN4 ....57 F5
Malia Rd *CHNE* S41 ....188 A3
Malinda St *OWL* S3.................125 H2
Malinder Cl *ECK/KIL* S21 ......168 B2
Malin Rd *RHAM/THRY* S65 ....107 F1
Malin St *ATT* S4 ....86 B5
Malkin St *CHNE* S41 ....6 H3
Mallard Av *ARMTH* DN3 ....29 F1
Mallard Cl *DONS/BSCR* DN4...71 F2
KIMB S61 ....105 E5
Mallard Ct *STV/CWN* S43 * ...182 B4
Mallard Dr *ECK/KIL* S21 ....167 H1
Mallin Cft *HOY* S74 ....62 A2
Mallory Av *RAW* S62.................85 E5
Mallory Cl *CHNE* S41 ....179 E3
Mallory Dr *MEX/SWTN* S64 ...67 H2
Mallory Rd
RHAM/THRY S65 ....107 E1
Mallory Wy *CUD/GR* S72........17 E5
Malon Wy *HAN/WDH* S13......143 F1
Malson Wy *CHNE* S41 ....187 F3
Maltby St *DARN/MH* S9 ....116 C5
Malthouse La *RCH* S42 ....194 B4
Malthouse Rd
BSLYN/ROY S71 * 3 H5
Malting La *ATT* S4....................11 K1
Maltings Ct *ARMTH* DN3 ....29 F2
The Maltings *RHAM* S60...........9 F7
Maltkiln St *RHAM* S60 ....9 E4
Malton Dr *AU/AST/KP* S26 ....145 G5
Malton Pl *BSLYN/ROY* S71 .....14 C5
WHHL DN2 ....41 F5
Malton St *ATT* S4 ....115 G5
Maltravers Cl
SHEF/MNR S2........................127 E5
Maltravers Crs
SHEF/MNR S2........................126 D4
Maltravers Pl
SHEF/MNR S2........................127 E4
Maltravers Rd
SHEF/MNR S2........................127 E5
Maltravers Ter
SHEF/MNR S2........................127 E5
Maltravers Wy
SHEF/MNR S2........................127 E4
Malvern Av *BTLY* DN5..............39 E5
Malvern Cl *DOD/DAR* S75 ....18 D5
Malvern Dr *MALT* S66 ....108 B2
Malvern Rd *CHSW* S40 ....4 C2
DARN/MH S9 ....127 H2
WHHL DN2 ....57 G1
Malvern Wy *MALT* S66...........108 B2
Manchester Rd *FUL* S10........124 A4
STKB/PEN S36 ....76 B1
Mandeville St *DARN/MH* S9..128 A2
Mangham Rd *KIMB* S61 ....97 H5
Mangham Wy *KIMB* S61..........97 H5
Manifold Av *STV/CWN* S43 ...189 H1
Manknell Rd *CHNE* S41..........187 G1
Mannering Rd
DONS/BSCR DN4 ....71 E2
Manners St *OWL* S3................125 H1
Manor Ap *KIMB* S61...............104 D2
Manor Av *DEARNE* S63 ....37 G5
STV/CWN S43 ....188 D2
Manor Cl *RHAM/THRY* S65 ....107 F1
STV/CWN S43 ....188 D2
Manor Ct *RHAM* S60 ....191 H1
Manor Court Rd *BSVR* S44 ....196 C1
Manor Crs *CHSW* S40............191 H1
CUD/GR S72..............................17 H4
DRON S18 ....170 D2
RHAM S60 ....118 B4
Manor Dr *AU/AST/KP* S26 ....147 F5
BTLY DN5...................................69 F3
CHSW S40 ....191 H1
DIN S25 ....134 C3
RHAM S60 ....120 A3
STV/CWN S43 ....188 D2
WMB/DAR S73 ....7 J4
Manor End *BTLY* DN5...............26 B3
Manor Farm Cl
AU/AST/KP S26.....................131 F5
AWLS/ASK DN6 ....25 F1
BSLYN/ROY S71 ....15 H4
Manor Farm Ct
ECK/KIL S21 ....168 B3
MOS S20 * 157 G2
RHAM S60 ....99 H2
Manor Farm Dr
MEX/SWTN S64 ....86 A1
Manor Farm Gdns *DIN* S25...148 B4
Manor Farm Ms
MOS S20 * 157 G2
Manor Flds *RHAM* S60 ....9 H5
Manor Gdns *BSLYN/ROY* S71..33 G2
BTLY DN5...................................54 B4
Manor Gv *BSLYN/ROY* S71 .....15 F1
CUD/GR S72..............................17 H4
STV/CWN S43 ....177 E4
Manor House Cl *HOY* S74.......62 A2
Manor House Ct *BTLY* DN5.....39 F1
Manor House Rd *KIMB* S61 ...104 C1

Manor Laith Rd
SHEF/MNR S2........................126 D5
Manor La *DIN* S25..................135 E3
MEX/SWTN S64 ....67 E1
SHEF/MNR S2........................141 E1
Manor Oaks Cl
SHEF/MNR S2........................127 E4
Manor Oaks Ct
SHEF/MNR S2........................126 D4
Manor Oaks Dr
SHEF/MNR S2........................126 D4
Manor Oaks Gdns
SHEF/MNR S2........................126 D4
Manor Oaks Pl
SHEF/MNR S2........................127 E5
Manor Oaks Rd
SHEF/MNR S2........................126 D4
Manor Occupation Rd
BSLYN/ROY S71 ....12 B5
Manor Park Av
SHEF/MNR S2........................141 F1
Manor Park Centre
SHEF/MNR S2........................141 F1
Manor Park Cl
SHEF/MNR S2........................141 F1
Manor Park Ct
SHEF/MNR S2........................141 F1
Manor Park Crs
SHEF/MNR S2........................141 F1
Manor Park Dr
SHEF/MNR S2........................141 F1
Manor Park Pl
SHEF/MNR S2........................141 F1
Manor Park Ri
SHEF/MNR S2........................127 F5
Manor Park Rd
RAW S62 ....98 C1
Manor Park Wy
SHEF/MNR S2........................141 F1
Manor Pl *RAW* S62...................98 C1
Manor Rd *AU/AST/KP* S26.....159 F2
BTLY DN5...................................26 C3
CHSW S40 ....191 G1
CUD/GR S72..............................21 G1
DEARNE S63 ....37 G2
DEARNE S63 ....64 A1
DIN S25 ....134 C3
ECK/KIL S21 ....168 B5
MALT S66 ....111 E3
MEX/SWTN S64 ....86 B1
RHAM S60 ....118 B4
STV/CWN S43 ....177 E4
STV/CWN S43 ....182 A4
Manor Sq *DEARNE* S63............36 D2
Manor St *BSLYN/ROY* S71 ......15 H4
Manor Vw *CUD/GR* S72...........17 H4
MOS S20 * 157 F3
Manor Wy *AU/AST/KP* S26 ...147 F5
DEARNE S63 ....53 F5
HOY S74 ....62 A2
Manse Cl *DONS/BSCR* DN4.....58 C5
Manse Farm Ms
CUD/GR S72..............................16 D5
Mansel Av *SHEFN* S5..............101 G3
Mansel Crs *SHEFN* S5............101 G3
Mansel Rd *SHEFN* S5.............101 G3
Mansfeldt Crs *CHNE* S41 ......187 E3
Mansfeldt Dr *CHNE* S41 ....42 B3
Mansfield Dr *HACK/IN* S12...141 H4
Mansfield Rd
AU/AST/KP S26.....................158 D2
BSLYN/ROY S71 ....14 D4
BSVR S44 ....197 E5
CHNE S41 ....193 F5
ECK/KIL S21 ....168 D2
HACK/IN S12 ....141 H4
RHAM S60 ....9 G5
Manton St *SHEF/MNR* S2 ....11 H7
Manvers Cl
AU/AST/KP S26.....................145 F3
DIN S25 ....148 B1
Manvers Pk *DEARNE* S63.......66 A2
Manvers Rd
AU/AST/KP S26.....................145 F3
BSVR S44 ....197 E5
MEX/SWTN S64 ....66 C3
MOS S20 * 157 G2
ST/HB/BR S6.........................114 A5
Manvers Wy *DEARNE* S63.......66 E1
Maori Av *DEARNE* S63 ....52 C3
Maple Av *DONS/BSCR* DN4.....58 B5
MALT S66 ....110 B3
Maplebeck Dr
DARN/MH S9 ....117 G2
Maplebeck Rd
DARN/MH S9 ....117 G2
Maple Cl *BSLY* S70 ....32 B3
Maple Croft Crs
DARN/MH S9 ....116 B1
Maple Croft Rd
DARN/MH S9 ....116 B1
Maple Dr *ECK/KIL* S21 ....168 A3
MALT S66 ....108 B3
Maple Gv *CHPT/GREN* S35 .....94 A2
CONI DN12 ....89 E5
DARN/MH S9 ....128 C4
STKB/PEN S36 ....76 B5
Maple Pl *AU/AST/KP* S26.......145 F3
DOD/DAR S75 ....60 B5

Maple St *STV/CWN* S43 ....189 F1
Maplewood Av *MALT* S66 .....108 B1
Mapperley Rd *DRON* S18 ......170 A4
Mappin St *SHEF* S1 ....10 D3
Mappin's Rd *RHAM* S60 ....129 G2
Mapplebeck Dr
CHPT/GREN S35 ....80 C4
Mapplewell Dr
DOD/DAR S75 ....14 A4
Maran Av *WMB/DAR* S73 ....35 G5
Marbeck Cl *DIN* S25 ....134 B4
Marcham Dr *MOS* S20...........157 G1
March Ga *CONI* DN12 ....89 E2
March St *CONI* DN12 ....89 E1
DARN/MH S9 ....116 D5
March Vale Ri *CONI* DN12 ......89 E2
Marchwood Av
ST/HB/BR S6..........................124 A1
Marchwood Cl *CHSW* S40 ....4 C2
Marchwood Dr
ST/HB/BR S6..........................113 E5
Marchwood Rd
ST/HB/BR S6..........................113 E5
Marcliff Cl *MALT* S66.............107 H5
Marcliff Crs *MALT* S66 ....107 H5
Marcliff La *MALT* S66 ....107 H5
Mardale Cl *CHNE* S41 ....179 E5
Marden Rd *ABRD* S7 ....139 G4
Margaret Cl
AU/AST/KP S26.....................145 F4
WMB/DAR S73........................34 D5
Margaret Rd *WMB/DAR* S73..34 D5
Margaret St *MALT* S66 ....111 F5
SHEF S1 ....11 G7
Margate St *ATT* S4 ....115 H4
Margetson Crs *SHEFN* S5......101 H3
Margetson Dr *SHEFN* S5.......101 H3
Margetson Rd *SHEFN* S5.......101 H3
Marian Rd *ARMTH* DN3 ....29 E5
Marigold Cl *SHEFN* S5...........116 A1
Marina Ri *WMB/DAR* S73........34 C5
Marine Dr *CHNE* S41..................5 K4
Marion Rd *ST/HB/BR* S6........113 H4
Markbrook Dr
CHPT/GREN S35 ....80 A3
Market Cl *BSLYN/ROY* S71 ....3 J5
Market Hl *BSLY* S70 ....3 F4
Market Pde *BSLY* S70 ....3 G4
Market Pl *BSVR* S44 ....196 D2
CHSW S40 ....191 G1
CUD/GR S72..............................16 D5
DON DN1 ....6 D2
SHEF S1 ....11 H2
The Market Pl *MOS* S20 * 157 E3
Market Rd *DON* DN1 ....6 F3
Market Sq *RHAM/THRY* S65 * ..9 F3
Market St *AWLS/ASK* DN6 .....25 F5
BSLY S70 ....3 F4
CHPT/GREN S35 ....94 B1
CUD/GR S72..............................16 D5
DEARNE S63 ....37 G2
ECK/KIL S21 ....166 D5
HOY S74 ....62 A2
MEX/SWTN S64 ....66 C3
RHAM S60 ....50 B1
STKB/PEN S36 ....44 D3
STV/CWN S43 ....182 A4
Markfield Dr *MALT* S66..........108 B3
Markham Av *ARMTH* DN3.......42 C3
CONI DN12 ....88 C1
Markham Cottages
CONI DN12 * 88 C1
Markham Ct *CONI* DN12 * 88 C1
Markham Crs
STV/CWN S43 ....182 B4
Markham Rd *CHSW* S40 ....4 E5
Markland Av *STV/CWN* S43 ..185 G2
Markland Crs *STV/CWN* S43..185 G2
Markland La *STV/CWN* S43 ..185 G2
Mark La *FUL* S10 ....137 E4
Mark St *BSLY* S70 ....3 G6
Marlborough Av *BTLY* DN5.....55 F2
Marlborough Cl
DEARNE S63 ....37 E2
DIN S25 ....148 B1
Marlborough Ri
AU/AST/KP S26.....................145 G4
Marlborough Rd *FUL* S10 .....125 E4
WHHL DN2 ....7 J2
Marlborough Ter *BSLY* S70 * ..2 E6
Marlcliffe Rd *ST/HB/BR* S6 ...113 G2
Marlfield Cl
CHPT/GREN S35 ....102 B1
Marlow Cl *MALT* S66..............108 C1
WHHL DN2 ....41 G5
Marlowe Dr
RHAM/THRY S65 ....106 D4
Marlowe Rd
RHAM/THRY S65 ....106 D4
Marlow Rd *WHHL* DN2 ....41 G5
Marples Cl *SHEFS* S8 ....139 H3
Marples Dr *SHEFS* S8 ....139 H3
Marrick Ct *CHPT/GREN* S35 ...93 H1
Marri Av *RAW* S62 ....85 G5
Marriott La *ABRD* S7 ....152 B2
Marriott Pl *RAW* S62 ....85 G5
Marriott Rd *ABRD* S7 ....152 B2
MEX/SWTN S64 ....66 C4
Marrison Dr *ECK/KIL* S21 .....168 A2
Marr Ter *FUL* S10 ....138 B1

Marsala Wk *WMB/DAR* S73 ....**34** D4
Marsden La *OWL* S3 ....**10** E2
Marsden Pl *CHSW* S40 * **4** A5
  CHSW S40 * **5** F2
Marsden Rd
  STKB/PEN S36 * **77** E2
Marsden St *CHSW* S40 ....**5** F3
Marshall Av
  DONS/BSCR DN4 ....**71** G1
Marshall Cl *RAW* S62 ....**98** B2
Marshall Gv *DEARNE* S63 .....**65** F3
Marshall Rd *SHEFS* S8 ....**152** D3
Marsh Av *DRON* S18 ....**163** F5
Marsh Cl *MOS* S20 ....**166** C2
Marshfield *SHEFS* S70 ....**47** H4
Marshfield Gv
  STV/CWN S43 ....**182** C4
Marsh Ga *BTLY* DN5 ....**6** A1
Marsh House Rd *ECC* S11 ....**138** B5
Marsh La *ARMTH* DN3 ....**28** C1
  BTLY DN5 ....**5** G3
  FUL S10 ....**124** B4
Marsh Rd *BTLY* DN5 ....**39** H5
Marsh St *RHAM* S60 ....**8** D7
  STKB/PEN S36 ....**77** F2
  WMB/DAR S73 ....**50** C2
Marsh Vw *ECK/KIL* S21 ....**174** B1
Marson Av *AWLS/ASK* DN6 ....**24** D2
Marston Cl *DRON* S18 ....**170** B3
Marston Crs *BSLYN/ROY* S71..**19** H1
Marstone Crs
  STV/CWN S43 ....**181** G5
Marston Rd *FUL* S10 ....**124** D3
Martin Cl *ECK/KIL* S21 ....**166** C5
Martin Crs *SHEFN* S5 ....**102** B3
Martindale Cl
  STV/CWN S43 ....**181** C5
Martin La *HOY* S74 ....**48** D4
Martin Ri *ECK/KIL* S21 ....**166** C5
  KIMB S61 ....**82** C5
Martins Rd *BSLYN/ROY* S71 ...**21** E4
Martin St *ST/HB/BR* S6 ....**10** B1
Marton Rd *BTLY* DN5 ....**26** B2
Marvell Rd *BTLY* DN5 ....**38** D4
Mary Ann Cl *BSLYN/ROY* S71..**20** D5
Mary Ann St *CHNE* S41 ....**179** E2
Maryhill Cl *RHAM* S60 ....**130** B3
Mary La *WMB/DAR* S73 ....**35** F5
Mary St *CUD/GR* S72 ....**36** A4
  ECK/KIL S21 ....**166** D5
  RHAM S60 ....**8** D3
  SHEFP/MNR S2 ....**11** G7
Mary's Pl *DOD/DAR* S75 ....**18** D5
Masbrough St *RHAM* S60 ....**8** B5
Masefield Cl *DIN* S25 ....**135** E5
Masefield Rd *DEARNE* S63 ....**64** C1
  HAN/WDH S13 ....**142** A3
  WHHL DN2 ....**41** G3
Masham Ct *DONS/BSCR* DN4..**58** A5
Masham Rd
  DONS/BSCR DN4 ....**74** A1
Mason Av *AU/AST/KP* S26 ....**145** F1
Mason Crs *HAN/WDH* S13 ....**142** B3
Mason Dr *AU/AST/KP* S26 ....**145** F1
Mason Gv *HAN/WDH* S13 .....**142** B4
Mason Lathe Rd *SHEFN* S5 ..**103** E4
Mason St *DEARNE* S63 ....**37** G5
Masons Wy *BSLY* S70 ....**32** C4
Mason Wy *HOY* S74 ....**61** H1
Massey Rd *HAN/WDH* S13 ....**143** H5
Masson Cl *CHSW* S40 ....**186** D4
Mastall La *BTLY* DN5 ....**27** C5
Masters Crs *SHEFN* S5 ....**102** B4
Masters Rd *SHEFN* S5 ....**102** B4
Mastin Av *STV/CWN* S43 ......**184** C1
Mather Av *DARN/MH* S9 ....**127** H5
Mather Cl *DARN/MH* S9 ....**127** H4
Mather Crs *DARN/MH* S9 ....**127** H4
Mather Dr *DARN/MH* S9 ....**127** H4
Mather Rd *DARN/MH* S9 ....**127** H4
Matilda La *SHEF* S1 ....**11** H6
Matilda St *SHEF* S1 ....**11** F5
Matilda Wy *SHEF* S1 ....**11** F5
Matlock Dr *STV/CWN* S43 .....**189** E4
Matlock Rd *BSLYN/ROY* S71 ...**20** B1
  RCH S42 ....**191** C5
  ST/HB/BR S6 ....**125** E2
Mattersey Cl
  DONS/BSCR DN4 ....**74** A3
Matthew Gap
  STKB/PEN S36 ....**64** D2
Matthews Av *DEARNE* S63 ....**64** D2
Matthews Cl *DEARNE* S63 ....**64** D3
Matthews Dr *MALT* S66 ....**121** F1
Matthews Fold *SHEFS* S8 .....**153** G4
Matthews La *SHEFS* S8 ....**153** G4
Matthew St *OWL* S3 ....**10** E1
Maugerhay *SHEFS* S8 ....**153** G4
Maulays Ct *NROS/TKH* DN11..**91** H3
Mauncer Crs
  HAN/WDH S13 ....**143** F3
Mauncer Dr *HAN/WDH* S13 ...**143** F4
Mauncer La *HAN/WDH* S13 ...**143** F4
Maun Wy *SHEFN* S5 ....**115** G1
Maurice St *RAW* S62 ....**98** B3
Mawfa Av *GLV* S14 ....**153** H5
Mawfa Crs *GLV* S14 ....**153** H5
Mawfa Dr *GLV* S14 ....**153** H5
Mawfa La *GLV* S14 ....**153** H5
Mawfa Rd *GLV* S14 ....**153** H5
Mawfield Rd *DOD/DAR* S75 ....**18** B3

Maxey Pl *SHEFS* S8 ....**140** A4
Maxfield Av *FUL* S10 ....**125** E4
Maxwell St *ATT* S4 ....**126** C1
Maxwell Wy *ATT* S4 ....**126** C1
May Av *CHNE* S41 ....**180** A3
  DONS/BSCR DN4 ....**70** G2
Maycock Av *KIMB* S61 ....**96** B4
May Day Gn *BSLY* S70 ....**3** G4
May Day Green Ar *BSLY* S70 *..**3** G4
Mayfield *BSLYN/ROY* S71 ....**20** B3
  STKB/PEN S36 ....**45** H5
Mayfield Crs *BSLY* S70 ....**31** G4
  NROS/TKH DN11 ....**91** F3
Mayfield Rd *BTLY* DN5 ....**39** C5
  CHSW S40 ....**191** G2
  FUL S10 ....**137** E3
Mayfields *BTLY* DN5 ....**38** D1
Mayflower Ct *HACK/IN* S12 ...**141** H4
Mayflower Rd
  DONS/BSCR DN4 ....**70** C3
Mayflower Wy
  WMB/DAR S73 ....**50** C3
Maynard Rd *CHSW* S40 ....**4** A7
  RHAM S60 ....**120** A1
May Rd *ST/HB/BR* S6 ....**113** H4
May Ter *BSLY* S70 ....**2** A4
Maythorne Cl *DOD/DAR* S75 ..**14** A4
May Tree Cl *MOS* S20 ....**157** E4
Maytree Cl *WMB/DAR* S73 .....**51** E1
May Tree Cft *MOS* S20 ....**157** E4
May Tree La *MOS* S20 ....**157** E4
McConnel Crs
  NROS/TKH DN11 ....**90** D2
McGregor's Wy *CHSW* S40 ...**195** H1
McIntyre Rd *STKB/PEN* S36 ...**76** D3
McKenzie Wy
  AU/AST/KP S26 ....**159** H3
McLaren Crs *MALT* S66 ....**111** E4
McLintock Wy *BSLY* S70 ....**2** D4
McLoughlin Wy
  AU/AST/KP S26 ....**159** H3
McMahon Av *STV/CWN* S43..**189** F3
Meaburn Cl
  DONS/BSCR DN4 ....**74** B1
Meadow Av *CUD/GR* S72 ....**22** B3
  RAW S62 ....**84** D4
Meadow Bank Av *ABRD* S7 ...**137** F5
Meadowbank Cl *KIMB* S61 ...**105** E5
Meadow Bank Rd *ECC* S11 ..**139** F3
  KIMB S61 ....**104** A5
Meadow Cl *BSVR* S44 ....**196** D4
  DRON S18 ....**163** G4
  RHAM/THRY S65 ....**99** C5
  STV/CWN S43 ....**177** C5
  STV/CWN S43 ....**180** B4
Meadow Ct *BSLYN/ROY* S71 ...**15** H1
Meadowcourt
  DARN/MH S9 ....**116** D2
Meadow Crs *BSLYN/ROY* S71..**12** D5
  CUD/GR S72 ....**17** H5
  MOS S20 * **166** B1
Meadow Cft *ARMTH* DN3 ....**29** C5
  BTLY DN5 ....**54** C5
  CUD/GR S72 ....**17** E1
  MEX/SWTN S64 ....**86** A3
Meadowcroft Cl *RHAM* S60 ..**119** H4
Meadowcroft Gdns
  MOS S20 ....**157** E5
Meadowcroft Gld *MOS* S20 ..**157** E5
Meadowcroft Ri *MOS* S20 ....**157** E5
Meadow Dr *BSLYN/ROY* S71 ...**20** D3
  CHPT/GREN S35 ....**93** C1
  MEX/SWTN S64 ....**86** A1
Meadowfield Dr *HOY* S74 ....**62** A4
Meadow Field Rd
  ARMTH DN3 ....**29** C1
  WMB/DAR S73 ....**51** E4
Meadow Gate Av *MOS* S20 ..**157** H2
Meadow Gate Cl *MOS* S20 ...**157** H3
Meadow Gate La *MOS* S20 ...**157** H4
Meadowgate Pk
  ECK/KIL S21 ....**168** A1
Meadowgates *DEARNE* S63 ...**53** E2
Meadow Gv *TOT/DORE* S17 ..**161** E4
Meadow Grove Rd
  TOT/DORE S17 ....**160** D4
Meadowhall Rd
  DARN/MH S9 ....**116** D2
  KIMB S61 ....**104** B4
Meadowhall Wy
  DARN/MH S9 ....**116** D2
Meadowhead *SHEFS* S8 ....**152** D5
Meadow Head Av
  SHEFS S8 ....**162** C1
Meadow Head Dr
  SHEFS S8 ....**152** D5
Meadow House Dr *FUL* S10 ..**137** H1
Meadowland Ri
  CUD/GR S72 ....**22** A2
Meadowlands *BSVR* S44 ....**197** F2
Meadow La *MALT* S66 ....**111** E4
  MEX/SWTN S64 ....**67** E5
  WMB/DAR S73 ....**35** F5
Meadow Pk *BSLYN/ROY* S71..**15** H1
Meadows Ct
  NROS/TKH DN11 ....**91** H3
Meadowside Cl *RCH* S42 .....**195** G5
Meadows Rd *DEARNE* S63 .....**65** H2
The Meadows
  AU/AST/KP S26 ....**147** E5
  DOD/DAR S75 ....**18** A3

Meadow St *BSLYN/ROY* S71 ....**3** H2
  DIN S25 ....**134** A3
  KIMB S61 ....**105** E3
  OWL S3 ....**10** D1
Meadow Ter *ECC* S11 ....**139** E2
The Meadow *BTLY* DN5 ....**54** C4
Meadow Vw *BSLY* S70 ....**32** A5
  CHSW S40 ....**191** E4
  STV/CWN S43 ....**185** F3
Meadow View Cl *HOY* S74 .....**61** H3
Meadow View Dr
  RHAM/THRY S65 ....**109** E1
Meadow View Rd
  MEX/SWTN S64 ....**86** B3
  SHEFS S8 ....**152** D5
Meadow Wk *ARMTH* DN3 ......**29** C4
Meadow Wy
  MEX/SWTN S64 ....**66** D4
Meadstead Dr
  BSLYN/ROY S71 ....**15** F1
Meadstead Fold
  BSLYN/ROY S71 ....**15** F1
The Meads *SHEFS* S8 ....**153** F5
The Meadway
  TOT/DORE S17 ....**160** D1
Meakin St *CHNE* S41 ....**193** F4
Mears Cl *STKB/PEN* S36 ....**18** A2
The Mede *AWLS/ASK* DN6 .....**24** D2
Medina Wy *DOD/DAR* S75 ......**18** A2
Medley Vw *CONI* DN12 ....**89** F2
Medlock Cl *HAN/WDH* S13 ...**129** E5
Medlock Cft *HAN/WDH* S13 ..**129** E5
Medlock Crs *HAN/WDH* S13 .**129** E5
Medlock Dr *HAN/WDH* S13 ...**129** E5
Medlock Rd *CHSW* S40 ....**191** C4
  HAN/WDH S13 ....**129** E5
Medway Cl *DOD/DAR* S75 .....**18** B2
Medway Pl *WMB/DAR* S73 .....**50** D4
Meersbrook Av *SHEFS* S8 ....**139** H5
Meersbrook Park Rd
  SHEFS S8 ....**139** H5
Meersbrook Rd *SHEFS* S8 ....**140** B5
Meetinghouse Cft
  HAN/WDH S13 ....**143** G4
Meetinghouse La
  HAN/WDH S13 ....**143** G4
  SHEF S1 ....**11** G2
Mekyll Cl *MALT* S66 ....**108** B3
Melbeck Ct *CHPT/GREN* S35..**93** G1
Melbourne Av
  AU/AST/KP S26 ....**145** G2
  DEARNE S63 ....**52** D3
  FUL S10 ....**125** E5
Melbourne Rd
  DONS/BSCR DN4 ....**71** E2
  STKB/PEN S36 ....**76** C2
Melbourn Rd *FUL* S10 ....**125** E2
Melciss Rd *MALT* S66 ....**108** A5
Melford Dr
  DONS/BSCR DN4 ....**71** G4
Melfort Gln *FUL* S10 ....**124** A4
Melia Av *HOY* S74 ....**61** H2
Melling Av *BTLY* DN5 ....**55** F2
Melling Cl *CHSW* S40 ....**192** B4
Melling Ct *CHSW* S40 ....**192** B4
Mellington Cl *SHEFS* S8 ......**153** G3
Mellor Lea Farm Cha
  CHPT/GREN S35 ....**94** B4
Mellor Lea Farm Dr
  CHPT/GREN S35 ....**94** B4
Mellor Lea Farm Garth
  CHPT/GREN S35 ....**94** B4
Mellor Rd *WMB/DAR* S73 ....**50** B3
Mellor Wy *CHSW* S40 ....**192** C5
Mellow Fields Rd *DIN* S25 ....**134** B1
Mellwood Gv
  WMB/DAR S73 ....**50** A5
Melrose Cl *CHSW* S40 ....**191** G1
  DONS/BSCR DN4 ....**71** E1
  MALT S66 ....**132** D1
Melrose Gv *RHAM* S60 ....**119** G2
Melrose Rd *OWL* S3 ....**126** B1
Melrose Wy *BSLYN/ROY* S71..**20** D5
Meltham Av *CHNE* S41 ....**187** H3
Melton Av *DEARNE* S63 ....**37** C5
  WMB/DAR S73 ....**51** F5
Melton Ct *AU/AST/KP* S26 ...**146** A3
Meltonfield *DEARNE* S63 ......**37** H5
Meltonfield Cl *ARMTH* DN3 ...**43** E5
Melton Gdns *BTLY* DN5 ....**54** B4
Melton Gn *DEARNE* S63 ....**37** C5
Melton Gv *MOS* S20 ....**156** A3
Melton High St *DEARNE* S63..**64** C2
Melton Rd *BTLY* DN5 ....**54** B4
  MEX/SWTN S64 ....**67** F5
Melton St *MEX/SWTN* S64 .....**67** F5
Melton Ter *BSLY* S70 ....**32** C5
Melton Wood Gv *BTLY* DN5 ...**34** B4
Melville Av *DONS/BSCR* DN4..**71** G1
Melville Crs *STV/CWN* S43 ...**188** D5
Melville Dr *SHEFP/MNR* S2 ..**141** G2
Melville St *WMB/DAR* S73 ......**54** A1
Melvinia Crs *DOD/DAR* S75 ...**19** F5
Melwood Ct *ARMTH* DN3 ....**59** E1
Mendip Cl *BTLY* DN5 ....**39** E5
  DOD/DAR S75 ....**18** D5
Mendip Crs *CHSW* S40 ....**186** B5
Mendip Ri *RHAM* S60 ....**118** D3
Merbeck Dr *CHPT/GREN* S35..**80** B5
Merbeck Gv *CHPT/GREN* S35..**80** B5
Mercaston Cl *CHSW* S40 .....**186** A4

Mercel Av *ARMTH* DN3 ....**43** E2
Merchants Wy *WHHL* DN2 ....**41** G1
Mercia Dr *TOT/DORE* S17 ....**161** E2
Meredith Crs
  DONS/BSCR DN4 ....**71** H2
Meredith Rd *ST/HB/BR* S6 ...**113** H4
Mere Gv *ARMTH* DN3 ....**42** C3
Mere La *ARMTH* DN3 ....**42** C3
Merlin Av *BSVR* S44 ....**196** C1
Merlin Cl *AWLS/ASK* DN6 ....**25** F1
  BSLY S70 ....**47** H5
Merlin Wy *KIMB* S61 ....**82** C5
  SHEFN S5 ....**115** G1
Merrian Cft *STV/CWN* S43 *..**180** C5
Merrick Cl *CHSW* S40 ....**186** D4
Merrill Rd *DEARNE* S63 ....**37** E1
Merton La *DARN/MH* S9 ....**103** H5
Merton Ri *DARN/MH* S9 ....**103** H5
Merton Rd *DARN/MH* S9 ....**103** H5
Metcalfe Av *ECK/KIL* S21 .....**168** A2
Methley Cl *HACK/IN* S12 ......**141** F4
Methley St *CUD/GR* S72 ....**21** H1
Mexborough Rd
  DEARNE S63 ....**53** F4
Meynell Cl *CHSW* S40 ....**191** G2
Meynell Crs *SHEFN* S5 ....**101** F5
Meynell Rd *SHEFN* S5 ....**101** F5
Michael Cl *RCH* S42 ....**195** G2
Michael Cft *DEARNE* S63 ....**64** D2
Michael Rd *BSLYN/ROY* S71 ...**21** E5
Mickelden Wy
  DOD/DAR S75 ....**30** C1
Micklebring Gv *CONI* DN12 ....**88** C3
Mickleburn Wy *MALT* S66 ...**109** H2
Mickley La *TOT/DORE* S17 ...**161** F4
Middle Av *RAW* S62 ....**85** F5
Middle Bank
  DONS/BSCR DN4 ....**56** C5
Middleburn Cl *BSLY* S70 ....**32** A3
Middlecliff Rd *MOS* S20 ....**157** E4
Middlecliff Cl *MOS* S20 ....**157** E4
Middlecliff La *CUD/GR* S72 ....**36** A3
  CUD/GR S72 ....**36** A3
Middlecliff Rd *MOS* S20 ....**157** E4
Middlecroft Rd
  STV/CWN S43 ....**189** C2
Middle Dr *RHAM* S60 ....**119** F3
Middlefield Cl
  TOT/DORE S17 ....**160** C1
Middlefield Cft
  TOT/DORE S17 ....**160** C2
Middlefield Rd
  DONS/BSCR DN4 ....**73** H1
  RHAM S60 ....**119** G2
Middlefields Dr *RHAM* S60 ...**120** A3
Middlegate *BTLY* DN5 ....**38** D1
Middleham Rd
  DONS/BSCR DN4 ....**74** A1
Middle Hay Cl *GLV* S14 ....**141** H5
Middle Hay Pl *GLV* S14 ....**141** E5
Middle Hay Ri *GLV* S14 ....**141** H5
Middle Hay Vw *GLV* S14 ......**154** A1
Middle La *CHPT/GREN* S35 ....**92** D5
  RHAM/THRY S65 ....**9** K3
  ST/HB/BR S6 ....**124** C1
Middle La South
  RHAM/THRY S65 ....**106** C3
Middle Ox Cl *MOS* S20 ....**167** F2
Middle Ox Gdns *MOS* S20 ...**167** F2
Middle Pavement
  CHSW S40 * **5** F4
Middle Rd *RHAM/THRY* S65..**106** D2
Middlesex St *BSLY* S70 ....**31** H3
Middle St *BSVR* S44 ....**197** F4
Middleton Av *DIN* S25 ....**134** C5
  STV/CWN S43 ....**189** F4
Middleton La
  CHPT/GREN S35 ....**101** F1
Middleton Rd
  RHAM/THRY S65 ....**9** K4
Middletown Mdw
  STV/CWN S43 ....**177** C5
Middlewood Cha
  ST/HB/BR S6 ....**113** C1
Middlewood Dr *KIMB* S61 ......**96** A4
  ST/HB/BR S6 ....**113** C1
Middlewood Dr East
  ST/HB/BR S6 ....**100** B5
Middlewood Rd
  ST/HB/BR S6 ....**113** C1
Middlewood Rd North
  CHPT/GREN S35 ....**100** B4
Middlewoods
  DOD/DAR S75 ....**30** C3
Middlewoods Wy
  BSLYN/ROY S71 ....**15** F4
Midfield Rd *FUL* S10 ....**124** C3
Midhill Rd *SHEFP/MNR* S2 ...**140** B3
Midhope Wy *DOD/DAR* S75 ...**30** C1
Midhurst Gv *DOD/DAR* S75 ...**30** C1
Midhurst Rd *ST/HB/BR* S6 ...**100** D4
Midland Ct *CHNE* S41 ....**192** D5
Midland Rd *BSLYN/ROY* S71 ...**12** D5
  KIMB S61 ....**8** A4
  MEX/SWTN S64 ....**3** G4
  RAW S62 ....**98** A4
  SHEF S1 ....**11** C7
Midland Ter *CHNE* S41 *.......**192** D5
Midland Wy *STV/CWN* S43 ...**184** A1
Midvale Av *ST/HB/BR* S6 .....**125** C2
Midvale Cl *ST/HB/BR* S6 .....**125** C2
Milano Ri *WMB/DAR* S73 ....**34** D5

Milbanke St *DON* DN1 ....**6** E1
Milburn Ct *MOS* S20 ....**157** G4
Milburn Gv *MOS* S20 ....**157** G4
Milden Pl *BSLY* S70 ....**32** A4
Milden Rd *ST/HB/BR* S6 ....**113** C2
Milefield La *CUD/GR* S72 ....**17** C5
Milefield Vw *CUD/GR* S72 .....**17** H5
Miles Cl *SHEFN* S5 ....**80** C4
Miles Rd *CHPT/GREN* S35 .....**80** C4
  SHEFN S5 ....**114** D3
Mileswood Cl *CUD/GR* S72 ...**23** H4
Milethorn La *DON* DN1 ....**40** B5
Milford Av *HOY* S74 ....**62** D2
Milford Rd *STV/CWN* S43 .....**189** G4
Milford St *DARN/MH* S9 ....**116** D4
Milgate St *BSLYN/ROY* S71 ...**12** D5
Milgrove Crs
  CHPT/GREN S35 ....**80** B3
Milking La *STV/CWN* S43 .....**184** B3
Millais Ri *MALT* S66 ....**108** B2
Millard La *MALT* S66 ....**111** E4
Millbank Cl *CHPT/GREN* S35..**80** B5
Mill Cl *RHAM* S60 ....**105** G5
Mill Ct *BSLY* S70 ....**32** A5
  CHPT/GREN S35 ....**94** A5
Milldale Cl *CHSW* S40 ....**186** C4
Milldale Rd *TOT/DORE* S17 ..**161** F3
Milldyke Cl *RHAM* S60 ....**120** B3
Millennium Wy *CHNE* S41 ...**179** E5
Miller Av *STV/CWN* S43 ....**185** E2
Miller Cft *HAN/WDH* S13 ......**143** E4
Miller Dale Dr *RHAM* S60 *...**118** D5
Miller Rd *ABRD* S7 ....**139** H3
Millers Dl *BSLY* S70 ....**48** A1
Miller St *STKB/PEN* S36 ....**77** H2
Mill Field Ct *ARMTH* DN3 ....**29** C1
Millfield Rd *BTLY* DN5 ....**40** A2
Mill Ga *BTLY* DN5 ....**39** H2
Mill Gn *STV/CWN* S43 ....**181** H4
Mill Green Wy
  STV/CWN S43 ....**185** E2
Mill Hvn *DIN* S25 ....**148** B3
Millhill *ARMTH* DN3 ....**59** E1
Mill Hl *RHAM* S60 ....**120** A3
  WMB/DAR S73 ....**49** H1
Mill Hill Cl *BTLY* DN5 ....**55** F2
Mill Hills *AU/AST/KP* S26 .....**147** F5
Millhouses Cl *ECC* S11 ....**151** H1
Millhouses Gln *ECC* S11 ......**151** H1
Millhouses La *ABRD* S7 ....**152** A2
  ECC S11 ....**138** C5
Millhouses St *HOY* S74 ....**62** A3
Millicent Sq *MALT* S66 ....**111** E4
Millindale *MALT* S66 ....**111** E4
Mill La *AWLS/ASK* DN6 ....**25** F1
  BSVR S44 ....**196** D1
  BTLY DN5 ....**70** B1
  CHSW S40 ....**4** A5
  DEARNE S63 ....**53** E5
  DIN S25 ....**148** B3
  DONS/BSCR DN4 ....**70** C2
  DRON S18 ....**171** F2
  ECK/KIL S21 ....**175** C1
  RAW S62 ....**82** B1
  RHAM S60 ....**129** H3
  STKB/PEN S36 ....**77** H2
  TOT/DORE S17 ....**161** F3
Mill Meadow Gdns
  MOS S20 ....**157** H4
Millmoor La *RHAM* S60 ....**8** B5
Millmoor Rd
  DONS/BSCR DN4 ....**58** A5
  WMB/DAR S73 ....**50** D1
Millmount Rd *HOY* S74 ....**62** B2
  SHEFS S8 ....**139** H5
Millrace Dr *DEARNE* S63 ....**53** E1
Mill Rd *CHPT/GREN* S35 ....**94** B5
  ECK/KIL S21 ....**167** E4
  RHAM S60 ....**129** H3
Mill Road Cl *CHPT/GREN* S35..**94** B5
Millsands *OWL* S3 ....**11** H1
Millside *CUD/GR* S72 ....**17** E1
Millside Ct *BTLY* DN5 ....**39** H2
Millside Wk *CUD/GR* S72 ......**17** E1
Millstone Cl *DRON* S18 ....**170** B1
Millstone Dr
  AU/AST/KP S26 ....**145** F3
Millstream Cl *BTLY* DN5 ....**54** D4
Mill Stream Cl *CHSW* S40 ....**191** G3
Mill St *ARMTH* DN3 ....**42** D4
  CHNE S41 ....**5** H4
  KIMB S61 ....**97** F2
  RHAM S60 ....**8** F7
  STV/CWN S43 ....**185** G2
Millthorpe Rd *SHEFN* S5 .....**102** D5
Mill Vw *DEARNE* S63 ....**52** D4
Mill Wk *BSVR* S44 ....**196** D1
Millwood Rd
  DONS/BSCR DN4 ....**71** F3
Mill Wood Vw
  ST/HB/BR S6 ....**112** C5
Milner Av *STKB/PEN* S36 ....**44** B3
Milner La *MALT* S66 ....**109** E5
Milner Gate Ct *CONI* DN12 ....**89** F1
Milner Rd
  DONS/BSCR DN4 ....**71** F1
Milnes Cl *BSLY* S70 * **3** J7
Milne St *DOD/DAR* S75 ....**18** A3
Milnrow Crs *SHEFN* S5 ....**101** H1
Milnrow Dr *SHEFN* S5 ....**101** H1
Milnrow Rd *SHEFN* S5 ....**101** H1
Milton Av *BTLY* DN5 ....**55** F'

Milton Cl *HOY* S74 ....62 B1
   KIMB S61 ....97 F2
   WMB/DAR S73 ....51 F5
Milton Ct *MEX/SWTN* S64 ....66 A5
Milton Crs *CHSW* S40 ....192 C4
   HOY S74 ....62 A3
Milton Gv *ARMTH* DN3 ....42 D4
   WMB/DAR S73 ....50 C3
Milton La *OWL* S3 ....10 E6
Milton Pl *STV/CWN* S43 ....182 B5
Milton Rd *ABRD* S7 ....139 G5
   ARMTH DN3 ....59 C4
   CHPT/GREN S35 ....93 F1
   DIN S25 ....135 E5
   HOY S74 ....62 A4
   MEX/SWTN S64 ....67 E3
   RHAM/THRY S65 ....9 J1
Milton St *CUD/GR* S72 ....23 H5
   MALT S66 ....110 D4
   MEX/SWTN S64 ....66 A5
   OWL S3 ....10 D6
   RHAM S60 ....8 D1
Milton Wk *DON* DN1 ....6 C5
Minden Cl *MALT* S66 ....108 B5
Minden Ct *BTLY* DN5 ....39 H2
Minimum Ter *CHSW* S40 ....4 C6
Minna Rd *OWL* S3 ....115 F5
Minneymoor Hl *CONI* DN12 ....69 F5
Minneymoor La *CONI* DN12 ....89 F1
Minster Cl *CHPT/GREN* S35 ....102 C1
   DONS/BSCR DN4 ....74 C1
Minster Rd
   CHPT/GREN S35 ....102 C1
Minster Wy *BSLYN/ROY* S71 ....20 D4
Minto Rd *ST/HB/BR* S6 ....113 H3
Miriam Av *CHSW* S40 ....191 E4
Mission Fld *WMB/DAR* S73 ....51 E5
Mitchell Cl *BSLY* S70 ....32 D5
Mitchell Rd *SHEFS* S8 ....152 D3
   WMB/DAR S73 ....34 A5
Mitchell St *OWL* S3 ....10 C2
   STV/CWN S43 ....185 F2
Mitchells Wy
   WMB/DAR S73 ....50 A1
Mitchell Wy *STV/CWN* S43 ....180 C3
Mitchell's St *BSLY* S70 ....33 E5
Mitchelson Av
   DOD/DAR S75 ....30 A3
Moat Cl *MALT* S66 ....108 C2
Moat Cft *BTLY* DN5 ....39 F1
Moat Hills Ct *BTLY* DN5 ....39 G1
Moat House Wy *CONI* DN12 ....69 F5
Moatlands *MALT* S66 ....121 G2
Moat La *MALT* S66 ....121 G3
Modena Ct *WMB/DAR* S73 ....34 C4
Moffat Gdns *WHHL* DN2 ....41 H1
Moffatt Rd *SHEF/MNR* S2 ....140 B3
Molineaux Cl *SHEFN* S5 ....102 D4
Molineaux Rd *SHEFN* S5 ....102 C3
Molineux Av *STV/CWN* S43 ....181 H5
Molloy Pl *SHEFS* S8 ....140 A4
Molloy St *SHEFS* S8 ....140 A5
Mona Av *FUL* S10 ....125 E3
Mona Rd *DONS/BSCR* DN4 ....55 H5
   FUL S10 ....125 E2
Monckton St *DOD/DAR* S75 ....2 C3
Monckton Rd *SHEFN* S5 ....116 B1
Moncrieffe Rd *ABRD* S7 ....139 G4
Monksbridge Rd *DIN* S25 ....134 A4
Monks Cl *KIMB* S61 ....96 A4
Monkspring *BSLY* S70 ....32 C5
Monks Wy *BSLYN/ROY* S71 ....20 D4
Monk Ter *BSLYN/ROY* S71 ....21 E2
Monkton Wy
   BSLYN/ROY S71 ....12 C4
Monkwood Rd *CHNE* S41 ....186 D1
   RAW S62 ....85 E4
Monmouth Rd *WHHL* DN2 ....41 H4
Monmouth St *FUL* S10 ....10 C5
Monnies End *STV/CWN* S43 ......184 C1
Monsal Crs *BSLYN/ROY* S71 ....15 E5
   STV/CWN S43 ....189 F3
Monsal St *DEARNE* S63 ....37 E2
Montague Av *CONI* DN12 ....68 C5
Montague St *CUD/GR* S72 ....17 E4
   DON DN1 ....6 E1
   ECC S11 ....139 G1
Montagu Rd *BTLY* DN5 ....55 E3
Montagu St *MEX/SWTN* S64 ....58 D3
Monteney Crs *SHEFN* S5 ....102 A1
Monteney Gdns *SHEFN* S5 ....102 A2
Monteney Rd *SHEFN* S5 ....102 A2
Montfort Dr *OWL* S3 ....126 B1
Montgomery Dr *ABRD* S7 ....139 G3
Montgomery Gdns
   WHHL DN2 ....41 G5
Montgomery Rd *ABRD* S7 ....139 G3
   DEARNE S63 ....65 E2
Montgomery Terrace Rd
   OWL S3 ....125 H2
Montrose Av *WHHL* DN2 ....41 F5
Montrose Rd *DRON* S18 ....170 B1
Montrose Rd *ABRD* S7 ....139 E5
Monument Dr *CUD/GR* S72 ....17 H2
Monyash Cl *STV/CWN* S43 ....189 G2
Moonpenny Wy *DRON* S18 ....171 E2
Moonshine La *SHEFN* S5 ....114 D1
Moonshine Wy *SHEFN* S5 ....114 D2
Moorbank Cl *DOD/DAR* S75 ....19 E3
   FUL S10 ....123 H4
   WMB/DAR S73 ....49 H1
Moorbank Dr *FUL* S10 ....124 A4

Moorbank Rd *FUL* S10 ....123 H4
   WMB/DAR S73 ....33 H5
Moorbank Vw
   WMB/DAR S73 ....33 H5
Moorbridge Crs
   WMB/DAR S73 ....51 F4
Moorcroft Cl *FUL* S10 ....137 F3
Moorcroft Dr *FUL* S10 ....137 F3
Moorcroft Rd *FUL* S10 ....137 F3
Moordale Vw *RAW* SG2 ....86 A4
Moore End Rd *FUL* S10 ....125 E3
Moore St *SHEF* S1 ....10 E6
Moore Street Jct *OWL* S3 ....10 D7
Moor Farm Av *DIN* S25 ....156 B5
Moor Farm Garth *MOS* S20 ......156 B5
Moor Farm Ri *MOS* S20 ....156 B5
Moorfield Av *BSVR* S44 ....197 E3
   RHAM/THRY S65 ....108 D2
Moorfield Cl
   RHAM/THRY S65 ....108 D2
Moorfield Dr *ARMTH* DN3 ....42 D5
Moorfield Gv
   RHAM/THRY S65 ....108 D2
Moorfield Sq *BSVR* S44 ....197 E3
Moorgate Av *FUL* S10 ....125 F3
   RHAM S60 ....106 A5
Moorgate Cha *RHAM* S60 ....9 G7
Moorgate Crs *DRON* S18 ....171 F3
Moorgate Rd *RHAM* S60 ....106 A5
Moorgate La *RHAM* S60 ....106 A5
Moorgate Rd *RHAM* S60 ....9 F6
   RHAM S60 ....119 G2
Moorgate St *RHAM* S60 ....9 F4
Moor Green Cl
   DOD/DAR S75 ....18 C5
Moorhay Cl *CHNE* S41 ....186 B2
Moor Head *SHEF* S1 ....11 F5
Moorhead Wy *MALT* S66 ....109 F4
Moorhouse Cl *RHAM* S60 ....120 B3
Moorhouse La *RHAM* S60 ....120 A3
Moorland Av *BSLY* S70 ....30 D2
Moorland Ct *STKB/PEN* S36 ....76 C2
Moorland Gv
   DONS/BSCR DN4 ....57 G4
Moorland Pl *ST/HB/BR* S6 ....123 E4
Moorlands *MALT* S66 ....107 H5
Moorlands Crs *RHAM* S60 ....120 A3
Moorland Ter *CUD/GR* S72 ....22 A2
Moorland Vw
   AU/AST/KP S26 ....145 G3
   DEARNE S63 ....51 G5
   DRON S18 ....172 C2
   HACK/IN S12 ....154 C3
Moorland View Rd
   CHSW S40 ....191 G3
Moorland View *DEARNE* S63 ....51 G5
Moor La North
   RHAM/THRY S65 ....108 D1
Moor La South
   RHAM/THRY S65 ....108 D2
Moorlawn Av *RCH* S42 ....190 C5
Moor Oaks Rd *FUL* S10 ....125 E4
Moorpark Av *CHSW* S40 ....191 G4
Moorroyd St *BSLY* S70 ....65 F1
   RHAM/THRY S65 ....106 D3
Moorside *FUL* S10 ....137 E2
Moorside Av *STKB/PEN* S36 ....44 C4
Moorside Cl *MOS* S20 ....156 C5
Moorsyde Av *FUL* S10 ....124 D2
Moorsyde Crs *FUL* S10 ....124 D2
The Moor *SHEF* S1 ....11 F6
Moorthorpe Dell *MOS* S20 ....156 B4
Moorthorpe Gdns
   MOS S20 ....156 A3
Moorthorpe Gn *MOS* S20 ....155 H3
Moorthorpe Ri *MOS* S20 ....156 B4
Moorthorpe Vw *MOS* S20 ....156 A3
Moortop Rd *DRON* S18 ....172 D2
Moortown Av *DIN* S25 ....149 E1
Moor Va *MOS* S20 ....155 H3
Moor Vw *ARMTH* DN3 ....59 F3
Moorview *KIMB* S61 ....104 B3
Moorview Cl *RCH* S42 ....195 G4
Moorview St *STV/CWN* S43 ....188 B2
Moor View Dr *SHEFS* S8 * 152 C3
Moor View Rd *SHEFS* S8 ....152 C3
   STV/CWN S43 ....182 C4
Moor View Ter *ECC* S11 ....138 A5
Moorwinstow Cft
   TOT/DORE S17 ....161 E1
Moorwood La
   ST/HB/BR S6 ....122 B3
Moorwoods Av
   CHPT/GREN S35 ....81 E5
Moorwoods La
   CHPT/GREN S35 ....93 H1
Moray Pl *DRON* S18 ....170 B1
Mordaunt Rd
   SHEF/MNR S2 ....141 F4
Morgan Av *SHEFN* S5 ....114 C1
Morgan Cl *SHEFN* S5 ....114 C1
Morgan Rd *SHEFN* S5 ....114 C2
   WHHL DN2 ....57 J1
Morland Cl *GLV* S14 ....154 B2

Morland Dr *GLV* S14 ....154 B2
Morland Pl *GLV* S14 ....154 B2
Morland Rd *GLV* S14 ....154 A2
Morley Av *CHSW* S40 ....186 C5
Morley Cl *DRON* S18 ....170 A2
Morley Pl *CONI* DN12 ....88 D2
Morley Rd *DON* DN1 ....40 C5
   KIMB S61 ....96 C5
Morley St *RAW* S62 ....98 B2
   ST/HB/BR S6 ....113 H5
Morpeth Gdns *OWL* S3 ....10 D1
Morpeth St *OWL* S3 ....10 D1
   RHAM/THRY S65 ....9 G3
Morrall Rd *SHEFN* S5 ....101 H2
Morrell St *MALT* S66 ....111 E4
Morris Av *CHNE* S41 ....187 E4
   RAW S62 ....85 F3
Morrison Av *MALT* S66 ....111 E2
Morrison Dr
   NROS/TKH DN11 ....91 F3
Morrison Pl *WMB/DAR* S73 ....35 E4
Morrison Rd *WMB/DAR* S73 ....34 D4
Mortain Rd *RHAM* S60 ....119 F3
Mortains *AU/AST/KP* S26 ....147 F4
Morthcroft *CUD/GR* S72 ....17 E2
Morthen Hall La *MALT* S66 ....121 G5
Morthen La *MALT* S66 ....131 F1
Morthen Rd *MALT* S66 ....121 F1
Morven Av *BSVR* S44 * 197 E4
Mosborough Hall Dr
   MOS S20 ....167 G3
Mosborough Moor
   MOS S20 ....156 B5
Mosbrough Rd
   HAN/WDH S13 ....141 H3
Mossbrook Rd *MOS* S20 ....156 D5
Mossdale Av *BTLY* DN5 ....39 E3
Moss Dr *ECK/KIL* S21 ....168 B3
Mossfoot Ct
   ECK/KIL S21 ....167 E4
Moss Gv *HACK/IN* S12 ....156 D1
Moss Rd *TOT/DORE* S17 ....160 B4
Moss Vw *MOS* S20 ....166 B2
Moss Wy *MOS* S20 ....156 D3
Motehall Dr
   SHEF/MNR S2 ....141 G1
Motehall Pl *SHEF/MNR* S2 ....141 H1
Motehall Wy
   SHEF/MNR S2 ....141 G1
The Motte *KIMB* S61 ....104 D1
Mottram St *BSLYN/ROY* S71 ....3 G3
Mound Rd *CHSW* S40 ....192 C3
Mount Av *CUD/GR* S72 ....36 A1
Mountbatten Dr
   CHPT/GREN S35 ....93 F1
Mountcastle St *CHNE* S41 * 187 F1
Mount Cl *BSLY* S70 ....31 H5
Mount Crs *HOY* S74 ....61 H2
Mounteney Rd *RHAM* S60 ....9 F7
Mountfield Wy *DIN* S25 ....134 A3
Mountford Cft
   TOT/DORE S17 * 161 E3
Mount Pleasant *BSLY* S70 ....48 B1
   CHNE S41 * 179 G3
   DONS/BSCR DN4 ....71 G1
Mount Pleasant Cl
   CHPT/GREN S35 ....81 E5
Mount Pleasant Rd
   DEARNE S63 ....65 F4
   ECC S11 ....139 H2
   KIMB S61 ....8 A2
Mount Rd *CHPT/GREN* S35 ....80 B5
   OWL S3 ....114 D5
Mount St *BSLY* S70 ....2 E7
   BSLYN/ROY S71 ....33 F2
   ECC S11 ....139 H1
   KIMB S61 ....8 A2
Mount Ter *DEARNE* S63 ....64 C2
   WMB/DAR S73 ....50 A2
The Mount *ARMTH* DN3 ....42 C1
   MALT S66 ....108 C2
Mount Vernon Av *BSLY* S70 ....31 H3
Mount Vernon Crs *BSLY* S70 ......32 A4
Mount Vernon Rd *BSLY* S70 ....31 H4
Mount View Av *SHEFS* S8 ....153 E2
Mount View Gdns
   SHEFS S8 * 153 E2
Mount View Rd *SHEFS* S8 ....153 E3
Mousehole Cl
   RHAM/THRY S65 ....99 G5
Mousehole La
   RHAM/THRY S65 ....99 G5
Mowbray Gdns
   RHAM/THRY S65 ....107 E1
Mowbray Pl
   RHAM/THRY S65 ....107 E1

Mowbray St *OWL* S3 ....126 A2
   RHAM/THRY S65 ....106 D1
Moxon Cl *STKB/PEN* S36 ....77 F3
Mucky La *BSLYN/ROY* S71 ....33 G1
   STKB/PEN S36 ....76 B4
Muglet La *MALT* S66 ....111 F4
Muirfield Av
   DONS/BSCR DN4 ....74 D2
   MEX/SWTN S64 ....86 C1
Muirfield Cl *CHNE* S41 ....187 H3
Mulberry Cl *BTLY* DN5 ....38 D5
   DEARNE S63 ....37 E5
   RAW S62 ....98 B3
   RCH S42 ....195 G3
   WMB/DAR S73 ....50 E1
Mulberry Dr *DONS/BSCR* DN4 ....70 D1
Mulberry Cft *STV/CWN* S43 ......181 E5
Mulberry Rd *DIN* S25 ....148 C2
   ECK/KIL S21 ....174 B1
Mulberry St *SHEF* S1 ....11 H5
Mulberry Wy *ARMTH* DN3 ....58 D1
   ECK/KIL S21 ....167 H3
Mulehouse Rd *FUL* S10 ....124 C3
Mundella Pl *SHEFS* S8 ....153 E2
Munsbrough La *KIMB* S61 ....97 E4
Munsbrough Ri *KIMB* S61 ....97 F5
Murdoch Pl *BSLYN/ROY* S71 ......14 D5
Murdock Rd *SHEFN* S5 ....101 H5
Murrayfield Dr *MOS* S20 ....167 G2
Murray Rd *ECC* S11 ....138 C4
   ECK/KIL S21 ....168 C1
   RAW S62 ....85 G2
Musard Pl *STV/CWN* S43 ....181 H5
Musgrave Crs *SHEFN* S5 ....115 E3
Musgrave Dr *SHEFN* S5 ....115 E3
Musgrave Pl *SHEFN* S5 ....115 E3
Musgrave Rd *SHEFN* S5 ....114 D3
Mushroom La *FUL* S10 ....10 A3
Muskoka Av *ECK/KIL* S21 ....138 A5
Muskoka Dr *ECK/KIL* S21 ....138 A4
Mutual St *DONS/BSCR* DN4 ....55 H3
Myers Gv La
   ST/HB/BR S6 ....113 E5
Myers Grove La
   ST/HB/BR S6 ....112 A1
Myers St *WMB/DAR* S73 ....50 A1
Mylnhurst Rd *ECC* S11 ....151 H1
Mylor Ct *BSLYN/ROY* S71 ....20 C4
Mylor Rd *ECC* S11 ....150 C1
Myrtle Crs *MALT* S66 ....108 C4
Myrtle Gv *AU/AST/KP* S26 ....159 G3
   STV/CWN S43 ....181 E5
Myrtle Rd *SHEFP/MNR* S2 ....140 A2
   WMB/DAR S73 ....50 A2
Myrtle Springs Dr
   HACK/IN S12 ....141 F5
Myrtle St *DOD/DAR* S75 ....2 B3
Mysten Cft *DOD/DAR* S75 ....19 F3
Myton Rd *DARN/MH* S9 ....127 G3

N

Nabeel Ct *RHAM* S60 ....9 H7
Nairn Dr *DRON* S18 ....170 B2
Nairn St *FUL* S10 ....124 D4
Nancy Crs *CUD/GR* S72 ....23 F1
Nancy Rd *CUD/GR* S72 ....23 F1
Nanny Hl *STKB/PEN* S36 ....77 E2
Napier Mt *BSLY* S70 ....31 H4
Napier St *ECC* S11 ....139 G1
Narrow La *DIN* S25 ....148 C3
Naseby Av *BTLY* DN5 ....38 D4
Naseby St *ATT* S4 ....116 C2
Nathan Ct *MOS* S20 ....157 F4
Nathan Dr *MOS* S20 ....157 F3
Nathan Gv *MOS* S20 ....157 E3
Navan Rd *SHEFP/MNR* S2 ....141 G3
Navigation Wy
   WMB/DAR S73 ....51 E4
Navvy La *BSLYN/ROY* S71 ....12 D2
Naylor Gv *DOD/DAR* S75 ....30 B3
Naylor St *RAW* S62 ....98 B2
Neale Bank *STV/CWN* S43 ....188 B2
Neale Rd *WHHL* DN2 ....41 F2
Neale St *STV/CWN* S43 ....185 F2
Nearcroft Rd *KIMB* S61 ....104 D1
Nearfield Rd
   DONS/BSCR DN4 ....73 H2
Needham Wy *ABRD* S7 ....139 E5
Needlewood *DOD/DAR* S75 ....30 B4
Neepsend La *OWL* S3 ....125 C1
Neild Rd *HOY* S74 ....62 C2
Neill Rd *ECC* S11 ....139 E2
Nelson Av *BSLYN/ROY* S71 ....20 A3
Nelson Cl *RHAM* S60 ....118 D4
Nelson Pl *CHPT/GREN* S35 ....93 F1
Nelson Rd *MALT* S66 ....108 C3
   ST/HB/BR S6 ....124 B1
Nelson St *BSLY* S70 ....3 F5
   CHNE S41 ....187 G3
   DONS/BSCR DN4 ....6 E7
   RHAM/THRY S65 ....9 H4
Nemesia Cl *DIN* S25 ....148 A4
Nesbit St *BSVR* S44 ....197 E4
Nesfield Cl *CHNE* S41 ....186 D1
Nesfield Wy *SHEFN* S5 ....102 D5
Nether Av *CHPT/GREN* S35 ....93 F5
   ECK/KIL S21 ....168 A2
Nether Cantley La
   ARMTH DN3 ....58 D3

Nether Cl *RCH* S42 ....195 G5
Nether Crs *CHPT/GREN* S35 ....93 F5
Nethercroft *DOD/DAR* S75 ....18 A2
Nether Croft Rd
   STV/CWN S43 ....188 C2
Netherdene Rd *DRON* S18 ....171 F4
Nether Edge Rd *ECC* S11 ....139 G5
Nether Farm Cl
   STV/CWN S43 ....188 D4
Netherfield *HOY* S74 ....62 B2
Netherfield Cl
   STKB/PEN S36 ....77 H2
   STV/CWN S43 ....182 L4
Netherfield Cft *CUD/GR* S72 ......16 D2
Netherfield La *RAW* S62 ....98 B2
Netherfield Rd *CHSW* S40 ....191 E4
   FUL S10 ....124 D2
Netherfields Crs *DRON* S18 ......171 E3
Netherfield Vw
   RHAM/THRY S65 ....107 F1
Nethergate *ST/HB/BR* S6 ....123 F2
Nethergreen Av
   ECK/KIL S21 ....168 B1
Nethergreen Ct
   ECK/KIL S21 ....168 B1
Nethergreen Gdns
   ECK/KIL S21 ....168 B1
Nethergreen Rd *ECK/KIL* S21 ....138 A2
   ECK/KIL S21 ....168 B1
Nether Hall Rd *DON* DN1 ....6 D3
Nether La *CHPT/GREN* S35 ....94 B4
Netherleigh Rd *CHSW* S40 ....191 F1
Nether Ley Av
   CHPT/GREN S35 ....94 A1
Nether Ley Ct
   CHPT/GREN S35 ....94 A1
Nether Ley Cft
   CHPT/GREN S35 ....94 A1
Nether Ley Gdns
   CHPT/GREN S35 ....94 A1
Nethermoor Av
   ECK/KIL S21 ....168 B1
Nethermoor Cl
   ECK/KIL S21 ....168 B1
Nethermoor Dr
   ECK/KIL S21 ....168 B1
   MALT S66 ....121 G2
Nethermoor La
   ECK/KIL S21 ....168 B1
Nethermoor Rd *RCH* S42 ....195 G5
Nether Oak Cl *MOS* S20 ....157 H3
Nether Oak Dr *MOS* S20 ....157 H3
Nether Oak Vw *MOS* S20 ....157 H3
Nether Shire La *SHEFN* S5 ....102 C2
Nether Springs Rd
   BSVR S44 ....196 C1
Netherthorpe
   STV/CWN S43 ....182 C4
Netherthorpe Cl
   ECK/KIL S21 ....168 A1
   STV/CWN S43 ....182 B5
Netherthorpe La
   ECK/KIL S21 ....168 A1
Netherthorpe Pl *OWL* S3 ....10 D1
Netherthorpe Rd *OWL* S3 ....10 C3
   STV/CWN S43 ....182 B4
Netherthorpe St *OWL* S3 ....10 D1
Netherthorpe Wk *OWL* S3 ....10 C1
Netherthorpe Wy *DIN* S25 ....148 C1
Netherwood Rd
   WMB/DAR S73 ....34 B5
Nettleham Rd *SHEFS* S8 ....152 D2
Neville Av *BSLY* S70 ....32 D3
   OWL S3 ....126 B2
   WMB/DAR S73 ....49 H1
Neville Ct *WMB/DAR* S73 ....49 H1
Neville Crs *BSLY* S70 ....32 D3
Neville Dr *OWL* S3 ....126 B1
Neville Rd *KIMB* S61 ....96 D5
Neville St *RHAM* S60 ....8 E3
Nevis Cl *CHSW* S40 ....186 D5
Newark *MOS* S20 * 157 E5
Newark Rd *MEX/SWTN* S64 ....66 C3
Newark St *DARN/MH* S9 ....116 C5
   NROS/TKH DN11 ....91 E2
New Barborough Cl
   STV/CWN S43 ....184 D1
New Beetwell St *CHSW* S40 ....5 F4
Newbiggin Cl *RAW* S62 ....98 A2
Newbiggin Dr *RAW* S62 ....98 A2
Newbiggin Av *CHNE* S41 ....187 E3
Newbold Back La
   CHSW S40 ....186 D4
Newbold Dr *CHNE* S41 ....187 E3
Newbold La *CHNE* S41 ....4 E1
Newbolt Ter *BTLY* DN5 ....39 F4
Newbolt Rd
   DONS/BSCR DN4 ....71 H2
Newbould Crs *MOS* S20 ....156 D3
Newbould La *FUL* S10 ....125 E5
Newbridge Ct *CHNE* S41 ....179 C5
Newbridge Dr
   STV/CWN S43 ....188 B1
Newbridge Gv
   BSLYN/ROY S71 ....20 B4
Newbridge La *CHNE* S41 ....179 H5
   STV/CWN S43 ....188 B1
Newburn Dr *DARN/MH* S9 ....117 G2
Newbury Rd *FUL* S10 ....124 D3
Newbury Wy *BTLY* DN5 ....38 C4
Newby Crs
   DONS/BSCR DN4 ....71 G3
Newby Rd *CHNE* S41 ....186 C1

Newcastle Cl *DIN* S25 ....148 C1
Newcastle St *SHEF* S1 ....10 E3
New Chapel Av
  STKB/PEN S36 ....44 C5
Newcomen Rd *BTLY* DN5....39 G5
Newcroft Cl *MOS* S20 ....157 H2
New Cross Dr
  HAN/WDH S13 ....143 E4
New Cross Wy
  HAN/WDH S13 ....143 E4
Newdale Av *CUD/GR* S72 ......21 G3
New Droppingwell Rd
  KIMB S61 ....103 H3
Newent La *FUL* S10.............124 D3
Newfield Av *BSLYN/ROY* S71...20 D3
Newfield Crs *DEARNE* S63 ......64 D3
  TOT/DORE S17 ....160 C1
Newfield Cft
  TOT/DORE S17 ....160 C1
Newfield Farm Cl *GLV* S14...141 E5
Newfield Green Rd
  SHEFP/MNR S2...........140 D4
Newfield La *TOT/DORE* S17..160 C1
Newfield Pl *TOT/DORE* S17..160 C1
Newgate Cl
  CHPT/GREN S35 ....80 B4
Newhall Av *MALT* S66.........121 G2
New Hall Crs *STKB/PEN* S36...76 B1
New Hall La *STKB/PEN* S36...76 A2
New Hall Rd *CHSW* S40........191 H2
Newhall Rd *ARMTH* DN3.........29 C4
  ATT S4 ....116 A4
  DARN/MH S9 ....116 B5
Newhaven Cl *CHSW* S40......191 F5
Newhill Rd *BSLYN/ROY* S71...20 A4
  DEARNE S63................64 D3
New Ings *ARMTH* DN3............42 A4
Newington Av *CUD/GR* S72...16 D4
Newington Dr
  AU/AST/KP S26...........145 G3
Newington Rd *ECC* S11 ......139 E2
Newland Av *CUD/GR* S72......21 G1
  MALT S66....................5 G1
Newland Cl *CHNE* S41 ....5 G1
Newland Gdns *CHNE* S41 ....187 E4
Newland Rd
  BSLYN/ROY S71 ....14 C5
Newlands Av *CHSW* S40......191 G1
  HACK/IN S12 ....141 G4
Newlands Cl
  DONS/BSCR DN4............74 B1
Newlands Dr *BTLY* DN5.........39 F5
  HACK/IN S12 ....141 G4
Newlands Gv *HACK/IN* S12...141 H4
Newlands Rd *HACK/IN* S12...141 G4
Newlands Wy
  DOD/DAR S75 ....51 E4
New La *BTLY* DN5.................54 A4
  NROS/TKH DN11............91 G2
New Lodge Crs
  BSLYN/ROY S71 ....14 C3
Newlyn Dr *BSLYN/ROY* S71...20 B4
Newlyn Pl *SHEFS* S8...........152 D2
Newlyn Rd *SHEFS* S8 ....152 D2
Newman Av
  BSLYN/ROY S71 ....15 G3
Newman Cl *DARN/MH* S9 ....103 H5
Newman Dr *RHAM* S60.........119 G2
Newman Dr *DARN/MH* S9 ...103 G5
Newman Rd *DARN/MH* S9 ...116 C1
  RHAM S60 ....119 G2
Newmarch St
  DARN/MH S9 ....117 G1
Newmarket Rd
  DONS/BSCR DN4............57 H3
New Mdw *RAW* S62 ....84 D3
New Queen St *CHNE* S41 ....4 E1
New Rd *DEARNE* S63 ....65 F2
  DIN S25 ....148 A2
  DOD/DAR S75 ....14 A3
  DOD/DAR S75 ....60 B3
  DRON S18 ....172 C2
  KIMB S61 ....103 H4
  RCH S42 ....195 E4
  STKB/PEN S36 ....77 F2
  STV/CWN S43.............117 F2
  WMB/DAR S73 ....63 F1
Newsam Rd *MEX/SWTN* S64...86 B2
New School Cl *MOS* S20.....166 C1
New School La *MOS* S20.....166 C1
New School Rd *MOS* S20.....166 C1
Newsham Rd *SHEFS* S8.......139 H5
New Smithy Av
  STKB/PEN S36 ....44 A2
New Smithy Dr
  STKB/PEN S36 ....44 A2
Newsome Av
  WMB/DAR S73 ....49 H2
New Station Rd *BSVR* S44...196 C3
  MEX/SWTN S64 ....66 C5
Newstead Av *HACK/IN* S12 ..155 G3
Newstead Cl *DRON* S18.......170 A2
  HACK/IN S12 ....155 F2
Newstead Gv *HACK/IN* S12..155 G2
Newstead Pl *HACK/IN* S12...155 G3
Newstead Ri *HACK/IN* S12...155 G3
Newstead Rd
  BSLYN/ROY S71 ....14 C4
  BTLY DN5...................39 F1
  HACK/IN S12 ....155 G2
Newstead Wy *HACK/IN* S12..155 G3

New St *BSLY* S70 ....3 F6
  BSLY S70 ....48 C1
  BSLYN/ROY S71 ....15 G1
  BSLYN/ROY S71 ....33 E2
  BSVR S44 ....196 C3
  BTLY DN5...................39 G2
  CHPT/GREN S35 ....80 B3
  CHSW S40 ....5 F6
  CUD/GR S72 ....23 E1
  DEARNE S63................53 F4
  DIN S25 ....134 C1
  DOD/DAR S75 ....30 B4
  DON S1 ....6 C7
  KIMB S61 ....95 F2
  KIMB S61 ....97 F2
  MEX/SWTN S64 ....67 H3
  MOS S20 ....157 G5
  RAW S62 ....98 B1
  RHAM S60 ....129 H1
  SHEF S1 ....11 G2
  WMB/DAR S73 ....62 D1
New Street Bus Link
  MOS S20 ....157 G5
New Street La
  SHEFP/MNR S2............11 K2
Newton Av *STKB/PEN* S36...76 B1
Newton Chamber Rd
  CHPT/GREN S35 ....80 D3
Newton Chambers Rd
  CHPT/GREN S35 ....80 D4
Newton Cl *CHPT/GREN* S35...81 E4
Newton Dr *BTLY* DN5............55 F2
  RHAM/THRY S65 ....106 C3
Newton Gdns
  CHPT/GREN S35 ....81 E4
Newton La *BTLY* DN5............55 F2
  SHEF S1 ....11 G6
  STKB/PEN S36 ....76 B1
Newton Pl *KIMB* S61............95 F3
Newton Rd *CHPT/GREN* S35...80 C5
Newtons Croft Crs
  STV/CWN S43.............177 F5
Newton St *BSLY* S70 ....2 D4
  RHAM/THRY S65 ....106 C3
Newton V *CHPT/GREN* S35...80 D4
Newtown
  BSLYN/ROY S71 ....12 B5
  CUD/GR S72 ....21 H2
Newtown Gn *CUD/GR* S72...21 H2
New Wortley Rd *KIMB* S61 ....8 B3
Niagara Rd *ST/HB/BR* S6 ....114 A1
Nicholas La *DEARNE* S63........37 E5
Nicholas St *BSLY* S70 ....2 D5
  CHNE S41 ....193 F5
Nicholson Av *DEARNE* S63...64 D3
  DOD/DAR S75 ....18 A3
Nicholson Pl *SHEFS* S8 ....140 A4
Nicholson Rd
  DONS/BSCR DN4............55 G4
  SHEFS S8 ....140 A4
Nichols Rd *ST/HB/BR* S6 .....124 C2
Nickerwood Dr
  AU/AST/KP S26...........145 F4
Nickleby Cl *RHAM* S60........129 F1
Nidderdale Pl *MALT* S66......108 D3
Nidderdale Rd *KIMB* S61......96 D3
Nidd Rd *DARN/MH* S9 ....127 G2
Nidd Rd East *DARN/MH* S9...127 G2
Nightingale Cl *CHNE* S41 ....5 F2
  RHAM S60 ....9 F7
Nightingale Ct *RHAM* S60......9 F6
Nightingale Cft *RHAM* S61...82 C5
Nightingale Rd
  CHPT/GREN S35 ....101 F1
Nikolas Rd *ECK/KIL* S21 ......175 H2
Nile St *FUL* S10..................125 E5
Nine Trees *MALT* S66..........121 H4
Ninian Gv *DONS/BSCR* DN4...58 A5
Nobel Wy *DIN* S25..............134 B3
Noble St *HOY* S74 ....62 B3
Noblethorpe Rd
  MEX/SWTN S64 ....86 D4
Nodder Rd *HAN/WDH* S13 ...142 A3
Noehill Pl *SHEFP/MNR* S2....141 H1
Noehill Rd *SHEFP/MNR* S2...141 H1
Nookery Cl *MALT* S66..........111 F2
Nooking Cl *ARMTH* DN3........43 E4
Nook La *ST/HB/BR* S6..........123 C1
  STKB/PEN S36 ....45 E5
The Nook *FUL* S10..............124 D3
Nora St *DEARNE* S63.............37 H4
Norborough Rd
  DARN/MH S9 ....117 G2
  WHHL DN2 ....40 D5
Norbreck Rd
  DONS/BSCR DN4............70 C3
Norbriggs Rd *STV/CWN* S43..183 E4
Norbrook Wy *RHAM* S60.....120 B3
Norburn Dr *ECK/KIL* S21......168 B2
Norbury Cl *CHSW* S40.........186 B4
  DRON S18 ....170 B2
Norcroft *BSLY* S70 ....31 H4
Norcross Gdns
  WMB/DAR S73 ....35 F5
Norfolk Cl *BSLYN/ROY* S71...20 B3
  RCH S42 ....191 F4
Norfolk Ct
  RHAM/THRY S65 ....9 G3
Norfolk Dr *DIN* S25.............148 C2
Norfolk Hl *CHPT/GREN* S35...93 E5
Norfolk Hill Cft
  CHPT/GREN S35 ....93 E5
Norfolk La *SHEF* S1 ....11 G4

Norfolk Park Av
  SHEFP/MNR S2............140 D1
Norfolk Park Dr
  SHEFP/MNR S2............140 C1
Norfolk Park Rd
  SHEFP/MNR S2............140 C1
Norfolk Pl *MALT* S66 ....111 E3
Norfolk Rd *CUD/GR* S72........36 A1
  DONS/BSCR DN4............71 H2
  SHEFP/MNR S2............11 K5
Norfolk Rw *SHEF* S1 ....11 G3
Norfolk St *RHAM/THRY* S65....9 G3
  SHEF S1 ....11 G4
Norfolk Wy *RHAM* S60........119 G2
Norgreave Wy *MOS* S20......167 E1
Norman Cl *BSLY* S70.............32 A5
  BSLYN/ROY S71 ....20 C3
Norman Ct *BTLY* DN5............38 D3
  NROS/TKH DN11............91 E2
Normancroft Crs
  SHEFP/MNR S2............142 A1
Normancroft Dr
  SHEFP/MNR S2............141 H1
Normancroft Wy
  SHEFP/MNR S2............141 H1
Normandale Av
  ST/HB/BR S6...............112 D4
Normandale Rd
  ST/HB/BR S6...............114 B5
Norman St *DARN/MH* S9.....116 C5
  DEARNE S63................37 G2
Normanton Gdns *ATT* S4...115 G5
Normanton Gv
  HAN/WDH S13 ....142 D4
Normanton
  Hl *HACK/IN* S12 ....142 A4
Normanton Spring Ct
  HAN/WDH S13 ....142 A5
Normanton Spring Rd
  HAN/WDH S13 ....142 C5
Normanville Av *RHAM* S60...118 B3
Norrels Dr *RHAM* S60..........106 B5
Norrel's Cft *RHAM* S60........106 B5
Norris Rd *ST/HB/BR* S6........113 H4
Norroy St *ATT* S4...............126 D1
Norstead Crs *MALT* S66 ......109 E3
Northampton Rd
  WHHL DN2 ....41 G5
North Bridge Rd *BTLY* DN5....6 B2
North Church St *SHEF* S1 ....11 G2
North Cliff Rd *CONI* DN12....68 D5
North Cl *BSLYN/ROY* S71 ......15 C1
  DRON S18 ....172 A5
Northcote Av
  SHEFP/MNR S2............140 B4
Northcote Rd
  SHEFP/MNR S2............140 B4
Northcote Ter
  DOD/DAR S75 ....2 A3
North Crs *ECK/KIL* S21........158 C5
  RHAM/THRY S65 ....106 C2
North Dr *RHAM* S60................8 E1
Northern Av
  SHEFP/MNR S2............141 E3
Northern Common
  DRON S18 ....161 H5
North Farm Ct
  AU/AST/KP S26...........145 H2
Northfield Av *FUL* S10........124 D3
  RAW S62 ....85 F4
Northfield Cl *FUL* S10.........125 E2
Northfield Ct *MALT* S66......108 A4
Northfield La *MALT* S66......108 A4
Northfield Rd *BTLY* DN5.......55 H1
  FUL S10 ....124 D3
  RHAM S60 ....9 F2
Northfields *STV/CWN* S43...185 F3
Northgate *DOD/DAR* S75 ......19 E4
North Ga *MEX/SWTN* S64......67 G3
North Hill Rd *SHEFN* S5.......101 H5
Northlands *BSLYN/ROY* S71...12 C5
Northlands Rd *SHEFN* S5.....101 H5
Northmoor Cl
  STV/CWN S43 *............188 D2
North Moor Vw
  STV/CWN S43.............188 D2
North Pitt St *KIMB* S61.......104 D3
North Pl *DOD/DAR* S75........18 D4
  RHAM/THRY S65 ....106 C2
North Qd *SHEFN* S5............102 D5
North Rd *BSLYN/ROY* S71......12 D5
  BSVR S44 ....193 H1
  RHAM/THRY S65 ....106 D2
  STV/CWN S43.............185 G2
North Royds Wd
  BSLYN/ROY S71 ....14 D3
Northside Rd *DEARNE* S63....65 F2
North St *DONS/BSCR* DN4.......6 E7
  MEX/SWTN S64 ....66 C5
  RAW S62 ....85 H4
  RAW S60 ....98 D1
  WMB/DAR S73 ....35 G4
North Swaithe Cl *BTLY* DN5..26 C5
North Ter *CHNE* S41 *..........192 D5
Northumberland Av
  HOY S74......................62 A1
  WHHL DN2 ....40 D1
Northumberland Rd
  FUL S10 ....125 E4
Northumberland Wy
  BSLYN/ROY S71 ....33 F2
North View St *BSVR* S44.....196 B3
Northwood *ST/HB/BR* S6.....100 C5

Northwood Dr
  ST/HB/BR S6...............100 B5
Northwood Pl
  ST/HB/BR S6...............113 F1
Norton Av *CHSW* S40..........191 E4
  GLV S14 ....153 H4
  HACK/IN S12 ....154 B3
Norton Church Glebe
  SHEFS S8 ....153 F4
Norton Church Rd
  SHEFS S8 ....153 F4
Norton Green Cl *SHEFS* S8..153 G4
Norton Hammer La
  SHEFS S8 ....152 C1
Norton La *SHEFS* S8...........163 E1
Norton Lees Cl *SHEFS* S8 *...153 E2
Norton Lees Crs *SHEFS* S8...153 E1
Norton Lees La *SHEFS* S8....152 D1
Norton Lees Rd *SHEFS* S8...139 H5
Norton Lees Sq *SHEFS* S8...153 E1
Norton Ms *SHEFS* S8...........153 G5
Norton Park Av *SHEFS* S8...153 F5
Norton Park Crs *SHEFS* S8...153 E5
Norton Park Dr *SHEFS* S8....153 F5
Norton Park Rd *SHEFS* S8....163 E1
Norton Park Vw *SHEFS* S8...153 E5
Norton Rd *DEARNE* S63.........64 D1
  GLV S14 ....154 A3
  WHHL DN2 ....41 F5
Norville Crs *WMB/DAR* S73...35 F4
Norwich Rd *WHHL* DN2........41 E3
Norwich Rw *SHEFP/MNR* S2..11 K4
Norwith Rd
  DONS/BSCR DN4............73 H2
Norwood Av *CHNE* S41.......193 F5
  MALT S66 ....110 D2
  SHEFN S5 ....115 F3
Norwood Cl *MALT* S66........110 D2
  SHEFN S5 ....115 F3
Norwood Crs
  AU/AST/KP S26...........159 G4
  ECK/KIL S21 ....168 D1
Norwood Dr *BTLY* DN5.........26 C4
  DOD/DAR S75 ....18 C3
  SHEFN S5 ....115 F3
Norwood Grange Dr
  SHEFN S5 ....115 F2
Norwood Pl *ECK/KIL* S21.....168 D1
Norwood Rd *CONI* DN12.......88 D1
  SHEFN S5 ....115 F3
Norwood St
  RHAM/THRY S65 ....99 F5
Nostell Fold *DOD/DAR* S75...30 B4
Nostell Pl *DONS/BSCR* DN4...73 H2
Nottingham Cliff *OWL* S3....126 A1
Nottingham Cl
  BSLYN/ROY S71 ....33 C3
  BTLY DN5...................38 D4
  DIN S25 ....148 B5
  RCH S42 ....195 H4
Nottingham Dr *RCH* S42.....195 H4
Nottingham St *OWL* S3.......115 F5
  RHAM/THRY S65 ....9 G3
Notton La *HOR/CROF* WF4...12 C2
Novara Cl *BSLY* S70.............32 B2
Novello St *MALT* S66...........111 G4
Nowill Ct *SHEFS* S8............140 A4
Nowill Pl *SHEFS* S8.............140 A4
Nunnery Crs *RHAM* S60......129 C1
Nunnery Dr
  SHEFP/MNR S2............127 F3
Nunnery Sq
  SHEFP/MNR S2 *...........127 E4
Nunnery Ter
  SHEFP/MNR S2............127 E4
Nunnington Wy
  ARMTH DN3 ....29 E3
Nursery Crs *DIN* S25...........148 B2
Nursery Dr *BSVR* S44..........196 C2
  CHPT/GREN S35 ....102 B1
  RHAM S60 ....129 C1
Nursery Gdns *BSLY* S70........33 E3
Nursery Gv
  CHPT/GREN S35 ....102 B1
Nursery La *BTLY* DN5............70 A1
  OWL S3 ....126 B2
Nursery St *SHEFP/MNR* S2.....3 F7
  OWL S3 ....126 B2
Nuttall Pl *SHEFP/MNR* S2...126 D4
Nutwell Cl *DONS/BSCR* DN4..74 A2
Nutwell La *ARMTH* DN3........42 D4

O

Oadby Dr *CHNE* S41............193 E5
Oak Av *DEARNE* S63.............65 C3
Oak Bank Av *CHNE* S41......179 H3
Oakbank Cl *MEX/SWTN* S64...86 B3
Oakbank Ct
  TOT/DORE S17 *............161 E3
Oakbrook Rd *ECC* S11.........138 B2
Oak Cl *ECK/KIL* S21.............168 A3
  HOY S74......................61 G3
  MALT S66 ....108 B3
  MEX/SWTN S64 ....66 C3
  STV/CWN S43.............188 B2
Oakwood Dr *DONS/BSCR* DN4..72 A3
  MEX/SWTN S64 ....66 C3
Oates Av *RAW* S62...............98 C3

Oak Crs *HOR/CROF* WF4........13 H1
  RCH S42 ....195 H4
Oakcrest *DONS/BSCR* DN4....74 D4
Oakdale *BSLY* S70.................32 B5
Oakdale Cl *ARMTH* DN3.........42 B1
Oakdale Pl *KIMB* S61...........104 D3
Oak Dale Rd
  DONS/BSCR DN4............70 C4
Oakdale Rd *DIN* S25............148 D3
  ECC S11 ....139 F4
  KIMB S61 ....104 D4
Oakdell *DRON* S18..............163 H5
Oakdene *NROS/TKH* DN11.....91 F3
Oak Dr *ARMTH* DN3..............42 C2
Oaken Wood Cl *KIMB* S61.....95 C1
Oaken Wood Rd *KIMB* S61...95 F1
Oakes Gn *DARN/MH* S9 ......127 F1
Oakes Park Vw *GLV* S14......153 H3
Oakes St *DARN/MH* S9 ....103 H5
Oakfern Gv *CHPT/GREN* S35...80 B3
Oakfield Av *CHSW* S40........191 F5
Oakfield Wk *DOD/DAR* S75...18 D5
Oak Gv *CONI* DN12 ....88 D2
Oakham Dr *OWL* S3.............125 H1
Oakham Pl *DOD/DAR* S75 ......2 A1
Oak Haven Av *CUD/GR* S72...36 A3
Oakhill Rd *ABRD* S7.............139 F4
  DRON S18 ....169 G2
  WHHL DN2 ....41 F4
Oakholme Ms *FUL* S10........139 E1
Oakholme Rd *FUL* S10.........139 E1
Oakland Rd *ST/HB/BR* S6.....113 H4
Oaklands *DONS/BSCR* DN4.....75 E3
  MALT S66 ....121 G2
Oaklands Av
  BSLYN/ROY S71 ....20 C3
Oaklands Dr
  DONS/BSCR DN4............57 H5
Oaklands Gdns
  DONS/BSCR DN4............73 H1
Oaklands Pl *DEARNE* S63......65 E3
Oaklea *BSLY* S70..................48 C1
  DEARNE S63................53 F3
Oak Lea *KIMB* S61................97 F3
Oak Lea Av *DEARNE* S63.......64 C1
Oakley Av *CHSW* S40.............4 C2
Oakley Rd *HAN/WDH* S13...128 C3
Oak Lodge Rd
  CHPT/GREN S35 ....80 A4
Oak Mdw *RHAM/THRY* S65...106 D1
Oak Pk *FUL* S10 ....124 B5
Oak Park Ri *BSLY* S70............32 A3
Oak Rd *ARMTH* DN3..............42 C2
  CUD/GR S72 ....17 F2
  DEARNE S63................63 C3
  DEARNE S63................65 C3
  HACK/IN S12 ....154 C3
  MALT S66 ....110 B3
  MEX/SWTN S64 ....66 C3
  MOS S20 ....157 F1
Oakroyd Crs *CUD/GR* S72......23 E1
Oaks Av *STKB/PEN* S36.........76 C2
Oaks Cl *DEARNE* S63.............65 G4
Oaks Crs *BSLY* S70................32 C2
Oaks Fold *SHEFN* S5............103 E3
Oaks Fold Av *SHEFN* S5.......103 E4
Oaks Fold Rd *SHEFN* S5.......103 E4
Oaks La *BSLY* S70.................96 A5
  KIMB S61 ....96 A5
  SHEFN S5 ....103 E4
Oak St *BSLY* S70.....................2 D5
  CUD/GR S72 ....23 F2
  MOS S20 ....157 G5
  SHEFS S8 ....140 A3
  STV/CWN S43.............181 E5
Oak Ter *AU/AST/KP* S26.......144 D2
  DON DN1 ....56 A4
Oak Tree Av *CUD/GR* S72......16 D5
Oaktree Cl *MALT* S66..........108 C4
Oak Tree Rd *ARMTH* DN3......59 G4
  STV/CWN S43.............185 E4
Oakwell Cl *MALT* S66..........111 E2
Oakwell La *BSLYN/ROY* S71...3 J5
Oakwell Ter *BSLYN/ROY* S71...3 K6
Oakwell Vw *BSLYN/ROY* S71...3 K5
  BSLYN/ROY S71 ....32 B1
Oakwood Av
  BSLYN/ROY S71 ....12 B5
  SHEFN S5 ....101 H2
Oakwood Cl *BSLY* S70............48 C1
Oakwood Crs
  BSLYN/ROY S71 ....15 E5
  RAW S62 ....85 E4
Oakwood Dr *ARMTH* DN3......42 C5
  RHAM S60 ....119 G1
Oakwood Gv *RHAM* S60......106 D5
Oakwood Hall Dr
  RHAM S60 ....119 F2
Oakwood Rd
  BSLYN/ROY S71 ....12 B5
  DONS/BSCR DN4............71 F1
Oakwood Rd East
  RHAM S60 ....119 G1
Oakwood Rd West
  RHAM S60 ....119 F1
Oakwood Wy
  STV/CWN S43.............182 D2
Oakworth Cl *DOD/DAR* S75...18 U4
  MOS S20 ....167 E2
Oakworth Dr *MOS* S20........166 D2
Oakworth Gv *MOS* S20........166 D2
Oakworth Vw *MOS* S20.......166 D2

Oates Cl KIMB S61....105 E2
Oates St KIMB S61....105 E2
Oats Orch MOS S20....166 D2
Oberon Cres WMB/DAR S73....34 D4
Oborne Cl RHAM/THRY S65....109 E1
Occupation Cl
STV/CWN S43....177 E5
Occupation La
HACK/IN S12....155 H2
ST/HB/BR S6....112 U5
Occupation Rd CHNE S41....187 F1
RAW S62....81 H2
Ochre Dike La DEARNE S63....65 F2
Ochre Dike La MOS S20....156 D3
Octavia Cl RHAM S60 *....118 C2
Odeon Ar DON DN1 *....6 D4
Odom Ct SHEFP/MNR S2....140 B4
Offridge Cl STV/CWN S43....185 F4
Ogden Rd WHHL DN2....41 H2
Oil Mill Fold RHAM S60....9 F5
Oldale Cl HAN/WDH S13....143 C5
Oldale Ct HAN/WDH S13....143 G4
Oldale Gv HAN/WDH S13....143 G4
Old Anna Lane or
Long La STKB/PEN S36....44 A2
Old Bakery Ct CHNE S41....179 G4
Old Brick Works La
CHNE S41....187 G3
Old Clifton La
RHAM/THRY S65....9 J5
Oldcoates Cl DIN S25....134 D3
Oldcotes Rd DIN S25....135 E2
Old Cottage Cl
HAN/WDH S13....143 H3
Old Cross La DEARNE S63....65 F2
Old Doncaster Rd
DEARNE S63....65 H2
Old Farm Ct MEX/SWTN S64....66 C2
Oldfield Av CONI DN12....88 B1
ST/HB/BR S6....123 H1
Oldfield Cl HOY S74....62 A2
Oldfield Gv ST/HB/BR S6....123 H2
Oldfield Rd
RHAM/THRY S65....107 F2
ST/HB/BR S6....123 H2
Old Fulwood Rd FUL S10....137 H3
Old Garden Dr
RHAM/THRY S65....9 K2
Oldgate La RHAM/THRY S65....99 C5
Old Guildhall Yd DON DN1 *....6 E3
Old Hall Cl BTLY DN5....54 C5
DIN S25....134 B1
MALT S66....108 D4
Old Hall Dr MALT S66....108 D4
Old Hall Ms MALT S66....108 D4
Old Hall Pl BTLY DN5....39 H2
Old Hall Rd BSLY S70....47 F3
BTLY DN5....39 H2
CHSW S40....191 H2
DARN/MH S9....116 C5
Old Hall Wk CUD/GR S72 *....36 A1
Oldhay Cl TOT/DORE S17....160 D2
Old Hay Gdns
TOT/DORE S17....160 C2
Old Hay La TOT/DORE S17....160 C2
Old Hexthorpe
DONS/BSCR DN4....55 F4
Old House Cl WMB/DAR S73....63 E1
Old House Rd CHSW S40....186 D3
Old La MOS S20....167 F1
Old Manor Dr
STKB/PEN S36....45 H5
Old Mill Dr CHNE S41....186 A2
Old Mill La BSLY S70....3 F2
Old Mill Rd CONI DN12....89 F1
Old Oak Vw BSLY S70....32 C2
Old Park Av SHEFS S8....162 B1
Old Park Rd SHEFS S8....162 B1
Old Pheasant Ct CHSW S40....191 E2
Old Quarry Av
AU/AST/KP S26....147 F5
Old Quarry Cl
STV/CWN S43....177 F5
Old Retford Rd
HAN/WDH S13....143 G1
Oldridge Cl CHSW S40....186 A3
Old Rd BSLYN/ROY S71....20 A2
CHSW S40....191 G1
CONI DN12....88 B3
Old School Cl ARMTH DN3....42 D4
HOY S74....62 A1
KIMB S61....97 G2
RCH S42....174 A4
Old School Ct DOD/DAR S75....18 A2
Old School Dr SHEFS S8....102 B4
Old School La BSVR S44....193 H2
RHAM S60....129 H1
Old School Wy WHHL DN2....40 C5
Old Sheffield Rd RHAM S60....8 E7
Old Ship La CHSW S40....7 H1
Old Station Dr ABRD S7....152 B2
Old St SHEFP/MNR S2....126 C3
Old Town Hall RHAM S60....9 F3
Old Warren V RAW S62....84 C4
Oldwell Cl TOT/DORE S17....160 D4
Old Whittington La
DRON S18....172 A5
Old Wortley Rd KIMB S61....104 C1
Olive Cl AU/AST/KP S26....145 F3
Olive Crs HACK/IN S12....154 C3

Olive Grove Rd
SHEFP/MNR S2....140 B2
Olive Rd MOS S20....166 D1
STKB/PEN S36....76 D2
Oliver Rd ABRD S7....152 A1
DONS/BSCR DN4....71 G1
Olivers Dr DARN/MH S9....128 B3
Olivers Mt DARN/MH S9....128 C3
Oliver St MEX/SWTN S64....66 C3
Olivers Wy RHAM S60....118 B5
Olivet Rd SHEFS S8....152 D3
Ollerton Rd BSLYN/ROY S71....14 D4
Onchan Rd ST/HB/BR S6....124 A2
Onslow Rd ECC S11....138 D3
Orange St SHEF S1....10 E3
Orchard Av DIN S25....148 C1
Orchard Cl ARMTH DN3....29 E3
BSLYN/ROY S71....20 C2
BSVR S44....197 E3
MEX/SWTN S64....67 E3
RHAM S60....129 H1
SHEFN S5....102 B2
STV/CWN S43....185 E3
Orchard Crs SHEFN S5....102 B2
Orchard Cft
AU/AST/KP S26....159 F2
DOD/DAR S75....37 G4
Orchard Flatts Crs KIMB S61....97 E4
Orchard Gdns DIN S25....148 B4
Orchard Gv MALT S66....110 B2
Orchard La AU/AST/KP S26....159 F3
MOS S20....157 F3
SHEF S1....11 F3
Orchard Lea Dr
AU/AST/KP S26 *....145 F3
Orchard Ms BTLY DN5....39 F5
DEARNE S63....64 D2
ECK/KIL S21....168 B2
RHAM S60....8 C4
Orchard Pl CUD/GR S72....22 A2
DEARNE S63....64 D2
ECK/KIL S21....168 B2
RHAM S60....8 C4
Orchard Sq DRON S18....170 B1
SHEF S1....11 G5
Orchard St DEARNE S63....63 G1
DONS/BSCR DN4....55 H4
SHEF S1....11 G5
STKB/PEN S36....77 H3
WMB/DAR S73....50 B3
Orchards Wy DARN/MH S9....191 C5
The Orchard DEARNE S63....37 E3
DIN S25....148 C2
Orchard Vw BSVR S44....196 B4
Orchard View Rd
CHSW S40....186 C5
Orchard Vls
RHAM/THRY S65 *....99 H3
Orchard Wy BSLYN/ROY S71....3 G1
Orchard Wy DEARNE S63....37 F2
RHAM S60....118 C5
Orchard Wls MALT S66....108 C5
Orchid Wy DIN S25....148 A4
Ordnance Ter WMB/DAR S73 *....104 D3
Orgreave Cl HAN/WDH S13....143 G1
Orgreave Crs
HAN/WDH S13....143 G1
Orgreave Dr HAN/WDH S13....143 E1
Orgreave La HAN/WDH S13....143 E1
Orgreave Pl HAN/WDH S13....129 F5
Orgreave Ri HAN/WDH S13....143 H2
Orgreave Rd RHAM S60....129 G2
Orgreave Wy
HAN/WDH S13....143 G2
Oriel Rd FUL S10....137 G3
Oriel Wy BSLYN/ROY S71....20 D4
Ormesby Cl DRON S18....170 A2
Ormesby Crs BTLY DN5....39 E5
Ormesby Wy MALT S66....109 E4
Ormes Meadow MOS S20....156 C3
Ormond Cl RCH S42....191 F5
SHEFS S8....163 F2
Ormond Dr SHEFS S8....163 F2
Ormond Rd SHEFS S8....163 F2
Ormond Wy SHEFS S8....163 F1
Ormsby Cl DONS/BSCR DN4....71 G4
Ormsby Rd CHNE S41....187 F2
Orpen Dr GLV S14....154 A3
Orpen Wy GLV S14....154 A3
Orwell Cl WMB/DAR S73....50 D4
Osberton Pl ECC S11....139 E2
Osberton St RAW S62....85 H5
RHAM/THRY S65....99 E5
Osbert Rd RHAM S60....119 H1
Osborne Av
AU/AST/KP S26....145 G2
ECC S11....139 E3
WHHL DN2....27 H1
Osborne St BSLY S70 *....3 K6
Osgathorpe Crs ATT S4....115 G4
Osgathorpe Dr ATT S4....115 H4
Osgathorpe Rd ATT S4....115 G4
Osmaston Rd SHEFS S8....152 D3
Osmond Dr BSLY S70....32 A5
Osmond Pl BSLY S70 *....32 A5
Osmond Wy BSLY S70....32 A5
Osmund Rd ECK/KIL S21....166 B5
Osprey Av AWLS/ASK DN6....25 F1
Osprey Cl AWLS/ASK DN6....47 H5

Osprey Gdns
SHEFP/MNR S2....127 E5
Osprey Rd AU/AST/KP S26....145 G4
Oswestry Rd SHEFN S5....102 C5
Oswin Av DONS/BSCR DN4....55 F5
Otley Cl CONI DN12....89 F1
Otter St DARN/MH S9....127 F1
Oughtibridge La
CHPT/GREN S35....100 A2
Oughton Wy ATT S4....115 H5
Oulton Av MALT S66....109 F3
Oulton Dr CUD/GR S72....17 E5
Oulton Ri MEX/SWTN S64....67 H2
Ouseburn Cft DARN/MH S9....127 G2
Ouseburn Rd DARN/MH S9....127 G2
Ouseburn St DARN/MH S9....127 G2
Ouse Rd DARN/MH S9....127 G2
Ouselthwaite Ct BSLY S70....31 G4
Ouson Gdns BSLYN/ROY S71....15 G3
Outgang La DIN S25....134 A2
MALT S66....111 F5
Outram St CHNE S41....187 F3
Outwood Rd SHEFN S5....127 E5
Oval Rd RHAM S60....106 D2
The Oval AWLS/ASK DN6....24 D1
CONI DN12....69 E5
DIN S25....148 C2
DONS/BSCR DN4....57 C4
HOR/CROF WF4....3 E5
SHEFS S5....115 G1
Overcroft Ri
TOT/DORE S17....160 C4
Overdale Av BSLY S70....32 B4
Overdale Gdns
TOT/DORE S17....160 C2
Overdale Ri TOT/DORE S17....160 C2
Overdale Rd WMB/DAR S73....50 C4
Overend Cl GLV S14....153 H1
Overend Dr GLV S14....153 H1
Overend Rd GLV S14....153 H1
Overend Wy GLV S14....153 H1
Oversley Rd MALT S66....110 B2
Oversley St DARN/MH S9....127 G2
Overton Cl STV/CWN S43....182 B3
Overton Rd ST/HB/BR S6....113 H2
Owen Cl RHAM/THRY S65....9 H1
SHEFN S5....101 F3
Owen Falls Av CHNE S41....5 A3
Owen Pl SHEFN S5....101 F3
Owlcotes Vw BSVR S44....196 D4
Owler Car La DRON S18....164 A3
Owler La ATT S4....115 H3
Owlings Pl ST/HB/BR S6....113 G4
Owlings Rd ST/HB/BR S6....113 G4
Owlthorpe Av MOS S20....156 B5
Owlthorpe Cl MOS S20....156 B5
Owlthorpe Greenway
MOS S20....157 E4
Owlthorpe Gv MOS S20....156 B5
Owlthorpe La MOS S20....156 B5
Owlthorpe Ri MOS S20....156 B5
Owram St WMB/DAR S73 *....35 E5
Ox Carr ARMTH DN3....42 C4
Ox Close Av KIMB S61....96 C5
TOT/DORE S17....161 G3
Oxclose Dr DRON S18....170 A2
Oxclose La DRON S18....170 A2
Oxclose Park Gdns
MOS S20....167 F2
Oxclose Park Rd MOS S20....167 F2
Oxclose Park Rd North
MOS S20....167 F2
Oxclose Park Vw MOS S20....167 F2
Oxcroft La BSVR S44....197 E5
Oxcroft Wy STV/CWN S43....184 B1
Oxford Cl KIMB S61....97 G3
Oxford Pl BSLYN/ROY S71....33 E2
DON DN1....6 C6
Oxford Rd STV/CWN S43....188 D1
Oxford St BSLY S70....32 A3
BSLYN/ROY S71....33 E2
MEX/SWTN S64....66 C3
NROS/TKH DN11....91 E2
RHAM/THRY S65....106 C2
ST/HB/BR S6....10 B1
Oxford Vls
RHAM/THRY S65 *....106 C2
Ox Hl MOS S20....167 G3
Oxley Cl STKB/PEN S36....76 C2
Oxley Ct RHAM S60....106 B5
Oxley Gv RHAM S60....106 B5
Oxspring Bank SHEFN S5....114 B2
Oxspring La STKB/PEN S36....45 H5
Oxted Rd DARN/MH S9....116 C2
Oxton Dr DONS/BSCR DN4....70 D2
Oxton Rd BSLYN/ROY S71....15 C3

P

Packer's Rw CHSW S40....5 G4
Pack Horse La
CHPT/GREN S35....80 C3
Packington Rd
DONS/BSCR DN4....74 C1
Packman Rd DEARNE S63....64 B3
Packman Wy DEARNE S63....64 B3
Packwood Cl MALT S66....111 E2
Paddington Cl DIN S25....134 A3

Paddock Cl BTLY DN5....39 E5
DOD/DAR S75....36 D4
RCH S42....195 F4
Paddock Crs
SHEFP/MNR S2....141 E5
Paddock Cft
MEX/SWTN S64....65 H5
Paddock Dr MALT S66....108 C2
Paddock Rd CUD/GR S72....17 E5
Paddock Wy DRON S18....171 F1
Padley Cl DOD/DAR S75....30 A3
Padley Wy SHEFN S5....102 C5
Padua Ri WMB/DAR S73....34 D5
Page Hall Rd SHEFN S5....115 H3
Pagenall Dr
AU/AST/KP S26....145 F2
Paget St DARN/MH S9....116 B5
Pagnell Av DEARNE S63....36 D3
Paisley Cl STV/CWN S43....189 G1
Palermo Fold
WMB/DAR S73....34 D4
Palgrave Crs SHEFN S5....101 C5
Palgrave Rd SHEFN S5....101 F5
Pallington Gv
DONS/BSCR DN4....58 A4
Pall Ml BSLY S70....3 F5
Pall Mall AU/AST/KP S26....147 E5
Palm Av DARN/MH S9....128 B3
Palmer Cl STKB/PEN S36....44 C5
Palmer Crs DRON S18....171 F2
Palmer Rd DARN/MH S9....128 A1
Palmerston Av MALT S66....110 C2
Palmerston Rd FUL S10....10 A4
Palmer St DARN/MH S9....127 F2
Palmers Wy MALT S66....132 C1
Palm Gv CONI DN12....88 C3
Palm Hollow Cl MALT S66....107 H5
Palm La ST/HB/BR S6....125 E1
Palm St DOD/DAR S75....2 C1
ST/HB/BR S6....125 E1
Palterton La BSVR S44....196 A5
Pamela Dr DONS/BSCR DN4....70 C2
Pangbourne Rd
DEARNE S63....36 D3
Pantry Gn BSLY S70 *....48 C1
Pantry Hl BSLY S70....32 C5
Pantry Well BSLY S70....48 C1
Paper Mill Rd SHEFN S5....102 D2
The Parade HOY S74....61 H3
RAW S62....85 E4
Paradise La SHEF S1....11 G2
Paradise Sq SHEF S1....11 G2
Paradise St SHEF S1....11 G2
Parish Wy BSLYN/ROY S71....20 D4
Park Av ARMTH DN3....42 B3
BSLY S70....14 D5
BSLYN/ROY S71....33 E5
BTLY DN5....54 C4
CHPT/GREN S35....94 A2
CONI DN12....89 E2
CUD/GR S72....16 D5
DIN S25....148 C1
DRON S18....171 F2
FUL S10....138 D2
MEX/SWTN S64....67 E3
RHAM S60....8 D3
STKB/PEN S36....44 C3
Park Cl ARMTH DN3....42 D4
BTLY DN5....54 C4
CHSW S40....192 C5
DOD/DAR S75....36 D4
MEX/SWTN S64....65 E5
RHAM/THRY S65....99 H4
Park Ct DEARNE S63....37 F2
Park Crs BSLYN/ROY S71....15 H1
CHPT/GREN S35....102 B1
DEARNE S63....53 F5
DONS/BSCR DN4....70 C3
FUL S10....10 A6
Park Dr STKB/PEN S36....76 D2
AU/AST/KP S26....144 D3
BTLY DN5....54 C4
CHNE S41....187 F2
Parkdrive DOD/DAR S75....46 D1
Park Drive Wy
SHEFS S8....76 D1
Park End Rd DEARNE S63....53 F1
Parker Av BSVR S44....193 H1
Parkers La TOT/DORE S17....150 C5
Parker St BSLY S70....2 E6
Parker's La FUL S10....125 E4
Parker's Rd FUL S10....125 E4
Park Farm DRON S18....170 A1
Park Farm Ms ECK/KIL S21....176 B2
Parkfield Ct RAW S62....98 B3
Parkfield Rd RHAM/THRY S65....99 H4
Parkgate DEARNE S63....37 H5
DRON S18....171 G1

Parkgate Av CONI DN12....88 C1
Parkgate Cl MOS S20....156 A5
Parkgate Cft MOS S20....156 A5
Parkgate Dr MOS S20....156 A4
Parkgate La ECK/KIL S21....180 C5
Park Grange Cft
SHEFP/MNR S2....140 C1
Park Grange Dr
SHEFP/MNR S2....140 C2
Park Grange Mt
SHEFP/MNR S2....140 C2
Park Grange Ri
SHEFP/MNR S2....140 C2
Park Grange Rd
SHEFP/MNR S2....140 B1
Park Grange Vw
SHEFP/MNR S2....140 C2
Park Gv BSLY S70....2 E7
MALT S66....108 D4
RAW S62....85 F4
STKB/PEN S36....76 D1
Park Hall Rd RCH S42....191 E4
Park Hall Cl RCH S42....191 F5
Park Hall Gdns RCH S42....191 F4
Parkhall La ECK/KIL S21....176 B1
Parkhead Cl
BSLYN/ROY S71....12 A5
Parkhead Ct ECC S11....151 F1
Parkhead Crs ECC S11....151 F1
Parkhead Rd ECC S11....151 F2
Park Hl ARMTH DN3 *....29 G2
AU/AST/KP S26....144 D3
ECK/KIL S21....167 E5
Park Hill Gdns
WMB/DAR S73....144 D3
Parkhill Rd WMB/DAR S73....50 C2
Park Hollow WMB/DAR S73....50 C3
Park House La
DARN/MH S9....117 H4
Parkinson St DON DN1....40 B5
Parkland Dr
NROS/TKH DN11....91 H2
RCH S42....195 G5
Parklands ARMTH DN3....42 B1
Parklands Av DIN S25....134 C5
Parklands Cl
NROS/TKH DN11....91 G2
Parklands Vw
AU/AST/KP S26....145 G5
Parkland Vw
BSLYN/ROY S71....21 F2
Park La CHNE S41....187 F2
CHPT/GREN S35....77 F1
CUD/GR S72....23 E4
DIN S25....134 A3
DONS/BSCR DN4....57 G3
FUL S10....10 A6
RHAM/THRY S65....99 H4
STKB/PEN S36....50 C3
Park Lane Ct
RHAM/THRY S65....99 H3
Park Mt RHAM/THRY S65....9 H5
Park Nook RHAM/THRY S65....99 C4
Park Pl RHAM/THRY S65....106 D2
Park Rd BSLY S70....31 G3
BTLY DN5....39 G1
CHSW S40....5 F5
CONI DN12....88 D2
DEARNE S63....37 E2
DEARNE S63....65 E3
DON DN1....6 E3
MEX/SWTN S64....86 A1
RHAM/THRY S65....106 C2
ST/HB/BR S6....124 B1
Park Side CHNE S41 *....187 G2
Parkside BSLYN/ROY S71....15 H3
DOD/DAR S75....19 F3
Parkside La ST/HB/BR S6....123 H2
Parkside Ms BSLY S70....32 A5
Parkside Rd HOY S74....61 F4
ST/HB/BR S6....114 A3
Parkside Vw CHNE S41....186 B3
Parkson Rd RHAM S60....119 H2
Park Spring Dr
SHEFP/MNR S2....140 C2
Park Spring Pl
SHEFP/MNR S2....140 C2
Park Spring Rd CUD/GR S72....22 D5
Park Spring Wy
SHEFP/MNR S2....140 C2
Park Sq CHPT/GREN S35....80 D4
Park Square Jct
SHEFP/MNR S2....11 J5
Parkstone Crs MALT S66....109 H5
Parkstone Delph
HACK/IN S12....154 C3
Parkstone Wy WHHL DN2....41 H4
Park St AU/AST/KP S26....145 E3
BSLY S70....2 E7
CHSW S40....192 C5
KIMB S61....8 A3
RAW S62....85 F5
STV/CWN S43....177 H4
WMB/DAR S73....50 C3
Park Ter CHPT/GREN S35....94 B2
DON DN1....6 E3
RHAM/THRY S65 *....99 H4
Park Vale Dr
RHAM/THRY S65....99 H4
Parkview BSLY S70....32 B5
Park Vw AWLS/ASK DN6....25 F1
BSLYN/ROY S71....12 D5
CHNE S41....193 F5

CUD/GR S72 ....17 E1
DOD/DAR S75 ....30 B3
KIMB S61 ....97 F3
MALT S66 ....111 F5
STV/CWN S43 ....177 F4
Park View Av MOS S20 ....167 E1
Park View Rd
  CHPT/GREN S35 ....94 A2
  DOD/DAR S75 ....14 A3
  KIMB S61 ....104 A3
  ST/HB/BR S6 ....106 A3
Park Wy AWLS/ASK DN6 ....25 F1
Parkway ARMTH DN3 ....26 C3
Parkway Av DARN/MH S9 ....127 F3
Parkway Cl DARN/MH S9 ....127 F3
Parkway Dr DARN/MH S9 ....127 G4
Parkway North WHHL DN2 ....40 D4
Parkway South WHHL DN2 ....41 E4
Parkwood Ri ARMTH DN3 ....29 G2
Parkwood Rd OWL S3 ....114 C5
Parliament St ECC S11 ....139 G1
Parma Ri WMB/DAR S73 ....34 C5
Parsley Hay Cl
  HAN/WDH S13 ....142 D1
Parsley Hay Dr
  HAN/WDH S13 ....142 D1
Parsley Hay Gdns
  HAN/WDH S13 ....142 D1
Parsley Hay Rd
  HAN/WDH S13 ....142 D1
Parsonage Cl MOS S20 ....166 D2
Parsonage Crs
  ST/HB/BR S6 ....125 E1
Parsonage St ST/HB/BR S6 ....125 E1
Parson Cross Rd
  ST/HB/BR S6 ....101 E5
Partridge Cl ECK/KIL S21 ....166 B5
Partridge Flatt Rd
  DONS/BSCR DN4 ....74 B2
Partridge Pl
  AU/AST/KP S26 ....145 G4
Partridge Ri
  DONS/BSCR DN4 ....74 B2
Partridge Vw
  SHEFP/MNR S2 ....127 E5
Parwich Cl CHSW S40 ....186 A4
Pashley Ct WMB/DAR S73 ....49 H3
Passfield Rd
  NROS/TKH DN11 ....91 G3
Passhouses Rd ATT S4 ....115 F4
Pasture Cl ARMTH DN3 ....42 C5
Pasture Gv ECK/KIL S21 ....166 C5
Pasture La BTLY DN5 ....51 H1
Pastures Br
  MEX/SWTN S64 * 67 G3
Pastures Ct MEX/SWTN S64 ....67 H3
  NROS/TKH DN11 ....91 H5
Pastures La BTLY DN5 ....68 C1
Pastures Rd
  MEX/SWTN S64 ....68 A3
The Pastures
  AU/AST/KP S26 ....147 E5
  MEX/SWTN S64 ....67 H3
Paternoster Rw SHEF S1 ....11 H5
Paterson Cl STKB/PEN S36 ....76 C1
Paterson Ct STKB/PEN S36 ....76 C1
Paterson Cft STKB/PEN S36 ....76 C1
Paterson Gdns
  STKB/PEN S36 ....76 C1
Paterson Rd DIN S25 ....135 E4
Patmore Rd SHEFN S5 ....102 D5
Paton Gv STV/CWN S43 ....188 B1
Patrick Stirling Ct
  DONS/BSCR DN4 ....55 C4
Patterdale Cl DRON S18 ....170 C2
Patterdale Wy DIN S25 ....148 D2
The Pavement
  SHEF S1 ....11 K3
Pavilion Cl STV/CWN S43 ....185 E4
Pavilion Rd RHAM S60 ....118 B2
Pavilion Wy SHEFS S8 ....102 D5
Pavillion Cl CONI DN12 ....70 C5
Paxton Crs ARMTH DN3 ....42 B3
Paxton Rd CHSW S40 * 188 A4
Payler Cl SHEFP/MNR S2 ....141 G3
Payne Crs RAW S62 ....85 E4
Peacock Cl ECK/KIL S21 ....168 A2
  KIMB S61 ....82 B5
Pea Fields La
  CHPT/GREN S35 ....79 F1
Peakdale Crs HACK/IN S12 ....142 C5
Peake Av CONI DN12 ....88 C1
Peak La MALT S66 ....110 C5
Peak Vw STV/CWN S43 ....188 A1
Peak View Rd CHSW S40 ....186 D5
Pearce La RCH S42 ....194 C4
Pearce Rd DARN/MH S9 ....128 A4
Pearce Wk DARN/MH S9 ....128 A4
Pearl St ECC S11 ....139 G2
Pearmain Dr MALT S66 ....110 B1
Pea Royd La STKB/PEN S36 ....77 E1
Pearson Crs WMB/DAR S73 ....49 H1
Pearson Gdns DSVR S44 ....196 B4
Pearson Pl SHEFS S8 ....152 D1
Pearsons Cft CHNE S41 ....186 C3
Pearson St STKB/PEN S36 ....76 D1

Pearson's Cl
  RHAM/THRY S65 ....107 E5
Pearson's Fld
  WMB/DAR S73 ....50 B2
Pear St ECC S11 ....139 G1
Peartree Av MALT S66 ....195 E4
  DEARNE S63 ....37 E2
Pear Tree Av MALT S66 ....108 C4
Pear Tree Cl CUD/GR S72 ....23 H5
  ECK/KIL S21 ....168 A3
  RHAM S60 ....118 D4
  STV/CWN S43 ....189 E1
Peartree Orch
  BSLYN/ROY S71 ....12 D4
Pear Tree Rd SHEFN S5 ....102 D3
Pearwood Crs
  DONS/BSCR DN4 ....71 F3
Peasehill Cl BSLY S70 ....3 F6
Peashill St RAW S62 ....98 B1
Peatfield Rd ECK/KIL S21 ....168 D1
Peckham Rd
  CHPT/GREN S35 ....80 B5
Pedley Av MOS S20 ....157 E4
Pedley Cl MOS S20 ....157 E5
Pedley Dr MOS S20 * 157 E5
Pedley Gv MOS S20 ....157 E4
Peel Cl MALT S66 ....110 C2
Peel Pde BSLY S70 ....2 E4
Peel Pl BSLYN/ROY S71 ....20 A4
Peel Sq BSLY S70 ....3 F4
Peel St BSLY S70 ....2 E4
  FUL S10 ....125 E5
Peel Ter FUL S10 ....10 B4
Peggars Cl STV/CWN S43 ....177 F5
Pell's Cl DON DN1 * 5 F3
Pembrey Ct MOS S20 ....157 G3
Pengeston Rd
  STKB/PEN S36 ....44 B4
Penistone Boundary Wk
  STKB/PEN S36 ....45 G1
Penistone Ct
  STKB/PEN S36 * 45 E3
Penistone Rd
  CHPT/GREN S35 ....93 E5
  OWL S3 ....125 G1
  ST/HB/BR S6 ....114 A3
Penistone Rd North
  ST/HB/BR S6 ....114 A1
Penistone St DON DN1 ....6 E2
Penley St ECC S11 ....139 G2
Penmore Gdns CHNE S41 ....193 E4
Penmore La CHNE S41 ....193 E4
Penmore St CHNE S41 ....193 E4
Pennine Gdns MALT S66 ....110 B2
Pennine Vw CHSW S40 ....186 C4
  DOD/DAR S75 ....18 D5
Pen Nook Cl STKB/PEN S36 ....77 F4
Pen Nook Ct STKB/PEN S36 ....77 G4
Pen Nook Dr STKB/PEN S36 ....77 G4
Pen Nook Gdns
  STKB/PEN S36 ....77 G4
Pen Nook Gld
  STKB/PEN S36 ....77 G4
Penns Rd SHEFP/MNR S2 ....140 C4
Penny Engine La
  ECK/KIL S21 ....167 G4
Pennyfields DEARNE S63 ....52 D3
Penny Hill La
  AU/AST/KP S26 ....131 H3
  MALT S66 ....132 C3
Penny La TOT/DORE S17 ....160 C5
Penny Piece La DIN S25 ....148 B2
Penny Piece Pl DIN S25 ....148 B2
Pennywell Dr RCH S42 ....190 B5
Penrhyn Rd ECC S11 ....139 E3
Penrhyn Wk
  BSLYN/ROY S71 ....33 G2
Penrith Cl SHEFN S5 ....114 C2
Penrith Crs SHEFN S5 ....114 C2
Penrith Gv BSLYN/ROY S71 ....33 F2
Penrith Rd SHEFN S5 ....114 C2
Penrose Pl HAN/WDH S13 ....143 E4
Penthorpe Cl HACK/IN S12 ....141 G4
Pentland Cl CHSW S40 ....186 E4
Pentland Gdns MOS S20 ....156 D3
Pentland Rd DRON S18 ....170 B2
Penton St SHEF S1 * 11 F3
Penwood Wk MALT S66 ....108 B1
Penyghent Cl
  CHPT/GREN S35 ....80 D5
Pepper Cl KIMB S61 ....96 B3
Pepper St HOY S74 ....49 E5
Percy St OWL S3 ....125 H2
  RHAM/THRY S65 ....9 G4
Peregrine Dr RSLY S70 * 40 H5
Perigree Rd SHEFS S8 ....152 C2
Periwood Av SHEFS S8 ....152 C2
Periwood Cl SHEFS S8 ....152 C2
Periwood Dr SHEFS S8 ....152 C2

Periwood Gv SHEFS S8 ....152 C2
Periwood La SHEFS S8 ....152 C2
Perkyn Rd SHEFN S5 ....102 C2
Perkyn Ter SHEFN S5 ....102 C2
Perran Gv BTLY DN5 ....39 F5
Perseverance St BSLY S70 ....2 C1
Persimmon Cl
  NROS/TKH DN11 ....91 F4
Perth Cl MEX/SWTN S64 ....67 G2
Petal Cl MALT S66 ....111 F2
Peterborough Cl FUL S10 ....137 E2
Peterborough Dr FUL S10 ....137 E1
Peterborough Rd FUL S10 ....137 E1
Peterdale Cl STV/CWN S43 ....188 C1
Peterdale Rd STV/CWN S43 ....188 C1
Peterfoot Wy
  BSLYN/ROY S71 ....15 F3
Petersgate BTLY DN5 ....39 F2
Peter St KIMB S61 ....104 C2
  MALT S66 ....133 E1
Peters Yd KIMB S61 * 104 C2
Petre Dr ATT S4 ....116 A4
Petre St ATT S4 ....115 H5
Pettyclose La CHNE S41 ....188 B4
Petworth Cft
  BSLYN/ROY S71 ....12 B5
Petworth Dr ECC S11 ....151 F3
Pevensey Av CHNE S41 ....187 E5
Peveril Crs BSLYN/ROY S71 ....15 E5
Peveril Rd BSVR S44 ....196 C1
  CHNE S41 ....187 F2
  ECC S11 ....138 D3
  ECK/KIL S21 ....167 E4
Pexton Rd ATT S4 ....115 G4
Pheasant Bank
  NROS/TKH DN11 ....91 G2
Pheasant Cl
  ST/HB/BR S6 ....125 G2
Philadelphia Dr
  ST/HB/BR S6 ....125 G2
Philadelphia Gdns
  ST/HB/BR S6 ....125 G2
Philadelphia Gv
  ST/HB/BR S6 ....125 G2
Philip Rd BSLY S70 ....32 D5
Phillimore Rd DARN/MH S9 ....127 H1
Phillips Rd ST/HB/BR S6 ....112 D3
Phoenix Ct HACK/IN S12 ....155 G4
Phoenix Gv DEARNE S63 ....37 G3
Phoenix La DEARNE S63 ....37 G3
Phoenix Rd DARN/MH S9 ....117 G1
  HACK/IN S12 ....155 G4
Piccadilly BTLY DN5 ....39 G2
  CHNE S41 ....5 J5
Piccadilly Rd CHNE S41 ....5 J5
  MEX/SWTN S64 ....86 A2
Pickard Crs HAN/WDH S13 ....142 B2
Pickard Dr HAN/WDH S13 ....142 B2
Pickburn La BTLY DN5 ....24 A4
Pickering Crs
  AU/AST/KP S26 ....145 E4
  OWL S3 ....114 D5
Pickering Rd BTLY DN5 ....26 C4
  OWL S3 ....114 D5
Pickering St
  DARN/MH S9 * 116 D4
Pickhill's Av DEARNE S63 ....37 H4
Pickmere Rd FUL S10 ....124 D3
Pickton Cl CHSW S40 ....191 H1
Pickup Crs WMB/DAR S73 ....50 B4
Pickwick Dr RHAM S60 ....129 F1
Piece End CHPT/GREN S35 ....80 B3
Piece End Cl
  CHPT/GREN S35 ....80 B3
The Pieces North
  RHAM S60 ....119 H4
The Pieces South
  RHAM S60 ....119 H4
Pigeon Bridge Wy
  AU/AST/KP S26 ....145 H4
Pighills La DRON S18 ....163 F4
Pike Cl CHSW S40 ....186 B4
Pike Lowe Gv
  RHAM S60 ....14 B4
Pike Rd RHAM S60 ....118 C3
Pilgrim St OWL S3 ....115 F5
Pilley Gn DOD/DAR S75 ....60 B3
Pilley Hl DOD/DAR S75 ....30 B4
Pilley La DOD/DAR S75 ....60 B2
Pinchfield Cl MALT S66 ....121 F1
Pinchfield Holt MALT S66 ....121 F1
Pinchfield La MALT S66 ....121 F1
Pinchmill Hollow MALT S66 ....121 F2
Pinch Mill La RHAM S60 ....120 C3
Pinchwell Vw MALT S66 ....121 F1
Pindale Av STV/CWN S43 ....189 G2
Pindar Oaks Cottages
  BSLY S70 ....32 B2
Pindar Oaks St BSLY S70 * 3 J7
Pindar St BSLY S70 ....32 B2
Pine Av DIN S25 ....148 B5
Pine Cl BSLY S70 ....32 C4
  ECK/KIL S21 ....168 A3
  HOY S74 ....62 A3
  MALT S66 ....108 C3
Pine Cft CHPT/GREN S35 ....94 A2
Pinecroft Wy
  CHPT/GREN S35 ....94 A2
Pinefield Av ARMTH DN3 ....29 G1
Pinefield Rd ARMTH DN3 ....29 G1
Pine Gv CONI DN12 ....88 C3
Pinehall Dr BSLYN/ROY S71 ....20 D3
Pine Hall Rd ARMTH DN3 ....29 G1
Pinehurst Ri MEX/SWTN S64 ....86 B1
Pine Rd DONS/BSCR DN4 ....58 B5
The Pines FUL S10 ....137 E2

Pine St STV/CWN S43 ....189 E1
Pine Vw CHSW S40 ....191 F1
Pine Wk MEX/SWTN S64 ....86 B3
Pinewood Av ARMTH DN3 ....42 D2
  DONS/BSCR DN4 ....71 E3
Pinewood Cl CUD/GR S72 ....23 H4
Pinfold Cl BSLYN/ROY S71 ....33 E2
  MEX/SWTN S64 ....86 A1
  RCH S42 ....190 C4
Pinfold Ct ARMTH DN3 ....29 F1
Pinfold Gdns CUD/GR S72 ....22 A2
Pinfold Hl BSLY S70 ....32 A4
Pinfold Lands
  MEX/SWTN S64 ....67 F4
Pinfold La BSLYN/ROY S71 ....15 G2
  OWL S3 ....115 E5
  RHAM S60 ....9 H6
  WMB/DAR S73 ....35 F5
Pinfold St ECK/KIL S21 ....166 D5
  SHEF S1 ....11 F5
Pingle Av ABRD S7 ....152 A2
Pingle Gra STV/CWN S43 ....188 C2
Pingle Rd ABRD S7 ....152 A2
  ECK/KIL S21 ....168 C1
Pingles Crs
  RHAM/THRY S65 ....99 G4
Pinner Rd ECC S11 ....139 E3
Pinstone St SHEF S1 ....11 G4
Pioneer Cl DEARNE S63 ....66 A2
Pipe House La RAW S62 ....85 F4
Piper Cl SHEFN S5 ....115 E1
Piper Ct SHEFN S5 ....115 E1
Piper Crs SHEFN S5 ....115 E1
Pipering Lane (East)
  BTLY DN5 ....39 F3
Pipering Lane (West)
  BTLY DN5 ....39 E3
Piper La AU/AST/KP S26 ....145 H2
  RCH S42 ....190 C1
Pipeyard La ECK/KIL S21 ....166 C5
Pipworth Gv
  SHEFP/MNR S2 ....142 A1
Pipworth La ECK/KIL S21 ....167 F4
Pisgah House Rd FUL S10 ....125 E4
Pitch Cl STV/CWN S43 ....185 E4
Pitchford La FUL S10 ....137 H1
Pithouse La
  AU/AST/KP S26 ....158 B3
  MOS S20 ....158 A2
Pit La HACK/IN S12 ....141 G4
  KIMB S61 ....95 F3
  RHAM S60 ....130 B3
Pitman Rd CONI DN12 ....68 A5
Pitsmoor Rd OWL S3 ....126 A1
Pittam Cl ARMTH DN3 ....42 D4
Pitt Cl SHEF S1 ....10 D4
Pitt La SHEF S1 * 10 D4
Pitt St BSLY S70 ....3 H5
  ECK/KIL S21 ....174 C1
  KIMB S61 ....104 D3
  MEX/SWTN S64 ....67 G3
  SHEF S1 ....10 D4
  WMB/DAR S73 ....34 C5
Pitt St West BSLY S70 ....2 D5
Plane Cl DONS/BSCR DN4 ....58 B5
Plane Dr MALT S66 ....108 C4
Plane Tree Wy EPW DN9 ....75 H5
Plank Ga CHPT/GREN S35 ....100 A1
  STKB/PEN S36 ....78 A4
Plantation Av
  BSLYN/ROY S71 ....15 H1
  DIN S25 ....134 D4
  DONS/BSCR DN4 ....74 D4
Plantation Cl CHSW S40 ....186 A4
  MALT S66 ....110 D2
Plantation Ct DIN S25 ....134 D4
Plantation Rd
  DONS/BSCR DN4 ....72 A4
  SHEFS S8 ....140 A4
Plantin Ri MOS S20 * 167 E1
The Plantin MOS S20 ....167 E1
Platts Dr MOS S20 ....157 G1
Platts La CHPT/GREN S35 ....100 A2
Platt St OWL S3 ....126 A1
Pleasant Av BSVR S44 ....197 E5
Pleasant Cl HACK/IN S12 ....141 H4
Pleasant Pl CHSW S40 * 4 A4
Pleasant Vw CUD/GR S72 ....22 A3
Pleasley Rd AU/AST/KP S26 ....131 E3
  RHAM S60 ....119 H4
Plover Ct NROS/TKH DN11 ....91 G2
  SHEFP/MNR S2 ....127 E5
Plover Cft KIMB S61 ....82 C5
Plover Rd BSLY S70 ....47 H5
Plover Wy BSVR S44 ....193 H1
Plowright Cl GLV S14 ....140 D5
Plowright Dr GLV S14 ....140 D5
Plowright Mt GLV S14 ....140 D5
Plowright Wy GLV S14 ....140 D5
Plumber St BSLY S70 ....2 D4
Plumbley Hall Ms MOS S20 ....166 C2
Plumbley Hall Rd MOS S20 ....166 C2
Plumbley La MOS S20 ....166 B2
Plumb Leys RHAM S60 ....130 A3
Plum La OWL S3 ....11 G1
Plumper's Rd DARN/MH S9 ....117 F2
Plumpton Av
  MEX/SWTN S64 ....67 G2
Plumpton Gdns
  DONS/BSCR DN4 ....74 C2

Plumpton Pk CUD/GR S72 ....17 E2
Plumpton Park Rd
  DONS/BSCR DN4 ....74 C3
Plum St OWL S3 ....11 G1
Plunket Rd WHHL DN2 ....7 J1
Plymouth Rd ABRD S7 ....139 G5
Pocket Handkerchief La
  DIN S25 ....147 F2
Pocknedge La RCH S42 ....190 B3
Pogmoor La DOD/DAR S75 ....18 C5
Pogmoor Rd DOD/DAR S75 ....2 A2
Polka Ct OWL S3 ....126 A1
Pollard Av SHEFN S5 ....114 C1
Pollard Crs SHEFN S5 ....114 C1
Pollard Rd SHEFN S5 ....114 C1
Pollard St KIMB S61 ....104 C3
Pollitt St DOD/DAR S75 ....2 D1
Pollyfox Wy DOD/DAR S75 ....30 A3
Polyfields La BSVR S44 ....197 E4
Pomona St ECC S11 ....139 G1
Pond Cl ST/HB/BR S6 ....123 H1
Pond Hl SHEF S1 ....11 J3
Pond La RCH S42 ....195 E3
Pond Rd ST/HB/BR S6 ....123 H1
Pond Sq SHEF S1 ....11 J4
Pond St BSLY S70 ....3 F6
  CHSW S40 ....5 H5
  SHEF S1 ....11 H5
Pondwell Dr STV/CWN S43 ....188 C2
Pontefract Rd
  BSLYN/ROY S71 ....3 J5
  CUD/GR S72 ....17 E3
  DEARNE S63 ....64 B1
Pool Dr DONS/BSCR DN4 ....74 D2
Poole Pl DARN/MH S9 ....128 A3
Poole Rd DARN/MH S9 ....128 A3
Pools La BSLYN/ROY S71 ....16 A1
Pool Sq SHEF S1 ....11 G3
Pope Av CONI DN12 ....88 B1
Poplar Av CHSW S40 ....191 F3
  CUD/GR S72 ....17 E2
  DEARNE S63 ....37 G5
  MOS S20 ....144 B5
  RHAM/THRY S65 ....99 G4
  STKB/PEN S36 ....76 D3
Poplar Cl ARMTH DN3 ....59 F4
  DRON S18 ....171 G4
  ECK/KIL S21 ....168 A3
  MEX/SWTN S64 ....66 D2
Poplar Dr DEARNE S63 ....65 F4
  RHAM S60 ....118 B4
Poplar Gld MALT S66 ....108 C4
Poplar Gv BSLYN/ROY S71 ....21 E5
  CONI DN12 ....88 D2
  DONS/BSCR DN4 ....70 C4
  MEX/SWTN S64 * 66 B5
  RHAM/THRY S65 ....109 E1
Poplar Pl ARMTH DN3 ....42 D4
  CHNE S41 * 5 F2
Poplar Ri MALT S66 ....110 B2
Poplar Rd ECK/KIL S21 ....174 C1
  WMB/DAR S73 ....50 C3
Poplars Rd BSLY S70 ....32 B3
The Poplars CONI DN12 ....88 D2
Poplar St CUD/GR S72 ....23 F2
Poplar Ter BSLYN/ROY S71 ....12 D5
  BTLY DN5 ....39 H2
Poplar Wy RHAM S60 ....129 G2
Popple St ATT S4 ....116 A3
Poppyfields Wy
  ARMTH DN3 ....75 E1
Porter Av DOD/DAR S75 ....2 A2
Porter Brook Vw ECC S11 ....139 F2
Porter St STV/CWN S43 ....182 A4
Porter Ter DOD/DAR S75 ....18 D5
Portland Av
  AU/AST/KP S26 ....145 G3
  BSVR S44 ....197 E3
Portland Buildings
  ST/HB/BR S6 * 125 G2
Portland Cl CHNE S41 ....5 F2
  DIN S25 ....134 C5
Portland Ct ST/HB/BR S6 ....125 C1
Portland Crs BSVR S44 ....197 E3
Portland La SHEF S1 ....10 D4
Portland Pl DON DN1 ....6 C5
  MALT S66 ....111 E3
Portland Rd MOS S20 ....157 G3
  NROS/TKH DN11 ....91 H4
Portland St BSLY S70 ....32 B2
  MEX/SWTN S64 ....86 B1
  ST/HB/BR S6 ....125 G2
  STV/CWN S43 ....185 G2
Portobello St SHEF S1 ....10 D3
Portsea Rd ST/HB/BR S6 ....113 H4
Pot House La
  STKB/PEN S36 ....76 D3
Potterdyke Av RAW S62 ....85 F3
Potter Hl KIMB S61 ....95 E3
Potter Hill La
  CHPT/GREN S35 ....80 A4
Potteric Carr Rd
  DONS/BSCR DN4 ....56 C4
Potters Cl CHNE S41 ....179 H4
Potters Ga CHPT/GREN S35 ....80 A4
Pottery Cl RAW S62 ....98 B1
Pottery La East CHNE S41 ....187 G2
Pottery La West CHNE S41 ....187 G2
Pottery Rd KIMB S61 ....105 E4
Poucher St KIMB S61 ....104 A3
Poulton St BSLYN/ROY S71 ....20 D1

Powder Mill La *BSLY* S70.......48 C2
Powell Dr *ECK/KIL* S21......168 A2
Powell St *BSLY* S70.......48 B1
   OWL S3.................10 B2
Power Station Rd *BTLY* DN5.....55 H1
Powley Rd *ST/HB/BR* S6......101 E4

Poynton Av
   AU/AST/KP S26..........131 G4
Poynton Dr *DIN* S25......134 D3
Poynton Wy *AU/AST/KP* S26..131 G4
Poynton Wood Crs
   TOT/DORE S17.........161 G2
Poynton Wood Gld
   TOT/DORE S17.........161 G2
Prescott Rd *ST/HB/BR* S6......113 G2
President Wy *ATT* S4.......126 C2
Preston Av *HOY* S74........62 C1
Preston St *SHEFS* S8.......140 A3
Preston Wy *BSLYN/ROY* S71...20 D1
Prestwich St *DARN/MH* S9....103 H5
Prestwold Wy *CHNE* S41.....193 E5
Priest Croft La
   BSLYN/ROY S71.........34 D2
Priestfield Gdns *CHNE* S41...186 B2
Priestley Av *RAW* S62.......85 H4
Priestley Cl *DONS/BSCR* DN4..71 F3
Priestley St *SHEFP/MNR* S2....140 B1
Primrose Av *RHAM* S60......118 D5
   SHEFS S5...............103 E5
   WMB/DAR S73...........34 D5
Primrose Cir
   NROS/TKH DN11.........91 G3
Primrose Cl *ECK/KIL* S21....168 C1
Primrose Crs *MOS* S20.....157 F2
Primrose Dr
   CHPT/GREN S35........102 B1
   ST/HB/BR S6..........125 C1
Primrose La *ECK/KIL* S21...158 C5
Primrose Pk *RHAM* S60 *......8 D1
Primrose Pl
   DONS/BSCR DN4.........57 F5
Primrose Wy *HOY* S74.......62 A3
Primulas Cl *DIN* S25.......148 A4
Prince Arthur St
   DOD/DAR S75............2 C2
Princegate *DON* DN1..........6 D4
Prince of Wales Rd
   DARN/MH S9...........128 A4
   SHEFP/MNR S2.........141 G3
Princess Cl *DEARNE* S63.....52 D3
Princess Gv *SHEFP/MNR* S2...141 H2
Princess Dr *DEARNE* S63......37 G3
   STKB/PEN S36..........77 F5
Princess Gdns
   WMB/DAR S73...........50 B3
Princess Gv *DOD/DAR* S75....60 A5
Princess Rd *DEARNE* S63....155 G1
   DRON S18.............171 E1
   MEX/SWTN S64..........67 F3
Princess St *ATT* S4.......126 C2
   AWLS/ASK DN6..........25 F3
   BSLY S70................2 E5
   CHNE S41................4 E1
   CUD/GR S72............23 E1
   DEARNE S63...........64 D1
   DIN S25..............134 A3
   HOY S74...............61 F3
   STV/CWN S43.........180 D5
   WMB/DAR S73...........50 A2
Princes St *RHAM* S60........8 B4
Prince's St *MEX/SWTN* S64....66 B4
Prince's Crs *CONI* DN12......70 B5
Prince's Rd *DONS/BSCR* DN4...29 F3
Prince's Sq *ARMTH* DN3.......29 F3
Prince's St *DON* DN1.........6 E4
Pringle Rd *RHAM* S60.......118 B3
Printing Office St *DON* DN1....6 C4
Prior Rd *CONI* DN12.........88 D2
Priory Av *ECC* S11.........139 H2
Priory Cl *BSLY* S70.........47 H3
   CHPT/GREN S35.........94 A5
   CONI DN12.............69 E5
   MEX/SWTN S64 *........67 G4
Priory Crs *BSLYN/ROY* S71...21 E4
Priory Pl *ABRD* S7.........139 H2
   BSLYN/ROY S71.........21 E5
   DON DN1................7 F2
Priory Rd *ABRD* S7.........139 G3
   BSLYN/ROY S71.........21 E5
   CHPT/GREN S35.........94 A5
   DEARNE S63............53 E3
Priory Wk *DON* DN1..........6 D4
Priory Wy *AU/AST/KP* S26...145 G3
Pritchard La *HACK/IN* S12...156 B2
Private Dr *STV/CWN* S43....189 E1
Probert Av *DEARNE* S63......37 G5
Proctor Pl *ST/HB/BR* S6....114 A4
Progress Dr *MALT* S66.....108 D5
Prominence Wy *MALT* S66...108 B1
Prospect *STKB/PEN* S36......44 A3
Prospect Cl *MALT* S66.....108 D5
Prospect Ct *TOT/DORE* S17..161 F1
Prospect Pl *DON* DN1........6 C6
   TOT/DORE S17.........161 G2
Prospect Rd *BTLY* DN5......26 C5
   CHNE S41.............179 F4
   DEARNE S63...........53 E2
   DRON S18............163 G5
   SHEFP/MNR S2.........140 A3
   TOT/DORE S17.........161 G3
Prospect St *BSLY* S70........2 D1
   CUD/GR S72............16 D5

Prospect Ter *CHSW* S40.......4 C1
Providence Ct *BSLY* S70.......3 F7
Providence Rd
   ST/HB/BR S6.........124 D1
Providence St *KIMB* S61.....97 G3
   RHAM S60..............50 D1
   WMB/DAR S73..........50 D1
Psalter La *ECC* S11.........138 D3
Psalters Dr *STKB/PEN* S36....45 G5
Psalters La *KIMB* S61......104 D2
Pullman Cl *STV/CWN* S43....182 B3
Pump Houses
   STV/CWN S43 *........183 E4
Purbeck Av *CHSW* S40......186 D5
Purbeck Ct *MOS* S20........156 D3
Purbeck Gv *MOS* S20.......156 D3
Purbeck Rd *MOS* S20.......156 D3
Purcell Cl *MALT* S66.......111 G4
Purslove Cl *MALT* S66.....109 G5
Pye Bank Cl *OWL* S3.......126 A1
Pye Bank Dr *OWL* S3.......126 A1
Pye Bank Rd *OWL* S3.......126 A1
Pym Rd *MEX/SWTN* S64......67 G3
Pynot Rd *CHNE* S41........179 H4

Q

The Quadrant
   TOT/DORE S17.........161 E3
Quail Ri *SHEFP/MNR* S2....127 E5
Quaker Cl *DEARNE* S63......64 D3
Quaker La *BSLYN/ROY* S71....33 F2
   DONS/BSCR DN4.........70 D2
Quantock Wy *CHSW* S40....186 B4
Quarry Bank Cl
   CUD/GR S72............21 H1
Quarry Bank Rd *CHNE* S41....5 K6
Quarry Cl *RHAM* S60.......118 A4
Quarryfield La *MALT* S66...110 D1
Quarryfield La *MALT* S66...121 F2
Quarry Flds *MALT* S66.....121 F1
Quarry Hi *ECK/KIL* S21....173 F1
   HACK/IN S12..........156 A5
   RHAM S60.............118 A4
Quarry Hill Ct *DEARNE* S63...65 E4
Quarry Hill Rd *DEARNE* S63...65 E4
Quarry La *ARMTH* DN3.......59 F5
   AWLS/ASK DN6..........25 E3
   CHSW S40............191 G2
   DIN S25..............148 B2
   ECC S11..............139 E4
   KIMB S61...............8 C1
Quarry Rd *BSVR* S44.......196 D1
   DRON S18.............172 C2
   ECK/KIL S21..........168 A1
   HAN/WDH S13.........128 C4
   HOY S74...............48 D4
   TOT/DORE S17.........161 E3
Quarry St *BSLY* S70.........3 H6
   BSLYN/ROY S71.........20 A2
   CUD/GR S72............16 D5
   MEX/SWTN S64..........67 F4
   RAW S62...............85 F5
Quarry Vale Gv
   HACK/IN S12..........155 E1
Quarry Vale Rd
   HACK/IN S12..........155 E1
Queen Av *MALT* S66.......111 E4
   NROS/TKH DN11........91 E2
Queen Gdns *WMB/DAR* S73...50 B3
Queen Mary Cl
   SHEFP/MNR S2.........141 G3
Queen Mary Crs
   ARMTH DN3............29 F3
   SHEFP/MNR S2.........141 G2
Queen Mary Gv
   SHEFP/MNR S2.........141 G3
Queen Mary Ms
   SHEFP/MNR S2.........141 G3
Queen Mary Ri
   SHEFP/MNR S2.........141 G2
Queen Mary Rd *CHSW* S40...191 F3
   SHEFP/MNR S2.........141 F2
Queen Mary's Rd
   SHEFP/MNR S2.........141 F2
Queen Mary's Rd
   NROS/TKH DN11........91 E2
Queens Acre
   MEX/SWTN S64 *........66 B5
Queens Av *AU/AST/KP* S26..131 F2
Queensberry Rd *WHHL* DN2...57 G1
Queens Crs *HOY* S74.........61 E3
Queens Dr *DOD/DAR* S75......2 B1
   DOD/DAR S75..........19 E4
Queens Gdns *DOD/DAR* S75....2 B1
   HOY S74...............61 H5
Queensgate
   CHPT/GREN S35 *......101 F1
   DON DN1................6 D5
Queens Pk *CONI* DN12......70 B5
Queens Rd *AU/AST/KP* S26..145 E5
   BSLYN/ROY S71.........3 H4
   CUD/GR S72............23 F1
   SHEFP/MNR S2.........140 B3
Queen St *BSLY* S70..........3 G4
   CHPT/GREN S35.........81 G5
   CHSW S40...............4 C1
   DEARNE S63............37 G5
   DIN S25..............134 D3
   DONS/BSCR DN4.........55 H5
   ECK/KIL S21..........167 E5

Queen St North *CHNE* S41...187 G1
Queensway *BSLY* S70........49 B1
   BSLYN/ROY S71.........12 C5
   CUD/GR S72............23 E1
   DOD/DAR S75...........19 E4
   HOY S74...............62 B2
   RHAM S60.............119 F2
Queenswood Cl
   ST/HB/BR S6..........113 F1
Queenswood Dr
   ST/HB/BR S6..........113 F1
Queenswood Ga
   ST/HB/BR S6..........113 F1
Queenswood Rd
   ST/HB/BR S6..........113 F1
Queen Victoria Rd
   TOT/DORE S17.........161 F3
Queen's Av *CUD/GR* S72......35 H3
   DOD/DAR S75...........2 C2
   MEX/SWTN S64..........66 B4
Queen's Crt *BTLY* DN5.......39 G4
Queen's Crs *CONI* DN12......70 B5
Queen's Dr *BTLY* DN5.......39 G4
   CUD/GR S72............16 D1
   DOD/DAR S75...........19 E4
Queen's Rd *CUD/GR* S72......17 E3
   DON DN1................7 F1
   MOS S20.............157 F1
Queen's Row *OWL* S3........10 C1
Queen's Ter *MEX/SWTN* S64...67 E3
Quern Wy *WMB/DAR* S73......35 F4
Quest Av *WMB/DAR* S73......49 H5
Quiet La *FUL* S10..........137 F4
Quilter Rd *MALT* S66......111 G4
Quintec Ct *KIMB* S61.......98 A5
Quoit Gn *DRON* S18.........171 F2
Quorn Dr *CHSW* S40........186 A4

R

Raby Rd *WHHL* DN2..........40 D5
Raby St *DARN/MH* S9.......117 G1
Racecommon La *BSLY* S70....31 F3
Racecommon Rd *BSLY* S70.....2 C7
Racecourse Mt *CHNE* S41...187 F1
Racecourse Rd *CHNE* S41...187 F1
   MEX/SWTN S64..........66 B5
Race St *BSLY* S70...........2 E5
Racker Wy *ST/HB/BR* S6....113 H5
Rackford Rd *DIN* S25......148 C3
Radburn Rd
   NROS/TKH DN11........91 E4
Radcliffe Cl *BTLY* DN5......39 E1
Radcliffe La *BTLY* DN5......39 E1
Radcliffe Rd *BSLYN/ROY* S71..14 D4
   BTLY DN5..............26 C5
Radford Cl
   RHAM/THRY S65.......109 E1
Radford St *OWL* S3.........10 D2
Radley Av *MALT* S66.......108 A4
Radnor Cl *MOS* S20........157 C5
Radnor Wy *WHHL* DN2.......41 E5
Raeburn Cl *GLV* S14.......154 A3
Raeburn Pl *GLV* S14.......154 A2
Raeburn Wy *GLV* S14......154 A3
Ragusa Dr *NROS/TKH* DN11...91 H4
Rail Mill Wy *RAW* S62......98 B4
Rails *ST/HB/BR* S6.........123 E3
Railway Av *RHAM* S60.......8 D4
Railway Ct *CHNE* S41 *.....192 D5
   RHAM S60...............8 D4
Railway Vw *DEARNE* S63.....37 G5
Rainborough Ct
   DEARNE S63............63 H2
Rainborough Ms
   DEARNE S63............64 B1
Rainborough Rd
   DEARNE S63............64 B2
Rainbow Av *HACK/IN* S12...156 C1
Rainbow Crs *HACK/IN* S12...156 C1
Rainbow Dr *HACK/IN* S12...156 C1
Rainbow Gv *HACK/IN* S12...156 C1
Rainbow Pl *HACK/IN* S12...156 C1
Rainbow Wy *HACK/IN* S12...156 C1
Rainford Dr *BSLYN/ROY* S71..20 D1
Rainford Sq *ARMTH* DN3.....29 F2
Rainton Dr *DOD/DAR* S75....18 C1
Rainton Rd *DON* DN1........7 F6
Raintree Ct *BTLY* DN5.......39 F5
Raisen Hall Pl *SHEFN* S5...115 E2
Raisen Hall Rd *SHEFN* S5...115 E2
Rake's La *NROS/TKH* DN11...73 E5
Raleigh Ct *WHHL* DN2.......57 F2
Raleigh Dr *CHPT/GREN* S35...93 F1
Raleigh Rd *SHEFP/MNR* S2...140 A3
Raleigh Ter *DONS/BSCR* DN4..71 E2
Raley St *BSLY* S70...........2 A7
Ralph Ellis Dr *STKB/PEN* S36..76 D3
Ralph Rd *STV/CWN* S43.....182 C4

Ralston Ct *MOS* S20.......166 D2
Ralston Cft *MOS* S20......167 E2
Ralston Gv *MOS* S20.......166 D2
Ramper Av *STV/CWN* S43....185 E4
Rampton Rd *ABRD* S7......139 H3
Ramsay Crs *BTLY* DN5.......39 F4
Ramsden Rd
   DONS/BSCR DN4.........55 G3
   RHAM S60...............9 H7
Ramsey Av *MEX/SWTN* S64..191 H5
Ramsey Rd *FUL* S10.......125 E3
Ramshaw Cl *CHNE* S41.....188 C2
Ramshaw Rd *DRON* S18.....172 A5
Ramsker Dr *ARMTH* DN3......42 D5
Ramsworth Cl *BTLY* DN5.....39 E5
Ranby Rd *ECC* S11.........138 D3
Randall Pl *SHEFP/MNR* S2...139 H2
Randall St *ECK/KIL* S21....174 B1
   SHEFP/MNR S2.........140 A1
Randerson Dr
   MEX/SWTN S64..........86 C2
Rands La *ARMTH* DN3.......43 E3
Ranelagh Dr *ECC* S11......138 D5
Raneld Mt *CHSW* S40......191 G4
Ranfield Ct
   RHAM/THRY S65.......109 E1
Rangeley Rd *ST/HB/BR* S6...124 C2
Ranmoor Cliffe Rd *FUL* S10..138 A1
Ranmoor Cl *CHNE* S41 *....193 E4
Ranmoor Crs *FUL* S10......138 B1
Ranmoor Park Rd *FUL* S10..138 B1
Ranmoor Ri *FUL* S10.......138 B1
Ranmoor Rd *FUL* S10.......138 B1
Ranskill Ct *DARN/MH* S9...117 E5
Ranworth Rd *MALT* S66....109 E4
Ranyard Rd
   DONS/BSCR DN4.........71 F1
Raseby Av *MOS* S20.......157 E3
Raseby Cl *MOS* S20.......157 E3
Raseby Pl *MOS* S20.......157 E3
Rasen Cl *MEX/SWTN* S64.....67 F2
Ratcliffe Cl *CHNE* S41......5 H5
Ratcliffe Rd *ECC* S11.....139 F2
Ratten Rw *DOD/DAR* S75.....30 A4
Ravencar Rd *ECK/KIL* S21..166 B5
Ravencarr Pl
   SHEFP/MNR S2.........141 G1
Ravencarr Rd
   SHEFP/MNR S2.........141 G1
Raven Dr *KIMB* S61.........82 C5
Raven Edge
   RHAM/THRY S65.......108 D3
Ravenfield Cl *MOS* S20....156 A3
Ravenfield Dr
   BSLYN/ROY S71.........20 A1
Ravenfield Rd *ARMTH* DN3...43 E5
Ravenfield St *CONI* DN12....68 B5
Ravenholt *BSLY* S70.........48 A1
Raven La *CUD/GR* S72.......13 G3
Raven Mdw *MEX/SWTN* S64...86 A3
Ravenna Cl *BSLY* S70........32 B2
Raven Rd *ABRD* S7.........137 H4
Raven Royd *BSLYN/ROY* S71..14 D3
Ravenscar Cl *CONI* DN12....68 B5
Ravenscourt *BSLY* S70......48 B1
Ravenscroft Av
   HAN/WDH S13.........142 C2
Ravenscroft Cl
   HAN/WDH S13.........142 C2
Ravenscroft Ct
   HAN/WDH S13.........142 C2
Ravenscroft Crs
   HAN/WDH S13.........142 C2
Ravenscroft Dr
   HAN/WDH S13.........142 C2
Ravenscroft Ov
   HAN/WDH S13.........142 C2
Ravenscroft Pl
   HAN/WDH S13.........142 C2
Ravenscroft Rd
   HAN/WDH S13.........142 C2
Ravenscroft Wy
   HAN/WDH S13.........142 C2
Ravensdale Cl
   STV/CWN S43.........189 G3
Ravensdale Rd *DRON* S18...170 A2
Ravenshaw Cl
   DOD/DAR S75...........18 D4
Ravensmead Ct
   DEARNE S63............53 E3
Ravens Wk *CONI* DN12......89 G1
Ravenswood Dr *MALT* S66...108 A4
Ravensworth Rd *CHSW* S40..186 A4
Ravensworth Rd *DON* DN1....7 F4
The Ravine *SHEFN* S5......103 E2
Rawmarsh HI *RAW* S62.......98 B2
Rawmarsh Rd *RHAM* S60......9 F1
Rawson Cl *DONS/BSCR* DN4...58 B4
Rawsons Bank
   CHPT/GREN S35........102 B1
Rawson Spring Rd
   ST/HB/BR S6..........114 B2
Rawson Spring Wy
   ST/HB/BR S6..........114 B2
Raybould Rd *MALT* S66......96 D5
Rayleigh Av *STV/CWN* S43..188 B1
Rayls Ri *AU/AST/KP* S26...147 F5
Rayls Rd *AU/AST/KP* S26...147 F5
Raymond Av *CUD/GR* S72....23 E1
Raymond Rd *BSLY* S70.......32 D3
   BTLY DN5..............39 F4
Raynald Rd *SHEFP/MNR* S2...141 G1
Reader Crs *MEX/SWTN* S64...66 B4

Reaper Crs *CHPT/GREN* S35...80 C5
Reasbeck Ter
   BSLYN/ROY S71.........19 H2
Reasby Av
   RHAM/THRY S65.......108 D1
Reavill Cl *DIN* S25........134 D3
Rebecca Ms *BSLY* S70........3 G7
Rebecca Rw *BSLY* S70........3 G7
Recreation Av *MALT* S66...133 F1
Recreation Cl
   STV/CWN S43.........185 E2
Recreation La
   NROS/TKH DN11........91 E2
Recreation Rd
   AWLS/ASK DN6..........25 F3
   DEARNE S63............65 F1
   STV/CWN S43.........188 D4
Rectory Cl *BSLYN/ROY* S71...15 H3
   DEARNE S63............36 D2
   ECK/KIL S21..........167 E4
   STKB/PEN S36..........77 E4
   WMB/DAR S73..........50 B3
Rectory Dr *RCH* S42.......194 D3
Rectory Gdns *DON* DN1.......7 G1
Rectory La *DEARNE* S63......36 D2
Rectory Ms *BTLY* DN5.......54 B5
Rectory Rd *ECK/KIL* S21...168 B2
   STV/CWN S43.........182 A4
   STV/CWN S43.........185 E2
Rectory St *RAW* S62........98 B2
Rectory Wy *BSLYN/ROY* S71...20 D4
Redacre Dr *BSVR* S44......197 F2
Redbourne Rd *BTLY* DN5.....39 H1
Redbrook Av *CHNE* S41....192 D4
Redbrook Ct *DOD/DAR* S75...19 E3
Redbrook Cft *MOS* S20.....156 A2
Redbrook Gv *MOS* S20......156 A2
Redbrook Rd *DOD/DAR* S75...18 C3
Redbrook Vw
   DOD/DAR S75...........19 E3
Redbrook Wk
   DOD/DAR S75...........19 E3
Redcar Cl *CONI* DN12.......88 A1
Redcar Rd *FUL* S10.......125 E4
Redcliffe Cl *DOD/DAR* S75...18 D3
Redfearn St *BSLYN/ROY* S71...3 H2
Redfern Av *MOS* S20.......156 D4
Redfern Ct *MOS* S20.......156 D4
Redfern Dr *MOS* S20.......156 D4
Redfern Gv *MOS* S20.......156 D4
Red Fern Gv *STKB/PEN* S36...76 D3
Redgrave Pl *MALT* S66.....108 B3
Redgrove Wy *CHSW* S40....191 G4
Redhall Cl *ARMTH* DN3......29 G3
Red Hi *OWL* S3.............10 E2
Redhill Av *BSLY* S70........32 C5
Redhouse Ct *STV/CWN* S43..180 B2
Red House La
   AWLS/ASK DN6..........24 B1
Redland La *ABRD* S7......152 B2
Redland Wy *MALT* S66.....110 C2
Red La *CHNE* S41.........180 A5
   FUL S10..............136 B1
Red Lion Yd *RHAM* S60......9 F4
Redmarsh Av *RAW* S62......85 F4
Redmires La *FUL* S10......136 B1
Redmires Rd *FUL* S10......136 D1
Rednall Cl *CHSW* S40......186 A4
Red Oak La *ST/HB/BR* S6...111 C5
Redrock Rd *RHAM* S60.....119 G2
Redscope Crs *KIMB* S61.....96 B4
Redscope Rd *KIMB* S61......96 B5
Redthorne Wy *CUD/GR* S72...16 D1
Redthorn Rd
   HAN/WDH S13.........142 D2
Redthorpe Crest
   DOD/DAR S75...........18 C3
Redvers Buller Rd
   CHSW S40............192 C3
Redwood Av
   BSLYN/ROY S71.........15 G1
   ECK/KIL S21..........168 A3
Redwood Cl *HOY* S74........61 H3
   STV/CWN S43.........189 E1
Redwood Dr *MALT* S66.....110 A3
Redwood Gln
   CHPT/GREN S35.........93 H2
Reedham Dr *MALT* S66.....109 H2
Reeves Wy *ARMTH* DN3......43 E4
Regent Ct *HOY* S74.........61 G3
Regent Av *BSLYN/ROY* S71...14 D5
Regent Gdns *BSLY* S70.......3 G3
Regent Gv *BTLY* DN5........39 F5
Regent Sq *DON* DN1.........6 E4
Regent St *BSLY* S70.........3 G3
   DONS/BSCR DN4.........71 C1
   HOY S74...............61 E3
   KIMB S61.............100 D3
   SHEFS S1.............103 D3
   STV/CWN S43.........184 D2
Regent St South *BSLY* S70 *...3 G3
Regents Wy
   AU/AST/KP S26........145 G3
Regent Ter *DON* DN1........7 F4
   OWL S3................10 C3
Regina Crs *CUD/GR* S72.....17 G1
Reginald Rd *BSVR* S44.....197 G2
   WMB/DAR S73 *.........50 D3
Rembrandt Dr *DRON* S18...170 A2
Remington Av *SHEFN* S5...101 H2
Remington Dr *SHEFN* S5...101 H2
Remington Rd *SHEFN* S5...101 H2

Remington Rd SHEFN S5......101 H3
Remount Rd KIMB S61......96 B4
Remount Wy KIMB S61......96 B4
Rempstone Dr CHNE S41...192 D5
Renathorpe Rd SHEFN S5...102 D3
Rencliffe Av RHAM S60......119 F1
Reneville Cl RHAM S60......105 H5
Reneville Ct SHEFN S5......102 A1
Reneville Crs SHEFN S5......102 A1
Reneville Dr RHAM S60......105 H5
Reneville Rd RHAM S60......105 H5
Reney Av SHEFS S8......162 B2
Reney Crs SHEFS S8......162 B2
Reney Dr SHEFS S8......162 B2
Reney Rd SHEFS S8......162 B2
Renishaw Av RHAM S60......119 H2
Renishaw Rd STV/CWN S43..183 E1
Renshaw Cl
 CHPT/GREN S35......80 A3
Renshaw Rd ECC S11......138 C4
Renville Cl RAW S62......85 E4
Renway Rd RHAM S60......106 C5
Repton Cl CHSW S40......186 A4
Repton Pl DRON S18......170 A2
Reresby Crs RHAM S60......120 A2
Reresby Dr RHAM S60......120 A2
Reresby Rd RHAM S60......119 H2
Reservoir Rd
 AU/AST/KP S26......131 E3
 FUL S10......125 E4
Reservoir Ter CHSW S40......4 C1
Retford Rd HAN/WDH S13...143 E1
Retford Wk
 NROS/TKH DN11......91 H2
Revell Cl RHAM/THRY S65...107 F2
Revill Cl MALT S66......110 D2
Revill Ct DIN S25......134 D3
Revill La HAN/WDH S13......143 E4
Rex Av ABRD S7......151 H1
Rex Cnr DON DN1 *......4 G2
Reynard Crs ECK/KIL S21...175 H5
Reynard La ST/HB/BR S6...123 F2
Reynolds Cl DRON S18......170 C3
 MALT S66......108 B4
Rhodes Av CHNE S41......187 E4
 KIMB S61......96 C4
Rhodes Cottages
 STV/CWN S43......185 F2
Rhodes Dr RHAM S60......120 A2
Rhodesia Rd CHSW S40......191 F2
Rhodes St WMPN/MNR S2...11 K4
Rhodes Ter BSLY S70......3 J6
Ribble Cl CHPT/GREN S35...80 D5
Ribblesdale Dr
 HACK/IN S12......155 H4
Ribble Wy SHEFN S5......115 C1
Riber Cl BSLYN/ROY S71...15 E5
Riber Cl ST/HB/BR S6......112 D5
 STV/CWN S43......189 C4
Riber Ter CHSW S40......4 C6
Ribston Ct DARN/MH S9...127 C2
Ribston Ms DARN/MH S9...127 H3
Ribston Pl DARN/MH S9...127 H3
Ribston Rd DARN/MH S9...127 C3
Richard Av BSLYN/ROY S71...20 A1
Richard La NROS/TKH DN11...91 E2
Richard Rd BSLYN/ROY S71...20 A1
 RHAM S60......9 H7
Richards Ct
 SHEFP/MNR S2 *......140 E4
Richards Rd SHEFP/MNR S2..140 A3
Richard St BSLY S70......2 D5
Richards Wy RAW S62......85 C5
Rich Farm Cl BTLY DN5......27 F4
Richmond Av
 HAN/WDH S13......142 C2
Richmond Cl CHSW S40...192 A4
Richmond Ct
 HAN/WDH S13......142 B3
Richmond Farm Ms
 HAN/WDH S13......142 B3
Richmond Gv
 HAN/WDH S13......142 C1
Richmond Hall Av
 HAN/WDH S13......142 B2
Richmond Hall Crs
 HAN/WDH S13......142 B3
Richmond Hall Dr
 HAN/WDH S13......142 B2
Richmond Hall Rd
 HAN/WDH S13......142 B2
Richmond Hall Wy
 HAN/WDH S13......142 B3
Richmond Hill Rd
 BTLY DN5......55 E3
 HAN/WDH S13 *......142 B4
Richmond Park Av
 HAN/WDH S13......128 C5
 KIMB S61......104 B3
Richmond Park Cl
 HAN/WDH S13......142 C1
Richmond Park Crs
 HAN/WDH S13......128 C5
Richmond Park Cft
 HAN/WDH S13......128 B5
Richmond Park Dr
 HAN/WDH S13......142 C1
Richmond Park Gv
 HAN/WDH S13......142 B1
Richmond Park Ri
 HAN/WDH S13......128 B5
Richmond Park Rd
 HAN/WDH S13......142 C1

Richmond Park Vw
 HAN/WDH S13......142 C1
Richmond Park Wy
 HAN/WDH S13......142 C1
Richmond Pl
 HAN/WDH S13......142 B3
Richmond Rd BTLY DN5......38 D3
 DEARNE S63......37 E2
 HAN/WDH S13......142 A4
 KIMB S61......104 C3
Richmond St BSLY S70 *......2 C5
 OWL S3......126 B1
Richworth Rd
 HAN/WDH S13......142 D2
Rickley Pitt Cottages
 DOD/DAR S75 *......47 F3
Ricknald Cl AU/AST/KP S26...131 F5
Ridal Av STKB/PEN S36......76 C1
Ridal Cl STKB/PEN S36......76 C1
Ridal Cft STKB/PEN S36......76 C1
Riddings Cl MALT S66......133 F1
 SHEFP/MNR S2......141 G3
Riddings Cft CHNE S41......186 C3
Ridd Wy RCH S42......195 G4
Rider Rd ST/HB/BR S6......114 A4
Ridge Balk La
 AWLS/ASK DN6......24 D2
Ridgedale Rd BSVR S44......196 D4
Ridgehill Av HACK/IN S12...141 G5
Ridgehill Gv HACK/IN S12...141 F5
Ridge Rd AWLS/ASK DN6......25 F5
 ECK/KIL S21......173 C1
 RHAM/THRY S65......9 H3
The Ridge FUL S10......137 G1
Ridge View Cl
 DARN/MH S9......116 C1
Ridge View Dr
 DARN/MH S9......116 C1
Ridgewalk Wy BSLY S70......31 H4
Ridgeway DRON S18......163 H5
 RHAM/THRY S65......107 E2
 STV/CWN S43......185 F3
Ridgeway Av RHAM S60......197 E2
Ridgeway Cl MALT S66......109 C5
 RHAM/THRY S65......107 F2
Ridgeway Crs
 BSLYN/ROY S71......15 C3
 HACK/IN S12......141 C4
 HACK/IN S12......141 C5
Ridgeway Dr HACK/IN S12...141 C4
Ridgeway Moor
 HACK/IN S12......165 C3
Ridgeway Rd HACK/IN S12...141 C5
 RHAM S60......118 B4
 SHEFP/MNR S2......141 C3
Ridgeway West
 STV/CWN S43......185 E4
Ridgewood Av ARMTH DN3...42 B1
Ridgway Av WMB/DAR S73...35 E4
Riding Cl DONS/BSCR DN4...74 D2
 MALT S66......108 A4
Ridings Av BSLYN/ROY S71...20 D5
The Ridings BSLYN/ROY S71...20 C2
Rig Cl KIMB S61......96 D5
Rig Dr MEX/SWTN S64......65 C5
Riggs High Rd
 ST/HB/BR S6......122 D2
Riggs Low Rd
 ST/HB/BR S6......122 D2
Riley Av DONS/BSCR DN4...71 F2
Riley Rd DEARNE S63......65 F3
Rimington Rd
 WMB/DAR S73......50 B2
Rimini Ri WMB/DAR S73......34 C5
Ringer La STV/CWN S43......185 E3
Ringer Wy STV/CWN S43......185 E3
Ringinglow Rd ECC S11......150 B1
Ringstead Av FUL S10......124 A5
Ringstead Crs FUL S10......124 B5
Ringway DEARNE S63......52 D3
Ringwood Av CHNE S41......187 E2
 STV/CWN S43......189 C1
Ringwood Crs MOS S20......157 C3
Ringwood Dr MOS S20......157 C3
Ringwood Gv MOS S20......157 C3
Ringwood Rd MOS S20......157 C3
 STV/CWN S43......188 D1
Ringwood Vw
 STV/CWN S43......188 D2
Ripley Gv DOD/DAR S75......18 D3
Ripley St ST/HB/BR S6......114 A5
Ripon Dr DARN/MH S9......127 F2
Ripon Wy AU/AST/KP S26...145 E3
Rippon Cl RAW S62......85 F4
Rippon Crs ST/HB/BR S6...113 H4
Rippon Rd ST/HB/BR S6...113 H4
Risedale Rd DEARNE S63...53 F2
The Rise CUD/GR S72......17 H2
 DIN S25......148 C3
 MEX/SWTN S64......64 D5
Rising St OWL S3......126 B1
Rivelin Bank ST/HB/BR S6...113 H4
Rivelin Mill Br ST/HB/BR S6..123 E4
Rivelin Park Crs
 ST/HB/BR S6......124 B1
Rivelin Park Dr
 ST/HB/BR S6......124 B1
Rivelin Park Rd
 ST/HB/BR S6......124 C1
Rivelin Rd ST/HB/BR S6......124 C1
Rivelin St ST/HB/BR S6......124 C1
Rivelin Ter ST/HB/BR S6...124 C1

Rivelin Valley Rd
 ST/HB/BR S6......123 E4
River Bank
 CHPT/GREN S35......100 A2
Riverdale Av FUL S10......138 B2
Riverdale Dr FUL S10......138 C1
Riverdale Pk
 STV/CWN S43 *......182 C3
Riverdale Rd BTLY DN5......39 F2
 FUL S10......138 C2
Riverhead BTLY DN5......54 B4
Riverside Cl CONI DN12......69 E5
 DONS/BSCR DN4......75 F4
 ST/HB/BR S6......113 F4
 WMB/DAR S73......35 C4
Riverside Ct DIN S25......134 A2
Riverside Crs RCH S42......190 B5
Riverside Dr BTLY DN5......54 C4
Riverside Gdns DEARNE S63...53 F4
 EPW DN9......75 H1
Riverside Prec RHAM S60......8 E4
Riverside Wy RHAM S60......8 C7
River Ter ST/HB/BR S6......114 A4
River Vw CHSW S40 *......5 H7
River Wy EPW DN9......75 H1
Riviera Mt BTLY DN5......39 H5
Riviera Pde BTLY DN5......39 H5
Rix Rd MEX/SWTN S64......86 B3
Roache Dr DEARNE S63......53 E1
Roach Rd ECC S11......139 E2
Robert Av BSLYN/ROY S71...20 D5
Robert Cl DRON S18......179 E1
Robert Rd SHEFS S8......162 D1
Roberts Av CONI DN12......89 F2
Roberts Gv AU/AST/KP S26...145 C3
Robertson Crs
 STKB/PEN S36......77 F3
Robertson Dr ST/HB/BR S6...124 C1
Robertson Rd
 ST/HB/BR S6......124 C2
Roberts Rd DONS/BSCR DN4...6 A7
Roberts St CUD/GR S72 *......16 D5
 WMB/DAR S73 *......50 A3
 RHAM S60......8 B4
Robey St ATT S4......115 H3
Robincroft CHSW S40......192 B5
Robincroft Rd RCH S42......194 D3
Robinets Rd KIMB S61......97 E3
Robin Hood Av
 BSLYN/ROY S71......12 D5
Robin Hood Cha
 ST/HB/BR S6......112 C5
Robin Hood Crs ARMTH DN3...42 C1
Robin Hood Rd ARMTH DN3...42 B1
 DARN/MH S9 *......103 C5
Robin La BSLYN/ROY S71...12 D5
 MOS S20......157 F1
Robin Pl AU/AST/KP S26...145 C4
Robins Rd AU/AST/KP S26...145 C5
Robinson Rd
 SHEFP/MNR S2......126 C5
Robinson St RHAM S60......105 H5
Rob Royd DOD/DAR S75......30 B4
Rob Royd La BSLY S70......31 F4
Roche MOS S20 *......157 E5
Roche Cl BSLYN/ROY S71...14 A4
Roche End AU/AST/KP S26...147 E5
Rocher Av CHPT/GREN S35...101 G2
Rocher Cl CHPT/GREN S35...101 G2
Rocher Gv CHPT/GREN S35...101 G2
Rochester Cl FUL S10......137 E1
Rochester Dr FUL S10......137 E1
Rochester Rw BTLY DN5......38 D5
Rochester Rd
 BSLYN/ROY S71......20 B3
 DIN S25......148 B5
 FUL S10......137 E1
Rockcliffe Houses
 RAW S62 *......98 A2
Rockcliffe Rd RAW S62......98 B2
Rockingham Cl BSLY S70......60 C2
Rockingham Cl BSLY S70......60 C2
 DOD/DAR S75......191 G1
 DRON S18......170 A2
 SHEF S1......11 F6
Rockingham Ct
 BSLYN/ROY S71......3 J4
Rockingham Ga SHEF S1...11 F5
Rockingham La SHEF S1...11 F4
Rockingham Rd
 DOD/DAR S75......30 C5
 MEX/SWTN S64......65 H5
 RAW S62......85 G5
Rockingham Rw BSLY S70...60 D2
Rockingham St BSLY S70......60 D2
 HOY S74......61 E2
 SHEF S1......10 E3
Rockingham Wy SHEF S1...11 F5
Rockland Vls
 RHAM/THRY S65 *......99 G4
Rockley Cl MEX/SWTN S64...86 A1
Rockley Av BSLY S70......47 G4
 WMB/DAR S73......49 H4
Rockley Cl CHSW S40......192 B5
Rockley Crs BSLY S70......60 C1
Rockley La DOD/DAR S75...47 E2
Rockley Mdw BSLY S70......31 E3
Rockley Nook WHHL DN2...41 F3
Rockley Rd ST/HB/BR S6...113 H2
Rockley Vw DOD/DAR S75...60 B2

Rockliffe Av
 DONS/BSCR DN4......71 E2
Rock Mt HOY S74......62 B2
Rock Mount Rd
 DARN/MH S9......103 H5
Rockside STV/CWN S43 *...185 E2
Rock Side Rd STKB/PEN S36...44 A3
Rock St BSLY S70......126 B2
 OWL S3......126 B2
Rockwood Cl
 CHPT/GREN S35......93 G1
Roddis Cl DIN S25......134 B4
Roden Wy RAW S62......84 C3
Rodge Cft CHNE S41......179 G5
Rodger Rd HAN/WDH S13...143 H3
Rodger St KIMB S61......8 B2
Rodman Dr HAN/WDH S13...143 H2
Rodman St HAN/WDH S13...143 H2
Rod Moor Rd
 TOT/DORE S17......161 H4
Rodney Hl ST/HB/BR S6...112 D4
Rodsley Cl CHSW S40......186 B4
Rodwell Cl RHAM S60......118 A3
Rodwood Av
 STV/CWN S43......177 E4
Roebuck Hl HOY S74......49 F5
Roebuck Rd ST/HB/BR S6...125 F3
Roebuck St WMB/DAR S73...50 C4
Roecar Cl CHNE S41......179 H4
Roe Croft Cl DIN S25......54 B3
Roehampton Ri
 BSLYN/ROY S71......20 D5
 BTLY DN5......38 D5
 DARN/MH S9......118 A3
Roe La OWL S3......115 F4
Roger Rd BSLYN/ROY S71...21 E5
Rojean Rd CHPT/GREN S35...101 F1
Rokeby Dr SHEFN S5......102 A3
Rokeby Rd SHEFN S5......102 A3
Rolleston Av MALT S66......110 C5
Rolleston Dr SHEFN S5......102 C5
Rollin Dr ST/HB/BR S6......113 H5
Rolling Dales Cl MALT S66...110 C1
Rolls Crs RAW S62......84 C3
Roman Ct MALT S66......104 C3
Roman Crs RAW S62......85 E5
 RHAM S60......118 C3
Romandale Gdns
 SHEFP/MNR S2......142 A1
Roman Rdg AWLS/ASK DN6...24 D3
Roman Ridge Rd
 DARN/MH S9......116 D1
Roman Rd WHHL DN2......7 G5
Roman St DEARNE S63......37 G1
Romeley Crs STV/CWN S43...184 D3
Romeley La BSVR S44......184 A4
Romney Cl MALT S66......108 B5
Romney Dr DRON S18......170 C2
Romney Gdns
 SHEFP/MNR S2......140 B4
Romsdal Rd FUL S10 *......125 E3
Romwood Av
 MEX/SWTN S64......65 G5
Ronald Rd DARN/MH S9...128 A3
 DONS/BSCR DN4......55 G5
Ronksley Crs SHEFN S5......102 D3
Ronksley La ST/HB/BR S6...102 D5
Ronksley Rd SHEFN S5......102 D5
Rood La STV/CWN S43......185 G3
Rookdale Cl DOD/DAR S75...18 D3
Rookery Bank
 STKB/PEN S36......77 H3
Rookery Cha STKB/PEN S36...77 H3
Rookery Cl AU/AST/KP S26...159 G2
 STKB/PEN S36......77 H3
Rookery Dell STKB/PEN S36...77 H3
Rookery Ri STKB/PEN S36...77 H3
Rookery Rd MEX/SWTN S64...85 H1
The Rookery STKB/PEN S36...77 H3
Rookery V STKB/PEN S36...77 H3
Rook Hl BSLY S70......32 C5
Roper Hl FUL S10......136 B3
Rosamond Av
 TOT/DORE S17......161 G2
Rosamond Cl
 TOT/DORE S17......161 G2
Rosamond Dr
 TOT/DORE S17......161 G3
Rosamond Gld
 TOT/DORE S17......161 G2
Rosamond Pl
 TOT/DORE S17......161 G2
Rosa Rd FUL S10......125 E3
Roscoe Bank ST/HB/BR S6...124 B2
Roscoe Dr ST/HB/BR S6...124 B2
Roscoe Mt ST/HB/BR S6...124 B2
Roscoe Rd OWL S3......125 H2
Rose Av DONS/BSCR DN4...55 H5
 MOS S20......157 E2
 STV/CWN S43......185 G1
 WMB/DAR S73......34 C3
Roseberry Cl HOY S74......62 A4
Rosebery St BSLY S70......32 D2
Rosebery Cl RHAM S60......118 D5
Rosebery Ter BSLY S70 *......3 J6
Rose Cl RHAM S60......118 D5
Rose Ct DONS/BSCR DN4...55 H5
 MALT S66......108 A3
Rose Crs BTLY DN5......39 E3
 RAW S62......85 H5
 STV/CWN S43......185 G1
Rosedale Av CHSW S40...192 D4
 RAW S62......85 F5

Rosedale Gdns BSLY S70......2 B4
 ECC S11......139 F1
Rosedale Rd AU/AST/KP S26..145 G2
 BTLY DN5......38 D3
 ECC S11......139 F1
Rosedale Vw RCH S42......191 F5
Rosedale Wy MALT S66......108 C3
Rose Dr MALT S66......108 B4
Rose Garth Av
 AU/AST/KP S26......145 G2
Rosegarth Cl BTLY DN5......39 E3
Rosegreave DEARNE S63......37 F5
Rose Gv ARMTH DN3......23 G4
 WMB/DAR S73......49 H1
Rose Hl CHSW S40......4 E4
 DONS/BSCR DN4......57 G4
 MOS S20......156 B5
Rose Hill Av MOS S20......156 B5
Rose Hill Cl MOS S20......156 B5
 STKB/PEN S36......44 C4
Rosehill Cottages
 DOD/DAR S75 *......30 C4
Rosehill Ct BSLY S70......3 F2
 BSVR S44......196 D3
Rose Hill Dr DOD/DAR S75...30 B3
 MOS S20......156 B5
Rose Hl East CHSW S40......5 F4
Rose Hill Ms MOS S20......156 B5
Rose Hill Ri DONS/BSCR DN4...57 G3
Rosehill Rd RAW S62......85 F5
Rose Hill Vw MOS S20......156 B5
Rose Hl West CHSW S40......4 E4
Rose La DIN S25......133 H1
Roselle St ST/HB/BR S6......114 A4
Rosemary Gv BTLY DN5......69 F3
Rosemary Rd MALT S66......108 A4
 MOS S20......157 F1
Rose PI WMB/DAR S73......50 A1
Rose Tree Av CUD/GR S72...16 D5
Rose Tree Cl CUD/GR S72...16 D5
Rose Wy ECK/KIL S21......168 B3
Rosewell Ct
 RHAM/THRY S65......106 C1
Roslin Rd FUL S10......125 E4
Rossendale Cl CHSW S40...192 A4
Rosser Av HACK/IN S12......154 D3
Rossetti Mt MALT S66......108 B3
Rossington Br
 DONS/BSCR DN4......74 D4
Rossington Rd ECC S11......139 C2
Rossington St CONI DN12...68 B4
Rosslyn Av AU/AST/KP S26...145 G2
Rosslyn Crs BTLY DN5......26 D5
Ross St DARN/MH S9......128 B3
Rosston Rd MALT S66......111 F3
Roston Cl DRON S18......170 B2
Rothay Cl DRON S18......170 C3
Rothay Rd ATT S4......116 B4
Rothbury Cl MOS S20 *......157 G3
Rothbury Ct MOS S20......157 G3
Rothbury Wy RHAM S60......118 C3
Rother Av STV/CWN S43...188 D1
Rother Cl CHSW S40......192 A4
Rother Crs RHAM S60......130 A3
Rother Cft HOY S74......62 A2
Rotherham Rd
 AU/AST/KP S26......145 E3
 BSLYN/ROY S71......20 A1
 BSVR S44......197 G5
 DEARNE S63......64 B2
 DIN S25......134 A3
 ECK/KIL S21......167 F5
 ECK/KIL S21......169 E4
 HAN/WDH S13......129 F5
 MALT S66......110 A3
 MOS S20......167 F1
 RHAM S60......98 A5
 RHAM S60......129 H1
 WMB/DAR S73......35 H5
Rotherham Rd North
 MOS S20......167 F1
Rotherham Roundwalk
 KIMB S61......96 A2
 RAW S62......83 F3
 RHAM S60......119 E1
 RHAM/THRY S65......119 E2
Rotherham St
 DARN/MH S9 *......116 C5
Rotherhill Cl
 RHAM/THRY S65......106 C2
Rothermoor Av
 AU/AST/KP S26......159 G3
Rother Rd RHAM S60......118 C3
Rotherside Rd ECK/KIL S21...167 F4
Rotherstoke Cl RHAM S60...118 B3
Rother St WMB/DAR S73...51 E5
Rother Ter RHAM S60......118 D1
Rothervale Cl MOS S20......157 G1
Rothervale Rd CHSW S40...5 J9
Rother Valley Wy MOS S20..157 H5
Rother View Gdns
 AU/AST/KP S26......144 C3
Rother View Rd RHAM S60..118 D1
Rother Wy CHNE S41......187 H3
 MALT S66......109 C3

Rotherway RHAM S60...........119 E4
Rotherwood Av
  HAN/WDH S13...........143 H2
Rotherwood Cl BTLY DN5....38 D4
Rotherwood Crs MALT S66...133 E1
Rotherwood Rd
  ECK/KIL S21...........168 C1
Rothesay Cl BTLY DN5.......39 F5
Roughbirchworth La
  STKB/PEN S36...........45 H5
Rough La CHPT/GREN S35....78 C3
  CHPT/GREN S35...........92 D5
Roughwood Rd KIMB S61....96 C4
Roundel St DARN/MH S9...127 F2
Round Green La
  DOD/DAR S75...........46 D1
Roundhill Cottages
  ECK/KIL S21 *...........166 B4
Roundhill Ct
  DONS/BSCR DN4...........57 F5
Roundwood Ct BSLY S70....48 A1
Roundwood Gv RAW S62....98 C1
Roundwood Wy
  WMB/DAR S73...........34 D5
Rowan Cl BSLY S70...........31 H3
  CHPT/GREN S35...........94 A2
  DEARNE S63...........37 E5
Rowan Ct WHHL DN2...........41 G4
Rowan Dr DEARNE S63.......37 E5
  DOD/DAR S75...........108 C4
  MALT S66...........108 C4
Rowan Garth BTLY DN5......39 G4
Rowan Mt WHHL DN2.........41 F4
Rowan Ri MALT S66...........110 B3
Rowan Rd ECK/KIL S21......174 B2
  STV/CWN S43...........183 E3
Rowan Tree Dell
  TOT/DORE S17...........161 E5
Rowan Tree Rd
  ECK/KIL S21...........167 H2
Rowborn Dr
  CHPT/GREN S35...........100 B5
Rowdale Crs HACK/IN S12..142 B5
Rowell La ST/HB/BR S6....112 B5
Rowena Av ARMTH DN3.......42 B1
Rowena Dr BTLY DN5.........38 C4
Rowena Rd CONI DN12 *....88 D1
Rowernfields DIN S25......149 F1
Rowland Pl DON DN1...........6 C5
Rowland Rd
  SHEFP/MNR S2...........140 A2
Rowland St BSLYN/ROY S71..12 D5
  OWL S3...........126 A2
Rowley Wy MALT S66.........108 B1
Rowms La MEX/SWTN S64...144 A5
Rowsley Crs STV/CWN S43..189 G1
Rowsley St SHEFP/MNR S2..140 B1
Roxby Ct DONS/BSCR DN4....73 H5
Roxby Rd DONS/BSCR DN4....73 H5
Roxton Rd SHEFS S8.........152 C4
Royal Av DON DN1...........7 F2
Royal Ct DOD/DAR S75.......18 A1
  HOY S74...........62 B2
Royale Cl ECK/KIL S21.....167 E5
Royal Oak St STV/CWN S43..183 E2
Royal St BSLY S70...........3 F4
Royd Av CUD/GR S72.........21 H1
Royd Cl BSLY S70...........47 H1
Royd Ct STKB/PEN S36.......77 F4
Roydfield Cl MOS S20......156 D3
Roydfield Dr MOS S20......156 D3
Roydfield Gv MOS S20......156 D3
Royd La STKB/PEN S36.......77 F4
Roydmoor Ct STKB/PEN S36..156 A2
Royds Av RHAM S60...........120 A2
Royds Close Crs
  RHAM/THRY S65...........99 G4
Royds La HOY S74...........63 E5
Royds Moor Hl RHAM S60...120 C3
The Royd STKB/PEN S36.....77 F4
Roy Kilner Rd
  WMB/DAR S73...........49 H1
Royston Av BTLY DN5.......39 G3
  MOS S20...........156 A3
Royston Cl MOS S20........156 A3
Royston Cft MOS S20.......156 A3
Royston Gv MOS S20........156 A3
Royston Hl HOY S74.........61 H2
Royston La BSLYN/ROY S71..15 G2
Royston Rd CUD/GR S72.....16 C3
Rubens Cl DRON S18.........170 D2
Rubens Rw SHEFP/MNR S2..126 C4
Rud Broom Cl
  STKB/PEN S36...........44 B4
Rud Broom La
  STKB/PEN S36...........44 B3
Rudyard Rd ST/HB/BR S6...114 A4
Rufford Av BSLYN/ROY S71..15 E4
Rufford Cl CHSW S40...........4 C7
  HOR/CROF WF4...........9 F1
Rufford Ct MOS S20.........157 G3
Rufford Ri DEARNE S63......53 E1
  MOS S20...........157 G3
Rufford Rd DONS/BSCR DN4....7 J7
Rufus La NROS/TKH DN11...90 D2
Rugby St OWL S3...........126 A1
Rundle Dr ABRD S7.........139 G3
Rundle Rd ABRD S7.........139 G3
  DIN S25...........76 D2
Runnymede Rd WHHL DN2...57 F2
Rupert Rd ABRD S7.........139 G5
Rural Crs ARMTH DN3.........59 F5
Rural La ST/HB/BR S6......113 F2

Ruscombe Pl
  BSLYN/ROY S71...........15 G3
Rushby St ATT S4...........116 A3
Rushdale Av SHEFS S8.....140 A5
Rushdale Mt SHEFS S8.....140 A5
Rushdale Rd SHEFS S8.....140 A5
Rushdale Ter SHEFS S8....140 A5
Rushen Mt CHSW S40.......195 F1
Rushey Cl RAW S62...........85 E3
Rushley Av TOT/DORE S17..150 D5
Rushley Cl TOT/DORE S17..150 D5
Rushley Dr TOT/DORE S17..150 D5
Rushley Rd TOT/DORE S17..160 D1
Rushton Dr BSLYN/ROY S71..12 C5
Ruskin Av MEX/SWTN S64....67 F2
Ruskin Cl DEARNE S63.......64 C1
Ruskin Dr ARMTH DN3.......43 E4
Ruskin Rd DONS/BSCR DN4..71 G2
Ruskin Sq SHEFS S8.........140 A4
The Rusk STV/CWN S43 *...177 F5
Russell Cl AU/AST/KP S26..144 D3
  BSLYN/ROY S71...........20 D3
Russell Ct ECC S11.........151 G3
Russell Pl MALT S66.......111 E2
Russell Rd MEX/SWTN S64...86 C4
Russell St OWL S3...........126 A2
  RHAM/THRY S65...........9 H1
Russett Ct MALT S66.......110 B2
Rustlings Rd ECC S11......138 C2
Ruston Cl CHSW S40........186 B3
Ruston Dr BSLYN/ROY S71...12 C5
Ruthin St ATT S4...........116 A4
Ruth Sq FUL S10...........10 B5
Ruthven Dr
  DONS/BSCR DN4...........70 D1
Ruthyn Av STV/CWN S43....177 E4
Rutland Av BSVR S44.......196 C3
  DIN S25...........148 B1
Rutland La NROS/TKH DN11...90 D2
Rutland Pk FUL S10.........125 E5
Rutland Pl WMB/DAR S73....49 H3
Rutland Rd CHSW S40.........34 D4
  OWL S3...........126 A1
Rutland St CHNE S41.......179 G4
  DON DN1 *...........7 F2
  OWL S3...........126 A1
Rutland Wy DOD/DAR S75.....2 A1
  OWL S3...........125 H2
Ryan Dr HAN/WDH S13......144 A3
Ryan Pl RAW S62...........98 B2
Rydal Cl DEARNE S63.........53 E4
  DRON S18...........170 B2
  STKB/PEN S36...........44 D2
Rydal Ct DONS/BSCR DN4....71 G4
Rydal Crs CHNE S41........187 E1
Rydalhurst Av
  ST/HB/BR S6...........113 F2
Rydal Rd BTLY DN5...........39 F2
Rydal Rd DIN S25...........148 D1
  SHEFS S8...........139 G5
Rydal Ter BSLYN/ROY S71.....3 J5
Rydal Wy MEX/SWTN S64.....67 G2
Rye Bank RHAM S60.........120 B3
Rye Cft BSLYN/ROY S71.....20 A1
  CONI DN12...........89 G1
Ryecroft Bank HOY S74......61 H1
Ryecroft Glen Rd
  TOT/DORE S17...........151 G5
Ryecroft Rd RAW S62.......86 A5
Ryecroft Vw
  TOT/DORE S17...........150 D5
Ryefield Gdns ECC S11.....138 C5
Rye Flatt La CHSW S40.....191 F5
Ryegate Crs FUL S10.......124 C4
Ryegate Rd FUL S10.......124 C4
Ryehill Av CHSW S40.......191 E2
Ryeview Gdns KIMB S61.....97 F4
Ryhill Dr MOS S20.........156 A3
Rykneld Ri RCH S42........195 H4
Ryle Rd ABRD S7...........139 G4
Rylstone Cl HACK/IN S12..156 B3
Rylstone Gv HACK/IN S12..156 B3
Rylstone Wk BSLY S70.......32 D4
Ryton Av WMB/DAR S73......50 D4
Ryton Cl MALT S66.........111 E3
Ryton Rd DIN S25.........148 B3
Ryton Wy DONS/BSCR DN4...74 C2

S

Sackerville Ter ECK/KIL S21..167 H1
Sackville Cl RCH S42......191 F4
Sackville Rd FUL S10......124 D3
Sackville St BSLY S70......2 E5
Saddler Av MOS S20........156 D4
Saddler Cl MOS S20........156 D4
Saddler Gn MOS S20........156 D4
Saddler Gv MOS S20........156 D4
Saddletree Vw
  STV/CWN S43...........182 D2
Sadler Ga BSLY S70...........3 F3
Sadler's Ga WMB/DAR S73...50 A1
Saffron Ct WMB/DAR S73....50 C3
St Agnes' Rd
  DONS/BSCR DN4...........7 K6
St Aidan's Av
  SHEFP/MNR S2...........140 D2
St Aidan's Cl
  SHEFP/MNR S2...........141 E1
St Aidan's Dr
  SHEFP/MNR S2...........141 E1

St Aidan's Mt
  SHEFP/MNR S2...........141 E2
St Aidan's Pl
  SHEFP/MNR S2...........141 E2
St Aidan's Rd
  SHEFP/MNR S2...........140 D1
St Aidan's Wy
  SHEFP/MNR S2...........141 E2
St Albans Cl FUL S10......137 G1
St Albans Ct MALT S66....108 B5
St Albans Dr FUL S10......197 F1
St Albans Rd FUL S10......137 F1
St Alban's Wy MALT S66...108 B5
St Andrew Rd
  STKB/PEN S36...........77 G3
St Andrews Cl
  DONS/BSCR DN4...........74 D2
  MALT S66...........108 C2
St Andrews Crs HOY S74....62 A2
St Andrews Rd CHSW S40 *..191 G4
St Andrews Rd HOY S74......62 A2
St Andrews Wk RHAM S60..118 A3
St Andrews Wy
  BSLYN/ROY S71...........33 G3
St Andrew's Cl ECC S11...139 F3
  MEX/SWTN S64...........86 B2
St Andrew's Rd CONI DN12..88 D2
  ECC S11...........139 F3
St Andrew's Sq
  DEARNE S63...........53 E3
St Andrew's Ter
  DONS/BSCR DN4...........7 F7
St Andrew's Wy
  ARMTH DN3...........29 F1
St Annes Dr BSLYN/ROY S71..15 H5
St Anne's Rd
  DONS/BSCR DN4...........57 E3
St Ann's Rd RHAM/THRY S65...9 G1
  STKB/PEN S36...........77 F2
St Ann's Rbt
  RHAM/THRY S65...........9 H2
St Anthony Rd FUL S10....124 C3
St Augustines Av
  CHSW S40...........192 C3
St Augustines Dr
  CHSW S40...........192 C3
St Augustines Mt
  CHSW S40...........192 C3
St Augustines Ri
  CHSW S40...........192 C4
St Augustines Rd
  CHSW S40...........192 B4
  DONS/BSCR DN4...........57 G4
St Austell Dr DOD/DAR S75..18 A3
St Barbara's Cl MALT S66..110 C4
St Barbara's Rd
  WMB/DAR S73...........34 D5
St Barnabas La
  SHEFP/MNR S2...........140 A2
St Barnabas Rd
  SHEFP/MNR S2...........140 A2
St Bartholomews Ri
  DONS/BSCR DN4...........57 H4
St Bartholomew's Cl
  MALT S66 *...........110 C4
St Barts Ter BSLY S70.....3 F3
St Bede's Rd RHAM S60......8 C4
St Benedicts Ct
  SHEFP/MNR S2...........140 D2
St Catherines Wy
  DOD/DAR S75...........18 D5
St Catherine's Av
  DONS/BSCR DN4...........55 H5
St Cecilia's Rd
  DONS/BSCR DN4...........7 K7
St Chad's Wy BTLY DN5.....54 C5
  CHNE S41...........187 G1
St Charles St DARN/MH S9..127 E1
St Christophers Cl
  BSLYN/ROY S71...........33 G3
St Christopher's Crs
  BTLY DN5...........39 E4
St Clements Cl
  BSLYN/ROY S71...........33 G3
  BTLY DN5 *...........38 D4
St David Rd STKB/PEN S36..77 G2
St Davids Dr BSLYN/ROY S71..33 F2
  RHAM S60...........118 A5
  BTLY DN5...........38 D4
  DIN S25...........148 B5
St David's Ri CHSW S40...191 H4
St David's Rd CONI DN12...88 D2
St Dominic's Cl BTLY DN5..54 B5
St Edmund's Av MALT S66..133 E2
St Edwards Av BSLY S70.....2 C7
St Elizabeth Cl
  SHEFP/MNR S2...........140 B2
St Eric's Rd DONS/BSCR DN4..57 H5
St Francis Bvd
  BSLYN/ROY S71...........33 F2
St Francis Cl FUL S10.....124 A5
  MALT S66...........108 C2
St George Ga DON DN1.......4 E5
St George Rd STKB/PEN S36..77 G3
St Georges Cl OWL S3......10 D3
St Georges Dr RHAM S60...118 A3
St George's
  MEX/SWTN S64...........65 H5
St George's Cl OWL S3.....10 D3
St George's Rd BSLY S70....2 E5
St George's Ter OWL S3....10 D3
St Giles Cl CHSW S40......192 D4
St Giles Ga BTLY DN5.......38 D5

St Giles Sq CHPT/GREN S35..93 H1
St Helen Rd STKB/PEN S36...77 G3
St Helens Av
  BSLYN/ROY S71...........20 B1
St Helens Bvd
  BSLYN/ROY S71...........20 B1
St Helens Cl DEARNE S63....36 D2
  RHAM S60...........130 B4
St Helens Ct HOY S74 *.....62 C2
St Helens Wy
  BSLYN/ROY S71...........20 D2
St Helen's Bvd
  BSLYN/ROY S71...........20 B1
St Helen's Cl CHNE S41......5 F2
St Helen's Rd
  DONS/BSCR DN4...........7 K6
St Helen's Sq ARMTH DN3...29 F3
St Helen's St CHNE S41......5 F1
  HOY S74...........62 C2
St Helier Dr DOD/DAR S75...18 D5
St Hilda Av BSLY S70........2 A4
St Hilda Cl STKB/PEN S36...77 G4
St Hildas Cl DEARNE S63....37 G1
St Hilda's Rd
  DONS/BSCR DN4...........7 K6
St James Av DIN S25.......148 B4
St James Cl ARMTH DN3.....29 F3
  CHNE S41...........193 E5
St James Gdns
  DONS/BSCR DN4...........55 H4
St James's Br
  DONS/BSCR DN4...........6 B6
St James' St SHEF S1.......11 G3
St Joan Av STKB/PEN S36...77 G4
St Johns Av MALT S66......108 C3
St Johns Rd RCH S42......191 F5
St Johns Rd STV/CWN S43..181 G5
St Johns Ris CUD/GR S72 *..21 H1
St Johns Wk
  BSLYN/ROY S71...........15 H1
St John's Av DOD/DAR S75...18 A3
  RHAM S60...........8 B4
St John's Cl DOD/DAR S75...30 A4
St John's Cl DIN S25......134 C1
St John's Crs STV/CWN S43..185 F3
St John's Mt CHNE S41.....187 F1
St John's Rd BSLY S70......3 F7
  CHNE S41...........187 F1
  CUD/GR S72 *...........21 H1
  DIN S25...........134 C1
  DONS/BSCR DN4...........55 C5
  DRON S18...........172 A3
  MEX/SWTN S64...........66 A5
  RHAM/THRY S65...........106 C1
  STKB/PEN S36...........77 H3
St John's Ct DIN S25......134 C1
  MALT S66...........108 C3
St Joseph's Cl DIN S25....134 D4
St Joseph's Gdns BSLY S70..32 B2
St Joseph's Rd
  HAN/WDH S13...........128 D5
St Lawrence Av BSVR S44..197 F4
St Lawrence Ct
  AWLS/ASK DN6...........25 E1
St Lawrence Glebe
  DARN/MH S9...........117 G2
St Lawrence Rd
  DARN/MH S9...........117 G1
St Leger Cl DIN S25.......134 A3
St Leger Wy DIN S25.......134 D3
St Leonards Ct SHEFN S5...115 F1
St Leonards Dr CHNE S41..193 E3
St Leonards Wy
  BSLYN/ROY S71...........33 G3
St Leonard's Av
  RHAM/THRY S65...........99 H4
St Leonard's Cl DIN S25...134 C5
St Leonard's Cft
  RHAM/THRY S65...........99 H4
St Leonard's La
  RHAM/THRY S65...........9 K2
St Leonard's Lea BTLY DN5..39 E4
St Leonard's Pl
  RHAM/THRY S65...........9 K2
St Leonard's Rd
  RHAM/THRY S65...........9 H3
St Lukes Wy
  BSLYN/ROY S71 *...........20 C4
St Margaret Av
  STKB/PEN S36...........77 G3
St Margaret's Dr CHSW S40...4 E3
  MEX/SWTN S64...........65 H5
St Margaret's Rd
  CHPT/GREN S35...........102 B1
  DONS/BSCR DN4...........7 K6
St Mark St STKB/PEN S36...77 G3
St Mark's Crs FUL S10.....125 F5
St Mark's Rd CHSW S40......4 B4
St Martin Cl STKB/PEN S36..77 G3
St Martins Cl CHSW S40...187 E4
  DOD/DAR S75...........18 D5
St Martin's Av BTLY DN5...39 F5
St Martin's Cl CHNE S41...186 D3
St Mary Crs STKB/PEN S36..77 G4
St Marys Rd WMB/DAR S73...50 A3

St Mary's Cl CHPT/GREN S35..94 A5
St Mary's Crs DON DN1......7 F1
  MEX/SWTN S64...........66 A5
St Mary's Dr ARMTH DN3....43 E4
  RHAM S60...........129 G1
St Mary's Gdn BSLY S70....48 A3
St Mary's Ga CHPT/GREN S35..3 F3
  CHNE S41...........5 H5
  SHEFP/MNR S2...........10 E7
St Mary's La
  CHPT/GREN S35...........94 A5
St Mary's Pl BSLY S70......3 F3
St Mary's Rd DEARNE S63...37 H4
  DON DN1...........40 C5
  RAW S62...........98 C1
  SHEF S1...........11 G7
  WMB/DAR S73...........35 F5
St Mary's Sq SHEF S1......10 E6
St Mary's St STKB/PEN S36..77 G4
St Mary's Vw KIMB S61......97 F3
St Mary's Wk BTLY DN5.....54 B5
St Matthews Cl
  ECK/KIL S21...........175 H2
St Matthews Wy
  BSLYN/ROY S71...........20 C4
St Matthias Rd
  STKB/PEN S36...........77 G3
St Michaels Av
  BSLYN/ROY S71...........20 D1
  NROS/TKH DN11...........91 G1
St Michaels Cl DEARNE S63..37 F5
St Michael's Av
  MEX/SWTN S64...........66 B4
St Michael's Cl
  CHPT/GREN S35 *...........102 B1
St Michael's Crs
  CHPT/GREN S35...........102 B1
St Michael's Rd
  CHPT/GREN S35...........102 B1
  DONS/BSCR DN4...........57 G5
St Nicholas Cl ARMTH DN3..29 E5
St Nicolas Rd RAW S62.....85 G5
St Oswald's Dr ARMTH DN3..29 E5
St Owens Dr DOD/DAR S75..18 D5
St Pancras Cl DIN S25....134 A3
St Patrick Rd STKB/PEN S36..77 G3
St Patrick's Rd WHHL DN2...7 K1
St Patrick's Wy BTLY DN5..38 D4
St Paul Cl AU/AST/KP S26..147 E5
  STKB/PEN S36...........77 G3
St Pauls Cl DIN S25.......134 A2
St Pauls Pde
  BSLYN/ROY S71...........11 G4
  SHEF S1...........11 G4
St Pauls Rd DOD/DAR S75...2 B1
  DOD/DAR S75...........19 E4
St Paul's Pde BTLY DN5....38 D5
St Peter Av STKB/PEN S36..77 H3
St Peter's Cl RHAM S60...118 A4
  SHEF S1...........11 G2
St Peter's Ga DEARNE S63..37 E1
St Peter's Rd CONI DN12...71 E1
St Peter's Ter BSLY S70....3 J6
St Philip's Dr CHNE S41..192 D4
St Philip's Rd OWL S3.....10 C1
St Phillip's Cl MALT S66 *..110 C4
St Quentin Cl
  TOT/DORE S17...........161 G3
St Quentin Dr
  TOT/DORE S17...........161 H3
St Quentin Mt
  TOT/DORE S17...........161 H3
St Quentin Ri
  TOT/DORE S17...........161 H3
St Quentin Vw
  TOT/DORE S17...........161 H3
St Ronan's Rd ABRD S7...139 H3
St Sepulchre Ga DON DN1...6 C4
St Sepulchre Ga West
  DONS/BSCR DN4...........6 B6
St Stephens Wk BTLY DN5...39 E5
St Stephen's Dr
  AU/AST/KP S26...........145 F2
St Stephen's Rd
  RHAM/THRY S65...........9 H2
St Stephen's Wk OWL S3...10 D3
St Thomas Rd FUL S10.....124 D4
St Thomas St SHEF S1 *....10 E5
St Thomas's Cl
  DONS/BSCR DN4...........71 G2
St Thomas's Rd
  DOD/DAR S75...........18 C3
St Thomas's Rd CHSW S40..191 G2
St Ursula's Rd
  DONS/BSCR DN4...........7 K6
St Veronica Rd
  STKB/PEN S36...........77 G4
St Vincent Av
  AWLS/ASK DN6...........24 D1
  DON DN1...........7 F2
St Vincent's Av ARMTH DN3..75 E1
St Wandrilles Cl
  CHPT/GREN S35...........94 A5
St Wilfrid's Rd
  DONS/BSCR DN4...........57 G4
  SHEFP/MNR S2...........140 A2
St Withold Av MALT S66...133 E1
Salcey Sq CHSW S40........4 A7
Salcombe Cl DOD/DAR S75...14 A4
Sale Hl FUL S10...........124 D5
Salerno Wy WMB/DAR S73...34 C4

Sale St *HOY* S74.................................**61** E3
Salisbury Av *CHNE* S41.....**187** E2
  DRON S18...............................**171** E3
Salisbury Crs *CHNE* S41.....**187** F2
Salisbury Rd
  DONS/BSCR DN4...........**55** G4
  DRON S18...............................**171** H4
  FUL S10................................**124** D4
  MALT S66.............................**110** D2
Salisbury St *DOD/DAR* S75........**2** D1
  DOD/DAR S75......................**19** F4
Salt Box Gv
  CHPT/GREN S35..............**101** E2
Salt Box La
  CHPT/GREN S35..............**101** E2
Saltergate *CHSW* S40.................**4** D3
Salter Oak Cft
  BSLYN/ROY S71...............**15** G3
Saltersbrook *DEARNE* S63...**37** F5
Saltersbrook Rd
  WMB/DAR S73......................**34** D3
Salter's Wy *STKB/PEN* S36....**44** D4
Salvin Crs *STV/CWN* S43.......**185** E2
Samson St *SHEFP/MNR* S2....**126** C5
Samuel Ct *SHEFP/MNR* S2....**140** D3
Samuel La *SHEFP/MNR* S2....**140** D3
Samuel Pl *SHEFP/MNR* S2....**140** D3
Samuel Rd *DOD/DAR* S75......**18** D4
  SHEFP/MNR S2...................**140** D3
Samuel Sq *DOD/DAR* S75......**18** D4
Samuel St *DONS/BSCR* DN4....**71** F2
Sanctuary Flds *DIN* S25........**148** A1
Sandal Ct *KIMB* S61..................**8** B2
Sandall Beat La *WHHL* DN2...**41** H4
Sandall Beat Rd *WHHL* DN2....**57** G2
Sandall Carr Rd *ARMTH* DN3...**29** E4
Sandall La *ARMTH* DN3...........**28** D3
Sandall Pk *WHHL* DN2 *...........**41** G2
Sandall Park Dr *WHHL* DN2...**41** G3
Sandall Ri *WHHL* DN2...............**41** F4
Sandall Stones Rd
  ARMTH DN3.........................**28** D4
Sandall Vw *DIN* S25..............**134** A2
Sandall Rd *CONI* DN12.............**88** C2
Sandalwood Cl *WHHL* DN2....**41** G3
Sandalwood Ri
  MEX/SWTN S64.................**86** B3
Sandbeck Ct
  NROS/TKH DN11...................**91** G3
Sandbeck Pl *ECC* S11............**139** F3
Sandbeck Rd
  DONS/BSCR DN4.....................**7** J6
Sandbeck Wy *MALT* S66......**109** G3
Sandbed Rd *OWL* S3..............**114** C5
Sandbergh Rd *KIMB* S61.........**96** C4
Sandby Ct *GLV* S14..............**154** A3
Sandby Cft *GLV* S14.............**154** A3
Sandby Dr *GLV* S14...............**154** A3
Sandcliffe Rd *WHHL* DN2.......**41** F4
Sandcroft Cl *HOY* S74.............**61** G3
Sandeby Dr
  RHAM/THRY S65...............**108** D2
Sanderson St *DARN/MH* S9...**116** B5
Sandford Cl *BSLY* S70................**2** D6
Sandford Grove Rd
  ABRD S7.............................**139** G4
Sandford Rd
  DONS/BSCR DN4.................**71** G2
Sandhill Cl *RAW* S62................**85** H4
Sandhill Ri *EPW* DN9...............**75** H1
Sandhill Rd *RAW* S62..............**85** H5
Sandhills Rd *BSVR* S44.........**197** E3
Sandhurst Rd
  DONS/BSCR DN4.................**74** C1
Sandiway *CHSW* S40............**191** G4
Sandown Cl *ECK/KIL* S21......**166** B5
Sandown Gdns
  DONS/BSCR DN4.................**57** H3
Sandown Rd
  MEX/SWTN S64...................**67** F2
Sandpiper Rd *KIMB* S61.........**82** B5
Sandpit Hl *ARMTH* DN3..........**59** F5
Sandringham Av
  RHAM S60.........................**119** H3
Sandringham Cl *CHNE* S41...**187** F1
  STKB/PEN S36......................**44** A2
  STV/CWN S43....................**188** D5
Sandringham Pl *FUL* S10.....**136** D2
  RHAM/THRY S65................**108** D1
Sandringham Rd
  DARN/MH S9.....................**103** G5
  WHHL DN2.................................**7** K3
Sandrock Dr
  DONS/BSCR DN4.................**74** A1
Sands Cl *GLV* S14.................**154** A1
Sandstone Av
  DARN/MH S9.....................**116** B2
  RCH S42..............................**191** F4
Sandstone Cl *DARN/MH* S9...**116** C1
Sandstone Dr
  DARN/MH S9.....................**116** B2
Sandstone Rd
  DARN/MH S9.....................**116** B2
Sandwith Rd
  AU/AST/KP S26.................**147** G5
Sandy Acres Cl *MOS* S20.....**157** F4
Sandy Acres Dr *MOS* S20.....**157** G4
Sandybridge La
  CUD/GR S72..........................**13** H5
Sandycroft Cft
  DONS/BSCR DN4.................**71** G2
Sandy Flat La *MALT* S66.......**121** F2

Sandygate *DEARNE* S63.........**65** F4
Sandygate Grange Dr
  FUL S10.............................**124** A5
Sandygate Gv *FUL* S10........**123** H5
Sandygate Pk *FUL* S10........**123** G5
Sandygate Park Crs
  FUL S10.............................**123** H5
Sandygate Park Rd
  FUL S10.............................**123** H4
Sandygate Rd *FUL* S10.......**123** H5
Sandy La *DONS/BSCR* DN4........**7** K7
  HOY S74...............................**49** E3
Sandymount Rd
  DEARNE S63........................**65** G3
Sanforth St *CHNE* S41.........**187** G5
Sankey Sq *DEARNE* S63.........**37** F5
Sarah Ct *ARMTH* DN3.............**43** G3
Sarah St *KIMB* S61....................**8** A5
  MEX/SWTN S64....................**67** E4
Sargeson Rd *ARMTH* DN3......**42** B4
Sark Rd *SHEFP/MNR* S2.......**140** A3
Saundby Cl *DONS/BSCR* DN4...**73** G1
Saunderson Rd
  STKB/PEN S36......................**44** B2
Saunders Pl
  SHEFP/MNR S2...................**127** E4
Saunders Rd
  SHEFP/MNR S2...................**127** E4
Saunders Rw
  WMB/DAR S73......................**50** A3
Savage La *TOT/DORE* S17.....**160** D1
Savile St *ATT* S4....................**126** C2
Savile St East *ATT* S4..........**126** D1
Savile St Sct *OWL* S3...........**126** D1
Saville Hall La *DOD/DAR* S75..**30** B4
Saville Rd *DEARNE* S63..........**65** E3
  DOD/DAR S75........................**30** C4
  RHAM S60.........................**119** H3
Saville St *CUD/GR* S72............**16** D5
  RHAM/THRY S65...................**99** E5
Saville Ter *BSLY* S70...................**3** F7
Sawdon Rd *ECC* S11.............**139** C1
Sawn Moor Av *MALT* S66.....**133** F1
Sawn Moor Rd *MALT* S66.....**133** F2
Sawston Cl *DONS/BSCR* DN4...**71** G4
Saxon Cl *DONS/BSCR* DN4.....**74** B2
Saxon Crs *BSLY* S70.................**32** A5
Saxonlea Av
  SHEFP/MNR S2...................**142** A1
Saxonlea Ct
  SHEFP/MNR S2...................**142** A1
Saxonlea Crs
  SHEFP/MNR S2...................**142** A1
Saxonlea Dr
  SHEFP/MNR S2...................**141** H1
Saxon Rd *KIMB* S61..............**104** B3
  SHEFS S8...........................**140** A4
Saxon Rw *CONI* DN12..............**89** G1
Saxon St *CUD/GR* S72.............**21** H1
  DEARNE S63.........................**56** C5
Saxton Av *DONS/BSCR* DN4....**57** G5
Saxton Cl *CHNE* S41.............**193** E4
  HOY S74................................**62** D1
Saxton Dr *RHAM* S60............**119** F3
Sca Fell Pl *DIN* S25..............**148** D2
Scaftworth Cl
  DONS/BSCR DN4.................**73** G1
Scammadine Cl *RHAM* S60..**118** C4
Scarborough Cl *DIN* S25......**148** C1
Scarborough La
  NROS/TKH DN11...................**90** D2
Scarborough Rd
  DARN/MH S9.....................**128** A2
  MALT S66...........................**108** B4
Scarbrough Crs *MALT* S66...**111** E4
Scarfield Cl *BSLYN/ROY* S71...**33** F2
Scargill Cft *OWL* S3................**11** G2
Scar La *BSLYN/ROY* S71.........**33** F2
Scarlett Oak Meadow
  ST/HB/BR S6.......................**123** G1
Scarll Rd *DONS/BSCR* DN4.....**57** G5
Scarsdale Cl *DRON* S18.......**171** F3
Scarsdale Crs
  STV/CWN S43.....................**188** B2
Scarsdale Cross *DRON* S18..**171** F2
Scarsdale Rd *CHNE* S41......**187** G1
  DRON S18...........................**171** F2
  SHEFS S8...........................**152** D2
Scarsdale St *BSVR* S44........**196** B4
  DIN S25.............................**135** C4
Scarth Av *DONS/BSCR* DN4....**55** H5
Scawsby La *BTLY* DN5............**38** B2
Scawthorpe Av *BTLY* DN5.....**38** D1
Sceptone Gv *CUD/GR* S72......**17** E1
Schofield Dr *WMB/DAR* S73...**35** E4
Schofield Pl *WMB/DAR* S73....**35** E4
Schofield Rd *STKB/PEN* S36..**77** F2
  WMB/DAR S73......................**35** E4
Schofield St *MEX/SWTN* S64..**66** D3
Scholar Av *STKB/PEN* S36.....**44** C5
Schole Hill La *STKB/PEN* S36..**44** E4
Scholes La *KIMB* S61...............**95** H3
Scholes Ri *CHPT/GREN* S35..**102** B1
Scholes Vw *CHPT/GREN* S35..**94** B5
Scholey Rd *MALT* S66..........**108** B4
Scholfield Crs *MALT* S66.....**111** F4
School Av *MOS* S20...............**167** E1
School Board La *CHSW* S40......**4** B4
School Cl *AU/AST/KP* S26....**159** F2
  MOS S20.............................**167** F1
School Ct *DON* DN1 *..................**6** E1
Schoolfield Dr *RAW* S62........**85** F4

Schoolfield Cl *BSVR* S44......**197** F3
School Green La *FUL* S10....**137** F3
School Gv *AU/AST/KP* S26...**145** G3
School Hl *CUD/GR* S72............**16** D5
  RHAM S60.........................**119** H3
School La *ARMTH* DN3............**58** D5
  CHPT/GREN S35...................**93** E5
  DRON S18...........................**171** E2
  ECK/KIL S21......................**165** G5
  RAW S62..............................**98** A3
  RHAM/THRY S65...................**99** H3
  SHEFP/MNR S2...................**126** C4
  SHEFS S8...........................**153** G2
  ST/HB/BR S6......................**123** G2
School Lane Cl *SHEFS* S8....**153** G4
School Rd *AU/AST/KP* S26...**159** E3
  CHNE S41..........................**187** G2
  CHPT/GREN S35...................**80** C4
  DIN S25.............................**134** B1
  FUL S10.............................**124** D4
  MALT S66...........................**133** F1
  MOS S20.............................**157** G2
School St *AU/AST/KP* S26....**145** E3
  BSLY S70...............................**32** D2
  CUD/GR S72..........................**16** D4
  CUD/GR S72..........................**23** H5
  DEARNE S63.........................**37** F2
  DEARNE S63.........................**56** C5
  DIN S25.............................**134** D4
  DOD/DAR S75........................**25** G3
  DOD/DAR S75........................**14** A3
  ECK/KIL S21......................**166** D5
  RHAM/THRY S65...................**99** G4
  WMB/DAR S73......................**63** E1
School Wk *CONI* DN12.............**68** B4
  SHEFS S8...........................**140** D3
Scotia Cl *SHEFP/MNR* S2.....**141** F2
Scotia Dr *SHEFP/MNR* S2.....**141** F2
Scotland St *OWL* S3.................**10** E1
Scot La *DON* DN1.........................**5** H3
Scott Av *CONI* DN12................**88** C2
Scott Cl *MALT* S66...............**133** E1
Scott Crs *ARMTH* DN5............**29** E4
Scott Hl *BTLY* DN5...................**54** B5
Scott Rd *ATT* S4...................**115** G4
Scott St *ATT* S4....................**116** A4
  OWL S3..............................**110** B2
Scott Wy *CHPT/GREN* S35......**93** H2
Scovell Av *RAW* S62...............**85** E4
Scowerdons Cl
  HACK/IN S12......................**142** D5
Scowerdons Dr
  HACK/IN S12......................**142** D5
Scraith Wood Dr *SHEFN* S5...**114** B2
Scrooby Dr *KIMB* S61...............**97** G3
Scrooby La *KIMB* S61..............**97** H3
Scrooby Ri *KIMB* S61...............**97** H3
Scrooby St *KIMB* S61...............**97** G3
Seabrook Rd
  SHEFP/MNR S2...................**154** D1
Seagrave Av *HACK/IN* S12...**154** D1
Seagrave Crs *HACK/IN* S12..**154** C2
Seagrave Dr *CHNE* S41........**193** E5
  HACK/IN S12......................**154** C2
Seagrave Rd *HACK/IN* S12...**154** C1
Searby Rd *MALT* S66............**108** D2
Searson Av *BSVR* S44...........**196** D3
Seaton Cl *SHEFP/MNR* S2....**127** F5
Seaton Crs *SHEFP/MNR* S2..**127** F5
Seaton Gdns
  NROS/TKH DN11...................**91** F4
Seaton Pl *SHEFP/MNR* S2....**127** F5
Seaton Wy *SHEFP/MNR* S2..**127** F5
Sebastion Vw *RHAM* S60......**118** C2
Second Av *AWLS/ASK* DN6......**25** F3
Second La *DIN* S25..............**148** C5
  MALT S66...........................**121** G2
Sedan St *ATT* S4..................**115** G5
Sedbergh Crs *CHNE* S41......**186** D2
Sedge Cl *MALT* S66..............**108** D5
Sedgefield Wy
  MEX/SWTN S64...................**67** F2
Sedgemoor Cl *CHSW* S40.....**186** B5
Sedgley Rd *ST/HB/BR* S6.......**56** B4
Sefton Rd *FUL* S10..............**138** A3
Selborne Rd *FUL* S10..........**124** C4
Selborne St
  RHAM/THRY S65.....................**9** G1
Selbourne Cl *DOD/DAR* S75...**18** A2
Selby Cl *AU/AST/KP* S26.....**145** E3
  CHSW S40..........................**191** G4
Selby Rd *BSLYN/ROY* S71 *....**14** D5
  SHEFN S5...........................**115** H3
  WHHL DN2...........................**41** E5
Selhurst Crs
  DONS/BSCR DN4.................**74** A1
Selhurst Rd *CHNE* S41........**187** H4
Selkirk Rd *WHHL* DN2.............**41** G4
Sellars Rd *KIMB* S61..............**96** D5
Selly Oak Gv *SHEFS* S8........**163** G2
Selly Oak Rd *SHEFS* S8........**163** G2
Selmer Ct *STV/CWN* S43......**188** B1
Selwood Flats
  RHAM/THRY S65......................**9** K2
Selwyn St *BSVR* S44............**197** F4
  RHAM/THRY S65......................**9** H1
Senior Rd *DARN/MH* S9........**128** A3
  DONS/BSCR DN4.................**58** C5
Seniors Pl *CHPT/GREN* S35...**80** D5
Sennen Cft *BSLYN/ROY* S71...**20** B4
Setcup La *ECK/KIL* S21........**174** C1
Seth Ter *BSLY* S70......................**3** K6

Setts Wy *RCH* S42................**195** H3
Sevenairs Fold *MOS* S20.....**157** E2
Sevenairs Rd *MOS* S20........**157** E2
Sevenairs Vw *MOS* S20.......**157** E2
Sevenfields Ct
  ST/HB/BR S6.......................**113** G3
Sevenfields La
  ST/HB/BR S6.......................**113** G3
Severn Ct *FUL* S10...............**125** F4
Severn Rd *FUL* S10...............**125** F4
Severnside Dr
  HAN/WDH S13....................**143** E3
Severnside Gdns
  HAN/WDH S13....................**143** E3
Severnside Pl
  HAN/WDH S13....................**143** E3
Sewell Rd *MOS* S20..............**167** F2
Sexton Dr *MALT* S66............**108** D5
Seymore Rd
  AU/AST/KP S26.................**145** F4
Seymour La *STV/CWN* S40.....**4** A3
Seymour Rd *SHEFP/MNR* S2..**111** F4
Shackleton Dr *WHHL* DN2.....**41** H1
Shackleton Vw
  STKB/PEN S36......................**44** C4
Shady Side *DONS/BSCR* DN4..**55** G4
Shaftesbury Av *CHSW* S40......**4** A3
  WHHL DN2...........................**57** F2
Shaftesbury Dr *HOY* S74.......**61** H3
Shaftesbury St *HOY* S74........**32** D2
Shaftholme La *BTLY* DN5.......**27** E1
Shaftholme Rd *BTLY* DN5......**27** E1
Shafton Hall Dr *CUD/GR* S72...**16** D1
Shafton Rd *RHAM* S60..........**119** H3
Shaftsbury Av
  AWLS/ASK DN6....................**24** D2
Shaftsbury Sq
  RHAM/THRY S65......................**9** G2
Shakespeare Av *BTLY* DN5.....**55** F1
Shakespeare Crs
  DRON S18...........................**171** G3
Shakespeare Dr *DIN* S25.....**135** E5
Shakespeare Rd *BTLY* DN5...**39** H1
  DEARNE S63.........................**64** D1
Shaldon Gv *AU/AST/KP* S26..**145** F3
Shalesmoor *OWL* S3................**11** F1
Shalesmoor Jct *OWL* S3......**125** H2
Shambles St *BSLY* S70...............**2** E4
The Shambles *CHSW* S40.........**5** C4
Shamrock Pl *STV/CWN* S43..**183** G2
Shap Cl *CHSW* S40...............**186** C4
Shardlow Gdns
  DONS/BSCR DN4.................**74** B2
Sharlston Gdns
  NROS/TKH DN11...................**91** H2
Sharman Cl *DRON* S18.........**172** C2
Sharpe Av *SHEFS* S8............**152** C5
Sharpfield Av *RAW* S62.........**85** E3
Sharrard Cl *HACK/IN* S12....**141** H5
Sharrard Dr *HACK/IN* S12....**141** H5
Sharrard Gv *HACK/IN* S12....**141** H4
Sharrard Rd *HACK/IN* S12....**141** H5
Sharrow La *ECC* S11............**139** G2
Sharrow Vw *ABRD* S7.............**139** G2
Sharrow Vale Rd *ECC* S11...**139** E2
Shaw Ct *ARMTH* DN3..............**43** E5
Shawfield Cl *ARMTH* DN3......**29** C1
Shawfield Rd
  BSLYN/ROY S71...................**20** C1
Shaw La *BSLY* S70......................**2** C5
  DOD/DAR S75........................**14** A3
  WHHL DN2...........................**41** H2
Shaw Rd *CONI* DN12................**70** B5
  RHAM/THRY S65.................**106** C1
Shawsfield Rd *RHAM* S60....**106** B5
Shaw St *BSLY* S70......................**2** C5
  CHNE S41..........................**187** G1
Shaw Wood Wy *WHHL* DN2...**41** H3
Shaw's Rw *CHSW* S40..........**191** H2
Shay House La
  STKB/PEN S36......................**76** D3
Shay Rd *STKB/PEN* S36.........**76** D2
The Shay *DONS/BSCR* DN4.....**74** A1
Sheaf Bank *SHEFP/MNR* S2..**140** A3
Sheaf Cl *CONI* DN12................**89** F2
Sheaf Crs *DEARNE* S63..........**53** F4
Sheaf St *SHEF* S1.....................**11** J4
Sheardown St
  DONS/BSCR DN4.....................**6** A5
Sheards Cl *DRON* S18..........**170** D2
Sheards Dr *DRON* S18..........**170** C2
Sheards Wy *DRON* S18.........**170** C2
Shearman Av *KIMB* S61..........**96** C4
Shearwood Rd *FUL* S10.........**10** A4
Sheep Bridge La
  NROS/TKH DN11...................**91** H1
Sheepcote Rd *ECK/KIL* S21..**168** A2
Sheep Cote Rd *RHAM* S60...**120** B1
Sheep Dike La *MALT* S66.....**121** G4
Sheerien Cl *BSLYN/ROY* S71...**14** C4
Sheffield La *RHAM* S60........**129** G2
Sheffield Pkwy
  SHEFP/MNR S2...................**126** D3
Sheffield Rd *BSLY* S70................**3** H6
  BSLY S70...............................**60** D1
  CHNE S41...............................**5** G1
  CONI DN12..........................**69** H5
  DARN/MH S9.....................**117** E3

Sheffield Round Wk
  ECC S11.............................**150** C2
  SHEFS S8...........................**152** B5
Sheldon Av *CONI* DN12..........**89** F2
Sheldon La *ST/HB/BR* S6.....**123** G2
Sheldon Rd *ABRD* S7...........**139** G4
  CHSW S40..........................**186** B4
  STKB/PEN S36......................**76** D2
Sheldon Rw *OWL* S3................**11** J1
Sheldon St *SHEFP/MNR* S2..**140** A1
Sheldrake Cl *KIMB* S61...........**95** F1
Shelley Av *DONS/BSCR* DN4..**71** H2
Shelley Cl *STKB/PEN* S36......**44** D2
Shelley Dr *ARMTH* DN3...........**43** E5
  BSLYN/ROY S71...................**14** D5
  DIN S25.............................**135** F5
  DRON S18...........................**171** G4
  RHAM/THRY S65.................**106** D4
Shelley Gv *BTLY* DN5..............**55** F1
Shelley Ri *AWLS/ASK* DN6......**25** E2
Shelley Rd
  RHAM/THRY S65.................**106** D4
Shelley Wy *DEARNE* S63........**64** C1
Shenstone Dr
  RHAM/THRY S65.................**106** D5
Shenstone Rd
  RHAM/THRY S65.................**106** D5
  ST/HB/BR S6.......................**113** H2
Shepcote La *DARN/MH* S9...**117** E5
Shepcote Ter *BSLY* S70 *.........**32** D2
Shepcote Wy *DARN/MH* S9..**117** E5
Shephard's Cl *CONI* DN12......**68** B3
Shepherd Dr
  CHPT/GREN S35...................**80** C5
Shepherd La *DEARNE* S63.....**37** F3
Shepherd St *OWL* S3...............**10** E1
Shepley Cft *CHPT/GREN* S35..**80** C5
Shepley St *CHSW* S40...............**4** A5
Sheppard Rd
  DONS/BSCR DN4.................**71** G1
Shepperson Rd
  ST/HB/BR S6.......................**113** H3
Sherbourne Av *CHNE* S41....**187** E1
Sherburn Ga
  CHPT/GREN S35...................**80** D5
Sherburn Rd
  BSLYN/ROY S71...................**14** C5
Sherde Rd *ST/HB/BR* S6......**125** F1
Sheridan Av
  DONS/BSCR DN4.................**72** A2
Sheridan Ct *BSLYN/ROY* S71...**20** B4
Sheridan Dr
  RHAM/THRY S65.................**107** E3
Sheringham Cl
  CHPT/GREN S35...................**80** B4
Sherwood Av *ARMTH* DN3......**29** F5
  BTLY DN5..............................**38** D4
  CONI DN12............................**88** C2
Sherwood Crs *RHAM* S60.........**9** G5
Sherwood Dr
  DONS/BSCR DN4.................**71** E3
Sherwood Gln *ABRD* S7.......**151** H4
Sherwood Pl *DRON* S18.......**170** B2
Sherwood Rd *DRON* S18......**170** B2
  ECK/KIL S21......................**168** C1
  NROS/TKH DN11...................**91** G3
Sherwood St
  BSLYN/ROY S71.......................**3** H4
  BSVR S44...........................**197** E4
  CHSW S40..........................**192** D3
Sherwood Wy *CUD/GR* S72....**16** C5
Shetland Rd *DRON* S18........**171** F5
Shield Av *BSLY* S70...................**31** H5
Shinwell Av *STV/CWN* S43...**189** F2
Ship Hl *RHAM* S60.......................**9** F5
Shipman Ct *MOS* S20...........**166** D1
Shipton St *ST/HB/BR* S6......**125** C2
Shirburn Gdns
  DONS/BSCR DN4.................**58** A4
Shirebrook Rd *SHEFS* S8.....**140** A4
Shirecliffe Cl *OWL* S3..........**115** F5
Shirecliffe La *OWL* S3..........**115** E5
Shiregreen La *SHEFN* S5.....**103** E5
Shiregreen Ter *SHEFN* S5....**102** D4
Shirehall Crs *SHEFN* S5.......**102** D2
Shirehall Rd *SHEFN* S5........**102** D3
Shire Oak Dr *HOY* S74.............**62** D3
Shireoaks Rd *DRON* S18......**171** G1
Shireoaks Wy *CUD/GR* S72....**17** H4
Shires Cl *BTLY* DN5.....................**7** J2
Shirewood Cl *DEARNE* S63.....**63** H2
Shirland Av *BSLYN/ROY* S71..**20** A1
Shirland Ct *DARN/MH* S9.....**127** F1
Shirland La *DARN/MH* S9.....**127** F1
Shirland Ms *DARN/MH* S9....**127** F2
Shirland Pl *DARN/MH* S9.....**127** H2
Shirland St *CHNE* S41...............**5** G1

Shirley Cl CHSW S40 ....186 B4
Shirley Rd DONS/BSCR DN4 ....55 G4
Shooters Hill Dr
 NROS/TKH DN11 ....91 H3
Shoreham Dr RHAM S60 ......119 F3
Shoreham Rd RHAM S60 ......119 F3
Shoreham St SHEF S1 ....11 H5
 SHEFP/MNR S2 ....140 A2
Shore La FUL S10 ....124 C5
Shorland Dr RHAM S60 ....130 A3
Shortbrook Bank MOS S20 ...157 E5
Shortbrook Cl MOS S20 ....157 E5
Shortbrook Cft MOS S20 * ...157 F5
Shortbrook Dr MOS S20 ......157 E5
Shortbrook Rd MOS S20 ......157 E5
Shortbrook Wy MOS S20 ......157 E5
Short Cl RCH S42 ....190 B5
Shortfield Ct
 BSLYN/ROY S71 ....14 C4
Short La DONS/BSCR DN4 .....73 F1
 ST/HB/BR S6 ....122 C2
Short Rd WHHL DN2 ....57 G1
Shorts La TOT/DORE S17 ....160 B2
Short Wood La BSLY S70 .....47 H4
Shotton Wk DON DN1 ....6 C6
Shrewsbury Cl
 MEX/SWTN S64 ....66 D3
 STKB/PEN S36 ....44 D3
Shrewsbury Rd
 SHEFP/MNR S2 ....11 J6
 STKB/PEN S36 ....44 D3
Shrewsbury Ter KIMB S61 ...104 D3
Shroggs Head Cl
 WMB/DAR S73 ....35 F4
Shrogswood Rd RHAM S60 ...120 B1
Shubert Cl HAN/WDH S13 ....143 F2
Shude Hl SHEF S1 ....11 J3
Shunters Drift
 STV/CWN S43 ....177 F5
Shuttle Cl NROS/TKH DN11 ...91 G3
Shuttleworth Cl
 NROS/TKH DN11 ....91 G3
Sicey Av SHEFN S5 ....102 D5
Sicey La SHEFN S5 ....102 D5
Sicklebrook La DRON S18 ....164 A4
Sidcop Rd CUD/GR S72 ....16 D4
Siddall St SHEF S1 ....10 D3
Sidings Ct DONS/BSCR DN4 ...56 C5
The Sidings Rbt
 DONS/BSCR DN4 ....6 E7
Sidlaw Cl CHSW S40 ....186 C4
Sidney Rd WHHL DN2 ....57 F1
Sidney St MEX/SWTN S64 ....66 B5
 SHEF S1 ....11 G6
Sidons Cl KIMB S61 ....96 C4
Siemens Cl DARN/MH S9 ....117 G2
Siena Cl WMB/DAR S73 ......34 C4
Sike La STKB/PEN S36 ....44 A5
Sikes Rd DIN S25 ....148 B3
Silkstone Cl DOD/DAR S75 ...60 B3
 HACK/IN S12 ....155 G1
Silkstone Crs HACK/IN S12 ...155 G1
Silkstone Dr HACK/IN S12 ...155 F1
Silkstone Pl HACK/IN S12 ...155 G1
Silkstone Rd HACK/IN S12 ...155 G1
Silkstone Vw HOY S74 ....49 E5
Silver Birch Av FUL S10 ....137 G3
Silverdale Cl ARMTH DN3 ....59 G5
 CHNE S41 ....179 E5
 ECC S11 ....138 C5
Silverdale Cft ECC S11 ......151 E1
Silverdale Dr
 BSLYN/ROY S71 ....20 D2
Silverdale Gdns ECC S11 ....151 E1
Silverdale Gld ECC S11 ......151 G1
Silverdale Rd ECC S11 ......151 G1
Silverdales DIN S25 ....135 E4
Silver Hill Rd ECC S11 ......138 D5
Silver Jubilee Cl WHHL DN2 ...41 G4
Silver Mill Rd
 SHEFP/MNR S2 ....140 A2
Silvermoor Dr
 RHAM/THRY S65 ....108 D1
Silverstone Av CUD/GR S72 ...17 E5
Silver St BSLY S70 ....3 F6
 DOD/DAR S75 ....30 B4
 DON DN1 ....6 D3
 RHAM/THRY S65 ....99 G4
 SHEF S1 ....11 G2
Silver Street Head SHEF S1 ..11 F2
Silver Well Dr
 STV/CWN S43 ....189 H1
Silverwood Cl MALT S66 ....108 B2
Silverwood Ct DEARNE S63 ...65 H1
Simcrest Av ECK/KIL S21 ....168 B3
Simmonite Rd KIMB S61 ......96 D5
Simons Wy WMB/DAR S73 ....33 H5
Simpson Pl MEX/SWTN S64 ...66 D3
Sims Cft CHNE S41 ....180 A3
Sims St SHEF S1 ....11 F2
Sincil Wy DONS/BSCR DN4 ...74 A1
Singleton Crs ST/HB/BR S6 ...114 A5
Singleton Gv ST/HB/BR S6 ...114 A5
Singleton Rd ST/HB/BR S6 ...114 A5
Sitka Cl BSLYN/ROY S71 .....15 F2
Sitwell MOS S20 ....157 E5
Sitwell Av CHSW S40 ....192 B3
Sitwell Gv MEX/SWTN S64 ...86 B1
 RHAM S60 ....119 G2

Sitwell La MALT S66 ....121 F1
Sitwell Park Rd RHAM S60 ...120 B1
Sitwell Pl ABRD S7 ....139 H2
Sitwell Rd ABRD S7 ....139 H2
Sitwell St ECK/KIL S21 ......174 C1
Sitwell V RHAM S60 ....119 F1
Sitwell Vw RHAM S60 ....120 B3
Sivilla Rd MEX/SWTN S64 ....86 B3
Skeldale Dr CHSW S40 ......192 D4
Skelton Cl HAN/WDH S13 ....143 G5
Skelton Gv HAN/WDH S13 ...143 F4
Skelton La HAN/WDH S13 ....143 F4
 MOS S20 ....157 F2
Skelton Rd SHEFS S8 ....140 A5
Skelwith Cl ATT S4 ....116 A3
 CHNE S41 ....186 D1
Skelwith Dr ATT S4 ....116 B3
Skelwith Rd ATT S4 ....116 B3
Skew Hill La
 CHPT/GREN S35 ....100 D1
Skiddaw Cl CHSW S40 ....186 D2
Skiers Hall HOY S74 ....62 B4
Skiers Vw HOY S74 ....61 G3
Skiers Wy HOY S74 ....61 G3
Skinnerthorpe Rd ATT S4 ...115 H3
Skipton Cl CONI DN12 ....68 A3
Skipton Rd ATT S4 ....115 G4
 AU/AST/KP S26 ....145 E3
Skipwith Gdns
 NROS/TKH DN11 ....91 E3
Skye Edge Av
 SHEFP/MNR S2 ....126 D5
Skye Edge Rd
 SHEFP/MNR S2 ....126 D5
Slack La CHSW S40 ....191 F1
 CUD/GR S72 ....13 H4
Slade Rd MEX/SWTN S64 ....86 A3
Slag La STV/CWN S43 ....173 F5
Slaidburn Av
 CHPT/GREN S35 ....80 D5
Slate St SHEFP/MNR S2 .....140 A3
Slayleigh Av FUL S10 ....137 G2
Slayleigh Delph FUL S10 ....137 G2
Slayleigh Dr FUL S10 ....137 G2
Slayleigh La FUL S10 ....137 G2
Slayley Hl STV/CWN S43 ....184 C2
Slayley Vw STV/CWN S43 ...184 C1
Slayley View Rd
 STV/CWN S43 ....177 F5
Sleaford St DARN/MH S9 * ..127 F1
Sledgate Dr MALT S66 ......120 D1
Sledgate La MALT S66 ......120 D1
Sledmere Rd BTLY DN5 ......39 E4
Slinn St FUL S10 ....125 E3
Slitting Mill La DARN/MH S9 ..127 F1
Sloade La HACK/IN S12 .....165 F1
Smallage La HAN/WDH S13 ..144 C1
Smalldale Rd HACK/IN S12 ..155 F1
Smawell La HOR/CROF WF4 ...12 B2
Smeaton Cl
 RHAM/THRY S65 ....108 D1
Smeaton St ABRD S7 ....139 H2
Smeckley Wood Cl
 CHNE S41 ....178 C3
Smelter Wood Av
 HAN/WDH S13 ....142 C3
Smelter Wood Cl
 HAN/WDH S13 * 142 C3
Smelter Wood Crs
 HAN/WDH S13 ....142 C3
Smelter Wood Dr
 HAN/WDH S13 ....142 C3
Smelter Wood La
 HAN/WDH S13 ....142 C3
Smelter Wood Pl
 HAN/WDH S13 ....142 D3
Smelter Wood Rl
 HAN/WDH S13 ....142 D3
Smelter Wood Rd
 HAN/WDH S13 ....142 C3
Smelter Wood Wy
 HAN/WDH S13 ....142 C3
Smillie Rd NROS/TKH DN11 ...91 G3
Smith Av STV/CWN S43 .....189 F2
Smith Crs CHNE S41 ....193 F3
Smithey Cl CHPT/GREN S35 ...80 B5
Smithfield OWL S3 ....11 F1
Smithfield Rd HACK/IN S12 ..154 C3
Smithies La DOD/DAR S75 ....19 G3
Smithies Rd MEX/SWTN S64 ..59 H4
Smithies St BSLYN/ROY S71 ..19 G3
Smithley La WMB/DAR S73 ...49 G1
Smith Rd STKB/PEN S36 ......76 C2
Smithson Av BSVR S44 ......197 G3
Smith Sq DONS/BSCR DN4 ...71 F1
Smith St CHPT/GREN S35 ....94 A1
 DONS/BSCR DN4 ....71 F1
 WMB/DAR S73 ....50 C2
Smithy Bridge La
 WMB/DAR S73 ....63 F1
Smithy Brook Rd
 ECK/KIL S21 ....176 A3
Smithy Carr Av
 CHPT/GREN S35 ....93 H1
Smithy Carr Cl
 CHPT/GREN S35 ....93 H1
Smithy Cft DRON S18 ....170 A1
Smithy Fold La *
 CHPT/GREN S35 ....79 E4
Smithy Moor La
 STKB/PEN S36 ....76 A1

Smithy Wood Crs SHEFS S8 ..152 C1
Smithy Wood La
 DOD/DAR S75 ....30 B4
Smithy Wood Rd
 CHPT/GREN S35 ....94 C2
 SHEFS S8 ....152 C1
Snail Hl RHAM S60 ....9 F4
Snailsden Wy DOD/DAR S75 ..14 B4
Snaithing La FUL S10 ....138 A1
Snaithing Park Cl
 FUL S10 * 138 A1
Snaithing Park Rd
 FUL S10 ....138 A1
Snake La CONI DN12 ....89 F2
Snape Hl DRON S18 ....171 E4
Snape Hill Crs DRON S18 ...163 E5
Snapehill Crs DRON S18 ....171 E1
Snape Hill Dr DRON S18 * ..163 E5
Snape Hill La DRON S18 ....171 E1
Snape Hill Rd
 WMB/DAR S73 ....35 E5
Snelston Cl DRON S18 ......170 A2
Snetterton Cl CUD/GR S72 ...17 F5
Snig Hill OWL S3 ....11 H2
Snipe Cl RCH S42 ....190 B5
Snowberry Cl
 MEX/SWTN S64 ....86 A3
Snowden Ter
 WMB/DAR S73 ....50 B2
Snowdon La ECK/KIL S21 ....164 D5
Snowdon Wy RHAM S60 .....118 D5
Snow La OWL S3 ....11 F1
Snydale Rd CUD/GR S72 .....16 D5
Soaper La DRON S18 ....171 E1
Soap House La
 HAN/WDH S13 ....144 A3
Society St DON DN1 ....6 D4
Sokell Av WMB/DAR S73 .....50 A3
Solly St OWL S3 ....10 D2
Solway Ri DRON S18 ....170 B1
Somercotes Rd
 HACK/IN S12 ....142 B5
Somersall Cl CHSW S40 .....191 E4
Somersall La CHSW S40 .....191 E4
Somersall Park Rd
 CHSW S40 ....191 E3
Somersall Willows
 CHSW S40 ....191 E3
Somersby Av BTLY DN5 ......55 F1
 RCH S42 ....191 F5
Somerset Dr STV/CWN S43 ..188 D1
Somerset Rd DON DN1 ....6 E6
 OWL S3 ....126 B1
Somerset St BSLY S70 * 2 D3
 CUD/GR S72 ....21 H1
 MALT S66 ....111 F4
 OWL S3 ....126 B1
Somerton Dr
 DONS/BSCR DN4 ....74 A1
Somerville Ter
 RHAM/THRY S65 ....125 F1
Somin Ct DONS/BSCR DN4 ...72 A3
Sopewell Rd KIMB S61 ......104 B3
Sorby Rd AU/AST/KP S26 ...144 D5
Sorby St ATT S4 ....126 C2
Sorby Wy MALT S66 ....121 F1
Soresby St CHSW S40 ....5 F4
Sorrel Rd MALT S66 ....108 C3
Sorrelsykes Cl RHAM S60 ...119 H4
Sorrento Wy
 WMB/DAR S73 ....34 D4
Sothall Cl MOS S20 ....157 F2
Sothall Ct MOS S20 ....157 F2
Sothall Gn MOS S20 ....157 F2
Sothall Ms MOS S20 ....157 F2
Sough Hall Av KIMB S61 ....95 F1
Sough Hall Cl KIMB S61 ....95 F1
Sough Hall Crs KIMB S61 ...95 F1
Sough Hall Rd KIMB S61 ....95 F1
Soughley La
 CHPT/GREN S35 ....78 A1
 FUL S10 ....136 C2
Sousa St MALT S66 ....111 G4
Southall St SHEFS S8 ....140 A4
South Av MEX/SWTN S64 ....85 H1
Southbourne Rd FUL S10 ...125 E5
South Cl BSLYN/ROY S71 ....15 G2
 DRON S18 ....172 A5
Southcote Dr DRON S18 ....170 B2
South Cft TOT/DORE S17 * ..161 E1
South Crs BSVR S44 ....197 E3
 DOD/DAR S75 ....30 B4
 ECK/KIL S21 ....168 C1
 RHAM/THRY S65 ....106 D2
South Cft CUD/GR S72 ......17 E1
Southcroft Gdns ABRD S7 ...114 B3
Southdown Av CHSW S40 ...186 C5
South Dr BSLYN/ROY S71 ....15 G2
 DEARNE S63 ....52 D4
Southend Pl
 SHEFP/MNR S2 ....127 E5
Southend Rd
 SHEFP/MNR S2 ....127 E5
Southey Av SHEFN S5 ....115 E1
Southey Cl SHEFN S5 ....114 D1
Southey Ct MALT S66 ....111 G3
 SHEFN S5 ....114 D1
Southey Dr SHEFN S5 ....115 E1
Southey Green Cl
 SHEFN S5 ....114 D1
Southey Green Rd
 SHEFN S5 ....101 F5
Southey Hall Dr SHEFN S5 ..114 D1

Southey Hall Rd SHEFN S5 ..114 D1
Southey Hl SHEFN S5 ....101 C5
Southey Ri SHEFN S5 ....114 D1
Southey Rd MALT S66 ......111 G3
Southfield Crs DEARNE S63 ...36 D3
Southfield Dr DRON S18 ....171 G3
Southfield La DRON S18 ....36 D3
Southfield Mt DRON S18 ....171 G3
Southfield Rd ARMTH DN3 ...42 D4
 CUD/GR S72 ....22 A3
Southfields STV/CWN S43 ...185 F5
Southgate CUD/GR S72 .....17 F2
 DRON S18 ....19 E4
 ECK/KIL S21 ....167 E5
 HOY S74 ....62 A3
 STKB/PEN S36 ....45 E4
Southgate Ct ECK/KIL S21 ..167 E5
Southgate Crs
 STV/CWN S43 ....185 F1
Southgate Wy
 STV/CWN S43 ....181 F2
South Grimesthorpe Rd
 ATT S4 ....126 C1
Southgrove Rd FUL S10 ....139 F1
Southlands
 AU/AST/KP S26 ....145 G3
South La SHEF S1 ....11 F7
Southlea Av HOY S74 ....62 B3
Southlea Cl HOY S74 ....62 B3
Southlea Dr HOY S74 ....62 A3
Southlea Rd HOY S74 ....62 A2
South Lodge Ct CHSW S40 ..191 F1
Southmoor Av ARMTH DN3 ...42 C5
Southmoor Cl
 STV/CWN S43 ....188 D5
Southmoor La ARMTH DN3 ...42 C5
South Pde DON DN1 ....7 F4
 OWL S3 ....126 A2
South Pl CHSW S40 ....5 C5
 DOD/DAR S75 ....18 D4
 WMB/DAR S73 ....49 H2
South Rd CHPT/GREN S35 ...80 B4
 KIMB S61 ....104 C3
 ST/HB/BR S6 ....125 E1
Southsea Rd
 HAN/WDH S13 ....143 E4
South St AWLS/ASK DN6 ....25 C5
 BSLY S70 ....2 B4
 CHSW S40 ....5 C5
 DIN S25 ....134 C4
 DOD/DAR S75 ....30 B4
 DONS/BSCR DN4 ....6 E7
 KIMB S61 ....104 C4
 MALT S66 ....133 F1
 RAW S62 ....85 G5
 STV/CWN S43 ....35 E5
South St North
 STV/CWN S43 ....180 B2
South Street Pk
 SHEFP/MNR S2 ....11 K3
South Ter RHAM S60 * 9 F5
South Vw MOS S20 ....167 G1
 STV/CWN S43 ....35 E5
South View Cl
 ST/HB/BR S6 ....113 E3
South View Crs ABRD S7 ...139 H3
South View Ri
 ST/HB/BR S6 ....113 E3
South View Ter RHAM S60 ..129 G2
Southwell Gdns
 AU/AST/KP S26 ....144 C3
Southwell Ri
 MEX/SWTN S64 ....67 F2
Southwell Rd ATT S4 ....116 B3
 RAW S62 ....85 H5
Southwell St DOD/DAR S75 ..18 D4
Southwood Av DRON S18 ...171 E4
Southwood Dr
 STV/CWN S43 ....185 F3
Southwood Gv
 ST/HB/BR S6 ....113 G1
Spa Brook Cl HACK/IN S12 ..155 H1
Spa Brooke Dr
 HAN/WDH S13 ....142 D5
Spa La CHNE S41 ....5 H4
 HAN/WDH S13 ....143 G5
Spa Lane Cft
 HAN/WDH S13 ....143 G5
Spalton Rd RAW S62 ....98 B2
Spansyke St
 DONS/BSCR DN4 ....6 A5
Spark La DOD/DAR S75 ......14 A4
Sparrowbusk Cl
 STV/CWN S43 ....177 F5
Spartan Vw MALT S66 ......110 B1
Spa View Av HACK/IN S12 ..155 H2
Spa View Cl HACK/IN S12 ...155 H2
Spa View Dr HACK/IN S12 ...155 H2
Spa View Pl HACK/IN S12 ...155 H2
Spa View Rd HACK/IN S12 ..155 H2
Spa View Ter HACK/IN S12 ..155 H2
Spa View Wy HACK/IN S12 ..155 H2
Spa Well Crs RHAM S60 ....114 B4
Speetley Vw STV/CWN S43 ..177 F4
Speeton Rd ST/HB/BR S6 ...114 A5
Speighthill Crs RCH S42 ....195 E3
Spencer Av STV/CWN S43 ..182 D4

Spencer Ct RHAM S60 ......120 B3
Spencer Dr
 RHAM/THRY S65 ....108 D1
Spencer Gn RHAM S60 .....120 B3
Spencer Rd SHEFP/MNR S2 ..140 A3
Spencer St BSLY S70 ....2 E7
 BSVR S44 ....196 C4
 CHSW S40 ....5 F2
 MEX/SWTN S64 ....66 C3
Spenser Rd
 RHAM/THRY S65 ....106 C4
Spey Cl DOD/DAR S75 ....14 A5
Spilsby Cl DONS/BSCR DN4 ...74 C2
Spink Hall Cl STKB/PEN S36 ..77 E3
Spink Hall La STKB/PEN S36 ..76 D3
Spinkhill Av HAN/WDH S13 ..142 A2
Spinkhill Dr HAN/WDH S13 ..142 B2
Spinkhill La ECK/KIL S21 ....176 A1
Spinkhill Rd ECK/KIL S21 ...175 H2
 HAN/WDH S13 ....142 B3
Spinkhill Vw ECK/KIL S21 ...175 H2
Spinner Cft CHSW S40 ......5 G7
Spinners Rd WHHL DN2 .....40 C3
Spinney Cl RHAM S60 ......119 G1
Spinney Hl BTLY DN5 ....54 B5
The Spinney ARMTH DN3 ...29 C1
 DONS/BSCR DN4 ....71 F3
Spital Brook Cl CHNE S41 ..193 E3
Spitalfields OWL S3 ....126 B2
Spital Gdns CHNE S41 ......5 K7
Spital La NROS/TKH DN11 ...91 C4
Spital Hl ATT S4 ....126 C2
Spital La CHNE S41 ....5 J5
 OWL S3 ....126 B2
Spital St OWL S3 ....126 B2
Spittal Gn BSVR S44 ....196 D4
Spofforth Rd DARN/MH S9 ..127 C2
Spooner Dr ECK/KIL S21 ....168 A2
Spooner Rd FUL S10 ....125 G4
Spoon Gld ST/HB/BR S6 ....123 C4
Spoonhill Rd ST/HB/BR S6 ..123 E1
Spoon La ST/HB/BR S6 .....123 E1
Spoon Ms ST/HB/BR S6 ....123 C1
Spoon Wy ST/HB/BR S6 ....123 C1
Spotswood Cl GLV S14 .....141 E5
Spotswood Mt GLV S14 ....153 H1
Spotswood Pl GLV S14 .....153 H1
Spotswood Rd GLV S14 ....153 H1
Spout La ST/HB/BR S6 ......112 B5
Spout Spinney
 ST/HB/BR S6 ....123 F1
Springbank WMB/DAR S73 ..35 F5
Springbank Cl
 BSLYN/ROY S71 ....15 G4
Spring Bank Rd CHSW S40 ...4 D3
 CONI DN12 ....88 D3
Spring Cl ECK/KIL S21 ......154 B1
Spring Close Dell GLV S14 ..154 A1
Spring Close Mt GLV S14 ...154 A1
Spring Close Vw GLV S14 ...154 A1
Spring Crs BTLY DN5 ....54 B4
Spring Cft KIMB S61 ....96 D5
Springcroft Dr BTLY DN5 ...39 E5
Spring Dr WMB/DAR S73 ....51 E5
Spring Farm
 HOR/CROF WF4 ....12 A3
Springfield DEARNE S63 * ...52 C3
Springfield Av CHSW S40 ....4 A3
 ECC S11 ....139 E1
Springfield Cl ABRD S7 .....152 A1
 ARMTH DN3 ....43 E5
 ECK/KIL S21 ....166 C5
 KIMB S61 ....97 H5
 STV/CWN S43 ....35 F5
 WMB/DAR S73 ....35 F5
Springfield Ct BTLY DN5 ....39 E5
Springfield Crs BSVR S44 ...196 C1
 HOY S74 ....61 G3
 WMB/DAR S73 ....35 F5
Springfield Gln ABRD S7 ....151 H1
Springfield Pl BSLY S70 * 2 C4
Springfield Rd ABRD S7 .....152 A1
 CUD/GR S72 ....17 H5
 HOY S74 ....61 F3
 MALT S66 ....108 A4
 MEX/SWTN S64 ....86 C4
Springfields DOD/DAR S75 ...18 C3
Springfield St BSLY S70 .....35 E5
Spring Gdns
 BSLYN/ROY S71 ....20 C3
 DON DN1 ....6 C4
 HOY S74 ....61 G3
Spring Gv BSLYN/ROY S71 ...15 H4
Spring Hl FUL S10 ....125 G5
Springhill Av WMB/DAR S73 ..51 E5
Spring Hill Cl BTLY DN5 ....54 B4
Spring Hill Rd FUL S10 .....125 G5
Spring House Rd FUL S10 ...125 G5
Spring La BSLYN/ROY S71 ...15 G4
 BTLY DN5 ....54 B1
 SHEFP/MNR S2 ....141 E3
Spring Pl CHSW S40 * 3 F6
Spring St BSLY S70 ....3 F6
 RHAM/THRY S65 ....9 H3
Spring Vale Av BSLY S70 ....47 H1
Springvale Cl MALT S66 ....110 D2
 MALT S66 ....121 G2
Springvale Gv
 STKB/PEN S36 ....35 F5
Springvale Rd CUD/GR S72 ..22 D2
 FUL S10 ....125 F3

Spring Vale Rd
  STV/CWN S43 ....**188** C1
Springvale Wk
  ST/HB/BR S6 ....**125** F2
Spring View Rd *FUL* S10 ....**125** E3
Spring Wk *RHAM/THRY* S65 ....**9** G3
Spring Water Av
  HACK/IN S12 ....**155** H2
Spring Water Cl
  HACK/IN S12 ....**155** H1
Spring Water Dr
  HACK/IN S12 ....**155** H1
Springwell Cl *MOS* S20 ....**157** E1
Springwell Cl *MALT* S66 ....**111** F2
Springwell Crs *MOS* S20 ....**157** E1
Springwell Dr *MOS* S20 ....**157** E1
Springwell Gdns
  DONS/BSCR DN4 ....**71** F2
Springwell Vw *MOS* S20 ....**157** E1
Springwell La
  STV/CWN S43 ....**71** F3
Springwell Park Dr
  STV/CWN S43 ....**189** G2
Springwood Av
  AU/AST/KP S26 ....**145** E1
Springwood Cl *ARMTH* DN3 .....**59** G5
Spring Wood Cl *CHNE* S41 ....**186** C1
Springwood Ct
  AU/AST/KP S26 ....**145** F1
  STV/CWN S43 * **180** B2
Springwood Gv
  DEARNE S63 ....**37** E3
Springwood La
  CHPT/GREN S35 ....**80** A5
Springwood Rd *BTLY* DN5 ....**39** E2
  HOY S74 ....**61** G3
  SHEFS S8 ....**140** A4
Springwood Vw
  STKB/PEN S36 ....**45** F4
Sprotbrough Rd *BTLY* DN5 .....**55** F2
Spruce Av *BSLYN/ROY* S71 ......**15** F1
  MALT S66 ....**108** B4
Spruce Ri *ECK/KIL* S21 ....**168** A3
Spurley Hey Gv
  STKB/PEN S36 ....**77** E3
Spurr St *SHEFP/MNR* S2 ....**140** B2
The Square *BSLY* S70 ....**2** C7
  CUD/GR S72 ....**23** F1
  RAW S62 ....**81** H2
The Square West *MALT* S66 ...**108** B2
Stables Ct *BSVR* S44 ....**197** F3
The Stables *MEX/SWTN* S64 .....**64** A5
Stacey Crs *CUD/GR* S72 ....**17** H5
Stacey Dr *RHAM* S60 ....**119** H1
Stacye Av *HAN/WDH* S13 ....**143** H4
Stacye Ri *HAN/WDH* S13 ....**143** H4
Stadium Ct *RAW* S62 ....**98** A4
Stadium Wy *DARN/MH* S9 .....**127** F2
  RHAM S60 ....**98** A5
Stafford Cl *DRON* S18 ....**170** A1
Stafford Crs *RHAM* S60 ....**119** F3
Stafford Dr *RHAM* S60 ....**119** F3
Stafford Gv *BSLY* S70 ....**60** D3
Stafford La *SHEFP/MNR* S2 ....**126** D5
  SHEFP/MNR S2 ....**126** D5
Stafford St *SHEFP/MNR* S2 ....**126** C5
Stafford Wy
  CHPT/GREN S35 ....**93** H1
Stag Cl *RHAM* S60 ....**120** A1
Stag Crs *RHAM* S60 ....**120** A1
Stag La *RHAM* S60 ....**119** H1
Stag Willow Cl *RHAM* S60 ....**106** D5
Stainborough Cl
  DOD/DAR S75 ....**30** B4
Stainborough La
  DOD/DAR S75 ....**46** A5
Stainborough Rd
  DOD/DAR S75 ....**30** B4
Stainborough Vw *BSLY* S70 ...**31** H5
  DOD/DAR S75 ....**60** B2
Staindrop Cl
  CHPT/GREN S35 ....**80** D4
Staindrop Vw
  CHPT/GREN S35 ....**81** E5
Stainley Cl *DOD/DAR* S75 ....**18** D3
Stainmore Av *MOS* S20 ....**157** G3
Stainton Av *BSLYN/ROY* S71 ...**19** C1
Stainton La *MALT* S66 ....**170** A1
Stainton Rd *ECC* S11 ....**138** D2
Stainton St *CONI* DN12 ....**68** B5
Stairfoot Wy *BSLY* S70 ....**33** E3
Stair Rd *ATT* S4 ....**115** C4
Stalker Lees Rd *ECC* S11 ....**139** F2
Stamford Rd *MALT* S66 ....**108** B1
Stamford St *DARN/MH* S9 .....**116** B5
Stampers Hi *BSLY* S70 ....**47** F3
Stanage Ri *HACK/IN* S12 ....**142** B5
Stanbury Cl *DOD/DAR* S75 ......**18** D4
Stancil La *NROS/TKH* DN11 .....**90** A4
Standhill Crs
  BSLYN/ROY S71 ....**14** C5
Standish Av *SHEFN* S5 ....**115** G4
Standish Bank *SHEFN* S5 ....**115** G4
Standish Cl *SHEFN* S5 ....**115** G4
Standish Dr *SHEFN* S5 ....**115** G4
Standish Gdns *SHEFN* S5 ......**115** G3
Standish La *SHEFN* S5 ....**115** G3
Standish Wy *SHEFN* S5 ....**115** G3
Standon Crs *DARN/MH* S9 .....**103** F4

Standon Dr *DARN/MH* S9 ......**103** F4
Standon Rd *DARN/MH* S9 ......**103** G4
Stand Pk *CHNE* S41 * **187** C2
Stand Rd *CHNE* S41 ....**187** F2
Staneford Ct *MOS* S20 ....**156** D4
Stanford Cl *MALT* S66 ....**111** G4
Stanford Rd *DRON* S18 ....**170** A2
Stanford Wy *RCH* S42 ....**191** F4
Stanhope Gdns
  DOD/DAR S75 ....**2** B1
Stanhope Rd *DON* DN1 ....**40** C5
  HACK/IN S12 ....**142** A5
Stanhope St *BSLY* S70 ....**2** C4
Stanier Wy *ECK/KIL* S21 ....**175** H3
Staniforth Av *ECK/KIL* S21 ....**166** B5
Staniforth Crs
  AU/AST/KP S26 ....**147** E5
Staniforth Rd
  DARN/MH S9 ....**127** G2
Stanley Av *STV/CWN* S43 ......**189** F2
Stanley Gdns
  DONS/BSCR DN4 ....**6** A7
Stanley La *AU/AST/KP* S26 ....**145** G2
Stanley La *OWL* S3 ....**126** B2
Stanley Rd *BSLY* S70 ....**33** E2
  BTLY DN5 ....**38** D3
  CHPT/GREN S35 ....**80** C5
  SHEFS S8 ....**140** B5
  STKB/PEN S36 ....**77** E3
Stanley Sq *ARMTH* DN3 ....**29** F3
Stanley St *BSLY* S70 ....**2** D4
  CHNE S41 ....**5** K6
  CUD/GR S72 ....**22** A2
  ECK/KIL S21 ....**168** B1
  OWL S3 ....**126** B2
Stanley Ter *MALT* S66 ....**110** B4
Stannington Gln
  ST/HB/BR S6 ....**124** A1
Stannington Ri
  ST/HB/BR S6 ....**113** G5
Stannington Rd
  ST/HB/BR S6 ....**123** F1
Stannington View Rd
  FUL S10 ....**124** C3
Stanton Crs *HACK/IN* S12 ......**155** F1
Stanwell Av *DARN/MH* S9 .....**103** G5
Stanwell St *DARN/MH* S9 ......**103** G5
Stanwood Av *ST/HB/BR* S6 ...**124** B1
Stanwood Crs
  ST/HB/BR S6 ....**124** B1
Stanwood Dr *RCH* S42 ....**191** F4
  ST/HB/BR S6 ....**124** B1
Stanwood Ms
  ST/HB/BR S6 ....**124** B1
Stanwood Rd *ST/HB/BR* S6 ...**124** B1
Stapleton Rd
  DONS/BSCR DN4 ....**70** D3
Star La *BSLY* S70 ....**2** E4
Starling Md
  SHEFP/MNR S2 ....**127** E5
Starnhill Cl *CHPT/GREN* S35 ...**94** C5
Station La *ATT* S4 ....**116** C2
  CHNE S41 ....**179** G4
  CHPT/GREN S35 ....**100** A1
  STV/CWN S43 ....**180** B4
Station Rd *ARMTH* DN3 ....**29** F1
  AU/AST/KP S26 ....**159** H3
  BSLY S70 ....**13** D5
  BSLY S70 ....**48** C1
  BSLYN/ROY S71 ....**12** B5
  BSLYN/ROY S71 ....**21** F2
  BSVR S44 ....**196** B2
  BTLY DN5 ....**27** F5
  CHNE S41 ....**5** H4
  CHNE S41 ....**187** H1
  CHPT/GREN S35 ....**94** C5
  CONI DN12 ....**69** E5
  DARN/MH S9 * **128** A3
  DEARNE S63 ....**37** F2
  DEARNE S63 ....**65** F2
  DIN S25 ....**134** A2
  DOD/DAR S75 ....**30** A3
  ECK/KIL S21 ....**175** F1
  HAN/WDH S13 ....**143** H3
  MEX/SWTN S64 ....**67** E4
  MOS S20 ....**166** D1
  NROS/TKH DN11 ....**91** G2
  RHAM S60 ....**8** B4
  RHAM S60 ....**129** G1
  STKB/PEN S36 ....**78** A2
  STV/CWN S43 ....**185** E2
  STV/CWN S43 ....**188** A1
  WMB/DAR S73 ....**50** C2
Station St *MEX/SWTN* S64 ....**66** B5
Station Wy *DIN* S25 ....**134** A2
Staton Av *MOS* S20 ....**157** G1
Staton La *DRON* S18 ....**172** C2
The Statutes *RHAM* S60 ....**8** D4
Staunton Av *CHSW* S40 ....**195** G1
Staunton Rd
  DONS/BSCR DN4 ....**74** C1
Staveley La *ECK/KIL* S21 ....**174** A4
  STV/CWN S43 ....**181** F1
Staveley Rd *SHEFS* S8 ....**140** A3
  STV/CWN S43 ....**180** C3
Staveley St *CONI* DN12 ....**70** B5
Steade Rd *ABRD* S7 ....**139** H3
Steadfield Rd *HOY* S74 ....**61** F4
Steadfold Gdns *MALT* S66 ....**133** G1
Steadfolds Cl *MALT* S66 ....**133** G1
Steadfolds La *MALT* S66 ....**133** F1
Steadfolds Ri *MALT* S66 ....**133** G1
The Steadlands *RAW* S62 ....**84** D1

Stead La *HOY* S74 ....**61** F3
Stead St *ECK/KIL* S21 ....**166** D5
Steele Av *STV/CWN* S43 ....**189** F5
Steele St *HOY* S74 ....**61** E3
Steel Hi *CHPT/GREN* S35 ....**101** E2
Steelhouse La *OWL* S3 ....**11** G1
Steel La *BSVR* S44 ....**197** E2
Steel Rd *ECC* S11 ....**139** E2
Steel St *KIMB* S61 ....**105** E4
Steep La *RCH* S42 ....**194** A3
  STKB/PEN S36 ....**45** F2
Steeplegate *CHSW* S40 ....**5** G4
Steeton Ct *HOY* S74 ....**62** C2
Stemp St *ECC* S11 ....**139** H2
Stenton Rd *SHEFS* S8 ....**162** D1
Stephen Dr
  CHPT/GREN S35 ....**100** D1
  FUL S10 ....**124** B4
Stephen Hi *FUL* S10 ....**124** B4
Stephen Hill Rd *FUL* S10 ....**124** B4
Stephen La
  CHPT/GREN S35 ....**100** D1
Stephenson Pl *CHSW* S40 ....**5** G4
Stephenson Rd
  STV/CWN S43 ....**182** A5
Stepney St *SHEFP/MNR* S2 .....**11** K2
Stepping La *CHPT/GREN* S35 ...**92** D5
Sterland St *CHSW* S40 ....**4** C4
Sterry Cl *STV/CWN* S43 ....**185** E4
Steven Cl *CHPT/GREN* S35 ....**93** H2
Steven Crs *CHPT/GREN* S35 .....**93** H1
Steven Pl *CHPT/GREN* S35 ....**93** H2
Stevenson Dr *DOD/DAR* S75 ...**18** A3
  RHAM/THRY S65 ....**106** D4
Stevenson Rd
  DARN/MH S9 ....**127** C1
  DONS/BSCR DN4 ....**71** H2
Stevenson Wy
  DARN/MH S9 ....**127** C1
Stevens Rd *DONS/BSCR* DN4 ...**55** H4
Stewart Rd *ECC* S11 ....**139** F2
Stewarts Rd *RAW* S62 ....**85** G5
Stewart St *DON* DN1 ....**6** B5
Sticking La *DEARNE* S63 ....**66** C1
Stillman Cl *CHNE* S41 ....**193** E4
Stirling Cl *HOY* S74 ....**62** C2
Stirling St *DON* DN1 ....**6** C6
Stockarth Cl
  CHPT/GREN S35 ....**100** B5
Stockarth La
  CHPT/GREN S35 ....**100** A5
Stockarth Pl *ST/HB/BR* S6 ....**100** B5
Stockbridge Av *BTLY* DN5 ....**39** G3
Stockbridge La *BTLY* DN5 ....**27** C5
Stockbridge Works
  STKB/PEN S36 ....**77** F1
Stockil Rd *DONS/BSCR* DN4 .....**7** G6
Stockport La *BSVR* S44 ....**197** E4
Stock Rd *SHEFP/MNR* S2 ....**141** E1
Stocks Green Ct
  TOT/DORE S17 ....**160** C4
Stocks Green Dr
  TOT/DORE S17 ....**160** D4
Stocks Hi *CHPT/GREN* S35 ......**94** A5
Stockton Cl *OWL* S3 * **126** B1
Stockwell Av
  AU/AST/KP S26 ....**159** G4
Stockwell Gn
  BSLYN/ROY S71 ....**20** A3
Stockwell La
  AU/AST/KP S26 ....**159** F4
Stock's La *DOD/DAR* S75 ....**2** B4
  RAW S62 ....**98** B1
Stoken La *AU/AST/KP* S26 .....**131** H2
Stokewell Rd *DEARNE* S63 ....**64** C1
Stoneacre Av *HACK/IN* S12 ...**156** B2
Stoneacre Cl *HACK/IN* S12 ....**156** B3
Stoneacre Ri *HACK/IN* S12 ....**156** B3
Stonebridge La *CUD/GR* S72 ...**36** A1
Stonecliffe Dr
  STKB/PEN S36 ....**76** D4
Stonecliffe Pl
  SHEFP/MNR S2 ....**141** C1
Stonecliffe Rd
  SHEFP/MNR S2 ....**141** C1
Stone Cl *DRON* S18 ....**165** G5
Stone Close Av
  DONS/BSCR DN4 ....**55** H3
Stone Crs *MALT* S66 ....**108** B4
Stonecroft Rd
  TOT/DORE S17 ....**161** E3
Stone Cross Dr *BTLY* DN5 ....**54** B3
Stonecross Gdns
  DONS/BSCR DN4 ....**58** C5
Stonedale Cl *MOS* S20 ....**166** D1
Stone Delf *FUL* S10 ....**137** C1
Stone Font Gv
  DONS/BSCR DN4 ....**74** B1
Stonegarth Cl *CUD/GR* S72 .....**21** H1
Stonegravels La *CHNE* S41 ...**187** C4
Stonegravels Wy *MOS* S20 ...**167** F2
Stone Gv *FUL* S10 * **125** F4
Stonehill *CHPT/GREN* S35 ....**61** C1
Stone Hill Dr
  AU/AST/KP S26 ....**145** E3
Stonehill Ri *BTLY* DN5 ....**38** D2
  CUD/GR S72 ....**21** H1
  STKB/PEN S36 ....**44** C5

Stone La *HAN/WDH* S13 ....**143** E5
  STV/CWN S43 ....**180** B2
Stone Leigh *DOD/DAR* S75 ....**60** B4
Stoneleigh Cl *DIN* S25 ....**149** F1
Stoneleigh Cft *BSLY* S70 * **31** H5
Stoneley Cl *HACK/IN* S12 ......**154** C4
Stoneley Crs *HACK/IN* S12 ....**154** B3
Stoneley Dell *HACK/IN* S12 ...**154** D4
Stoneley Dr *HACK/IN* S12 ......**154** D4
Stonelow Crs *DRON* S18 ....**171** H1
Stonelow Rd *DRON* S18 ....**171** F1
Stoney Brook *MALT* S66 ....**108** D3
Stone Moor Rd
  STKB/PEN S36 ....**76** C4
Stone Park Cl *MALT* S66 * **111** F3
Stone Rd *DRON* S18 ....**163** G4
Stone Row Ct *DOD/DAR* S75 ...**60** B4
Stonerow Wy *RHAM* S60 ....**98** B5
Stone St *BSLYN/ROY* S71 ....**19** C3
  MOS S20 ....**166** D1
Stonewood Ct *FUL* S10 ....**123** H5
Stonewood Gv *FUL* S10 ....**123** H5
  HOY S74 ....**61** H4
Stoney Cft *HOY* S74 ....**61** F3
Stoneycroft La *RCH* S42 ....**194** A3
Stoney Ga *CHPT/GREN* S35 .....**80** B3
Stoney Royd
  BSLYN/ROY S71 ....**14** D3
Stonyford Rd
  WMB/DAR S73 ....**50** D1
Stoops Cl *CHSW* S40 ....**186** D3
Stoops La *DONS/BSCR* DN4 .....**73** F1
Stoops Rd *DONS/BSCR* DN4 ....**73** H1
Stopes Rd *ST/HB/BR* S6 ....**123** E1
Store St *SHEFP/MNR* S2 ....**140** B1
Storey Cl *MEX/SWTN* S64 ....**66** A5
Storey's Ga *WMB/DAR* S73 ......**49** H2
Storforth La *CHNE* S41 ....**193** E5
  CHSW S40 ....**192** C5
Storforth Lane Ter
  CHNE S41 ....**193** E4
Storrs Br *ST/HB/BR* S6 ....**112** A3
Storrs Bridge La
  ST/HB/BR S6 ....**112** A3
Storrs Hall Rd
  ST/HB/BR S6 ....**124** D1
Storrs La *CHPT/GREN* S35 ....**79** H1
  ST/HB/BR S6 ....**112** B5
Storrs Mill La
  BSLYN/ROY S71 ....**22** C5
Storrs Rd *CHSW* S40 ....**191** F2
Storrs Wood Vw
  CUD/GR S72 ....**22** B3
Storth Av *FUL* S10 ....**138** A2
Storth La *AU/AST/KP* S26 ......**159** C2
  FUL S10 ....**138** A1
Stortholme Ms *FUL* S10 ....**138** B1
Storth Pk *FUL* S10 ....**137** H3
Stotfold Dr *DEARNE* S63 ....**37** E2
Stothard Rd *FUL* S10 ....**124** D3
Stottercliffe Rd
  STKB/PEN S36 ....**44** B3
Stour Cl *STV/CWN* S43 ....**188** C1
Stour La *ST/HB/BR* S6 ....**113** F2
Stovin Cl *DARN/MH* S9 ....**127** H1
Stovin Dr *DARN/MH* S9 ....**127** H1
Stovin Gdns *DARN/MH* S9 ....**116** D5
Stow Bridge La *RHAM* S60 ....**131** C1
Stowe Av *ABRD* S7 ....**152** A1
Stradbroke Av
  HAN/WDH S13 ....**142** B3
Stradbroke Cl
  HAN/WDH S13 ....**142** C3
Stradbroke Crs
  HAN/WDH S13 ....**142** C3
Stradbroke Dr
  HAN/WDH S13 ....**142** B3
Stradbroke Pl
  HAN/WDH S13 ....**142** C3
Stradbroke Ri *CHSW* S40 ....**191** G4
Stradbroke Rd
  HAN/WDH S13 ....**142** B3
Stradbroke Wy
  HAN/WDH S13 ....**142** C3
Strafford Av *BSLY* S70 ....**33** H4
  HOY S74 ....**62** C2
Strafford Pl *KIMB* S61 ....**95** E1
Strafford Rd *KIMB* S61 ....**96** A4
Strafford Wk *DOD/DAR* S75 .....**30** B4
Strafford La *DEARNE* S63 ....**37** C5
Strafford Rd *FUL* S10 ....**137** H1
Strafford Wy *MALT* S66 ....**109** E5
Strathmore Gv
  DEARNE S63 ....**65** F2
Strathmore Rd *WHHL* DN2 ....**7** K3
Strathtay Rd *ECC* S11 ....**138** D3
Stratton Rd *BSVR* S44 ....**196** D2
Strauss Crs *MALT* S66 ....**111** H4
Strawberry Av *SHEFN* S5 ......**102** B3
Strawberry Gdns
  BSLYN/ROY S71 ....**12** C5
Strawberry Lee La
  TOT/DORE S17 ....**160** B3
Straw La *ST/HB/BR* S6 * **125** C2
Streatfield Crs
  NROS/TKH DN11 ....**91** E3
Streetfield Crs *MOS* S20 ....**166** D2
Streetfields *MOS* S20 ....**167** E2
Street La *RAW* S62 ....**83** G1
Strelley Av *SHEFS* S8 ....**152** C4
Strelley Rd *BSLYN/ROY* S71 ....**14** C4
  SHEFS S8 ....**152** B4

Stretton Cl *DONS/BSCR* DN4 ..**58** C5
Stretton Rd *BSLYN/ROY* S71 ...**20** A2
  ECC S11 ....**139** E3
The Stride *CHSW* S40 * **192** B5
Stringers Cft *RHAM* S60 ....**128** D3
Struan Rd *ABRD* S7 ....**138** B5
Strutt Rd *OWL* S3 ....**115** E5
Stuart Cl *CHNE* S41 ....**188** A3
Stuart Gv *CHPT/GREN* S35 ......**94** B3
Stuart Rd *CHPT/GREN* S35 .....**94** B2
Stuart St *DEARNE* S63 ....**37** G2
Stubbin Cl *RAW* S62 ....**84** D4
Stubbing House La
  CHPT/GREN S35 ....**100** C2
Stubbing La
  CHPT/GREN S35 ....**112** C1
Stubbing Rd *CHSW* S40 ....**192** B5
Stubbin La *RAW* S62 ....**84** D3
  SHEFN S5 ....**102** C5
Stubbin Rd *RAW* S62 ....**84** B4
Stubbs Crs *KIMB* S61 ....**96** D5
Stubbs Rd *WMB/DAR* S73 ....**50** A3
Stubley Cl *DRON* S18 ....**170** C1
Stubley Cft *DRON* S18 ....**170** C1
Stubley Dr *DRON* S18 ....**170** C1
Stubley Hollow *DRON* S18 .....**170** C1
Stubley La *DRON* S18 ....**170** B1
Stubley Pl *DRON* S18 ....**170** C1
Studfield Crs *ST/HB/BR* S6 ....**113** F3
Studfield Dr *ST/HB/BR* S6 .....**113** F4
Studfield Gv *ST/HB/BR* S6 .....**113** F3
Studfield Hi *ST/HB/BR* S6 ......**113** F3
Studfield Rd *ST/HB/BR* S6 .....**113** F4
Studley Ct *DARN/MH* S9 * **128** A3
Studley Gdns *ARMTH* DN3 ......**29** E3
Studmoor Rd *KIMB* S61 ....**96** A5
Stump Cross Gdns
  DEARNE S63 ....**52** D3
Stump Cross Rd
  DEARNE S63 ....**65** E3
Stumperlowe Av *FUL* S10 .....**138** A2
Stumperlowe Cl *FUL* S10 ......**138** A2
Stumperlowe Crescent Rd
  FUL S10 ....**137** H2
Stumperlowe Cft *FUL* S10 ....**137** H1
Stumperlowe Hall Cha
  FUL S10 ....**137** H1
Stumperlowe Hall Rd
  FUL S10 ....**137** H3
Stumperlowe La *FUL* S10 ......**137** H2
Stumperlowe Park Rd
  FUL S10 ....**137** H1
Stumperlowe Vw *FUL* S10 .....**137** H1
Stupton Rd *DARN/MH* S9 ....**116** C2
Sturge Cft *SHEFP/MNR* S2 ....**140** B4
Sturton Cl *DONS/BSCR* DN4 ....**73** G2
Sturton Cft *RHAM/THRY* S65 ..**99** C5
Sturton Rd *ATT* S4 ....**115** G4
Sudbury Cl *CHSW* S40 ....**186** B4
Sudbury Dr *AU/AST/KP* S26 ..**145** G3
Sudbury St *OWL* S3 ....**125** H2
Sudhall Cl *CHNE* S41 ....**186** D1
Suffolk Cl *DIN* S25 ....**148** C2
Suffolk Rd *DONS/BSCR* DN4 ....**71** H2
  SHEFP/MNR S2 ....**11** H5
Sulby Gv *BSLY* S70 ....**32** D4
Summerdale Rd
  CUD/GR S72 ....**21** G2
Summerfield
  RHAM/THRY S65 ....**9** H4
Summerfield Crs
  STV/CWN S43 ....**188** C1
Summerfield Rd
  CHSW S40 ....**4** E7
  DRON S18 ....**168** B5
Summerfield St *ECC* S11 ....**10** C7
Summer La *BSLYN/ROY* S71 ....**12** B5
  DOD/DAR S75 ....**2** C2
  TOT/DORE S17 ....**160** C4
  WMB/DAR S73 ....**49** C3
Summerley Lower Rd
  DRON S18 ....**172** A1
Summerley Rd *DRON* S18 .....**172** A1
Summer Rd *BSLYN/ROY* S71 ...**12** B5
Summerskill Gn
  STV/CWN S43 ....**189** G2
Summer St *BSLY* S70 ....**2** D3
  OWL S3 ....**10** B2
Summer Vw *BSLYN/ROY* S71 ..**15** F1
Summerwood Cft
  DRON S18 ....**170** D1
Summerwood La
  DRON S18 ....**162** D5
Summerwood Pl
  DRON S18 ....**170** D1
Sumner Rd
  RHAM/THRY S65 ....**9** J1
Sunderland St *ECC* S11 ....**139** G1
Sunderland Ter *BSLY* S70 ....**3** K6
Sundew Cft *CHPT/GREN* S35 ...**80** B3
Sundew Gdns
  CHPT/GREN S35 ....**80** B2
Sundown Pl *HAN/WDH* S13 ...**142** D2
Sundown Rd
  HAN/WDH S13 ....**142** D2
Sun Lea Flats
  RHAM/THRY S65 * **9** J3
Sunningdale Cl *CHSW* S40 ....**192** A5
  DONS/BSCR DN4 ....**74** D2
  MEX/SWTN S64 ....**82** B2
Sunningdale Dr *CUD/GR* S72 ..**17** C3
Sunningdale Mt *ECC* S11 ....**138** D5

Sunningdale Ri CHSW S40 ....191 G4
Sunningdale Rd DIN S25....148 D1
  WHHL DN2 ....41 E5
Sunny Bank FUL S10 ....10 C7
  HOY S74...........................62 B2
Sunnybank Crs RHAM S60....118 C4
Sunny Bank Dr
  CUD/GR S72 ....21 H3
Sunny Bank Ri HOY S74........62 C2
Sunny Bank Rd
  STKB/PEN S36 ....77 E5
Sunny Bar DON 6 D3
Sunnybrook Cl HOY S74........62 A4
Sunny Brook Cl
  STV/CWN S43..................185 E3
Sunnyside ARMTH DN3 ....29 E5
  ARMTH DN3 ....59 G5
Sunnyside Cl DIN S25 ....148 C2
Sunny Springs CHNE S41........5 C1
Sunnyvale Av
  TOT/DORE S17 ....160 D4
Sunnyvale Rd
  TOT/DORE S17 ....160 D4
Surbiton St DARN/MH S9..116 D4
Surrey La BSLY S70.............31 H3
Surrey La SHEF S1 ....11 H5
Surrey Pl SHEF S1 ....11 H5
Surrey Rd DONS/BSCR DN4...71 H1
  SHEF S1 ....11 G4
Surtees Cl MALT S66 ....110 C1
Sussex Av ATT S4 ....126 C2
  CHPT/GREN S35 ....94 A1
Sussex St ATT S4 ....126 C3
  OWL S3 ....126 C2
Suthard Cross Rd
  FUL S10 * 124 D3
Sutherland Rd ATT S4 ....126 C1
Sutherland St ATT S4...........126 C1
Sutton Av BSLYN/ROY S71....14 C4
Sutton Crs STV/CWN S43 ....189 G2
Sutton Hall Rd BSVR S44 ....196 B4
Sutton Rd ARMTH DN3.........29 F2
Sutton St OWL S3 ....10 C3
Sutton Vw BSVR S44...........197 E4
Swaddale Av CHNE S41.......187 H3
Swaddale Cl CHNE S41.......187 H3
Swaith Av BTLY DN5...........39 F3
Swaithe Cl BTLY DN5...........39 F3
Swaithedale BSLY S70 ....32 D5
Swaithe Vw BSLY S70...........32 D5
Swale Cl DEARNE S63 ....11 K5
Swaledale Dr WMB/DAR S73..50 C2
Swaledale Rd ABRD S7.........139 F5
Swale Dr CHPT/GREN S35....93 C1
Swale Gdns DARN/MH S9....128 A3
Swale Rd KIMB S61 ....97 E3
Swallow Cl BSLY S70...........32 D5
Swallow Ct NROS/TKH DN11..91 G2
Swallow Crs RHAM S60.........32 D5
Swallow La AU/AST/KP S26...145 G4
Swallow Wood Cl
  RHAM S60 ....130 A3
Swallowwood Ct
  DEARNE S63 ....63 H2
Swallow Wood Ct
  HAN/WDH S13 ....143 E4
Swallow Wood Rd
  AU/AST/KP S26 ....144 C3
Swamp Wk ST/HB/BR S6..114 B5
Swanbourne Pl SHEFN S5 ....102 C5
Swanbourne Rd SHEFN S5....102 C4
Swanee Rd BSLY S70...........32 B4
Swannington Cl
  DONS/BSCR DN4 ....74 C1
Swan Rd AU/AST/KP S26...145 G4
Swan St BTLY DN5 ....39 H1
  RHAM S60 ....130 A3
Swanwick St CHNE S41........179 G4
Swarcliffe Rd DARN/MH S9..127 G2
Swathwick Cl RCH S42.........195 E3
Swathwick La RCH S42.........194 C3
Sweyn Cft BSLY S70 * 32 A5
Swifte Rd RHAM S60 ....119 G1
Swift Ri KIMB S61...........82 C5
Swift Rd DOD/DAR S75...........2 D2
Swift Wy SHEF/MNR S2.......127 E5
Swinburne Av
  AWLS/ASK DN6 ....25 E2
  DONS/BSCR DN4 ....71 H2
Swinburne Pl
  RHAM/THRY S65 ....106 D4
Swinston Hill Gdns
  DIN S25 ....135 E5
Swinston Hill Rd DIN S25 ....149 G2
Swinton St MEX/SWTN S64...66 B4
Swinton St OWL S3 ....126 A2
Swithland Cl CHNE S41 ....192 D5
Sycamore Av ARMTH DN3.....43 E3
  AU/AST/KP S26 ....159 F3
  CHSW S40.......................4 B7
  CUD/GR S72 ....16 D5
  CUD/GR S72 ....23 F2
  DRON S18.......................163 E5
  MALT S66...................64 C2
Sycamore Cl BSVR S44 ....197 F2
Sycamore Ct ECC S11 ....139 E3
  MEX/SWTN S64 ....66 C3
Sycamore Crs DEARNE S63...65 F3
Sycamore Dr
  BSLYN/ROY S71 ....15 E1
  BSVR S44 ....193 F1
  ECK/KIL S21...................168 A3

Sycamore Farm Cl
  MALT S66...................121 F1
Sycamore Gv CONI DN12......88 C2
  DONS/BSCR DN4 ....58 B5
Sycamore House Rd
  SHEFN S5...................103 F3
Sycamore La STV/CWN S43..177 F5
  STV/CWN S43...................181 E5
Sycamore Rd
  CHPT/GREN S35 ....102 B1
  MEX/SWTN S64 ....66 C3
  RHAM/THRY S65 ....98 D5
  STKB/PEN S36 ....76 C3
  STV/CWN S43...................180 D5
The Sycamores BTLY DN5....38 C2
Sycamore St DOD/DAR S75....2 B3
  MOS S20...................156 C5
Sycamore Vw BTLY DN5.......54 B4
Sycamore Wk STKB/PEN S36..44 D3
Syday La ECK/KIL S21.........176 B2
Sydney Rd ST/HB/BR S6.......125 F3
Sydney St CHSW S40.............4 B4
Syke Cft BSLYN/ROY S71.......12 C4
Sykes Av DOD/DAR S75.........2 D2
Sykes Ct MEX/SWTN S64......86 B2
Sykes St BSLY S70...........31 F3
Sylvan Cl CHNE S41.........192 D5
  MALT S66...................111 F2
Sylvester Av
  DONS/BSCR DN4 ....56 A4
Sylvester Gdns SHEF S1......11 G6
Sylvester St SHEF S1 ....11 F7
Sylvestria Ct
  NROS/TKH DN11...........91 G2
Sylvia Cl HAN/WDH S13 *...143 H1
Sylvia Rd DRON S18...........178 D1
Symes Gdns
  DONS/BSCR DN4 ....74 C2
Symonds Av RAW S62.........84 C3
Symons Crs SHEFN S5 ....101 H4

T

Tadcaster Cl CONI DN12.......88 A1
Tadcaster Crs SHEFS S8 ....152 D1
Tadcaster Rd SHEFS S8......152 D1
Tadcaster Wy SHEFS S8......152 D1
Taddington Rd CHSW S40 *..186 B4
Talbot Crs CHNE S41.........193 F5
  SHEFP/MNR S2..................11 K5
Talbot Gdns SHEFP/MNR S2..11 K5
Talbot Pl SHEFP/MNR S2.....126 C5
Talbot Rd MEX/SWTN S64.....66 D5
  SHEFP/MNR S2..................126 C4
  STKB/PEN S36 ....44 C3
Talbot St CHNE S41.........193 F5
  SHEFP/MNR S2..................11 K5
Tallys End STV/CWN S43 ....177 E5
Talmont Rd ECC S11 ....138 D4
Tamar Cl DOD/DAR S75........14 A4
Tanfield Cl BSLYN/ROY S71...12 A5
Tanfield Rd ST/HB/BR S6.....114 B3
Tanfield Wy MALT S66.........108 B5
Tankersley La HOY S74........60 D4
Tank Rw BSLYN/ROY S71.....32 D1
Tannery Cl HAN/WDH S13....143 F4
Tannery Rd HAN/WDH S13...143 F4
Tansley Dr CHSW S40.........186 A4
  DARN/MH S9...................103 H5
Tansley St DARN/MH S9......103 H5
Tansley Wy STV/CWN S43....189 G3
Tap La CHSW S40.................4 C4
Taplin Rd ST/HB/BR S6.......113 H4
Tapton Bank FUL S10 ....124 C4
Tapton Crescent Rd
  FUL S10...................124 D5
Tapton Hill Rd FUL S10......124 C4
Tapton House Rd FUL S10...124 D5
Tapton La CHNE S41 ....5 H3
Tapton Ms FUL S10...........124 D5
Tapton Lock Hl CHNE S41...187 H3
Tapton Park Mt FUL S10.....138 B1
Tapton Park Rd FUL S10....138 B1
Tapton Ter CHNE S41.........5 H2
Tapton V CHNE S41...........188 A4
Tapton View Rd CHNE S41...187 F4
Taptonville Crs FUL S10......125 E5
Taptonville Rd FUL S10......125 E4
Tarleton Cl ARMTH DN3......188 D5
Tasker Rd FUL S10...........124 D4
Tasman Gv MALT S66.........110 C2
Tatenhill Gdns
  DONS/BSCR DN4 ....74 C2
Taunton Av DARN/MH S9....116 D1
Taunton Gdns
  MEX/SWTN S64 ....67 G2
Taunton Gv MEX/SWTN S64..67 G2
Taverner Cl CHPT/GREN S35..80 B2
Taverner Cft
  CHPT/GREN S35 ....80 C3
Taverner Wy
  CHPT/GREN S35 ....80 C3
Tavy Cl DONS/BSCR DN4....7 J7
Tay Cl DOD/DAR S75...........14 A5
  DRON S18...................170 B1
Taylor Crs CHNE S41.........193 F5
  CUD/GR S72 ....23 E2
Taylor Rw BSLY S70.............3 H6
  DEARNE S63 *...............64 D4

Taylors Cl RAW S62...........98 A4
Taylors Ct RAW S62...........98 A4
Taylors La RAW S62...........98 A3
Taylor St CONI DN12...........89 F1
Tay St ST/HB/BR S6...........10 A1
T Benedict Ct
  SHEFP/MNR S2 *...........140 D2
Teesdale Rd HACK/IN S12...155 H4
  KIMB S61...................96 D3
Teeside Cl BTLY DN5...........58 D2
Telford Crs STV/CWN S43...192 H4
Telford Rd BTLY DN5...........39 F5
Telson Cl MEX/SWTN S64....65 G5
Temperance St
  MEX/SWTN S64 ....86 B1
Tempest Av BTLY DN5.........55 F1
Templar Cl MALT S66.........132 D1
Temple Crs MALT S66.........108 D5
Temple Gdns
  DONS/BSCR DN4 ....74 B1
Temple Rd RHAM S60.........117 H1
Templestowe Ga CONI DN12..89 C1
Temple Wy BSLYN/ROY S71..20 D4
Ten Acre Rd KIMB S61.......104 D1
Tenby Gdns
  DONS/BSCR DN4 ....71 G1
Ten Lands La
  HOR/CROF WF4 ....13 F2
Tennyson Av ARMTH DN3.....35 E3
  BTLY DN5...................55 F1
  CHSW S40.......................4 B3
  MEX/SWTN S64 ....86 B1
Tennyson Cl DIN S25.........135 E5
  STKB/PEN S36 ....44 D2
Tennyson Ri DEARNE S63....64 C1
Tennyson Rd
  BSLYN/ROY S71 ....20 B3
  BTLY DN5...................39 H1
  MALT S66...................111 E4
  RHAM/THRY S65 ....106 D3
  ST/HB/BR S6...................125 F1
Ten Pound Wk
  DONS/BSCR DN4 ....56 B5
Tenter Balk La
  AWLS/ASK DN6 ....25 E2
Tenterden Rd SHEFN S5.....103 F5
Tenter Hl STKB/PEN S36......44 A2
Tenter La DONS/BSCR DN4...70 C2
Tenter Rd DONS/BSCR DN4...70 C2
Tenters Gn BSLY S70...........47 H1
  SHEF S1...................11 F2
Terminus Rd RHAM S60......152 A2
Terrace Rd RAW S62...........98 B2
Terrey Rd TOT/DORE S17....161 E3
Terry St DARN/MH S9.........116 D5
Tetney Rd FUL S10...........138 B1
Tewitt Rd BTLY DN5...........26 C3
Teynham Dr SHEFN S5.......114 D2
Teynham Rd SHEFN S5......114 C2
Thackeray Av RAW S62.......85 H4
Thames St RHAM S60...........8 D3
Theably Gdns
  DONS/BSCR DN4 ....73 G1
Theatre La CHNE S41...........5 H3
Thellusson Av BTLY DN5......38 C4
Theobald Av
  DONS/BSCR DN4 ....7 H6
Theobald Cl
  DONS/BSCR DN4 ....7 G7
Thicket Dr MALT S66.........111 F2
Thicket La ST/HB/BR S6......48 C1
Third Av AWLS/ASK DN6.....25 G3
Thirlmere Dr DIN S25.........148 D2
  DRON S18...................171 E1
Thirlmere Rd ABRD S7.......139 F5
  BSLYN/ROY S71 ....3 J4
  CHNE S41...................186 C2
Thirlwall Av CONI DN12......88 C1
Thirlwell Rd SHEFS S8......140 A4
Thirsk Cl CONI DN12...........88 A1
Thistley Ct CUD/GR S72......17 H4
Thomas St AU/AST/KP S26..159 H3
  BSLY S70...................3 G6
  BSLY S70...................32 A5
  MEX/SWTN S64 ....86 C4
  SHEF S1...................10 E5
  WMB/DAR S73...................54 C3
Thompson Cl CHNE S41......187 G1
  MALT S66...................110 C1
  RAW S62...................84 C3
Thompson Dr
  MEX/SWTN S64 ....86 A2
Thompson Gdns
  CHPT/GREN S35 ....80 A3
Thompson Rd ECC S11......139 F1
  WMB/DAR S73...................50 B3
Thompson St CHNE S41.....187 G1
Thomson Av
  DONS/BSCR DN4 ....71 F1
Thomson Cl DEARNE S63....65 F2
Thoresby Av
  BSLYN/ROY S71 ....20 D4
  DONS/BSCR DN4 ....7 J7
  STV/CWN S43...................185 G2
Thoresby Cl
  AU/AST/KP S26 ....145 H3
Thoresby Pl
  STV/CWN S43 * 189 G3
Thoresby Rd
  ST/HB/BR S6...................114 A5

Thornborough Cl
  SHEFP/MNR S2...........140 C3
Thornborough Pl
  SHEFP/MNR S2...........140 C3
Thornborough Rd
  SHEFP/MNR S2...........140 B3
Thornbridge Av
  HACK/IN S12...............155 F2
Thornbridge Cl
  HACK/IN S12...............155 F2
Thornbridge Crs CHSW S40..195 F1
  HACK/IN S12...............155 G2
Thornbridge Dr
  HACK/IN S12...............155 F2
Thornbridge Gv
  HACK/IN S12...............155 F2
Thornbridge La
  HACK/IN S12...............155 G2
Thornbridge Pl
  HACK/IN S12...............155 G2
Thornbridge Ri
  HACK/IN S12...............155 G2
Thornbridge Rd
  HACK/IN S12...............155 F2
Thornbridge Wy
  HACK/IN S12...............155 G2
Thornbrook Cl
  CHPT/GREN S35 ....81 E5
Thornbrook Gdns
  CHPT/GREN S35 ....81 E5
Thornbrook Ms
  CHPT/GREN S35 ....81 E5
Thorncliffe Cl
  AU/AST/KP S26 ....144 D4
Thorncliffe La
  CHPT/GREN S35 ....80 D4
Thorncliffe Rd
  CHPT/GREN S35 ....81 E3
Thorncliffe Vw
  DOD/DAR S75...................60 C3
Thorndale Rd RHAM S60....118 D4
Thorndon Cl CHNE S41......187 F3
Thorne Cl BSLYN/ROY S71...14 C5
Thornely Av DOD/DAR S75...30 B2
Thorne Rd ABRD S7...........139 G5
  ARMTH DN3...................29 F5
  DON DN1...................41 J4
  WHHL DN2...................41 E4
Thornfield Av CHSW S40....191 F3
Thorn Garth BTLY DN5.......39 G4
Thornham Cl ARMTH DN3.....42 D5
Thornham La ARMTH DN3.....43 H4
Thornhill Av RHAM S60......118 D5
  WHHL DN2...................41 F4
Thornhill Edge RHAM S60....8 C3
Thorn La WHHL DN2...........28 D5
Thornley Brook
  DEARNE S63...................36 D2
Thornley Sq DEARNE S63....36 D2
Thorn Rd RHAM/THRY S65...86 B2
Thornsett Gdns
  TOT/DORE S17...............161 F1
Thornsett Rd ABRD S7.......139 G5
Thorntondale Rd BTLY DN5..38 D4
Thornton Pl DRON S18.......170 A2
Thornton Rd BSLY S70........32 C3
Thornton St CHNE S41......104 C4
Thornton Ter BSLY S70.......32 C3
Thorntree La HAN/WDH S13..95 F3
Thorntree La DOD/DAR S75...2 C2
Thornwell Gv CUD/GR S72...21 G1
Thornwood Cl DEARNE S63...82 E5
Thorpe Gn MOS S20...........156 D3
Thorpehall Rd ARMTH DN3...29 G4
Thorpe House Av SHEFS S8..153 F1
Thorpe House Ri SHEFS S8..153 F1
Thorpe House Rd
  SHEFS S8...................153 F1
Thorpe La BTLY DN5...........54 B4
Thorpe St KIMB S61...........95 E1
Thorpleigh Rd
  STV/CWN S43...................182 D1
Three Hills Cl
  RHAM/THRY S65 ....99 H3
Three Nooks La CUD/GR S72..16 D3
Threshfield Wy
  HACK/IN S12...............156 B2
Thrumpton Rd
  BSLYN/ROY S71 ....14 D3
Thrush Av RHAM S60.........118 D4
Thrush St ST/HB/BR S6......124 D1
Thrybergh Ct CONI DN12....17 E4
Thrybergh Hall Rd RAW S62..85 H5
Thundercliffe Rd KIMB S61..103 H2
Thurbrook Gdns MALT S66..133 G1

Thurnscoe La CUD/GR S72...36 B1
Thurnscoe Rd DEARNE S63...53 E3
Thurstan Av SHEFS S8......152 C5
Tiber Vw RHAM S60...........118 C2
Tickhill Rd DONS/BSCR DN4...7 F3
Tickhill Sq CONI DN12.........68 B5
Tickhill St CONI DN12.........68 B4
Tickhill Wy SHEFN S5........91 G3
Tideswell Cl STV/CWN S43..189 G1
Tideswell Rd SHEFN S5.....102 D5
Tiercel Ms DIN S25...........134 C4
Tilford Rd HAN/WDH S13...143 G4
Tillotson Cl SHEFS S8.......140 A4
Tillotson Ri SHEFS S8.......140 A4
Tilts La BTLY DN5...........27 F1
Timothy Wood Av BSLY S70..47 H5
Tingle Bridge Av
  WMB/DAR S73...................63 E1
Tingle Bridge Crs
  WMB/DAR S73...................63 E1
Tingle Bridge La
  WMB/DAR S73...................63 E1
Tingle Cl WMB/DAR S73......63 E1
Tinker La FUL S10...........124 D2
  HOY S74...................61 E2
Tinker Rd RAW S62...........85 G5
Tinsley Park Cl
  DARN/MH S9...................117 E5
Tinsley Park Rd
  DARN/MH S9...................116 D5
Tinsley Rd HOY S74...........61 H1
Tippit La CUD/GR S72.........22 A2
Tipton St DARN/MH S9......103 H5
Tissington Ct CHSW S40....186 B4
Tithe Barn Av
  HAN/WDH S13 ....143 F3
Tithe Barn Cl
  HAN/WDH S13 ....143 G3
Tithe Barn Ct
  MEX/SWTN S64 ....53 H5
Tithe Barn La
  HAN/WDH S13 ....143 G4
Tithe Barn Wy
  HAN/WDH S13 ....143 F3
Tithe Laithe HOY S74.........62 A2
Titterton Cl DARN/MH S9...127 G1
Titterton St DARN/MH S9...127 G1
Tiverton Cl MEX/SWTN S64..86 B1
Toad La MALT S66...........132 D2
Tockwith Rd DARN/MH S9..127 H2
Todmorden Cl CONI DN12...68 A5
Todwick Rd
  AU/AST/KP S26 ....147 G2
  SHEFS S8...................152 C1
Tofts La ST/HB/BR S6.......123 G3
Toftstead ARMTH DN3.........42 D5
Toftwood Av FUL S10.......124 D3
Toftwood Rd FUL S10.......124 D3
Togo St DEARNE S63...........37 E3
Toll Bar Av HACK/IN S12 *..141 E5
Toll Bar Cl HACK/IN S12....141 E5
Toll Bar Dr HACK/IN S12....141 E5
Toll Bar Rd HACK/IN S12...141 E5
  MEX/SWTN S64 ....65 H5
  RHAM/THRY S65 ....107 C5
Tollbridge Rd
  STV/CWN S43...................182 D4
Tollgate Cl CUD/GR S72......17 F2
Toll House Md MOS S20....166 C5
Tom La FUL S10...........124 D3
Tomlinson Rd HOY S74.......62 B2
Tompson Hi
  CHPT/GREN S35 ....79 H4
Tooker Rd RHAM S60...........9 G6
Topcliffe Rd BSLYN/ROY S71..20 A2
Top Field La
  RHAM/THRY S65 ....107 F1
Top Fold BSLYN/ROY S71 *...33 G2
Top Hall Rd DONS/BSCR DN4..74 B3
Toppham Dr SHEFS S8.......162 D2
Toppham Rd SHEFS S8......162 D2
Toppham Wy SHEFS S8......162 D2
Top Pingle Cl STV/CWN S43..188 C2
Top Rd BSVR S44...........193 H2
Top Rw BSLYN/ROY S71 *....33 G2
Top Side CHPT/GREN S35....92 D5
Top Tree Wy
  RHAM/THRY S65 ....99 H3
Torbay Rd ATT S4...........114 C1
Tor Cl BSLYN/ROY S71........20 B2
Torksey Cl DONS/BSCR DN4..74 A2
Torksey Rd SHEFN S5.......102 D5
Torne Cl DONS/BSCR DN4...74 C2
Torry Cl HAN/WDH S13.......143 G4
Tortmayns AU/AST/KP S26..147 E5
Torver Dr DEARNE S63........53 E4
Tor Wy RHAM S60...........118 D5
Torwood Dr SHEFS S8.......162 C1
Totley Brook Cl
  TOT/DORE S17 * 160 D3
Totley Brook Cft
  TOT/DORE S17 ....160 D3
Totley Brook Gln
  TOT/DORE S17 ....160 D3
Totley Brook Gv
  TOT/DORE S17 ....160 D3
Totley Brook Rd
  TOT/DORE S17 ....160 D3
Totley Brook Wy
  TOT/DORE S17 ....160 D3
Totley Grange Cl
  TOT/DORE S17 * 160 D4

Totley Grange Rd
TOT/DORE S17 ....160 D4
Totley Hall Cft
TOT/DORE S17 ....160 D5
Totley Hall Dr
TOT/DORE S17 ....160 D4
Totley Hall La
TOT/DORE S17 ....160 D5
Totley Hall Md
TOT/DORE S17 ....160 D5
Totley Mt STV/CWN S43 ...188 B1
Towcester Wy
MEX/SWTN S64 ....67 C2
Tower Cl BTLY DN5 ....38 D1
SHEFP/MNR S2 ....140 C2
Tower Crs BSVR S44 ....197 E4
Tower Dr SHEFP/MNR S2 ...140 C2
Tower St BSLY S70 ....31 G3
DRON S18 ....172 B2
Town End BSVR S44 ....196 D2
DRON S18 ....172 B2
Town End Av
AU/AST/KP S26 ....145 F2
Townend
RHAM/THRY S65 ....99 G4
Townend Cl RHAM S60 .....130 A3
Townend La STKB/PEN S36 ...77 G4
Town End Rd
CHPT/GREN S35 ....101 H1
Townend St FUL S10 ....125 E3
Town Flds DON DN1 * 7 F4
Townfield Vls DON DN1 * 7 F3
Towngate STKB/PEN S36 ....44 A2
Townhead Rd
TOT/DORE S17 ....160 C1
Townhead St SHEF S1 ......11 F3
Townlands Cl
WMB/DAR S73 ....50 D1
Town La KIMB S61 ....96 B4
Town Moor Av WHHL DN2 ...7 H2
Town St DARN/MH S9 ......117 F1
RHAM S60 ....105 H5
Town View Av BTLY DN5 .....38 A2
Town Wells Ct DIN S25 .....148 B3
Toyne St FUL S10 ....125 E4
Trafalgar St ST/HB/BR S6 ...101 E5
Trafalgar St SHEF S1 ....10 E4
Traffic Ter CHNE S41 * 192 D5
STV/CWN S43 ....181 F2
Trafford Ct DON DN1 * 6 B4
Trafford Wy DON DN1 ....6 B4
Tranmoor Av
DONS/BSCR DN4 ....74 A1
Tranmoor Ct HOY S74 ....61 F3
Trans Pennine Trail
BSLY S70 ....47 H1
BTLY DN5 ....69 G2
CHPT/GREN S35 ....93 E3
DARN/MH S9 ....116 B5
DEARNE S63 ....52 A4
DOD/DAR S75 ....60 A4
ECK/KIL S21 ....175 G3
MOS S20 ....144 A5
RHAM S60 ....8 C6
SHEFN S5 ....101 H4
STKB/PEN S36 ....44 A3
STV/CWN S43 ....182 B3
Trap La ECC S11 ....138 A4
Travey Rd SHEFP/MNR S2 ...141 G3
Travis Gdns
DONS/BSCR DN4 ....55 F4
Travis Pl FUL S10 ....10 C6
Tredis Cl BSLYN/ROY S71 ...20 B4
Treecrest Rd DOD/DAR S75 ...19 G3
Treefield Cl KIMB S61 ....97 E3
Treelands DOD/DAR S75 ....18 D4
Treeneuk Cl CHSW S40 ....191 H4
Tree Root Wk FUL S10 .....125 E4
Treeton La RHAM S60 ......129 H2
Treetown Crs RHAM S60 ...130 A2
Treherne Rd RHAM S60 ......9 J7
Trelawney Wk BSLY S70 ....31 H5
Trent Cl CHNE S41 ....4 E1
Trent Gdns ARMTH DN3 .....29 F2
Trent Gv DRON S18 ....168 F5
Trentham Ct RHAM S60 ....118 D4
Trenton Cl HAN/WDH S13 ..143 H4
Trenton Ri HAN/WDH S13 ..143 H4
Trent St DARN/MH S9 ......127 F2
Trent Ter CONI DN12 * 69 E5
Treswell Crs ST/HB/BR S6 * ...114 A4
Trevorrow Crs CHSW S40 ....5 G7
Trewan Ct BSLYN/ROY S71 ...20 B4
Trickett Rd CHPT/GREN S35 ...80 A3
ST/HB/BR S6 ....114 A5
Trinity Cl CHNE S41 ....4 E1
Trinity St OWL S3 ....11 F1
Trippet La SHEF S1 ....11 F3
Tristford Cl RHAM S60 ......129 H1
Troon Cl CHSW S40 ....191 G4
Troon Wk DIN S25 ....134 D5
Troughbrook Rd
STV/CWN S43 ....181 F5
Troutbeck Cl DEARNE S63 ...37 E3
Troutbeck Rd ABRD S7 .....152 C1
Trowell Wy BSLYN/ROY S71 ...14 D4
Trueman Gn MALT S66 .....110 C2
Trueman Ter
BSLYN/ROY S71 ....21 E5
Truman Gv STKB/PEN S36 ...77 H2

Truman St BTLY DN5 ....39 G1
Truro Av WHHL DN2 ....41 G2
Truro Ct BSLYN/ROY S71 ....20 B4
Truswell Av FUL S10 ....124 C3
Truswell Rd FUL S10 ....124 C4
Tudor Ct CUD/GR S72 ....23 E1
Tudor Rd AWLS/ASK DN6 ....25 G4
WHHL DN2 ....57 F1
Tudor St DEARNE S63 ....37 G2
NROS/TKH DN11 ....91 F3
STV/CWN S43 ....182 B4
Tudor Wy BSLY S70 ....32 A5
Tuffolds Cl SHEFP/MNR S2 ...141 G3
Tulip Tree Cl MOS S20 ......144 C5
Tullibardine Rd ECC S11 ....138 D4
Tumbling La BSLYN/ROY S71 ...21 F1
Tummon Rd
SHEFP/MNR S2 ....127 E5
Tummon St KIMB S61 ....8 A5
Tune St BSLY S70 ....3 J7
WMB/DAR S73 ....50 A3
Tunstall Gn CHSW S40 ....4 A7
Tunstall Wy CHSW S40 ....4 A7
Tunwell Av SHEFN S5 ....102 B2
Tunwell Dr SHEFN S5 ....102 B2
Tunwell Greave SHEFN S5 ...102 B2
Turie Av SHEFN S5 ....102 A3
Turie Crs SHEFN S5 ....102 A3
Turnberry Cl CHSW S40 .....191 G4
Turnberry Ct BTLY DN5 ......39 G2
Turnberry Gv CUD/GR S72 * ...17 E3
Turnberry Wy DIN S25 ......148 D1
Turnbull Cl CHSW S40 ......192 B3
Turner Av WMB/DAR S73 ....49 H4
Turner Cl DRON S18 ....170 D2
RAW S62 ....98 C2
Turner Dr STV/CWN S43 ...189 F2
Turner La RHAM S60 ....119 H5
Turners La FUL S10 ....125 E5
Turner St CUD/GR S72 ....36 A1
SHEFP/MNR S2 ....11 H5
Turner's Cl HOY S74 ....62 B1
Turnesc Gv DEARNE S63 ....37 F3
Turnoaks La CHSW S40 .....192 C5
Turnpike Cft
CHPT/GREN S35 ....93 E5
Turnshaw Av
AU/AST/KP S26 ....145 E1
Turnshaw Farm
AU/AST/KP S26 ....131 H4
Turton Rd RHAM/THRY S65 ...109 F1
Tuscany Gdns BSLY S70 .....32 B2
Tutbury Gdns
DONS/BSCR DN4 ....74 C1
Tuxford Crs BSLYN/ROY S71 ...20 D5
Twelve Lands Cl
DOD/DAR S75 ....60 C3
The Twenty Lands
RHAM S60 ....130 A4
Twentywell Dr
TOT/DORE S17 ....161 H2
Twentywell La
TOT/DORE S17 ....161 G1
Twentywell Ri
TOT/DORE S17 ....161 H1
Twentywell Rd
TOT/DORE S17 ....161 H3
Twentywell Vw
TOT/DORE S17 ....161 H3
Twibell St BSLYN/ROY S71 ...3 J1
Twickenham Cl MOS S20 ...167 E3
Twickenham Ct MOS S20 ...167 E3
Twickenham Crs MOS S20 ...167 E3
Twickenham Gld MOS S20 ...167 E3
Twickenham Gln MOS S20 ...167 E3
Twickenham Gv MOS S20 ...167 E2
Twigg Ct MEX/SWTN S64 ....86 D2
Twitchill Dr HAN/WDH S13 ..143 F4
Twyford Cl MEX/SWTN S64 ...65 G5
Tyas Pl MEX/SWTN S64 * ...67 G3
Tyas Rd MOS S20 ....102 A2
Tye Rd MOS S20 ....157 G2
Tyers Hill Cottages
BSLYN/ROY S71 * 34 B2
Tyler St DARN/MH S9 ....116 D1
Tyler Wy DARN/MH S9 ......116 D1
Tylney Rd CHSW S40 ....191 F5
SHEFP/MNR S2 ....140 D1
Tynedale Ct ARMTH DN3 ....29 C3
Tynker Av MOS S20 ....157 G2
Tyzack Rd SHEFS S8 ....152 C3

U

Ulley Crs HAN/WDH S13 .....141 H3
Ulley La AU/AST/KP S26 .....145 G2
Ulley Rd HAN/WDH S13 .....141 H3
Ulley Vw AU/AST/KP S26 ....131 F5
Ullswater Av MOS S20 ......167 E2
Ullswater Cl DEARNE S63 ....53 E4
DRON S18 ....148 C1
DRON S18 ....170 C1
MOS S20 ....167 E2
Ullswater Dr DRON S18 .....170 C2
Ullswater Pl DRON S18 .....170 C1
Ullswater Rd
BSLYN/ROY S71 ....33 H2
MEX/SWTN S64 ....67 H2
Ulrica Dr MALT S66 ....133 E1
Ulverston Rd CHNE S41 ....186 D2
SHEFS S8 ....152 C1

Undercliffe Rd
ST/HB/BR S6 ....124 B2
Undergate Rd DIN S25 ......134 C3
Underhill BSLY S70 ....48 B1
Underhill La ST/HB/BR S6 ...100 D4
Underhill Rd ST/HB/BR S6 ..177 F5
Underwood Av BSLY S70 .....32 B4
Underwood Rd SHEFS S8 ..152 D1
Union Ct BSLY S70 ....3 H6
Union Dr ECC S11 ....139 F4
Union Rd ABRD S7 ....139 F4
ECC S11 ....139 F4
Union St BSLY S70 ....3 G6
DON DN1 ....6 C5
KIMB S61 ....98 D5
SHEF S1 ....11 G5
Union Wk CHSW S40 * 5 J2
Unity Pl RHAM S60 ....9 F5
University Sq Jct OWL S3 ...10 C3
Unstone-Dronfield By-Pass
CHNE S41 ....178 C2
DRON S18 ....162 D5
Unstone Hl DRON S18 ......171 H3
Unstone La CHNE S41 ......179 F1
Unstone St SHEFP/MNR S2 ...140 A1
Unwin Crs STKB/PEN S36 ....44 D4
Unwin St STKB/PEN S36 .....44 D4
Upland Ri CHSW S40 ....191 H5
Uplands Rd ARMTH DN3 .....43 E4
Uplands Wy RAW S62 ....43 E5
Upper Albert Rd SHEFS S8 ..140 B5
Upper Allen St OWL S3 ....10 D2
Upper Clara St KIMB S61 ...104 D3
Upper Cliffe Rd
DOD/DAR S75 ....30 A2
Upper Croft Cl
STV/CWN S43 ....188 C2
Upperfield Cl MALT S66 ....110 D2
Upperfield Rd MALT S66 ....110 C1
Upper Folderings
DOD/DAR S75 ....30 B3
Upper Forest Rd
BSLYN/ROY S71 ....14 D4
Upper Gate Rd
ST/HB/BR S6 ....123 F2
Upper Hanover St FUL S10 ...10 C4
OWL S3 ....10 C5
Upper Hoyland Rd HOY S74 ...61 G1
Upper Ley Ct
CHPT/GREN S35 ....94 A1
Upper Ley Dell
CHPT/GREN S35 ....94 A1
Upper Lum Cl CHNE S41 ...193 F2
Upper Lunns Ct
BSLYN/ROY S71 ....16 A1
Upper May Day Green Ar
BSLY S70 ....3 G4
Upper Millgate RHAM S60 ....9 F4
Upper Moor St
CHSW S40 ....191 F2
Upper Newbold Cl
CHNE S41 ....186 B2
Upper New St BSLY S70 ......3 G6
Upper Rye Cl RHAM S60 ....20 D3
Upper School La DRON S18 ...171 E2
Upper Sheffield Rd
BSLY S70 ....32 A4
Upperthorpe ST/HB/BR S6 ..125 F2
Upperthorpe Gln
ST/HB/BR S6 ....125 F2
Upperthorpe Rd
ECK/KIL S21 ....168 B3
ST/HB/BR S6 ....125 G2
Upper Valley Rd SHEFS S8 ..140 A5
Upper Whiston La
RHAM S60 ....120 A5
Upperwood Hall
WMB/DAR S73 * 34 D4
Upperwood Rd
WMB/DAR S73 ....34 C4
Upper Wortley Rd
KIMB S61 ....95 E2
Upton Cl MALT S66 ....110 C1
WMB/DAR S73 ....49 H1
Upwell Hl ATT S4 ....116 A3
Upwell La ATT S4 ....116 A3
Upwell St ATT S4 ....116 A3
Upwood Cl CHSW S40 ......186 A4
Upwood Rd ST/HB/BR S6 ..113 H5
Urban Rd DONS/BSCR DN4 ...55 H4
Urch Cl CONI DN12 ....89 E2
Uttley Cl MALT S66 ....127 H1
Uttley Cft DARN/MH S9 .....127 H1
Uttley Dr DARN/MH S9 ......127 H1
Uttoxeter Av MEX/SWTN S64 ...67 G2

V

Vaal St BSLY S70 ....32 B2
Vainor Rd ST/HB/BR S6 .....113 G2
Vale Av RHAM/THRY S65 ....99 H4
Vale Cl BSVR S44 ....196 D3
DRON S18 ....171 F2
Vale Ct RHAM/THRY S65 ....99 H4
Vale Crs RHAM/THRY S65 ...99 H4
Vale Gv ST/HB/BR S6 ....113 F4
Valentine Cl SHEFN S5 ......102 C4
Valentine Crs SHEFN S5 .....102 C4
Valentine Rd SHEFN S5 .....102 C4
Vale Rd OWL S3 ....114 D5
RHAM/THRY S65 ....99 H4

Valiant Gdns BTLY DN5 ....55 E2
Valley Crs CHNE S41 ....5 K6
Valley Dr ARMTH DN3 ....59 F5
DEARNE S63 ....63 F2
ECK/KIL S21 ....168 B1
Valley Gv BSLYN/ROY S71 ....21 F2
Valley Rd BSVR S44 ....196 D4
CHNE S41 ....5 K6
CHPT/GREN S35 ....80 C5
ECK/KIL S21 ....168 B1
HACK/IN S12 ....156 C3
MEX/SWTN S64 ....86 C4
SHEFS S8 ....140 A4
STV/CWN S43 ....183 E2
WMB/DAR S73 ....50 C1
Valley Vw BSVR S44 * 197 E5
Valley View Cl CHNE S41 ...193 G5
ECK/KIL S21 * 174 C1
Valley Wy HOY S74 ....62 A3
WMB/DAR S73 ....50 C3
Vancouver Dr DEARNE S63 ...52 D3
Varley Gdns MALT S66 ......108 B3
Varney Rd DEARNE S63 ......65 E3
Vaughan Av DON S6 ....6 E2
Vaughan Rd DOD/DAR S75 ...18 D4
Vauxhall Cl DARN/MH S9 ...103 H5
Vauxhall Rd DARN/MH S9 ...103 H5
Velvet Wood Cl
DOD/DAR S75 ....18 C4
Venetian Crs
WMB/DAR S73 ....34 D5
Ventnor Cl DONS/BSCR DN4 ...71 F1
Ventnor Pl ABRD S7 ....139 H2
Venture Wy CHNE S41 ......179 F5
Venus Ct RHAM S60 ....118 C2
Verdant Wy SHEFS S8 ......102 D4
Verdon St OWL S3 ....126 B2
Verelst Av AU/AST/KP S26 ...145 F1
Vere Rd ST/HB/BR S6 ....114 A2
Verger Cl NROS/TKH DN11 ...91 G2
Vernon Cl BSLY S70 ....31 H3
Vernon Crs BSLY S70 ....31 H3
Vernon Delph FUL S10 ......124 B4
Vernon Dr CHPT/GREN S35 ...80 D5
Vernon Rd BSLY S70 ....31 H5
CHSW S40 ....4 A4
RHAM S60 ....119 H1
TOT/DORE S17 ....161 E2
Vernon St BSLY S70 ....60 D2
BSLYN/ROY S71 ....3 H2
HOY S74 ....61 G3
Vernon St North
BSLYN/ROY S71 ....3 H2
Vernon Ter FUL S10 ....124 C5
Vernon Wy DOD/DAR S75 ...18 D4
MALT S66 ....110 C2
Verona Ri WMB/DAR S73 ....35 E5
Vesey St RAW S62 ....98 B2
Vicarage Cl
CHPT/GREN S35 ....101 E1
DONS/BSCR DN4 ....74 C1
HOY S74 ....62 A2
MEX/SWTN S64 ....67 G4
RHAM/THRY S65 ....107 F1
Vicarage Crs
CHPT/GREN S35 ....101 E1
Vicarage La BSLYN/ROY S71 ...15 G1
RHAM/THRY S65 ....9 F4
TOT/DORE S17 ....160 D1
Vicarage Rd
CHPT/GREN S35 ....101 E1
DARN/MH S9 ....116 B5
Vicarage Wy STKB/PEN S36 ...44 D3
Vicarage Wy BTLY DN5 ......17 F5
Vicar Crs WMB/DAR S73 ....35 F5
Vicar La CHSW S40 ....5 G4
HAN/WDH S13 ....143 F3
SHEF S1 ....11 G2
Vicar Rd DEARNE S63 ....64 D1
WMB/DAR S73 ....35 F5
Vickers Dr SHEFN S5 ....115 H1
Vickers Rd CHPT/GREN S35 ...80 B4
SHEFN S5 ....115 H2
Victoria Av RHAM/THRY S65 ...9 K5
STV/CWN S43 ....182 B3
Victoria Cottages
MEX/SWTN S64 * 66 C3
Victoria Ct ECC S11 ....139 F4
Victoria Crs BSLY S70 ....60 C1
DOD/DAR S75 ....2 D2
Victoria Crs West
DOD/DAR S75 ....2 D2
Victoria Gv STV/CWN S43 ...188 D4
Victoria Ms NROS/TKH DN11 ...91 H2
Victorian Crs WHHL DN2 ......7 H1
Victoria Park Rd
STV/CWN S43 ....188 C4
Victoria Quays
SHEFP/MNR S2 * 11 J2
Victoria Rd AWLS/ASK DN6 ...25 H1
BSLY S70 ....2 D2
BSLYN/ROY S71 ....12 D5
BTLY DN5 ....38 D5
CONI DN12 ....84 D1
DEARNE S63 ....63 D1
DONS/BSCR DN4 ....55 G5
FUL S10 ....10 B7
MEX/SWTN S64 ....66 A1
MOS S20 ....157 F1
RAW S62 ....98 B2
STKB/PEN S36 ....77 E2
WMB/DAR S73 ....50 A2

Victoria Station Rd
SHEFP/MNR S2 ....11 J1
Victoria St BSLY S70 ....2 E3
BSVR S44 ....197 E4
CHNE S41 ....5 F2
CUD/GR S72 ....16 D5
DEARNE S63 ....37 G5
DIN S25 ....135 E4
DRON S18 ....170 D1
HOY S74 ....62 B2
MALT S66 ....111 E5
MEX/SWTN S64 ....86 C4
OWL S3 ....10 D4
RHAM S60 ....8 B5
RHAM S60 ....129 H1
STKB/PEN S36 ....44 D1
STKB/PEN S36 ....76 D2
STV/CWN S43 ....180 D5
WMB/DAR S73 ....35 F4
Victoria St North
CHNE S41 ....5 F2
Victoria St West CHSW S40 ...191 G2
Victoria Ter BSLY S70 ....3 J7
Victoria Vls CHNE S41 * 187 F1
Victoria Wy MALT S66 ......110 B2
Victor Rd TOT/DORE S17 ...161 F1
Victor St ST/HB/BR S6 ......114 B5
Victor Ter BSLY S70 ....3 K6
Viewland Cl CUD/GR S72 ....22 A2
Viewlands Cl MALT S66 .....109 E5
View Rd RHAM/THRY S65 ...106 C1
SHEFP/MNR S2 ....140 A3
View Tree Cl RAW S62 ....81 H2
Vikinglea Cl
SHEFP/MNR S2 ....141 G2
Vikinglea Dr
SHEFP/MNR S2 ....141 H1
Vikinglea Gld
SHEFP/MNR S2 ....141 H1
Vikinglea Rd
SHEFP/MNR S2 ....141 H1
Villa Gdns BTLY DN5 ....26 C2
Village Ct CUD/GR S72 ....17 E5
Village St AWLS/ASK DN6 * ...25 H1
Villa Park Rd
DONS/BSCR DN4 ....58 A5
Villa Rd AWLS/ASK DN6 ......25 F2
Villas Rd BSVR S44 ....196 B3
Villiers Cl SHEFP/MNR S2 ...141 E4
Villiers Dr SHEFP/MNR S2 ...141 E4
Vincent Crs CHSW S40 .....191 F2
Vincent La CHSW S40 ....191 F2
Vincent Rd ABRD S7 ....139 H2
BSLYN/ROY S71 ....21 E4
MALT S66 ....108 D2
Vine Cl BSLYN/ROY S71 ......20 C3
RHAM S60 ....8 C4
Viola Bank SHEFP/MNR S36 ...76 D2
Violet Av MOS S20 ....157 E2
Violet Bank Rd ABRD S7 ...139 G4
Vivian Rd SHEFN S5 ....115 H1
Vizard Rd HOY S74 ....62 B2
Vulcan Rd DARN/MH S9 ....116 D3

W

Wadbrough Rd ECC S11 .....139 F1
Waddington Rd
DOD/DAR S75 ....18 D5
Waddington Wy
RHAM/THRY S65 ....98 C4
Wade Cl RHAM S60 ....106 B5
Wade Meadow
ST/HB/BR S6 ....113 G3
Wade St ATT S4 ....116 A3
DOD/DAR S75 ....18 D5
Wadsley La ST/HB/BR S6 ...113 G2
Wadsley Park Crs
ST/HB/BR S6 ....113 G3
Wadsworth Av
HACK/IN S12 ....142 A5
Wadsworth Cl
HACK/IN S12 ....142 B5
Wadsworth Dr
HACK/IN S12 ....142 B4
RAW S62 ....84 C3
Wadsworth Rd
HACK/IN S12 ....142 A5
MALT S66 ....108 D2
Wadworth Av
NROS/TKH DN11 ....91 H2
Wadworth Ri
RHAM/THRY S65 ....99 G5
Wadworth St CONI DN12 ....68 C4
Wagon Rd KIMB S61 ....97 F3
Wain Av CHNE S41 ....5 J4
Waingate OWL S3 ....11 H2
Wainwright Av
HAN/WDH S13 ....142 B2
WMB/DAR S73 ....49 H2
Wainwright Crs
HAN/WDH S13 ....142 A2
Wainwright Pl
WMB/DAR S73 ....49 H2
Wainwright Rd
DONS/BSCR DN4 ....7 G6
KIMB S61 ....96 D5
Wakefield Rd
BSLYN/ROY S71 ....19 H1
Wakelam Dr ARMTH DN3 ....42 B4

Wake Rd *ABRD* S7................139 G3
Walbank Rd *ARMTH* DN3.......43 E4
Walbank Av *DEARNE* S63........37 E3
Walbrook *BSLY* S70...................48 B1
Walden Av *BTLY* DN5................39 E1
Walden Rd *CHSW/MNR* S2....140 B3
Walders Av *ST/HB/BR* S6.......113 G2
Walders La *STKB/PEN* S36......77 E5
Walesmoor Av
  AU/AST/KP S26.................199 G3
Wales Pl *ST/HB/BR* S6............125 F1
Wales Rd *AU/AST/KP* S26.......159 F3
Waleswood Vw
  AU/AST/KP S26.................145 F4
Waleswood Rd *MOS* S20........158 A1
Waleswood Wy
  AU/AST/KP S26.................158 D2
Walford Rd *ECK/KIL* S21.........168 A1
Walgrove Av *CHSW* S40.............4 A7
Walgrove Rd *CHSW* S40..........191 H2
Walker Cl *CHPT/GREN* S35......93 H2
Walker Pl *RHAM/THRY* S65........9 G3
Walker Rd *DOD/DAR* S75..........60 D3
  KIMB S61................................96 D5
Walkers La *ECK/KIL* S21..........168 B2
Walker St *MEX/SWTN* S64........66 C5
  OWL S3....................................126 B2
  RAW S62...................................85 H5
Walker Vw *RAW* S62..................85 H5
Walkley Bank Cl
  ST/HB/BR S6.........................114 A5
Walkley Bank Rd
  ST/HB/BR S6.........................124 D1
Walkley Crescent Rd
  ST/HB/BR S6.........................124 D1
Walkley La *ST/HB/BR* S6........114 A5
Walkley Rd *ST/HB/BR* S6........125 E1
Walkley St *ST/HB/BR* S6.........125 F2
Walkley Ter *ST/HB/BR* S6.......124 C1
The Walk *BSLY* S70...................60 C2
Wallace Rd *DONS/BSCR* DN4..74 D7
  OWL S3....................................114 D5
Waller Rd *ST/HB/BR* S6..........124 C2
Walling Rd *DARN/MH* S9.........116 D2
Walling Rd *DARN/MH* S9.........116 D2
Wallsend Cottages
  CHNE S41 *..........................187 E4
Wall St *BSLY* S70........................3 F7
Walney Fold
  BSLYN/ROY S71....................20 D1
Walnut Cl *BSLY* S70 *...............31 H3
Walnut Dr *DIN* S25..................134 D5
  ECK/KIL S21..........................168 A3
Walnut Gv *MEX/SWTN* S64......64 B3
Walpole Cl *DONS/BSCR* DN4....71 F3
Walpole Gv *AU/AST/KP* S26....145 F1
Walsker La
  AU/AST/KP S26.....................169 G1
Walsham Dr *BTLY* DN5..............39 E1
Walstow Crs *ARMTH* DN3..........42 A4
Walters Rd *MALT* S66...............111 F3
Walter St *RHAM* S60....................8 C3
  ST/HB/BR S6.........................114 B1
Waltham Cft *CHNE* S41...........193 E5
Waltham Gdns *MOS* S20.........157 G3
Waltham St *BSLY* S70..................3 H6
Waltheof Rd
  SHEFP/MNR S2....................141 G2
Walton Back La *RCH* S42........190 D4
Walton Cl *CHPT/GREN* S35......80 A3
  CHSW S40.............................191 H4
  DRON S18.............................170 A1
Walton Crs *CHSW* S40.................4 A7
Walton Dr *CHSW* S40...................4 B7
Walton Drive Ct *CHSW* S40........4 B7
Walton Fields Rd
  CHSW S40.............................191 H2
  ECC S11.................................139 F1
Walton St *CHSW* S40................191 H5
Walton St North
  DOD/DAR S75........................18 D4
Walton Wk *RCH* S42..................4 C6
Wannop St *RAW* S62..................98 B3
Wansfell Rd *ATT* S4.................116 B3
Wansfell Ter *BSLYN/ROY* S71...3 J5
The Wapping
  RHAM/THRY S65....................87 G4
Warburton Cl
  SHEFP/MNR S2....................140 B3
Warburton Gdns
  SHEFP/MNR S2....................140 C3
Warburton Rd
  SHEFP/MNR S2....................140 C3
Ward Cl *STKB/PEN* S36............44 D4
Warde-Aldam Crs
  MALT S66..............................108 A4
Warde Av *DONS/BSCR* DN4......71 F3
Warden Cl
  DONS/BSCR DN4....................58 C5
Warden St *RHAM* S60..............118 D1
Wardgate Wy *CHSW* S40........186 A4
Ward La *STV/CWN* S43............177 F3
Wardlow Cl *CHSW* S40............192 B4
Wardlow Rd *HACK/IN* S12.......142 B5
Ward Pl *ABRD* S7.....................139 H2
Wardsend Rd *ST/HB/BR* S6....114 B2
Wardsend Road North
  ST/HB/BR S6.........................114 A1
Ward St *STKB/PEN* S36............44 D4

Wareham Ct *MOS* S20.............157 G3
Wareham Gv *DOD/DAR* S75......30 C2
Warehouse La *DEARNE* S63......65 E2
Warley Rd *SHEFP/MNR* S2......141 E1
Warminster Cl *SHEFS* S8.........153 F1
Warminster Crs *SHEFS* S8.......153 F1
Warminster Dr *SHEFS* S8........153 F1
Warminster Pl *SHEFS* S8..........153 F1
Warminster Rd *SHEFS* S8........153 E1
Warmsworth Halt
  DONS/BSCR DN4....................70 B4
Warmsworth Rd
  DONS/BSCR DN4....................71 E2
Warner Av *DOD/DAR* S75.........18 D5
Warner Pl *DOD/DAR* S75............2 A2
Warner Rd *DOD/DAR* S75.........18 D5
  ST/HB/BR S6.........................113 H5
Warner St *CHNE* S41...................5 J7
Warnington Dr
  DONS/BSCR DN4....................74 C3
Warning Tongue La
  DONS/BSCR DN4....................74 D4
Warren Av *RAW* S62...................85 E4
Warren Cl *BSLYN/ROY* S71......12 D4
  DONS/BSCR DN4....................70 C2
  WHHL DN2.............................57 E1
Warren Crs *BSLY* S70.................31 H3
  ECK/KIL S21.........................173 G1
Warren Dr *KIMB* S61................104 D1
Warreners Dr
  RHAM/THRY S65....................99 H4
Warren Gdns
  CHPT/GREN S35....................81 E3
Warren Hl *KIMB* S61................104 A1
Warren House Cl *MALT* S66....108 D3
Warren La *CHPT/GREN* S35......80 D2
  DONS/BSCR DN4....................74 B3
Warren Mt *KIMB* S61...............104 D1
Warren Pl *BSLY* S70..................31 H3
Warren Quarry La *BSLY* S70 *....3 G7
Warren Ri *DRON* S18................163 G5
Warren Rd *MALT* S66...............108 B4
Warren St *ATT* S4....................126 D2
The Warren
  NROS/TKH DN11.....................91 C1
Warren V *MEX/SWTN* S64.........85 G2
  RAW S62...................................85 G4
Warren Vale Rd
  MEX/SWTN S64......................65 C5
Warren Vw *BSLY* S70...................3 G7
  HOY S74...................................61 G4
Warrington Rd *FUL* S10...........125 F3
Warris Cl *KIMB* S61....................96 C5
Warris Pl *SHEFP/MNR* S2.......126 D4
Warsop Rd *BSLYN/ROY* S71.....14 C3
Warwick Rd *BSLYN/ROY* S71...20 B4
  MALT S66..............................110 A3
  WHHL DN2.............................41 F5
Warwick St *CHSW* S40............125 H3
Warwick St South
  CHSW S40.................................9 H6
Warwick Ter *FUL* S10..............125 E3
Warwick Wy *DIN* S25..............148 C2
Wasdale Av *MOS* S20..............167 E2
Wasdale Cl *MOS* S20...............167 E2
Washfield Crs *MOS* S20...........130 A3
Washfield La *RHAM* S60..........110 A3
Washford Rd *DARN/MH* S9.....127 E1
Wash House La *CHSW* S40......191 G2
Washington Av *CONI* DN12......88 B1
  WMB/DAR S73.......................49 H3
Washington Cl *DIN* S25...........134 B5
Washington Gv *BTLY* DN5.........39 C3
Washington St
  MEX/SWTN S64......................67 F3
Wasteneys Rd
  AU/AST/KP S26.....................147 F5
Watch House La *BTLY* DN5.......39 F4
Watchley Gdns *DEARNE* S63....37 E5
Watch St *HAN/WDH* S13..........143 H2
Waterdale Dr *DON* DN1..............6 D5
Waterdale Cl *BTLY* DN5.............39 E4
Waterdale Rd *BSLY* S70.............47 H1
Waterfield Ms *MOS* S20...........157 E4
Waterfield Pl *BSLY* S70.............33 E2
Waterford Rd *OWL* S3.............114 C5
Water Hall La *STKB/PEN* S36....44 D2
Waterhall Vw
  STKB/PEN S36.......................44 D2
Waterhouse Cl
  RHAM/THRY S65....................99 GG
Wateringbury Gv
  STV/CWN S43.......................182 B4
Watering Place Rd
  STKB/PEN S36.......................44 A3
Water La *BSVR* S44..................196 B4
  RAW S62...................................62 C5
  RHAM S60.................................8 E6
  TOT/DORE S17......................161 F1
Waterloo Ct *DIN* S25...............134 A2
Waterloo Rd *BSLY* S70................2 C5
Waterloo Wk *OWL* S3..............125 H1
Watermead *DEARNE* S63...........53 F4
Watermeade *ECK/KIL* S21.......174 B1
Water Meadow La
  CHNE S41..............................106 D3

Water Royd Dr
  DOD/DAR S75..........................30 B3
Waterside Dr *MALT* S66..........108 C1
Waterside Pk
  WMB/DAR S73 *......................50 C2
Waterside Vw *CONI* DN12.........69 E5
Water Slacks Cl
  HAN/WDH S13.....................143 F4
Water Slacks Dr
  HAN/WDH S13.....................143 F4
Water Slacks Rd
  HAN/WDH S13.....................143 F4
Watersmeet Rd
  ST/HB/BR S6.........................113 H5
Water St *OWL* S3........................11 G1
  RHAM/THRY S65......................9 F3
Waterthorpe Cl *MOS* S20 *.....157 F5
Waterthorpe Crs *MOS* S20.....157 F5
Waterthorpe Gdns
  MOS S20...............................157 E5
Waterthorpe Gln *MOS* S20.....157 F5
Waterthorpe Glen *MOS* S20...157 F5
Waterthorpe Greenway
  MOS S20...............................156 D2
Waterthorpe Ri *MOS* S20........157 F5
Watery St *OWL* S3....................125 H2
Wath Rd *ABRD* S7....................139 G4
  DEARNE S63.............................54 A1
  HOY S74...................................62 C4
  MEX/SWTN S64......................66 D4
  WMB/DAR S73.......................50 D4
Wath Wood Bottom
  DEARNE S63...........................65 E5
Wath Wood Dr
  MEX/SWTN S64......................65 F5
Wath Wood Rd *DEARNE* S63....65 F4
Watkinson Gdns *MOS* S20.......157 E3
Watnall Rd
  BSLYN/ROY S71.....................14 D3
Watson Cl *KIMB* S61................104 D1
Watson Gln *KIMB* S61..............104 A1
Watson La *RCH* S42..................194 C4
Watson Rd *FUL* S10..................125 E5
  KIMB S61..............................104 D1
Watson St *HOY* S74....................61 F3
Watt La *FUL* S10......................124 B5
Waveney Dr *DOD/DAR* S75.......18 A4
Waverley Av *CONI* DN12...........89 E1
  DONS/BSCR DN4....................71 E1
  MALT S66..............................133 F1
Waverley Cottages
  HAN/WDH S13.....................128 D4
Waverley Ct *KIMB* S61.............104 A1
Waverley Rd *DARN/MH* S9.....128 A3
Waverley Vw *RHAM* S60............88 C2
Waycliffe *BSLYN/ROY* S71.........20 C4
Wayford Av *CHNE* S41.............192 D3
  MALT S66..............................109 E3
Wayland Av *BSLY* S70................31 H5
Wayland Rd *ECC* S11...............139 F2
Wayside *HAN/WDH* S13..........143 F2
Wayside Ct *STV/CWN* S43......188 B1
The Way *CHSW* S40..................191 H4
Weakland Cl *HACK/IN* S12.....155 H2
Weakland Crs *HACK/IN* S12....155 H2
Weakland Dr *HACK/IN* S12.....155 H2
Weakland Wy *HACK/IN* S12....155 H2
Weaver Cl *DOD/DAR* S75.........18 A4
Weavers Cl *CHPT/GREN* S35....93 H1
Webb Av *STKB/PEN* S36............77 G3
Webbs Av *ST/HB/BR* S6...........124 A1
Webster Cl *KIMB* S61...............104 A1
Webster Ct *CHSW* S40............187 E4
Webster Crs *KIMB* S61.............104 D1
Webster Cft *CHNE* S41............179 H4
Webster St *DARN/MH* S9........116 D3
Wedgewood Cl *RAW* S62...........98 B1
Weedon St *DARN/MH* S9........116 D2
Weet Shaw Cl *CUD/GR* S72......17 E2
Weet Shaw La *CUD/GR* S72.....16 C3
Weetwood Dr *ECC* S11............138 C5
Weetwood Rd *RHAM* S60.........119 G2
Weigh La *SHEFP/MNR* S2 *.....126 C4
Weir Cl *HOY* S74.........................62 A3
Weir Head *DARN/MH* S9.........116 D3
Welbeck Cl *DRON* S18.............170 A1
Welbeck Ct *STV/CWN* S43......185 F3
Welbeck Dr *AU/AST/KP* S26...145 H3
  RCH S42.................................190 C3
Welbeck Ms *MALT* S66............121 F1
Welbeck Rd *BSVR* S44.............197 E3
  DONS/BSCR DN4......................7 H5
  ST/HB/BR S6.........................124 D1
Welbeck St *DOD/DAR* S75........2 C2
Welbeck Vis *BSVR* S44.............197 F2
Welbury Gdns *MOS* S20...........167 E2
Welby Pl *SHEFS* S8..................152 D1
Welbourne Cl
  CHPT/GREN S35....................94 C2
Wellcarr Rd *SHEFS* S8.............153 E3
Wellcliffe Cl *MALT* S66............108 C3
Well Court La *CUD/GR* S72......36 B4

Wellcroft Cl *WHHL* DN2............41 G4
Wellcroft Gdns *MALT* S66.......109 E5
Wellesley Rd *FUL* S10...............10 A4
Wellfield Cl *HACK/IN* S12.......155 G4
  ST/HB/BR S6...........................10 A1
Wellfield Gdns
  BSLYN/ROY S71.....................12 D3
Wellfield Rd *STKB/PEN* S36.....44 D1
  KIMB S61................................96 C4
  ST/HB/BR S6.........................125 F2
Wellgate *CONI* DN12.................89 E1
  RHAM S60..................................9 E4
Wellgate Mt *RHAM* S60..............9 E5
Wellgate Ter *RHAM* S60.............9 E5
Well Green Rd
  ST/HB/BR S6.........................123 F2
Wellhead Rd *SHEFS* S8...........140 A4
Well Hill Gv *BSLYN/ROY* S71....12 C5
Well House La
  STKB/PEN S36.......................44 D1
Wellhouse Wy
  STKB/PEN S36.......................44 D1
Wellingley Rd
  DONS/BSCR DN4....................72 A3
Wellington Av *DIN* S25............148 B1
Wellington Cl
  BSLYN/ROY S71.....................20 B3
Wellington Crs *BSLY* S70...........32 C5
Wellington Gv *BTLY* DN5...........39 G3
Wellington Pl *BSLY* S70 *............2 C3
Wellington Rd
  ST/HB/BR S6.........................124 A2
Wellington St *BSLY* S70...............3 F4
  DEARNE S63...........................53 C1
  MEX/SWTN S64......................67 E3
  SHEF S1...................................10 E5
  STV/CWN S43.......................180 B2
Welling Wy *KIMB* S61..............104 C2
Well La *AU/AST/KP* S26...........131 E5
  BSLYN/ROY S71.....................20 C2
  CHPT/GREN S35...................102 B1
  RHAM S60..............................130 A3
  ST/HB/BR S6.........................124 D1
Well Meadow Dr *OWL* S3.........10 D2
Well Meadow St *OWL* S3..........10 D1
Well Pl *SHEFS* S8....................140 A4
Wells Ct *DOD/DAR* S75............14 A4
Wellspring Cl *RCH* S42............195 H3
  STV/CWN S43.......................177 F5
Well Spring Cl
  STV/CWN S43.......................188 C2
Wells Rd *WHHL* DN2..................40 D4
Wells St *BSVR* S44...................197 F4
  CUD/GR S72............................21 H1
The Wells *DIN* S25...................148 B5
Well St *BSLY* S70.........................3 G5
Well View Rd *KIMB* S61...........104 B1
The Wellway *MALT* S66............108 B2
Welney Pl *ST/HB/BR* S6...........101 E5
Welshpool Pl *CHSW* S40 *..........4 A4
Welton Cl *DONS/BSCR* DN4.....73 C2
Welwyn Cl *MOS* S20................191 H1
  HACK/IN S12.......................154 D1
Welwyn Rd *HACK/IN* S12........154 D1
Wembley Av *CONI* DN12...........88 C1
Wembley Cl *HACK/IN* S12.........41 G5
Wendel Gv *HOY* S74..................62 D2
Wenlock Cl *STV/CWN* S43.......186 D5
Wenlock Crs *CHSW* S40..........186 C5
Wenlock St
  HAN/WDH S13 *..................142 D1
Wensley Ct *ATT* S4..................116 A3
Wensley Dr
  DONS/BSCR DN4....................74 D1
Wensley Cft *ATT* S4.................116 A2
Wensley Dale Dr
  RHAM S60..............................118 D5
Wensleydale Rd *BTLY* DN5........38 D3
  KIMB S61................................96 D3
Wensley Gdns *ATT* S4..............116 A2
Wensley Gn *ATT* S4.................116 A2
Wensley Rd *BSLYN/ROY* S71...14 C3
Wensley St *ATT* S4...................116 A2
  DEARNE S63...........................36 D2
Wensley Wy *STV/CWN* S43....189 G1
Wentworth Av
  AU/AST/KP S26.....................145 H4
  CHSW S40.............................192 A4
  ECC S11.................................151 F5
Wentworth Cl *KIMB* S61............95 E1
Wentworth Ct *KIMB* S61...........97 F2
Wentworth Crs
  DOD/DAR S75..........................14 A4
  STKB/PEN S36.......................44 D3
Wentworth Dr
  DOD/DAR S75 *.......................14 A4
  RAW S62...................................98 B2
Wentworth Gdns
  MEX/SWTN S64......................86 A3
Wentworth Mdw
  STKB/PEN S36.......................44 C2
Wentworth Ms
  DOD/DAR S75..........................14 A4
  STKB/PEN S36.......................44 D3
Wentworth Pl *KIMB* S61............95 E1
Wentworth Rd *BSLY* S70............48 D2
  DOD/DAR S75..........................14 A4
  DRON S18.............................170 A2
  HOY S74...................................61 H4
  KIMB S61................................95 F1
  RAW S62...................................84 D5

  STKB/PEN S36.......................44 C2
  WHHL DN2.............................40 C5
Wentworth St *BSLY* S70............60 C1
  BSLYN/ROY S71.....................19 G4
Wentworth Vw *HOY* S74............62 A3
  WMB/DAR S73.......................50 B4
Wentworth Wy *DIN* S25..........149 H1
  DOD/DAR S75..........................30 B4
  DOD/DAR S75..........................60 B4
Wescoe Av *CUD/GR* S72...........36 A1
Wesley Av *AU/AST/KP* S26.....145 F2
Wesley Ct *KIMB* S61...................95 F1
Wesley La *FUL* S10..................124 D4
Wesley Pl *DIN* S25...................148 B4
Wesley Rd *AU/AST/KP* S26.....159 H2
  CHPT/GREN S35....................80 A4
Wesley St *BSLY* S70.....................3 G5
Wessenden Cl *DOD/DAR* S75...30 C1
Wessex Cl *STV/CWN* S43........188 D1
Wessex Gdns
  TOT/DORE S17......................160 D3
Wessington Dr
  STV/CWN S43.......................189 G1
West Acre *STKB/PEN* S36.........45 E3
West Av *AWLS/ASK* DN6...........24 D3
  DEARNE S63...........................52 D4
  RAW S62...................................85 F5
  WMB/DAR S73.......................49 H2
Westbank Cl *DRON* S18...........163 F4
West Bank Ri *DIN* S25.............148 B4
West Bar *OWL* S3......................11 G2
West Bars *CHSW* S40..................4 A4
West Bawtry Rd *RHAM* S60....118 D3
Westbourne Gdns
  DONS/BSCR DN4....................71 F2
Westbourne Gv *CHSW* S40.....191 F1
  DOD/DAR S75..........................19 F4
Westbourne Rd *FUL* S10.........139 E1
Westbourne Ter *BSLY* S70..........2 B4
Westbridge Rd
  STV/CWN S43.......................177 E4
Westbrook Bank *ECC* S11.......139 F2
Westbrook Cl *CHSW* S40.........190 D2
Westbrook Dr *CHSW* S40........190 D2
Westbrook Rd
  CHPT/GREN S35....................94 A1
Westbury Av
  CHPT/GREN S35....................94 B2
Westbury Cl *DOD/DAR* S75......18 D3
Westbury St *DARN/MH* S9......127 F2
Westby Cl *RHAM/THRY* S65....109 E1
West Carr Rd *DIN* S25.............134 B4
West Cl *KIMB* S61....................104 C1
West Crs *STKB/PEN* S36............45 G4
  STKB/PEN S36.......................76 C2
West Croft Ct
  STV/CWN S43.......................189 F4
Westcroft Crs *MOS* S20...........157 E5
Westcroft Dr *MOS* S20.............157 E5
Westcroft Gdns *MOS* S20........157 E5
Westcroft Gln *MOS* S20...........167 E1
Westcroft Gv *MOS* S20.............167 E1
West Don St *ST/HB/BR* S6.......125 G1
West End *STV/CWN* S43..........177 E4
West End Av
  BSLYN/ROY S71.....................15 E1
  BTLY DN5................................39 E1
West End Bungalows
  STV/CWN S43.......................177 E4
West End Crs
  BSLYN/ROY S71.....................15 E1
West End La
  NROS/TKH DN11.....................90 D1
West End Rd *DEARNE* S63........64 B1
West End Vw *ECK/KIL* S21......174 C1
Westerdale Rd *BTLY* DN5..........38 B4
Western Av *DIN* S25.................134 D5
Western Bank *FUL* S10.............10 A4
Western Cl *DIN* S25..................134 D5
Western Rd *FUL* S10................124 C5
  RHAM/THRY S65..................106 C2
Western St *BSLY* S70....................2 E2
Western Ter *WMB/DAR* S73......50 A2
Westerton Dr *MALT* S66...........109 E5
West Farm La
  RHAM/THRY S65..................107 F1
Westfield Av
  AU/AST/KP S26.....................145 E1
  CHSW S40.............................191 F3
  HACK/IN S12.......................156 C2
  STKB/PEN S36.......................44 C3
West Field Bank
  STV/CWN S43.......................177 E4
Westfield Centre *MOS* S20......157 E5
Westfield Cl *CHSW* S40............191 F2
Westfield Crs *DEARNE* S63.......53 C5
  MOS S20...............................156 D5
Westfield Cft *DEARNE* S63.......64 A1
Westfield Gdns *CHSW* S40......191 F3
Westfield Gv *HACK/IN* S12......156 B2
Westfield La *ECK/KIL* S21........173 G3
  STKB/PEN S36.......................44 C3
  STV/CWN S43.......................176 D4
Westfield Northway
  MOS S20...............................157 E5
Westfield Rd *ARMTH* DN3.........42 C4
  DEARNE S63...........................64 A3
  DONS/BSCR DN4....................55 H4

DRON S18...............171 G3
ECK/KIL S21............168 A3
MALT S66................108 D4
RAW S62...................98 A2
WMB/DAR S73..........64 A1
Westfields BSLYN/ROY S71...12 A5
Westfield Southway
MOS S20..................157 E5
Westfield St BSLY S70.....2 C4
Westfield Ter SHEF S1....10 E4
West Garth Cl DIN S25....134 D4
Westgate BSLY S70.........2 E4
BSLYN/ROY S71............20 B3
West Ga MEX/SWTN S64....9 F5
Westgate RHAM S60.........9 F5
STKB/PEN S36.............44 D4
West Green Av
BSLYN/ROY S71............21 F1
West Green Dr ARMTH DN3...29 E3
West Gv BSLYN/ROY S71....12 A5
WHHL DN2..................41 G5
Westhaven CUD/GR S72 *...22 A2
West Hl KIMB S61.........104 A3
Westhill La OWL S3........10 D4
Westholme Rd
DONS/BSCR DN4.............6 A7
West Kirk La CUD/GR S72...36 A3
West Laith Ga DON DN1.....6 C4
Westland Cl MOS S20......157 E5
Westland Gdns MOS S20....157 E5
Westland Gv MOS S20......157 E5
Westland Rd MOS S20......157 E5
West La AU/AST/KP S26....144 D1
West Lea CHSW S40........191 F2
STV/CWN S43..............184 D2
Westlea Vw STV/CWN S43..184 D2
Westleigh Ct CHSW S40......4 C1
West Ml MOS S20..........157 E5
Westminster Av FUL S10...137 F1
Westminster Buildings
DON DN1 *..................6 D3
Westminster Cl FUL S10...137 F1
MALT S66.................109 E5
Westminster Crs FUL S10..137 F1
WHHL DN2..................41 G5
West Moor Crs
DOD/DAR S75...............18 D5
West Moor La ARMTH DN3....43 F3
Westmoor Rd
STV/CWN S43..............188 D5
Westmore Cl DEARNE S63...37 E5
Westmoreland St
ST/HB/BR S6.............125 G2
Westmorland St
DONS/BSCR DN4............71 F2
Westmorland Wy BTLY DN5..54 A4
Westmount Av DEARNE S63..51 C5
Westnall Rd SHEFN S5....102 D2
Westnall Ter SHEFN S5...102 D2
Weston Cl CHSW S40......186 A3
Westongales Wy BTLY DN5..39 G2
Weston Rd DONS/BSCR DN4..71 H2
Weston St OWL S3..........10 C4
Weston Vw FUL S10.......125 E4
Westover Rd FUL S10.....124 A5
West Park Dr
AU/AST/KP S26...........144 D3
West Pinfold
BSLYN/ROY S71............15 G1
Westpit Hl DEARNE S63....39 G1
West Pl BTLY DN5.........39 H1
West Qd DOD/DAR S75......18 D5
MEX/SWTN S64.............66 D5
Westside Gra
DONS/BSCR DN4............55 G5
West St BSLY S70.........48 B1
BSLYN/ROY S71............12 D5
CHSW S40...................4 D2
CONI DN12.................89 C4
DEARNE S63...............37 G4
DIN S25..................65 E2
DON DN1...................6 B4
DRON S18................170 D1
ECK/KIL S21.............174 C1
HOY S74...................61 G2
MEX/SWTN S64.............66 E4
MOS S20.................157 F2
SHEF S1...................10 E4
STV/CWN S43.............185 G1
WMB/DAR S73..............24 A3
West Street La SHEF S1...11 F3
Westthorpe Fields Rd
ECK/KIL S21.............168 A4
Westthorpe Rd
ECK/KIL S21.............168 B3
West Vale Gv
RHAM/THRY S65............99 H4
West Vw BSLY S70...........2 E5
BSVR S44.................197 E4
CUD/GR S72...............22 A2
STV/CWN S43.............181 H5
West View Cl
TOT/DORE S17...........161 D2
West View Crs DEARNE S63..53 E1
West View La
TOT/DORE S17...........161 F2
West View Rd CHNE S41...187 E3
KIMB S61................104 A4
MEX/SWTN S64.............67 E4
Westville Rd DOD/DAR S75...2 C1

West Wy BSLY S70...........2 E5
Westwell Pl MOS S20.....166 D2
Westwick Crs SHEFS S8...162 B1
Westwick Gv SHEFS S8....162 B1
Westwick La RCH S42.....190 B2
Westwick Rd SHEFS S8....162 B1
Westwood Av
ST/HB/BR S6.............113 H4
STV/CWN S43.............189 G1
Westwood Ct ST/HB/BR S6.113 F1
STV/CWN S43.............189 G4
Westwood Ct BSLY S70.....2 E2
CHPT/GREN S35...........80 B3
Westwood Dr
STV/CWN S43.............189 G4
Westwood Drive Gdns
STV/CWN S43.............189 F4
Westwood La
STV/CWN S43.............188 D5
Westwood New Rd
CHPT/GREN S35...........80 A4
DOD/DAR S75.............60 B5
Westwood Rd BSVR S44...189 E5
ECC S11.................138 B2
Wetherby Cl BTLY DN5....38 D5
Wetherby Ct DARN/MH S9.128 A3
Wetherby Dr
AU/AST/KP S26...........145 E3
MEX/SWTN S64............67 F2
Wetlands La CHNE S41....188 C5
Wet Moor La DEARNE S63...64 D1
Whaley Rd DOD/DAR S75....18 B2
Wharf Cl MEX/SWTN S64...66 C5
Wharfedale Dr
CHPT/GREN S35...........93 G1
Wharfedale Rd
DOD/DAR S75.............18 C4
Wharf La CHNE S41..........5 G1
STV/CWN S43.............182 B3
Wharf Rd DARN/MH S9....117 F1
DON DN1...................6 A5
MEX/SWTN S64............40 B5
Wharf St BSLYN/ROY S71....3 J1
MEX/SWTN S64............66 C5
SHEFP/MNR S2.............11 J2
Wharncliffe Av
AU/AST/KP S26...........145 G2
DEARNE S63..............65 F2
Wharncliffe Cl HOY S74...61 H4
RAW S62..................84 D3
Wharncliffe Hl
RHAM/THRY S65 *...........9 G3
Wharncliffe Rd
CHPT/GREN S35...........80 B4
FUL S10..................10 C6
Wharncliffe St BSLY S70.15 H4
BSLYN/ROY S71............15 H4
DONS/BSCR DN4...........55 G3
Wharton Av
AU/AST/KP S26...........145 F1
Wharton Dr CHNE S41......5 J3
Wheatacre Rd
STKB/PEN S36............77 E2
Wheata Dr SHEFN S5.....102 A2
Wheata Pl SHEFN S5.....102 A3
Wheata Rd SHEFN S5.....102 A3
Wheatbridge Rd CHSW S40...4 C4
Wheat Cft CONI DN12......89 G1
Wheatcroft Rd RAW S62...85 H5
Wheatcrofts SPRO S7......2 C4
Wheatfield Cl ARMTH DN3..29 G1
Wheatfield Crs SHEFN S5.102 D3
Wheatfield Dr DEARNE S63.37 F3
Wheathill Cl STV/CWN S43.188 C5
Wheathill La STV/CWN S43.188 C5
Wheatlands Rd RCH S42...195 G3
Wheatley Cl
BSLYN/ROY S71............19 H3
Wheatley Gv
HAN/WDH S13............142 C1
Wheatley Hall Rd
DONS/BSCR DN4...........40 D4
Wheatley La DON DN1........6 E1
Wheatley Pl CONI DN12 *..68 B5
Wheatley Rd BSLY S70....33 E3
BTLY DN5.................26 C5
KIMB S61.................96 C5
MEX/SWTN S64............86 C4
Wheatley St CONI DN12....68 B5
Wheeldon Crs
STV/CWN S43.............188 B2
Wheeldon St OWL S3.......10 D3
Wheel La CHPT/GREN S35.101 G1
The Wheel CHPT/GREN S35.101 G1
Wheldrake Rd SHEFN S5..115 H2
Whernside Av
CHPT/GREN S35...........80 D5
Whinacre Cl SHEFS S8...163 F2
Whinacre Pl SHEFS S8...163 F2
Whinby Cft DOD/DAR S75...30 B3
Whinby Rd DOD/DAR S75...30 A2
The Whines KIMB S61......97 C1
Whinfell Cl AWLS/ASK DN6.25 F1
Whinfell Ct ECC S11....151 E3
Whin Gdns DEARNE S63....37 F1
Whin Hill Rd
DONS/BSCR DN4...........57 H5
Whinmoor Rd
CHPT/GREN S35...........80 A4
SHEFN S5................116 B1
Whinside Crs DEARNE S63..37 E1
The Whins RAW S62........84 C5

Whiphill Cl DONS/BSCR DN4..74 A1
Whiphill La ARMTH DN3....43 E5
Whiphill Top La ARMTH DN3..59 C5
Whirlow Court Rd ECC S11.151 F3
Whirlowdale Cl ECC S11..151 E3
Whirlowdale Crs ABRD S7.151 F2
Whirlowdale Ri ECC S11..151 E3
Whirlowdale Rd ECC S11..151 F3
Whirlow Grange Av
ECC S11.................151 E3
Whirlow Grange Dr
ECC S11.................151 E3
Whirlow Gn ECC S11.....151 E3
Whirlow Gv ECC S11.....151 E3
Whirlow La ECC S11......151 E2
Whirlow Ms ECC S11 *...151 E2
Whirlow Park Rd ECC S11.151 F4
Whisperwood Dr
DONS/BSCR DN4...........71 H4
Whiston Brook Vw
RHAM S60................120 A3
Whiston Gra RHAM S60...119 G3
Whiston Gn RHAM S60....119 H4
Whiston Grange Rd RHAM S60.106 B5
Whiston V RHAM S60.....119 H4
Whitaker Cl
NROS/TKH DN11...........91 F4
Whitbourne Cl
BSLYN/ROY S71............19 H2
Whitburn Rd DON DN1......6 E6
Whitby Rd DARN/MH S9...127 H3
NROS/TKH DN11...........91 E2
Whitcomb Dr
NROS/TKH DN11...........91 F4
Whitebank Cl CHNE S41..192 D3
Whitecotes Cl CHSW S40.194 A4
Whitecotes La CHSW S40.194 A4
Whitecotes Pk CHSW S40.194 B4
White Cft SHEF S1........10 E2
Whitecroft Crs RHAM S60.118 C4
White Cross Av CUD/GR S72..21 H2
White Cross Ct CUD/GR S72..21 H2
White Cross La BSLY S70..32 D5
White Cross Mt CUD/GR S72..21 H2
White Cross Ri BSLY S70..32 D5
White Cross Rd CUD/GR S72..32 D5
White Edge Cl CHSW S40.186 D4
White Ga DIN S25.......148 D2
White Hart Cnr
ECK/KIL S21.............167 E4
Whitehead Av
STKB/PEN S36............77 F3
Whitehead Cl DIN S25...134 C5
Whitehead St
STV/CWN S43............182 B4
White Hill Av BSLY S70...30 C1
Whitehill Av RHAM S60..118 C4
Whitehill Dr RHAM S60..118 C5
White Hill Gv BSLY S70...30 D1
Whitehill La RHAM S60..118 C3
Whitehill Rd RHAM S60..118 C4
White Hill Ter BSLY S70..30 C1
Whitehouse La
ST/HB/BR S6............125 F1
Whitehouse Rd
ST/HB/BR S6............125 F1
Whitehouses CHNE S41.....5 J7
White La CHPT/GREN S35..81 F4
HACK/IN S12............154 C2
Whitelea Gv
MEX/SWTN S64............66 D4
White Leas CHSW S40....186 B5
Whitelee Rd
MEX/SWTN S64............66 C5
Whiteley La FUL S10....137 G3
Whiteley Wood Cl ECC S11.138 A3
Whiteley Wood Rd
ECC S11..................11 A3
Whitelow La
TOT/DORE S17...........160 A1
White Rose Ct BTLY DN5..40 A1
White Rose Wy
DONS/BSCR DN4...........56 C5
Whites Croft Vw
STV/CWN S43.............177 E5
White Thorns Cl SHEFS S8.163 F2
White Thorns Dr SHEFS S8.163 F3
White Thorns Vw
SHEFS S8................163 F2
Whiteways Cl ATT S4....115 H4
Whiteways Dr ATT S4....115 H4
Whiteways Gv ATT S4....115 H4
Whiteways Rd ATT S4....115 H4
Whitewood Cl
BSLYN/ROY S71............15 F1
White's La SHEF/MNR S2.126 D4
Whitfield Gdns WRKN S81.149 H4
Whitfield Rd FUL S10...137 C5
RAW S62..................84 C3
Whiting St SHEFS S8....140 A4
Whitley Carr
CHPT/GREN S35...........93 G4
Whitley Cft CHPT/GREN S35.94 B4
Whitley La CHPT/GREN S35.93 F5
Whitley Vw CHPT/GREN S35.94 B4
Whitley View Rd KIMB S61.103 H4
Whitney Cl DONS/BSCR DN4.71 E3
Whittier Rd
DONS/BSCR DN4...........71 G2
EPW DN9..................85 F2
Whittington Hl CHNE S41.179 G5
Whittington La DRON S18.179 F1

Whittington Rd
STV/CWN S43.............180 C2
Whittingtons Ct WHHL DN2..41 G2
Whittington St DON DN1...40 B5
Whittington Wy CHNE S41.179 G5
Whitting Valley Rd
CHNE S41................179 G5
Whitton Cl DONS/BSCR DN4.73 G2
Whitwell Crs STKB/PEN S36.76 D2
Whitwell La STKB/PEN S36..76 D2
Whitwell St DARN/MH S9..128 B3
Whitwell Vw
NROS/TKH DN11...........91 H2
Whitworth La
DARN/MH S9..............116 C5
Whitworth Rd CHNE S41..187 F3
FUL S10..................138 A1
Whitworth St DEARNE S63..37 C5
Whitworth Wy DEARNE S63..65 E1
Whybourne Ter RHAM S60 *...9 G5
Whyn Vw DEARNE S63......37 E2
Wicker OWL S3............11 J1
Wicker La OWL S3.........11 J1
Wickersley Rd RHAM S60.106 C5
Wickethern Rd ARMTH DN3..43 E4
Wicket Wy CONI DN12......70 C5
Wickfield Cl HACK/IN S12.142 C5
Wickfield Dr HACK/IN S12.155 C1
Wickfield Gv HACK/IN S12.142 C5
Wickfield Pl HACK/IN S12.142 C5
Wickfield Rd HACK/IN S12.155 H1
Wickins Pl STV/CWN S43..182 B5
Wicklow Rd WHHL DN2.....41 E5
Widdop Cl HAN/WDH S13..142 B2
Widdop Cft HAN/WDH S13.142 B2
Wigfield Dr BSLY S70.....31 H5
Wigfull Rd ECC S11.....139 E1
Wigley Rd STV/CWN S43..189 E3
Wignall Av MALT S66....107 H5
Wikeley Wy STV/CWN S43.188 B2
Wike Rd BSLYN/ROY S71...21 E5
Wilberforce Rd DIN S25.148 B3
WHHL DN2.................41 H1
Wilbrook Ri DOD/DAR S75..18 C3
Wilby Carr Gdns
DONS/BSCR DN4...........58 B4
Wilby La BSLY S70.........3 J6
Wilcox Cl ST/HB/BR S6..101 F4
Wilcox Rd ST/HB/BR S6..101 F4
Wild Av RAW S62..........84 C4
Wilden Cft STV/CWN S43.129 G2
Wildene Dr MEX/SWTN S64..67 E2
Wildflower Cl
NROS/TKH DN11...........91 E4
Wilding Wy KIMB S61....104 C1
Wilfred Cl DARN/MH S9..127 G2
Wilford Rd BSLYN/ROY S71..14 C5
Wilfred Cl DARN/MH S9...127 G2
Wilfred St RHAM S60.......9 F5
Wilfrid Rd DARN/MH S9..127 G2
Wilkinson Av
NROS/TKH DN11...........91 G3
Wilkinson Cl CHSW S40..195 G1
Wilkinson Dr STV/CWN S43.189 F2
Wilkinson La FUL S10.....10 C4
Wilkinson Rd HOY S74....62 C3
Wilkinson St BSLY S70....3 H7
FUL S10..................10 B4
William Cl MOS S20 *....166 D1
Williams Gv
MEX/SWTN S64............66 C5
William Crs MOS S20....166 D1
William La NROS/TKH DN11.90 D2
Williamson Rd ECC S11..139 F3
Williams Rd BTLY DN5....39 F4
William St BSLY S70.......32 A5
CHNE S41................187 G3
DEARNE S63..............37 E5
DEARNE S63..............65 F2
ECK/KIL S21............166 D5
FUL S10..................10 B4
MEX/SWTN S64............66 C5
RAW S62..................98 C2
RHAM S60..................9 H5
WMB/DAR S73.............24 A3
William St North CHNE S41.179 F1
Willingham Cl MOS S20..157 G4
Willingham Gdns
MOS S20 *................157 G3
Willington Rd SHEFN S5.102 C5
Willis Rd ST/HB/BR S6..113 H5
Willman Rd
BSLYN/ROY S71............21 F4
Willoughby St ATT S4...115 H2
Willow Av DONS/BSCR DN4.58 B5
RAW S62..................98 C2
Willow Bank
BSLYN/ROY S71............19 F5
RHAM/THRY S65.........106 D1
Willow Beck
HOR/CROF WF4............12 A2
Willow Cl CUD/GR S72....16 D5
DIN S25.................148 B5
HOY S74..................61 G3
MALT S66.................108 C3
RHAM S60................118 D5
Willow Ct MALT S66......108 B3
Willow Crs CHPT/GREN S35.94 A2

Willow Dr CONI DN12......70 C5
DARN/MH S9.............128 C4
MALT S66................108 C3
MEX/SWTN S64............66 D3
STV/CWN S43.............183 E2
Willow Dro HOR/CROF WF4.13 H1
Willow Garth RAW S62....85 C5
Willowgarth Av RHAM S60.118 C5
Willowgarth Cl
HOR/CROF WF4............13 G1
Willow Garth Rd CHNE S41.186 C1
Willow Gv AU/AST/KP S26.145 H2
Willow La DEARNE S63....53 F4
NROS/TKH DN11...........91 G2
Willowlees Ct
DONS/BSCR DN4...........74 A1
Willow Rd ARMTH DN3.....43 E3
DEARNE S63...............37 F2
DEARNE S63...............65 G4
ECK/KIL S21............168 A3
MALT S66................110 B3
STKB/PEN S36............76 D4
The Willows KIMB S61....96 B4
Willow Sq DEARNE S63....45 H5
Willow St BSLY S70.......2 D6
CONI DN12................89 F1
Willow Tree Dr
STV/CWN S43.............185 F4
Willow Vw BTLY DN5 *....26 C4
Wilmington Dr
DONS/BSCR DN4...........72 D1
Wilsden Gv DOD/DAR S75..18 D3
Wilson Av RAW S62........85 C5
STKB/PEN S36............44 D4
STV/CWN S43.............185 G1
Wilson Dr RHAM/THRY S65..99 G5
Wilson Gv BSLYN/ROY S71..21 F3
Wilson Pl SHEFS S8.....140 A4
Wilson Rd DRON S18.....163 G4
ECC S11.................139 E2
STKB/PEN S36............77 H3
Wilson St DRON S18.....171 F3
OWL S3...................126 A1
WMB/DAR S73.............24 B3
Wilthorpe Av
BSLYN/ROY S71............33 G3
Wilthorpe Crs DOD/DAR S75..19 E3
Wilthorpe Farm Rd
DOD/DAR S75.............19 E3
Wilthorpe Gdns MOS S20.156 A3
Wilthorpe Gn DOD/DAR S75..19 E3
Wilthorpe La DOD/DAR S75..18 D3
Wilthorpe Rd DOD/DAR S75..18 D3
Wilton Ct RAW S62........98 B1
Wilton Cl KIMB S61.....105 E2
Wilton Gdns KIMB S61...105 E2
Wilton La KIMB S61.....105 E3
Wilton Pl FUL S10........10 B6
Wiltshire Rd WHHL DN2...57 G1
Wimborne Crs CHNE S41..187 E2
Winberry Av DIN S25....148 C3
Wincanton Cl
MEX/SWTN S64............67 E2
Winchester Av FUL S10..137 F2
WHHL DN2.................41 E4
Winchester Ct
RHAM/THRY S65 *..........9 G3
Winchester Crs FUL S10.137 F2
Winchester Dr FUL S10 *.137 F2
Winchester Rd CHNE S41.187 E2
FUL S10.................137 F2
Winchester Wy
BSLYN/ROY S71............33 G3
BTLY DN5.................38 D4
RHAM S60................118 A3
Wincobank Av SHEFN S5..116 A1
Wincobank Cl SHEFN S5..116 B1
Wincobank La ATT S4....116 B3
Wincobank Rd SHEFN S5..116 B1
Windermere Av DRON S18.170 C2
WHHL DN2.................41 G5
Windermere Ct DIN S25.148 C2
Windermere Crs
ARMTH DN3................29 F5
Windermere Rd ABRD S7.139 G5
BSLYN/ROY S71............3 J4
STKB/PEN S36............186 C2
Winders Cnr STV/CWN S43.184 B1
Winders Pl WMB/DAR S73..50 B3
Windgate Hl CONI DN12....69 F5
Windham Cl BSLYN/ROY S71..3 G1
Windhill Av MEX/SWTN S64..67 G3
Windhill Crs MEX/SWTN S64.67 G3
Windhill La MEX/SWTN S64.67 G3
Windhill Ter MEX/SWTN S64.67 G3
The Windings DEARNE S63..37 G5
Windle Rd DONS/BSCR DN4..55 G4
Windle Sq ARMTH DN3.....29 F5
Windmere Av DEARNE S63..53 G1
Windmill Av CONI DN12....89 F2
CUD/GR S72...............17 H4
Windmill Balk La
AWLS/ASK DN6.............25 F3
Windmill Cl BSVR S44...196 D1
Windmill Ct AWLS/ASK DN6..25 F1
KIMB S61.................95 G3
WMB/DAR S73.............49 H3
Windmill Greenway
MOS S20.................167 G3
Windmill Hill La
CHPT/GREN S35...........93 G2
Windmill La DRON S18...172 C5
SHEFN S5................116 A1
STKB/PEN S36............44 A3

Windmill Rd *DIN* S25 ....**148** C2
  WMB/DAR S73 ....**49** H3
Windmill Wy *STV/CWN* S43 ....**188** A1
Windsor Av *STKB/PEN* S36 ......**44** A2
Windsor Cl *CHSW* S40 ....**191** C3
  MALT S66 ....**108** D3
Windsor Crs *BSLYN/ROY* S71 ...**20** B4
  CUD/GR S72 ....**67** G2
Windsor Dr *DOD/DAR* S75 * **30** B3
  DRON S18 ....**170** A2
  MEX/SWTN S64 ....**49** G1
Windsor Gdns *DEARNE* S63 ......**37** C2
Windsor Rd *AU/AST/KP* S26 .....**145** G4
Windsor Ri *CONI* DN12 * **68** C5
  KIMB S61 ....**95** F2
  SHEFS S8 ....**139** H4
  WHHL DN2 ....**7** H1
Windsor Sq *DEARNE* S63 ....**37** C2
Windsor St *ATT* S4 ....**126** D1
  DEARNE S63 ....**37** C2
  HOY S74 ....**61** H1
Windsor Wk *BTLY* DN5 ....**39** E4
  CHNE S41 ....**193** E3
  DIN S25 ....**148** A5
Windy Fields Rd *RCH* S42 ....**190** B5
Windy House La
  SHEFP/MNR S2 ....**141** F3
Windy Rdg *AU/AST/KP* S26 .....**145** E1
Winfield Rd *DEARNE* S63 ....**65** F3
Wingerworth Av *SHEFS* S8 ....**162** B4
Wingerworth Wy
  CHSW S40 ....**192** B5
Wingfield Cl *DRON* S18 ....**170** A3
  KIMB S61 ....**97** E3
Wingfield Crs *HACK/IN* S12 ....**142** B5
Wingfield Rd
  BSLYN/ROY S71 ....**20** A1
  KIMB S61 ....**96** C3
Winholme *ARMTH* DN3 ....**42** D4
Winifred St *RHAM* S60 ....**103** E4
Winkley Ter *SHEFN* S5 ....**103** E4
Winlea Av *RHAM/THRY* S65 ....**107** G5
Winnat Pl *STV/CWN* S43 ....**189** G2
Winnats Cl *CHSW* S40 ....**186** C4
Winn Cl *ST/HB/BR* S6 ....**113** H1
Winn Dr *ST/HB/BR* S6 ....**113** H1
Winn Gdns *ST/HB/BR* S6 ....**113** H1
Winn Gv *ST/HB/BR* S6 ....**100** C5
Winnipeg Rd *BTLY* DN5 ....**39** H1
Winsford Rd *ST/HB/BR* S6 ......**101** E4
Winster Cl *BSLY* S70 ....**47** H5
Winster Rd *ST/HB/BR* S6 ....**114** A3
  STV/CWN S43 ....**189** C1
Winter Av *BSLYN/ROY* S71 ......**12** C4
  DOD/DAR S75 ....**2** A2
Wintersett Dr
  DONS/BSCR DN4 ....**57** F5
Winter St *OWL* S3 ....**10** B2
Winter Ter *DOD/DAR* S75 ....**2** A2
Winterton Cl
  DONS/BSCR DN4 ....**73** H2
Winterton Gdns
  HACK/IN S12 ....**156** C2
Winterwell Rd *DEARNE* S63 .....**64** C1
Winton Cl *BSLY* S70 ....**32** A3
Winton Rd *WHHL* DN2 ....**57** F1
Wisbech Cl *CHSW* S40 ....**192** A4
Wisconsin Dr
  DONS/BSCR DN4 ....**73** E1
Wiseton Rd *ECC* S11 ....**139** E1
Wisewood Av
  ST/HB/BR S6 ....**113** G4
Wisewood La
  ST/HB/BR S6 ....**113** G4
Wisewood Pl
  ST/HB/BR S6 ....**113** G4
Wisewood Rd
  ST/HB/BR S6 ....**113** G4
Wishing Well Gn
  AU/AST/KP S26 ....**144** D3
Wiston Wy *CHNE* S41 ....**193** E5
Witham Cl *CHNE* S41 ....**188** A3
Witham Ct *CHSW* S40 ....**191** C1
  DOD/DAR S75 ....**18** A4
Witham Rd *FUL* S10 ....**125** E5
Withens Av *ST/HB/BR* S6 ......**113** H2
Witney St *SHEFS* S8 ....**140** A3
Wivelsfield Rd
  DONS/BSCR DN4 ....**70** D1
Woburn Cl *DONS/BSCR* DN4 ...**71** E3
  ECC S11 ....**151** F3
Woburn Pl *DOD/DAR* S75 ....**30** B4
Wolfe Cl *CHSW* S40 ....**191** H4
Wolfe Dr *ST/HB/BR* S6 ....**101** F4
Wolfe Rd *ST/HB/BR* S6 ....**101** F4
Wollaton Av
  TOT/DORE S17 ....**161** G3
Wollaton Cl
  BSLYN/ROY S71 ....**21** E5
Wollaton Dr *TOT/DORE* S17 ...**161** G3
Wollaton Rd
  TOT/DORE S17 ....**161** F4
Wolseley Rd *SHEFS* S8 ....**139** H3
Wolsey Av *WHHL* DN2 ....**57** H1
Woodacre Rd
  HAN/WDH S13 ....**143** E4
Wombwell Av *DEARNE* S63 ......**65** E3

Wombwell La *BSLY* S70 ....**33** F3
  HOY S74 ....**48** D3
Wombwell Rd *HOY* S74 ....**62** A1
Wood Acres *DOD/DAR* S75 ......**18** C3
Woodall La *AU/AST/KP* S26 ...**169** G2
Woodall Rd *ECK/KIL* S21 ....**168** D3
  RHAM/THRY S65 ....**107** E4
Woodall Rd South
  RHAM/THRY S65 ....**107** E4
Woodbank Crs *SHEFS* S8 ......**139** H5
Woodbank Rd
  ST/HB/BR S6 ....**122** D3
Woodbine Rd
  DARN/MH S9 ....**116** B5
Woodbourne Gdns
  DOD/DAR S75 ....**60** C3
Woodbourn Hl
  DARN/MH S9 ....**127** F2
Woodbourn Rd
  DARN/MH S9 ....**127** F3
Woodburn Dr
  CHPT/GREN S35 ....**94** B1
Woodbury Cl *DARN/MH* S9 ....**153** G3
Woodbury Rd
  DARN/MH S9 ....**103** G4
Wood Cliffe *FUL* S10 ....**137** F4
Wood Cl *CHPT/GREN* S35 ....**94** C2
  RAW S62 ....**80** A5
  RCH S42 ....**194** D3
  RHAM/THRY S65 ....**107** F4
Woodcock Cl *KIMB* S61 ....**96** D4
Woodcock Pl
  SHEFP/MNR S2 ....**126** D4
Woodcock Rd *HOY* S74 ....**62** A3
Wood Cft *KIMB* S61 ....**96** D5
Woodcross Av
  DONS/BSCR DN4 ....**74** C1
Wood End Av *STKB/PEN* S36 ...**44** C5
Woodend Cl *ST/HB/BR* S6 ......**113** C5
Woodend Ct *DOD/DAR* S75 ......**30** C4
Woodend Dr *ST/HB/BR* S6 ......**113** C5
Woodfarm Av
  ST/HB/BR S6 ....**124** A1
Woodfarm Cl *ST/HB/BR* S6 ....**124** A1
Woodfarm Dr
  ST/HB/BR S6 ....**124** A1
Woodfarm Pl *ST/HB/BR* S6 ....**124** A1
Woodfield Av
  MEX/SWTN S64 ....**67** F3
Woodfield Cl
  WMB/DAR S73 ....**35** E4
Woodfield Rd *ARMTH* DN3 ......**43** E5
  DEARNE S63 ....**64** B2
  DONS/BSCR DN4 ....**71** G1
  FUL S10 ....**124** D3
Wood Flds *MALT* S66 ....**109** E5
Woodfield Wy *RHAM* S60 * **106** A5
Woodfield Wy
  DONS/BSCR DN4 ....**71** H4
  DONS/BSCR DN4 ....**72** C2
Wood Fold *OWL* S3 ....**115** E5
Woodfoot Rd *RHAM* S60 ....**119** F3
Woodgrove Rd
  DARN/MH S9 ....**103** H4
  RHAM/THRY S65 ....**107** G2
Woodhall Cl *WMB/DAR* S73 .....**35** E4
Woodhall Ri
  MEX/SWTN S64 ....**86** B1
Woodhall Rd
  WMB/DAR S73 ....**35** E4
Woodhead Dr *HOY* S74 ....**48** D4
Woodhead La *HOY* S74 ....**49** E4
Woodhead Rd
  CHPT/GREN S35 ....**78** D2
  SHEFP/MNR S2 ....**140** A2
Woodholm Pl *ECC* S11 ....**138** D5
Woodholm Rd *ECC* S11 ....**138** D5
Woodhouse Av *MOS* S20 ....**157** F1
Woodhouse Cl *RAW* S62 ....**84** D5
Woodhouse Ct *MOS* S20 ....**144** A5
Woodhouse Crs *MOS* S20 ......**157** F1
Woodhouse La *BSVR* S44 ....**196** B1
  MOS S20 ....**144** A5
  STV/CWN S43 ....**183** E1
Woodhouse Rd
  HACK/IN S12 ....**141** H4
  HOY S74 ....**61** H3
  WHHL DN2 ....**40** C4
Woodkirk Cl *STKB/PEN* S36 ....**45** F4
Woodknot Ms
  DONS/BSCR DN4 ....**71** H4
Woodlaithes Rd *MALT* S66 .....**81** G5
Woodland Av *DIN* S25 * **148** C3
Woodland Cl *MALT* S66 ....**121** G1
  RHAM S60 ....**129** F2
Woodland Dr *BSLY* S70 ....**30** D2
  DIN S25 ....**148** C3
  HACK/IN S12 ....**154** D3
Woodland Gdns *MALT* S66 .....**111** F3
Woodland Gv *DEARNE* S63 ......**65** F4
  STV/CWN S43 ....**177** E5
  STV/CWN S43 ....**185** G2
Woodland Pl
  TOT/DORE S17 ....**161** F3
Woodland Rd
  DEARNE S63 ....**65** F4
  SHEFS S8 ....**153** F2
Woodlands *STV/CWN* S43 ......**188** B2
Woodlands Av *MOS* S20 ....**144** B5
Woodlands Cl
  AU/AST/KP S26 ....**145** F1
Woodlands Crs
  MEX/SWTN S64 ....**85** G1

Woodlands Farm
  RHAM S60 ....**130** A3
Woodlands Rd
  AWLS/ASK DN6 ....**25** F3
  HOY S74 ....**49** E5
The Woodlands
  ARMTH DN3 ....**43** E3
Woodlands Vw
  AWLS/ASK DN6 * **25** E3
  HOY S74 ....**62** A1
  WMB/DAR S73 ....**49** G5
Woodland Ter *CUD/GR* S72 .....**23** H2
Woodland Vw *CUD/GR* S72 .....**21** H2
  HACK/IN S12 ....**154** D3
  MEX/SWTN S64 ....**67** G4
Woodland View Rd
  ST/HB/BR S6 * **124** C1
Woodland Vls
  CUD/GR S72 * **23** F1
  DOD/DAR S75 * **60** C3
Woodland Wy
  RHAM/THRY S65 ....**107** G5
Wood La *BSLYN/ROY* S71 ....**14** C2
  BSLYN/ROY S71 ....**118** A5
  MALT S66 ....**121** G1
  MALT S66 ....**132** C2
  RHAM S60 ....**130** B4
  ST/HB/BR S6 ....**124** B1
Wood Lane Cl
  ST/HB/BR S6 ....**124** A1
Woodlea Gdns
  DONS/BSCR DN4 ....**74** B1
Woodlea Gv *ARMTH* DN3 ....**42** D4
Woodlea Wy *WHHL* DN2 ....**41** G3
Woodleys Av *RAW* S62 ....**85** E3
Woodman Dr
  MEX/SWTN S64 ....**85** C1
Woodmere Dr *CHNE* S41 ....**180** A2
Woodmoor St
  BSLYN/ROY S71 ....**15** H4
Woodnook Gv *ECK/KIL* S21 ...**173** C1
Wood Park Vw
  BSLYN/ROY S71 ....**14** D3
Woodpecker Cl
  AU/AST/KP S26 ....**145** G4
Wood Rd *KIMB* S61 ....**96** D5
  ST/HB/BR S6 ....**113** H4
Woodrove Av
  HAN/WDH S13 ....**141** H3
Woodrove Cl
  HAN/WDH S13 ....**141** H3
Woodroyd Av
  BSLYN/ROY S71 ....**15** C3
Woodroyd Ct
  BSLYN/ROY S71 ....**15** C3
Wood Royd Rd
  STKB/PEN S36 ....**77** G2
Wood Seats
  CHPT/GREN S35 ....**93** F3
Woodseats Cl *SHEFS* S8 ......**152** C1
Woodseats House Rd
  SHEFS S8 ....**152** D3
Woodseats Rd *SHEFS* S8 ......**152** C1
Woodsetts Rd *DIN* S25 ....**148** C2
Woodsett Wk *CONI* DN12 ....**69** C5
Woodside Av *DEARNE* S63 ......**65** F3
  ECK/KIL S21 ....**168** D1
Woodside Cl
  AWLS/ASK DN6 ....**25** E3
  MALT S66 ....**121** G1
Woodside La
  CHPT/GREN S35 ....**93** E5
  OWL S3 ....**126** A1
Woodside Rd
  AWLS/ASK DN6 ....**25** E3
  BTLY DN5 ....**39** H5
Woodside Vw *DEARNE* S63 .....**53** F3
Woodside Wk *KIMB* S61 ....**97** E4
Wood Spring Ct *ATT* S4 ....**116** A4
Woodstock Dr *CHNE* S41 ......**193** H4
Woodstock Gdns
  DONS/BSCR DN4 ....**71** E2
Woodstock Ri *CHNE* S41 ....**193** H4
Woodstock Rd *ABRD* S7 ....**139** G4
  DOD/DAR S75 ....**19** F3
  DONS/BSCR DN4 ....**71** E2
  ST/HB/BR S6 ....**113** H2
Wood St *BSLY* S70 ....**3** C7
  DON DN1 ....**5** D3
  MEX/SWTN S64 ....**66** B5
  RHAM/THRY S65 ....**99** G4
  ST/HB/BR S6 ....**125** G1
  WMB/DAR S73 ....**35** E4
Wood Syke *DOD/DAR* S75 ......**30** C3
Wood Ter *RHAM* S60 ....**118** D1
Woodthorpe Crs
  HAN/WDH S13 ....**142** A2
Woodthorpe Rd
  HAN/WDH S13 ....**142** A3
  STV/CWN S43 ....**183** E4
Woodvale Cl *CHSW* S40 ....**191** B4
Woodvale Rd *FUL* S10 ....**138** D1
Woodview *BTLY* DN5 ....**54** B4
Wood Vw *CONI* DN12 ....**89** G2
  HOY S74 ....**62** C3
Woodview Ct *RCH* S42 ....**195** F4
Woodview La
  DOD/DAR S75 ....**18** A4
Wood View Pl *RHAM* S60 ......**118** D1
Woodview Rd
  ST/HB/BR S6 ....**114** A5
Woodview Ter *ECC* S11 ....**138** A2

Wood Wk *BSLYN/ROY* S71 ......**12** C4
  HOY S74 ....**49** E5
  MEX/SWTN S64 ....**66** D2
  WMB/DAR S73 ....**49** G5
The Woodway *MALT* S66 ....**108** B2
Wood's Riding *WHHL* DN2 ......**57** H1
Woofindin Av *ECC* S11 ....**138** A3
Woofindin Rd *FUL* S10 ....**137** H5
Woxdale Cl *MOS* S20 ....**156** A5
Woodale Cft *MOS* S20 ....**156** A5
Woodale Dr *MOS* S20 ....**156** A5
Wooldale Gdns *MOS* S20 ......**156** A5
Wooley Av *WMB/DAR* S73 ......**50** A3
Woolley Rd *STKB/PEN* S36 .....**76** C2
Woolley Wood Rd
  SHEFN S5 ....**103** E2
Wootton Ct
  RHAM/THRY S65 ....**99** G4
Worcester Av *DARN/MH* DN2 ...**40** D3
Worcester Cl *FUL* S10 ....**137** F1
Worcester Dr *FUL* S10 ....**137** F1
Worcester Rd *FUL* S10 ....**137** G1
Wordsworth Av *DIN* S25 ....**135** F5
  SHEFN S5 ....**114** C1
  STKB/PEN S36 ....**44** C4
Wordsworth Crs
  SHEFN S5 ....**101** G5
Wordsworth Dr *BTLY* DN5 ......**55** F1
  SHEFN S5 ....**106** C3
  SHEFN S5 ....**101** G5
Wordsworth Pl *DRON* S18 ....**171** G4
Wordsworth Rd
  BSLYN/ROY S71 ....**20** B3
  CHNE S41 ....**187** F1
  DEARNE S63 ....**64** C1
Work Bank La
  STKB/PEN S36 ....**44** B2
Workhouse La *OWL* S3 ....**11** G1
Worksop Rd
  AU/AST/KP S26 ....**145** F3
  AU/AST/KP S26 ....**146** B3
  DARN/MH S9 ....**127** G1
  DIN S25 ....**148** C4
  STV/CWN S43 ....**182** D3
Works Rd *STV/CWN* S43 ....**181** F3
Worral Av *RHAM* S60 ....**130** A3
Worral Cl *BSLY* S70 ....**31** H4
Worral Ct *ARMTH* DN3 ....**29** C5
Worrall Rd *CHPT/GREN* S35 ....**80** C5
  ST/HB/BR S6 ....**113** F2
Worry Goose La *RHAM* S60 ...**120** A2
Worsborough Vw
  DOD/DAR S75 ....**60** B2
Worsbrough Rd *BSLY* S70 ....**47** H5
  HOY S74 ....**48** D4
Worsley Cl *BSLY* S70 ....**32** B4
Worthing Crs *CONI* DN12 ....**89** F1
Worthing Rd *DARN/MH* S9 ....**128** A2
Wortley Av *MEX/SWTN* S64 ....**86** B1
  WMB/DAR S73 ....**49** H1
Wortley Dr
  CHPT/GREN S35 ....**100** A2
Wortley Ms *KIMB* S61 ....**95** F2
Wortley Rd
  CHPT/GREN S35 ....**80** A3
  KIMB S61 ....**104** C1
  STKB/PEN S36 ....**77** H2
Wortley St *BSLY* S70 ....**3** F5
Wortley Vw *HOY* S74 ....**48** D4
Wostenholm Rd *ABRD* S7 .....**139** H3
Wragby Rd *ECC* S11 ....**138** C2
Wragg Rd *SHEFP/MNR* S2 ......**127** E5
Wreakes La *DRON* S18 ....**168** D5
Wrelton Cl *BSLYN/ROY* S71 ....**15** F1
Wren Bank
  SHEFP/MNR S2 ....**127** E5
Wren Park Cl *CHSW* S40 ....**192** B5
  HACK/IN S12 ....**155** C5
Wrenpark Rd *RCH* S42 ....**194** D3
Wrens Wy *BSLY* S70 ....**47** H5
Wright Crs *WMB/DAR* S73 ......**50** B3
Wrightson Av
  DONS/BSCR DN4 ....**70** C3
Wrightson Ter *BTLY* DN5 ....**39** H4
Wright St *DIN* S25 ....**148** C2
Wright's Hl *ECC* S11 ....**139** H1
Wroxham Cl *MALT* S66 ....**109** E4
Wroxham Dr *MALT* S66 ....**109** E4
Wroxham Wy *BTLY* DN5 ....**39** E5
  MALT S66 ....**109** E4
Wulfric Cl *SHEFP/MNR* S2 .....**141** F2
Wulfric Pl *SHEFP/MNR* S2 .....**141** F2
Wulfric Rd *ECK/KIL* S21 ....**166** C5
  SHEFP/MNR S2 ....**141** F3
Wyatt Av *ECC* S11 ....**139** E4
Wybourn House Rd
  SHEFP/MNR S2 ....**127** E4
Wybourn Ter
  SHEFP/MNR S2 ....**127** E4
Wychwood Cl
  DONS/BSCR DN4 ....**71** H4
Wychwood Cft *MOS* S20 ......**157** G3
Wychwood Gln *MOS* S20 ......**157** G3
Wychwood Gv *MOS* S20 ....**157** G3
Wycombe St
  BSLYN/ROY S71 ....**21** E5
Wyedale Cft *MOS* S20 ....**157** F1
The Wynd *ECK/KIL* S21 ....**175** H4
Wyndthorpe Av
  DONS/BSCR DN4 ....**74** A1
Wyn Gv *WMB/DAR* S73 ....**64** A1

Wynmoor Crs
  WMB/DAR S73 ....**51** E5
Wynyard Rd *ST/HB/BR* S6 .....**113** H3
Wythburn Rd *CHNE* S41 ....**186** C2
Wyvern Gdns
  TOT/DORE S17 ....**161** E2

Y

Yarborough Ter *BTLY* DN5 ......**39** H5
Yardley Sq *OWL* S3 * **10** B2
Yarmouth St *DARN/MH* S9 .....**116** D3
Yarncliff Cl *CHSW* S40 ....**186** D4
Yarwell Dr *MALT* S66 ....**110** C2
Yates Cl *MALT* S66 ....**121** E1
Yealand Cl *AWLS/ASK* DN6 .....**25** F1
Yearling Cha
  MEX/SWTN S64 ....**65** H5
Yeldersley Cl *CHSW* S40 ....**186** B4
Yeomans Rd *ST/HB/BR* S6 .....**125** G2
Yewdale *BSLY* S70 ....**32** B5
Yew Greave Crs *SHEFN* S5 ...**101** H2
Yew La *SHEFN* S5 ....**101** G2
Yews Av *BSLY* S70 ....**32** B3
Yews La *BSLY* S70 ....**32** B4
Yews Pl *BSLY* S70 ....**32** B4
The Yews *RHAM/THRY* S65 * **9** K2
Yew Ter *CONI* DN12 * **69** C5
Yew Tree Av *DIN* S25 ....**148** D3
Yew Tree Crs
  NROS/TKH DN11 ....**91** G1
Yew Tree Dr *CHSW* S40 ....**191** E4
  DARN/MH S9 ....**117** H3
  ECK/KIL S21 ....**168** A3
Yew Tree Rd *MALT* S66 ....**110** A2
Yezedale Av
  CHPT/GREN S35 ....**80** C5
York Gdns *DONS/BSCR* DN4 ...**57** H4
York La *MALT* S66 ....**121** F5
York Ms *DEARNE* S63 ....**37** G2
York Ri *AU/AST/KP* S26 ....**25** H5
York Rd *AWLS/ASK* DN6 ....**25** H5
  BTLY DN5 ....**38** D2
  DARN/MH S9 ....**128** A2
  RHAM/THRY S65 ....**9** H2
  STKB/PEN S36 ....**76** D2
Yorkshire Wy *ARMTH* DN3 ....**43** F4
York St *BSLY* S70 ....**2** E5
  CHNE S41 ....**193** E5
  CUD/GR S72 ....**37** G1
  DEARNE S63 ....**37** G1
  HOY S74 ....**62** A1
  MEX/SWTN S64 ....**66** A3
  NROS/TKH DN11 ....**91** E1
  SHEF S1 ....**11** G2
  WMB/DAR S73 ....**50** B2
Youlgreave Dr
  HACK/IN S12 ....**142** B5
Young St *DON* DN1 ....**6** D4
  SHEF S1 ....**10** E6
Yvonne Gv *WMB/DAR* S73 ......**49** H2

Z

Zamor Crs *MALT* S66 ....**133** E2
Zetland Rd *HOY* S74 ....**62** D3
  WHHL DN2 ....**7** J1
Zion La *DARN/MH* S9 ....**127** F1
Zion Pl *DARN/MH* S9 ....**127** F1
Zion Ter *BSLY* S70 ....**33** E3

Abbeydale Golf Club
TOT/DORE S17 ....161 H1
Abbeydale
Grange School
ABRD S7 ....152 B1
Abbeydale Park
Sports Club
TOT/DORE S17 ....161 G1
Abbeydale Primary
School
ABRD S7 ....139 H4
Abbey Lane Primary
School
SHEFS S8 ....152 C3
Abbey Special School
KIMB S61 ....104 A2
Abercrombie Primary
School
CHNE S41 ....5 F1
ACE Business Centre
OWL S3 ....126 B2
Acorn Business Park
SHEFS S8 ....152 C1
Acres Hill Primary School
DARN/MH S9 ....127 H4
Adult & Community
Learning Unit
ST/HB/BR S6 ....10 A1
Adwick Leisure Centre
AWLS/ASK DN6 ....25 F3
Adwick Park Junior School
AWLS/ASK DN6 ....25 F2
Adwick Washington Infant
School
AWLS/ASK DN6 ....25 G3
Aldham Industrial
Estate
WMB/DAR S73 ....34 A5
The Alhambra Shopping
Centre
BSLY S70 ....3 C5
All Saints Catholic High
School
SHEFP/MNR S2 ....11 K7
Alma Leisure Park
CHSW S40 ....5 H7
Amber Business Centre
RHAM S60 ....9 F2
Ambergate Clinics
KIMB S61 ....105 F3
Anchorage Lower School
BTLY DN5 ....39 E4
Anchorage Upper School
BTLY DN5 ....38 C4
Anns Grove J & I School
SHEFS S8 ....140 A3
Anston Brook Primary
School
DIN S25 ....148 B3
Anston Greenlands J & I
School
DIN S25 ....148 B1
Anston Hillcrest Primary
School
DIN S25 ....148 B4
Anston Park J & I School
DIN S25 ....148 D1
Apperknowle Community
Primary School
DRON S18 ....172 B2
Arbourthorne Community
Primary School
SHEFP/MNR S2 ....140 D4
Ardsley House Hotel
BSLYN/ROY S71 ....33 G2
Arksey Primary School
BTLY DN5 ....27 F5
Armthorpe Community
Centre
ARMTH DN3 ....42 D4
The Armthorpe School
ARMTH DN3 ....42 C3
Armthorpe Southfield
Primary School
ARMTH DN3 ....42 D5
Armytage Industrial
Estate
CHNE S41 ....179 G5
Ashdell Preparatory
School
FUL S10 ....124 D5
Ashgate Croft Special
School
CHSW S40 ....186 C5
Ashley Industrial Estate
RHAM S60 ....9 F2
Ash Lodge Medical
Centre
CHSW S40 ....191 H2
Ashville Medical Centre
BSLY S70 ....32 D2
Aston CE Primary School
AU/AST/KP S26 ....145 G3
Aston Comprehensive
School
AU/AST/KP S26 ....144 D1
Aston Fence J & I School
HAN/WDH S13 ....144 C2
Aston Hall CC
AU/AST/KP S26 ....146 A3
Aston Lodge Primary
School
AU/AST/KP S26 ....145 G4

Aston Springwood
Primary School
AU/AST/KP S26 ....145 G2
Athersley North Primary
School
BSLYN/ROY S71 ....14 C4
Athersley South Primary
School
BSLYN/ROY S71 ....14 D5
Athron Industrial Estate
DON DN1 ....6 E1
Atlas Business Park
CHPT/GREN S35 ....94 C5
Attercliffe Cemetery
DARN/MH S9 ....116 B5
Aughton Primary School
AU/AST/KP S26 ....145 F1
Badsley Moor Infant
School
RHAM/THRY S65 ....106 D3
Bailey House
(Council Building)
RHAM S60 ....8 E2
Balby Carr Community
Sports College
DONS/BSCR DN4 ....72 A2
Balby Street J & I School
CONI DN12 ....68 D5
Ballifield Primary School
HAN/WDH S13 ....143 E2
Bankwood Lane
Industrial Estate
NROS/TKH DN11 ....90 D1
Bankwood Primary School
GLV S14 ....140 D5
Barbot Hall
Industrial Estate
KIMB S61 ....97 H5
Barlborough Hall School
STV/CWN S43 ....177 F2
Barlborough Primary
School
STV/CWN S43 ....177 H4
Barnsley Business
Innovation Centre
CUD/GR S72 ....16 D5
Barnsley Cemetery
BSLY S70 ....3 K7
Barnsley College
BSLY S70 ....3 F2
STKB/PEN S36 ....44 D3
Barnsley College
(Belle Vue)
DOD/DAR S75 ....3 F1
Barnsley District
General Hospital
DOD/DAR S75 ....2 A2
Barnsley FC
(Oakwell Stadium)
BSLYN/ROY S71 ....3 K4
Barnsley Municipal
Golf Club
DOD/DAR S75 ....14 A2
Barnsley Private Clinic
DOD/DAR S75 ....2 E1
Barrow Hill
STV/CWN S43 ....181 E3
Barrow Hill Primary
School
STV/CWN S43 ....181 F3
Barrow Hill Railway
Centre
STV/CWN S43 ....181 E3
The Base
BSLY S70 ....3 G5
Beauchief Golf Club
SHEFS S8 ....151 H4
The Beauchief Hotel
ABRD S7 ....151 H4
Beevor Industrial Estate
BSLYN/ROY S71 ....20 B5
Beighton Cemetery
MOS S20 ....157 H2
Beighton Health Centre
MOS S20 ....157 F1
Beighton Infant School
MOS S20 ....157 H2
Belgrave Medical Centre
SHEFP/MNR S2 ....140 A2
Bentley Colliery CC
BTLY DN5 ....26 D5
Bentley Health Centre
BTLY DN5 ....39 G1
Bentley High Street
Primary School
BTLY DN5 ....39 H2
Bentley New Village
Primary School
BTLY DN5 ....26 D5
Bents Green Special School
ECC S11 ....138 A5
Bessacarr Primary School
DONS/BSCR DN4 ....57 G5
Best Western Elton Hotel
MALT S66 ....108 D3
Best Western Mosborough
Hall Hotel
MOS S20 ....166 D2
Best Western
The Consort Hotel
MALT S66 ....121 H5
Birch Hall Golf Club
DRON S18 ....179 E1

Birdholme Infant School
CHSW S40 ....192 C5
Birdwell Health Centre
BSLY S70 ....60 D2
Birdwell Primary School
BSLY S70 ....60 D1
Birkdale Preparatory
School
FUL S10 ....139 E1
Birkdale School
FUL S10 ....139 E1
Birk Hill Infant School
ECK/KIL S21 ....174 B1
Birkwood Primary School
CUD/GR S72 ....22 A2
Birley Community College
HACK/IN S12 ....155 F3
Birley Community
Primary School
HACK/IN S12 ....155 F2
Birley Health Centre
HACK/IN S12 ....155 F3
Birley Spa Community
Primary School
HACK/IN S12 ....155 H1
Birleywood Golf Club
HACK/IN S12 ....155 G3
Blackburn Primary School
KIMB S61 ....103 H3
Bluebell Medical Centre
SHEFN S5 ....116 B1
Bolsover Business Park
BSVR S44 ....196 B2
Bolsover Castle
BSVR S44 ....196 D2
Bolsover CE Junior School
BSVR S44 ....196 D2
Bolsover Clinic
BSVR S44 ....197 E3
Bolsover Infant School
BSVR S44 ....197 E2
Bolsover Local Hospital
BSVR S44 ....197 F2
Bolton Medical Centre
DEARNE S63 ....53 E3
Bolton upon Dearne
Cemetery
DEARNE S63 ....53 E2
Bolton upon Dearne
Infant School
DEARNE S63 ....53 E3
Bonaroma Training
Academy
RHAM/THRY S65 ....99 H3
Boythorpe Cemetery
CHSW S40 ....4 C7
Bracken Moor
Sports Club
STKB/PEN S36 ....77 E3
Bradmarsh Business Park
RHAM S60 ....8 D7
Bramley Grange
Primary School
MALT S66 ....109 E3
Bramley Sunnyside Infant
School
MALT S66 ....108 C3
Brampton Cortonwood
Infant School
WMB/DAR S73 ....51 E5
Brampton Ellis CE
Infant School
DEARNE S63 ....64 C2
Brampton Ellis CE Junior
School
DEARNE S63 ....64 B1
Brampton Primary School
CHSW S40 ....4 B4
Brantwood School
for Girls
ECC S11 ....139 F3
Brightside Infant School
DARN/MH S9 ....116 D2
Brimington Cemetery
STV/CWN S43 ....188 B2
Brimington Clinic
STV/CWN S43 ....188 C1
Brinsworth Clinic
RHAM S60 ....118 B3
Brinsworth
Comprehensive School
RHAM S60 ....118 A4
Brinsworth Howarth
Primary School
RHAM S60 ....118 C5
Brinsworth Manor Junior
School
RHAM S60 ....118 B3
Brinsworth Medical
Centre
RHAM S60 ....118 A3
Brinsworth Whitehill
Primary School
RHAM S60 ....118 C5
Brockwell Primary
School
CHSW S40 ....186 D5
Brookfield Community
School
CHSW S40 ....191 E2
Brookhouse Junior
School
MOS S20 ....157 H2

Broombank Road
Industrial Estate
CHNE S41 ....178 C3
Broomhill Clinic
FUL S10 ....125 E5
Broomhill Infant School
FUL S10 ....125 E5
Broomhill Medical Centre
FUL S10 ....125 F5
Broom Lane Medical
Centre
RHAM S60 ....119 G1
Broom Valley J&I School
RHAM S60 ....106 A4
Brunswick Primary School
HAN/WDH S13 ....143 H3
Burncross Cemetery
CHPT/GREN S35 ....93 H1
Burngreave Cemetery
ATT S4 ....115 G5
Burns Medical Centre
DONS/BSCR DN4 ....58 A5
Burton Road Business Park
BSLYN/ROY S71 ....21 E2
Burton Road Primary
School
BSLYN/ROY S71 ....20 A4
Business & Innovation
Barnsley Centre
DOD/DAR S75 ....18 D3
Business Training Centre
DON DN1 ....6 D7
Busk Meadow Infant
School
SHEFN S5 ....115 E2
Byron Wood Primary
School
OWL S3 ....115 F5
Calow CE Primary School
CHNE S41 ....193 H1
Calow Lane Industrial
Estate
CHNE S41 ....193 G4
The Campanile Hotel
DONS/BSCR DN4 ....57 F4
Canklow Meadows
Industrial Estate
RHAM S60 ....118 D3
Canklow Woods J & I
School
RHAM S60 ....118 D2
Cantley Health Centre
DONS/BSCR DN4 ....58 B5
Cantley Sycamore Primary
School
DONS/BSCR DN4 ....74 A1
Carbrook Hall Industrial
Estate
DARN/MH S9 ....116 D3
Carfield Primary School
SHEFS S8 ....140 B5
Caribbean Sports Club
CHPT/GREN S35 ....102 C1
Carlton Industrial Estate
BSLYN/ROY S71 ....15 G4
Carlton Park Hotel
RHAM S60 ....106 A5
Carlton Primary School
BSLYN/ROY S71 ....15 H4
Carrfield Medical Centre
SHEFP/MNR S2 ....140 B4
Carr House Centre
DONS/BSCR DN4 ....7 J6
Carter Knowle Junior
School
ABRD S7 ....139 F5
Castle Hills Primary School
BTLY DN5 ....39 E2
Castle Industrial Estate
BSVR S44 ....196 B2
Castle Market
SHEFP/MNR S2 ....11 J2
Castle Street Medical
Centre
BSVR S44 ....196 C2
Catcliffe Primary School
RHAM S60 ....129 H1
Cathedral Church of
St Peter & St Paul
SHEF S1 ....11 G2
Cavendish Junior School
CHNE S41 ....187 F1
Cedar School
DONS/BSCR DN4 ....71 F2
Centenary Industrial
Park
SHEFS S8 ....139 G5
Central Business Park
RHAM S60 ....8 D4
Centre in the Park
SHEFP/MNR S2 ....140 D2
Centurion Business Park
KIMB S61 ....105 E4
Centurion Retail Park
BTLY DN5 ....39 H5
Century Business Centre
DEARNE S63 ....51 G4
Chapel Green Community
College
CHPT/GREN S35 ....80 D5
Charles Clifford
Dental Hospital
FUL S10 ....10 A4

Charnock Hall Primary
School
HACK/IN S12 ....154 D3
Charter Gallery Museum
CONI DN12 ....88 D1
Chaucer School
SHEFN S5 ....101 G4
Chesterfield &
North Derbyshire
Royal Hospital
STV/CWN S43 ....193 G1
Chesterfield Bowl
CHSW S40 ....192 D5
Chesterfield Caravan &
Leisure Centre
CHNE S41 ....179 E3
Chesterfield College
CHNE S41 ....5 G2
Chesterfield Crematorium
STV/CWN S43 ....188 B3
Chesterfield FC
(Recreation Ground)
CHSW S40 ....4 D2
Chesterfield Golf Club
RCH S42 ....191 H5
Chesterfield Museum
CHNE S41 ....5 H4
Chesterfield Newspaper
Office
CHNE S41 ....5 H4
Chesterfield RFC
CHNE S41 ....187 G4
Chesterfield Small
Business Centre
CHNE S41 ....187 G2
Chesterfield Trading Estate
CHNE S41 ....178 B3
Childrens Hospital
FUL S10 ....10 A4
Child Welfare & School
Clinic
RHAM/THRY S65 ....9 K1
Christ Church CE Primary
School
CHNE S41 ....187 G4
Cineworld
CHSW S40 ....5 H7
DARN/MH S9 ....117 E4
City Road Cemetery
SHEFP/MNR S2 ....141 E1
City Road Crematorium
SHEFP/MNR S2 ....141 E2
Civic Theatre
BSLY S70 ....3 G4
Claremont Hospital
FUL S10 ....123 H5
Clarence Industrial
Trading Estate
CHNE S41 ....187 G1
Claycliffe Business Park
DOD/DAR S75 ....18 A2
Clayfield Industrial Estate
DONS/BSCR DN4 ....71 G2
Clifford CE Infant School
ECC S11 ....139 F2
Clifford Dental Hospital
FUL S10 ....10 A4
Clifford Lister Business
Centre
MALT S66 ....108 A5
Clifton-A Community
Arts School
RHAM/THRY S65 ....106 B2
Clifton Park Museum
RHAM/THRY S65 ....9 H4
Clocktower Business
Centre
STV/CWN S43 ....181 E3
Clough House Medical
Centre
SHEF S1 ....11 G7
Clowne Cemetery
STV/CWN S43 ....184 C1
Clowne Infant School
STV/CWN S43 ....185 E3
Clowne Junior School
STV/CWN S43 ....185 E3
Clowne Welfare Sports
Club
STV/CWN S43 ....184 D3
Coit Primary School
CHPT/GREN S35 ....94 A2
Coleridge Primary School
RHAM/THRY S65 ....106 C1
The Colonnades Shopping
Centre
DON DN1 ....6 C4
Concord Junior School
SHEFN S5 ....103 F5
Concord Park Golf Club &
Sports Centre
SHEFN S5 ....103 E4
Conisbrough Castle
CONI DN12 ....89 E1
Conisbrough Cemetery
CONI DN12 ....88 D3
Contour Health Centre
RHAM S60 ....9 F6
Copley Junior School
BTLY DN5 ....54 B5
Courtyard by Marriott
Hotel
RHAM S60 ....119 E3

Crooked Spire Church
CHSW S40 ....5 G4
Crookes Cemetery
FUL S10 ....124 C4
Crookhill Park Municipal
Golf Club
CONI DN12 ....89 H4
Crucible Theatre
SHEF S1 ....11 H3
Crystal Peaks Shopping &
Leisure Centre
MOS S20 ....157 E3
Cudworth Churchfield
Primary School
CUD/GR S72 ....16 D5
Cudworth Pontefract Road
Primary School
CUD/GR S72 ....16 D4
Curlew Junior School
WHHL DN2 ....41 G1
Cusworth Country Park
BTLY DN5 ....54 D1
Cutlers Hotel
SHEF S1 ....11 H3
Dalton Foljambe Primary
School
RHAM/THRY S65 ....99 G5
Dalton Health Centre
RHAM/THRY S65 ....99 F5
Dalton Listerdale Primary
School
RHAM/THRY S65 ....107 G5
Danum Hotel
DON DN1 ....6 D4
Danum School Technology
College
WHHL DN2 ....41 H5
Darfield All Saints CE
Primary School
WMB/DAR S73 ....35 F5
Darfield CC
WMB/DAR S73 ....35 F4
Darfield Health Centre
WMB/DAR S73 ....35 F5
Darfield Upperwood J & I
School
WMB/DAR S73 ....34 D4
Darfield Valley Primary
School
WMB/DAR S73 ....50 D1
Darnall Cemetery
DARN/MH S9 ....128 A2
Darnall Health Centre
DARN/MH S9 ....128 A2
Days Inn
AU/AST/KP S26 ....169 F3
Dead Earnest Theatre
ST/HB/BR S6 ....125 E1
Dearne Carrfield Primary
School
DEARNE S63 ....53 E1
Dearne Highgate Primary
School
DEARNE S63 ....37 E5
Dearne High School
DEARNE S63 ....53 G1
Dearne Valley College
DEARNE S63 ....66 A3
Dearne Valley College
(Rockingham Centre)
DEARNE S63 ....65 E2
Deepcar St Johns CE
Junior School
STKB/PEN S36 ....77 G3
Deer Park Primary School
RCH S42 ....195 H4
Denaby Ings Visitor
Centre
MEX/SWTN S64 ....68 B2
Denaby Lane Industrial
Estate
CONI DN12 ....68 A5
Denaby Main Primary
School
CONI DN12 ....68 B4
Department for Education
& Skills
SHEF S1 ....10 E7
Devonshire Green Medical
Centre
OWL S3 ....10 E4
Dinnington Business
Centre
DIN S25 ....134 C3
Dinnington Clinic
DIN S25 ....134 D5
Dinnington
Comprehensive School
DIN S25 ....134 D3
Dinnington Primary
School
DIN S25 ....134 D4
Dinnington RFC
DIN S25 ....135 F4
Dinnington St Joseph's RC
Primary School
DIN S25 ....134 D4
Dobcroft Infant School
ECC S11 ....151 H1
Dobcroft Junior School
ABRD S7 ....151 H2
Dodworth CE School
DOD/DAR S75 ....30 A4

Dodworth Health Centre
DOD/DAR S75 ....30 B3
Dodworth Keresforth
Road Primary School
DOD/DAR S75 ....30 C4
Dodworth Primary School
DOD/DAR S75 ....30 B3
The Dome Leisure Centre
DONS/BSCR DN4 ....57 F4
Doncaster Balby Central
First School
DONS/BSCR DN4 ....55 G4
Doncaster Civic Theatre
DON DN1 ....6 E4
The Doncaster Clinic
WHHL DN2 ....57 E2
Doncaster Colege
DON DN1 ....6 D1
Doncaster College & School
for the Deaf
WHHL DN2 ....7 K4
Doncaster Gate Hospital
RHAM/THRY S65 ....9 G4
Doncaster Golf Club
DONS/BSCR DN4 ....74 C3
Doncaster Leisure Park
DONS/BSCR DN4 ....57 F4
Doncaster Museum &
Art Gallery
DON DN1 ....6 E4
Doncaster Old (Hyde Park)
Cemetery
DON DN1 ....6 C7
Doncaster Racecourse
WHHL DN2 ....57 F3
Doncaster Racecourse
Exhibition Centre
WHHL DN2 ....57 E2
Doncaster Railport
DONS/BSCR DN4 ....56 B5
Doncaster Road Junior
School
MEX/SWTN S64 ....67 G4
Doncaster Road Primary
School
BSLY S70 ....3 J6
Doncaster Rovers FC
DONS/BSCR DN4 ....57 E3
Doncaster Royal Infirmary
WHHL DN2 ....41 G5
Doncaster Town CC
WHHL DN2 ....7 G4
Doncaster Town Moor
Golf Club
DONS/BSCR DN4 ....57 E3
Don Valley School &
Performing Arts College
BTLY DN5 ....38 D2
Don Valley Stadium
DARN/MH S9 ....127 G1
Dore House Farm
Industrial Estate
HAN/WDH S13 ....143 G1
Dore Primary School
TOT/DORE S17 ....160 D2
Dore & Totley Golf Club
TOT/DORE S17 ....162 A3
Dorothy Hyman Stadium
CUD/GR S72 ....22 A1
Drake House Retail Park
MOS S20 ....156 D2
Dronfield Cemetery
DRON S18 ....171 F3
The Dronfield Henry
Fanshawe School
DRON S18 ....171 F1
Dronfield Junior School
DRON S18 ....171 E2
The Dronfield School
DRON S18 ....170 C1
Dronfield Sports Centre
DRON S18 ....170 D2
Dunstan Primary School
CHNE S41 ....186 D1
Dunston Trading Estate
CHNE S41 ....179 E4
Dykebull Medical Centre
ST/HB/BR S6 ....113 H3
East Dene Primary School
RHAM/THRY S65 ....106 C1
East Herringthorpe
Cemetery
RHAM/THRY S65 ....107 F3
East Hill Secondary
School
SHEFP/MNR S2 ....140 C2
Eastwood Trading Estate
RHAM/THRY S65 ....98 C5
Ecclesall CE Junior School
ECC S11 ....138 B4
Ecclesall Infant School
ECC S11 ....138 B4
Ecclesall Medical Centre
ECC S11 ....138 D5
Ecclesfield Cemetery
CHPT/GREN S35 ....93 H5
Ecclesfield Comprehensive
School
CHPT/GREN S35 ....94 A3
Ecclesfield Health Centre
CHPT/GREN S35 ....94 B3
Ecclesfield Primary School
SHEFN S5 ....102 A4

Eckington Camms CE
Primary School
ECK/KIL S21 ....166 D4
Eckington Cemetery
MOS S20 ....167 E3
Eckington Health Centre
ECK/KIL S21 ....167 E5
Eckington Junior School
ECK/KIL S21 ....166 D5
Eckington School
ECK/KIL S21 ....166 A5
Eckington Swimming Pool
ECK/KIL S21 ....167 E5
Edenthorpe
Canon Popham CE
Primary School
ARMTH DN3 ....29 F4
Edenthorpe Hall Primary
School
ARMTH DN3 ....29 G5
Edlington Victoria Primary
School
CONI DN12 ....70 A5
The Edmunds Primary
School
BSLY S70 ....32 B5
Edward Sheerien
Secondary School
BSLYN/ROY S71 ....20 B1
Ellesmere Teaching School
ATT S4 ....126 C1
The Ellis CE Primary
School
WMB/DAR S73 ....50 A5
The Elmhirst School
BSLY S70 ....48 D1
Elsecar CE Primary School
HOY S74 ....62 D3
Elsecar Heritage Centre
HOY S74 ....62 C4
Elsworth House School
MALT S66 ....109 G3
Emmanuel Anglican-
Methodist Junior School
MOS S20 ....156 D4
EPPIC Theatre
SHEF S1 ....102 A1
Euro Link Business Park
DONS/BSCR DN4 ....56 C4
Fan Road Industrial Estate
STV/CWN S43 ....182 B4
Far Lane Medical Centre
ST/HB/BR S6 ....113 H3
Ferham House Clinic
KIMB S61 ....105 E3
Ferham Primary School
KIMB S61 ....8 A5
Fernbank School
AWLS/ASK DN6 ....25 C1
Fields End Business Park
DEARNE S63 ....37 G2
Fire Police Museum
OWL S3 ....11 F2
Firs Hill Community
Primary School
ATT S4 ....115 H4
Firth Park Medical Centre
SHEFN S5 ....115 H1
Firth Park School &
Community College
SHEFN S5 ....102 D4
Fir Vale School
ATT S4 ....115 H3
Flanderwell J & I School
MALT S66 ....108 B3
The Foulstone School
WMB/DAR S73 ....35 F5
Foundry Street Industrial
Estate
CHNE S41 ....187 G1
Foxhill Medical Centre
ST/HB/BR S6 ....101 F3
Fox Hill Primary School
ST/HB/BR S6 ....101 F3
Foxwood Industrial Park
CHNE S41 ....179 F5
Frenchgate Shopping
Centre
DON DN1 ....6 C3
Fullerton House School
CONI DN12 ....68 B5
The Garrison Hotel
ST/HB/BR S6 ....114 B4
Gateway Industrial
Estate
RAW S62 ....98 A4
Gawber Primary School
DOD/DAR S75 ....38 C4
Gilbert Heathcote Infant
School
CHNE S41 ....187 F1
Gillott Industrial Estate
BSLY S70 ....2 D3
Gladys Buxton School
DRON S18 ....171 G1
Gleadless Clinic
HACK/IN S12 ....154 D2
Gleadless Primary School
HACK/IN S12 ....141 H5
Globe Business Centre
ST/HB/BR S6 ....125 H2
Goldthorpe Health Centre
DEARNE S63 ....53 F1

Goldthorpe Industrial
Estate
DEARNE S63 ....52 D1
Goldthorpe Primary
School
DEARNE S63 ....37 G5
Gooseacre Primary School
DEARNE S63 ....37 G1
Gorseybrigg Infant School
DRON S18 ....170 B2
Gorseybrigg Primary
School
DRON S18 ....170 B2
Grand St Leger Hotel
DONS/BSCR DN4 ....7 J5
Grange Lane Industrial
Estate
BSLYN/ROY S71 ....33 E2
Grange Lane Infant School
NROS/TKH DN11 ....90 D3
Grange Park Golf Club
KIMB S61 ....95 C5
Grasmere School
BSLY S70 ....33 E2
Graves Art Gallery
SHEF S1 ....11 G4
Greasbrough Lane
Cemetery
RAW S62 ....98 A1
Greasbrough Health Centre
KIMB S61 ....97 F3
Greasbrough J & I School
KIMB S61 ....97 F3
Great Houghton Cemetery
CUD/GR S72 ....23 H5
Great Houghton Clinic
CUD/GR S72 ....36 A1
Greenacre School
BSLY S70 ....31 E3
Green Arbour Special
School
MALT S66 ....133 E1
Greendale Shopping
Centre
DRON S18 ....171 F1
Greenfield Primary School
HOY S74 ....62 B2
Greengate Lane Primary
School
CHPT/GREN S35 ....80 C4
Greenhill Health Centre
SHEFS S8 ....162 C1
Greenhill Primary School
SHEFS S8 ....162 C1
Greenlands J & I School
DARN/MH S9 ....127 H3
Greensprings Touring Park
DOD/DAR S75 ....47 E4
Greenway Natural Health
Centre
TOT/DORE S17 ....161 E4
Grenoside Crematorium
CHPT/GREN S35 ....100 D2
Grenoside Primary School
CHPT/GREN S35 ....93 E5
Greystones First School
ECC S11 ....138 C3
Greystones Medical
Centre
ECC S11 ....138 D3
Greystones Primary
School
ECC S11 ....138 D3
Grimethorpe Cemetery
CUD/GR S72 ....23 F2
Grimethorpe Hall
CUD/GR S72 ....17 H4
Grimethorpe Ladywood
Primary School
CUD/GR S72 ....23 F1
Grove Street Primary
School
BSLYN/ROY S71 ....3 J4
Gunhills Lane Industrial
Estate
ARMTH DN3 ....43 E3
Hackenthorpe Medical
Centre
HACK/IN S12 ....156 A2
Hady Primary School
CHNE S41 ....193 F2
Halfway Infant School
MOS S20 ....167 E1
Halfway Junior School
MOS S20 ....167 E1
Hallam FM Arena
DARN/MH S9 ....116 D5
Hallam Primary School
FUL S10 ....137 G1
Hallamshire Business
Park
ECC S11 ....10 C7
Hallamshire Golf Club
FUL S10 ....123 G5
Hallamshire Natural
Health Centre
ECC S11 ....139 E2
Hall Cross Lower School
DONS/BSCR DN4 ....57 F5
Hall Cross School
DON DN1 ....7 G2
Hallowes Golf Club
DRON S18 ....171 F4

Handsworth Branch Clinic
HAN/WDH S13 ....142 D1
Handsworth Cemetery
HAN/WDH S13 ....129 E5
Handsworth Christian
School
HAN/WDH S13 ....128 D5
Handsworth Road
Medical Centre
HAN/WDH S13 ....142 D1
Hanover Medical Centre
FUL S10 ....10 C6
Hartington Industrial
Estate
STV/CWN S43 ....182 A2
Hasland Hall Community
School
CHNE S41 ....193 F5
Hasland Infant School
CHNE S41 ....193 E4
Hasland Junior School
CHNE S41 ....193 E5
Hatchell Wood Primary
School
DONS/BSCR DN4 ....74 C2
Hatfield Primary School
SHEFN S5 ....102 A4
Haugh Road Cemetery
RAW S62 ....85 E5
Havercroft Health Centre
HOR/CROF WF4 ....13 H1
Hawthorn Primary School
DONS/BSCR DN4 ....58 A4
Hayfield Lane Primary
School
EPW DN9 ....75 H4
The Hayfield School
EPW DN9 ....75 H4
Heather Garth Primary
School
DEARNE S63 ....52 D2
Heeley Business Centre
SHEFP/MNR S2 ....140 A2
Heeley City Farm
SHEFP/MNR S2 ....140 A3
Heeley Retail Park
SHEFS S8 ....152 D2
Hellaby Hall Hotel
MALT S66 ....109 H4
Hellaby Industrial Estate
MALT S66 ....109 G3
Henry Bradley Infant
School
STV/CWN S43 ....188 D1
Heritage Community
School
STV/CWN S43 ....184 D2
Heritage Park Community
School
SHEFP/MNR S2 ....140 C1
Herringthorpe J & I School
RHAM/THRY S65 ....106 D5
Herringthorpe Leisure
Centre
RHAM S60 ....106 C5
Herringthorpe Stadium
RHAM S60 ....106 C5
Hexthorpe Business Park
DONS/BSCR DN4 ....6 A5
Hexthorpe Primary
School
DONS/BSCR DN4 ....55 F4
Highfield Hall Primary
School
CHNE S41 ....187 F3
Highfields Primary School
AWLS/ASK DN6 ....25 F5
High Greave Primary
School
RHAM/THRY S65 ....107 E1
High Green Health Centre
CHPT/GREN S35 ....80 B3
High Green Primary School
CHPT/GREN S35 ....80 B3
High Hazels Golf Club
DARN/MH S9 ....128 B3
High Storrs School
ECC S11 ....138 B4
High Street Cemetery
RAW S62 ....98 A2
High Street Medical Centre
STV/CWN S43 ....182 A4
High View Primary
Learning Centre
WMB/DAR S73 ....49 H2
Highwoods Infant School
MEX/SWTN S64 ....66 C2
Hill House St Marys School
DON DN1 ....7 G2
DONS/BSCR DN4 ....57 H5
Hill Primary School
DEARNE S63 ....37 G1
Hillsborough Barracks
Shopping Mall
ST/HB/BR S6 ....114 B4
Hillsborough Golf Club
ST/HB/BR S6 ....113 E1
Hillsborough Health
Centre
ST/HB/BR S6 ....114 A5
Hillsborough Leisure
Centre
ST/HB/BR S6 ....114 B3

Hillsborough Primary
School
ST/HB/BR S6 ....114 A3
Hilstown Business Centre
BSVR S44 ....197 E5
Hilltop Special School
MALT S66 ....110 B2
Hinde House School
SHEFN S5 ....103 E5
HM Prison
BTLY DN5 ....55 H2
Holgate Meadows
Community Special
School
SHEFN S5 ....102 A4
Holgate School Sports
College
BSLY S70 ....2 B5
Holiday Inn
ATT S4 ....11 K1
Hollies Medical Centre
ECC S11 ....139 F3
Hollingwood Primary
School
STV/CWN S43 ....181 E5
Hollis Hospital
ECC S11 ....151 E3
Holly House School
CHNE S41 ....179 G3
Hollywood Bowling
DARN/MH S9 ....116 D4
Holme Hall Primary School
CHSW S40 ....186 B4
Holmescarr Junior Mixed
School
NROS/TKH DN11 ....91 E2
Holt House Infant School
ABRD S7 ....152 B1
Holy Cross Deanery CE
Primary School
BSLYN/ROY S71 ....20 B1
Holy Rood Catholic Primary
School
BSLY S70 ....2 C6
Hoober Stand
RAW S62 ....83 H1
Hotel Ibis
CHNE S41 ....5 H5
MALT S66 ....109 F4
SHEF S1 ....11 J2
STV/CWN S43 ....177 E5
Houghton Main Welfare &
Sports Club
CUD/GR S72 ....36 A3
Hound Hill
BSLY S70 ....31 F5
Hoyland Cemetery
HOY S74 ....61 G2
Hoyland Common Primary
School
HOY S74 ....61 E3
Hoyland St Helens RC
Primary School
HOY S74 ....61 H2
Hoyland Sports Centre
HOY S74 ....61 G2
Hoyland Springwood
Primary School
HOY S74 ....61 H3
HSBC Sports Club
TOT/DORE S17 ....150 D4
Hucklow Primary School
SHEFN S5 ....115 G2
Hungerhill School
ARMTH DN3 ....29 E5
Hunloke Park Primary
School
RCH S42 ....195 G3
Hunningley Primary
School
BSLY S70 ....33 E3
Hunters Bar Primary
School
ECC S11 ....139 E2
Hutcliffe Wood Cemetery
SHEFS S8 ....152 B3
Hutcliffe Wood
Crematorium
SHEFS S8 ....152 B3
Hyde Park Industrial
Estate
DONS/BSCR DN4 ....6 E7
Immaculate Conception
Catholic Primary School
ECK/KIL S21 ....176 A1
Inkersall Primary School
STV/CWN S43 ....189 G2
Inland Revenue Office
SHEF S1 ....10 E7
Intake Cemetery
HACK/IN S12 ....142 A4
Intake Primary School
HACK/IN S12 ....141 H4
Ireland Industrial Estate
STV/CWN S43 ....182 B5
Ironbridge Industrial
Estate
HAN/WDH S13 ....143 G2
Ivanhoe J & I School
CONI DN12 ....88 C2
Jaunty Springs Health
Centre
HACK/IN S12 ....154 D1

Jordanthorpe Health
Centre
SHEFS S8 ....163 F2
Jump Cemetery
HOY S74 ....62 C1
Junction 34 Industrial
Estate
DARN/MH S9 ....117 F3
Kelham Island Museum
OWL S3 ....126 A2
Kendray Hospital
BSLY S70 ....32 C2
Kendray Infant School
BSLY S70 ....32 B3
Kendray Primary School
BSLY S70 ....32 C3
Killamarsh County J & I
School
ECK/KIL S21 ....168 C1
Killamarsh Leisure Centre
ECK/KIL S21 ....168 B1
Killamarsh Medical Centre
ECK/KIL S21 ....168 A1
Kilnhurst Business Park
MEX/SWTN S64 ....86 C5
Kilnhurst J & I School
MEX/SWTN S64 ....86 D4
Kimberworth Cemetery
KIMB S61 ....104 D3
Kimberworth Infant
School
KIMB S61 ....104 D2
Kimberworth Park Clinic
KIMB S61 ....96 C5
Kimberworth Park
Medical Centre
KIMB S61 ....104 C5
King Edward VII Lower
School
FUL S10 ....124 C5
King Edward VII School
FUL S10 ....125 F5
King Egbert Secondary
School
TOT/DORE S17 ....160 D2
Kingfisher Primary School
WHHL DN2 ....41 E3
Kings Oak Primary
Learning Centre
WMB/DAR S73 ....50 C3
The Kingstone School
BSLY S70 ....2 A7
Kirk Balk School
HOY S74 ....61 G2
Kirkby Avenue Primary
School
BTLY DN5 ....39 G4
Kirk Sandall Industrial
Estate
ARMTH DN3 ....28 D5
Kirk Sandall J & I School
ARMTH DN3 ....29 F4
Kiveton Park Meadows
Junior School
AU/AST/KP S26 ....159 G2
Lacewood Primary
School
DEARNE S63 ....53 F3
Lakeside First School
DONS/BSCR DN4 ....56 D4
Lakeside Village Shopping
Outlet
DONS/BSCR DN4 ....56 D5
Lantern Theatre
ABRD S7 ....139 G2
Laughton J & I School
DIN S25 ....134 B1
Lees Hall Golf Club
SHEFS S8 ....153 G3
Lenthall Infant School
DRON S18 ....163 F5
Library, Art Gallery &
Regimental Museum
RHAM/THRY S65 ....9 G3
Limpsfield Junior School
DARN/MH S9 ....116 C2
Listerdale Shopping
Centre
RHAM/THRY S65 ....107 G5
Little Theatre
DEARNE S63 ....36 D3
Littleworth Grange
Primary Learning Centre
BSLYN/ROY S71 ....20 D5
Lodge Moor Medical
Centre
FUL S10 ....137 E1
Longcar Primary School
BSLY S70 ....2 D6
Longley Park Sixth Form
College
SHEFN S5 ....115 G1
Longley Primary School
SHEFN S5 ....115 E2
Lound Infant School
CHPT/GREN S35 ....80 D5
Lound Junior School
CHPT/GREN S35 ....81 E5
Lowedges Primary School
SHEFS S8 ....162 D1
Lower Meadows Primary
School
SHEFS S8 ....163 H1

Lowfield Primary School
SHEFS S8 ....140 A3
Low Valley Industrial
Estate
WMB/DAR S73 ....50 B3
Loxley Primary School
ST/HB/BR S6 ....112 D3
The Lyceum Theatre
SHEF S1 ....11 H4
Lydgate Infants School
FUL S10 ....124 C4
Lydgate Junior School
FUL S10 ....124 C5
Macdonald St Paul's Hotel
SHEF S1 ....11 G4
Magna Science Adventure
Centre
RHAM S60 ....105 E5
Malin Bridge Primary
School
ST/HB/BR S6 ....113 H4
The Mallard Primary
School
DONS/BSCR DN4 ....71 E2
Maltby Cemetery
MALT S66 ....111 F3
Maltby Comprehensive
School
MALT S66 ....110 D3
Maltby Crags J & I School
MALT S66 ....111 E4
Maltby Hall Infant School
MALT S66 ....110 C3
Maltby Health Centre
MALT S66 ....110 D3
Maltby Lilly Hall Junior
School
MALT S66 ....110 C3
Maltby Manor Primary
School
MALT S66 ....110 D3
Maltby Redwood JMI
School
MALT S66 ....110 A3
Maltby St Mary's RC
Primary School
MALT S66 ....111 F4
Maltby Sports Centre &
Swimming Pool
MALT S66 ....110 D3
Manor Clinic
SHEFP/MNR S2 ....141 F4
Manor College
CHSW S40 ....4 D3
Manor Infant School
STV/CWN S43 ....188 D4
Manor Lodge Middle
School
SHEFP/MNR S2 ....141 E1
Manor Lodge Primary
School
SHEFP/MNR S2 ....141 E1
Manor Park Medical
Centre
SHEFP/MNR S2 ....127 G5
Manor Top Medical Centre
SHEFP/MNR S2 ....141 G4
Mansion House
DON DN1 ....6 C3
Maple Industrial Estate
DOD/DAR S75 ....14 B4
Mapplewell Primary
School
DOD/DAR S75 ....14 A3
Marcliffe Primary School
ST/HB/BR S6 ....113 H2
Marriott Hotel
ECC S11 ....139 F3
Marsden Industrial
Estate
HAN/WDH S13 ....128 D5
Marshgate Industrial
Estate
BTLY DN5 ....6 A2
Marsh Lane Primary
School
ECK/KIL S21 ....165 G5
Mary Swanick Primary
School
STV/CWN S43 ....179 G3
The McAuley Catholic
High School
DONS/BSCR DN4 ....58 C5
Meadow Bank Industrial
Estate
KIMB S61 ....104 D3
Meadowbrook Industrial
Estate
MOS S20 ....157 G5
Meadowhall Junior
School
KIMB S61 ....104 C3
Meadowhall Retail Park
DARN/MH S9 ....117 E4
Meadowhall Shopping
Centre
DARN/MH S9 ....117 E1
Meadowhead Secondary
School
SHEFS S8 ....163 E1
Meadows Community
School
CHNE S41 ....179 H3

Meadowview Industrial
Estate
ARMTH DN3 ....43 F3
Meersbrook Bank Primary
School
SHEFS S8 ....139 H5
Merlin Theatre
ABRD S7 ....139 F3
ST/HB/BR S6 ....113 E3
Metrodome Sports &
Leisure Complex
BSLYN/ROY S71 ....3 J3
Metropolitan Shopping
Centre
BSLY S70 ....3 G4
Mexborough Business
Centre
MEX/SWTN S64 ....67 F3
Mexborough Bus Station
MEX/SWTN S64 ....67 E4
Mexborough Cemetery
MEX/SWTN S64 ....67 E2
Mexborough Park Road
Infant School
MEX/SWTN S64 ....67 E3
Mexborough School
MEX/SWTN S64 ....66 D2
Middlecroft Leisure Centre
STV/CWN S43 ....189 H2
Miefield Primary School
CUD/GR S72 ....17 H5
Millennium Galleries
SHEF S1 ....11 H5
Millfield Industrial Estate
BTLY DN5 ....40 A1
Mill Trading Estate
BSLYN/ROY S71 ....32 B1
Milton Special School
MEX/SWTN S64 ....66 A5
Monk Bretton Cemetery
BSLYN/ROY S71 ....20 C3
Monk Bretton Health
Centre
BSLYN/ROY S71 ....20 C3
Monk Bretton Priory
BSLYN/ROY S71 ....21 E5
Monksbridge Trading
Estate
DIN S25 ....134 A3
Monkwood Health Centre
RAW S62 ....85 E4
Montagu Hospital
MEX/SWTN S64 ....67 E2
Montagu Junior School
MEX/SWTN S64 ....67 E2
Monteney Primary School
SHEFN S5 ....102 A2
Montgomery Theatre
SHEF S1 ....11 G3
Moorgate Business Centre
RHAM S60 ....9 G5
Moorgate Cemetery
RHAM S60 ....105 H5
Morley Place Junior
School
CONI DN12 ....88 D1
Mosborough Medical
Centre
MOS S20 ....166 C1
Mosborough Primary
School
MOS S20 ....166 D1
Mossbrook First & Middle
School
SHEFS S8 ....153 G5
Mount Osborne Industrial
Park
BSLYN/ROY S71 ....32 B1
Mount St Marys College
ECK/KIL S21 ....176 A1
Mount Vernon Hospital
BSLY S70 ....31 H4
Myers Grove School
ST/HB/BR S6 ....113 G5
Mylnhurst RC School
ECC S11 ....151 H1
Nether Green Infant
School
FUL S10 ....137 H2
Nether Green Junior
School
FUL S10 ....138 A2
Netherthorpe Primary
School
OWL S3 ....10 D1
Netherthorpe School
STV/CWN S43 ....182 C4
Newbold CE Primary
School
CHNE S41 ....187 E2
Newbold Community
School
CHSW S40 ....186 D3
New Bolsover Primary
School
BSVR S44 ....196 C3
Newfield Secondary
School
SHEFS S8 ....153 G2
The New Indoor Market
MALT S66 ....111 E3
Newman Special School
RHAM S60 ....119 G3

New Park Spring
CUD/GR S72 ....23 F3
New Street Health Centre
BSLY S70 ....3 F6
Newton Business Centre
BTLY DN5 ....55 F2
New Whittington
Community Primary
School
STV/CWN S43 ....180 B3
New Whittington Infant
School
STV/CWN S43 ....180 B2
Nine Trees Trading Estate
MALT S66 ....121 H4
Nook Lane Junior School
ST/HB/BR S6 ....112 C5
Norfolk Community
Primary School
SHEFP/MNR S2 ....141 E2
Norfolk Park Community
Special School
SHEFP/MNR S2 ....140 C1
Norfolk Park Health
Centre
SHEFP/MNR S2 ....140 C1
North Anston Business
Centre
DIN S25 ....134 A3
North Anston Trading
Estate
DIN S25 ....147 H2
Northcliffe School
CONI DN12 ....68 C5
North Derbyshire Tertiary
College
BSVR S44 ....196 D3
CHSW S40 ....4 C3
STV/CWN S43 ....185 E2
North Doncaster
Technology College
AWLS/ASK DN6 ....25 F2
Northern General Hospital
SHEFN S5 ....115 G2
Northfield Junior School
DRON S18 ....163 G5
Northlands Community
Health Centre
SHEFN S5 ....101 H5
Northpoint Industrial
Estate
DARN/MH S9 ....116 D1
Norton Oakes CC
SHEFS S8 ....153 H4
Norwood Industrial Estate
ECK/KIL S21 ....158 C5
Notre Dame High School
FUL S10 ....138 C1
Novotel
SHEF S1 ....11 G4
Oakes Park School & Talbot
Secondary School
SHEFS S8 ....153 G3
Oakhill Primary School
BSLY S70 ....33 E2
Oaks Business Park
BSLYN/ROY S71 ....32 D1
Oakwell Business Centre
BSLYN/ROY S71 ....32 B1
Oakwood Comprehensive
School
RHAM S60 ....119 E1
Oakwood Swimming
Baths
RHAM S60 ....119 F1
Oakwood Technology
College
RHAM S60 ....119 E1
Octagon Centre
FUL S10 ....10 B4
Odeon Cinema
BSLY S70 ....3 G3
DON DN1 ....6 E4
SHEF S1 ....11 H3
Old College of Technology
BSLY S70 ....3 F3
Old Forge Business Park
SHEFP/MNR S2 ....140 A3
The Old Hall Centre
BTLY DN5 ....39 H2
Old Hall Junior School
CHSW S40 ....191 G2
Old Moor Nature Reserve
Visitors Centre
WMB/DAR S73 ....51 G4
Open College of the Arts
DOD/DAR S75 ....18 D3
Orchard Infant School
BTLY DN5 ....54 B5
Orchard Square Shopping
Centre
SHEF S1 ....11 G3
Our Lady of Mount Carmel
RC Primary School
WHHL DN2 ....41 F5
Our Lady of Perpetual Help
Catholic Primary School
BTLY DN5 ....39 H1
Our Lady of Sorrows VA RC
Primary School
ARMTH DN3 ....42 C3
Oxspring Primary School
STKB/PEN S36 ....45 H5

Parkgate Business Park
  RAW S62 ....98 B4
Parkgate Medical Centre
  RAW S62 ....98 B2
Park Health Centre
  SHEFP/MNR S2 ....11 K4
Park Hill Primary School
  SHEFP/MNR S2 ....11 K4
Park Primary School
  WHHL DN2 ....40 D4
Parkside Community
  School
  CHSW S40 ....4 D7
Parkside Shopping Centre
  ECK/KIL S21 ....168 B1
Parkwood High School
  SHEFN S5 ....114 C2
Parson Cross Primary
  School
  ST/HB/BR S6 ....101 F5
Pastures Hotel
  MEX/SWTN S64 ....68 B3
The Pavement Shopping
  Centre
  CHSW S40 ....5 F4
Peacock Trading Estate
  ST/HB/BR S6 ....114 C4
Pearsons Trading Estate
  SHEF S1 ....187 H1
Penistone Cemetery
  STKB/PEN S36 ....44 C3
Penistone Grammar
  School
  STKB/PEN S36 ....44 C1
Penistone St John the
  Baptist CE Infant School
  STKB/PEN S36 ....44 C4
Penistone St John the
  Baptist CE Junior School
  STKB/PEN S36 ....44 C4
Penistone Sports Centre
  STKB/PEN S36 ....44 C2
Penistone Springvale
  Primary School
  STKB/PEN S36 ....45 F3
Penmore Business Centre
  CHNE S41 ....193 E4
The Petersgate Medical
  Centre
  BTLY DN5 ....39 E2
Pheasant Bank Junior
  School
  NROS/TKH DN11 ....91 E2
Phillimore Park Primary
  School
  DARN/MH S9 ....127 H1
Phoenix Golf Club
  RHAM S60 ....118 B2
Pipworth Junior School
  SHEFP/MNR S2 ....142 A1
Pitt Street Infant School
  MEX/SWTN S64 ....67 G4
Platts Common Industrial
  Estate
  HOY S74 ....61 G3
Plumb Estates
  ARMTH DN3 ....28 D5
Pomegranate Theatre
  CHNE S41 ....5 H4
Ponds Forge International
  Sports Centre
  SHEF S1 ....11 J3
Porter Croft CE Primary
  School
  ECC S11 ....139 G1
Portland Business Park
  HAN/WDH S13 ....142 C1
Potteric Carr Nature
  Reserve
  DONS/BSCR DN4 ....73 E2
Premier Inn
  CHNE S41 ....5 G2
  DARN/MH S9 ....116 D4
  DOD/DAR S75 ....60 A5
  DONS/BSCR DN4 ....56 D5
  RHAM/THRY S65 ....107 G5
  SHEF S1 ....11 H2
  WMB/DAR S73 ....51 F4
Prince Edward Primary
  School
  SHEFP/MNR S2 ....141 G3
Prince of Wales Road
  Medical Centre
  DARN/MH S9 ....128 A4
Priory School & Sports
  College
  BSLYN/ROY S71 ....20 D2
Pye Bank Infant School
  OWL S3 ....126 E1
Queens Medical Centre
  MALT S66 ....111 E3
Queens Park Leisure
  Centre
  CHSW S40 ....4 E5
Queens Park Sports
  Ground
  CHSW S40 ....4 E6
Queens Retail Park
  SHEFP/MNR S2 ....140 D2
Queens Road Clinic
  BSLYN/ROY S71 ....3 H4
Queen Street J & I School
  MEX/SWTN S64 ....66 B3

Railwaymens Sports Club
  BSLYN/ROY S71 ....13 E5
Railway Staff Social &
  Sports Club
  STV/CWN S43 ....180 D1
Rands Lane Industrial
  Estate
  ARMTH DN3 ....43 F3
Ravenside Retail Park
  CHSW S40 ....6 G6
Rawmarsh Ashwood
  Primary School
  RAW S62 ....98 B3
Rawmarsh Community
  School & Sports College
  RAW S62 ....85 E5
Rawmarsh CC
  RAW S62 ....98 C2
Rawmarsh Leisure Centre
  RAW S62 ....98 C2
Rawmarsh Monkwood
  Infant School
  RAW S62 ....85 E4
Rawmarsh Monkwood
  Junior School
  RAW S62 ....84 D4
Rawmarsh Rosehill Junior
  School
  RAW S62 ....85 F4
Rawmarsh St Josephs RC
  Primary School
  RAW S62 ....98 C1
Rawmarsh St Marys CE
  Primary School
  RAW S62 ....98 B1
Rawmarsh Shopping
  Centre
  RAW S62 ....98 A1
Rawmarsh Thorogate
  J & I School
  RAW S62 ....85 F4
RC Cemetery
  ST/HB/BR S6 ....124 C2
Redbrook Business Park
  DOD/DAR S75 ....18 D2
Red Lion Hotel
  AU/AST/KP S26 ....147 F4
Reflex Theatre
  SHEFS S8 ....140 A4
Regent Hotel
  DON DN1 ....6 E4
Reignhead Primary School
  MOS S20 ....157 F2
Renishaw Park Golf Club
  ECK/KIL S21 ....175 G1
Renishaw Primary School
  ECK/KIL S21 ....175 H3
Restover Lodge Hotel
  MALT S66 ....109 G4
Retail World
  RHAM S60 ....98 B5
Revolution House
  CHNE S41 ....179 G3
Richard Newman Primary
  School
  BSLYN/ROY S71 ....14 D5
Richmond Hill Primary
  School
  BTLY DN5 ....55 E2
Richmond Medical Centre
  HAN/WDH S13 ....142 A3
Ridgeway Medical Centre
  RHAM/THRY S65 ....107 E2
Ridgeway Primary School
  HACK/IN S12 ....155 G5
Ridgewood School
  BTLY DN5 ....38 C4
Ringwood Hall Hotel
  STV/CWN S43 ....189 E1
Rivelin Primary School
  ST/HB/BR S6 ....113 H5
The Robert Ogden School
  DEARNE S63 ....37 G3
Rockingham Business Park
  BSLY S70 ....60 D2
Rockingham J & I School
  KIMB S61 ....96 D3
Rosedale Primary School
  BTLY DN5 ....38 C3
Rose Hill Cemetery
  DONS/BSCR DN4 ....58 A4
Rose Hill Crematorium
  DONS/BSCR DN4 ....58 A4
The Rose Hill Crematorium
  BSLYN/ROY S71 ....33 G3
Rossington All Saints VA
  School
  NROS/TKH DN11 ....91 G4
Rossington St Michaels CE
  Primary School
  NROS/TKH DN11 ....91 H2
Rossington Swimming
  Pool
  NROS/TKH DN11 ....91 F2
Rotherham Art Gallery
  RHAM/THRY S65 ....9 G3
Rotherham Civic Theatre
  RHAM/THRY S65 ....9 G4
Rotherham College (Clifton)
  RHAM/THRY S65 ....9 F4
Rotherham College
  (Howard)
  RHAM S60 ....9 F4

Rotherham College of Arts
  & Technology
  BSLYN/ROY S71 ....9 G3
Rotherham College of Art
  & Technology
  RHAM/THRY S65 ....9 G3
Rotherham College of Art
  & Technology
  DIN S25 ....134 D3
Rotherham
  Crematorium
  RHAM/THRY S65 ....107 F3
Rotherham General
  Hospital
  RHAM S60 ....119 F2
Rotherham Golf Club
  RHAM/THRY S65 ....9 H1
Rotherham Road Medical
  Centre
  BSLYN/ROY S71 ....20 A1
Rotherham RUFC
  RHAM S60 ....8 B6
Rotherham Town CC
  RHAM/THRY S65 ....9 J6
Rotherham Town Hall
  RHAM S60 ....9 F5
Rotherham United FC
  (Millmoor Ground)
  KIMB S61 ....8 B5
Rother Junior School
  CHSW S40 ....192 C4
Rother Valley Country
  Park
  AU/AST/KP S26 ....158 C4
Rother Valley Golf Club
  AU/AST/KP S26 ....158 D4
Rotunda
  Business Centre
  CHPT/GREN S35 ....80 D3
Roughwood Primary
  School
  KIMB S61 ....96 C4
Rowan Primary School
  TOT/DORE S17 ....161 E2
Rowena Infant School
  CONI DN12 ....88 D1
Royal Hallamshire
  Hospital
  FUL S10 ....10 A5
Royal Hallamshire Hospital,
  Jessop Wing
  FUL S10 ....125 F5
Royd Infant School
  STKB/PEN S36 ....77 F3
Royston Cemetery
  BSLYN/ROY S71 ....15 C1
Royston Clinic
  BSLYN/ROY S71 ....15 C1
Royston High School
  BSLYN/ROY S71 ....12 C5
Royston Meadstead
  Primary School
  BSLYN/ROY S71 ....15 F1
Royston Parkside Primary
  School
  BSLYN/ROY S71 ....12 C5
Royston Summerfields
  Primary School
  BSLYN/ROY S71 ....12 C5
Rudston Preparatory
  School
  RHAM S60 ....9 K7
Ruskin Gallery
  SHEF S1 ....11 G4
Rustlings Road Medical
  Centre
  ECC S11 ....138 C2
Rutland Business Park
  OWL S3 ....125 H1
Ryecroft Infant School
  RAW S62 ....85 G5
Sacred Heart Catholic
  Primary School
  DEARNE S63 ....37 G4
  ST/HB/BR S6 ....114 A5
St Albans CE Primary
  School
  MALT S66 ....108 B5
St Albans RC J & I School
  CONI DN12 ....68 C5
St Andrews CE Methodist
  Primary School
  DRON S18 ....170 B2
St Anns J & I School
  RHAM/THRY S65 ....9 J2
St Anns Medical Centre
  RHAM S60 ....9 F2
St Anns Primary School
  STKB/PEN S36 ....76 D3
St Bedes RC Primary
  School
  KIMB S61 ....104 C1
St Bernard's Catholic High
  School
  RHAM/THRY S65 ....107 E4
St Catherines RC Primary
  School
  SHEFN S5 ....115 E4
St Francis Xavier Catholic
  Primary School
  DONS/BSCR DN4 ....6 A7
St Georges Church
  OWL S3 ....10 D3
St Giles CE Primary
  School
  ECK/KIL S21 ....168 A2

St Helens Primary School
  BSLYN/ROY S71 ....20 D2
St James Swimming Pool
  DON DN1 ....6 D5
St John Baptist CE VA Primary
  School
  BSLYN/ROY S71 ....15 G1
St John Fisher RC Primary
  School
  HACK/IN S12 ....156 A2
St Johns CE Primary
  School
  MEX/SWTN S64 ....67 F2
  SHEFP/MNR S2 ....126 D4
St Joseph & St Teresas
  Catholic Primary School
  AWLS/ASK DN6 ....25 G3
St Josephs Convent School
  CHSW S40 ....4 E2
St Josephs RC Primary
  School
  HAN/WDH S13 ....128 D5
St Josephs RC Primary
  School
  NROS/TKH DN11 ....91 F2
  STV/CWN S43 ....189 H1
St Marie RC Cathedral
  SHEF S1 ....11 G3
St Maries Catholic Primary
  School
  FUL S10 ....138 C1
St Marys Catholic Primary
  School
  RHAM/THRY S65 ....107 E3
St Mary's CE Primary
  School
  DOD/DAR S75 ....2 B3
St Mary School
  ST/HB/BR S6 ....125 E2
St Marys CE Primary
  School
  ST/HB/BR S6 ....125 F1
St Marys High Green RC
  Primary School
  CHPT/GREN S35 ....80 C3
St Marys RC High School
  CHNE S41 ....186 C2
St Marys RC Primary
  School
  CHSW S40 ....4 E2
St Matthews Infant School
  DOD/DAR S75 ....2 B1
St Michael & All Angels
  Catholic Primary School
  WMB/DAR S73 ....50 D1
St Michaels C & CE High
  School
  BSLYN/ROY S71 ....15 G5
St Oswald's RC Primary
  School
  SHEFP/MNR S2 ....127 F5
St Patricks Catholic
  Primary School
  SHEFN S5 ....102 C5
St Peter & St Paul School
  CHNE S41 ....193 E1
St Peters Catholic Primary
  School
  DONS/BSCR DN4 ....57 E4
St Peters CE Primary
  School
  DOD/DAR S75 ....60 C3
St Theresas Catholic
  Primary School
  SHEFP/MNR S2 ....141 H3
St Thomas CE Primary
  School
  MEX/SWTN S64 ....86 C3
St Thomas More RC
  Primary School
  CHPT/GREN S35 ....101 F2
St Thomas of Canterbury
  RC Primary School
  SHEFS S8 ....152 D4
St Thomas's Cemetery
  BSLY S70 ....32 B5
Saint Vincent Medical
  Centre
  DON DN1 ....7 G2
St Wilfrids Catholic
  Primary School
  ABRD S7 ....152 A1
St Wilfrids Primary School
  ARMTH DN3 ....59 F5
Saltergate Health Centre
  CHSW S40 ....5 F3
Saltergate Junior School
  BTLY DN5 ....39 E4
Sandall Wood School
  WHHL DN2 ....41 H5
Sandhill Golf Club
  CUD/GR S72 ....35 H2
Sandhill JMI School
  RAW S62 ....86 A5
Sandhill Primary School
  CUD/GR S72 ....36 A1
Sandpiper Hotel
  CHNE S41 ....179 E2
Sandringham Primary
  School
  WHHL DN2 ....41 H4
Scawthorpe Clinic
  BTLY DN5 ....39 F3

Scawthorpe Sunnyfields
  Primary School
  BTLY DN5 ....39 E3
School of Nursing &
  Midwifery (University
  of Sheffield)
  ST/HB/BR S6 ....10 A2
School of Nursing
  (Sheffield University)
  WHHL DN2 ....40 D5
Shafton Primary School
  CUD/GR S72 ....17 F2
Shardlows Sports Club
  CHPT/GREN S35 ....94 B4
Sharrow Infant School
  ABRD S7 ....139 H2
Sharrow Junior School
  ABRD S7 ....139 H2
Shaw Lane Industrial
  Estate
  WHHL DN2 ....42 A2
Shaw Wood Primary
  School
  ARMTH DN3 ....42 C2
Sheaf Gardens Industrial
  Estate
  SHEFP/MNR S2 ....11 H7
Sheepbridge Business
  Centre
  CHNE S41 ....179 E4
Sheffield Area Health
  Authority Sports &
  Social Club
  FUL S10 ....137 H3
Sheffield Airport Business
  Park
  DARN/MH S9 ....116 D1
Sheffield City Airport
  DARN/MH S9 ....128 D1
Sheffield College
  HACK/IN S12 ....155 E1
  SHEF S1 ....11 J3
  SHEFN S5 ....101 H2
  ST/HB/BR S6 ....113 F5
  STKB/PEN S36 ....77 H3
The Sheffield College
  (Castle College-
  Northside)
  SHEFP/MNR S2 ....11 K6
The Sheffield College
  (Castle College-
  Southside)
  SHEFP/MNR S2 ....11 K7
The Sheffield College
  (Hillsborough College)
  ST/HB/BR S6 ....114 B4
The Sheffield College
  (Norton College)
  SHEFS S8 ....163 F1
The Sheffield College
  DARN/MH S9 ....117 E2
  MOS S20 ....157 F5
Sheffield Eagles RLFC
  DARN/MH S9 ....116 C5
Sheffield General
  Cemetery
  ECC S11 ....139 G2
Sheffield Hallam
  University
  ECC S11 ....138 D3
  FUL S10 ....10 A7
  SHEF S1 ....11 H5
Sheffield High School
  Junior Department
  FUL S10 ....125 E5
Sheffield Newspaper
  Offices
  SHEF S1 ....11 H2
Sheffield Park Hotel
  SHEFS S8 ....163 E2
Sheffield Ski Village
  OWL S3 ....114 C5
Sheffield Sports
  Stadium
  ST/HB/BR S6 ....114 B3
Sheffield Technology
  Park
  DARN/MH S9 ....127 G1
Sheffield United CC
  DARN/MH S9 ....117 H3
Sheffield United FC
  (Bramall Lane)
  SHEF S1 ....140 A1
Sheffield Wednesday FC
  (Hillsborough)
  ST/HB/BR S6 ....114 A2
Shirecliffe Junior School
  SHEFN S5 ....114 C2
Shiregreen Cemetery
  SHEFN S5 ....103 F5
Shire Green Medical
  Centre
  SHEFN S5 ....103 E3
Shooters Grove Primary
  School
  ST/HB/BR S6 ....113 F5
Short Brook Primary
  School
  MOS S20 ....157 F5
Showroom Cinema
  SHEF S1 ....11 H5
Shrewsbury Hospital
  SHEFP/MNR S2 ....126 C5

Silverdale School
ECC S11 ....138 A5
Sir Harold Jackson
Primary School
TOT/DORE S17 ....161 H3
Sitwell Arms Hotel
ECK/KIL S21 ....175 G2
Sitwell J & I School
RHAM S60 ....119 H1
Sitwell Park Golf Club
RHAM S60 ....120 C1
Skate Central
SHEFP/MNR S2 ....11 J7
Sothall Leisure Centre
MOS S20 ....157 F2
Sothall Medical Centre
MOS S20 ....157 F3
Southey Green Infant
School
SHEFN S5 ....101 H5
Southey Green Medical
Centre
SHEFN S5 ....114 D1
South Yorkshire Business
Centre
RAW S62 ....98 A4
South Yorkshire
(Redbrook) Industrial
Estate
DOD/DAR S75 ....18 C2
Speedwell Industrial
Estate
STV/CWN S43 ....182 A5
Speedwell Infant School
STV/CWN S43 ....182 A5
Spital Cemetery
CHNE S41 ....5 K5
Springbank Community
Centre
CHSW S40 ....4 C3
Springfield Primary School
OWL S3 ....10 D5
Springwell Community
School
STV/CWN S43 ....189 H2
Sprotbrough Health
Centre
BTLY DN5 ....55 E3
Stag Medical Centre
RHAM S60 ....120 A1
Stainborough Castle
DOD/DAR S75 ....46 B2
Staindrop Lodge Hotel
CHPT/GREN S35 ....81 E4
Stairfoot Health Centre
BSLY S70 ....32 D3
Stairfoot Industrial Estate
BSLYN/ROY S71 ....33 F2
Stannington Health
Centre
ST/HB/BR S6 ....123 G1
Stannington Infant
School
ST/HB/BR S6 ....123 G1
Station Lane Industrial
Estate
CHNE S41 ....179 H4
Station Rd Industrial
Estate
STV/CWN S43 ....185 G2
Station Road Industrial
Estate
WMB/DAR S73 ....50 C2
Station Road J & I School
CONI DN12 ....68 D5
Staveley Cemetery
STV/CWN S43 ....182 A5
Staveley Health Clinic
STV/CWN S43 ....182 A5
Staveley Junior School
STV/CWN S43 ....181 H5
Staveley Norbriggs
County Infants School
STV/CWN S43 ....183 E3
Stirling Primary School
DON DN1 ....6 C7
Stocksbridge Cemetery
STKB/PEN S36 ....77 E2
Stocksbridge & District
Golf Club
STKB/PEN S36 ....77 F4
Stocksbridge High School
STKB/PEN S36 ....76 D2
Stocksbridge Infant School
STKB/PEN S36 ....76 D2
Stocksbridge
Junior School
STKB/PEN S36 ....76 D3
Stocksbridge Leisure
Centre
STKB/PEN S36 ....76 C2
Stocksbridge RFC
STKB/PEN S36 ....76 D1
Stonelow Junior School
DRON S18 ....171 G1
Storforth Lane Trading
Estate
CHNE S41 ....192 D4
Stradbroke Primary
School
HAN/WDH S13 ....142 B3
Strafford Industrial Park
DOD/DAR S75 ....30 C5

Sues Health Centre
BSLYN/ROY S71 ....15 E4
Summer Lane Primary
School
DOD/DAR S75 ....2 B2
Superbowl 2000
KIMB S61 ....104 C1
Superintendent
Swimming Baths
CHPT/GREN S35 ....94 A1
Swallownest Health
Centre
AU/AST/KP S26 ....145 F3
Swallownest Primary
School
AU/AST/KP S26 ....144 D2
Swinton Brookfield
Primary School
MEX/SWTN S64 ....86 B1
Swinton Community
School
MEX/SWTN S64 ....86 A1
Swinton Fitzwilliam J & I
School
MEX/SWTN S64 ....85 H1
Swinton Meadows
Business Park
MEX/SWTN S64 ....66 D5
Swinton Meadows
Industrial Estate
MEX/SWTN S64 ....66 D5
Swinton Swimming Pool
MEX/SWTN S64 ....66 B5
Sycamore Hall
Preparatory School
DONS/BSCR DN4 ....71 G1
Talbot School
SHEFS S8 ....153 G4
Tankersley Manor Hotel
DOD/DAR S75 ....60 C5
Tankersley Park Golf Club
CHPT/GREN S35 ....81 E2
Tapton Park Golf Club
CHNE S41 ....188 A5
Templeborough Business
Centre
RHAM S60 ....105 G5
Tertiary College
ECK/KIL S21 ....166 D5
Thomas Rotherham
College
RHAM S60 ....106 A5
Thornbury Hospital
FUL S10 ....138 B1
Thornhill Industrial Estate
RHAM S60 ....8 D1
Thornhill Primary School
RHAM S60 ....8 C3
Thorpe Hesley Clinic
KIMB S61 ....95 F2
Thorpe Hesley Infant
School
KIMB S61 ....95 E2
Thorpe Hesley Junior
School
KIMB S61 ....95 F2
Thrybergh Comprehensive
School
RHAM/THRY S65 ....99 H3
Thrybergh Fullerton CE
Primary School
RHAM/THRY S65 ....99 H3
Thrybergh Medical
Centre
RHAM/THRY S65 ....99 H4
Thrybergh St Gerards RC
M & I School
RHAM/THRY S65 ....99 F4
Thurcroft Cemetery
MALT S66 ....133 F3
Thurcroft Infant School
MALT S66 ....133 G1
Thurcroft Junior School
MALT S66 ....133 F1
Thurlstone Primary
School
STKB/PEN S36 ....44 A2
Thurnscoe Business
Centre
DEARNE S63 ....37 G2
Thurnscoe Cemetery
DEARNE S63 ....36 D3
Tickhill Road Hospital
DONS/BSCR DN4 ....71 H3
Tinsley Industrial Estate
DARN/MH S9 ....128 A1
Tinsley Infant School
DARN/MH S9 ....117 G2
Tinsley Junior School
DARN/MH S9 ....117 G3
Tinsley Park Cemetery
DARN/MH S9 ....128 B1
Todwick JMI School
AU/AST/KP S26 ....147 F5
Toll Bar Primary School
BTLY DN5 ....26 C2
Tornedale Infant School
NROS/TKH DN11 ....91 F2
Totley All Saints CE
Primary School
TOT/DORE S17 ....160 C4
Town End Industrial Estate
BTLY DN5 ....55 G1

Townfield Primary School
DON DN1 ....7 G2
Trafalgar House Medical
Centre
ST/HB/BR S6 ....101 F5
Tramways Medical Centre
ST/HB/BR S6 ....114 A4
Tranmoor Infant & Junior
School
ARMTH DN3 ....42 D5
Travelodge
BSLY S70 ....33 E2
CHNE S41 ....187 G1
SHEFP/MNR S2 ....128 A5
Treeton CE Primary School
RHAM S60 ....130 A4
Trinity Croft Primary
School
RHAM/THRY S65 ....107 F1
Turner Museum of Glass
SHEF S1 ....10 E3
Turnoaks Business Park
CHSW S40 ....195 G1
TV Studios
SHEF S1 ....11 F5
UCI Cinema
MOS S20 ....157 E2
Ulley Country Park
AU/AST/KP S26 ....131 F3
University of Sheffield
FUL S10 ....10 A5
FUL S10 ....124 D5
FUL S10 ....138 C1
SHEF S1 ....10 E3
Unstone Junior School
DRON S18 ....172 A4
Unstone St Marys Infant
School
DRON S18 ....172 A3
Upperthorpe Healthy
Living Centre
ST/HB/BR S6 ....125 G2
Valley Park Community
Primary School
GLV S14 ....154 A3
Valley Park Industrial
Estate
WMB/DAR S73 ....51 E4
Vanguard Trading Estate
CHSW S40 ....192 C5
Verdon Recreation
Centre
OWL S3 ....126 B2
Victoria Hall
SHEF S1 ....11 H3
Victoria Quays Shopping
Centre
SHEFP/MNR S2 ....11 J2
Vue Cinema
DARN/MH S9 ....117 E2
DONS/BSCR DN4 ....57 E4
Wales High School
AU/AST/KP S26 ....159 G2
Wales J & I School
AU/AST/KP S26 ....159 F3
Walkley Medical Centre
ST/HB/BR S6 ....125 E1
Walkley Primary School
ST/HB/BR S6 ....114 B5
Waltheof Secondary
School
SHEFP/MNR S2 ....127 H5
Walton Holymoorside
Primary School
RCH S42 ....190 B5
Walton Hospital
CHSW S40 ....192 A5
Ward Green Primary
School
BSLY S70 ....31 H5
Wardsend Cemetery
SHEFN S5 ....114 C3
Warmsworth Halt
Industrial Estate
DONS/BSCR DN4 ....70 C4
Warmsworth Primary
School
DONS/BSCR DN4 ....70 C2
Warwick Street Industrial
Estate
CHSW S40 ....192 D4
Waterdale Centre
DON DN1 ....6 C4
Water Sports Centre
AU/AST/KP S26 ....158 B4
Waterthorpe Infant
School
MOS S20 ....157 E3
Wath Cemetery
DEARNE S63 ....65 G3
Wath Central Primary
School
DEARNE S63 ....65 E3
Wath CE Primary School
DEARNE S63 ....65 E1
Wath Comprehensive
School Language College
DEARNE S63 ....65 F1
Wath Golf Club
RAW S62 ....84 D1
Wath Our Lady & St Josephs
RC Primary School
DEARNE S63 ....65 F2

Wath RUFC
DEARNE S63 ....65 F1
Wath Victoria Primary
School
DEARNE S63 ....65 G2
Wath West Industrial
Estate
DEARNE S63 ....51 G5
Waverley Primary School
DONS/BSCR DN4 ....71 E2
Wentworth Castle
DOD/DAR S75 ....46 B2
Wentworth Castle College
of Education
DOD/DAR S75 ....46 B2
Wentworth CE Primary
School
RAW S62 ....82 C2
Wentworth Industrial
Park
RAW S62 ....60 C4
Westbourne School
FUL S10 ....125 E5
Westfield Health Centre
MOS S20 ....157 E5
Westfield Infant School
CHSW S40 ....191 F2
Westfield Secondary
School
MOS S20 ....156 D5
West Meadows Primary
School
HOY S74 ....61 G2
West Melton Primary
School
DEARNE S63 ....64 C1
Weston Park Hospital
FUL S10 ....125 F4
Weston Park Museum
FUL S10 ....10 A3
Westways Primary
School
FUL S10 ....125 E5
Westwood Country Park
CHPT/GREN S35 ....80 C2
Westwood Industrial
Estate
ARMTH DN3 ....43 E5
Wharncliffe Industrial
Complex
STKB/PEN S36 ....78 A2
Wheatbridge Retail Park
CHSW S40 ....4 D5
Wheatley Golf Club
WHHL DN2 ....41 H4
Wheatley Hall Business
Centre
WHHL DN2 ....41 E3
Whiston Grange School
RHAM S60 ....119 G3
Whiston Primary School
RHAM S60 ....119 H2
Whiston Worry Goose JMI
School
RHAM S60 ....120 B3
Whitecotes Primary
School
CHSW S40 ....192 B4
Whitelea Grove Trading
Estate
MEX/SWTN S64 ....66 C4
Whiteley Wood Clinic
FUL S10 ....138 A3
Whiteways Junior School
ATT S4 ....115 H4
Whitley Hall CC
CHPT/GREN S35 ....93 G5
Whitley Hall Hotel
CHPT/GREN S35 ....93 G4
Whittington Medical
Centre
CHNE S41 ....179 G3
Whittington Moor
Surgery
CHNE S41 ....187 H2
Wickersley Health Centre
MALT S66 ....108 B4
Wickersley School &
Sports College
MALT S66 ....108 C5
William Levick Infant
School
DRON S18 ....170 A1
William Levick Primary
School
DRON S18 ....170 A1
William Rhodes Primary
School
CHSW S40 ....4 C6
Wilthorpe Infant School
DOD/DAR S75 ....19 E3
Wilthorpe Junior School
DOD/DAR S75 ....19 E3
Wincobank Infant School
DARN/MH S9 ....103 G5
Windhill Primary School
MEX/SWTN S64 ....67 G2
The Winding Wheel
Theatre
CHNE S41 ....5 H2
Windmill Hill Primary
School
CHPT/GREN S35 ....93 H2

Wingfield Comprehensive
School
KIMB S61 ....97 E4
Winter Garden
SHEF S1 ....11 G4
Winterhill School
KIMB S61 ....104 C2
Wisewood Cemetery
ST/HB/BR S6 ....112 D4
Wisewood Primary School
ST/HB/BR S6 ....113 F3
Wisewood Secondary
School
ST/HB/BR S6 ....113 F3
Wombwell Cemetery
WMB/DAR S73 ....50 A2
Wombwell Clinic
WMB/DAR S73 ....50 A2
Wombwell CC
WMB/DAR S73 ....49 H3
Wombwell High School
WMB/DAR S73 ....50 C4
Wombwell Jump Primary
School
HOY S74 ....62 B2
Wombwell Park Street
Primary School
WMB/DAR S73 ....50 C3
Wombwell Public Baths
WMB/DAR S73 ....50 B3
Woodbourn Athletics
Centre
DARN/MH S9 ....127 F2
Woodbourn Road
Stadium
DARN/MH S9 ....127 F2
Woodfield Primary School
DONS/BSCR DN4 ....71 H2
Woodhouse Clinic
HAN/WDH S13 ....143 F4
Woodhouse Medical
Centre
HAN/WDH S13 ....143 F4
Woodlands Primary
School
AWLS/ASK DN6 ....25 E3
Woodseats Medical
Centre
SHEFS S8 ....152 D3
Woodseats Primary
School
SHEFS S8 ....152 D2
Woodthorpe CE Primary
School
STV/CWN S43 ....183 E5
Woodthorpe Community
Primary School
HAN/WDH S13 ....142 A3
Woolley Wood J & I School
SHEFN S5 ....103 E3
Wool Market
DON DN1 ....6 D3
Worsbrough Bank End
Primary School
BSLY S70 ....32 C4
Worsbrough Common
Primary School
BSLY S70 ....31 H4
Worsbrough Health Centre
BSLY S70 ....32 B5
Worsbrough Mill Country
Park
BSLY S70 ....47 G2
Worsbrough Mill Museum
BSLY S70 ....48 A2
Worsbrough St Marys CE
Primary School
BSLY S70 ....47 H4
Wybourn Primary School
SHEFP/MNR S2 ....126 D4
Yewlands School
CHPT/GREN S35 ....101 G2
York & Lancaster
Regimental Museum
RHAM/THRY S65 ....9 G3
York House Medical
Centre
SHEFP/MNR S2 ....141 F2
Yorkshire Neurology
Clinic
MALT S66 ....108 A5
Youth & Community
Centre
MALT S66 ....110 C3

Schools address data provided by Education Direct.

Petrol station information supplied by Johnsons

Garden centre information provided by

Garden Centre Association   Britains best garden centres

Wyevale Garden Centres

The statement on the front cover of this atlas is sourced, selected and quoted
from a reader comment and feedback form received in 2004

How do I find the perfect place?

 **Street by Street** QUESTIONNAIRE

Dear Atlas User
Your comments, opinions and recommendations are very important to us.
So please help us to improve our street atlases by taking a few minutes
to complete this simple questionnaire.

You do not need a stamp (unless posted outside the UK). If you do not want to remove this page from your street atlas, then photocopy it or write your answers on a plain sheet of paper.

Send to: Marketing Assistant, AA Publishing, 14th Floor Fanum House,
Freepost SCE 4598, Basingstoke RG21 4GY

ABOUT THE ATLAS...

Please state which city / town / county you bought:

_____

Where did you buy the atlas? (City, Town, County)

_____

For what purpose? (please tick all applicable)

To use in your local area ☐   **To use on business or at work** ☐

Visiting a strange place ☐   **In the car** ☐   **On foot** ☐

Other (please state)

_____

Have you ever used any street atlases other than AA Street by Street?

Yes ☐   No ☐

If so, which ones?

_____

Is there any aspect of our street atlases that could be improved?
(Please continue on a separate sheet if necessary)

_____
_____
_____

ML072y

continued overleaf

Please list the features you found most useful:

_____

_____

Please list the features you found least useful:

_____

_____

_____

LOCAL KNOWLEDGE...

Local knowledge is invaluable. Whilst every attempt has been made to make the information contained in this atlas as accurate as possible, should you notice any inaccuracies, please detail them below (if necessary, use a blank piece of paper) or e-mail us at *streetbystreet@theAA.com*

_____

_____

_____

ABOUT YOU...

Name (Mr/Mrs/Ms) _____

Address _____

Postcode _____

Daytime tel no _____

E-mail address _____

Which age group are you in?

Under 25 ☐   25-34 ☐   35-44 ☐   45-54 ☐   55-64 ☐   65+ ☐

Are you an AA member? YES ☐   NO ☐

Do you have Internet access? YES ☐   NO ☐

Thank you for taking the time to complete this questionnaire. Please send it to us as soon as possible, and remember, you do not need a stamp (unless posted outside the UK).

We may use information we hold about you to, telephone or email you about other products and services offered by the AA, we do NOT disclose this information to third parties.

Please tick here if you do not wish to hear about products and services from the AA. ☐